Ultimate Auto Album

An Illustrated History of the Automobile

6-CYL. 241.5 CID L-HEAD ENGINE

DE SOTO "CUSTOM AIRSTREAM"

1936

3.89 GEAR RATIO

RUMBLE SEAT AT REAR, FOR 2 EXTRA RIDERS

117" WHEELBASE
6.25×16" TIRES

OVERDRIVE AVAILABLE

ONLY 641 OF THESE CUSTOM AIRSTREAM R.S. COUPES BLT. (AT $795., f.o.b.)

LOWER-PRICED "DE LUXE" AIRSTREAM and ... AVAILABLE.

93 H.P.

© 3400 RPM ... (... + STR.)

Tad Burness

Published by

krause
publications

700 E. State Street • Iola, WI 54990-0001
Telephone: 715/445-2214

Please call or write for our free catalog of publications. Our toll-free
number to place an order or obtain a free catalog is
800-258-0929 or please use our regular business telephone,
715-445-2214.

Library of Congress Catalog Number: 2001096282
ISBN: 0-87349-369-9 Printed in the United States of America

Tad Burness welcomes mail from readers.
His address is "Auto Album,"
P.O. Box 247, Pacific Grove, CA 93950.
For a personal reply, please enclose
a stamped, self-addressed envelope.

Dedication

I dedicate this book to the three women in my life: my mother (Wallea Draper), my wife (Sandra), and my daughter (Tammy).

With love,
Tad Burness

Table of Contents

A Friendly Introduction

Thank you for selecting this big, new *Ultimate Auto Album*! I hope you'll enjoy browsing through it many times and that it will bring to fond remembrance the vehicles you're familiar with, others you've not seen for years, and even some oldies that may be new to you!

Since 1966, *Auto Album* has been giving newspaper readers a nostalgic little "car corner" where a different old automobile (or commercial vehicle) is presented each week. An illustrated panel (with certain vital specs) contains a detailed drawing of the featured vehicle, be it antique, classic, or otherwise. And, ever since January 30, 1972, a written column with further information has accompanied the illustrated panel.

In addition to the Fords, Chevrolets, Plymouths, Pontiacs, Ramblers, Jeeps, and Dodges that were such great sellers for so many years, you'll also see numerous other makes such as Studebaker, Hudson, Kaiser, Nash, Willys, Packard, and others of the so-called "independents" that were still selling back in the 1950s. Also represented are the import cars such as Volkswagen, M.G., Datsun, Mercedes-Benz, etc. ... and long-gone "orphan brands" like Pierce-Arrow, Whippet, Chandler, Marmon, Hupmobile, Stutz, etc. that your grandparents may have known and which are now the delight of car collectors!

I first got the idea for *Auto Album* in 1962, having been interested in cars ever since early childhood. (As a toddler, one of my earliest nightmares was of a mean man trying to run me down with a yellow '36 Auburn Speedster! Fortunately, nothing like that actually happened.) After four years, I was able to get *Auto Album* syndicated in the Spring of 1966. My first assignments: Get 18 complete new drawings ready within two weeks, in order to meet that first important newspaper deadline. By staying up 'til 1 or 2 a.m. each night, I was able to get those first 18 new drawings completed on time. But, when I wasn't so rushed, my later drawings were of a much better quality and more detailed. Quick-drying pens and ink and better paper now make production a great deal easier! An effort is made to continually improve the quality of my work.

This collection includes most *Auto Album* releases seen in newspapers between 1984 and 1993. If your local newspaper uses *Auto Album* each week, be sure to clip and save the current issues, which are not available in book form.

In addition to interesting and unusual old cars, you'll find old houses and buildings in some of the backgrounds. You will also see lists of old songs, old radio and TV shows, brands of many long-forgotten cars, and other memory-tickling tidbits of nostalgic pop culture in this new book! May it give to you much enjoyment!

Sincerely,

Tad

Tad Burness
Pacific Grove, California

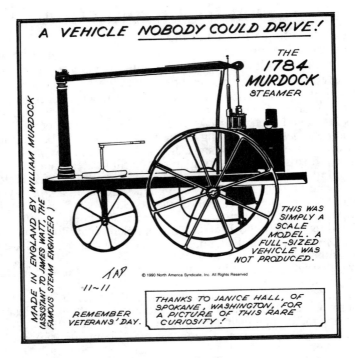

A VEHICLE *NOBODY COULD DRIVE!*

THE
1784
MURDOCK
STEAMER

MADE IN ENGLAND BY WILLIAM MURDOCK
(ASSISTANT TO JAMES WATT, THE
FAMOUS STEAM ENGINEER)

THIS WAS
SIMPLY A
SCALE
MODEL. A
FULL-SIZED
VEHICLE WAS
NOT PRODUCED.

© 1990 North America Syndicate, Inc. All Rights Reserved

REMEMBER
VETERANS' DAY.

THANKS TO JANICE HALL, OF
SPOKANE, WASHINGTON, FOR
A PICTURE OF THIS RARE
CURIOSITY!

1784 Murdock Steamer

We usually show more familiar vehicles in *Auto Album*—cars or trucks that many will remember. Obviously, nobody would remember a car that's over 200 years old, but it's fun to occasionally wander far back into the past to get a look at one of the earliest!

This is the second-oldest car ever seen in *Auto Album*. Only the 1769 Cugnot—shown some time ago in the series—is older than this one.

In fact, drawings of the 1769 Cugnot, made in France, inspired Mr. Murdock to create a steam vehicle of his own, in England.

Avoiding Cugnot's mistake of building a top-heavy, unbalanced machine that could easily overturn, Murdock mounted his steam engine over the rear wheels. "Spirits" (apparently alcohol) provided the fuel for the steam.

Unfortunately for future historians, Murdock built only a miniature steamer, so we don't know how the full-sized version would have performed.

The Murdock steamer is 100 years older than most other pioneer horseless carriages!

1802 Trevithick's Steam Carriage

This odd, simple-looking vehicle was tested near London, on a 10-mile stretch of road, shortly after it was built in 1802.

Until the very late 1800s, no automobiles were available for sale, anywhere, so this one-of-a-kind machine was nearly a century ahead of its time! Richard Trevithick designed it, but he built no more self-propelled vehicles after this, and he is virtually forgotten today.

Other very early experimental automobiles are the 1805 Orukter Amphibolos, 1840 "Exterminator" fire engine, and the 1863 Roper Steam Buggy (which had no brakes and required the driver to throw it into reverse in order to stop!).

Little is known of the history of Trevithick's Steam Carriage, and of course there is no horsepower rating, etc., on a vehicle this early. The patent drawings are still in existence, and the prototype was built and tested. We don't know what eventually became of the actual vehicle, and we can only hope that it was not completely dismantled and discarded long ago! Richard Trevithick may not have realized that, at the time, he was making history.

1859 American (Fisher) Steam Carriage

The automotive industry didn't begin—in any noticeable way—until the 1890s. The earlier exceptions were just a few individually built or experimental models that gained little attention.

When the auto industry began to grow in the 1890s and early 1900s, France had the jump on the United States and other nations, by a few years. The earliest horseless carriages on the market were often of French manufacture, and many early car dealers in America sold French cars in addition to domestic ones.

Yet, one of the earliest motor vehicles known to have been offered for sale to the public at a designated price was John Kenrick Fisher's American (Fisher) steam carriage. Fisher's total production figure could be counted on the fingers of one hand, and he reportedly failed to find buyers for his strange new creations. One of his most unusual is this 1859-1860 model, one with a very long wheelbase (exact figure not mentioned). The illustrated vehicle would carry up to 10 passengers, cozily, but hazardously, seated around the upright steam boiler. As such ancient boilers radiated much heat and belched sparks and soot from the smokestack, the safety of driver and passengers left much to be desired.

It would be another four decades before most other horseless carriages would begin to appear on the roads. Even until the days of World War I, a good number of horse-drawn buggies and wagons could be seen in any town or city.

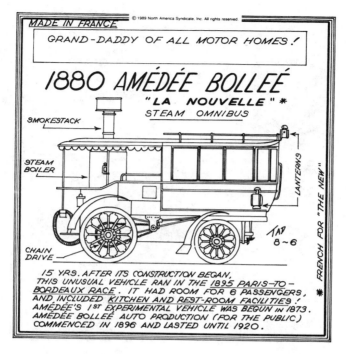

MADE IN FRANCE

© 1989 North America Syndicate, Inc. All rights reserved.

GRAND-DADDY OF ALL MOTOR HOMES!

1880 AMÉDÉE BOLLEÉ
"LA NOUVELLE" *
STEAM OMNIBUS

SMOKESTACK

STEAM BOILER

CHAIN DRIVE

LANTERNS

FRENCH FOR "THE NEW"

TAP 8~6

15 YRS. AFTER ITS CONSTRUCTION BEGAN, THIS UNUSUAL VEHICLE RAN IN THE 1895 PARIS-TO-BORDEAUX RACE. IT HAD ROOM FOR 6 PASSENGERS, AND INCLUDED KITCHEN AND REST-ROOM FACILITIES! AMÉDÉE'S 1ST EXPERIMENTAL VEHICLE WAS BEGUN IN 1873. AMÉDÉE BOLLEÉ AUTO PRODUCTION (FOR THE PUBLIC) COMMENCED IN 1896 AND LASTED UNTIL 1920.

1880 Amédée Bolleé Omnibus

Back in the 1880s, self-propelled vehicles were usually railroad locomotives, and all were steam-powered. Electric and gasoline-powered automobiles had not yet reached the market. This 1880 Amédée Bolleé steam omnibus was the predecessor of the modern-day motor home, because it was equipped inside with both kitchen and toilet facilities. In 1895, it was entered in the 1,200-kilometer Paris-to-Bordeaux race in France, and it was named La Nouvelle (the new), even though the vehicle was already some fifteen years old. It finished the race in ninth place.

This oddity may remind some of a cross between a locomotive and a stagecoach. In those days, bodies of such vehicles were constructed of wood, though the steam boiler and most mechanical parts were of steel, iron, brass, etc. Notice that the drive wheels (powered) are larger than the dummy wheels (unpowered).

Ninety-seven vehicles were originally signed for the race, but only twenty-two actually started. Of that number, only nine actually managed to finish. This La Nouvelle omnibus was the only one of the steam-powered vehicles that completed the race.

Coming in first was a Panhard & Levassor, but a Peugeot won on a technicality. The Amédée Bolleé La Nouvelle would have done much better if it hadn't had trouble with a tight connecting rod that overheated. Wet rags were applied to keep the rod cool, but the rags became entangled in the mechanism, causing several stops for repairs. A powerful steamer, this vehicle had been ahead of the others in the early part of the race.

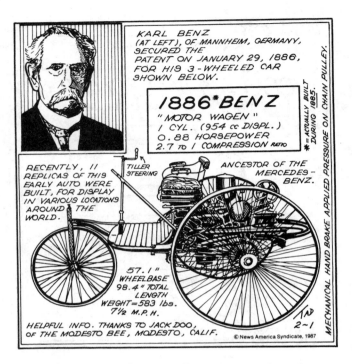

1886 Benz

This pioneer Benz "Motor Wagen" was built during 1885, but it's considered an 1886 car by its successor, Mercedes-Benz of Germany, because it was patented in 1886.

The original car is on display in the Deutsches Museum in Munich, Germany. But, in the 1980s, Mercedes-Benz officials wished that this famous old vehicle could be seen throughout the entire world, so they commissioned eleven replicas to be built by young Mercedes-Benz apprentices.

Over a period of two years, 10,000 hours were spent in the building of the eleven replicas, all copied carefully from the original. The apprentices used nothing but authentic tools and materials used a century ago. Two of these replicas have been displayed in the U.S.A., one of them at the Modesto Concours of 1986 in Modesto, Calif., after which it was later scheduled to be on permanent display at Mercedes-Benz's American headquarters at Montvale, N.J.

Mercedes-Benz celebrated its Centennial Year in 1986, and therefore the touring displays of the replicas.

In 1901, Mercedes pioneered a touring car with a hood and radiator in front, which looked several years ahead of its time. Most autos of the early 1900s were buggy-like horseless carriages.

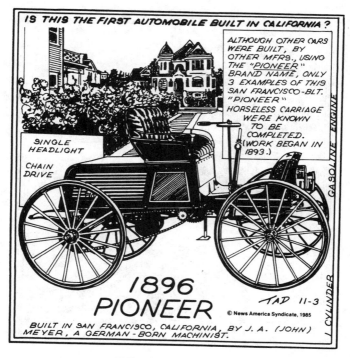

IS THIS THE FIRST AUTOMOBILE BUILT IN CALIFORNIA?

ALTHOUGH OTHER CARS WERE BUILT, BY OTHER MFRS., USING THE "*PIONEER*" BRAND NAME, ONLY 3 EXAMPLES OF THIS SAN FRANCISCO-BLT. "PIONEER" HORSELESS CARRIAGE WERE KNOWN TO BE COMPLETED. (WORK BEGAN IN 1893.)

SINGLE HEADLIGHT

CHAIN DRIVE

GASOLINE ENGINE

1 CYLINDER

1896 PIONEER

TAD 11-3

© News America Syndicate, 1985

BUILT IN SAN FRANCISCO, CALIFORNIA, BY J. A. (JOHN) MEYER, A GERMAN-BORN MACHINIST.

1896 Pioneer

Several years ago, this rare Pioneer horseless carriage was acquired by the Oakland (Calif.) Museum for display in its Cowell Hall of California History. It is believed that this San Francisco-built car may be the earliest gasoline-powered automobile built and sold in California! Only three of these Pioneers were known to have been built. It is reported that the illustrated one served heroically in the disastrous 1906 San Francisco fire and earthquake, passing through ravaged streets where horses feared to enter!

The two other Pioneer cars, built after the illustrated model, were sold to Dr. J. W. Jesse of Santa Rosa, Calif. (for making house calls), and to George Colgate (publisher of the *Orland Register*).

Were any additional Pioneer cars built and sold? Perhaps not, but unfortunately, some of the valuable historical information pertaining to this manufacturing enterprise was lost in the 1906 fire and quake. But, at least Albert Meyer (son of John Meyer, the founder), managed to retain some information. He also kept the first of the three known Pioneer cars, which he eventually sold to the Oakland Museum.

DETAILS THANKS TO
BILL MUNSON,
MUNCIE, INDIANA

FACTORY

THE MUNSON COMPANY

1900 MUNSON
HORSELESS CARRIAGE
7-HP GAS-ELECTRIC
4 SPEEDS:
2, 4, 8, and
16 M.P.H.

WT. 2000 LBS.

MFD. BY THE
MUNSON CO.
LA PORTE, INDIANA

SLOGAN:
"THE HORSELESS VEHICLE IS A COMMERCIAL SUCCESS"

1900 Munson

According to various reports, the Munson Company of La Porte, Ind. produced motor vehicles sometime between 1896 and 1902—but not for that entire timespan. We DO know that there was a 1900 Munson, and we're grateful to William B. (Bill) Munson of Muncie, Ind. for sending detailed information on the car and its manufacturer, including a reprint of an original sales catalog!

The Munson gas-electric was driven by a self-starting electric motor, but also used a gasoline engine to generate power for recharging the battery.

In addition to operating the factory in La Porte, various Munsons were instrumental in establishing and maintaining auto dealerships throughout the state of Indiana, with affiliations in Virginia, North Carolina, and elsewhere.

At one time or another, Munson dealerships have sold Allens, AMC cars, Buicks, Cadillacs, Chevrolets, Chrysler Corp. cars and trucks, Datsuns, Federal trucks, Fords, Graham-Paiges and Grahams, Hudsons, Jeeps, Lincolns, Mack trucks, Nashes, Packards, Pierce-Arrows, Pontiacs, Studebakers, Willys-Overland products, and others! Some of the Munson dealerships are still going strong today.

The first Munsons to establish a dealership were Burr N. Munson and Gael D. Munson (Allen Cars, 1916, at Warsaw, Ind.). In 1931, Burr Munson also introduced his invention of a chrome wheel trim cover to enhance the appearance of ordinary wood-spoked wheels; at that time, he was selling Studebakers.

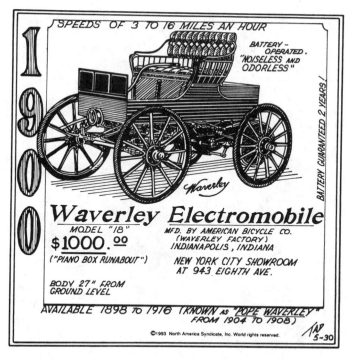

SPEEDS OF 3 TO 16 MILES AN HOUR

BATTERY – OPERATED. "NOISELESS AND ODORLESS"

BATTERY GUARANTEED 2 YEARS!

Waverley Electromobile

MODEL "18"

$1000.00

("PIANO BOX RUNABOUT")

MFD. BY AMERICAN BICYCLE CO. (WAVERLEY FACTORY) INDIANAPOLIS, INDIANA

NEW YORK CITY SHOWROOM AT 943 EIGHTH AVE.

BODY 27" FROM GROUND LEVEL

AVAILABLE 1898 TO 1916 (KNOWN AS "POPE WAVERLEY" FROM 1904 TO 1908)

1900 Waverley Electromobile

Detroit, Baker, Ohio, Rauch & Lang, Milburn, and Waverley were among the more popular brands of electrics produced during the antique car era. Many of the electric cars built in the years between 1910 and 1920 were tall, comfortable, wooden-bodied closed cars that resembled stagecoaches. However, this turn-of-the century Waverley Electromobile Model 18 was an earlier, simpler-looking affair, built like an open buggy. With a top speed of only sixteen miles per hour, it could barely outrun a man on foot!

Nevertheless, this horseless carriage was advertised in 1900 as "a new departure in electric vehicle construction: light, safe, noiseless, odorless, clean, durable, comfortable, [and] simple in operation."

Surely, the solid rubber tires did nothing to increase the riding comfort. Because such vehicles were driven slowly on city streets, one need not call them "boneshakers."

The Pope automobile-manufacturing conglomerate had control of Waverley before 1904, and the car was known as the Pope Waverley Electric from 1904 to 1908. But, sales were better when the name Waverley was used alone. In 1908, the Indianapolis factory was in receivership and was sold that September to a group of local businessmen. W. B. Cooley, W. C. Johnson, and H. H. Rice were among those purchasers who had already been with the company. When they reorganized, they shortened the name of the car to "Waverley" again and enjoyed a few years of comparative success.

THE FIRST FRANKLIN!

1902 FRANKLIN

RUNABOUT
10 H.P.

1903 SIMILAR,
BUT HAS
WOOD-SPOKED
WHEELS.

BLT. IN SYRACUSE, NEW YORK 1902 TO 1934

HAVE A

HAPPY 4TH OF JULY!

TAP
7-1

FRANKLIN CARS had a WOODEN CHASSIS FRAME!

1.7-LITRE OVERHEAD VALVE AIR-COOLED 4-CYLINDER ENGINE MOUNTED CROSSWISE.

BORE and STROKE 3 1/4" x 3 1/4"

ORIGINAL COST:
$1200.
F.O.B.

News America Syndicate
© News Group Chicago, Inc., 1984

1902 Franklin

Next to the Volkswagen "Beetle," the Franklin was the most successful air-cooled car ever built. The Franklin automobile remained in production from 1902 to 1934, in an era when many other air-cooled cars were introduced only to fail.

The driving force behind the Franklin Automobile Company was its founder, Herbert H. Franklin (1866-1956). H. H. Franklin got a job in a sleigh-building shop at age 19. Later, he went to work for a newspaper, and within six years he was in charge. In 1893, he founded his H. H. Franklin Company in Syracuse, pioneering in the manufacture of small, die-cast metal objects.

Later, Franklin collaborated with John Wilkinson, a young Cornell graduate who had built a four-cylinder air-cooled car. He incorporated many of Wilkinson's ideas in what was to become the early Franklin.

One characteristic long peculiar to the Franklin was its hardwood chassis frame. Franklin persisted with this idea years after other cars had standardized on heavy steel-girder under frames.

The early model Franklins had transverse-mounted (crosswise) engines, generations before this idea became universally popular, in order to provide more legroom in front. The four-cylinder Franklin engine provided greater smoothness than the bucking, noisy, one-cylinder engines found in so many other pioneer cars.

Only thirteen Franklins were built in 1902, but production "soared" to 184 the following year!

Top speed of the illustrated car was about 30 m.p.h. These early Franklins were superior to many horseless carriages, and some have survived to this very day!

Field Enterprises, Inc., 1983

1902 ½ *
HAYNES –
APPERSON
"PHAETON" (A
RUNABOUT WITH TOP)
2 CYLS. (190 CID)
9 H.P.
3-SP. TRANS.
CHAIN DRIVE
ORIG. PRICE
$1500.⁰⁰
BUILT AT KOKOMO,
INDIANA

THANKS TO MRS. L.A.
GERSZEWSKI, SEATTLE,
FOR A PICTURE OF
HER 1902-BUILT
HOUSE.

TAP
10-23

* EARLIER 1902 MODELS
HAD TILLER-CONTROLLED STEERING.

1902 1/2 Haynes-Apperson

This little gas buggy doesn't look like it was ever capable of winning any races or endurance runs, but in 1902 Haynes-Apperson Co. of Kokomo, Indiana, chalked up many such victories!

On April 25, 1902, on Long Island, N.Y., a Haynes-Apperson won a 100-mile nonstop run (the Long Island Endurance Contest), and won another 100-mile nonstop test, "as usual," on May 30.

A Haynes-Apperson won a five-mile speed run at the Fort Erie Track in Buffalo, N.Y. on Sept. 27, and finished first in a ten-mile speed run at the Grosse Pointe Track near Detroit on Oct. 10.

Two Haynes-Apperson cars achieved the highest averages of any American-built car in the 1902 New York-Rochester Endurance Contest, and Haynes-Apperson won a gold medal at the Pan-American Exposition.

In a July 1, 1902, advertisement in *Cycle and Automotive Trade Journal*, Haynes-Apperson pointed with pride that they made "the only automobile that has won every endurance contest in America." Their 1902 slogan: "The most practical automobile in the world."

During 1902, the Apperson Bros., having dissolved their partnership with Elwood Haynes, formed their own Apperson Bros. Automobile Co., which lasted until 1926. During the year of 1904, Haynes dropped the "Apperson" name and continued his line of cars simply as Haynes until 1925.

In 1903, Haynes-Apperson cars were restyled and had steering wheels as standard equipment. Earlier 1902 models resembled the illustrated subject, but had tiller (lever-controlled) steering. So, this is a rare, transitional "1902 1/2!"

1902 Milwaukee Steam

W. H. Starkweather, Herman Pfiel, and W. G. Smith organized the Milwaukee Automobile Co. in December 1899 for the cost of $100,000. They chose to produce a steam car, because steam was an older and more "proven" method of propulsion than gasoline or electricity. Bronze bearings were used instead of ball bearings, because they, too, were "time-proven." But, by June 1902, the company was bankrupt with nearly $42,000 in debts. In July 1902, its assets were auctioned off.

Interestingly enough, this was not the only early automobile company to produce a "Milwaukee" car in that city. Back in 1878, a "Milwaukee Steamer" had been built in Sun Prairie to be entered in a State of Wisconsin contest. The contest was held in order to determine a practical method of horseless transportation other than railroads, which were already well established.

There was also a Milwaukee Automobile and Brass Specialty Company at Broadway, south of Biddle St. in Milwaukee (1901-1902), which was established for only $15,000 in September 1901. A few runabouts, phaetons, and delivery wagons were built before the company folded for lack of finances. These cars were also sold under the name of Rosenbauer (one of the founders) for a brief time.

Another "Milwaukee" car was renamed the Ideal (1902-1903). Another was renamed Eagle (1906). There were others built by Milwaukee-named and/or Milwaukee-based auto manufacturers in the early years of the 20th century.

BUILT BY CREST MANUFACTURING COMPANY, CAMBRIDGE, MASS. (1900-1905)
AIR-COOLED 1-CYLINDER, 5-H.P. ENGINE
UP TO 30 MILES PER HR., 150 MILES ON TANKFUL OF GAS.

CAN BE STARTED FROM THE DRIVER'S SEAT!

© News America Syndicate, 1985

SHAFT DRIVE

1903

CRESTMOBILE

$750.

MODEL "D" 2-PASSENGER RUNABOUT

1903 Crestmobile

Originally known as the Crest, the Crestmobile was built in Cambridge, Mass. (with a branch plant at Dorchester, Mass.), starting in 1901. Early models were typical "horseless carriages," lacking the hood in front which graces the illustrated '03 model. At first, De Dion engines were used, but later Crestmobile developed an engine of its own design.

In addition to the Model D seen here, there were also the smaller 3 1/2-horsepower, 57-inch wheelbase Model C Runabout and Model F Touring in 1903, but these two were not continued in 1904.

In 1904-1905, the Model D continued, but with center-column steering, a longer (76-inch) wheelbase, and 8 1/2 horsepower. By the end of 1903, about 1,000 Crestmobiles had been built, no puny figure for those early days!

Crestmobile stuck with one-cylinder engines, though this may have led to its decline; many rivals offered two- or four-cylinder engines. In 1905, Alden-Sampson Manufacturing Co., a Pittsfield, Mass. builder of commercial vehicles, absorbed Crest Manufacturing Co. The branch plant at Dorchester was sold to Hub Motor Car Exchange, which then built the Dorchester in 1906 and the Hub in 1907.

Amazingly, several Crestmobiles have survived through the years, and they are in the hands of collectors. Moreover, a few Crestmobiles were exported and sold in England by O'Halloran Brothers. There, they were known as "OHB" cars, in reference to their distributor.

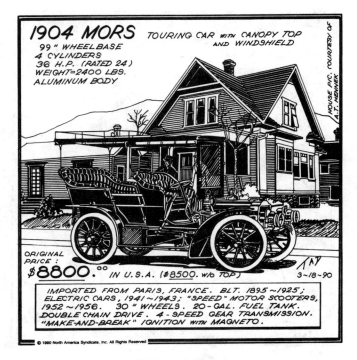

1904 MORS TOURING CAR with CANOPY TOP AND WINDSHIELD
99" WHEELBASE
4 CYLINDERS
36 H.P. (RATED 24)
WEIGHT=2400 LBS.
ALUMINUM BODY

HOUSE PIC. COURTESY OF A.T. HENNEK

ORIGINAL PRICE :
$8800.⁰⁰ IN U.S.A. ($8500. w/o TOP)
3~18~90

IMPORTED FROM PARIS, FRANCE. BLT. 1895~1925; ELECTRIC CARS, 1941~1943; "SPEED" MOTOR SCOOTERS, 1952~1956. 30" WHEELS. 20-GAL. FUEL TANK. DOUBLE CHAIN DRIVE. 4-SPEED GEAR TRANSMISSION. "MAKE-AND-BREAK" IGNITION with MAGNETO.

1904 Mors

Unless you happen to be an avid antique-car buff, it's likely that you've never heard of the Mors automobile (illustrated). However, it was a fairly popular import from France in the early years of this century.

But, it certainly was not cheap: The $8,800+ purchase price would buy a fine, new twelve-room house back then! As a matter of fact, the modest house you see in the background of this picture would probably have sold, then, for only a third to a fourth of the cost of a new Mors!

Although a few light cars like the Oldsmobile, the Brush, the Maxwell, etc. were popular in the pre-1910 era, it was Henry Ford's famous Model T that brought prices way down and helped to put most of America on wheels by the 1920s. During the 1920s, Ford's cheapest Model Ts (roadsters, without electric starters) were available, new, for as little as $290!

Notice the surrey-like, rigid "canopy top" on this Mors. The canopy top was installed on a number of 1904 touring cars, but since the sides and rear of the body were still open to the elements, this type could not be considered a truly "closed" car.

Before the mid-1920s—with few exceptions—fully closed cars were usually more expensive than open models. Most families and individuals purchased more affordable touring cars and roadsters. Later in the 'teens, glassed-in superstructures were available for installation on open cars, making them far more comfortable in bad weather. One such addition was the old "California Top."

1904 PIERCE STANHOPE
ORIGINAL PRICE:
$1200.
(TOP,
$100. EXTRA)

© News America Syndicate, 1986

TAP
5-11

1-CYL. WATER-COOLED ENGINE
8 H.P.   2-SPEED PLANETARY TRANS.
70" WHEELBASE   WT.=1200 lbs.
5 1/2-GAL. FUEL TANK
MFD. BY GEO. N. PIERCE CO. (LATER PIERCE-ARROW)
BUFFALO, N.Y.   (1901-1938)

VICTORIAN
1896-STYLE
HOUSE SHOWN
IN BACKGROUND.

1904 Pierce

Many readers have heard of the once-famous Pierce-Arrow, a luxury car manufactured until 1938. From 1914 on, most Pierce-Arrows were easily identifiable by their unusual headlights, which were sunken into the front fenders (though a few were sold after that time with conventional, bracket-mounted headlights—on special order).

Back in the early 1900s, the Pierce-Arrow name was yet to come, and this early model was, simply, the Pierce (though some other models were known as the "Arrow" or as the "Great Arrow").

The "Stanhope" name applied to the horseless carriage body with its then-stylish "Victoria" buggy top. A folding seat at the very front offered extra passenger space, but foolishly blocked the driver's view!

The standard color was a deep "Quaker Green." Four passengers could be carried (including driver), but when fully loaded, the little one-cylinder engine was held back. How fast would such an early automobile go? Perhaps it would get up to 30 to 35 m.p.h., if the driver was alone. With passengers, 15 to 25 m.p.h. would be more like it. In 1904, the horse still dominated America's byroads, and most horseless carriage trips were short local ones because mechanical problems were frequent. Also, tire trouble was an incessant problem, not to mention the primitive condition of inter-city roads.

This 1904 Pierce is not to be confused with the Pierce Steamer (West Virginia, 1895); the Pierce Electric (New Jersey, 1900-1904); or the Pierce Racine (Wisconsin, 1904-1911). These other enterprises were unrelated to Pierce-Arrow.

HAPPY NEW YEAR!

1904 STEVENS-DURYEA MODEL "L"

(C) Field Enterprises, Inc. 1983

TUBULAR FRAME AND WOOD BODY

69" WHEELBASE

28 x 3

2 CYLS.
7 H.P.
CHAIN DRIVE
WT.: 1350 lbs.
6-GALLON GAS TANK

$1300.
(WITH TOP)
WATER-COOLED
HORIZONTAL CYLINDERS.
JUMP-SPARK IGNITION.

TAP 1-2-83

MFD. BY J. STEVENS ARM and TOOL CO., CHICOPEE FALLS, MASS. (1902-1927)

1904 Stevens-Duryea

Charles E. Duryea and his brother Frank (J. Frank) Duryea planned and built one of America's pioneer automobiles, beginning in 1892. Though The Duryea car went into production and continued until 1917, younger brother Frank departed from the original company (Duryea Motor Wagon Co.; Duryea Power Co.) and in 1900 organized the Hampden Automobile and Launch Company in Springfield, Mass. His plan was to build a Hampden car, but, instead, in a year he joined with the J. Stevens Arms and Tool Co. to build the new Stevens-Duryea automobile. The factory where these cars were built was formerly the factory for the Overman car, of 1895 to 1898, in Chicopee Falls, Mass.

After 1906, the company name was changed to the Stevens-Duryea Co., and during the early 1920s, it became Stevens-Duryea Motors, Inc.

The illustrated 1904 Model L had a concealable folding front seat (shown in "open" position) for additional passengers. Fifty dollars could be reduced from the car's price if purchased without the folding, Victoria buggy-type top. Maroon was the most typical color of this Model L.

Tillers, rather than steering wheels, were often used to steer these early automobiles. The manufacturer oddly described the Model L Stevens-Duryea steering control as "one spoke of wheel steerer."

J. Frank Duryea lived until 1967. In his later years, he was acclaimed by many auto historians, finally getting the credit he deserved for having done much of the work behind the scenes, when his elder brother was getting most of the attention.

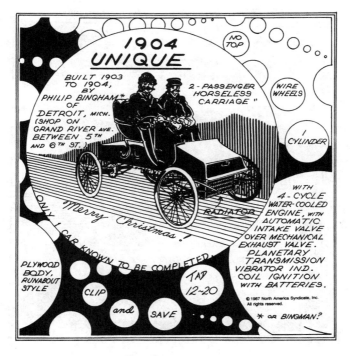

1904 Unique

For the thousands of different makes and models of cars and trucks that have been manufactured since the 1890s, there are still many thousands more which "never made it." Some, like this 1904 Unique, were actually built—though not duplicated. And, others were only dreams and plans. Some were simply stock promotion schemes that existed only on paper!

Philip Bingham (some say Bingman) built this lone Unique car between 1903 and 1904 at his shop in Detroit. His son helped him build it. And, in the 1970s, the builder's grandson, Thomas, worked in Chrysler Corporation's Styling Office. It was Thomas Bingham who brought this rare antique car to light once again through an old photograph and notes in his possession. F. Donald Butler wrote about it in the September 1974 newsletter of the *Society of Automotive Historians*.

Spare parts were reportedly made for the Unique car, but only the one car was completed and used.

1904 YALE "D"

PRICE = $1800.⁰⁰

MOST "CLOSED" CARS OF 1904 HAD A "CANOPY TOP" OF THIS TYPE.

2 CYLINDERS HORIZONTALLY-OPPOSED 16 HP

WT. 1850 LBS.

84" W.B.

WOOD BODY

PRODUCED BY THE KIRK MFG. CO., TOLEDO, OHIO (1902~1906)

"JUMP-SPARK" IGNITION WITH 2 SETS OF BATTERIES

© 1988 North America Syndicate, Inc. All rights reserved.

AN "AUTO ALBUM" SAFETY HINT :

WHEN THERE IS A STRONG GLARE FROM THE SUN (ESPECIALLY AT SUNRISE OR SUNSET,) MAKE SURE YOUR WINDSHIELD IS CLEAN – – – SO YOU WILL NOTICE PEDESTRIANS OR APPROACHING CARS.

TAP 8·14

CHAIN DRIVE, PLANETARY TRANSMISSION 2 SPEED

1904 Yale

There have been three different companies in the U.S.A. that have used the Yale name on cars produced from 1900 to 1918. The Kirk Mfg. Co. of 946 Oakwood Ave., Toledo, Ohio was the second. They built the car shown here.

The Kirk Mfg. Co. originally built bicycles and other products. Starting in the summer of 1902, they offered automobiles as well. Nearly all parts for the Yale car were built by its manufacturer, except for the differential and the oiler.

The illustrated 1904 model was priced $200 less ($1,600) without the rigid top (though some 1904 Yale advertisements give $1,500 as the base price). The tonneau (rear seat) section was detachable. One could change it from a touring car to a single-seat runabout and back to a touring car again in a fairly simple operation. The engine was water-cooled, and the fuel tank held twelve gallons of gasoline. There were "two brakes on differential gear, one on rear wheels." The standard color was a deep blue. Though the body was of wood, the chassis frame was made of angle steel. The Yale was advertised in 1904 as "a car with the doubt and the jar left out."

Kirk was a part of a three-company merger that resulted in the Consolidated Manufacturing Company. At the end of 1905, the new amalgamated firm announced that it was "too busy" manufacturing Yale and Snell bicycles, and other goods, to continue their line of autos. Consolidated slipped into bankruptcy in May of 1906.

"A CHICAGO CAR FOR CHICAGO PEOPLE"

JUMP SPARK IGNITION (12 BATTERIES)
SHAFT DRIVE WITH 3-SP. SLIDING-GEAR TRANS.

1905 BANKER

4 CYLS. (4 1/4" × 5") CAST IN PAIRS
25 TO 30 H.P.   TOP SPEED = 50
100" WHEELBASE   WEIGHT = 2000 lbs.
16-GALLON COPPER FUEL TANK

News America Syndicate
© News Group Chicago, Inc., 1984

$2250.
(WITH WOOD BODY)

9-16

BUILT (AND SOLD DIRECT TO BUYERS) BY THE
A.C. BANKER CO., CHICAGO (MFD. 1905 ONLY)
(NO DEALERSHIP REPRESENTATION)

1900s

1905 Banker

Can a car be sold successfully with no dealers to represent it? Officials of the A. C. Banker Co. of Chicago thought this would be possible. They hoped to eliminate the "middle man" by selling direct from factory to buyer. But, their idea didn't work. The Banker car was on the market for only one year (1905).

Banker did publish a four-page 1905 brochure, and it offered three models: the illustrated touring car with wood body; a $2,500 aluminum-bodied model with cape top; and a $3,000 limousine. A one-year guarantee was available for $5 per month.

The upholstery was hard buffed leather over "curled hair," and all exposed metallic parts were made of polished brass.

The standard paint scheme was a blue body with yellow gear, but other colors could be ordered if preferred.

Contracting band brakes on rear wheels were controlled by a side lever. There was also a band brake on the transmission shaft, and the application of either brake automatically withdrew the clutch. This wasn't so sensible for going down long grades, when the additional braking power of the engine would have helped.

The Banker car carried a tool set, tire repair kit and pump, two oil lamps, and two acetylene lamps, as well as a tail light.

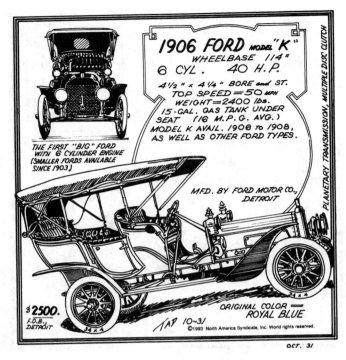

1906 FORD MODEL "K"
WHEELBASE 114"
6 CYL. 40 H.P.
4½" x 4¼" BORE and ST.
TOP SPEED = 50 MPH
WEIGHT = 2400 lbs.
15-GAL. GAS TANK UNDER
SEAT (16 M.P.G. AVG.)
MODEL K AVAIL. 1906 to 1908,
AS WELL AS OTHER FORD TYPES.

THE FIRST "BIG" FORD
WITH 6 CYLINDER ENGINE
(SMALLER FORDS AVAILABLE
SINCE 1903)

MFD. BY FORD MOTOR CO.,
DETROIT

PLANETARY TRANSMISSION, MULTIPLE DISC CLUTCH

$2500.
F.O.B.,
DETROIT

ORIGINAL COLOR =
ROYAL BLUE

TAP 10-31
©1993 North America Syndicate, Inc. World rights reserved.

OCT. 31

1906 Ford Model K

Ford's four-cylinder Model T (late 1908 to early 1927) was such a long-running series, so popular, and so lastingly remembered that many people think of it as Ford's first car. However, Ford produced and sold a variety of other models between 1903 and 1908—mostly small two- and four-cylinder cars, as well as the very large six-cylinder Model K (illustrated).

What specific models did Ford offer in the early 1900s? First, there was the initial Model A (not the later successor to the Model T). This pioneer Model A series was a small two-cylinder horseless carriage, available in 1903 and 1904.

The first Model B was offered 1904 to 1905 (four cylinder). The Model C was also available 1904 to 1905, but was a smaller, two-cylinder car. In 1905, there was a Model E two-cylinder Ford delivery truck (very rare!). Also, new for 1905 was the Model F (two-cylinder, also available in 1906). The Model N had four cylinders and was available from 1906 to 1908 (as was the illustrated Model K). There was a four-cylinder Model R in 1907 and a four-cylinder Model S (1907-1908).

Rare experimental Fords included an air-cooled four-cylinder model in 1904 (probably a Model D), and the six-cylinder Model J, circa 1910.

A special six-cylinder Model T was also built for Henry Ford's son, Edsel.

1907 Apperson "Jack Rabbit"

The Apperson Jack Rabbit was several years ahead of its time. A real sports car, in an era of primitive and clumsy "horseless carriages," the Jack Rabbit was much like the Stutz Bearcat, the Mercer Raceabout, and other such speedsters of the 1911-1915 period.

"In presenting the Jack Rabbit," the manufacturer stated, "we are catering to that limited class of owners who want a car that can be put to any service—racing or touring."

The manufacturer promised that "only 15 cars of this type will be built for 1907," thus insuring its exclusiveness. Construction was of "Krupp nickel steel throughout," and the transmission was four-speed. Chain drive was still in vogue on many cars of 1907.

The '07 model was the first Jack Rabbit. A full racing version was also offered, for $15,000—an unheard-of price back then.

In the early 'teens, Jack Rabbit became a model series of Apperson, also encompassing other body types (touring, coupe, town car, etc.). The Jack Rabbit series continued through 1913.

Notice the "rabbit-eared" Oliver typewriter in the illustration. Like the Apperson Jack Rabbit, this, too, has come to be a valuable collector's piece. Some of these Oliver typewriters—like one I bought secondhand some years ago—came in a metal carrying-case that resembled a gigantic lunch box.

I don't know the current value of an Oliver typewriter, but according to various books, an original Apperson Jack Rabbit, in excellent condition, would bring over $40,000.

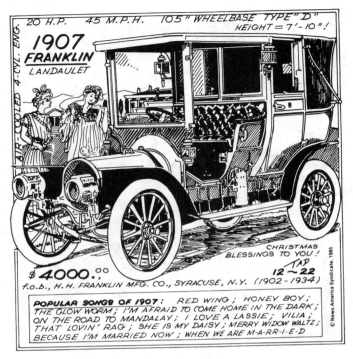

20 H.P.   45 M.P.H.   105" WHEELBASE TYPE "D"
HEIGHT = 7'-10"!

AIR-COOLED 4-CYL. ENG.

1907
FRANKLIN
LANDAULET

CHRISTMAS
BLESSINGS TO YOU!
TAD
12~22

$4000.°°
f.o.b., H.H. FRANKLIN MFG. CO., SYRACUSE, N.Y. (1902-1934)

POPULAR SONGS OF 1907:   RED WING ; HONEY BOY ;
THE GLOW WORM ; I'M AFRAID TO COME HOME IN THE DARK ;
ON THE ROAD TO MANDALAY ; I LOVE A LASSIE ; VILIA ;
THAT LOVIN' RAG ; SHE IS MY DAISY ; MERRY WIDOW WALTZ ;
BECAUSE I'M MARRIED NOW ; WHEN WE ARE M-A-RR-I-E-D

1907 Franklin

This Franklin Type D Laudaulet for 1907 had a convertible rear quarter section that could be folded down. Also, the windshield slid up into the roof over the driver's seat.

Franklin's claim to fame, in addition to an overhead-valve, air-cooled engine, was its light weight for a car its size. The Model D touring car, for example, weighed only 1,900 lbs. Considerable weight was saved by using a wooden (Ash) chassis frame instead of the usual cast-iron or steel type. The wooden frame was flexible, and it was advertised as "jarless." It was claimed that Franklin's light weight cut the usual fuel cost and tire cost "in half!"

In a 1906 endurance run, a Franklin traveled from San Francisco to New York in fifteen days, two hours, and twelve minutes, over a circuitous route that totaled about 4,000 miles!

Though an earlier "horseless carriage" type was continued to 1906, the uniquely-styled, round-radiator Franklin was offered, in various models, from 1905 to 1910. In 1911, Franklin was restyled with a sloping front like that of the French Renault (and a few others). Air-cooled, Franklin never had a genuine radiator as such, though for many years it did use a cooling fan.

The illustrated 1907 Landaulet is rare! The only one left that I know of was restored in 1975, after having been stored in the East in two separate halves (body and chassis) by a pair of co-owners who'd had a disagreement.

BY KLINK MOTOR CAR MFG. CO., DANSVILLE, N.Y. (1907~1910)

4 CYL. CONTINENTAL ENGINE "RENAULT-TYPE"

1907 Klink

MODEL "30"
ROADSTER

$2000.
WEIGHT = 1950 LBS.
108" WHEELBASE

RARE!!
ONLY 20 BELIEVED TO HAVE BEEN BLT. (RDSTRS. and TOUR. CARS), AND EACH CAR TOOK 6 WEEKS TO BUILD!

30 H.P.

THE 2 FINAL 1910 MODELS (6 CYL.) WERE UNSOLD
AND REMAINED IN
STORAGE AT KLINK
PHOTO STUDIO UNTIL
THEY WERE SCRAPPED
IN 1934!

HELPFUL DETAILS THANKS TO
JOSEPH C. KLINK, VACAVILLE, CALIF. and
ROBERT M. KLINK, DAYTON, OHIO.

TAP 6·7

1907 Klink

John F. Klink, a commercial photographer, in partnership with Charles Day, founded the Klink Motor Car Manufacturing Co. in March 1907. There were fifteen workers at the small Klink factory, with Charles Day as general superintendent. Shop foreman was Harvey Toms, a local bicycle repairman who had custom built a car for John Klink in 1906.

In May 1907, the first Klink automobile, a touring car, was completed. Initial cars were fours, but in 1909 a six-cylinder model was introduced.

During 1909, Charles Day quit the company after a dispute with John Klink. Day had plans to manufacture another car under his own name, but that never came to pass.

Short of working capital and new orders, John Klink shut down his factory in September 1909. Early in 1910, he re-hired two former employees to build two final Klink cars from leftover parts. Unable to sell his two 1910 models, Klink returned to photography and kept the pair of unsold, unused $2,000 Klink cars in a building behind his studio. They may have gathered dust, but the two rare old cars were still "new" when they were unceremoniously hauled off for scrap in 1934.

As for the illustrated 1907 roadster, this was the second car produced by Klink's company. Since there were various sizes and models of 1907-1910 Klink autos, and only about twenty units produced in all, few were alike.

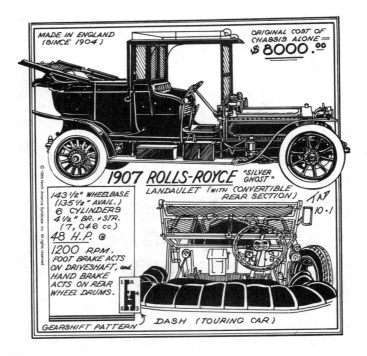

MADE IN ENGLAND
(SINCE 1904)

ORIGINAL COST OF
CHASSIS ALONE =
$8000.⁰⁰

1907 ROLLS-ROYCE "SILVER GHOST"
LANDAULET (WITH CONVERTIBLE REAR SECTION)

143 1/2" WHEELBASE
(135 1/2" AVAIL.)
6 CYLINDERS
4 1/2" BR. + STR.
(7,046 cc)
48 H.P. @
1200 RPM.
FOOT BRAKE ACTS
ON DRIVESHAFT, and
HAND BRAKE
ACTS ON REAR
WHEEL DRUMS.

TAP
10·1

GEARSHIFT PATTERN

DASH (TOURING CAR)

1907 Rolls-Royce

Entering the world market as a small but exceptionally fine car in 1904-1905, the Rolls-Royce soon grew to mammoth proportions as the Silver Ghost models were introduced for 1907.

Rolls-Royce soon earned its self-proclaimed title of "The best car in the world." The quality was impeccable. Legends abounded that no Rolls-Royce has ever worn out, and even that Rolls-Royces' hoods were sealed because one never needed to look at the engine. These were sheer exaggerations, but they added to the Rolls-Royce mystique. Few were ever scrapped. Most Rolls-Royce automobiles ever built are either in current use or in collections and museums.

In November 1906, a polished 1907 Silver Ghost chassis was placed on exhibit at England's annual Olympia Motor Show. It won much admiration for its fine workmanship, excellence of materials, and advanced mechanical features. The six-cylinder engine was cast in two blocks of three cylinders each. Each block had its own manifold (a dual exhaust system). The Silver Ghost got its name for its near-silent operation and the silver-plated metal parts and silver-aluminum body color of some examples.

The Landaulet (illustrated) body style is an interesting one—the opposite of a town car, which had closed rear quarters and open or convertible chauffeur's compartment. In a Landaulet, the passengers were the ones who could enjoy the sunshine if they so pleased. Many early limousines and Landaulets had open sides in the chauffeur's compartment, so at times the driver got a very windy ride!

1907 STUDEBAKER ELECTRIC MFD. BY STUDEBAKER AUTOMOBILE CO., SOUTH BEND, INDIANA $1910. f.o.b.

ALSO AVAIL.: ELECTRIC TRUCKS, AND MODEL F and G 4-CYL. GASOLINE CARS.

CLIP and SAVE

1907

ABOUT 18 M.P.H.

TAD 6-3

© News Group Chicago, Inc., 1984

(ILLUSTR.) VARIOUS STUDEBAKER ELECTRIC CARS of 1907:
22-A RUNABOUT = $1110.; 22-B STANHOPE = $1250.; 13-A HIGH-SPEED STANHOPE = $1650.; 16-A VICTORIA-PHAETON = $1750.; 20 SURREY = $2800.; 21 STATION WAGON = $3500.; 2006-E 14-PASSENGER OMNIBUS = $3000.

1907 Studebaker Electric

Many Americans under twenty-five years of age have never heard of a Studebaker car, since Studebakers have not been produced since 1966. Yet, there are many fiercely loyal Studebaker fans throughout the world that still drive their favorite cars and declare that they'd "rather fix than switch."

Before bowing out of the automotive market in '66, Studebaker enjoyed the honor of being the oldest company in the business (established 1852), though their early products were wheelbarrows and horse-drawn vehicles. It was in 1902 that Studebaker's first horseless carriages were produced. They were electrics, joined in 1904 by Studebaker's new gasoline-powered machines. The Studebaker electrics continued to 1912. Contrary to the stereotyped idea, early electric cars were not all closed models shaped like boxy stagecoaches and driven only by rich little old ladies. There were open models, like the illustrated "Runabout," resembling some of the "gas buggies" of their day.

In *Harper's Magazine* (March 1907), Studebaker advertised that, "Mechanically, the Studebaker is the most successful type of electric car. Its operation is within a child's understanding." Also, according to the ad, the weight of the batteries was distributed upon both pairs of springs, making the ride superior to electric cars that suspended the batteries below the springs.

Studebaker's 1907 sales slogan: "The automobile with a reputation behind it." John Studebaker once coined a wise motto: "Always Give More Than You Promise."

Studebaker electrics have always been scarce, and most early surviving Studebakers are the gasoline-powered types.

1908 Oldsmobile Model M

Later in 1908, Oldsmobile became a part of the brand new General Motors empire, which was pulled together by Billy Durant. However, the illustrated car is an early 1908 model, built in November 1907. This car does not have the square cowl lanterns found on many 1908 Oldsmobiles.

This Model M touring car was sometimes known as the "Palace Touring Car." In addition to this model, the 1908 Oldsmobile line also included the "M. R." Flying Roadster ($2,750); the "M" Limousine ($3,800); the "M" Landaulet ($4,000); and the new "Z" Sixty touring car ($4,200), a 6-cylinder model, with a big 130-inch wheelbase.

Oldsmobile production in 1908 was low with 1,055 cars built and sold. In 1907, Oldsmobile produced 1,200 cars; 1,600 were built and sold in 1906; 6,500 in 1905; and 5,508 in 1904—the year Oldsmobile had been America's top seller.

The situation improved in 1909, under General Motors' direction, when 6,575 Oldsmobiles were built and sold. A few leaner years followed until 1915 (7,696 sold) and 1916 (10,507 sold). In August 1915, Oldsmobile's first V-8 engines were available. Surprisingly, V-8 powered Oldsmobile series were available from the 1916 to the 1923 model years—which may surprise many who thought Olds only made fours and sixes in that era. A Viking V-8 automobile was marketed by GM's Oldsmobile Division in 1929 and early 1930. But, Oldsmobile's first truly successful V-8 models were the "88" and "98" series, which began in 1949.

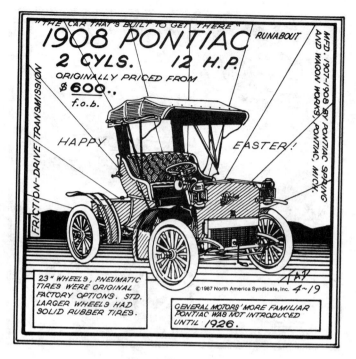

"THE CAR THAT'S BUILT TO GET THERE"

1908 PONTIAC RUNABOUT

2 CYLS. 12 H.P.

ORIGINALLY PRICED FROM $600.. f.o.b.

MFD. 1907-1908 BY PONTIAC SPRING AND WAGON WORKS, PONTIAC, MICH.

FRICTION-DRIVE TRANSMISSION

HAPPY EASTER!

23" WHEELS, PNEUMATIC TIRES WERE ORIGINAL FACTORY OPTIONS. STD. LARGER WHEELS HAD SOLID RUBBER TIRES.

© 1987 North America Syndicate, Inc. 4~19

GENERAL MOTORS' MORE FAMILIAR PONTIAC WAS NOT INTRODUCED UNTIL 1926.

1908 Pontiac

There were other cars bearing the Pontiac name long before the familiar General Motors version made its bow in 1926. In 1906, there had been a Pontiac Motor Co. in Pontiac, Mich. In 1913, a Pontiac Motor Car Co. was organized in the same city. Stock was reportedly issued, but no cars were known to have been built. In 1915, there was a Pontiac Chassis Co., also in Pontiac, Mich. Their initial product: a 106-inch wheelbase chassis fitted with a four-cylinder Perkins gasoline engine. No body was included.

A more successful enterprise was the Pontiac of 1908, built by the Pontiac Spring and Wagon Works (incorporated 1899). This company took over the manufacture of the Rapid truck in 1905, and in 1907 it decided to add cars to their line.

By late 1908, about thirty to forty Pontiac buggy-like autos had been built. But, in November of that year, the founders (Albert G. North and Harry G. Hamilton) sold out to the Motorcar Company of Detroit, builder of the more successful Cartercar.

Scarce as they had been from the start, at least four 1908 Pontiacs were known still to exist in the 1980s. One has been beautifully restored and featured in the November-December 1984 issue of *Antique Automobile* magazine. (Note: An odd feature of at least one of these remaining 1908 Pontiacs is a spike at the rear, which can be lowered so that the sharp tip digs into the ground and prevents the car from rolling backward on a hill!)

1909 Hamilton

Here's a rare antique car, one that few have ever heard of. It's the 1909 Hamilton, a two-cylinder, air-cooled vehicle with solid tires and an open-sided touring-car body. A windshield was not included.

We have automotive historian Arch Brown to thank for taking several good photos of what may be the only remaining example of a 1909 Hamilton and for publishing the photos, along with an interesting article, in *Cars & Parts* magazine.

The 1909 Hamilton was also described in the informative book *Standard Catalog of American Cars 1805-1942* (Krause Publications, 1985), which reports only twenty-five such Hamilton/Columbia motor buggies built.

The large wooden wheels and solid rubber tires made this car adaptable for backcountry use on small farms.

However, the Hamilton wasn't a very reliable machine. Ford's soon-to-become-famous Model T was also on the market in 1909; it was a much better engineered car for only a few dollars more.

Notice that the Hamilton has right-hand drive, as did many of the early horseless carriages. By the early 1910s, most American cars had switched to left-hand drive. But, a few makes continued with right-hand drive until the early 1920s.

The car shown here was originally purchased by a member of the Hershey family (famous for manufacturing chocolate). Later, the car went to a museum in Fairfax, Va. Then, in 1976, it was purchased by a collector in California who repainted it in its original colors of French Gray body, black fenders, and Automobile Red wheels and trim.

THE TALL RADIATOR FILLER SPOUT IDENTIFIES EARLY HUPMOBILES.

4 CYL. 16.9 TO 20 H.P. 86" W.B.
SLIDING-GEAR TRANSMISSION (2-SP.)
2-WHEEL MECHANICAL BRAKES

BOSHCH MAGNETO. STARTING CAR REQUIRED
HAND-CRANKING!

$750.00
(INCLUDING 3 OIL LAMPS,
BULB HORN
AND TOOLS)

1909
MODEL 20
Hupmobile

HUPP MOTOR CAR CO., DETROIT
(1909 — 1940)

1, 618 HUPMOBILES SOLD IN 1909; 5,340 IN 1910.

1909 Hupmobile

Robert Craig Hupp was the founder of the Hupp Motor Car Co. and producer of the Hupmobile. The first Model 20 Runabout (illustrated) was initially displayed at the Detroit Automobile Show in February 1909, and it went into regular production the following month. Until November 1910, no other Hupmobile body style, save this Runabout, was available—allowing the manufacturer to concentrate on one basic model and perfect it.

The 1909 Hupmobile won considerable acclaim in many events. It earned cups and perfect scores in the Baltimore and Detroit reliability and endurance runs. It "carried off the palm" in the Buffalo fuel economy contest. It won the six-hour race at Brighton Beach, and it did a mile in fifty-eight seconds at the Los Angeles Motordrome! In San Francisco, it made the fastest time and won a perfect score in the "200-mile Annual Mud Plug." It climbed to 9,000-foot elevations in the Colorado Rockies, was the first car to negotiate Stone Mountain in Georgia, and won other prizes and accolades in various events too numerous to mention here!

Proof of the quality lies is the fact that many 1909 and 1910 Hupmobile Runabouts have survived and are now in the hands of collectors, while most other 1909 cars are just "history."

It may surprise you to realize that in a 1986 price guide, the value of this car ranged from $2,000 for a well-worn specimen to $14,000 for a fully restored or perfect original specimen.

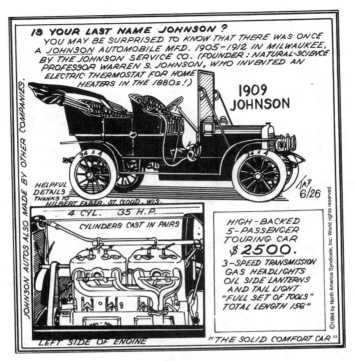

IS YOUR LAST NAME JOHNSON ?
YOU MAY BE SURPRISED TO KNOW THAT THERE WAS ONCE
A JOHNSON AUTOMOBILE MFD. 1905-1912 IN MILWAUKEE,
BY THE JOHNSON SERVICE CO. (FOUNDER : NATURAL-SCIENCE
PROFESSOR WARREN S. JOHNSON, WHO INVENTED AN
ELECTRIC THERMOSTAT FOR HOME
HEATERS IN THE 1880s !)

1909 JOHNSON

JOHNSON AUTOS ALSO MADE BY OTHER COMPANIES.

HELPFUL DETAILS THANKS TO HILBERT FABER, ST. CLOUD, WIS.

TAP 6/26

© 1994 by North America Syndicate, Inc. World rights reserved.

4 CYL. 35 H.P.
CYLINDERS CAST IN PAIRS

HIGH-BACKED
5-PASSENGER
TOURING CAR
$2500.
3-SPEED TRANSMISSION
GAS HEADLIGHTS
OIL SIDE LANTERNS
AND TAIL LIGHT
"FULL SET OF TOOLS"
TOTAL LENGTH 156"

LEFT SIDE OF ENGINE

"THE SOLID COMFORT CAR"

1909 Johnson

Milwaukee's Johnson Service Co. was the most successful of the various Johnson automotive ventures, producing cars from 1905 to 1912. This company built steam-powered automobiles as well as a line of gasoline cars (as illustrated). The 1909 selection included a variety of touring cars, runabouts, and even a limousine with fully enclosed rear quarters. Johnson also built a few trucks.

The 1909 Johnson catalog assured the reader, "The Johnson car is not made in the same way as those which were advertised to be sold in thousands. We do not care for the trade of thousands, but for a fair number of good people who want first-class cars. We make our cars in SERIES and not in FLOODS."

Johnson Service Co. claimed that they could make ongoing improvements in their line of cars as production continued. The Johnson catalog pointed out that competing makes of cars, 1909 models prematurely introduced in the summer of 1908, would have to have been planned at least a year before that time—in the summer of 1907.

Moreover, Johnson Service Co. "didn't waste money on advertising, on sponsoring races, or in building test tracks, etc., as some manufacturers did." These savings could be passed along to the customer.

But, the 1909 Johnson catalog was another story. It was an extremely long-winded document with 25 pages of self-complimentary prose before the cars were even illustrated!

The founder, Professor Warren S. Johnson, died on December 4, 1911, and without his leadership the company simply collapsed.

1909 PATERSON MOTOR BUGGY
MODEL 14

PLANETARY TRANSMISSION

INTRO. LATE IN 1908, THE 1909 PATERSON WAS A PRIMITIVE HIGH-WHEELED HORSELESS CARRIAGE, AS ILLUSTRATED. 64 OF THIS TYPE BUILT.

DOUBLE-CHAIN DRIVE

TILLER-CONTROL STEERING

2 CYL. AIR-COOLED ENGINE

WOOD-SPOKED BUGGY WHEELS, WITH SOLID RUBBER TIRES. 80" WHEELBASE

BY W.A. PATERSON CO. FLINT, MICHIGAN 1908 ~ 1923
(4 CYL. 1910 MODEL WAS A MORE CONVENTIONAL TYPE.)

14 HORSEPOWER

10~4

1909 Paterson Motor Buggy

Though the illustrated car looks as though it dates to the turn of the century, it's actually one of the sixty-four Model 14 motor buggies built in late 1908 and in 1909 by the W. A. Paterson Company of Flint, Mich. Flint is better known today as the home of the Buick automobile (since Buick's second year in 1904).

W. A. Paterson established a carriage-building business in Flint in 1869, when he was 31 years of age. His first production automobiles were of the illustrated type. By 1909, most other cars already came with much smaller wheels and pneumatic tires, runabout or touring car bodies, an engine, hood and radiator out front, and four fenders and a running board. So, in 1910, Paterson introduced a conventional-style touring car and discontinued the motor buggies as well as its line of horse-drawn vehicles.

From 1910 to 1916, four-cylinder models were produced. Starting in 1915, Paterson introduced a six. Paterson sedans joined the line in 1918, and coupes joined in 1920 (following the discontinuation of the Paterson roadster after 1919). Dependable Continental engines were used.

W. A. Paterson passed on in 1921. His son and an associate had difficulty in holding the business together because of the 1920-1922 recession. In July 1923, they sold out to Dallas Winslow, a prominent Dodge Bros. automobile dealer in Flint. Winslow at first had thoughts of having the Paterson redesigned and continued. But, he changed his mind. Concentrating on his prosperous Dodge dealership seemed the most sensible thing to do.

"Everyman's Car"
— — — SALES SLOGAN FOR THE

MODEL "D"

1910 BRUSH

ORIGINAL f.o.b. PRICE : $485.00

2-SPEED GEAR TRANS.

1 CYLINDER   10 H.P.

ROAD SPEED = 27 MILES PER HOUR (35 M.P.H. POSSIBLE)

DOUBLE CHAIN DRIVE

ORIGINAL COLOR SCHEME = MAROON -AND- BLACK

HELPFUL DATA THANKS TO BOB McCONNELL, PACIFIC GROVE, CALIF.

80 INCH W.B.

MFD. BY THE BRUSH RUNABOUT CO. 212 BALTIMORE AVE., DETROIT (1907 ~ 1911)   (REPL. BY 1912 LIBERTY-BRUSH)

© 1993 North America Syndicate, Inc. World rights reserved.

1910 Brush

Some time ago, Bob McConnell, of Pacific Grove, Calif., offered me some pieces of old, unused wallpaper that featured various old cars. It was a pleasant surprise to discover that the wallpaper segments contained reprints of original picture-and-text advertisements for various old cars! The wallpaper pieces contained a much-detailed and lengthy ad for a 1910 Brush.

The Brush was a popular small car in 1910, selling for under $500. During the first decade of the 20th century, some cars still resembled buggies. In comparison, the Brush had a sporty appearance!

The Brush people claimed their one-cylinder engine was as smooth running as a four, because of "one extra loaded balance gear, driven by a crankshaft gear." This balance gear was said to eliminate most vibration " ... theoretically, in better balance than a four-cylinder motor!"

The Brush was an early car to use a clutch pedal, instead of lever-actuated operation. The axles and frame were made of "oil-treated oak, hickory, and maple." "Spiral" springs were featured at all four corners. Before the mid-1930s, coil-spring suspension was rare indeed!

The tread was fifty-six inches, but sixty inches on cars to be sold in the South. Two oil lanterns were provided on the cowl, and one smaller tail lantern at left rear.

The typical Brush is a two-passenger open runabout, though optional "mother-in-law seats" could be added.

LEARN ABOUT AUTOMOTIVE HISTORY! COLLECT EACH OF THESE "AUTO ALBUM" PICTURES AND STORIES.

1910 BUICK MODEL "10" (TOURING CAR)
4 PASSENGER MODEL, AVAILABLE AS A $1050. "TOURABOUT" OR AS $1150. "TOY TONNEAU" (1730 LBS.)
92" WHEELBASE
4-CYL. OVERHEAD-VALVE ENGINE
165 C.I.D. (3 3/4" BORE and STROKE)
22 1/2 H.P. MARVEL CARBURETOR

10~5
© News America Syndicate. 1986

SOME CARS HAVE ROUND LANTERNS

30 × 3

MODELS F, 16, 17, 7, 19 AND 41 ALSO AVAIL. 1910.

THE FIRST BUICK WAS BUILT IN 1903.

1910 Buick

The 1910 Buick Model 10 was a popular car in its day (about 11,000 sold that year). Total sales of all models were nearly 30,000 (though some Model 14s built during 1910 were 1911 models); 27,377 is the reported "model year" production figure for Buick for 1910.

Buick made a name in racing in 1910 by establishing various speed records with the special "Buick Bug" racers. A time-trial record speed of 105.87 m.p.h. was amazing for those days. A stock 1910 Buick "10" would be winded at less than half that speed!

All cars built before World War I are rare these days, yet quite a few examples of the Buick Model 10 have survived, which is a lasting testimony to its durability. In 1910, there was no Chevrolet; so Buick was General Motors' best-selling car.

The windshield was optional on this Model 10. The 1910 "10" was little changed from its 1909 counterpart. The only closed car in the 1910 Buick line was the Model 41, a five-passenger limousine priced at $2,750.

Buick's pioneer year is traditionally 1903, and the Golden Anniversary was celebrated in 1953. However, no actual Buick sales took place until well into 1904.

Two former Buick executives who helped push Buick ahead and later founded their own automotive empires were Charles W. Nash and Walter P. Chrysler.

For nearly all of its history, Buick has used an overhead-valve engine. However, Buick's low-priced subsidiary, the 1930 Marquette, used an L-head.

1910s

100" WHEELBASE — *4 CYL. AIR-COOLED* — *18 H.P.*

1910 FRANKLIN

TAXICAB
MODEL K-3
$2850.⁰⁰
ORIGINAL PRICE, F.O.B. FACTORY
(WINDSHIELD WAS 45. EXTRA.)
OIL SIDE LAMPS
WEIGHT = 2250 LBS.
TAXI 10
STD. COLORS = "QUAKER GREEN" AND BLACK, BUT OTHER COLORS WERE OPTIONAL FOR $50.
MFD. BY H.H. FRANKLIN MFG. CO., SYRACUSE, N.Y. (1902 ~ 1934)
30 × 4" TIRES
MANY THANKS TO MRS. PEARL SLATER, OF OIL CITY, PA., FOR PHOTOCOPYING A 1910 FRANKLIN BROCHURE.
PICTURE MAY BE TINTED WITH CRAYONS, MARKERS, COLOR PENCILS, ETC.

1910 Franklin Taxicab

From the mid-1930s until well into the 1950s, Chrysler Corporation's DeSoto was the dominant choice of most taxi fleets. But, of course, there were many others, including Checker, Yellow (a GM subsidiary), Parmelee, Luxor, and various brands specializing in taxi production.

Even Franklin got into the act, in the early days. The Franklin was a high-quality, moderately-priced, air-cooled car. Like Pierce-Arrow, the Franklin was built in upstate New York.

After Franklin left the automobile business, the company continued to produce aircraft engines (a variation of which was used in the fabled postwar Tucker car).

This 1910 Franklin taxi was also illustrated and described in Franklin's 1910 sales brochure. Obviously, the cabdriver enjoyed few luxuries—not even a windshield, unless one was ordered for an additional $45. There were no side doors in front, and no top. In those days—long before seat belts—the driver's position in a 1910 Franklin taxi was definitely a hazardous one!

This primitive taxi didn't even have headlights, but only a pair of oil-fed cowl lanterns (plus a single taillight). Most early cabs were used primarily in large cities, where the streets were lighted after dark. Bright taxi headlights would only have added to the glare.

But, can you imagine how the driver of an open-front cab like this would feel if someone hailed him at night, during a rainstorm, and demanded, "Take me 100 miles out to my farm in the country!" The only possible consolation would be a big tip.

1911 Flanders "20"

"**S**ilent as an electric; amply efficient in its motive power; … the Flanders "20" Coupe is the ideal vehicle to carry Milady on her expeditions into the shopping district or on her round of social duties.

"Its comfort makes it a veritable drawing room on wheels.

"This Coupe is luxuriously equipped, is finished in dark green enamel with nickel trimmings, has English broadcloth upholstery, and is fitted with interior and exterior electric lights." So reads an original advertisement for this distinctive-looking car, from the December 24, 1910 *Collier's* magazine.

The fully enclosed Coupe, priced at only $975 for the early 1911 season, was a terrific bargain! As a rule, early closed cars were far costlier than open roadsters or touring cars, before the mid-1920s—but not in this case.

Interestingly, the Coupe body could be removed in summertime and be temporarily replaced by a Flanders runabout, suburban touring or roadster body.

The Flanders was built to compete with the Ford Model T. It could not do so for long, but over 31,000 Flanders cars were produced from 1910 to 1912. A Flanders Electric was also built (1912-1914), and for a very brief interval in 1913, a Flanders Six was available.

Most Flanders automobiles disappeared from the road by the end of World War I, yet they're still remembered by some readers. How much is this 1911 Flanders "20" Coupe worth today? Anywhere from $2,400 "as is" (needing considerable repairs) to $17,000 in excellent or restored condition.

A FOUR-WHEEL-DRIVE ANTIQUE CAR !!

1911 7-PASSENGER F.W.D. TOURING CAR 4 CYLS. 134" W.B.

5" x 5¾" BORE and STROKE (CYLS. CAST IN PAIRS)

ALUMINUM BODY

ORIGINAL PRICE $4500. ONLY 12 BUILT !

EARLY F.W.D FACTORY

FOUR WHEEL DRIVE AUTO CO.

15 M.P.G.

GAS HEAD-LIGHTS

OIL SIDE AND TAIL LAMPS

36 x 4½ FIRESTONE TIRES

3-SPEED GEARBOX with CHAIN DRIVE SUB-TRANS.

HAVE A HAPPY 4TH OF JULY !

MFD. BY 4 WHEEL DRIVE AUTO CO., CLINTONVILLE, WIS., WHICH HAS CONTINUED TO BUILD 4WD F.W.D. TRUCKS.

1911 F-W-D Touring Car

F-W-D has long been known as a quality make of four-wheel-drive heavy-duty trucks, a product of one of Wisconsin's leading manufacturers.

The F-W-D developed from the Four Wheel Drive Auto Co. of Clintonville, Wis. The company was generations ahead of its time when it built this 1911 model—unable to foresee the great four-wheel-drive car craze of the late 1980s and early 1990s!

In 1909, the company had built and extensively tested a pilot model, nicknamed "The Battleship." The illustrated car is the ensuing production model, available in 1911 and 1912, of which only a dozen were reportedly built.

Trucks came to be a staple of this company. In 1912, five trucks were built. In 1913, nineteen trucks were produced, and quickly took the place of the cars.

On March 23, 1915, the British government ordered fifty F-W-D trucks, and it wanted them within forty days! The pace of the small factory picked up to a fever pitch, and as World War I darkened Europe, orders for F-W-D military and heavy-duty trucks dramatically increased both overseas and in the United States.

On March 18, 1917, eighty-four F-W-D trucks were lost at sea when the Germans torpedoed the liner Vigilancia (with the trucks in the hold). During World War I, nearly 15,000 F-W-D trucks were built for the war effort, with the assistance of the Peerless, Kissel, Premier, and Mitchell companies, which built F-W-D trucks under special license, to get the job done.

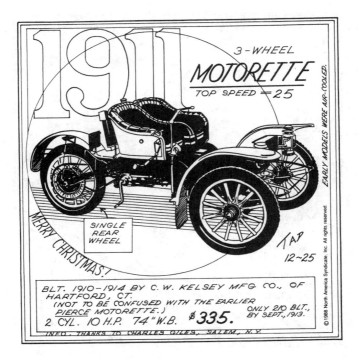

1911 Motorette

Perhaps the best known of the three-wheeled vintage cars was the British Morgan of the 1930s. But, long before that, there were many other three-wheeled cars built in the U.S.A. as well as overseas. Here is Kelsey's Motorette, a small car that C. W. Kelsey hoped to popularize in the early 1910s. Quite a few Motorettes were exported, including about a dozen "Motorette Rickshaws" for Japan.

The pilot model Motorettes overturned easily when cornering, so C. W. Kelsey developed a stabilizing anti-sway bar that solved the problem. That idea was later applied to many other cars.

One problem Kelsey could not overcome, however, was a rash of defective engines purchased for use in the 1912 models. Pistons seized, rendering the engines inoperable! Kelsey tried to make good on these "lemon" engines, but great damage was done to the reputation of the Motorette, and sales nose-dived.

By the age of 17, C. W. Kelsey had set up a complete machine shop at home, and he built a 5-h.p. engine. Then he built a car in which to install it. At 18, Kelsey and a friend built a three-wheeled car called the Auto-Tri, and they put more than 2,000 miles on it. The Smithsonian Institution eventually acquired this vehicle for its collection.

In 1910, Kelsey built a four-wheeled car called the Spartan. Then came the Motorette.

Kelsey later tried a line of six-cylinder friction-drive cars, but his real success was as president of the Rototiller Company, which he founded in 1930.

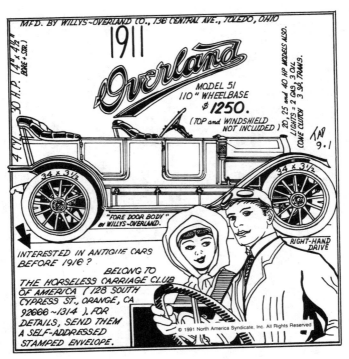

1911 Overland

The Overland may not be well remembered today, but in the 'teens and '20s it was an extremely popular, low-priced car, rivaling Ford, Chevrolet, Maxwell, Essex, etc.

The Standard Wheel Company built the first Overland in 1903 at Terre Haute, Ind. Two years later, the Overland Company, as it came to be known, relocated to Indianapolis.

In 1907, John North Willys, a prominent Elmira, N.Y., auto dealer, had put in a gigantic 500-car order but received nothing. Going to the factory at Indianapolis to investigate, Willys found affairs in total disarray because of the notorious "Panic of 1907" recession. Willys took charge of the Overland Company, and his dynamic leadership and high quotas got the organization rolling in high gear. When the move was made from Indianapolis, operations were transferred to the former Pope-Toledo factory in Toledo.

The 1911 Overlands came in four series, the illustrated "51" being in the second-to-top spot. Although this 1911 model had right-hand drive, it had the modern "center control"—the hand brake and gearshift levers were at the center of the floorboard, instead of outside the car as on some antique models.

A six-cylinder model was also offered from 1915 to 1918 and again in 1925 and 1926. Since 1914, Willys-Overland had also been building the larger Willys-Knight (with its unusual "sleeve-valve" Knight engine), and also, for a time, a Willys automobile with a conventional engine.

1911 Simplex

This mighty Simplex was a famous antique sports car! Imagine road speeds of over 80 miles an hour, when most other cars were putt-putting along at 45 or less. Stopping this car in a hurry was another thing, with the two-wheel mechanical brakes found on all domestic 1911 cars.

The Simplex, starting in 1907, was the follower of the old S&M (Smith & Mabley) car. Herman Broesel, a textile importer, had purchased the New York City factory and assets of S&M in 1907. The company's chief engineer, Edward Franquist, had just completed work on a powerful new 50-h.p. model. This was to be launched as the new Simplex Model 50. Production figures were very low for all Simplex models, never totaling above three figures!

Herman Broesel passed away in 1912, and in 1913 his sons sold the company to the Goodrich brothers (sons of tire maker B.F. Goodrich), though the Broesels and engineer Franquist remained with the company as employees. In 1914, the Goodrich brothers also purchased Henry Crane's Crane Motor Car Co. in Bayonne, N.J.

In 1916, Wright-Martin Aircraft Corp. acquired the Crane-Simplex industry, and after World War I began (in 1917), Hispano-Suiza aircraft engines were produced there, and soon Simplex car production was suspended.

One of the first cars ever to be exhibited as an antique, and most famous of all Simplexes, was the Speed Car on display at the Smithsonian in Washington, D.C., since about 1929!

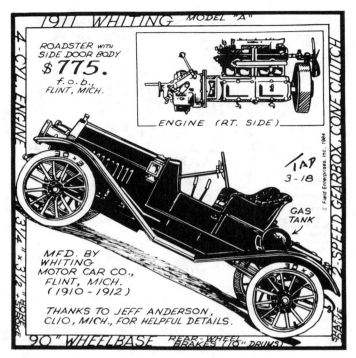

1911 Whiting

"Gentlemen: "In regard to service and durability of Whiting Model A Roadster, I would like to say that I have used one since spring on a rural mail route, and also in the livery business, making my route every day when the roads were fit for any machine and sometimes when the roads were bad.

"This machine has given the best satisfaction, and if I bought another roadster at anywhere near the price, I would buy a Whiting Model A.

"I tested my car four days and averaged 24 miles to a gallon of gasoline on a mail route, making 95 stops and starts, which I consider the hardest work on a machine and which few machines are able to stand ..."

Thus read a written testimonial of January 21, 1911 from A. A. Stewart, a satisfied Whiting automobile owner from St. Clair, Mich.

Top and windshield were sold separately, but all cars included two gas lamps, generator, two side lamps, tail lamp, horn, a complete set of tools, and a repair outfit.

Ignition was old-fashioned "jump-spark" type, with a Remy magneto and a set of dry cells. Engine lubrication on the roadster was "splash, automatic control."

The Sloan Museum in Flint, Mich. owns a rare Whiting automobile. Few exist today, and this is one that few have ever heard of. In spite of its age, it's not a bad-looking little car!

Dear Friends = **HAVE A HAPPY NEW YEAR!**

PULLMAN VENTILATORS IN ROOF

6 CYL. 60 HP

TAY 1~2~94

1912 ALCO *$* **7250.**
BERLINE LIMO.
134" WHEELBASE

BUILT 1905~1913 BY AMERICAN LOCOMOTIVE COMPANY, PROVIDENCE, R.I. (SALES OFFICE at 1893 BROADWAY, NYC) (ALCO BUILT RAILROAD LOCOMOTIVES, CARS, TAXIS AND TRUCKS.)

STEPS ARE LIGHTED WHEN DOORS ARE OPENED.

©1993 North America Syndicate, Inc. World rights reserved.

WHITE STRIPE AROUND BODY IDENTIFIES AN ALCO.

1912 Alco

A snowy scene was presented in an original 1912 magazine advertisement for Alco's new "Berline" limousine, an imposing-looking closed car deluxe. The Berline provided full side doors with glass windows, not only for the privileged passengers in back, but for the chauffeur as well.

Two-time winner of the Vanderbilt Cup Race (1909 and 1910), the Alco was built by the American Locomotive Company. Its railroad heritage was clearly reflected in the Berline's unusual Pullman-car roofline, with a raised clerestory section and its "Pullman ventilator" windows, which drew in fresh air without drafts. Wide 25 1/2-inch doors allowed easy access and exit. The broad, white beltline stripe around the body was a "badge of motor individuality" that identified the 1912 Alco.

There were Landaulets, Limousines, and Berline Limousines in Alco's luxury closed-car line for 1912 in both 40-h.p. four-cylinder and 60-h.p. six-cylinder series, with prices starting at $5,500 for a four-cylinder Landaulet or Limo. In both series, there were also Runabouts, Toy Tonneaus, and Touring Cars, with these open cars priced from $4,500.

The American Locomotive Company claimed proudly that its high quality automobiles required a total of 19 months to build, with the rear axle taking six months of work alone. Some 5,000 Alco autos were built from 1909 to 1913, but even though they were heralded at the time as America's "most expensive car," the manufacturer lost an average of $460 on each one built and decided in 1913 to drop its automotive sideline.

A few of these fabulous automobiles have survived to this day.

1912 Bessemer Truck

The screen-side delivery truck was a popular style of the 'teens and the early 1920s. Many commercial vehicle manufacturers (both small and large production companies) offered similar models in those days.

Some older readers may associate such a screen-side truck with a "dog-catcher's truck," for back in the old days, stray or unlicensed animals were frequently carted off to the pound in trucks that looked like this.

Bessemer trucks are rare. Most of them used Continental engines, as did many other small independent truck and auto manufacturers. Early Bessemers had chain drive to the rear wheels, but in 1916 a one-ton model with internal gear drive joined the Bessemer line, along with two, three and a half, and five-ton worm drive trucks.

The jerky-motion cone clutch gave way to a more modern dry-plate disc clutch, and in 1918 the remaining chain-drive Bessemers were discontinued.

A 1923 merger with American Motors Corp. of Plainfield, NJ. moved operations from Pennsylvania to Plainfield. And, soon a sixteen-passenger bus was added to the line.

Taking a cue from Reo's popular "Speed Wagon" series, Bessemer American Corp. introduced its own one-ton "speed truck" with six-cylinder Continental engine, shortly before operations ceased in 1926.

Not many extras were available for this Spartan-looking 1912 model, which didn't even have side doors or windows. However, each Bessemer truck of this type came equipped with "three lamps, a horn, and tools."

$1800.
f.o.b., DETROIT
TOP and WINDSHIELD,
$100. EXTRA

CHALMERS "30" and
"40" SERIES ALSO
AVAILABLE.

News America Syndicate
© News Group Chicago, Inc., 1985

1912 MODEL
INTRODUCED
JULY 8, 1911.

1912

CHALMERS "36"
5-PASSENGER TOURING CAR 115" WB
4 CYLINDERS 4 1/4" x 5 1/4" BORE and STR.
40 HORSEPOWER   4 SPEED TRANS.
COMPRESSED-AIR STARTER (new!)
CHALMERS MOTOR COMPANY, DETROIT (1908-1924)
PREDECESSOR TO THE CHRYSLER.

TAD
3-31

1912 Chalmers

A most notable feature of the 1912 Chalmers was the compressed-air self-starter. In prior years, one had to get out and crank a car in order to start it. Cranks could be treacherous; they could snap back suddenly and break someone's arm. This happened often, and there was also the possibility of the car breaking loose and rolling over the driver while he was in front of it!

Another quality feature on the new 1912 "36" was the four-speed transmission, heretofore found only on the most expensive cars. Fourth gear was direct-drive cruising speed, while third gear allowed for more torque and pulling power on hills.

The Model 36 had Bosch dual ignition, Solar brand gas lamps, and a Prest-O-Lite® tank, plus Continental demountable rims for ease of tire changing. The demountable rim was a good idea back in those days of terrible tires! Some motorists had flats and blowouts every few hours!

The glazed-enameled radiator emblem of the 1912 Chalmers was blue-and-white, and circular. In the inner circle was a large letter "C," wrapped around a smaller "M" over a smaller "C." The letters representing Chalmers Motor Company. And, "Chalmers Motor Co., Detroit, Mich. U.S.A." was inscribed around the outer ring of the emblem.

In the early 1920s, Walter P. Chrysler gained control of both Maxwell and Chalmers. He reorganized and revitalized these companies, merged them and then absorbed them into his new Chrysler Corporation. The final Chalmers was the early '24 model (built in 1923).

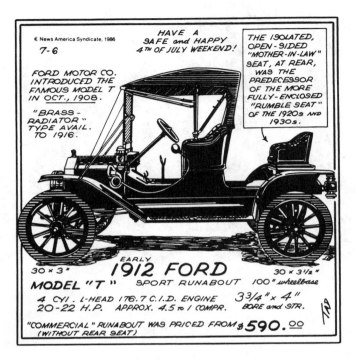

© News America Syndicate, 1986
7-6

HAVE A
SAFE and HAPPY
4TH OF JULY WEEKEND!

THE ISOLATED, OPEN-SIDED "MOTHER-IN-LAW" SEAT, AT REAR, WAS THE PREDECESSOR OF THE MORE FULLY-ENCLOSED "RUMBLE SEAT" OF THE 1920s AND 1930s.

FORD MOTOR CO. INTRODUCED THE FAMOUS MODEL T IN OCT., 1908.

"BRASS-RADIATOR" TYPE AVAIL. TO 1916.

EARLY
1912 FORD
MODEL "T"   SPORT RUNABOUT   100" *wheelbase*
30 × 3"   30 × 3½"
4 CYL. L-HEAD 176.7 C.I.D. ENGINE   3¾" × 4"
20-22 H.P.   APPROX. 4.5 TO 1 COMPR.   BORE and STR.

"COMMERCIAL" RUNABOUT WAS PRICED FROM $**590.**00
(WITHOUT REAR SEAT)

1912 Ford Model T

Some time ago in *Auto Album,* we presented a 1910 Ford Model T with a mother-in-law seat. This strange feature was still available in early 1912, though the idea was on its way out by then. In the mid 'teens, some sporty cars provided a precarious auxiliary seat at the side, over the running board (which was even more unsafe than the type illustrated).

The rumble seat did not become popular until the 1920s, but during the later 1920s and through most of the 1930s, rumble seats were found on many coupes and roadsters. In England, they were known as "Dickie-seats."

Though the Model T Ford was popular by 1912, less than 14,000 runabouts (roadsters) were sold by Ford that year.

Just eleven years later, nearly 300,000 Model T Ford roadsters were sold in the 1923 season alone!

Though comprehensive road tests in automotive magazines were yet in the future, a 1912 Model T Ford runabout was tested in 1951, in England, to determine its original performance. Top speed was 42 miles per hour. And, 35.8 seconds were required for the vintage vehicle to go from 0 to 40 miles per hour!

Average fuel consumption in the test was 28.5 miles per gallon, but in measured tests the Model T delivered 32 m.p.g. at a steady 30 m.p.h., and a thrifty 35 m.p.g. at a steady speed of 20. Fuel capacity of the test car was eight gallons.

1912 LION "40"

MODEL K TOURING CAR
4 CYL.   40 H.P.

BUILT 1910 TO 1912 BY
LION MOTOR CAR CO.,
106 FULTON ST.,
ADRIAN, MICHIGAN.
ON JUNE 2, 1912, THE FACTORY
BURNED, ALONG WITH OVER
150 NEW LION CARS. NOT
LONG AFTERWARD, WHAT WAS
LEFT OF THE COMPANY WAS
AUCTIONED OFF FOR ONLY
$7000.

ORIG. PRICE ABOUT $1600.

WITH
SELF-
STARTER

NOW
VALUED AT
$2400.
TO
17,000.
(DEPEND.
ON CAR'S
CONDITION.)

116" WHEELBASE

©1992 by North America Syndicate, Inc. World rights reserved.

1912 Lion Model K

"**M**easure the Lion '40' by the golden rule of goodness," proclaimed an ad in the January 1912 *Cosmopolitan*.

That ad listed the many features of the new Lion. The self-starter was a strong selling point. The Lion still used the old-fashioned gas headlights, with an acetylene storage tank visible on the right-hand running board (as illustrated).

The Lion is so rare that you've probably never heard of it unless you're an ardent student of antique car history! The company was founded in September 1909. The 1910 series was the Model A. For 1911, there was a Model A, B, C, and D. For 1912, the Model K touring (illustrated) or the Model L roadster was available.

When the Lion factory burned in June of 1912, it was a blow from which the company could not recover. Some items were rescued from the blazing factory, but the most valuable thing inside was a prototype of a new lower-priced 1913 model-to-be. Frantic workers were unable to save that 1913 pilot model, on which the Lion Motor Car Company had based its future hopes.

Lion was just one of several early makes of cars forced out of the market after a factory fire. To make matters worse, a considerably after-the-fact lawsuit was brought by the builders of a "gyroscopic" vertical automobile engine, which the Lion Co. had promised to order in quantity but never did. The $46,000 judgment was in favor of the plaintiff, against Fred Postal and Henry Bowen, co-founders of the defunct Lion Co.

1912 Reo

Ransom E. Olds, who had founded Oldsmobile, left his original company in 1904 and founded Reo, using his three initials to create the new name.

The illustrated 1912 model was known as Reo The Fifth. Olds wrote several advertisements for this car, proclaiming that it was his "farewell car," in that it was the very best he could ever achieve and no further improvements seemed possible! Such a proclamation seemed extremely shortsighted, as during the course of the "teen years" there were many changes in automotive design, and a typical car of 1910 would look nothing like one of 1920.

Though this Model 5-R was entitled Reo The Fifth, Mr. Olds stated that during twenty-five years of experience he had built twenty-three other models of cars, from one to six cylinders, and from six to 60 h.p. The new 1912 Reo was approaching perfection! It differed from the 1911 Reo in that the new one had left-hand drive, center-control gearshift, and foot control of both service and emergency brakes. Also new: a straight-line touring car body with all doors on the same level, sans the previous horizontal moldings between them. In spite of the numerous improvements, prices were lower than in 1911. A self-starter was optional for just $25.

In spite of the dramatic statements attributed to Olds in 1912, Reo The Fifth was not his final effort. He remained in control of the company until the mid 1920s, and returned again in '34 to take charge again in lean times.

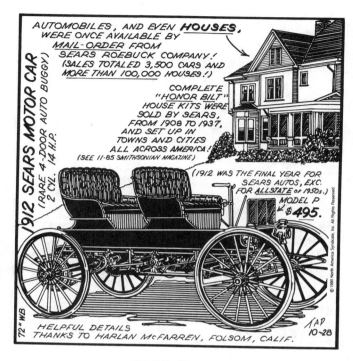

AUTOMOBILES, AND EVEN **HOUSES,** WERE ONCE AVAILABLE BY MAIL-ORDER FROM SEARS ROEBUCK COMPANY! (SALES TOTALED 3,500 CARS AND MORE THAN 100,000 HOUSES!)

COMPLETE "HONOR BILT" HOUSE KITS WERE SOLD BY SEARS, FROM 1908 TO 1937, AND SET UP IN TOWNS AND CITIES ALL ACROSS AMERICA! (SEE 11-85 SMITHSONIAN MAGAZINE)

1912 SEARS MOTOR CAR (RARE 4-DOOR AUTO BUGGY) 2 CYL. 14 H.P.

(1912 WAS THE FINAL YEAR FOR SEARS AUTOS, EXC. FOR ALLSTATE OF 1950s.) MODEL P $495.

© 1990 North America Syndicate, Inc. All Rights Reserved

72" WB

HELPFUL DETAILS THANKS TO HARLAN McFARREN, FOLSOM, CALIF.

AP 10-28

1912 Sears

Can you imagine ordering new cars—and even new houses—by mail order?

After a few years of selling their buggy-like cars, Sears discontinued the practice in 1912, because they were losing money with their extremely low prices. Raising prices would have lowered their competitive edge, so Sears Roebuck simply dropped out of the increasingly complex automobile business.

Sears re-entered the field in the early 1950s with its own version of Kaiser's compact Henry J car. The rare Sears Allstate version, with its own grille and other variations, is nearly as scarce as the much-older Sears auto buggies.

A 1912 advertising piece illustrated three models of Sears cars, heralded as "better than ever!" The two-passenger Model H runabout was priced at only $385. A similar-looking Model L, with heavier pneumatic (air-filled) tires, was $495. And, $495 also would buy the Model P four-passenger car, with solid tires (illustrated).

The sales flyer declared, "It will pay you to investigate the Sears before purchasing an automobile. We have issued a Handsome Special Automobile Catalog describing our complete line, and we will be glad to send this free upon request to anybody writing for it."

As for the Sears Honor Bilt kit houses, many sizes and varieties were available, from simple cabins to elegant city homes. One of the most impressive was the 10-room "Magnolia," Colonial-style, with a four-columned, two-story-high grand front porch and a magnificent facade. This one was introduced in the 1918 catalog, with a kit price of only $5,140!

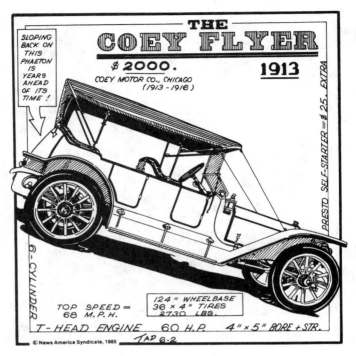

THE **COEY FLYER**

$ 2000. 1913

COEY MOTOR CO., CHICAGO
(1913 - 1916)

SLOPING BACK ON THIS PHAETON IS YEARS AHEAD OF ITS TIME !

PRESTO SELF-STARTER = $ 25. EXTRA

6 - CYLINDER

TOP SPEED = 68 M.P.H.

124" WHEELBASE
36 × 4" TIRES
2730 LBS.

T-HEAD ENGINE   60 H.P.   4" × 5" BORE + STR.

TAD 6-2

© News America Syndicate, 1985

1913 Coey Flyer

This is one of the most unusual and advanced American cars of 1913; yet it is virtually forgotten by all but a number of dedicated antique car enthusiasts.

The Coey flyer was advertised as "The World's Best Value" for $2,000: "a car at manufacturer's costs, plus a reasonable profit." Sales were direct from factory to buyer, so distribution was limited mostly to the greater Chicago area. The Flyer was attractive, with an "underslung" design and a sloping back.

Charles A. Coey was the founder of Coey Motor Co. and had been associated with automotive ventures since 1902 when he built and rented out small electric cars. He also operated a driving school in Chicago, and, for a time, sold Thomas automobiles.

In 1914, Coey also produced two models of cyclecars: the Coey Bear and the Coey Junior. The Junior was soon renamed the "C-A-C."

In addition to Coey White, the illustrated car was also available in "Bottle Green," "Golden Brown," or other colors on special order. If special colors were desired, the manufacturer warned that a waiting period of 30 days might be necessary. Car painting in those days was laborious—often done by hand brushing and hand rubbing, with a slow drying process between the many coats that were applied. Quick spraying was virtually unknown in that era.

Cars without dealerships have seldom stayed on the market for long. In 1916, Coey sold out to the Wonder Motor Truck Co., which produced a few more Flyers until sometime the following year.

1913 1/2 Imperial

The best-known pre-Chrysler Imperial was the one built at Jackson, Mich., from 1908 to 1916. The founders were the Campbell Brothers (T. A. and George N.), who'd been operating the Jackson Carriage Company.

Since there was already a well-known Jackson car built at Jackson, Mich., the Campbells decided to name their new line of automobiles the "Imperial."

In 1909, Jackson Carriage Company officially became the Imperial Automobile Co. The factory burned in the spring of 1912, but the Campbells bought Buick's former truck factory and were back in business.

Six-cylinder models joined the fours during 1913, and this 1913 1/2 model was Imperial's latest top-of-the-line offering, continuing into 1914.

In 1915, the Campbells decided to leave their company and join with Robert C. Hupp to produce a new, but unsuccessful economy car, the Emerson 4. Imperial merged with Marion of Indianapolis. The resulting combination became "Mutual Motors Corporation," which soon moved to the city of Jackson and discontinued the Imperial.

Before 1913, many cars had low hoods that extended to the flat wooden front (or dash) of the body. But, in 1913 and 1914, body and hood were usually separated by an awkward-looking small cowl section (as seen here). After 1915, most brands of cars raised the level of the top of the hood and the cowl to that of the body belt-line.

Note the impressive length of this illustrated 1913 1/2 Imperial, which rode on a generous 137-inch wheelbase. It looked comparable to other luxury cars that cost twice as much!

"ALL ROADS ARE LEVEL TO A MOYER."

TO HORSEPOWER @ 1600 RPM

4½" x 5¼" BR. + ST.

1913 MOYER 6 — MODEL "G" 7-PASS. TOURING CAR

6 CYL., CAST IN PAIRS — 135" WHEELBASE (WOODEN BODY!)

$ 3250.⁰⁰, f.o.b., SYRACUSE

ONLY ABOUT 400 CARS (4 and 6 CYL.) BUILT BY H.A. MOYER, SYRACUSE, N.Y., BETWEEN 1911 AND 1915 MODEL YEAR (SYRACUSE WAS ALSO THE HOME OF THE FRANKLIN.)

BUILT-IN AIR-COMPRESSOR INFLATES THE TIRES!

1913 Moyer 6

Many 1913 cars are easy to identify because 1913 was a transitional period between the old-fashioned separation of body and hood, and the more modern body silhouette, in which the hood lined up smoothly with body sides.

On the typical 1913 car, there was still a noticeable separation of hood from body. But, there was now a short cowl section in between, as seen here.

The Moyer automobile was the brainchild of Harvey Allen Moyer, a native of Clay, N.Y. In 1875, he built wagons in Cicero, and five years later he moved to Syracuse, where he continued to produce horse-drawn vehicles. In 1908, Moyer built his first experimental automobile, and in 1909 he revealed plans to build at least 200 more!

The 1911 was the first regular-production Moyer car. It was a four-cylinder machine on a 116-inch wheelbase. A six was added on a 121-inch wheelbase in 1912. In 1913 and later, the 121-inch wheelbase model was a four, and the six graduated to a 13.5-inch wheelbase, as seen here.

Moyer never incorporated as an officially organized company. Harvey Moyer preferred to run the business himself and maintain full control. He managed to produce about 400 cars before deciding to give it up in 1915. Remarkably, Moyer produced most of the parts for his cars, and full-pressure lubrication was an advanced feature of the Moyer engine.

Nearly all of the 400 Moyer cars were scrapped and forgotten by the late 1920s. No one thought they would ever be of any future value.

SILENT BUT SLOW!
TOP SPEED =
22!

COULD BE
CONTROLLED
FROM EITHER
FRONT or BACK
SEAT!
MAGNETIC
2-WH. BRAKES
TILLER STEER.
PRICED
FROM
$2900.⁰⁰

1913

OHIO
ELECTRIC

MFD. BY
OHIO ELECTRIC CAR CO.,
TOLEDO, OHIO (1910-1918)

© Field Enterprises, Inc. 1983

1913 Ohio Electric

"**T**his is the only five-passenger electric made that can be driven from both the front and rear seats. All passengers face forward," stated an original ad for this car (*Saturday Evening Post*, December 17, 1912). "When riding alone with your wife, sit beside her and drive from the rear seat. Don't sit in front and look like a hired chauffeur.

"When riding with three or four people, drive from the front seat and have an unobstructed view.

" ... Our handsome 1913 catalogue illustrates and explains in detail our complete line," concluded the ad, after mentioning that the car was now in its fourth successful year and that desirable territories were still open for established and responsible dealers.

Known as "the envied electric," the Ohio Electric was also advertised in various 1913 issues of *National Geographic* magazine, where inviting views of the comfortable, well-padded interiors of these cars were displayed. Some were known as "Viennese models," capitalizing on the charm of old Europe.

Though there were exceptions, most electric cars of the 'teens and early 1920s resembled old stagecoaches: unusually high and boxy, and built mostly of wood. Light weight was necessary in order to conserve the power of the batteries that propelled these electrics! Because their top speed was less than 25 m.p.h., and because their batteries needed recharging after fifty miles or so, electric cars never competed heavily with gas-driven models.

1910s

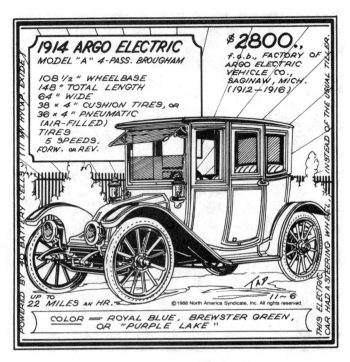

1914 ARGO ELECTRIC
MODEL "A" 4-PASS. BROUGHAM

108 1/2" WHEELBASE
148" TOTAL LENGTH
64" WIDE
38 × 4" CUSHION TIRES, OR
36 × 4" PNEUMATIC
(AIR-FILLED)
TIRES
5 SPEEDS,
FORW. OR REV.

$2800.,
f.o.b., FACTORY OF
ARGO ELECTRIC
VEHICLE CO.,
SAGINAW, MICH.
(1912-1916)

POWERED BY 30 BATTERY CELLS, (IN MY HYCAP. EXIDE)

THIS ELECTRIC CAR HAD A STEERING WHEEL, INSTEAD OF THE USUAL TILLER.

UP TO
22 MILES AN HR.
11-6
© 1988 North America Syndicate, Inc. All rights reserved.

COLOR = ROYAL BLUE, BREWSTER GREEN,
OR "PURPLE LAKE"

1914 Argo Electric

T his electric car is different from most other electric broughams made before World War I. The Argo Electric had a longer wheelbase than the ordinary electric car of its era, giving it a more rakish appearance (if a box on wheels can be considered "rakish")!

Another uncharacteristic touch was the Gemmer steering gear, with a conventional-type steering wheel. Many electric cars were still using the ancient "tiller" steering control.

The Argo Electric Vehicle Company was organized during 1910 and soon moved into the former factory of the Sommer Bros. Match Co., located at Jefferson & Atwater Streets in Saginaw, Mich. Because of various delays, no Argo electric cars were ready for the market until 1912.

In 1914, Argo merged with Broc and Borland electric car companies. The combined venture was named the American Electric Car Company, and soon all three makes were produced at Argo's factory. But, all three were discontinued in 1916. Later, the former Argo factory was used to produce the Yale 8 car—and still later, the Jumbo truck (a product of Nelson Motor Truck Co.).

Seventy years ago, several different makes of electric automobiles were in production, and a few can still be found in certain automobile museums. Electric cars ran smoothly and quietly, but their big drawback was their limited range, and the expense of replacing all the batteries when at last they were no longer rechargeable. Also, they were capable of speeds no higher than 20 to 25 m.p.h., in most cases.

IF YOUR NAME IS MITCHELL ....
YOU'LL BE INTERESTED TO SEE THIS
1914 Mitchell
"LITTLE SIX " 50 HP
TOURING CAR
$1895. fob.,
(WITH ELECTRIC STARTER)
4 CYL. and BIG 6 MODELS ALSO
132" WHEELBASE
MFD. BY MITCHELL-LEWIS MOTOR CO., RACINE, WIS.
AVAIL. 1903 TO 1923

© 1990 North America Syndicate, Inc. All Rights Reserved

1914 Mitchell

Mitchell cars, known today only to collectors, were once well known. Only eighty-two Mitchells were built in 1904, but by 1907 the production was up to 1,377, and by 1910 the yearly figure was 5,614 with over 6,000 built in 1912. These figures are low by today's standards, but back then the auto manufacturing pie was cut into so many dozens of tiny slivers that any figure above 2,000 a year was noteworthy.

The Mitchell was one of several well-known Wisconsin-built cars, also including the Jeffery and the Kissel Kar.

The 1914 Mitchell's selling points: electric starter and generator; electric lights; electric horn (squawking bulb horns were becoming outmoded); "electric magnetic exploring lamp"; speedometer; mohair top and dust cover; Jiffy quick-action side curtains; quick-action rain vision (horizontally split) windshield; and more. However, in 1914 windshield wipers were not required by law; they were an extra, found on only a few cars. Some early wipers were manually operated by a tiny inside crank.

Many small auto manufacturers hit the rocks in the early 1920s. Mitchell's downfall in 1923 was caused, in part, by the weird-looking 1920 model they built, aptly nicknamed The Drunken Mitchell. Odd back-slanting radiator, louvers, and windshield lacked sales appeal. In the conservative 1920s, it did not pay to buck the established trends. Chrysler was one of few that dared to be different in 1924 and made it! In 1924, the Mitchell factory was sold to Nash, which used it for the production of the low-priced Ajax 1925-1926.

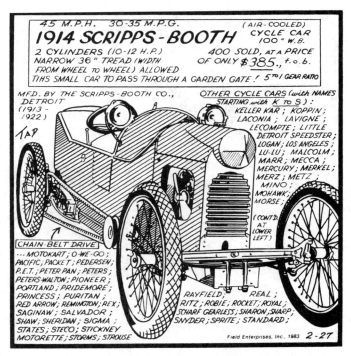

45 M.P.H.   30-35 M.P.G.   (AIR-COOLED)

1914 SCRIPPS-BOOTH   CYCLE CAR 100" W.B.

2 CYLINDERS (10-12 H.P.)   400 SOLD, AT A PRICE
NARROW 36" TREAD (WIDTH   OF ONLY $385., f.o.b.
FROM WHEEL TO WHEEL) ALLOWED
TIHS SMALL CAR TO PASS THROUGH A GARDEN GATE!   5 TO 1 GEAR RATIO

MFD. BY THE SCRIPPS-BOOTH CO.,   OTHER CYCLE CARS (with NAMES
DETROIT   STARTING with K TO S):
(1913-   KELLER KAR ; KOPPIN ;
1922)   LACONIA ; LAVIGNE ;
TAP   LECOMPTE ; LITTLE
DETROIT SPEEDSTER ;
LOGAN; LOS ANGELES ;
LU-LU ; MALCOLM ;
MARR ; MECCA ;
MERCURY ; MERKEL ;
MERZ ; METZ ;
MINO ;
MOHAWK;
MORSE ;

(CONT'D.
AT
LOWER
LEFT)

CHAIN-BELT DRIVE
...MOTOKART; O-WE-GO ;
PACIFIC; PACKET ; PEDERSEN ;
P.E.T. ; PETER PAN ; PETERS ;
PETERS-WALTON ; PIONEER ;
PORTLAND ; PRIDEMORE ;
PRINCESS ; PURITAN ;   RAYFIELD;   REAL ;
RED ARROW; REMINGTON; REX ;   RITZ ; ROBIE ; ROCKET ; ROYAL ;
SAGINAW ; SALVADOR ;   SCHARF GEARLESS; SHARON; SHARP;
SHAW ; SHERIDAN ; SIGMA ;   SNYDER ; SPRITE ; STANDARD ;
STATES ; STECO ; STICKNEY
MOTORETTE ; STORMS ; STROUSE   Field Enterprises, Inc., 1983   2-27

1914 Scripps-Booth Cyclecar

F unny face! "The little car with the big countenance!" That's what one might think when looking upon this strange, little critter! This Scripps-Booth Cyclecar seemed to have distinct facial features, and might call to mind later cars of that ilk (like the "buck-toothed" '50 Buick, the "frog-faced" '68 Subaru, the "bullet-nosed" '50-to-'51 Studebaker, etc.). You could call this the "Surprised Scripps-Booth," as it appeared to have a certain startled look! Some may call it "cute," others would say it's "weird," "grody," or just plain ugly. But, it was designed for economy.

The first Scripps-Booth Cyclecar was created during 1913, and long-time *Auto Album* readers may remember the 1913 "Bi-Autogo" by Scripps, a large and strange half-car, half-motorcycle.

Though today's presentation appeared first in 1913, it continued mostly in the 1914 model series. Four hundred sales was a low figure for a car that should have had wide popular appeal because of its low cost. As the cyclecar idea appeared to be a "flop," Scripps-Booth then turned to a more conventional type of automobile. In 1918, General Motors bought out the company, but continued to manufacture Scripps-Booth full-sized-cars until the 1923 models appeared.

In the text of the illustration, notice the many other brands of cycle cars listed (and these were only the names starting with K through S). Most of these flourished but briefly, during the mid-teens. Some got only as far as a pilot model or a stock promotion campaign. And, none ever achieved mass production.

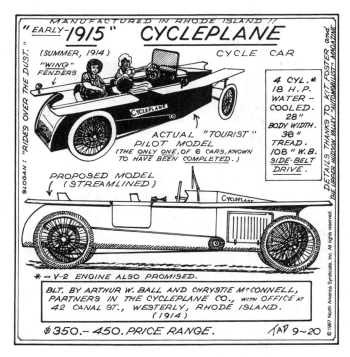

1915 Cycleplane

Though it was not a flying car, the name implied such. With its horizontal fender "wings," the Cycleplane looked as if it might take off. Not only were these flat, extended fenders simple to produce (no curved metal), but the manufacturer made the dubious claim that the fender wings helped to absorb shocks!

Billed as a 1915 model, the Cycleplane was produced during mid-1914. There is no proof that more than one car was ever completed and demonstrated. But, there were parts for more. Various one- and two-passenger models were planned and advertised to a limited extent, in two- or four-cylinder versions. The car in the upper half of the illustration was the one actually completed and demonstrated. The car appearing below it was one of the proposed models that

was advertised but probably never available. Some Cycleplane ads promised that cars would be ready by July 10, 1914, but that deadline was apparently missed.

Most of the flurry of activity for the Cycleplane Co. took place in 1914, and by early 1915 the venture was virtually "kaput." This happened despite an August 31, 1914 agreement between company founder Dr. Arthur W. Ball and Mr. Chrystie McConnell, in which Mr. McConnell was to take over the construction of additional Cycleplane cars and provide "skilled machinists" at 50 cents an hour and unskilled helpers at 25 cents an hour.

What became of the building that housed the Cycleplane business at 42 Canal St. in Westerly, R.I.? As of a recent report, it's serving as a hairdresser's shop.

1916 American Fiat

The Fiat is an Italian car, and it has been in production in Italy since 1899. Originally (until 1906) it was known as the "F.I.A.T." (an abbreviation of "Fabbrica Italiana Automobili Torino"). The founders were Giovanni Agnelli di Bricherasio and Count Carlo Biscaretti di Ruffia.

Luxury Fiats from Italy were first imported to America by O. H. Keep of New York City—followed by Hollander & Tangeman, also known as the "Hol-Tan" Company. Hol-Tan's Fiat-importing contract was cancelled in 1909, and a diamond importer named Ben Eichberg became the president of a new American Fiat company. The factory in Poughkeepsie, N.Y. was completed in the first half of 1910.

The Italian Fiat company received royalties for each car that American Fiat built. The Type 56 was a model produced and sold only in the U.S.A. All American Fiats (in various series) were large and luxurious! Back in Italy, Fiat built both large and small cars.

American Fiats were built between 1910 and early 1918. In February 1918, the Duesenberg brothers purchased the American Fiat factory in Poughkeepsie, but they moved all the machinery to Elizabeth, NJ.

Italian Fiat imports to the U.S.A. stopped in the early 1920s, but resumed in the later 1950s. Because of a low sales total of only 15,000 cars in America in 1982, Fiat stopped sending cars to the U.S. in the spring of 1983.

1916 HUDSON
"SUPER 6" 7-PASS. TOURING
125½" W.B.   (PHAETON)
new "YACHT-LINE" BODY
6 CYL.   288.6 CU. IN. DISPL.
76 HORSEPOWER

1350.⁰⁰
F.O.B., DETROIT

0-50 IN 16.2 SECONDS
75 MILES PER HR.
TAD
I-27
News America Syndicate
© News Group Chicago, Inc., 1985

1916 Hudson "Super Six"

Would you believe, a stock Hudson Super Six chassis reached a speed of 102.5 miles per hour at Ormond-Daytona Beach, Fla. on April 10, 1916! Even with a boxy, stock body attached, a 16 Super Six would do 75 m.p.h. or more!

Its manufacturer proclaimed the Super Six engine of 1916 as having defeated the finest and costliest engines in other cars—not only other sixes, but also mighty V-8s and V-12s!

"The Super Six motor (improved and patented as of December 28, 1915), is the same size as the Hudson '6-40' motor," read a Hudson advertisement. But, vibration had been reduced "to practically zero," and friction had been cut to only ten percent of what it had once been.

High compression and a finely balanced crankshaft were the secrets behind Hudson's improved engine, boosting efficiency by eighty percent.

Styling also took a great leap forward with the new "yacht-line" profile of the touring car (illustrated). This new styling appeared when the 1916 Hudsons were unveiled on June 15, 1915. The new touring car was heralded as "The Road Cruiser," with a new wider and higher rear seat and two auxiliary middle jump seats, which tucked away when not needed.

For 1916, an oven-baked "Ever-Lustre" paint finish was new. Some 15,000 Hudsons were sold during the 1914-1915 seasons, but production pulled ahead in 1916 as 25,772 were sold!

1916 1/2 Mid-Year Mitchell Submarine

T his custom-built 1916 1/2 mid-year Mitchell Submarine sporting car was produced for Carl H. Page, a New York City automobile dealer. It was displayed at Page's showroom and was personally used by Mr. Page for a time.

Nautical themes were popular with wealthy New Yorkers, many of whom owned estates along the New England or Long Island coasts. To carry this "ultra aquatic" styling to automobile design was to guarantee immediate attention in a crowd of conventional-looking cars!

Carrying capacity of the Submarine was six adults (plus "a child's seat under the cowl"). There were two outboard folding seats that were concealed behind doors in the body sides when not in use. These auxiliary seats hung over the running boards and guaranteed to either thrill or terrify the rider!

J. H. Clark, New York manager of the Page Company, designed the Submarine body. He supervised the construction as well. The paint scheme was white enamel on body, wheels, and radiator shell; the fenders, running gear, chassis apron, and leather upholstery were deep green.

In an era of dark, drab, clumsy-looking touring cars, this glamorous Mitchell Submarine was like a fresh breath of spring! Surely, Carl H. Page could have sold a number of these to well-heeled Mitchell buyers, but I have no record of any other such Submarine specials having been produced. I've seen no mention of this car since its initial review in the August 15, 1916 *Horseless Age.*

1910s

DEAR FRIENDS
Happy Easter!

1916 MONITOR
MODEL "M"   TOURING CAR
L-HEAD, 6-CYLINDER ENGINE *
(3" × 5" BORE and STR.)
40 H.P.   4.1 GEAR RATIO
            (2-WHEEL
115" WHEELBASE   MECHANICAL
                BRAKES)
(4-CYL. and V8 ALSO BUILT)

ORIGINAL 1916 PRICE =
$895., f.o.b.,
CUMMINS-MONITOR CO.,
COLUMBUS, OHIO
(MONITOR CARS AVAIL. 1915-1922)

*=CONTINENTAL ENGINE USED.

© News Group Chicago, Inc. 1984

TAP   4-22

1916 Monitor

Here's another in the long list of forgotten "orphan" brands. Few readers have ever seen or heard of the Monitor automobile of Ohio.

The four-cylinder Monitor "4-39" (1915) was joined for 1916 by the new six (illustrated).

Though its popularly supposed that most old cars like this were painted black, let me add that the 1916 Monitor touring car, illustrated here, had black fenders and chassis, but body color options included dark Brewster green or dark blue. Genuine leather upholstery was standard equipment. Yet, this car was priced under $1,000, in spite of the creeping inflation that immediately preceded World War I.

Rear tires were non-skid type, and the leaf springs were long to provide a smooth ride. The semi-elliptic front leaf springs were underslung and could "swivel on the axle" to reduce jolting and jouncing on rough unpaved roads. The propeller shaft was enclosed in a torque tube.

Outwardly, the Monitor Six looked a bit old fashioned for 1916, a time when many other marques were adopting higher hoods and straight-line profiles. But, the Monitor Six boasted one very advanced feature not generally seen for many years afterward—an extra water reservoir provided by a rearward extension of the top tank of the radiator.

1917 Cole

If you're interested in old cars, you're probably familiar with the Cole automobile. But, have you ever heard of the Cole Registry? That's a somewhat esoteric club for owners and fans of this rare but respected brand.

How many Cole automobiles remain today, from the more than 40,000 built? Not too many. There's one 1910 model, four 1911s, one 1912, four 1913s, three 1914s, five 1915s, four 1916s, four 1917s, one 1918, seven 1919s, seven 1920s, three 1921s, one 1922, two 1923s, and two 1924s. As might be expected, eleven of these forty-nine known Coles are located in their state of origin, Indiana. One car, a 1920 touring, is presently in Ecuador. Two are in Canada.

Researching and hunting for old cars is an enjoyable, constructive hobby, and there are literally thousands of different rare old makes and models that are nearly forgotten today!

We're much indebted to Leroy D. Cole of Cole's Machine Service, Inc. (201 W. Rising St., Davison, MI 48423) for his fine research work and his efforts to preserve the history of the Cole automobile. He owns two examples: a 1917 Toursedan of the type illustrated here and a rare 1923 five-window coupe.

Anyone interested in joining the Cole Registry may contact Norm Buckhart, 3165 California St., San Francisco, CA 94115.

FRANKLIN'S "SCIENTIFIC LIGHT WEIGHT"
PRODUCED **REMARKABLE FUEL AND TIRE**
ECONOMY!

1917 FRANKLIN SERIES 9
CENTER-DOOR SEDAN (WT. 2610 lbs.)
$2950. f.o.b.
SYRACUSE, N.Y.

115" WHEELBASE

6-CYL. AIR-COOLED ENGINE (OVERHEAD VALVES)

(MFD. BY FRANKLIN AUTOMOBILE CO., SYRACUSE, N.Y., 1902~1934)

5·22

ON JULY 13, 1917, IN A NATIONAL EFFICIENCY TEST, 179 FRANKLIN CARS, AT 179 DIFFERENT POINTS IN THE U.S.A., AVERAGED **40.3 MILES PER GALLON** OF GAS! AND A MODIFIED 1911 FRANKLIN ACHIEVED AN AMAZING 80 M.P.G.!
IN OWNER REPORTS OVER A 5-YEAR PERIOD, A SET OF TIRES LASTED AN AVERAGE OF 10,203 MILES... (NOT BAD, CONSIDERING THE LOW QUALITY OF MOST PRE-1925 CORD TIRES!)
(WOODEN CHASSIS FRAME!)

1917 Franklin

Franklin was the most popular of the early air-cooled automobiles built in the United States—and much of its good reputation rested on its fuel and tire economy. Franklin's "Scientific Light Weight" created this economy.

There was no radiator, thus no heavy gallons of water. The Franklin body, wooden-framed, was flexible and lightweight. And, the weight of the chassis frame was greatly reduced, because it was made of wood instead of steel.

A bit of aerodynamic design was featured on the Franklins that were built between 1911 and 1920, as those models had a hood that sloped forward (as on the French Renault). On this 1917 Franklin sedan, notice that the windshield was divided vertically in "V" fashion, bringing the superstructure of this car to a point in front, like the prow of a ship.

The center door looks strange today, but in 1917 it was not so unusual. And, most sedans of that era towered seven feet tall! Because of its weird looks, this 1917 Franklin sedan is easily recognizable.

As of April 1917, Franklin prices for its various body types were as follows, f.o.b., factory at Syracuse, N.Y.: Runabout, $1,900; Touring Car, 1,950; 4-passenger Roadster, 1,950; Cabriolet, 2,750; Brougham, 2,800; Sedan (illus.), 2,850 (increased $100 in midyear); Town Car, 3,100; Limousine, 3,100.

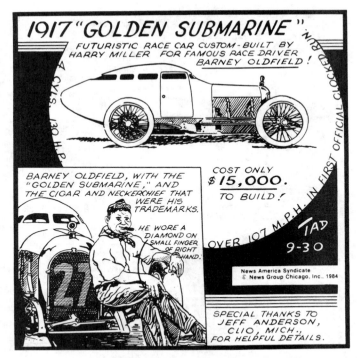

1917 "Golden Submarine"

Good news! Barney Oldfield's famous 1917 racecar, the "Golden Submarine," has recently been restored and now can be seen by the public—after having rusted in obscurity for many decades.

The Golden Submarine was unique: a super-streamlined, enclosed racing car in a day of antique, open speedsters. With its metallic-gold colored, egg-shaped aerodynamic body, the Golden Submarine was a futuristic sensation back in '17!

The car was designed in 1916 by Harry Miller, who also custom built it for Oldfield. It was revealed to an amazed public at Chicago's Maywood Stadium in June 1917.

Oldfield drove the car, and his mechanic (Waldo Stein) sometimes rode with him. Will Pickens was Oldfield's publicist, and he informed the press that the new racer would do "180 miles per hour," which was a highly exaggerated claim. In its first race at Maywood, the "Sub" clocked at 107.4 in the qualifying runs, and in the 250-mile initial race it was unable to finish because of engine problems.

The Golden Submarine won a few races, but one time at the Springfield track it hit a fence and overturned. Then it caught fire! Oldfield's shirt was aflame, and his hair was singed badly, but he managed to scramble out with minor injuries.

After '18, Oldfield left auto racing, becoming involved with Firestone Tires (where he headed the Oldfield Tire subsidiary for a time). He also tried producing a new automobile bearing his name. Only one known Oldfield car was completed: an attractive sport coupe.

1917 KENT 4 — $985.⁰⁰
TOURING CAR (ROADSTER, SAME PRICE)
4 CYL. CONTINENTAL ENGINE (3 3/4" x 5" BR. + ST.)
116" WHEELBASE   BOSCH MAGNETO IGNITION
ZENITH CARBURETOR   15-GALLON GAS TANK
STEWART VACUUM TANK FUEL FEED
BLT. IN NEWARK, N.J. FOR KENT MOTORS CORP.,
1790 BROADWAY, NYC (AN EXPORTER OF CARS TO LATIN
AMERICA) 1917 MODELS WERE ALL THE CARS BLT. BY
THIS COMPANY... (SEPT. 1916 TO MAY, 1917)

SONG HITS OF 1917 =   2-18-90
BELLS OF ST. MARY'S • DARKTOWN STRUTTER'S BALL •
FOR ME AND MY GAL • HAIL, HAIL, THE GANG'S ALL HERE •
I'M ALL BOUND 'ROUND WITH THE MASON DIXON LINE •
(BACK HOME IN) INDIANA • MacNAMARA'S BAND •
OH, JOHNNY, OH! • OUT WHERE THE WEST BEGINS •
THERE'S A LONG, LONG TRAIL A-WINDING • OVER THERE
• BEALE ST. BLUES • 'TIL THE CLOUDS ROLL BY

1917 Kent 4

Though its sales offices were in New York City, the Kent automobile was assembled in New Jersey in the Belleville section of Newark, overlooking the Passaic River.

Kent Motors Corp. exported cars to Latin America and had planned to establish an automobile factory in Havana, Cuba. But, instead, a factory was built and opened at the 16 1/2-acre site Kent had purchased in New Jersey.

The Kent was a rather ordinary "assembled" car with Continental engine and other popularly known components. Its most noteworthy feature was an eight-day clock, thrown in as standard equipment.

Only $200,000 was required to get the company started in Sept. 1916, and stock was offered for sale to the public to raise new funds for production.

But, the competition was stiff. In May 1917, a month after the United States had entered World War I, Kent Motors Corp. ran into financial difficulties so deep that "involuntary" bankruptcy was filed. Not long afterward, some Kent officials were indicted by a federal grand jury for stock promotion fraud. A conviction followed, but the report doesn't state whether these officials were issued their ball and chains, striped suits, and pickaxes. (Don't laugh! Prison life was no picnic in 1917.)

The Kent was just one of many long-forgotten makes that went belly-up during the turbulent 'teens.

4 CYLS. (3⁵/₈ × 4½")
185.8 CUBIC INCH DISPL.
25 H.P.

1917 MAXWELL
MODEL 25
CABRIOLET
103" WHEELBASE

CONVERTIBLE TOP CAN BE FOLDED DOWN, AND WINDOWS LOWERED INTO DOORS.

MAXWELL'S AVAIL. 1905-1925

30 × 3½" TIRES

TAD 3~1

$865. f.o.b.,
MAXWELL MOTOR CO., DETROIT

© News America Syndicate, 1987

1917 Maxwell

Beginning Sept. 13, 1916, Maxwell cars were improved for the coming year with a new windshield (on which the upper half overlapped the lower half for added rain protection); longer and more flexible springs; wider seats with deeper and softer cushions; a dash light; and a gas gauge on the dash at the left (filler cap was at opposite right).

The radiator design was interesting. As in 1916, the shell was rounded, with a heart-shaped dip at the center of the upper pan, creating the illusion of a costly V-shaped radiator!

Sales were good, and almost 600 cars a day could be produced on Maxwell's assembly line in Detroit.

Two cars in one: the illustrated cabriolet was fully convertible, combining the comfort of a closed coupe with the fun and airiness of an open roadster. The landau irons at the sides were functional in this case, helping to steady the top as it was folded up or down.

In 1925, it was decided that a second new model of Chrysler, the Chrysler Four, would replace the Maxwell in mid-year. And in turn, the 4-cylinder Chrysler series (successively 58, 50, and 52 models) was replaced in June 1928 by the new Chrysler-Plymouth (name shortened to Plymouth as the actual calendar year of 1929 began).

What is this little 1917 Maxwell cabriolet worth today? An absolutely perfect specimen in like-new condition could bring up to $20,000, 10 times the value of one in poor condition.

MFD. IN DETROIT, MICH.
BY
PAIGE-DETROIT
MOTOR CAR COMPANY
(1909 TO 1927)
SUCCEEDED 1928 BY
GRAHAM PAIGE.

6 CYL. 127" W.B.

AB 7-24

1917 PAIGE "6-51"
4-PASSENGER COUPE PRICE $2100.
DESIGNED BY ANDREW BACHLE, PAIGE DETROIT

1917 Paige

There were three series of Paige automobiles for the 1917 model year: the 6-39, the 6-46 (117-inch wheel base), and the larger 6-51 (127-inch w.b.), of which the Coupe is illustrated here.

Quoting from an original ad (November 1916, for the 1917 season), we read: "Our chief designer, Mr. Andrew Bachle, has put his ripest art into these exquisite models. As a result we offer a Coupe, Limousine, Sedan, and Town Car that will compare favorably with the finest productions of European makers.

"Every detail of the upholstering and general equipment has received painstaking care. Without regard to cost, we have deliberately set out to produce the smartest closed cars that can be found on the American market."

Notice the rakish slant of the windshield on this 1917 Paige. Most closed cars of other brands had absolutely vertical windshields and boxier lines. This Paige was a style-setter! The radiator front was pleasingly V-shaped, too.

In 1917, Paige was advertised as "The Most Beautiful Car In America." This claim may have been an exaggeration, but the Paige was certainly among the better-styled cars, if not the best.

In addition to model numbers, the open cars in the Paige line also had model names, such as the 6-39 Linwood touring or Dartmoor roadster.

For the 1918 and 1919 seasons, Paige produced a 6-55 Essex seven-passenger touring car, but when Hudson introduced its new low-priced, four-cylinder Essex subsidiary car in 1919, Paige decided to drop its own Essex model name.

1917
$860.,
f.o.b., YORK, PA.

4-CYL. L-HEAD ENG. 32 H.P.
3 3/4" x 4 1/4"
BR. + STR.

Pullman
4-PASS.
CLUB ROADSTER

TAP
8-18

© News America Syndicate, 1985

17 GALLON REAR FUEL TANK

114" WHEELBASE

MFD. 1903-1917 BY PULLMAN MOTOR CAR CO., YORK, PA.

1917 Pullman

The year 1917 was an interesting one for automobiles. Many makes were available, and it was a time when four-passenger "club roadsters" like this were in vogue.

What about the Pullman automobile? The first model (1903) was a strange, unsuccessful six-wheeler. The inventor was Albert P. Broomwell.

On the 1917 Pullman four-passenger roadster (illustrated), red-wall Firestone tires were used. Body color: Pullman green with black fenders and chassis. Electric horn button, according to original literature, was located not on the steering wheel but on the left-hand door! The dash was made of metal with a rubberized enamel finish and an inset instrument panel that included a speedometer with trip and season odometers; ammeter; oil gauge; lockup electric lighting switch; fuse box; carburetor choke; and electric dash light. Brakes were two-wheel mechanical with 12-inch-diameter drums. Fuel was drawn to the carburetor (Stromberg) through a Carter vacuum tank. The main gas tank at the rear had a visible fuel gauge on top.

The ignition was by Dixie waterproof, high-tension magneto. The oiling system was combined force-feed and splash, with indicator on dash. Thermosyphon cooling system made a water pump unnecessary. Front springs were 30-inch half-elliptic with 50 1/2-inch full cantilever springs at the rear. The seventeen-inch diameter steering wheel was of natural wood finish.

A total of about 15,000 Pullman autos were built, 1905-1917.

What is the illustrated roadster worth to collectors today? One up-to-date, reliable source gives a range of about $3,000 to $22,000, depending on the condition of the car.

"THE MOST FOR THE MONEY IN AMERICA!"

1917 RUSH
LIGHT DELIVERY TRUCK

MFD. 1915-1918 BY RUSH MOTOR TRUCK CO., PHILADELPHIA, PA.

CHASSIS $750. ($845. w. OPEN SIDED EXPRESS BODY)

WITH CONE CLUTCH

3½" x 5" BORE and STROKE LYCOMING ENGINE

WITH 4 CYLINDER

AS ILLUSTRATED, WITH PANEL BODY
870.
f.o.b., factory

105" W.B.

3½x4

1/2 TON CAPACITY

AD
3/21

©1993 North America Syndicate, Inc. World rights reserved.

1917 Rush Light Delivery Truck

A few *Auto Album* readers have suggested that I feature the Rush delivery truck, and it's surprising that this vehicle is remembered anymore, because it was discontinued after 1918, and on the market only four seasons.

During the late 'teens and early '20s, many truck manufacturers came out with peppy, lightweight delivery models such as this type shown here. Reo was one of the most successful, with its "Speed Wagon" canopy express.

One of the features of this little Rush truck was its smooth-performing Lycoming engine with counter-balanced crankshaft. The Rush was a so-called "assembled" truck, meaning that it was made from components supplied by several different specialized manufacturers. Connecticut ignition, Splitdorf electrical system, Carter carburetor, Borg & Beck clutch, and

Lavine steering gear were used. Like other vehicles of the time, this truck has two-wheel mechanical brakes.

Notice the finned top tank of the radiator, similar to several other makes of trucks of that era. The Rush had both vertical and horizontal fins (or grooves, if you will), at the top of the radiator. This wasn't just for looks, even though the feature was attractive. The grooved/finned surfaces were supposed to dissipate heat more quickly and efficiently.

At the end of 1915, chassis price for the Rush was just $625. But, in two years, wartime inflation had driven that price up to $895, and the small Philadelphia manufacturer could no longer meet the fierce competition.

It's surprising that the 1917 Rush with canopy express (open-sided) body cost just $95 more than a bare chassis!

ALMOST FORGOTTEN, THIS WAS THE FIRST V-8 CHEVROLET... INTRO. DURING 1917, FOR THE 1918 SEASON. CHEVROLET'S V8 WAS DROPPED IN 1919, and NOT OFFERED AGAIN UNTIL 1955.... WHEN IT BECAME A GREAT SUCCESS!

ZENITH CARBURETOR • CONE CLUTCH • REMY IGNITION • AUTO-LITE STARTER • GENERATOR

4.5 GEAR RATIO • 20-GAL. GAS TANK

120" WHEELBASE

↑AP
1~13

© 1991 North America Syndicate, Inc. All Rights Reserved

WITH 90° OVERHEAD VALVE 288 C.I.D. V8 ENG. 3³⁄₈" × 4" BORE and STROKE

3100 lbs. TOTAL ROAD WT.

CHEVROLET D-5
1918
TOURING CAR
(D-4 4-PASS. ROADSTER ALSO AVAILABLE)
$1550.⁰⁰ FOB PRICE OF EITHER BODY TYPE

ORIGINAL COLOR = CHEVROLET GREEN BODY and BLACK CHASSIS AND TOP.

(4-CYL. "490" and "FA" MODELS ALSO)

1918 Chevrolet D-5

Many readers assume that Chevy's first V-8 was the popular 1955 model. That assumption isn't surprising, because Chevrolet's first V-8, back in 1918, was considered a flop and was soon forgotten.

Always a rare car, the "D" series Chevrolet V-8 was available only as a four-passenger "cloverleaf" roadster or a five-passenger touring car. Closed models were available only in the lower-priced four-cylinder lines, which seems paradoxical.

Why did Chevrolet introduce its early V-8? In the mid-'teen years there was a sudden and short-lived craze for "multi-cylinder" engines (V-8s and V-12s), with several manufacturers offering them. Chevrolet advertising for the "D" series claimed that a V-8 gave more power impulses per flywheel turn than did a four—and thus a smoother, steadier, more powerful performance.

The "D" series had a simple dash: round, black-faced speedometer/odometer at center, with a map light directly above. At either side was a slightly smaller round gauge.

The accelerator pedal was unusual: large and spade-shaped, instead of small and round like most pre-1932 accelerator pedals.

Ironically, "D" series advertising mentioned that the "full streamline idea had been carried out!" ("Yeah, carried out the door!" you might snicker on seeing the boxy profile.) But, we must remember that in 1915-1916, when hood and cowl were at last blended into one flowing unit, cars were thought to be fully streamlined!

V-8 engines were successful for Cadillac and others, but Chevrolet was expected to be an economy car. That early V-8 was expensive to feed and maintain, so in 1919 it got the gate.

RARE!

1918 JONES 6

MANUFACTURED BY

THE JONES MOTOR CAR CO.

WICHITA, KANSAS
1914 ~ 1920

JOHN J. JONES, FOUNDER

4-PASS. ROADSTER

$1675.

PRESENT VALUE OF THIS CAR : $2700. TO $20,000.

THE JONES HAD A REPUTATION FOR DURABILITY, AROUND KANSAS AND THE MID-WEST. ONE JONES AUTO WAS HURLED 300 FEET, AGAINST A POLE, DURING A TORNADO — — — IT WAS ABLE TO RUN UNDER ITS OWN POWER, AFTER THE STORM WAS OVER !

JONES

303./ CID 6-CYL. CONTINENTAL ENGINE
125" WHEELBASE

TAD 9~4

MUCH OF THE JONES FACTORY BURNED DOWN IN 1920.

HAVE A SAFE AND HAPPY LABOR DAY WEEK-END !!

1918 Jones Six

This four-passenger roadster, was a popular body style in the late 'teen years. In the 1920s, the two-passenger roadster with a rumble seat for extra passengers would gain favor. But, the four-passenger roadster was safer to ride in.

Also available as a touring car, and in other body styles, the Jones Six was an "assembled" car. In addition to the popular Continental engine, some earlier Jones cars have been found with the Rutenber engines (also six-cylinder). Bodies, however, were Jones-built.

In addition to black, many Jones models sported bright and varied colors. The manufacturer claimed that any color was available. Women were told that even the colors of their favorite dresses could be matched! Various shades of beige could be chosen by the customer in a simple, but most unusual way: The customer was given a cup of coffee and cream. Then he or she could add more cream if a lighter beige was wanted. When the creamed coffee was the desired color, it was taken to the paint shop for careful matching!

During the late 'teens, Jones also built a "G-31" four-cylinder, one-ton truck and an "Oil-Field Special" roadster with an oil-drill-bit "bed" in the back. But, on February 18, 1920, a fire leveled two of the five factory buildings and also destroyed fourteen complete new cars and 100 additional car bodies! Jones cars went out of production during the 1920-1921 recession.

From 1914 to 1920, about 3,000 Jones cars and trucks had been built. At least five Jones cars are known to exist today.

CONE CLUTCH
REMY IGNITION

KISSEL KAR

32 x 4½" TIRES

KNOWN SIMPLY AS "KISSEL," FROM 1919 ON.

KISSEL MOTOR CAR
COMPANY, OF
HARTFORD, WI.,
BEGAN WITH
1907 MODEL.
ITS FINAL CAR
WAS THE 1931
MODEL.

6 CYL. (3 5/16 x 5½")
(SIDE SEATS SLIDE OUT OF
DRAWERS, ABOVE RUNNING-
BOARDS!)

2 - WHEEL MECHANICAL BRAKES

124" WHEELBASE
PRESENT VALUE OF
$7500. TO $85,000.

TAD
7-16

KISSEL KAR "SILVER SPECIAL"

NAMED FOR C. T. SILVER (N.Y.C. DISTRIBUTOR
OF KISSELS AND OTHER AUTOMOBILES,) THIS NEW 2-PASS.
SPEEDSTER DEVELOPED INTO THE FAMOUS "GOLD BUG!"

1918 Kissel Kar "Silver Special"

Most car buffs have heard of the classic Kissel Speedsters of the 1920s, especially the flashy, yellow Gold Bug models.

The Kissel Speedster was first known (as illustrated) as the "C. T. Silver" or "Silver Special," named for Conover Thomas Silver, the New York dealer/distributor for Kissel. Silver designed the Speedster as a special-ticket item, using the six-cylinder Kissel "100-Point" chassis.

After early 1919, Silver gave up his distributorship, and Kissel began using its own name on the sport models. In 1919, Kissel began painting most of the single-seat Speedster in "Chrome Yellow" (usually with black fenders). Reportedly, the Gold Bug name came from a contest sponsored by Kissel, in which "Gold Bug" was picked over 500 other suggestions.

"Bullet-shaped" tapering headlight shells on the Kissels were years ahead of their time, as were the adjustable sliding front seats.

An odd (and dangerous) feature of the Speedster was the drawer-type aux-iliary seat (one on each side) that slid out of the body, just over the running boards. Passengers riding "outboard" may have experienced a few thrills, but they were risking their necks!

One other interesting Kissel model was the 1918 all-year "staggered-door" sedan. The front door was on the left, and the back door was on the right. It was a two-door sedan with door access directly to either seat (but with only one door on each side).

In addition to the sixes, Kissel also sold a V-12 series (1917 and 1918 only). Later in the 1920s, they moved from sixes to straight-eights.

BUILT BY THE LANE MOTOR TRUCK CO., KALAMAZOO, MICH.
(1916 — 1920)

1918 MODELS (AVAILABLE 5-18) AS OF			
1 1/4 TONS	4 CYL.	$1850	WITH CONTINENTAL ENGINE, ELECTRIC STARTING AND LIGHTING
2 1/2	6	2700	
3 1/2	6	3500	
5	6	4500	

SOLID RUBBER TIRES and TIMKEN WORM-DRIVE REAR AXLE

1918 LANE MOTOR TRUCK

RARE!

1918 Lane Motor Truck

This Lane truck is rare, but it's just one of many discontinued "orphan" trucks of long ago. As a sample of the numerous forgotten trucks that were once available, let's look at a list of other discontinued American brands of trucks beginning only with the letters "LA."

La France-Republic (Alma, Mich., 1929-1942); Lange (Pittsburgh, Pa., 1911-1931); Lampher (Carthage, Mo., 1910); Lansden Electric (Newark, Allentown, Brooklyn, and Danbury, 1905-1928); Lansing (Lansing, Mich., 1917-1920); Lapeer (Lapeer, Mich., 1916-1920); Larrabee (Larrabee-Deyo) (Binghamton, N.Y., 1916-1932); La Salle-Niagara (Niagara Falls, N.Y. 1906); Lauth (Chicago, Ill., 1908-1910); Lauth-Juergens (Fremont, Ohio, 1910-1915); Lavigne (Detroit, 1914-1915); L.A.W. (Findlay, Ohio, 1912-1913); Lawson (Pittsburgh, Pa., 1917-1918).

Space limitations prevent us from listing all the other discontinued trucks with "L" names, not to mention hundreds and even thousands of others as well!

Notice the cab on the illustrated truck. It's typical of the era. Most early trucks had simple, open-sided cabs made mostly of wood. Some early trucks were sold as chassis units, and the buyer had to order body and cab elsewhere. Most pre-1920 trucks bounded along slowly on solid rubber tires and were suitable only for use within cities, on farms, or around factories or heavy construction sites.

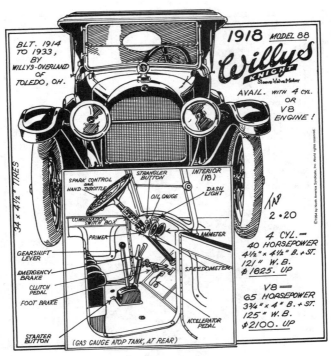

Figure labels (as shown in illustration):

BLT. 1914 TO 1933, BY WILLYS-OVERLAND OF TOLEDO, OH.

1918 MODEL 88

Willys KNIGHT Sleeve Valve Motor

AVAIL. WITH 4 CYL. OR V8 ENGINE!

34 x 4½" TIRES

SPARK CONTROL and HAND-THROTTLE — STRANGLER BUTTON — INTERIOR (V8) — DASH LIGHT — OIL GAUGE — COMBINATION SWITCH BOX — PRIMER — AMMETER — GEARSHIFT LEVER — EMERGENCY BRAKE — CLUTCH PEDAL — FOOT BRAKE — SPEEDOMETER — ACCELERATOR PEDAL — STARTER BUTTON

(GAS GAUGE ATOP TANK, AT REAR)

2•20

4 CYL.= 40 HORSEPOWER 4½" x 4½" B.+ ST. 121" W.B. $1025. UP

V8 = 65 HORSEPOWER 3¾" x 4" B.+ ST. 125" W.B. $2100. UP

1918 Willys-Knight "88"

W illys-Knight (1914-33) was the best known of all the cars that used a sleeve-valve Knight engine. Charles Y. Knight invented the double sleeve-valve engine.

It had no ordinary mushroom-shaped "poppet" valves for exhaust and intake, but instead had a pair of moving, slotted sleeves in each cylinder between the piston and cylinder wall. The sleeves were synchronized with the movement of the pistons, so as to serve as valves when their openings lined up to provide momentary intake or exhaust.

The Knight-type engine was said to be smooth, quiet, and to improve with use. A buildup of carbon deposits in a Knight engine was actually helpful—to a certain point. After about 50,000 miles, however, a Knight engine usually passed its peak of efficiency.

In addition to Willys-Knight, the following American cars used Knight engines during the years mentioned: Atlas-Knight (1912-1913); Brewster (1915-1925); Columbia (1912-1913); Edwards-Knight (1912-1914, predecessor to Willys-Knight); Falcon-Knight (1927-1928); Handley-Knight (1920, 1923); Knight Special (1917, pilot model only); Lyons-Knight (1913-1915); Moline-Knight (1914-1919); Porter-Knight (1915); Rauch & Lang (1930?); R&V (Root & Vandervoort) Knight (1920-24, successor to Moline-Knight); Silent Knight (1906-1908, 57 cars built by Charles Y. Knight); Silver-Knight (1916-1918?); Stearns-Knight (1912-1929); Sterling-Knight (1923-1925); Stoddard-Dayton Knight (1912).

Several other brands of Knight-engined cars were built in Europe, some even before Knight scored his first success with his engines in the United States.

1919 DORT
TOURING CAR
$925. f.o.b.
LYCOMING
4 CYL. ENG.
19.6 H.P.
105½" WB

BLT. 1915-1924 BY DORT MOTOR CAR CO., FLINT, MICH.

CURRENT VALUE:
$7000-19,000

SLOGAN: "QUALITY GOES CLEAR THROUGH"

TAD
1~14~90

1919 Dort

Even though the Dort was discontinued in the mid-1920s, there are readers who remember it. Several years ago, I drew a '24 Dort sedan in *Auto Album*. I also drew a 1921 Dort (the '21-'22 models had distinctive peaked radiator shells). I never released the '21 Dort drawing because I wasn't satisfied with it. But, sometime I'll try drawing that one again. Meanwhile, here's a close-up view of the 1919 version.

Some brief history: Back in 1886, William C. "Billy" Durant (later to found General Motors Corp.) and Josiah Dallas Dort teamed up to establish the Flint Road Cart Company, which later became the Durant-Dort

Carriage Co. When Durant made it big with G.M. in 1908, his good friend Dort remained in the carriage business, but kept in close touch. Witnessing Durant's success, Dort established the Dort Motor Car Co. in 1915. There was also a Canadian affiliate, for a time: the Gray-Dort, built up north by William Gray.

A four-cylinder Lycoming engine was standard Dort fare until '23, when a Falls 6 engine was introduced.

More than 107,000 Dort cars were built between 1915 and 1924. Though the junkyard circuit digested most of them in the 1920s and 1930s, a few examples escaped the wrecker's torch and have survived in antique car collections.

1919 Jordan Brougham

The Jordan, built in Cleveland, Ohio, was an "assembled" car, using components supplied by various specialized manufacturers. In 1919, its engine was an L-head, six-cylinder Continental. The Jordan was well built and well liked—though Jordan production was limited to a few thousand cars a year.

The first full year for Jordan automobile production was 1917, and by 1919 the small, independent company was rolling along very well. The famous Jordan "Playboy" roadster was conceived in 1919, as was the new Suburban Seven (seven-passenger) Sport Touring Car. Also available were a "Sport Marine" five-passenger touring car, a large sedan, and other types.

The illustrated Jordan Brougham was a new model in 1919. Jordan supplanted the Brougham in late 1919 (for 1920) with a "Silhouette Brougham," which had the vertical rear end of a two-door sedan or "coach."

Jordan's lightweight aluminum body (with wooden inner framework) was declared to be "virtually dust and rattle proof." The top half of the Brougham windshield could be opened, but the bottom half was stationary. The windshield was of the stylish "Brewster" type, markedly sloped with wedge-shaped front quarter windows between the windshield and each side door.

Doors on Jordans were "broad," for easy access to seats. Closed car windows operated with "improved lifts."

In addition to a dome light, there were individual "reading lamps." A clock was provided on the instrument board. The water temperature gauge was mounted up in front, atop the radiator cap.

HAPPY FATHER'S DAY!

1919 LOCOMOBILE

SPECIAL "GROWLER COUPE" *

* A TYPE ADAPTED FROM THE OLD
LONDON 4-WHEELER COACH.
(CHAUFFEUR-DRIVEN)

COST: $10,000.00 (f.o.b., approx.)

|◄——————142" wheelbase——————►| TAP 6/19

6 CYLINDERS (4½" × 5½") CAST IN PAIRS (100 H.P.)
2-WHEEL MECHANICAL BRAKES.   4-SPEED TRANSMISSION.
MFD. BY LOCOMOBILE CO. OF AMERICA,
BRIDGEPORT, CT. (1899-1929)

® Field Enterprises, Inc., 1983

1919 Locomobile "Growler Coupe"

G rowler Coupe—a great iron beast that lumbered along on a huge 142-inch wheelbase.

The very boxiness and baroque quaintness of this 1919 Locomobile Growler Coupe make it a prized treasure for any car collector fortunate enough to ever find one. Few ever existed, even though it was advertised in the August 1919 *National Geographic*.

With a removable canvas top over the driver's seat, this could be classified as a "town car." The chauffeur (or chauffeurs, as sometimes two were employed as a team) rode in semi-comfort with no side windows and chintzy little half-doors. The luxury-loving owners, however, reclined in lavishly upholstered, fully enclosed, rear quarters. Until the middle 1920s, most limousines, as well as taxicabs, did not provide fully enclosed front compartments.

Two spare tires were carried at the rear—and for good reason. The flimsy cord tires available in 1919 were terrible by today's standards. Blowouts were frequent.

In 1920, Locomobile, and also Mercer, were taken over by Hare's Motors, a receiving company. A few years later, Locomobile was absorbed into the Durant motor empire. In the Durant era, Locomobile produced a few smaller models (such as the Junior Eight, etc.), and yet the magnificent, old, large models were continued, in limited numbers, right up to the final year of the marque (1929).

1920 Lexington

The 1920 Lexington "Lex-sedan" was one of several early predecessors of the pillarless "four-door hardtop."

For 1920, Lexington offered a "greatly improved chassis," with a new feature called the "lexi-gasifier," incorporated into the combined intake and exhaust manifold. It served to completely "gasify" all fuel on its way to the combustion chamber, resulting in more power, less wasted fuel! Cable-operated mechanical brakes were an improvement over the old rod-operated type. (Later, in the 1930s, cable-operated mechanical brakes would be sometimes referred to as "steeldraulic," capitalizing on the rising popularity of genuine hydraulic brakes.)

The Lex-Sedan was claimed to be superior because the body was built for the top instead of vice versa. Thus the car was lighter than rival manufacturers' sedans, and also less top-heavy.

Still another feature of the 1920 Lexington was the vacuum-controlled, two-way headlamp system, which dipped the beam to a lower position instead of merely dimming it and losing road visibility ahead.

On the Lex-Sedan, the six side windows were of equal size, and could be partially lowered, or completely removed—along with the center-posts, as seen here.

"Unified frame" was another Lexington feature (continued from 1919), as was the "one-finger" emergency brake.

Later in 1920, Lexington Motor Company became a part of the United States Automotive Corporation. The winter of 1920-1921 was a recession period, and there were many failures, mergers, and takeovers. Only the stronger companies made it through the 1920s (not to mention the 1930s).

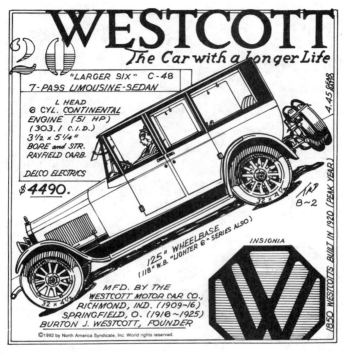

WESTCOTT *The Car with a longer Life*

"LARGER SIX" C-48
7-PASS LIMOUSINE-SEDAN

L HEAD
6 CYL. CONTINENTAL
ENGINE (51 HP)
(303.1 C.I.D.)
3½ x 5¼"
BORE and STR.
RAYFIELD CARB.

DELCO ELECTRICS

$4490.

4.45 GEAR

8~2

32 x 4½

125" WHEELBASE
(118" W.B. "LIGHTER 6" SERIES ALSO)

INSIGNIA

1850 WESTCOTTS BUILT IN 1920 (PEAK YEAR)

M.F.D. BY THE
WESTCOTT MOTOR CAR CO.,
RICHMOND, IND. (1909~16)
SPRINGFIELD, O. (1916~1925)
BURTON J. WESTCOTT, FOUNDER

32 x 4½

1920 Westcott

The Westcott Carriage Company was founded at Richmond, Ind. in 1896. In 1909, automobile production began at Westcott with a primitive motor buggy. The following year, a much-improved four-cylinder touring car was introduced, and the manufacturer's name was changed to Westcott Motor Car Co. In 1910, production was three cars a day.

In 1916, all of Westcott's operations moved to Springfield, and in 1921, Burton J. Westcott, company founder and president, won the mayoral election in that city.

After a 1920 peak sales year, however, Westcott sales declined. Even after numerous improvements (balloon tires, four-wheel brakes, etc.), the company went into receivership by January 1925—because of an $825,000 debt to various parts manufacturers. In

March 1925, Westcott lost his chief engineer, J. H. Tuttle, who left to take the same position with the up-and-coming Checker Cab Company of Kalamazoo, Mich. The following month, Westcott's factory was sold at auction. Westcott was allowed continued use of the factory for five more bleak months to complete about twenty-five more cars to fulfill orders.

A product of happier times for Westcott, the illustrated car was an interesting new addition to the line. Introduced during the summer of 1919, it was, technically, a 1920 model (since Westcott introduced its dual series of sixes for '20, and this sedan-limousine was a part of the larger series of sixes). A seven-passenger model, it included a pair of small auxiliary "jump seats," the tops of which can be seen just to the right of the rear side door in this picture.

1920 Winton Six

Alexander Winton came to the United States from Scotland in 1884 and established his first experimental motor vehicle. In 1897, he organized the Winton Motor Carriage Co. (later renamed) and built a second car; this two-cylinder vehicle managed to do over 33 m.p.h. on a racetrack.

In 1898, Winton began producing cars for sale to the public and made twenty-two sales that year. James Ward Packard bought the twelfth of these early Wintons. Packard soon offered Winton some suggestions, and Winton reportedly told Packard to go build his own cars if he thought he could do better. That's exactly what Packard did, giving birth to the legendary Packard Motor Car Company.

In 1919, a major restyling was in order. For the coming decade of the 1920s, the Winton got a new, higher straight-line hood with larger louvers and new body lines.

From 1921 on, Winton concentrated on only the 132-inch-wheelbase "25" series, renaming it the "40" in 1923 and cutting the base price for 1923 from $4,600 to $3,400. Alexander Winton wanted "no cheap cars" in his lineup, but the market in the Winton price range was very bleak when millions of Americans were buying new cars for less than $1,000.

When Winton passed away in 1932, he left an estate of $50,000. That was just one percent of the $5 million fortune he'd amassed some fifteen years earlier. Mr. Winton would have been amazed to know that someday just one of his cars, in like-new condition or totally restored, would be worth $50,000 at auction!

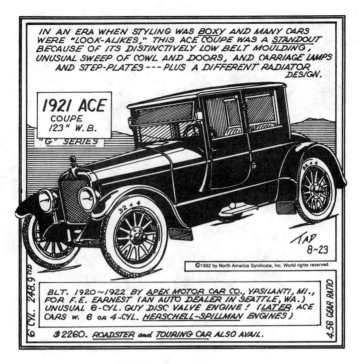

IN AN ERA WHEN STYLING WAS <u>BOXY</u> AND MANY CARS WERE "LOOK-ALIKES," THIS ACE COUPE WAS A <u>STANDOUT</u> BECAUSE OF ITS DISTINCTIVELY LOW BELT MOULDING, UNUSUAL SWEEP OF COWL AND DOORS, AND CARRIAGE LAMPS AND STEP-PLATES --- PLUS A DIFFERENT RADIATOR DESIGN.

1921 ACE
COUPE
123" W. B.
"G" SERIES

TAD
8~23

©1992 by North America Syndicate, Inc. World rights reserved.

6 CYL. 248.9 cu.in.

BLT. 1920~1922 BY <u>APEX MOTOR CAR CO.</u>, YPSILANTI, MI., FOR F.E. EARNEST (AN AUTO DEALER IN SEATTLE, WA.) UNUSUAL 6-CYL. GUY DISC VALVE ENGINE! (<u>LATER</u> ACE CARS w. 6 OR 4-CYL. <u>HERSCHELL-SPILLMAN</u> ENGINES)

4.56 GEAR RATIO

$2260. <u>ROADSTER</u> and <u>TOURING CAR</u> ALSO AVAIL.

1921 Ace Coupe

T his car is one of the most unique marques from the 1920s, with numerous odd mechanical and styling features. It looked very expensive, though in the upper middle-price range. Its Guy Disc-Valve engine was a bit weird and apparently not very durable. The engine promoters pulled out from Apex/Ace and went on their own. This was a mistake, because no other auto manufacturer seemed interested in the Guy Disc-Valve engine.

You'll be amazed at the large number of car makes available in the United States in 1921! The "top 40" were, 1-Ford 4; 2-Dodge Bros. 4; 3-Buick 4 & 6; 4-Chevrolet 4; 5-Studebaker 4 & 6; 6-Overland 4; 7-Nash 4 & 6; 8-Oldsmobile 6 & V-8; 9-Maxwell 4; 10-Essex 4; 11-Hupmobile 4; 12-Hudson 6; 13-Oakland 6; 14-Cadillac V-8; 15-Dort 4 & 6; 16-Paige 6; 17-Reo 4 & 6; 18-Willys-Knight 4; 19-Chandler 6; 21-Packard 6 & V-12; 22-Haynes 6 & V-12; 23-Velie 6.

LESS THAN 5000 SOLD, 24-Cleveland 6; 25-Gardner 4; 26-Briscoe 4; 27-Moon 6; 28-Chalmers 6; 29-Scripps-Booth 6; 30-Grant 6; 31-Jordan 6; 32-Stephens 6; 33-Mitchell 6; 34-Lexington 6; 35-Lincoln V8; 36-Columbia 6; 37-Cole V8; 38-Elcar 4 & 6; 39-Wills Sainte Claire V8; 40-Auburn 6.

We're grateful to Harlan E. Applequist for researching this list.

Also, tribute is due to the late Floyd Clymer, for publishing a picture, some years ago, of the rare Ace coupe! (This drawing was based on that illustration.) With his well-loved series of historical "Motor Scrapbooks," featuring early car advertisements and stories, Clymer did much to popularize the antique car hobby.

1921 Ferris 6

For the 1920 season, the Ohio Trailer Company of Cleveland, Ohio became the Ohio Motor Vehicle Company and began producing Ferris automobiles.

The Ferris car was named after William E. Ferris, Ohio's secretary-treasurer. The president of the Ohio Motor Vehicle Company was Charles Riegler, but, obviously, Ferris was an easier name to remember!

The Ferris was comparatively expensive for its day—over $3,000, though prices were later reduced. It was an "assembled" car with a Continental engine. Its bodywork was of unusually high quality, which contributed to the high price. The body was of aluminum sheathing over a formed wooden framework. The car was built for "the man who would not live on a street where all houses are alike."

The 1920-21 models were the "C-20" and "C-21," with choice of a six-passenger touring car, six-passenger Sport touring car (illustrated), or four-passenger Sedan (considerably higher-priced, approaching $5,000!).

Because of the 1920-1921 business recession that followed a brief postwar interlude of expansion and inflation, the Ohio Motor Vehicle Company went into receivership in mid-1921. However, production was allowed to continue for a short time, with two new series for 1922: the 60-h.p. "60," priced from $2,595, and the 70-h.p. "70," from $2,795. More body types were made available, including roadsters.

But, 1922 signaled the bitter end for the Ferris venture, with a grand total of only a few hundred sales. The Ferris was just one of many now forgotten makes of automobiles that failed commercially in the hard times of the early 1920s.

1921 Leach

The Leach-Biltwell, Leach Six, and Leach Power-Plus Six were expensive, top-quality cars of 1920 to 1923, manufactured in Southern California with the Hollywood set in mind. Priced well above $5,000, the Leach cars were available only as two-door or four-door hardtops! They had the look of a convertible, but featured open-sided stationary tops.

The new Leach had a solid, one-piece plate-glass sloping windshield with triangular side deflectors. Added ventilation was provided through a trap door at the top of cowl, though the massive windshield would open.

The steering wheel could be tilted and was also lockable. A Crosby directional signal box on the left rear fender was actuated by a control lever to the left of the steering column. The gas gauge on the dash was a feature found on few 1921 cars, and the dual dash lights and cigar lighter could be moved a considerable distance from the leather-padded dash!

Individual illuminated step plates took the place of running boards. The radiator was an oversized 400 cubic inches and four inches thick, while the heavy chassis frame was eight inches in thickness.

Goodrich Silvertown Cord tires were standard. Wire wheels were available on early Leaches, but disc wheels (as shown) became standard.

Only about 500 Leach autos were built, and few have been seen at all in recent decades. With only two California distributorships, sales were limited to the West Coast. Yet, in the top quality materials used and in its advanced design, the Leach rivaled the legendary Duesenberg!

1921 Monroe Model S

The Monroe Motor Co. and its Monroe car originated in Flint, Mich. in 1914. For its first few years, Monroe specialized in open roadsters with four-cylinder engines by Mason or Sterling. In 1917, other body styles were added.

In 1920-21, when the "S" series replaced the "M-6," no closed cars were listed, but a sedan returned for 1922, along with a new three-passenger coupe.

Early stockholders in the Monroe Motor Co. were also Chevrolet stockholders, and Monroe's early vice president was none other than William C. "Billy" Durant, who at two different periods was the head of General Motors Corp.

As of April 1916, Durant left Monroe, and President R. F. Monroe moved his company into the former Welch auto factory at Pontiac, Mich. In 1918, Monroe faced bankruptcy, and the William Small Co. in Indianapolis purchased the company assets.

Louis Chevrolet, a famed race driver and engineer for whom the Chevrolet car had been named, went to work for William Small to re-engineer the Monroe auto. He designed a few Monroe racecars, and Louis' brother Gaston Chevrolet scored a victory in a Monroe racer at the 1920 Indianapolis 500 race!

In spite of the great racing publicity, the Monroe organization went bust again, and in January 1922 its assets were sold for $175,000 to an Indianapolis bank. In 1923, the assets were resold to Frank Strattan, who planned to reintroduce the Monroe plus a second, lower-priced car bearing his own surname. Strattan sold Monroe to the Premier Co.

THIS CAR USUALLY PAINTED LIGHT BLUE, WITH BLACK CHASSIS.

WITH 6-CYLINDER
L-HEAD
CONTINENTAL
ENGINE (224 CID)
3 1/4" x 4 1/2" BORE & STROKE
(48 H.P.)
2-WHEEL MECH.
BRAKES
(AN "ASSEMBLED"
CAR, THE MOON
USED PARTS FROM
VARIOUS SPECIALIZED
MFRS.)

$ **2185.** 00
F.O.B., ST. LOUIS

THIS
PEAKED
"ROLLS ROYCE"
STYLE RADIA-
TOR USED ON
1919 TO
1926
MOONS.

122" WHEELBASE.

32 P.4

32 x 7

1921
MOON
TOURING CAR (6-48 SERIES)
MFR.: MOON MOTOR CAR CO., ST. LOUIS, MO.
(1905-1930)   (6-68 SERIES ALSO)

RAP
1-17

1921 Moon

The casual observer might mistake this Moon for an old Rolls-Royce because of the high-peaked radiator. (Roamer was another car in the 1920s that was sometimes mistaken on sight for a Rolls.)

Like many other long-gone "orphan" cars of the 1920s, the Moon was an assembled car. Moon's "Ten Proven Units" in 1921 were: a Continental engine, Delco starter and ignition, Timken axles, Spicer universal joints, Brownlipe transmission, Borg & Beck clutch, Rayfield carburetor, Exide battery, Fedders nickel-silver radiator, and Gemmer steering gear. (Disteel inwardly-curved disc wheels were used on many Moon models, but wood or wire wheels were also available if desired.)

Interestingly, the vent louvres on the sides of the hood on most Moon cars were punched inward rather than stamped outward as on other makes.

Though most auto historians trace Moon's origin to 1905, Moon advertising in the 1920s repeatedly claimed that the company was "founded 1907 by Joseph W. Moon." The company history actually went back to 1880, as Joseph Moon was originally a builder of horse-drawn coaches; some 1921 advertisements mentioned the company's 41-year history of coach building.

A sharp business recession in 1921 caused Moon prices to be cut more than once. In July, the touring car was reduced to $1,985. Moon changed the name of its cars to Windsor during 1929, and in 1930 collaborated with Kissel to manufacture the classic front-wheel-drive Ruxton automobile. But, 1930 was the first full year of the Great Depression, and Windsor/Ruxton production ceased within a few months.

THIS LUXURY CAR HAD A 404 C.I.D. V8 ENGINE !!

1922 DANIELS
V8

L-HEAD
V8 ENGINE
90
H.P.
(DANIELS-
BLT. ENG.)
132 OR
138-INCH
WHEELBASES
AVAIL.
ON
"D" SERIES
(ILLUSTRATED)

4-PASS.
SEDAN

2-WHEEL MECHANICAL BRAKES

© News America Syndicate, 1986

TAD
8-10

(SPEEDSTER
COULD REACH
90 MPH!)

OTHER
CARS IN
1920s WITH
V8 ENGINES
INCLUDED
CADILLAC,
LINCOLN, COLE,
WILLS SAINTE CLAIRE
PEERLESS, CUNNINGHAM,
OLDSMOBILE (SOME
MODELS) and OTHERS.

ORIG.
COST $ **7000.** ⁰⁰

MFD. IN READING, PENNSYLVANIA
(1915 — 1924)
BY THE DANIELS MOTOR CAR CO.
(EACH CAR CUSTOM-FINISHED TO
REQUIREMENTS OF ORDERING BUYER.)

1922 Daniels

On June 25, 1915, George E. Daniels incorporated his own automobile company in partnership with Neff E. Parish of Reading, Pa. The Model A Daniels automobile was built through 1917, powered by a Herschell-Spillman L-head V-8 (available in two sizes). In 1918 and early 1919, the Model B was produced, with a slightly altered engine. During 1919, the Daniels switched to an engine of its own design (the "D-19" V-8). The early models had used Fleetwood bodies.

Reportedly, 1,668 or more Daniels cars were built, and the venture did well until Daniels and Parish had a serious disagreement concerning a stock deal. Parish left the company, and Daniels was unable to find a competent partner to replace him. Without Parish to lend his leadership and financial support, the situation deteriorated. Daniels was forced to announce, on September 8, 1923, that the company would be sold to a receiver.

The following month, Levine Motors of Philadelphia bought up Daniels "lock, stock, and barrel." As late as 1927, the Daniels was listed as "still available," but the very few Levine-assembled models of 1924 were not up to the old high standard, yet cost $10,000 each.

When George Daniels had been in charge, he'd personally inspected each car, and even slashed the upholstery in one of them because he was dissatisfied with its installation!

According to a recent book, a 1922 Daniels four-passenger sedan, like the one illustrated, would be worth up to $40,000 now. A sporty Daniels two-passenger Speedster would be worth nearly twice that price!

FOLDING TOP CONCEALED IN DECK

note THE PORTHOLES IN PLACE OF HOOD LOUVRES.

TAP 6-17

DIXIE FLYER MODEL H

" FIREFLY " SPEEDSTER

$ *1395.*

112" W.B.   40 H.P.   4-CYL. HERSCHELL-SPILLMAN ENGINE

DIXIE FLYERS MFD. 1916~1923 BY KENTUCKY WAGON MFG. COMPANY, LOUISVILLE, KY. (ALSO THE BUILDER OF "OLD HICKORY" MOTOR TRUCKS)

1922 SERIAL NOS. 10300 ~ 12000

1920s

1922 Dixie Flyer

S outhern-built antique cars are interesting, and they're rare!

The Dixie Flyer was built by the Kentucky Wagon Manufacturing Co. (originally Kentucky Wagon Works, founded in 1878). About 10,000 Dixie Flyers were sold between 1916 and 1923. The manufacturer built Urban Electric and Old Hickory trucks, as well.

In 1949, restyled Buicks were graced with portholes along the front sides, and it was considered a new idea. Yet, for the 1922 season, the Dixie Flyer offered this novelty on certain models, even though it failed to set a trend. The only other thing remotely resembling portholes on other old cars in the United States was the bubble-shaped hood vents on the streamlined '34 and '35 La Salles or on the diminutive '35 and '36 Willys "77s." Plymouths had hood-side "portholes" in 1935, but they were crossed with horizontal chrome strips, and the real vents were concealed under the front fenders.

In 1923, Associated Motor Industries took control of Dixie Flyer, Jackson, and National, with the plan to continue only the National. It is reported that some of the final Dixie Flyers and Jacksons were sold bearing the National nameplate. But, after severe financial difficulties in 1923, National, too, was discontinued (1924).

As for the Kentucky Wagon Manufacturing Co., it continued its wagon making business until 1931.

1920s

THIS ESSEX 2-DOOR COACH WAS INSTRUMENTAL IN POPULARIZING CLOSED CARS, DURING THE 1920s, AS THE COACH PRICE WAS PERIODICALLY REDUCED, BRINGING IT DOWN TO THE PRICE OF AN OPEN CAR. DURING 1922, COACH PRICE WAS CUT FROM $1345 TO $1295, AND THEN TO $1245.

1922 Essex Coach

Dealers of rival makes of cars in the 1920s scoffed that the Essex had "the styling of a packing crate." But, many of these dealers envied Essex's increasing popularity during the early 1920s.

In 1922, Essex's new two-door coach (illustrated) sold in large numbers because it offered closed car comfort and convenience at little more than open car prices; and Essex prices were reduced at regular intervals to make the Essex more affordable.

"Why face winter in a cold and draughty touring car?" demanded one '22 Essex ad. "The comforts of a Coach cost but a trifle more. It means warm, snug travel in all weather." Another '22 Essex ad assured, "Controls are easy and natural … Gears shift as easily as lifting a fork at [a] table. …

"And so reliable that thousands go out from the salesrooms and drive for thousands of miles without returning for even a minor adjustment."

Like its parent car, the Hudson, the Essex had a unique oil-bathed clutch with cork inserts in the face disc, which lent added smoothness.

In June 1922, when the coach was priced at $1,345, the touring car was $1,095 and the cabriolet was $1,295. The "cabriolet" (not a convertible) was actually a two-passenger business coupe. Late in 1922, Essex reported that a fleet of sixty of these Essex "cabriolet" coupes had been sold to the sales department of the Sun-Maid Raisin Growers of Fresno, Calif. This fleet was to be used by Sun-Maid traveling salesmen in various regions of U.S.A. and Canada.

1922 Georges Irat

A rare French car, the Georges Irat was built from 1921 to 1946. You'll notice that in 1922, two different types of roadsters were offered (as illustrated). The antique-looking upper model was advertised in *L'Illustration* magazine, in France, in the March 25, 1922 issue. But, the "Tres Sport" type (lower left section of picture) was a more advanced-looking car, advertised in time for the Paris Motor Show of 1922.

Georges Irat cars participated in many vintage-era auto races and rallys, including Le Mans. And, in the Circuit des Routes Pavees, a Georges Irat won in 1923 and 1927.

The four-wheel Dewandre vacuum servo brakes were very advanced for 1921, when the marque began with a Georges Irat-designed overhead-valve four-cylinder engine. In 1927, the engine changed to a six, but with the same cylinder dimensions as before.

In 1935, the factory changed locations for the second time since '29, and a new front-wheel-drive small sports car was introduced (using a 1,100 c.c. Ruby engine). In 1939, came another front-wheel-drive model, with a Citroen engine. During World War II, small electric models were produced.

In 1946, a new prototype was shown with advanced features, but it never went into production. Instead, Georges Irat experimented with Diesel trucks and built engines for other cars.

Other similarly-named French cars: the Georges Richard (1897-1903), Georges Roy (1906-1929), and Georges Ville (1904-1909?).

The Georges Irat had no American dealers and, understandably, is quite rare outside of France. (You won't find many *there* either!)

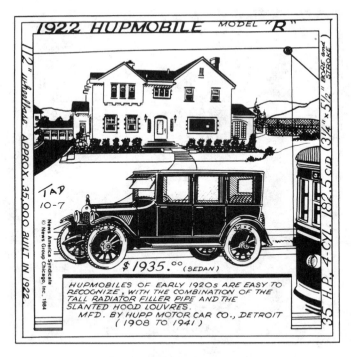

1922 Hupmobile

"In the Hupmobile's own plants, its motor and transmission, clutch and axles and other essential parts are built to Hupmobile designs and specifications, for the exclusive use of the Hupmobile.

"No compromise of good designing or fine manufacturing is ever forced upon our engineers. They are entirely free from the limitations they might meet if they were dependent, for some vital parts, on outside manufacturing sources."

We're quoting from an original Hupmobile advertisement of 1922, which assured the buyer that the Hupmobile was not merely an "assembled" car made of components from various other manufacturers.

Body types available from Hupmobile in 1922, in addition to the illustrated sedan: Touring Car $1,250; Roadster 1,250; Coupe (4-passenger) 1,835; and the new lightweight "Roadster-Coupe," which, as the name implied, was a two-passenger car on which the coupe top appeared to have been applied as an afterthought, though it was somewhat attractive.

Another Hupmobile ad (Feb. 4, 1922, *Saturday Evening Post*) assured the reader that Hupmobiles so well pleased their owners that few were ever advertised in the used-car columns in daily newspapers. Moreover, it was reported that "no less than half of all the Hupmobile sales in America are being made to owners of other [brands of] cars."

In addition to its American sales, 1922 Hupmobiles were shipped to Europe, Africa, South America, Australia, and Asia. According to Hupmobile advertising, its cars were popular in England, South Africa, India, Australia, Holland, and Belgium in particular. No doubt a few still remain in those overseas countries!

1922
VALVE-
IN-
HEAD
ENGINE
FROM $1240. (6)
OR $935. (4)

TOURING CAR
(6-691 OR
4-41 MODEL)

NASH

C Field Enterprises Inc 1983

IN
MID-
1917,
THE
NASH
REPLACED
THE
JEFFERY CAR , (WHICH IN TURN HAD
REPLACED THE RAMBLER IN 1914.)
FACTORY IN KENOSHA, WIS., BUT 4-
CYL. NASH BUILT IN MILWAUKEE.
CERTAIN DATA THANKS TO CARL G. FEIN, SEATTLE, WASH.

60 HP
248.9
C.I.D. 6,
OR 178.9
C.I.D. 4

121" OR
112"
WHEEL-
BASE
TAD
1-16

33 × 4

1922 Nash

"**N**ash Leads The World In Motorcar Value." That was the slogan in 1922, and that summer a magazine advertisement declared, "Early in April the 100,000th Nash left the factory, scarcely four and a half years since the first Nash made its appearance, and that is the most rapid production ever achieved by a car of the Nash class.

"During the past three months, the volume of purchasers has risen so swiftly that all previous sales records for any quarter have been surpassed and immediate expansion of our manufacturing capacity made imperative."

In addition to the successful six-cylinder line, Nash also built a four-cylinder model (1921 to 1924), which was built initially in Milwaukee rather than at the Kenosha factory. Both the Nash Four and the Nash Six had overhead-valve engines at that time.

Nash sales in 1922 amounted to 41,652, which was nearly twice the 1921 total. Nash introduced rubber engine mounts in 1922, and this greatly increased engine smoothness. In time, other auto manufacturers would also introduce such mounts.

The touring car was the most popular auto body type in the early 1920s, mainly because it cost much less than a closed sedan. But, early in 1922, Nash introduced a "Carriole" coach on its four-cylinder chassis; this was a simple, two-door sedan priced at $1,350. The 1922 season was the time that Hudson introduced its Hudson and its Essex coaches (two-door sedans), which were the most important factors in popularizing closed cars, as their prices were soon cut to equal the prices of open cars!

1920s

"3~35" SERIES

(36" WB)

(6-CYL. "SINGLE SIX" ALSO)

90 HP @ 2800 RPM

WITH **V-12 ENGINE!**

"SPECIAL" has NICKELED RADIATOR SHELL and DELUXE EQUIPMENT.

424.1 C.I.D. V-12 ENGINE (3"x5"b.s.)

PACKARD TWIN SIX

1922 TOURING CARS = $3850. and up

4.38 REAR AXLE RATIO

IN 3~5

© 1989 North America Syndicate, Inc. All rights reserved.

1922 Packard "Twin Six"

Packard's 12-cylinder Twin Six was its top-of-the-line series from 1916 to 1923.

The 1922 Twin Six smacked of quality. As a 1922 advertisement related, "What is it in the Packard Twin Six that has aroused in its owners an allegiance that any other car seems powerless to disturb?

"The fundamental cause is of course the unchanging excellence of Twin Six performance, but there are many other reasons than this.

"If you will think a moment, you will realize that you have never seen a Twin Six body that was anything but tight and sound and plumb.

"You will recall, again, that almost never have you seen a dilapidated Twin Six fender, nor a Packard wheel but ran staunchly and true.

"Twin Sixes that have years of service and tens of thousands of miles behind them still hold the deep lustre of their enamel and paint."

It was true … Most Twin Sixes received excellent care from their doting owners, and few ever met the fate of becoming a jalopy! Years later, surveys by the Packard Motor Car Company of their older models remaining in service, revealed a high percentage of survivors!

Interestingly, Packard's first Twin Six of 1916 is reported to have introduced aluminum pistons.

Although the Depression later spelled doom for some luxury car manufacturers, Packard assured its survival for many more years by introducing the 1935 "120" series, a full-sized Packard 8 at prices starting under $1,000!!

"ONCE AN OWNER — ALWAYS A FRIEND"

AUBURN

"THE SIX SUPREME"

BY AUBURN AUTOMOBILE CO., AUBURN, IND.
(1900 –1937)

1923 "6-63"

" 6 – 63 "
TOURING CAR
WITH PERMANENT TOP
(FOLDING TOP OPT.)
122 " W.B.
new OVERHEAD VALVE
248.9 c.i.d. 6 CYL.
ENGINE
(3¼" × 5" BORE £)
63 H.P.
70 MILES per HOUR
1 TO 50 M.P.H. IN
11 SECONDS.

AAP
5-15

$1650.,
f.o.b., FACTORY
$1965. ON
WEST COAST

M 739

1923 Auburn

C harles Eckhart worked for Stude-baker's wagon-building factory in South Bend, Indiana. But, in 1874 he moved to Auburn, where he established the Eckhart Carriage Company. In 1893, he retired, and his sons (Frank & Morris) took charge. In 1900, they built a one-cyclinder, tiller-controlled car and established the Auburn Automobile Company. Regular production for the public began in 1903.

In 1919, the Eckharts sold out to William Wrigley Jr. and a group of Chicago businessmen. The new owners offered the Auburn Beauty Six. The Beauty Six was nice looking, but it changed very little during the course of the early 1920s, and its sales were hurt by the 1920-1922 recession. The overhead-valve engine in this 1923 "6-63" was new, but by the time this car was built, only 15,000 Auburns had been sold since 1919.

In 1924, production was down to only six cars a day—with 700 unsold cars on hand outside the factory!!

Then, E. L. Cord offered to become Auburn's general manager for a special consideration: He'd draw no salary, but if he could get the company back on its feet, he was to have the option to buy a controlling interest in Auburn.

Cord succeeded in unloading the 700 excess cars by adding nickel plating and more attractive paint jobs. In 1925, he added a straight-8 engine to the Auburn line, plus all-new styling.

On the illustrated "6-63" touring car, the side curtains attached to the built-in windshield wings instead of to the windshield—this greatly increased the driver's visibility.

A CLASSIC HOME OF 1923 IN PIEDMONT, CALIF.

WITH
4 - CYL., L - HEAD
214 C.I.D. Lycoming ENG.
3 11/16" × 5" BR. + STR.
43 HP 112" wheelbase
4.8 TO I GEAR RATIO
WT. 2490 lbs.
COLOR LIMOUSINE BLUE
(LARGER 6 - CYL. and
STRAIGHT - 8 s AVAIL.
STARTING 1925)
$1145.00 f.o.b., ST. LOUIS

TAP 2-5

MFD. 1919 TO 1931 BY GARDNER MOTOR CO. ST. LOUIS, MO.

"The Guaranteed Car"

GARDNER

"RADIO SPECIAL" SPORT PHAETON

1923 Gardner Radio Special

If you've seen one of the rare, classic Gardners of the later 1920s at a car show or museum, you may have thought that Gardner was always a large, luxurious automobile. But, the Gardner was originally a small, four-cylinder car, from its 1919 introduction through 1924. In 1925, fours, sixes, and straight-eights were available, and the five-bearing four was discontinued for 1926 and afterward.

The illustrated "Radio Special" was new for 1923, available either as a sport roadster or sport phaeton (as seen). No car had a factory-installed radio in 1923, but this one was so named simply because radio was a popular and growing new medium of home entertainment and America's latest fad.

To quote an ad of May 1923: "No model in Gardner history has been so instantly welcomed, so widely desired, as this Radio Special.

"… The Radio Special awaits your inspection at the display rooms of more than 1,000 Gardner dealers the country over."

It's amazing that Gardner could claim 1,000 dealers in 1923, because some cars no less scarce than this were represented by dealers only in New York City, Chicago, and Los Angeles or San Francisco, without dealers or distributors between those points!

Gardners of 1923 carried a one-year written guarantee (given that year by "no other American automobile manufacturer"). The five-bearing crankshaft was new for '23 and was reported to be the first of its kind in a four-cylinder car.

1923 HAYNES "77" BLUE RIBBON SPEEDSTER
132" WHEELBASE
6 CYL. 70 HP
$3250.00
(FULLY EQUIPPED)
(REPLACES 1922 "75" SERIES.)
CAPABLE OF 80 M.P.H.!
HAYNES AUTOMOBILE CO., KOKOMO, IND.
BUMPERS INCLUDED ON 1923 MODEL.
INSIDE FUEL GAUGE
© News America Syndicate, 1986
TAD 8~31

1923 Haynes "77" Blue Ribbon Speedster

Very few of these illustrious speed-sters managed to survive the great scrapping sprees of the early 1930s and the World War II years of the early 1940s. According to a recent book, this car is now worth from $5,000 to $35,000, depending on the condition!

The Haynes began in 1898 as the Haynes-Apperson, becoming the Haynes during 1904. The name contin-ued until after 1925, a year that spelled financial disaster to the company. The founder, Elwood P. Haynes, succumbed to pneumonia in April 1925; no doubt his condition had been weakened by discouragement over business reverses and by the failure of the Haynes Auto-mobile Co.

For several years, Mr. Haynes had claimed that the Haynes was "America's First Car," though this was not actually so. Haynes had built an experimental car in conjunction with the Apperson Brothers in 1893, but it was not for sale. Moreover, John Lambert had built an earlier experimental car in 1891, so eventually Mr. Haynes made an agreement with Lambert to allow Haynes the coveted honor of being "first."

Meanwhile, George Selden had claimed that honor, as he had attempted to patent the *idea* of an internal-com-bustion automobile he'd designed in 1877.

Oldsmobile wins the title of the longest-established surviving make today, because not only did the Olds Motor Works go into business in 1897, but Ransom E. Olds built his first car (an experimental steamer) in 1887! Ford and Buick are runners-up in this category, having gone into production in 1903 and 1904, respectively.

185.8 CID, 4-CYL. L-HEAD ENG.
30 TO 32 H.P. @ 2150 RPM
3 5/8" x 4 1/4" BORE and STROKE
109" W.B.   50 M.P.H.
2-WHEEL MECHANICAL BRAKES
(55701 '23 MAXWELLS BLT.)

MAXWELL CARS
AVAIL. 1904 TO
1925.
DISC WHEELS

MAXWELL MOTOR CORP., DETROIT

$985.
2-PASS.
"CLUB COUPE"

1923 MAXWELL

© News America Syndicate, Inc. News Group Chicago, Inc. 1984

TAP 8-12

1923 Maxwell

In 1921, Walter P. Chrysler, who had just gained control of both the Maxwell and Chalmers Motor Car Corporations in Detroit, engineered vast improvements in each car. The 1921 and later "25" series of Maxwells were known as "The Good Maxwells," to signify the many mechanical improvements over their predecessors.

Club coupes are usually four-passenger or five-passenger models with a back seat inside the cab. However, in Maxwell's case, the so-called "Club Coupe" (illustrated) was a two-passenger model, not to be confused with Maxwell's four-passenger Coupe, which *did* have an inside back seat.

The 1923 Maxwell Club Coupe had a leather-upholstered seat with headliner in broadcloth. There was a locking trunk compartment in the rear deck. The left-side door locked by lever from the inside. The right-hand (curb-side) door was locked from the outside by a Yale key. A "ventilating-type" heater was included as standard equipment.

Maxwell's emblem: a shield with three arrows pointing downward, superimposed by a horizontal band bearing the Maxwell name.

Steel-disc wheels were more durable than the wooden-spoked types found on many other cars, but they provided less cross-ventilation for the two-wheel mechanical brakes, which lost most of their power when overheated. I learned this the hard way when a disc-wheeled '25 Dodge lost most of its braking force at a busy intersection and nearly ran into a bullet-nosed Studebaker! I had to run the Dodge off the road in order to avoid a collision.

A clean, original '23 Maxwell would now be worth $5,000, $7,500, $10,000, or possibly more!

1923 Peerless V-8

In Cleveland, Ohio, well over 100 different makes of cars were built at one time or another during the first three decades of the 20th century!

Among a few of the Cleveland-built old timers are the Baker Electric, Chandler, Cleveland, Grant, H.A.L., Jordan, Kurtz Automatic, Leon Rubay, Rollin, Stearns, Stearns-Knight, Templar, and Winton—not to mention the illustrated Peerless, plus dozens of lesser-known cars.

Peerless included a V-8 engine from 1916 to 1928 (also a six, from 1925 to 1929). In 1923, 5,700 Peerless cars were built. Peerless was doing well in those days, having built 3,500 cars in 1921 and 4,240 in 1922.

In 1929, Peerless continued the six for one more year, but dropped its own V-8 in favor of a Continental straight-8. In 1930 and 1931, only eight-cylinder Peerless automobiles were available: Standard 8, Master 8, and Custom 8.

Production shut down in June 1931, but for 1932 Peerless built its final, one-of-a-kind masterpiece: a sleek, Murphy-bodied sedan with many aluminum components, doors that curved into the roof, and a thundering 464 cubic-inch displacement V-16 engine that developed 173 h.p.

This 16-cylinder Peerless would do over 100 m.p.h., but it was only an experimental model. The lone specimen has been displayed, in excellent condition, at the Crawford Museum in Cleveland in recent years.

In the meantime, the Peerless Motor Car Company evolved into the manufacturer of Carlings beer and ale. So, in a sense, even after the Great Depression, something was still brewing at the Peerless factory!

1923 Studebaker "Big Six"

T he five-passenger coupe (illustrated) was a new model for Studebaker as 1923 began; though, because of its vertical back and separate, box-type trunk, it could better be described as a coach (two-door sedan). This new body model was available only in the Big Six series, though Studebaker offered four-passenger coupes in both Big Six and Special Six series.

The new five-passenger Big Six coupe featured squared, lantern-type parking lamps just ahead of the windshield, plus a courtesy light on the driver's side. There were front and rear bumpers (don't laugh; not all cars included these necessities in the 1920s) and a Motometer temperature gauge atop an ornamental radiator cap. A rearview mirror and automatic windshield wiper were included, as well as a heater. There were "opalescent" interior corner lights and an inside flower vase. The outside visor was of glare-proof glass. Upholstery: "velvety brown velour."

Radiator shell and bumpers were now nickel-plated, and disc wheels were available as illustrated (unless wood wheels were preferred).

The rear seat was full width, and the auxiliary front seat beside the driver was "In reality a cushioned armchair and will be found restful even in long-distance travel."

Nearly 50,000 of the Big Sixes were manufactured between November 1921 and July 1924, after which a totally restyled 1925 model appeared.

Old Big Sixes were durable! At the 1924 N.Y. Automobile Show, a 1918 Big Six with over 500,000 miles on it was displayed!

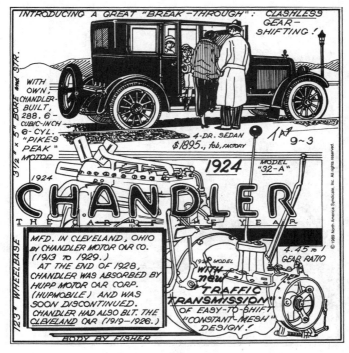

INTRODUCING A GREAT "BREAK-THROUGH": CLASHLESS GEAR-SHIFTING!

WITH OWN CHANDLER-BUILT, 288.6-CUBIC-INCH 6-CYL. "PIKES PEAK" MOTOR

3½" x 5" BORE and STR.

4-DR. SEDAN $1895., f.o.b. FACTORY

1924 MODEL "32-A"

1924

CHANDLER
THE CAR OF THE YEAR

MFD. IN CLEVELAND, OHIO BY CHANDLER MOTOR CAR CO. (1913 TO 1929.) AT THE END OF 1928, CHANDLER WAS ABSORBED BY HUPP MOTOR CAR CORP. (HUPMOBILE) AND WAS SOON DISCONTINUED. CHANDLER HAD ALSO BLT. THE CLEVELAND CAR (1919-1926.)

123" WHEELBASE

4.45 TO 1 GEAR RATIO

WITH new TRAFFIC TRANSMISSION OF EASY-TO-SHIFT "CONSTANT-MESH" DESIGN!

BODY BY FISHER

1924 Chandler

I f you've ever had to struggle with shifting the clashing gears in an antique or vintage car, you'd appreciate the 1924 Chandler. Though Cadillac lays claim to using the first truly Synchro-Mesh transmission (in its 1929 and later models), the "constant-mesh" Campbell-design Traffic Transmission introduced on the 1924 Chandler was almost as good.

Up to that time, it was almost impossible to down shift from high to second or from second to low without carefully and skillfully double-clutching. If you didn't depress the clutch pedal and rev the engine between down-shifts, you'd probably grind the gears. Such mistakes could cause serious damage, too. If teeth were torn from the gears, they could be tossed around in the transmission oil and shoved between teeth of

other gears in the gearbox, perhaps wrecking everything. But, with the remarkable 1924 Chandler, clash-less shifting became a startling reality.

Some 1924 Chandler advertisements assured husbands that their wives could enjoy driving a Chandler through heavy traffic or on steep hills "without the slightest worry." No longer was it necessary to have the skill of a professional truck driver to down shift while the car was in motion.

Though Fisher bodies have long been associated exclusively with General Motors cars (GM owns Fisher Body Company), a few other manufacturers purchased them from GM until the late 1920s. I once owned a 1928 Chrysler 72 sedan with a Fisher body, bearing the same Fisher body plate usually seen on Buicks.

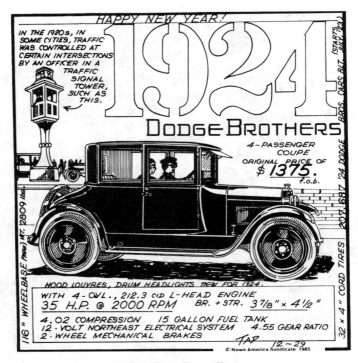

HAPPY NEW YEAR!

1924

IN THE 1920s, IN SOME CITIES, TRAFFIC WAS CONTROLLED AT CERTAIN INTERSECTIONS BY AN OFFICER IN A TRAFFIC SIGNAL TOWER, SUCH AS THIS.

DODGE BROTHERS

4-PASSENGER COUPE
ORIGINAL PRICE OF $1375. f.o.b.

116" WHEELBASE (new) WT. 2809 lbs.

'24 DODGE BROS. COST 6817 (STARTS JUNE '23)

32 × 4" CORD TIRES

HOOD LOUVRES, DRUM HEADLIGHTS new FOR 1924.
WITH 4-CYL., 212.3 CID L-HEAD ENGINE
35 H.P. @ 2000 RPM   BR. + STR. 3 7/8" × 4 1/2"
4.02 COMPRESSION   15 GALLON FUEL TANK
12-VOLT NORTHEAST ELECTRICAL SYSTEM   4.55 GEAR RATIO
2-WHEEL MECHANICAL BRAKES   TAP
12~29
© News America Syndicate, 1985

1924 Dodge Bros.

Dodge was not originally a part of the Chrysler Corp. family. The Dodge Brothers (John and Horace) made a fortune supplying parts to Oldsmobile and then to Ford. Eventually, they decided to manufacture their own car, beginning late in 1914 in Detroit. The Dodge Bros. car, rugged and reliable, was an immediate success.

John and Horace Dodge died in 1920, and their widows and associate ran the company until the mid-1920s, at which time they sold out to the New York banking house of Dillon, Read & Co. at a record price (then) of $146 million. In 1928, Dillon, Read & Co. sold Dodge Bros. to the up-and-coming Chrysler Corp. for $170 million in an exchange of stocks.

The big Dodge Bros. fours of the early- and mid-1920s were not hot performers. The 1926 coupe I owned in the 1950s would then do only 42 miles per hour, and at that spine-tingling speed it shot sparks and roared like an angry dragon! Stopping the car was another big problem: the two-wheel mechanical brakes were sheer terror above 20 m.p.h., as they merely *slowed* the car to a degree.

With proper adjustments, the old Dodge coupe might have improved slightly in performance, but I decided to buy a '29 Plymouth roadster for $35 and sold the Dodge to a friend for only $26!

The earliest Dodge Bros. cars were among the first to offer a welded steel body. Only a few Dodges ever used wood in the body framing!

OLDSMOBILE BROKE THE PRICE BARRIER FOR 6-CYLINDER CARS IN 1924 BY INTRODUCING ITS NEW SIX FOR ONLY

$750!

PRICE, f.o.b., LANSING, MICH., FOR TOURING CAR (ILLUSTRATED) OR ROADSTER.

(FIRST OLDS 6 SINCE 1921. 1922 + 1923 MODELS WERE 4s OR V-8s.)

1924 OLDSMOBILE NEW "30" SERIES WITH 70% L-HEAD 6 CYL. (169.3 C.I.D.) ENGINE (2 3/4" × 4 3/4" BORE + STR.) 42 HP @ 2600 RPM   25 MILES PER GALLON   110" W.B.

12 1/2-GAL. FUEL TANK

© News America Syndicate, 1987

1924 Oldsmobile

Many readers may be surprised to learn that some Oldsmobiles had V-8 engines in the early 1920s and, in fact, as early as the late-1915 introduction of the 1916 "Light Eight" series.

Olds stopped six-cylinder production in 1921, and for 1922 and 1923 only a four and the V-8 were offered. But, the six returned with a vengeance late in 1923 with the appearance of the popular, low-priced "30" series (illustrated), which placed a six below the price of many four-cylinder cars!

Motor World for Nov. 22, 1923, carried an ad on page 91 that described the recent "Coast-to-Coast in High Gear" 3,674-mile run of a new Oldsmobile 30 touring car driven by the famous "Cannonball" Baker. The trip lasted 12 1/2 days, through much rain, snow, and mud, over rocky and washed-out roads in many places, and over grades as steep as 17 percent! The test car, with a standard gear ratio rear axle, averaged an amazing 28.7 miles per gallon of gas with only 18 ounces of oil consumed! Perhaps there was coasting down hills to save fuel.

Available extras: bumpers ($15 each); radiator cap with bars ($2.50); spotlight ($5); windshield wiper, manual ($1.25); rearview mirror ($1.75); enameled steel trunk ($25); four trunk rails ($6.80); trunk platform ($7); sport tire carrier ($7.50); windshield vent wings ($17 per pair); running board step plates ($4.75). The Sport Touring Car included these extras, plus steel disc wheels.

The 1924 model was the last of the arched-radiator Oldsmobiles. For 1925-1927 came a new and ornate radiator design.

1924 Stutz Speedway 6

The Speedway 6 was an all-new, 1924 model from Stutz. The illustrated "Sportbrohm" (sport brougham) was one of few sedans in that era that included a trunk at the rear as standard equipment. The rear curve of the top was pleasingly modern and harmonized well with the rakish slant of the rear spare wheel.

The Speedway 6 differed in appearance from the Speedway 4, which did not have nickel plating on the radiator shell. The Special 6 did not have the three-piece Brewster windshield, as found on the Speedway.

Though $3,535 was the advertised price of this car in the spring of 1924, it could be purchased for $185 less without the optional balloon tires or hydraulic brakes. Bumpers were sold separately, as they were on many other cars of 1924.

Standard (non-balloon) tires on the Speedway 6 were 32 x 4 1/2 on open cars and 33 x 5 on closed models. The engine was Stutz-built, and the new Speedway 6 was a well-designed model but destined to be eclipsed two years later by the new straight-eight "Safety Stutz." In the September 1950 issue of *Mechanix Illustrated*, a Canadian owner of a Speedway 6 Sportbrohm submitted a photo of his car and advised *MI* editors that it was "still going strong."

The Speedway 6 was originally advertised, illustrated, and described in such publications as *Saturday Evening Post*, May 3, 1924, where it was claimed that 85.6 percent of all the Stutz cars produced during the last fourteen years were still in use!

"JUST A REAL GOOD CAR!"

109" WHEELBASE

1925 DURANT "A-22" SERIES

4 PASSENGER (VICTORIA) COUPE $**1160.**⁰⁰, f.o.b., LANSING

MFD. BY DURANT MOTORS, INC., NEW YORK CITY (1921—1932)
IN 1925, DURANT FACTORIES WERE LOCATED IN ELIZABETH, N.J.; LANSING, MICH.; OAKLAND, CALIF.; and TORONTO, ONT., CANADA.
DURANT MOTORS ALSO BUILT THE STAR CAR (1922-28.)
1925 SLOGAN: "IT'S A DELIGHT TO DRIVE A DURANT."

SPARE RIM RNGX

31 × 4

2 VICTORIA MECHANICAL BRAKES

4 CYLS. 37 H.P.

HAPPY THANKSGIVING!

© 1987 North America Syndicate, Inc. All rights reserved.

1925 Durant

Having founded General Motors in 1908 and having been GM's president on two different occasions, William C. "Billy" Durant had a world of automotive business experience behind him in 1921 when he launched Durant Motors, Inc.

Hoping to build another multi-car empire like GM's, Billy Durant offered other cars in addition to the Durant, once his company got rolling. In 1922, he added the low-cost Star, and later he introduced the medium-priced Flint Six and smaller Flint Junior. He bought out Locomobile in order to add that prestigious car to the top of his line.

Most popular of the additions was Durant's Star car, and in 1926-1927 the Star even replaced the Durant for several months. In 1928, however, the Durant nameplate returned, and the Star became the Durant-Star early in the year and was then replaced in turn by a low-cost Durant Four.

Most of the Durant cars existing today are 1928, 1929, or 1930 models, most of them sixes. These were apparently the best-built and longest-lasting models to bear Durant's name. Other year models, such as this illustrated 1925, are extremely scarce now.

During the spring of 1925, Durant Four prices were as follows: Touring Car, $830; 2-door Coach, $1,050; Sedan, $1,190; and, of course, this $1,160 four-passenger Coupe. To cut costs, a spare tire was an "extra."

Durant also built six-cylinder models, but in '25 only the four was produced. The Touring Car had "real leather" upholstery, while closed models were fitted with velvet-like mohair.

1925 Elcar 8-80

Notice the massive size and length of this leviathan-of-the-road Elcar 8-80! How did it feel to drive a car of this age and size? Well, it felt quite similar to driving a heavy-duty truck! Driver and passengers sat high—very high—off the road and could easily look over the tops of any of today's cars!

The interior of a car like this smelled like old-fashioned furniture. Cloth, mohair, and plenty of structural wood abounded. The body framework and floors were wooden in most 1925 cars. Seats were high and cushiony, almost like easy chairs!

To start a 1925 car, one usually flicked a dashboard ignition switch (some cars needed a key to unlock an ignition switch or transmission lock). Then you would step on the starter switch, on the sloping portion of the rubber-matted wooden floorboard. When the heavy, long, slow-revving engine came into action, it throbbed with the brute power of 65 horses or less, and the car vibrated slightly as the engine was "gunned."

Low and second gear had a deep, mighty growl, like that of a large truck transmission. Non-synchromesh gears required careful double-clutching foot-work when changing speeds, to avoid a noisy, grinding clash!

The old wooden steering wheels were rudimentary—no finger-dialing power steering in those days. The lights, hand-throttle, and spark controls were often on quadrants at the center of the steering wheel, along with the shiny, black, cork-like horn button. Most 1925 cars had motor-driven "ah-oogah!" horns.

1925 Ford Model T

As of August 1925, the 12-mil-lionth Ford motor was produced. Never was any American car as popular and as long-continued as the famous Model T Ford. In its long production run (fall 1908 to spring 1927), some 15 million were sold!

Henry Ford, founder of Ford Motor Co. in 1903, was destined to give the world's automobile buyers a low-priced, simple, dependable, and economical car at a bargain-basement price. By mass-producing the Model T and by continually finding new ways to simplify and economize that mass-production, Ford was able to periodically cut the price of a Model T so that in the mid-1920s, Ford Runabout prices started at only $260!

In the 1920s, General Motors' rival to the Ford—the Chevrolet—could not be sold for such a low figure. But, Chevrolet was gaining ground with the public by offering better styling, a more comfortable body by Fisher, and a choice of colors. So in 1926, Ford offered colors other than black, ending his long flirtation (since 1914) with black only as the standard Ford color. (It had been a part of Ford's simplification program.)

Henry Ford had stubbornly clung to his basic 1909-design, two-speed type of planetary band transmission, operated by foot pedals. By the 1920s, it seemed crude and flimsy. Legend has it that Henry Ford fired many a subordinate for suggesting that he drastically change or eliminate the Model T, but at last Henry "saw the light." Ford Motor Co. built its final Model Ts in 1927.

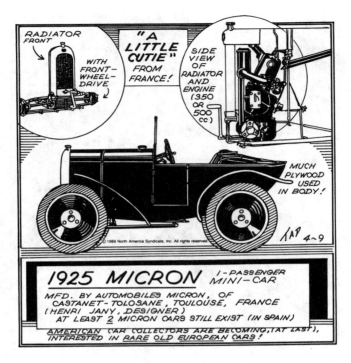

RADIATOR FRONT

WITH FRONT-WHEEL-DRIVE

"A LITTLE CUTIE" FROM FRANCE!

SIDE VIEW OF RADIATOR AND ENGINE (350 OR 500 cc)

MUCH PLYWOOD USED IN BODY!

© 1989 North America Syndicate, Inc. All rights reserved

LAP 4~9

1925 MICRON 1-PASSENGER MINI-CAR

MFD. BY AUTOMOBILES MICRON, OF CASTANET-TOLOSANE, TOULOUSE, FRANCE (HENRI JANY, DESIGNER)
AT LEAST 2 MICRON CARS STILL EXIST (IN SPAIN)

AMERICAN CAR COLLECTORS ARE BECOMING, (AT LAST), INTERESTED IN RARE OLD EUROPEAN CARS!

1925 Micron

France was an exciting place in the 1920s! Many American travelers visited that country in those days, and a number of American authors and show-business personalities made their homes there, either temporarily or permanently. The year 1925 was an especially exciting one in Paris—the year of a famous international exposition featuring the finest of modern art and design. It was also the year of this funny little Micron mini-car, made in France.

Small "cycle cars" were briefly popular in the United States from 1913 to 1916. And, interestingly, the cycle car—though virtually forgotten in the U.S.A. during the 1920s—flourished in Europe at that time. With such tiny cars, many people could now afford their own "wheels."

The typical cycle car has light weight, wire-spoked wheels with rather narrow tires (almost like motorcycle or bicycle wheels). But, this 1925 one-cylinder Micron used steel disc wheels, as seen here.

The Micron's engine was the ultimate in simplicity, and it had front-wheel drive. Top speed and fuel economy figures were not mentioned, but it's likely that this little vehicle would cruise at 25 or 30 m.p.h. and deliver 50 or more miles per gallon under favorable circumstances (such as a good wind behind it)!

A few years ago, American car collectors were almost exclusively interested in American-built cars. However, with more and more Americans traveling overseas in recent years, it's not surprising that car collectors would run across unusual foreign cars that interested them.

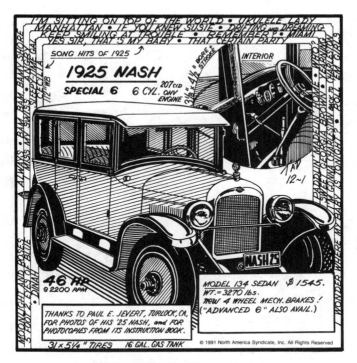

SONG HITS OF 1925

I'M SITTING ON TOP OF THE WORLD • UKULELE LADY • MANHATTAN • IF YOU KNEW SUSIE • DRIFTING and DREAMING • KEEP SMILING AT TROUBLE • REMEMBER? • MIAMI • YES SIR, THAT'S MY BABY • THAT CERTAIN PARTY

1925 NASH
SPECIAL 6   6 CYL. OHV   207 cid
ENGINE

3 3/8" x 4 1/2" BORE x STROKE

INTERIOR

112" WB

46 HP @ 2200 RPM

MODEL 134 SEDAN $1545.
WT.= 3270 lbs.
new 4 WHEEL MECH. BRAKES!
("ADVANCED 6" ALSO AVAIL.)

THANKS TO PAUL E. JEVERT, TURLOCK, CA, FOR PHOTOS OF HIS '25 NASH, and FOR PHOTOCOPIES FROM ITS INSTRUCTION BOOK.

31 x 5 1/4" TIRES   16 GAL. GAS TANK

1920s

1925 Nash Special 6

Everyone takes four-wheel brakes for granted now. But, back in the mid-1920s, it was something for auto dealers to boast about!

Until then, the average car had been equipped with comparatively ineffective two-wheel mechanical brakes, acting on the rear wheels only. These brakes could wear out fast and had a notorious tendency to "fade" when wet or overheated on long downgrades.

Nash advertised its new four-wheel mechanical brakes in 1925, as "The Industry's Greatest Four-Wheel Brake Achievement!" These Nash brakes were equalized to prevent swerving and "grabbing" and were proclaimed to be unaffected by extreme cold or hot weather. Sixty percent of the pressure was applied to rear wheels and only forty percent to front, so as not to interfere with "perfect steering."

By the end of the 1920s, four-wheel brakes were standard equipment on all new cars. Old models with two-wheel brakes were considered a safety hazard, and during the early 1930s, many Depression-weary cities and auto dealerships, sponsored the roundup of thousands of old jalopies and vented their frustrations on them.

Steel disc wheels were another feature of the 1925 Nash line. These would not break or rot as wood wheels sometimes did, and they were much easier to clean.

Smooth-rolling balloon tires were also featured.

In addition to the illustrated Special Six, there was also the big Nash "Advanced Six" (127-inch wheelbase). At midyear, Nash introduced a lower-priced third series, the Ajax Six. This $995 budget series had the four-wheel brakes but not the overhead-valve engine.

"THE MOLYBDENUM CAR " *
1925 WILLS SAINTE CLAIRE "B-68" $3880.
121" WHEELBASE with OVERHEAD-CAM V8 ENGINE (265 CU. IN. DISPLACEMENT) 3 1/4" × 4" BORE + STROKE 65 H.P. @ 2700 RPM
4.9 GEAR RATIO MFD. IN MARYSVILLE, MICH. BY WILLS SAINTE CLAIRE, INC. (1921-1927)

* - MADE USE OF THE "WONDER ALLOY," MOLYBDENUM STEEL.

THIS 4-DR. BROUGHAM has CLOSE-COUPLED BODY LIKE A VICTORIA CPE.

"GRAY GOOSE" MASCOT →

TAD 10-2

32 × 6 TIRES   HYDRAULIC BRAKES

(NEW 6-CYL. ALSO AVAILABLE)

THANKS TO VERN HANSEN, OF MEDFORD, OREGON, FOR HELPFUL DETAILS

© Field Enterprises, Inc., 1983

1925 Wills Sainte Claire B-68

The Wills Sainte Claire was the illustrious brainchild of C. H. (Childe Harold) Wills, founder of Wills Sainte Claire, Inc. in 1921.

Wills was a brilliant metallurgist who made use of special molybdenum steel alloys in much of his new car! The early Wills Sainte Claires were V-8s, and a six joined the line at the start of the 1925 season.

This illustrated 1925 model looks a good three years ahead of its time! The 1926 Wills Sainte Claires looked similar, except for having a taller radiator, smooth-topped full-crown fenders, etc. All Wills Sainte Claire automobiles had disc wheels and a rear-mounted spare.

The B-68 series included a two-door Victoria Coupe, which had a profile similar to this unusual four-door

brougham (except for the difference in number of side doors).

Before he'd gone on his own in the 1920s, Wills was a chief engineer and metallurgist for Henry Ford. Wills was a wealthy man when he resigned from Ford; he was not only able to establish a fine, new automobile factory, but he also built an up-to-date "company town" for his employees in Marysville, causing that town's population to leap from about 150 to a thriving 4,000-plus almost at once!

In 1975, a survey among Wills Sainte Claire fans turned up some eighty-four cars, and a list of eighty of these (and the names of their owners) was published. Three 1921 models remained; twenty-three 1922s; six 1923s; six 1924s; sixteen 1925s; and twenty-six 1926 models. None of the final 1927 models appeared on the list.

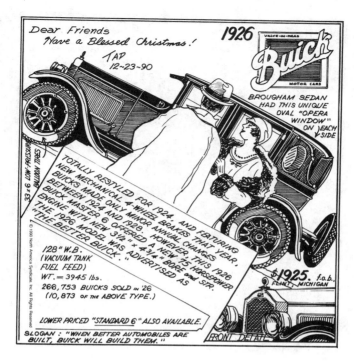

1926 Buick

When I was a boy in Oakland, Calif., a neighbor drove an ancient 1926 Buick to work, daily! It was the oldest vehicle in our neighborhood. The next-oldest vehicles around there were a couple of 1931 Model A Fords.

That old '26 Buick fascinated me. It was the illustrated Brougham sedan with the weird-looking oval rear-quarter windows. Its original green-and-black paint job was beginning to fade, and the car was getting noisy. It appeared, sadly, that its days of faithful service were drawing to an end. At that time, the only antique cars that collectors cared about were the horseless carriages from the early 1900s.

The 1924 through 1928 Buicks were part of a five-year styling cycle; their appearance had much in common. But, if you compare a '24 with a '28, you'll notice quite a few differences. Each year there had been some small changes and refinements. The '24 Buicks had been available as fours or sixes, but from '25 to '30 all Buicks were sixes. From 1931 to 1952, all Buicks were straight-eights. GM's Buick was a long-time champion of overhead-valve engines .

The '26 Buick still used an odd gear-shift pattern that was the mirror opposite of the standard American pattern. The following year, Buick introduced a quieter, "big-toothed" transmission gear design, and in '28 the standard shift pattern was adopted.

Buick set a sales record in 1926 that was not equaled for another fourteen years! In '26, some 266,753 new Buicks were sold, including 10,873 of these Model 51 Brougham Sedans.

INTERIOR
(5 WINDOW (COUPE)
(VICTORIA)

339.7 CID
6 CYL.
OVERHEAD VALVE
ENGINE
3¾" × 5⅛"
BORE and ST.
4.3 TO 1
COMPRESS.

88 HP
@
2800 RPM
4-WHEEL
MECHANICAL
BRAKES

32 × 6.20 TIRES

3 WINDOW
COUPE

STD.
COUPE
$3295.
(HAS RUMBLE
SEAT)

74 SERIES
1926 MARMON

136" WHEELBASE
3983 LBS.

BY MARMON MOTOR CAR
CO., INDIANAPOLIS
(CARS 1902~1933;
TRUCKS ONLY,•
1934 ON)
(• BUSES ALSO)

RADIATOR

"It's a Great Automobile"

1926 Marmon "74"

The 1926 Marmon "74" was a big car, on a 136-inch wheelbase, and retained the typical Marmon arched radiator shell with its odd, little triangular piece jutting out just above the nameplate. But, the 1926 model was loaded with features, some of them new for that year. In fact, the model was so improved that it was, as in 1925, called "The New Marmon," and the 1926 model was also sometimes called "The Greater New Marmon." The slogan, "It's a Great Automobile," certainly rang true.

The 1926 model had four-wheel mechanical brakes, centralized chassis lubrication, an efficient overhead-valve engine, and long, massive, steel-based running boards that also served as side bumpers and were claimed to give the car outstanding protection from major damage in side collisions. The special reinforced running boards ran all the way forward to the very short front fenders and even curved up at the front end to meet them (as illustrated here).

Two styles of coupes were offered. The two-passenger, three-window coupe had a very long cab with a leatherette-covered superstructure (over a structural frame of wood), decorative landau irons on either side, and a rumble seat. The Victoria coupe was somewhat similar in style, but had a half-arched rear quarter window on either side with additional back seating within the cab.

In its final years of producing automobiles (to 1933), Marmon built mostly straight-eight cars and a few magnificent V-16s. From 1934 on, the company was known as Marmon-Herrington and continued to produce trucks and buses only.

1926
RICKENBACKER
8
"SUPER
SPORT"
BOAT-TAILED
VICTORIA
COUPE
(DETROIT)
RARE! LESS THAN 3 DOZEN BUILT!
© News America Syndicate, 1987
TAD
2/8
STRAIGHT-8 ENG.
107 HP @ 3000 RPM
315 CID
90-95 MPH!
AIRPLANE
ORNAMENT
ON RADIATOR
CAP
CYCLE-TYPE FENDERS
121" W.B.
4-WHEEL BRAKES
COPPER TRIM!
RICKENBACKER CARS AVAIL. 1922-1927.
PRICE = $5000.

1926 Rickenbacker 8

As many might guess, the Rickenbacker automobile of the 1920s got its name from Captain Eddie Rickenbacker, former racing driver and World War I air ace. The "hat-in-the-ring" insignia used on this car was borrowed from the 94th Aero Pursuit Squadron, in which Captain Eddie had served.

In 1919, Rickenbacker went into business with two experienced automobile men (Byron F. "Barney" Everitt and Walter Flanders), and the Rickenbacker Motor Co. was founded. Two pilot models were built in 1920.

The 1922 Rickenbacker was a six with a 58 h.p. engine that featured a flywheel at either end of the crankshaft, for better balance. There were other good engineering features as well, and before long (mid-'23), four-wheel mechanical brakes were available. In August 1924, a straight-eight (Vertical 8) was added to the line. In 1925, came the four-door Coach-Brougham, a sedan with padded top, landau irons, and smart oval rear quarter windows.

The pièce de résistance of all Rickenbacker cars was the 1926 "Super Sport" Victoria coupe (illustrated) which startled the auto world with radically modern styling and a beefed-up straight-8 capable of up to 95 m.p.h. (stock)! More conventional models were also continued, but Rickenbacker had antagonized his dealers by forcing price cuts on them—in an attempt to increase sales by cutting profits. It didn't work; the dealers were mad because they were asked to cut prices on units already in stock. Trouble brewed within the company, and Eddie Rickenbacker resigned in 1926. The company went out of business in February 1927.

1920s

Labels within image:
1927 CHRYSLER "70" (NEW FINER TYPE)
218.6 C/D 6
68 HP @ 3000 RPM
THIS $1595. 4-PASS. COUPE WAS A SOURCE MODEL!
TOP SPEED = 70
("50", "60" and "IMPERIAL 80" CHRYSLERS ALSO AVAIL.)
new 18" WHEELS
(THE FIRST CHRYSLER WAS THE 1924 "6")
HYDRAULIC 4 WHEEL BRAKES
WALTER P. CHRYSLER (1875-1940) FOUNDER OF CHRYSLER CORPORATION
1927 "70" INTERIOR (new LOCK ON STEERING COLUMN)
new CLOCK
112 ¾" WHEELBASE
© 1991 North America Syndicate, Inc. All Rights Reserved

1927 Chrysler "New Finer 70"

The new Chrysler Corporation (a.k.a. Chrysler Motors) grew by leaps and bounds in the late 1920s. By 1927, Chrysler was in fourth place in sales among all U.S. makes! By '28, Chrysler briefly reached third place in sales. But, in midyear, Chrysler split into four different makes, having bought Dodge Bros. and introducing the new Plymouth and De Soto cars. Future Chrysler business was then, of necessity, divided four ways.

The "70" series developed from the first Chrysler Six. Model numbers designated the guaranteed top speed. In mid-1925, the new Chrysler Four (styled like the Six) replaced the former Maxwell car. In 1926, Chrysler added a small six (the "60") to the line, as well as the big Imperial 80. The Four became the Model 58. The four-cylinder line was downgraded in '27 and became the "50," with hydraulic brakes becoming an option on that model, instead of standard equipment.

For '27, the "70" was improved and became known as the "New Finer 70," making its debut in October 1926. The profile was improved with a forward-curving "military front and cadet visor" and smaller eighteen-inch wheels. Inside the improved "70," a clock was added to the oval instrument cluster, and a new lock on the steering column helped to foil would-be "car nappers."

The illustrated Victoria-style, four-passenger coupe was new to the "70" series. It was also available in the following 1928 "72" line, in the "75" for '29, and the 1930 "77." After that, a five-passenger coupe appeared in the new Chrysler 8 line for 1931.

DODGE'S NEW "FAST FOUR!" (MODEL 128)

INTRODUCED JULY, 1927 THIS COULD BE CONSIDERED A *1927½ DODGE BROS.*, BECAUSE THE EARLY '28 FOURS AFTER DEC., 1927 HAD 4-WHEEL BRAKES.

DODGE BROS. IN '27 WAS CONTROLLED BY THE NEW YORK BANKING FIRM OF DILLON, READ + CO., (FROM WHICH CHRYSLER CORP. PURCHASED DODGE IN MID-1928.) THE ILLUSTRATED CAR HAD A 4-CYL., *L-HEAD*, 212.3 C.I.D. ENGINE (3 7/8" × 4½") WITH 40 H.P. @ 2400 RPM. *new* SHORTER 108" WHEELBASE ENABLED CAR TO MAKE A U-TURN IN A 38-FT. STREET. TOP SPEED = 60 M.P.H. PLUS. COUPE WEIGHS 2428 lbs., COST $855., f.o.b.

* ALSO CONSIDERED AN "EARLY 1928"

MERRY CHRISTMAS!

3.8 TO 1 GEAR RATIO

5.00 X 19 TIRES

© Field Enterprises, Inc. 1982

12-19

1920s

1927 1/2 Dodge Fast Four

Until 1926, there was only one basic model series of the old Dodge Bros. The Four was a sturdy, large, steel-bodied car on a 116-inch wheelbase with a transmission that shifted in a pattern opposite to the usual, with low gear at the right and high at the left, and so forth. The old Dodge Bros. cars also had a remarkably quiet starter-generator unit and a 12-volt electrical system. The early 1927 model, however, differed from its predecessors in that closed models had a large, overhanging, French-style roof-visor with lower roofline.

In the spring of '27 came the 124 series, which, in the summer, made way for the all-new 128 series (illustrated). The years 1927 and 1928 saw a prolif-

eration of many varieties and variations of Dodges. In 1927, Dodge Bros. switched to a 6-volt electrical system and a conventional gearshift. The mid-year 1927s were frequently called "1928" Dodges, but fours actually built in 1928 had four-wheel brakes (after December, 1927). The illustrated model had two-wheel brakes.

Other Dodge Bros. models to appear in this era were the Senior Six (mid-1927), the Victory Six (1928), and the Standard Six (1928), which eventually took the place of the "128" four, which it resembled.

The 128 was known as the "Fast Four" or the "Mile-a-Minute Dodge" because it could travel at 60 miles per hour. That was an improvement over the lumbering earlier models.

THE MODEL T WAS DISCONTINUED AFTER SPRING, 1927, IN PREPARATION FOR THE ALL-NEW MODEL A FOR 1928.

1927 Ford Model T

S tarting July 1925, Ford Motor Company made great improvements in the famous Model T for 1926. By that time, the competition from GM's Chevrolet was growing.

In 1926, either wooden-spoke or wire wheels could be selected. In '27, Ford standardized on wire wheels. In 1926-1927, brakes were still two-wheel, but greatly improved. Other mechanical changes were made, with coupes and Tudor sedans getting a simple one-piece windshield.

Gunmetal Blue and Phoenix Brown were new '27 body colors for open Fords. Closed 1927 Ford bodies came in Highland Green, Royal Maroon, Fawn Gray, Drake Green, or the unglamorous-sounding "Moleskin."

Here's a list of the number of Ford Model T's produced, month-by-month, 1927: January—4,247;

February—139,442; March—88,499; April—76,049; May—72,504.

Ford T production had sharply declined late in '26, reaching its lowest point in January '27. As of June 1927, Ford production ceased for the summer while major retooling was under way for the vastly improved Model A. The great success of the Model A soon recovered the over $30 million loss in '27 that had been created by retooling costs and lack of sales while assembly lines were shut down.

Interestingly, long after the Model T was discontinued, Ford Motor Company built additional Model T replacement engines (from 12,000 a month in late '27, down to 100 a month in 1931). The final Model T engine was built on August 4, 1941! By that time, Model T's were seldom seen on the road.

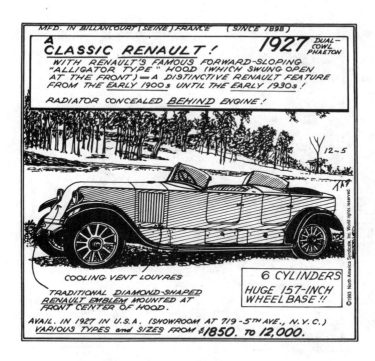

MFD. IN BILLANCOURT (SEINE) FRANCE   (SINCE 1898)

A **CLASSIC RENAULT !**   *1927* DUAL-COWL PHAETON

WITH RENAULT'S FAMOUS FORWARD-SLOPING "ALLIGATOR TYPE" HOOD (WHICH SWUNG OPEN AT THE FRONT) — A DISTINCTIVE RENAULT FEATURE FROM THE EARLY 1900s UNTIL THE EARLY 1930s !

RADIATOR CONCEALED *BEHIND* ENGINE !

12~5

COOLING VENT LOUVRES

TRADITIONAL *DIAMOND-SHAPED* RENAULT EMBLEM MOUNTED AT FRONT CENTER OF HOOD.

6 CYLINDERS HUGE 157-INCH WHEELBASE !!

AVAIL. IN 1927 IN U.S.A. (SHOWROOM AT 719-5ᵀᴴ AVE., N.Y.C.) VARIOUS TYPES and SIZES FROM $*1850.* TO *12,000.*

1927 Renault

Because of its uniquely shaped hood, you could always spot one of these classic Renaults three blocks away, if it were coming in your direction.

These older Renaults were water-cooled, but had a radiator mounted in back of the engine instead of in front. Before 1922, Renault hoods and cowls were distinctly separate and the radiator beyond the engine could clearly be seen. But, in 1922, the hood line was smoothed out to continue one level plane back to the windshield, thus hiding the radiator.

Louis Renault and his brothers Marcel and Fernand founded the Renault auto empire in 1898. At first, the company was known as Renault Freres (Renault Brothers), but in 1903 Marcel

Renault was killed in the Paris-Madrid auto race, and Fernand died in 1908. In 1909, the company was renamed SA des Usines Renault (until 1945).

And, what became of Louis Renault? He died in a French prison in 1944, following the liberation of France from Germany. Louis was incarcerated because leaders in the free French government believed he had not resisted the Nazis.

Renaults had been imported to the United States in limited numbers even before this illustrated 1927 model was produced. Mass imports of Renaults did not commence until after World War II, when small, rear-engined economy cars became the company's principal stock in trade.

new LOWER BELT MOULDING FOR 1927.

107" W.B. 2100 lbs.

© 1988 North America Syndicate, Inc. All rights reserved.

LATER '27 had BOWL-SHAPED LIGHTS.

80 x 4.75

30 x 4.75

EARLY *1927*
STAR 6 COUPE

2 3/4" x 4 3/4" BORE + STR.

ORIGINAL PRICE =
$**820.** f.o.b.

CONTINENTAL 14-L 6 CYL.
169.3 CID L-HEAD ENGINE
30 HP @ 2400 RPM
4.79 COMPR.

4.87 GEAR RATIO

Star 🟊 Cars

BUILT 1922-1928 BY DURANT MOTORS, INC.
(55,039 BLT. 1927)

1927 Star

The low-priced Star car was the mainstay of Durant Motors, from its 1922 introduction until early 1928. In '28, it became the Durant-Star for several weeks, and then it evolved into a low-priced model of the Durant.

Durant automobiles, introduced in 1921, continued to early 1932. Interestingly, William C. "Billy" Durant, who had founded General Motors in 1908, hoped to build a new auto empire of his own in the 1920s.

In the mid-1920s, the Star was a greater success than its parent car, the Durant—because of its lower price and its more extensive advertising campaign.

The illustrated coupe is a transitional type, as it continues the drum-type headlamps from the previous year but features a new, lower belt-line moulding, which the 1926 didn't

have. As 1927 progressed, bowl-type headlamps were adopted.

Because of the greater sales of the Star, the Durant nameplate was suspended for several months (1926-1927), but for 1928 the Durant returned with a vengeance—in various models—and soon replaced the Star. Durant had a good sales year in 1929, considering that it was a minor make. Although 1928 and 1930 were fairly good Durant years as well, sales slipped badly in 1931, even though some new models were available with a folding seat-bed (better known after 1935 as a Nash feature).

During the final years of Durant Motors, Billy Durant bowed out of the automobile business. In the 1930s and 1940s, he was involved with smaller enterprises, such as the operation of a bowling alley and a grocery store.

1928 Auburn

The convertible sedan (illustrated with top down) was a new model for Auburn—which received considerable advertising ballyhoo in 1928. "Heretofore obtainable only on special order from custom coach builders," the new phaeton sedan—as Auburn named it—was fitted with a fully convertible top and roll-up glass side windows.

Auburn claimed to have the strongest chassis frame of any car, and it had Lockheed four-wheel hydraulic brakes. The new, optional Dayton wire wheels were the racing type, which could speedily be changed, simply by removing the hubcap. New, heavy, ten-spoke wood artillery wheels were standard equipment.

Steel-based running boards did not rot or warp like the old-style wooden ones. All Auburns had Lycoming engines. Body styling was generally similar to what Auburn had introduced during 1925, though there were improvements to nearly every part on the 1928 models!

Strangely, the vertical windshield on the phaeton sedan was rigid, and it had a very narrow frame. It was adequate as long as no one was unfortunate enough to overturn the car.

At today's collector auction prices, a "115" phaeton sedan is worth $1,500 in junky, non-running, or incomplete condition and up to $50,000 in perfect condition. The "88" phaeton sedan is worth virtually the same. Most valuable of all '28 Auburns, however, is the two-passenger Speedster, a boat-tailed roadster, valued at up to $100,000 in perfect shape!

1928 Cadillac Town Car

First appearing in September 1927, and totally restyled for 1928, the new Cadillac "341" series was the best-looking and most modern-styled American car at that time—inside, as well as out! Most of the 341's styling features, including the glossy-black dash with small, separately mounted gauges, would be incorporated into most of GM's various makes of cars for the next four years.

At that time (1928), GM built the Cadillac, La Salle, Buick, Oakland, Oldsmobile, Pontiac, and Chevrolet. In 1929, GM added the Viking as a larger, V8-powered companion car to Oldsmobile, and in mid-1929 GM added the Marquette, as a smaller companion to the Buick.

Pontiac had appeared in '26 as a companion car to the larger Oakland, and by 1932, Pontiac replaced Oakland completely. After '30, both Viking and Marquette had been dropped. But, the La Salle continued as a lower-priced companion to Cadillac until 1940.

Cadillac advertising in 1928 was noteworthy for its majestic and glorious background scenes—bigger-than-life, colonnaded edifices that resembled heavenly mansions! These huge, temple-like structures had vast stairways and towering Gothic arches, with little groups of people strolling around on multiple levels. It had a thrilling, not-of-this-world appeal! The elaborate background shown here is similar to one in an original 1928 Cadillac advertisement.

The illustrated Town Car was usually an expensive body type, preferred by rich city dwellers who liked to display their chauffeurs. Sometimes they employed two: a driver and a footman to open doors and handle luggage.

1920s

1928 Chrysler "52"

C hrysler had a positively GREAT year in 1928! Beginning only in 1924, Chrysler—with its superior engineering and flashing performance—achieved such rapid and widespread popularity that for a time in '28 Chrysler had climbed to third place in nationwide sales of all makes of cars, approaching those top sellers, Chevrolet and Ford!

Illustrated here is the very rare Chrysler "52," which is a part of the transition between the old Maxwell of 1925 and the new Plymouth of 1929.

Mechanically, the Chrysler "52" has much in common with its Plymouth successor, but since it looks older, and since hydraulic brakes were not always found on the 4-cylinder Chryslers as they were on the Plymouth, the Chrysler "52" quickly grew dated and

disappeared from the roads of America while the early Plymouths survived.

Like the Plymouths until mid-1930, the Chrysler "52" had no fuel gauge on the dash, but, instead, a mechanical gauge out in back, atop the gas tank. This was most inconvenient on long trips, because the driver would have to stop the car and go back and look in order to determine how much gas was left. Also, there was no water temperature gauge on the dash; that was a luxury found on the larger "72" and "Imperial 80" models.

Notice, in the background, the typical glass-and-steel-frame service station of the late 1920s, with its tall "visible-supply" gasoline pump. Some of these big, glass-topped pumps were operated by a mechanical hand lever, and others were electrically controlled, when it came to pumping the gasoline.

1928 HUDSON
4-PASS. VICTORIA COUPE
(EARLY TYPE, W/O COWL LIGHTS
AND VISOR)
#128" W.B.   3775 lbs.
$1650., f.o.b., DETROIT
6-CYLINDER, F-HEAD ENG.
3½" x 5" BR. and STR.
288½ CID
90 HP
4.5 GEAR RATIO
4·1·88
new VERTICAL RADIATOR
SHUTTERS (1927 HUDSON HAD
HORIZONTAL SHUTTERS.)
#127⅜"
52,316 HUDSONS SOLD 1928.
TAD
10·2
© 1988 North America Syndicate, Inc. All rights reserved.

1928 Hudson Custom Victoria

This four-passenger Victoria coupe had the gracefulness of a coupe, coupled with the greater roominess of a two-door sedan! Yet, for some reason, the four-passenger coupe body type never caught on until the 1940s, when it became a "Club Coupe."

Hudson's mighty 1928 Custom Victoria appeared on Hudson's longer-wheelbase chassis. The car you see here was a rare early model, carrying a Motometer-type water temperature gauge on the radiator. Most 1928 Hudsons used a winged-goddess radiator cap ornament, because a water temperature gauge was made available on the dash, inside.

Some Custom Victorias were ordered with optional wire wheels and with fender-well spares. The Custom Victoria, typically, had a small outer sun visor.

Hudson patented its unusual "F-head" Super Six engine (Patent No. 1,656,051). The "F-head" was a sort of cross between an L-head and I-head (or overhead-valve) engine—the exhaust valves were mounted low, as on an L-head, and the intake valves were *overhead* (upside-down) and actuated by rocker arms and springs. Compression of the 1928 F-head Hudson engine was nearly 6 to 1—about 20 percent higher than the compression of the average 1928 automobile. Because of the high compression, fuel economy was slightly better than in other cars of Hudson's hefty size and weight. Fifteen to 18 m.p.g. was Hudson's official average in 1928, according to "many thousands of tests."

In addition to their long- and medium-wheelbase models, Hudson Motor Car Company also built a smaller Essex Super Six, priced from only $735. Hudson prices started at $1,250.

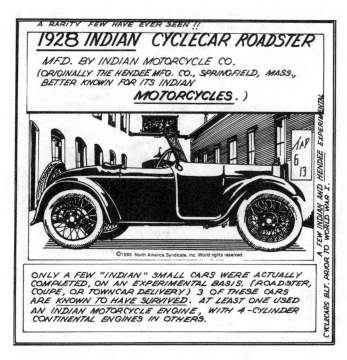

1928 Indian Cyclecar Roadster

The manufacturer of the Indian motorcycle had toyed with the idea of producing a light weight car since the early 1900s. As a matter of fact, a few "Hendee" automobiles were built and registered by Hendee/Indian before the 1920s.

The era between 1913 and 1916 was one that saw the introduction of many brands of small "cycle cars"—light-weight, narrow roadsters with small (one- to four-cylinder) engines, and bicycle- or motorcycle-type wire wheels. By 1927, the cycle-car craze was long forgotten, but the Indian Motorcycle Company got the idea once more to build a few such small cars. Between 1927 and 1929, a handful of pilot models were completed. These new cycle-car types were the brainchildren of Jack Bauer, son of the company's president.

Merrimac built the bodies for these Indian cars, and one had a Le Baron body. The development of these small cars cost $65,000.

Earlier, Indian had built a special factory in Springfield, Mass. for the production of automobiles. But, after it was completed, it was sold, and American Rolls-Royces were assembled there. (Rolls-Royce operated an American branch factory from the early 1920s to the early 1930s, and the American-built Rolls-Royces were usually longer and more ostentatious than their British counterparts.)

In 1929, Charles A. Levine gained control of the Indian company and curtailed all "unprofitable" activities, ending Indian's plans for a possible automotive sideline.

MFD. IN BINGHAMTON, N.Y. (1915~1932)
BY LARRABEE DEYO MOTOR TRUCK CO., INC.

$2050. PLUS COST OF CAB and BODY

SPARE TIRE RIM AT SIDE OF COWL

GRAVITY FUEL FEED

160" WHEELBASE

32 x 6" TIRES (METAL SPOKED WHEELS)

BREWSTER 4-PC. WINDSHIELD

SLANTING LOUVRES, ODD BODY DECORATION, REAR FENDERS, FULL-LENGTH RUNNING BOARDS, DISTINGUISHING FEATURES

4-SPEED TRANSMISSION
5.37 to 1 GEAR RATIO
(MFR. ALSO BUILT MAJESTIC TAXI CABS FOR USE IN N.Y.C.)

7~25

2-WHEEL BRAKES

1928 LARRABEE DEYO
MODEL "X-33" 1½ to 2 TON CAPACITY STAKE TRUCK
CONTINENTAL "8-R"
6-CYL. L-HEAD ENGINE
3 3/8" x 4 1/2" BORE and STR.
(CONTINENTAL ENGS. IN MOST MODELS
WEIGHT = 9900 lbs. WITH LOAD
CHASSIS WT. = 3800 lbs. ALONE
(4124 lbs. = ALTERNATE FIG.)

JULY 25   ©1993 North America Syndicate, Inc. World rights reserved.

1928 Larrabee Deyo Truck

This is a rare one, but easy to identify because of its unique styling! Larrabee Deyo continued this particular look for a few years, from the mid-1920s to 1929. In January 1929, a more up-to-date new model (the "50") joined the line, and in 1929 all models got Lockheed four-wheel hydraulic brakes as standard equipment.

The 1928 model shown here was one of six types, the other five being the A-3 (3/4 to 1 ton); X-21 (1 1/2 to 2 ton); XH-25 or XH-32 (each 2 1/2 to 3 tons); and the $3,900 XH-31 bus chassis. The price leader was the A-3 at $1,350.

These '28 models were replaced in 1929 by the new series "20," "30," "40," "50," "60," and "70" models (from 1 ton to 3 1/2 ton capacities).

The Larrabee Deyo trucks were named for company bosses and founders H. Chester Larrabee and R. Herbert Deyo. In 1929, the Binghamton, N.Y., company was producing 300 to 400 trucks per year. Some of the company's output, over the years, was labeled "Larrabee," others were "Larrabee Deyo."

The company's predecessor was the Sturtevant-Larrabee Company, builder of sleighs, wagons, and carriages, originating in 1881.

In the early '30s, Larrabee Deyo trucks were discontinued. But, R. H. Deyo maintained his Deyo Ice Cream Company, founded 1930. Deyo also sought good public relations with the Binghamton Police Dept. by sponsoring clambake parties for the police force. At one time, he gave each local policeman a personal bank account and passbook, since he felt the police were underpaid.

1928 Nash

Nash Motors sold 138,137 cars in 1928—a figure they would not surpass until 1949!

Nash had three types of front rooflines in 1928: the French roof, the overhanging roof, and the cadet-type visor with tilt-out front pillar. The last, shown in the lower center of the illustration, was the most up-to-date of three types. There were a few instances when a certain body type in one series would have the roofline characteristics of one of the two other series, as exemplified by the Special 6 Victoria coupe shown here. In November 1927, this particular model was introduced as a seven-window sedan with landau irons. Both were a part of the mid-range Special 6 line.

Nash cars in '28 were well appointed, with rich mohair upholstery, Colonial-pattern, silver-finished hardware, genuine walnut wood trim, and "handsome new steering wheel designs in solid walnut." Within two years, the traditional wooden-rimmed steering wheel would become a thing of the past. In accidents, wooden steering wheels could splinter into deadly spears!

Generally, 1928 Nashes were built lower than their predecessors, with smaller wheels, "in the newest vogue." The 1928 line was advertised as being the easiest of all cars to steer, and having a secret type of special-alloy springs, which, along with the shock absorbers, gave a smoother ride.

On February 1, 1928, C. W. Nash reduced the prices of his cars. A six-cylinder (seven-main-bearing engine) sedan was priced as low as $845, f.o.b., factory. Six of the twenty-four models were priced under $1,000!

LOWEST-PRICED SIX WITH A 7-BEARING CRANKSHAFT

new HIGHER RADIATOR

new "CADET" VISOR

5 PASS. COACH (2 DR.)
$695
f.o.b., FACTORY PRICE

28.5

109½" W. B.
2423 lbs.

WITH
4 WHEEL
MECHANICAL
BRAKES,
by BENDIX.

28 x
4.75
TIRES

4.89
GEAR
RATIO

THE "PERFECTED" 1928 ½ (APRIL, 1928)

Whippet Six

WITH A 178.3 CID L-HEAD 6,
(3⅛" x 3⅞")
WITH 43 HP @ 2800 RPM)

MOVED UP FROM
9TH PLACE IN 1927 TO
4TH PLACE IN '28 SALES!

171,958 SOLD
IN 10 MOS.

WHIPPET REPLACED THE OVERLAND IN MID-1926, WITH EARLY '27 MODEL. DISCONTINUED EARLY '31.

(4 CYL. MODELS ALSO)
MFD. BY WILLYS-OVERLAND, INC.,
TOLEDO, OHIO

TAP 7/12

1928 1/2 Whippet Six

Willys-Overland was late with its restyled 1928 Whippet Six. Not ready until April 1928, the "perfected" 98 series was, theoretically, a 1928 1/2 midseason model, and the earlier '28 Six was apparently a continuation of the smaller-looking '27.

Available as a four or six, the '27 Whippet featured an overhanging roof-visor ("French roofline") combination, while the illustrated '28 1/2 had a separate "Cadet" visor above the windshield. The '28 1/2 "98" series six had a new 178.3 c.i.d. engine that replaced the former 169.6 c.i.d. six (40 h.p.) of the '27 "93-A." Four-cylinder Whippets were designated the "96" series in both 1927 and 1928.

Some Whippet cars included a small, leaping-Whippet dog mascot attached to the radiator cap, but this accessory is rare. Both '27 and '28 Whippets had drum-type headlights, and the '27 had old-fashioned, raised crown panels atop the fenders.

Top speed was nothing to write home about—60 was "pushing it." The Whippet was relatively low-geared, and known for peppy pickup.

After the Whippets were dropped in 1931, no more four-cylinder Willys-Overland cars were built until the introduction of the 1933 Willys "77." The gap was filled by 1931 and 1932 Willys sixes and straight-eights.

Overland and Whippet cars were sometimes nicknamed "The Toledo Vibrators," but in truth their performance was comparatively smooth, especially with a seven-bearing crankshaft in the illustrated '28 1/2 six.

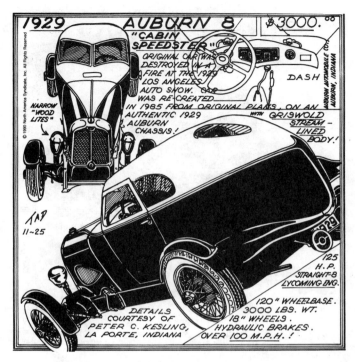

1929 Auburn "Cabin Speedster"

Dr. Peter C. Kesling deserves an enthusiastic vote of thanks for providing us with much information on the streamlined 1929 Auburn Cabin Speedster and its 1985 replica.

This was originally a show car, and Auburn intended to build more. However, the Cabin Speedster was displayed at the Los Angeles Automobile Show of 1929, and though it generated customer orders while there, a disastrous fire swept through the glittering display of classics, wiping out dozens of beautiful cars. The futuristic Cabin Speedster was reduced to a worthless, twisted wreck.

The Auburn Automobile Company, dismayed at the loss of their pilot model, dropped plans to duplicate it.

Extinct as it had become, the Cabin Speedster was a legend among classic car buffs. Finally, in 1985, Dr. Kesling located an authentic Auburn 8 chassis and had a duplicate made of the Cabin Speedster, using original plans.

The Cabin Speedster had an aluminum body formed over a framework of wood. The rear "periscope" window, as it was originally called, was not actually a periscope, and it was too high and too small to be practical. Rear visibility was poor to the point of being hazardous.

In a telephone conversation with me, Dr. Kesling said that the Cabin Speedster, sporty as it appeared, was exceedingly cramped, stuffy, and noisy. It was not a car to be recommended for continued driving. However, 100-plus miles per hour was a very impressive speed in 1929 and was seldom equaled by ordinary cars until the mid-1950s.

1929 DODGE SENIOR

THE "SENIOR" WAS DODGE'S LARGEST, MOST DELUXE SERIES --- AVAILABLE ONLY FROM 1927½ TO EARLY 1930. REPLACED BY DODGE 8.

5.56 COMPR.

78 HP @ 3000 RPM

15 GAL. GAS TANK

$1675.

COUPE (w. RUMBLE SEAT)
WOOD-AND-STEEL BODY
BY MURRAY (3358 lbs.)
(ALL-STEEL *BUDD* BODIES ON
LOWER PRICED STD. 6 and
VICTORY 6 DODGES)

6 CYL. L-HEAD ENG. (241.5 CID)
(3⅜ x 4½ B-ST.)

3/17

GEAR RATIO

4.45

6.00 x 19 " TIRES

120 " W.B.   HYDRAULIC BRAKES

1929 Dodge "Senior Six"

The Dodge Senior Six, launched in May 1927, was totally restyled in the summer of 1928 for the 1929 season. Interestingly, although Dodge Bros. had long used Budd all-steel bodies, this 1929 Senior featured a coach-built, composite, wood-framed Murray body (following a year of Seniors with Briggs or Murray bodies). The Senior also used a six-cylinder, Dodge-designed, but Continental-built engine.

The instrument panel was silver-faced with gauges behind glass in a new, somewhat bone-shaped configuration with a third "bulge" at the center, between the two at the ends.

The Senior Six has always been a rare model compared to other Dodges, and the enlarged '29-'30 style is apparently more scarce than the '27-'28 type. Reportedly, only about 7,000 of the '29-'30 Seniors left the factory before the Senior was phased out in May 1930.

Some of the late-model Senior Sixes were available with dash-mounted "Transitone" radios with the speaker mounted high in a small horn above the windshield! Beginning in 1929, the idea of cars with radios made a hit, and other manufacturers began offering optional radios in 1930.

Wire wheels were optional; Senior Sixes so equipped were "Sport" models.

Introduced September 1928, the 1929 Senior was available as a Roadster, Coupe, Victoria Brougham (actually a coach, or two-door sedan), four-door Sedan, and Landau Sedan (without rear quarter windows).

A grand total of 32,642 Senior Sixes were built between May 1927 and May 1930.

1929
ESSEX
COUPE

$695.
F.O.B.,
DETROIT

ESSEX MFD. 1919 TO 1933 AS LOW PRICED SUBSIDIARY OF
HUDSON.

160. 4 C.I.D. 6 CYL. ENGINE (2 3/4 × 4 1/2") TOP SPEED = OVER 70, IN SPITE OF VERY LOW - GEARED 5.60 TO 1 REAR AXLE RATIO!

110 1/2" WHEELBASE CORK - FACED CLUTCH

INSTRUMENT PANEL

55 H.P. @ 3600 RPM

© News America Syndicate, 1985

1929 Essex

Introduced for 1919, the Essex was Hudson's lower-priced companion all through the 1920s and into the early 1930s.

The 1929 Essex was known as the Challenger model. Unlike most other low-priced cars, the Essex included radiator shutters. (For quicker warm-ups in cold weather, and also for better looks.)

Chrome plating was now used on bright-work parts, having the bluish-silver look of stainless steel. Chrome plating maintained its shine without special maintenance much longer than nickel would.

The only drawback to the Essex cars of the later 1920s was the unusually low rear-axle ratio; 5.60-to-1 in high gear was nearly equivalent to second gear in some other cars! This meant that the little six-cylinder Essex engine raced needlessly at highway speeds.

Rod and bearing failures often resulted, and one was not wise to push the 1929 Essex to its limit, in spite of the advertisements that claimed the car could be driven 70 miles per hour and more.

"You may expect 18 to 20 miles to the gallon," the ads promised, in a day when gas was about 18 cents a gallon. Some Essex owners reported even more than 20 m.p.g.! Think what the Essex could have done with a higher-geared differential!

If one special-ordered any model, it could be built and shipped "within 48 hours." Hudson-Essex, in 1929, proclaimed itself to be the leading "independent" producer of cars in the U.S.A.

On the "H.N.C. Purchase Plan," monthly time payments were available, after a $245 to $295 down payment or trade-in of equivalent value.

$1195. f.o.b. DETROIT

NOTE THE DISTINCTIVE SUPPORT BRACKETS FOR SUN VISOR (6/2, 6/5)

HYDRAULIC BRAKES

4 SPEED TRANSMISSION (EXCEPT IN 6/2)

V SHAPED RADIATOR

AVAILABLE IN 5 SERIES

1929 GRAHAM-PAIGE

MODEL	CYLS.	H P	WHEELBASE	GEAR RATIO
6/2	6	62	112"	4.7
6/5	6	77	115"	(ILLUSTRATED) 3.92
62/	6	97	121"	3.4
8.27	8	123	127"	3.64
8.37	8	123	137"	3.92

FULL RANGE PRICES $895.~2495.

TAD 10-18

1929 Graham-Paige

During the 'teens and 1920s, the Paige automobile was a fairly popular marque from Detroit. In the 1920s, the three Graham Brothers had achieved considerable success in marketing Dodge Bros. trucks sold under the Graham Bros. name. And, in 1927, they bought up Paige (originally Paige-Detroit) from its founder, Harry Jewett.

The Paige was renamed Graham-Paige for 1928 and was totally restyled, with pleasing results! The car had a new emblem, bearing the likeness of the Graham Brothers (Joseph, Robert, and Ray) in open knight helmets.

Hydraulic brakes were an advanced feature of the Graham-Paige, and most models included a new four-speed Warner transmission with dual high range. Third gear was for quick acceleration on the road or for hill climbing, while fourth gear was a cruising range comparable to overdrive, providing higher speed with less work for the engine.

A great success at first, Graham-Paige sold nearly 74,000 units the first year, beating Pontiac's first-year model of 1926.

A minor styling change for Graham-Paige in 1929: thinner, Cadillac-style louvers set farther back along the sides of the hood, giving a costlier appearance. The gracefully curving visor brackets on some of the sixes were also pleasing in design, and one may wonder why they weren't reserved for the eights.

Early in 1930, the brand name was shortened to Graham. Paige commercial cars were offered for another couple of years.

Graham continued to build cars until 1940, and some of their final "Hollywood" models were prematurely tagged "1941s."

1929 ½ LINCOLN V8
384.8 CID V8 · 90 HP @ 2800 RPM
4.58 OR 4.9 GEAR RATIO

"CLUB ROADSTER"
(CABRIOLET) WITH
BODY BY LOCKE
225 BLT. $4900.

NOW WORTH UP TO $116,000.,
IF IN LIKE-NEW CONDITION !
(WORTH 5K IN POOR COND.)

4 WHEEL MECHANICAL BRAKES

136" W.B.

32 x 6.75 OR 7.00 x 20" TIRES

6800 TOTAL 29 LINCOLN SALES

RAP 8·25

CLASSIC LINCOLNS OFTEN USED BODIES BY
SUCH HANDCRAFT COACHBUILDERS AS
LE BARON, LOCKE, DIETRICH,
JUDKINS, WILLOUGHBY, BRUNN,
AND DERHAM. (ALL THESE
LISTED AS LINCOLN SUPPLIERS
DURING 1929.)

(SAFETY GLASS STANDARD)

1929 1/2 Lincoln "Club Roadster"

The Locke-bodied "Club Roadster" (illustrated) was advertised with wire wheels late in the 1929 season, but earlier 1929 models were pictured with wood-spoked artillery wheels and spare rims in the fenderwells.

Henry Ford bought the Lincoln Motor Co., founded by Henry Leland, in 1922. Fans of the popular Model A Ford will notice that it borrowed much of its styling from the Lincoln of the same era, unlike the boxy and rudimentary Model T Ford that was built until 1927.

Except for the 1921 and early 1922 models—the earliest Lincolns—Lincoln motor cars have always been built by the Ford Motor Company as their top-of-the-line product. Though Fords were inexpensive cars, no compromise with luxury was made in the classic Lincoln. During the 1920s, in fact, Lincoln quality continued to improve.

Lincoln mechanical precision was emphasized. As one 1929 advertisement mentioned, clearances between certain parts were as fine as "1/15th of a hair's breadth!" Yet, there was no initial "tightness" in a new 1929 Lincoln, and the owner could drive it at normal speeds even on the first day! No break-in period was necessary.

By 1929, many of the earlier Lincolns already had been driven over 250,000 miles and were still good! Lincolns did change year by year, but no yearly models were then announced—because "Lincoln's beauty was not to be branded with a date."

During the 1920s and 1930s, many older Lincolns were rehabilitated for use as tow trucks: a tribute to their durability!

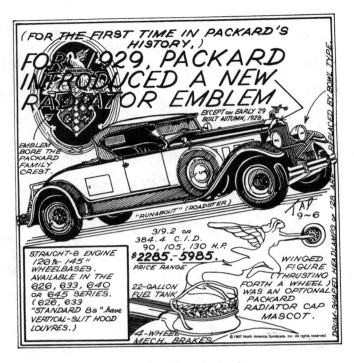

1929 Packard

Ever since 1904, Packard had been easily identified by its distinctive shape of radiator and hood. Over the years, the dimensions changed "as power plant needs increased," but a Packard was always recognizable. Because of this, a nameplate hardly seemed necessary. However, other cars bore radiator nameplates or emblems, and at last Packard briefly bowed to the popular custom. In 1929 a radiator crest appeared!

The new badge was designed to honor the late founders of the Packard Motor Car Company—James Ward Packard and his brother, William. The badge bore the coat of arms and crest of the old English family of Packard. *Country Life* (December 1928) and the *Saturday Evening Post* (October 27, 1928) each carried a Packard advertisement, discussing the new emblem, presenting it in color (red, gold, black, and chrome silver).

The Runabout (roadster) illustrated here was seen in color (orange, black, and sienna) in *Asia* magazine (June 1929) and in the May 25, 1929 *Saturday Evening Post*. There were variations during 1929, for the earlier '29 catalog for the Custom 8-40 series as well as the Standard Eight 6-26/6-33 series catalog illustrate the Runabouts as having a broadened section of the belt trim in the vicinity of the doors.

As in the previous year, the larger series Packards were fitted with four vent doors at either side of the hood, while the less-costly Standards had vertical louvre slots.

All 1929 Packards were powered by L-head, straight-eight engines. A six-cylinder Packard would not reappear until 1937.

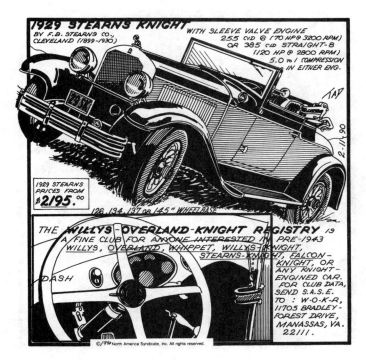

1929 Stearns-Knight

T he old-fashioned "sleeve-valve" Knight engine used movable sleeves between the pistons and cylinder walls. These sleeves (slotted with openings that lined up with openings in the cylinder walls when sleeves were in a certain position) served in place of valves.

There were many Knight-engined cars built from the early 'teens to the early '30s. Most common was the Willys-Knight. There was also the Stearns-Knight (illustrated), as well as the Falcon-Knight, Brewster-Knight, Columbia-Knight, British Daimler-Knight, Belgian Minerva-Knight, Federal-Knight truck, Handley-Knight, Moline-Knight, Sterling-Knight, R & V Knight, Russell-Knight, and others.

The 1933 Willys-Knight was the last Knight-engined car made in the USA,
since the Stearns-Knight was discontinued in 1930.

Most Knight engines were sixes or fours. However, the rare straight-eight Knight engine was available for this 1929 Stearns-Knight.

The dashboard design of the illustrated car was somewhat old fashioned, more typical of the Mid-1920s than of 1929. In 1929 and 1930, the instrument panels of some cars reflected the new vogue of Art Deco, which was evident in architecture, interior decoration, electrical appliances, etc.

What's a rare Stearns-Knight 1929 cabriolet, like this one, worth on the market today? Whether with six- or eight-cylinder engine, even a rough, unrestored specimen would be worth at least $5,000. One in perfect condition could bring $40,000, or even more!

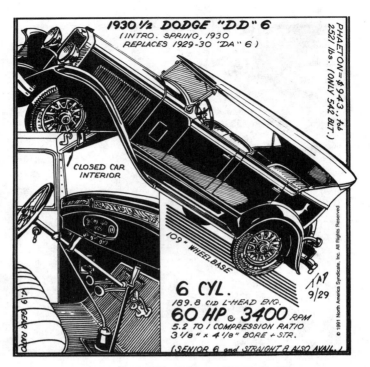

1930½ DODGE "DD" 6
(INTRO. SPRING, 1930
REPLACES 1929-30 "DA" 6)

PHAETON = $943.; fob
2521 lbs. (ONLY 542 BLT.)

CLOSED CAR
INTERIOR

109" WHEELBASE

4.19 GEAR RATIO

6 CYL.
189.8 CID L-HEAD ENG.
60 HP @ 3400 RPM
5.2 TO 1 COMPRESSION RATIO
3 1/8" x 4 1/8" BORE + STR.
(SENIOR 6 and STRAIGHT 8 ALSO AVAIL.)

© 1991 North America Syndicate, Inc. All Rights Reserved

1930 1/2 Dodge "DD" Six

In the late 1920s and early 1930s, Chrysler Corp. often introduced new models during the spring or summer. The Dodge "DD" Six, introduced in the spring of 1930, continued on into early 1931.

Back in the 'teens and early '20s, the four-door convertible touring car (a. k. a. phaeton) was the most popular body style of all. In the early 1930s, some buyers still selected roadsters or convertible coupes, but the four-door phaeton was out of fashion and becoming a very scarce model in new-car lineups.

Only 542 Dodge "DD" phaetons were built, and in 1931 there were but a mere forty-three Dodge phaetons produced, as Dodge dropped that body type. In '32 there would be a two-door Dodge convertible sedan, and in the mid-'30s Dodge would turn out a limited number of four-door convertible sedans (starting 1933), with roll-up glass windows in the doors.

Oddly, Chrysler Corp. phaetons had two-piece, horizontally-split ventilating windshields on most small- and mid-sized models (Chrysler, Plymouth, De Soto, Dodge) until mid-1930, though most other brands had gone to one-piece windshields on all body types back in the mid-1920s.

Where did all the old phaetons and touring cars go? In the middle and late 1930s (and in the early 1940s), many old phaetons wound up in the hands of high-school boys, who often adorned their old "jalopies" with crazy slogans painted on almost every part of the car body. Bare-bones transportation often acquired for $25, these jalopies led hard lives. When they were thoroughly worn out, the next stop was the junkyard!

PRODUCTION OF THIS UNUSUAL *2-DOOR* TOURING CAR BEGAN ON JUNE 3, 1930.

1930½ FORD MODEL **A**
"DELUXE PHAETON" TYPE 180A

$**625**, F.O.B., DEARBORN, MICH.
(PRICE CUT TO $580. IN 1931)

WITH 200½" CID L-HEAD ENGINE (3⅞" x 4¼" BORE and ST.)

3.7 GEAR RATIO
40 H.P.

HELPFUL DATA THANKS TO WESTON R. BRUSH, ALLYN, WA.

BODY BY BRIGGS

TAD 6~24

65 M.P.H. APPROX.
16 to 25 MILES PER GALLON

© 1990 North America Syndicate, Inc. All Rights Reserved

FORD'S DEPENDABLE MODEL A REPLACED THE FINAL 1927 MODEL T. 1928 and 1929 MODEL As HAD 21" WHEELS and A MORE ROUNDED, SMALLER RADIATOR THAN THE 1930 TO EARLY-1932 MODEL As. EARLY IN 1931, A REFINED RADIATOR SHELL APPEARED (WITH TOP FRONT SECTION PAINTED, and BEARING A STAINLESS-STEEL OVAL *Ford* EMBLEM INSTEAD OF BLUE ENAMELED TYPE).

1930s

1930 1/2 Model A Ford Deluxe Phaeton

One of the best-loved and most dependable of all vintage cars is Ford's second Model A series! This letter designation was originally used on Ford's very first production model of 1903. But, the better-known Model A is the series of 1928 to early 1932.

The Model A that was introduced in late '27 for the '28 model year offered four-wheel mechanical brakes, a doubling of horsepower (40 instead of 20), and a new sliding-gear manual transmission. The Model A was completely restyled for 1928, made to resemble a mini-version of Ford's top-line Lincoln automobile. More color choices were offered as well.

One of the most fascinating things about this Model A was the wide variety of body types and variations available at different periods of its 4 1/2-year run.

There were the Roadster (Standard or Deluxe); soft-top Sport Coupe (which resembled a convertible, but was not); the Convertible Cabriolet (with folding top and vertical windshield, or later slant-windshield type); Tudor (two-door) Sedan (and later Deluxe variations); Fordor (four-door) Sedan (in several types, with five or seven windows and soft- or steel-backed rear quarters, Standard or Deluxe); Victoria Coupe (1931, with soft- or steel-backed rear quarters); Convertible Sedan; rare luxury Town Car; Taxi; and Phaeton (four-door, convertible touring car). Also, the illustrated Deluxe Phaeton (the rare two-door variety, available from June 1930 on).

Over a million of the Model A Tudor Sedans were produced, yet the most commonly seen type is the steel-backed, five-window coupe.

1930 Hudson Great 8

For years, the Hudson "Super Six" had been a popular car—all through the 1920s, and even back to the mid-teens!

Thus, as America entered a bleak Depression era in 1930, it was unfortunate that Hudson would abandon a proven favorite and replace a hefty 92-horsepower six with a new and smaller straight-eight of 80 horsepower. It would not be a popular decision!

During the late 1920s, straight-eight engines had grown in public esteem, as their performance—with a long crankshaft and added bearings—seemed smoother than that of the average six and much smoother than a four!

True, eight cylinders consumed more gas, and there were more moving parts that could potentially break down. But, before the fateful stock market nosedive of October 29, 1929, Hudson's plans for the 1930 Great 8 were already a reality. Though many disappointed buyers cried "Bring back the Super Six," the Hudson Super Six would not be available as an alternate choice until the 1933 models arrived!

Though Hudson's "Great Eight" engine of 1930 was smaller and less powerful than the 1929 six, it was considered adequate because weight had been drastically reduced in the '30 models. Price was an attraction, as the two-passenger 1930 Hudson coupe was only $885, f.o.b. factory.

The eight grew in c.i.d. in 1931 and became the "Greater Eight," and it grew again in 1932. But, sales declined, and Hudson gave buyers a new choice of six or eight in 1933.

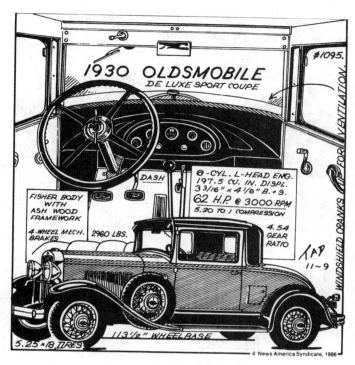

© News America Syndicate, 1986

1930s

1930 Oldsmobile

The 1930 Oldsmobile was a good car, but General Motors sold far more Chevrolets and Buicks at that time. In 1929 and 1930, to widen its buyer range, GM's Oldsmobile Division offered a second car as well: the very rare Viking V-8, a bigger car which bore a casual resemblance to Cadillac's subsidiary La Salle.

Oldsmobile, as most GM cars, featured a glossy black instrument panel with black gauges (round) in 1930. Wood-graining (either real or painted on) was "out" that year on GM cars, and yet the 1930 Viking did feature some wood-grain decoration on its dash.

Oldsmobile, in 1930, was proud of its extensive facility, the Olds Motor Works in Lansing, Mich. In a February 22, 1930 *Saturday Evening Post* ad (page 34), visitors were invited to come in for a factory tour. No appointment was necessary. Various factory scenes were included in some of Oldsmobile's other 1930 advertisements.

As for the '30 Oldsmobile, it featured finer upholstery, improved seat construction and springing, better carburetion, easier steering, fully enclosed mechanical brake cables, and slightly roomier, sleeker-looking bodies with a restyled belt moulding, and a new seven-degree slope to the windshield—to reduce nighttime glare. Incidentally, as illustrated, the windshield could be cranked up a few inches for ventilation, and some of this incoming air was directed downward, behind the dashboard gauges, toward the front floorboard.

To improve acceleration and hill-climbing, the 1930 Oldsmobile gear ratio was changed from 4.41-to-1 to 4.54-to-1, meaning a lower-geared car less suitable for highway cruising speeds.

3 5/16 x 3 7/8" BORE and STR.   60 HP @ 3000 RPM

OVAL REAR WINDOW, AS IN 1929.→

INDIAN-HEAD RADIATOR CAP MASCOT↘

L-HEAD ENG.

4.42 GEAR RATIO

AC FUEL PUMP

BODY BY FISHER
110-INCH WHEELBASE

6 CYL.

"NEW SERIES" 1930 PONTIAC BIG SIX

SPORT COUPE $825.

200 C.I.D.

GLOSSY BLACK DASH WITH 4 UNIFORMLY SIZED ROUND GAUGES

© 1989 North America Syndicate Inc. All rights reserved

IN ADDITION TO MOTOR VEHICLES, GM ALSO OFFERED *GENERAL MOTORS* RADIOS IN 1930! THIS GM "QUEEN ANNE" RADIO-PHONOGRAPH SOLD FOR $198.00 (w/o TUBES)

FRONT END

TAP 6-25

MIDLAND 4-WHEEL MECHANICAL BRAKES   13-GALLON GAS TANK

1930 Pontiac Sport Coupe

"Throughout its entire speed range there is an alluring new smoothness in the New Series Pontiac Big Six. A leisurely 'thirty' or brisk 'sixty'—either reveals a delightfully uniform absence of roughness and vibration. The basis of this increased smoothness is exceptionally fine engineering. The short, heavy crankshaft of Pontiac's 60-h.p. engine is dynamically balanced and fully counterweighted. It has a 'Harmonic Balancer' which prevents torsional vibration. The crankcase is much more rigid. And, Pontiac's power plant is now completely insulated from the frame by new-type rubber mountings." So declared an April 1930 advertisement by General Motors' Pontiac division.

Other Pontiac features for 1930: improved Lovejoy Hydraulic Shock Absorbers, new roller-bearing steering mechanism, improved non-squeak mechanical brakes, slightly sloped windshield to reduce glare, emergency brake that acted upon all four wheels, and more. Standard upholstery was of velvety mohair.

To protect the engine, a "gear-drive safety feature" immediately shut off the ignition if oil pressure should fail, preventing a driver from operating a "dry" engine and thus wrecking it.

The illustrated Sport Coupe also had a rumble seat for two extra passengers. Wire wheels were deluxe equipment; many '30 Pontiacs continued with the wood-spoked type.

The 1930 Pontiacs have been rare for many, many years. Though smooth-running and reasonably dependable, they had a wooden body framework, which was vulnerable to dry rot if not cared for properly. Therefore, a large number of these cars were scrapped during the late '30s or early '40s, when they were still in running condition.

1930

Stewart

1 - TON CANOPY TRUCK

WITH
199 C.I.D.,
4 - CYLINDER,
L-HEAD LYCOMING
"AFE" ENGINE
50 H.P. @ 2600 RPM
(3³/4" × 4¹/2" BORE + STROKE)
DELCO-REMY IGNITION   2905 lbs. (CHASSIS)
4-SPEED TRANS.   6.50 × 20 TIRES
BENDIX 4-WHEEL MECHANICAL BRAKES
MFD. BY STEWART MOTOR CORP., BUFFALO, N.Y.
(1912 - 1939)
130" wheelbase (120" on 140" AWHL.)
CHASSIS PRICE = $695. fob
2-19-84
© Field Enterprises, Inc., 1964

1930 Stewart Truck

If you're interested in buying or restoring an antique or classic car but discouraged by today's inflated prices, don't overlook the possibilities in an antique truck! Old trucks are less popular, and often priced less than cars of the same age. Yet, they are scarce, interesting, and can be useful as well as collectible!

This 1930 Stewart is a canopy truck, similar to a pickup except for the open-sided, built-on cover to protect the contents from inclement weather. Roll-down canvas curtains could be lowered from the roof, if desired. These canopy trucks were once popular with traveling fruit-and-vegetable peddlers, and were also known as "Peddler's wagons."

The illustrated Stewart truck used a four-cyclinder engine but was also available with a Lycoming six. Stewart's 1930 slogan: "Stewart trucks have won—by costing less to run."

In addition to the four- and six-cyclinder, one-ton models, in 1930 Stewart also supplied six-cylinder trucks in 1 1/4, 1 1/2, 2, 2 1/2, 3, 3 1/2, 5, and 6 to 7 ton capacities for up to $5,700 f.o.b. (out of Buffalo, N.Y.).

The six-spoke wheels on the illustrated truck were of metal, with demountable rims. Rear springs were 50 inches long by 2 1/2 inches wide, with 11 leaves.

Some 1918 Stewarts were still in service in 1930. Many Stewart trucks managed to survive much longer, and though they're rare today, a few have lasted long enough to be rescued and restored by appreciative collectors!

1930 Studebaker Commander 8

Studebaker is usually not thought of as a "classic" in the noble tradition of Packard, Pierce-Arrow, Duesenberg, etc. But, Studebaker's beautiful Commander 8 and President 8 roadsters deserve such a designation.

The 1930 Studebaker styling was only slightly changed from 1929. More models now included radiator shutters. Outside sun visors were eliminated on the Commander and President models. Studebaker's rectangular central instrument panel with its typical squared gauges was continued with little change.

During the '30 model year, Studebaker built the low-priced Erskine 6, replaced midseason by the 1930 1/2 Studebaker 6. Then there were the Dictator 6 and new Dictator 8, the Commander 6 and the new Commander 8 (illustrated), and the President 8 (available in two different wheelbase series).

The following features were included in the Commander 8 for 1930: coincidental steering-and-ignition lock; cam-and-lever steering; thermostatically-controlled radiator shutters; steel-core, thin-grip steering wheel; double-drop frame; composite bodies of steel sheathing over a hardwood framework; non-shatterable glass; Lanchester vibration dampeners; and much more.

By May 1930, Studebaker had built and sold a total of 100,000 straight-8s in less than three years.

Studebaker's brakes were mechanical. After unsuccessful experiments with hydraulic brakes a few years earlier, Studebaker returned to mechanicals and stuck with them until the mid-1930s.

What's this 1930 Studebaker Commander 8 roadster worth now? Even in poor condition, it could still be worth $3,500; and in like-new condition it's worth up to $32,000.

1930 WILLYS 6

WITH L-HEAD, 193 CID 6-CYL. ENG.

MFD. BY WILLYS-OVERLAND INC., TOLEDO, OHIO

2744 lbs.   110" W.B.   72 MPH

7-15 News America Syndicate, Inc., 1984 © News Group Chicago, Inc.

1930

SEDAN DE LUXE
$850.⁰⁰
F.O.B.

5.60 COMPRESSION
Auto Lite ELEC. SYSTEM
10 GAL. FUEL CAPACITY,
WITH VACUUM TANK SUPPLY
5.00 × 19 TIRES

4.09 GEAR RATIO

65 H.P. @ 3400 RPM   3 1/4" × 3 1/8" BORE + STR.

1930 Willys Six

The Willys Six was a new model for 1930. All through the 1920s, Willys-Overland had offered only their sleeve-valve Willys-Knight cars or lower-priced Overlands (and later, Whippets) with conventional poppet-valved engines. But, the Willys Six, and soon-to-be-introduced Willys straight-eight, had new poppet-valve engines and were price leaders that, within a year, would replace the Whippet series.

According to the January 1930 issue of *Motor* magazine (p. 146), "The new Willys Six … is a smooth, lively car with pleasing lines. According to factory figures, it has a maximum speed of 72 miles per hour, … and it has a speed of 50 m.p.h. in second."

Bendix four-wheel mechanical brakes were used. The Tillotson carburetor was fed via a Stewart vacuum tank.

As on the '29 Whippet, the new Six had "finger tip control" on the steering wheel. Early models of the '30 Willys Six had corrugated tubular bumpers, as illustrated. Later in the year, flat two-leaf bumpers were attached.

A stock Willys Six roadster, driven by W. F. Shepherd, raced around 203 curves on the 12 1/3-mile run to the top of Pike's Peak (elevation 14,109 feet above sea level) in 24 minutes, 18 1/2 seconds, setting a record at the time for stock cars priced below $1,000!

In the spring of 1930, the new Willys Eight joined the Six. In styling, the Eight was generally similar, but it was longer, had parking lamps on cowl, two-leaf bumpers, and a thin band of vertically-ribbed stampings (dark-colored) just below the upper plated radiator shell pan.

1930s

1930 Willys-Knight Great Six

The restyled Willys-Knight Great Six was introduced in 1929 and continued with few changes into 1930. Other body styles were available (coupe, sedan, and five-passenger coupe), and each type was priced, f.o.b. at factory, at $1,895. But, the illustrated roadster is particularly interesting because of the attractive sweep mouldings on cowl and body, and because of the novel checkerboard pattern on doors and surrounding sheet metal. This one is readily distinguishable from any other car!

In July 1929, the new Great Six was proclaimed to be "the most beautiful automobile that Willys-Overland's designers have ever created," and it bore little of the look of the older, smaller Willys-Knights. Vertical automatic radiator shutters were standard equipment, as were the new door vents on the sides of the hood. Wire wheels were standard equipment on the early Great Sixes of the 1929-1930 season, and early models (as illustrated) sported the tubular bumpers.

A striking car in any crowd, the roadster sported pale green fenders and chassis apron, which was unusual in an era when most cars had black fenders, or at least a darker color below. One reason dark tones were typical on fenders and chassis was because these areas would then be less likely to show stains from oil, dust, mud, etc.

Wire wheels and checkerboard strips were pale yellow on the Great Six roadster, with spares mounted in fender wells. In the years that have passed since it was new, this roadster has become a classic!

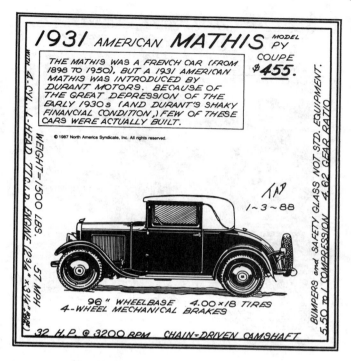

1931 AMERICAN **MATHIS** MODEL PY

COUPE $455.

THE MATHIS WAS A FRENCH CAR (FROM 1898 TO 1950), BUT A 1931 AMERICAN MATHIS WAS INTRODUCED BY DURANT MOTORS. BECAUSE OF THE GREAT DEPRESSION OF THE EARLY 1930s (AND DURANT'S SHAKY FINANCIAL CONDITION,) FEW OF THESE CARS WERE ACTUALLY BUILT.

WITH 4-CYL. L-HEAD 77 c.i.d. ENGINE (2¾" × 3¼" BORE)

WEIGHT = 1500 LBS.

57 MPH

TAD 1~3~88

BUMPERS and SAFETY GLASS NOT STD. EQUIPMENT.

5.50 TO 1 COMPRESSION 4.62 GEAR RATIO

96" WHEELBASE   4.00 × 18 TIRES
4-WHEEL MECHANICAL BRAKES

32 H.P. @ 3200 RPM   CHAIN-DRIVEN CAMSHAFT

1931 American Mathis

"Captive imports" are foreign cars sold by American manufacturers in the United States, often with the American brand name applied. These have been common in recent years.

But, Durant Motors tried a similar idea—as long ago as 1931! Durant sold fairly well in 1929 and early 1930, but things changed fast as the Depression got under way! What to do? Why not make a deal with the French Mathis company to make a clone of their light-weight 4-cylinder "PY" series for 1931? Arrangements were made in mid-1930 for Durant to produce an American Mathis, under license to the original company. A Franco-American car—predating the Renault Alliance by many decades!

Continental built engines for Durant cars, as well as for others, and it was planned that the American Mathis would use a Continental engine also. However, we don't know whether that came to pass, though reportedly Continental did supply both 6- and 8-cylinder engines to Mathis for use in their larger models sold in Europe.

Quite possibly, the few 1931 Mathis cars seen in the U.S.A. were actually built in France, though fitted with American (Goodyear) tires.

The American Mathis was displayed in January 1931 at the New York Automobile Show, and shortly afterward at the Chicago Automobile Show. The coupe (illustrated) and a $445 light-delivery car were presented. A roadster was promised, but never seen.

Durant Motors went into receivership in 1931, and the Mathis venture folded. There was a 1932 Durant, but very few were assembled before the towel was tossed into the ring.

1930s

A RARE BRITISH BEAUTY!

1931 BENTLEY
8 LITRE
CONVERTIBLE VICTORIA

$ 9000. CHASSIS PRICE!
£1850. IN ENGLAND

6 CYL. OVERHEAD CAM 487 CID
ENGINE 220 HP @ 3500 RPM
144 OR 156" WB

WITH RIGHT-HAND DRIVE

TAD 3-20

TOP SPEED = 102 MPH PLUS!

W. O. BENTLEY FOUNDED BENTLEY MOTORS, LTD. IN 1920. COMPANY SOLD TO ROLLS-ROYCE IN 1931. (BENTLEY AUTOMOBILES HAVE BEEN A PRODUCT OF ROLLS ROYCE SINCE THE EARLY '30s.)

A CLASSIC, WITH CHIC CUSTOM BODY BY MURPHY. (DISPLAYED AT THE 1987 CONCOURS D'ELEGANCE, PEBBLE BEACH, CALIF.)

7 x 21" TIRES

1931 Bentley "8 Litre"

From 1920 to 1931, Bentley Motors Ltd. was an independent British auto manufacturer, led by its founder, W. O. Bentley. Most early Bentley autos were touring cars, customarily painted in British Racing Green—and, indeed, the Bentley had an enviable racing record in the 1920s with many triumphs on the track.

Bentley's most luxurious model—while the company was still independent—was the 1930-31 8 Litre series, as shown. Amply powered by a huge (487 cubic-inch displacement) overhead-cam six, the Bentley 8L could do at least 100 miles an hour, even with a heavy closed body. A souped-up, open model achieved over 140 mph on one particular track!

Though classic beauties, Bentley's 8L models were too costly for those Depression times, and the company suffered as a result.

Bentley had offers to sell to either Napier or Rolls-Royce. Fortunately, Rolls-Royce won out; Napier had already been out of the automobile business for seven years in 1931 and had hoped to stage a comeback with the acquisition of Bentley—a comeback that may well have failed.

Rolls-Royce, on the other hand, was highly successful for years as the builders of "the best car in the world," and to this day has maintained an enviable reputation for quality.

From 1933 on, Bentley cars took on characteristics similar to Rolls-Royce, with few exceptions. Each has maintained its own distinctive radiator grille shape, an immediate badge of identity for either car. In 1960, Rolls-Royce and Bentley switched from six-cylinder engines to V-8s.

1931 Cunningham

T he classic Cunningham (since 1916) was powered by a 442 c.i.d. L-head V-8 engine. Though Cunningham did little advertising, its fame as a quality car spread during the 1920s in social circles. After 1919, the Cunningham was available on an elongated 142-inch wheelbase as well as on the 132-inch. Various custom bodies were applied to a purchaser's order, though Cunningham also built bodies.

The company was first incorporated in 1882, and it originally built carts, carriages, and other motorless vehicles. Its auto manufacturing began in 1907.

By the later 1920s, Cunningham had picked up a noteworthy list of clientele. Among the famous personalities who bought Cunningham automobiles:

Mary Pickford, Marshall Field, William Randolph Hearst, Philip Wrigley, Cecil B. De Mille, Harold Lloyd, and many other business, entertainment, and political figures.

After 1933, Cunningham ceased production of its own passenger car chassis and built bodies to be applied to Ford and other chassis. (Brewster was another respected East Coast manufacturer that did this.) Also, Cunningham continued a more lucrative sideline of ambulances and funeral vehicles.

Generally speaking, Curningham's heyday was in the 1920s. But, this 1931 model was one of its finest-looking creations, and that's why it was selected for *Auto Album*.

1931 Jordan "Speedway Ace" Roadster

Here's one of the rarest of classic cars: the magnificent Jordan "Speedway Ace," available for only a short time during the 1930-31 season.

Edward S. ("Ned") Jordan (b. 1882) attended the University of Wisconsin while working part-time as a newspaper reporter. Later, he married one of the daughters of Thomas B. Jeffery, manufacturer of the popular Rambler automobile and later the Jeffery. Through this marriage, Jordan gained the position of advertising manager for the Thomas B. Jeffery Automobile Co. Jordan was not mechanically inclined, but he was a very talented ad writer.

In 1916, Jordan established his own automobile company in Cleveland, Ohio. Jordan cars were assembled by various quality components supplied by specialized parts manufacturers. Jordan wrote the advertising, and it was effective. His 1923 "Somewhere West of Laramie" ad for the Jordan Playboy roadster is still an all-time classic of advertising prose and has been reprinted in many an English-class textbook as an example of effective copy!

Jordan sales were never voluminous. In 1926, sales marked the peak, with over 11,000 units built, and 1927 saw the introduction of the "Little Jordan," a well-designed small car that was a poor seller. In 1929 Jordan made his cars large again.

Note the narrow "Wood-lite" headlamps and fender parking lights on the illustrated roadster. Wood-lites were briefly in vogue on a few exclusive automobiles around 1930.

The streamlined pontoon running boards and the long, horizontal hood vent doors are distinctive features of the Speedway Jordans, not to mention the aeronautically-styled instrument panel!

DESIGNED FOR MILK ROUTES, NEWSPAPER DELIVERY, LAUNDRIES, GROCERS, FLORISTS, DEPT. STORES, BAKERIES, ETC.

new 6 CYLINDER 1931½

5.3

DRIVEN FROM EITHER STANDING OR SITTING POSITION.

White

MFD. BY THE WHITE CO., CLEVELAND, OHIO

MODEL "60 K" HOUSE-TO-HOUSE DELIVERY TRUCK 112" W.B. HYDRAULIC BRAKES

1931 1/2 White "60-K" Delivery Truck

How long since you've seen milk delivered on a neighborhood route? If you're under the age of forty, your answer may well be "never seen it." Generally speaking, house-to-house milk delivery routes ceased in the 1960s, the victim of supermarkets in suburban shopping centers.

Until the 1920s, milk had been delivered to homes by horse-drawn wagons; early trucks were too high and cumbersome for neighborhood use. But, in the 1920s, Reo and others introduced higher-speed, light weight trucks that were more suitable for delivery service.

According to an August 1931 ad, the new White 60-K "House-to-House" delivery truck was "a departure from the conventional type of delivery truck." Its drop-frame chassis design permitted driver or helper to step from the curb directly to the floor of the truck. Its peppy six-cylinder engine was "flexible" and time saving in its speed. The new model was designed to save "30 percent or more in delivery time," thus cutting the cost of serving outlying suburban areas.

Easy to handle, it could be driven from a standing or sitting position, with good driver visibility either way. The turning radius was short, and wide doors provided easy access. The standard wheelbase was 112 inches, but longer-wheelbase variations were available.

With "branches and dealers in all principal cities," the White Co. built "a complete line of trucks and busses," and once built cars as well.

In recent years, White has become affiliated with Volvo.

© News America Syndicate, 1985

78, 90, OR 104 HP

1932 **BUICK** SEDAN

TAD 8-4

INTERIOR

STRAIGHT 8 OVERHEAD-VALVE ENGINE 230.4, 272.6, OR 344.8 CID

$935.00 and up (f.o.b., FACTORY)

WOOD OR WIRE WHEELS

SERIES
50   114" WB
60   118"
80   126"
90   134"

18" WHEELS

MECHANICAL BRAKES

1932 Buick

Something new was added inside the 1932 Buick: swing-down sun visors and a glove compartment on the right side of the dash. The outside sunvisor was eliminated, door-type hood vents replaced former louvres, and chromed twin trumpet horns protruded below the headlights.

In the new 1932 Buick, there was "Free-Wheeling" (when engaged, it allowed the car to coast whenever the accelerator was released), a silent second gear on the Synchromesh transmission, and an automatic clutch. This improved system was labeled "Wizard Control" and was joined by a Ride Regulator attached to the left side of the steering column, enabling the driver to adjust the tension of the shock absorbers to meet various road conditions.

The gas gauge was changed from hydrostatic (thermometer type) to electric type with needle indicator. The speedometer now had a needle indicator instead of the former revolving drum. A vacuum booster pump kept windshield wipers from faltering when the car accelerated or pulled up a hill. There were 26 models, in four basic series, ranging from $935 to $2,055, f.o.b., Flint, Mich.

From November 14 to December 14, 1931, Buick dealers attracted prospects to their showrooms by means of an essay contest. Entrants were to write why they thought the new Buick was better, and first prize was $25,000. In those Depression days, that sum would buy a mansion!

Top speed of most models was over 80 m.p.h., and the 1932 Buicks were advertised to last for 200,000 miles and more.

SHEER LUXURY!

1932 CHRYSLER CUSTOM IMPERIAL EIGHT

CONVERTIBLE SEDAN with BODY BY LE BARON! WT.= 5125 LBS. ("CL" SERIES)

125 HP @ 3200 RPM

384.8 CID STRAIGHT-8 ENGINE (3½ x 5 BR. + STR.)

7.50 x 17

SELF-EQUALIZING HYDR. BRAKES with POWER BOOSTER.

"DUPLATE" SAFETY GLASS

146" WHEELBASE

ORIGINAL PRICE, f.o.b. $3595.00 WORTH 100 TIMES THAT, NOW!

A TRUE CLASSIC!

AP 12~4

1932 Chrysler Custom Imperial

If you could travel in time, you might be able to pick up a real bargain in a beautiful classic car of the 1930s—one like this Le Baron-bodied 1932 Chrysler Custom Imperial Eight. To buy a car like this today, in mint or completely restored condition, you'd need a few hundred thousand dollars!

Like old art treasures, the truly luxurious and inimitable classic automobiles of the 1930s have skyrocketed in value. By "classic," I mean such names as Duesenberg, Cord, Pierce-Arrow, Ruxton, Chrysler Custom Imperial, Marmon V-16, and expensive series of Packards, Cadillacs, and Lincolns, etc.

Chrysler began as a new make of car in 1924. In 1926, the Chrysler Imperial became a larger and separate series. The Imperial was a six until mid-1930. Beginning with the 1931 model year, it had a trunk at rear and a very long hood and was powered by a large straight-8 engine.

The 1931 Chryslers and Chrysler Imperials had hoods and front fenders that were unusually long and graceful. Instrument panels featured a row of circular gauges mounted on a long oval plate in the center of the dash. The 1931 and similarly styled 1932 Imperials had vertical hood louvers, but the 1932 Custom Imperial had a long 146-inch wheelbase and new door-type hood vents (as illustrated).

Because Le Baron bodies were handcrafted in limited numbers (only forty-nine of these 1932 Custom Imperial convertible sedans were built), they were often custom-built to buyers' orders. This convertible sedan, though on a huge 146-inch wheelbase, has a close-coupled body with extended trunk at rear and a very long hood in front.

1930s

1932 DE VAUX "80" CONVERTIBLE COUPE (CUSTOM SERIES)

RARE ! ORIGINAL PRICE = $**895.**

PRESENT VALUE $**4000.** TO **28,000.**, (DEPENDING ON CAR'S CONDITION)

15- GAL. FUEL TANK

5.50 × 17 TIRES

6 CYL. CONTINENTAL 214.7 CID LHEAD ENGINE (75 HP @3600 RPM)

114" WHEELBASE

12 ~ 3

ONLY 4,808 '31 MODELS, and 1,358 '32 MODELS

MFD. 1931~1932 BY DE VAUX-HALL MOTORS CORP., OAKLAND, CALIFORNIA AND GRAND RAPIDS, MICH. SUCCEEDED BY THE 1933 CONTINENTAL CAR.

TOP SPEED = 80 MECHANICAL BRAKES

1932 De Vaux "80"

Some time ago in *Auto Album,* I drew a 1931 De Vaux coupe and invited anyone who owns (or formerly owned) a De Vaux to write in and let us know. Surprisingly, I received letters from eighteen present or former De Vaux owners, from various parts of the United States!

One of these, a gentleman in Wisconsin, wrote that he was the original owner of a '31 De Vaux sedan, which he had hidden in like-new condition in a sealed garage behind his store—ever since 1937! He confided that no one in town knew he still owned this car, and he asked me not to reveal his name or address to anyone, since the car was not for sale and he didn't want to be pestered with inquiries. "But I thought you'd be interested to know I still own the car," he concluded.

The harp-shaped grille of the '31 model was continued on the '32 De Vaux, but the Hayes-built bodies were more streamlined for the new year. The Hayes bodies were of composite steel-over-wood-frame construction.

The De Vaux automobile, which first appeared in April 1931, offered many good features for a surprisingly low price. It was one of the first cars to have a "silent-second" transmission: That is, the second gear didn't whine and howl like that of a truck transmission.

The 1932 De Vaux was one of the rarest of all cars from the Depression era, and few are known to exist!

WITH L HEAD,
353 CU. INCH
V8 ENGINE
3 3/8 × 4 15/16"
BORE + 8TR.
115 HP @
3000 RPM

4.60 GEAR RATIO

FRONT VIEW

ONLY 3700 LA SALLES SOLD IN 1932.

CLASSIC *1932 LA SALLE V8* "345-B"
TOWN COUPE   130" W.B.
4695 lbs.
$2545.

RARE! —

PRESENT VALUE = $5000 TO 60,000!

TAD
© 1989 North America Syndicate, Inc. All rights reserved.
9 ~ 24

LA SALLE WAS A SUBSIDIARY OF
CADILLAC (GM) FROM 1927 TO 1940.

1930s

1932 La Salle

"**Y**ou'll drive for the joy of driving when you own a new La Salle." That was the heading of a 1932 La Salle advertisement, which continued:

"Again, Cadillac has made motoring more completely delightful than it has ever been before. Starting with the beautiful new La Salle, and ranging upward to the inimitable Cadillac V-16—Cadillac offers, literally, a new type of performance. Actually, you seem to float, rather than ride. The motor is quiet almost to the point of absolute silence. The gears—low, second, and high—are almost completely noiseless. You free wheel at the touch of a button—and shift without touching the clutch. You accelerate with incredible swiftness. You steer the car, and stop it, with the most delightful ease. In fact, it's the most entrancing performance since motor car history began. Will you confirm this with a La Salle—today? La Salle prices start at only $2,395, f.o.b., Detroit."

The Town Coupe (illustrated) was a close-coupled, two-door sedan with a built-in trunk. This pleasing body style was offered on some GM cars in 1932 and 1933 (and even later).

All '32 GM cars, from Chevrolet to Cadillac, bore the stylish vent doors along the sides of the hood, as did this La Salle.

Many buyers agreed that La Salle was Cadillac-built, of Cadillac quality and Cadillac style, and they felt it should also bear the Cadillac name. Thus in 1941, the La Salle was replaced by the new low-priced Cadillac 61 series, which sold for less than $1,500, f.o.b., factory.

1932 1/2 Packard "Light 8"

W hen I was 15, an older friend of the family owned a black 1932 1/2 Packard "Light 8" convertible like the one you see here.

The man was a heavy drinker, however, and one night when he'd had a few, he declared: "Tad, I know you're crazy about old cars, so as soon as I get myself a newer car for transportation, I'll let you have this old Packard."

You can imagine what a thrill that was to hear! He topped off the deal by saying, "Here's the key to the Packard. Go round up your friends and take it for a ride." The offer was gratefully taken.

The hood of the old Packard seemed extremely long, and the seat was low. This gave one the feel of an open-cockpit air-plane, with top down and the wind whipping through our hair! The car almost sounded like a plane, too, as its "Hollywood" muffler had a pleasing "rap" to it each time the gas pedal was released. That mellow exhaust rumbled powerfully each time we went down a long grade.

Our friend reluctantly agreed, on later occasions, that I could still have the Packard after he got another car. But, then he sold it! "Why should I give it to you, when I was able to get $350 cash for it?" he rationalized. "I didn't promise you the car. ' John Barleycorn' did!"

The new owner repainted the Packard light gray and installed a new white top. Obviously, it was getting better care than a 15-year-old could have afforded.

A VALUABLE "COLLECTOR'S CAR!"

REO FLYING CLOUD 1932 1/2

MODEL "S"

(INTRODUCED SPRING, 1932)
ORIGINAL f.o.b. PRICE = $1070.00 (SPORT COUPE)

6.00 x 17 TIRES

LANSING, MICH.

TAD 4~10

MOHAIR OR CLOTH UPH.

© 1988 North America Syndicate, Inc.
All rights reserved.

6 CYLINDERS
230 CU. IN. DISPL.
80 HP @ 3200 RPM
3 1/8" x 5"
BORE STROKE
117" WHEELBASE

DASH

AVAIL. W. FREE WHEELING,
RIDE CONTROL, STARTIX,
SAFETY GLASS WINDSHIELD,
TWIN HORNS,
TWIN WIPERS,
SPECIAL TRIM

REO MOTOR CAR CO.

1932 1/2 Reo "Flying Cloud S"

The 1932 1/2 Reo "Flying Cloud" Model S offered many features not found in the first Flying Cloud model of 1927, and for much less money! The new Model S had the streamlined styling of the awesome 1931 and 1932 Reo "Royale" luxury models, but prices for the S series started at only $995, f.o.b., Lansing, Mich., and there were several "extras" available for those willing to spend a few dollars more.

In one respect, the "S" was even more streamlined than the famed Royale, because it had a new grille that swept dramatically forward at the lower end (as did Packard's new "Light Eight" series).

Reo collectors and fans have a difficult time pinning down and identifying the many varieties of models Reo offered during 1931 and 1932 because there were many running changes in the various models and series during the two-year span. Some models had the streamlined Royale-style bodies and V-grilles; others had the streamlined bodies, but with flat radiators; others had the old boxy 1930-style bodies with modern V-grilles; and so on.

This 1932 "S" was fully streamlined, having the new Royale-style body, new grille, vent doors in hood, and wire wheels. One extra, "Startix," was a device that caused the engine to automatically restart if "killed" while the car was in motion.

Reo also built a popular line of trucks. No Reo cars were produced after 1936, but the trucks continued to 1967, when Reo combined with Diamond T to form Diamond-Reo.

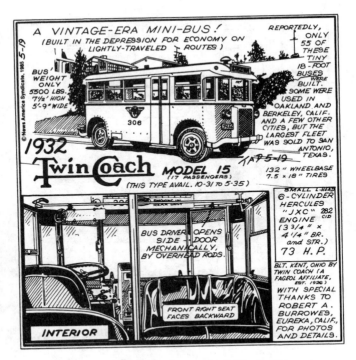

A VINTAGE-ERA MINI-BUS!
(BUILT IN THE DEPRESSION FOR ECONOMY ON LIGHTLY-TRAVELED ROUTES)

© News America Syndicate, 1985. 5-19

BUS' WEIGHT ONLY 5500 LBS. 7½' HIGH 5'-9" WIDE

306

REPORTEDLY, ONLY 55 OF THESE TINY 18-FOOT BUSES WERE BUILT. SOME WERE USED IN OAKLAND AND BERKELEY, CALIF. AND A FEW OTHER CITIES, BUT THE LARGEST FLEET WAS SOLD TO SAN ANTONIO, TEXAS.

1932
Twin Coach MODEL 15
(17 PASSENGERS)
(THIS TYPE AVAIL. 10-31 TO 5-35)

TAP 5-19

132" WHEELBASE
7.5 x 18" TIRES

SMALL L-HEAD
6-CYLINDER HERCULES "JXC" 282 CID ENGINE (3 3/4" x 4 1/4" BR. and STR.)
73 H.P.

BLT. KENT, OHIO BY TWIN COACH (A FAGEOL AFFILIATE, EST. 1926)
WITH SPECIAL THANKS TO ROBERT A. BURROWES, EUREKA, CALIF., FOR PHOTOS AND DETAILS.

BUS DRIVER OPENS SIDE DOOR MECHANICALLY, BY OVERHEAD RODS.

FRONT RIGHT SEAT FACES BACKWARD

INTERIOR

1932 Twin Coach Mini-Bus

Longtime residents of Oakland, Berkeley, San Antonio, Jacksonville, and a few other cities may be pleasantly surprised to see this vintage mini-bus in *Auto Album* today, as these rare little vehicles were used there in the 1930s and 1940s.

As a boy, I attended school for a year in Berkeley in the 1940s, and a school friend of mine lived up in the Grizzly Peak section of the Berkeley Hills. Occasionally, I'd ride one of those tiny Twin Coach mini-buses after school to go to his house. The fare was ten cents (or one token, which cost about seven cents).

Golden State Dairies, which brought milk to our door, had little delivery vans that resembled these diminutive buses.

Most of the buses in town were newer and much larger, and the first time I entered one of those tiny Model 15s, I wondered if it would actually make it up those steep hills!

The seats were upholstered in sweet-smelling black leather, and they were warm when it was sunny. The front right-hand seat was across from the driver and over the front right wheel, and it faced backward.

If the bus was not crowded (it usually wasn't), I'd try to get that choice front seat. By sitting sideways on the seat, I could see ahead. And, I probably asked the driver more questions than did the average kid. One time a barber threatened to stop my haircut and kick me out of his shop if I didn't sit still and shut up!

1932 Willys-Overland 8

T he 1932 Willys-Overland was similar in many ways to the 1931 Willys, though the Overland name, unused since the Whippet replaced it in mid-1926, was tacked on for '32.

On the 1932 models, the radiator filler cap was under the hood, and the radiator ornament was stationary. The hood was lengthened two inches, and the cowl was "shortened a like amount." Pleated and buttoned mohair replaced cloth upholstery in closed cars, and garnish moldings and instrument panels were "wood grained" with an imitation walnut finish. (Otherwise, instrument panels were quite similar to the 1931 type.) More sound-absorbent padding was glued to the inside of metal surfaces to improve the quietness of the Willys-Overland products.

Generally, the more expensive models had door-type hood vents, while others had horizontal slits of uneven lengths. There were certain exceptions to this rule during the '31-'32 season, so that some Willys-Overlands looked like Willys-Knights and vice versa. (I've seen original pictures showing the Willys-Overland 8-80 with both types of hoods. Also, some Willys-Overland eights had a figure "8" on the tie-bar ornament, while others had the words "Willys-Overland" to add to the confusion!)

During 1932, base price of the Willys-Overland 6 dropped to as low as $415, and the economy Model 95 of the Willys-Knight was available for as little as $745!

During the 1940s, most of the Willys cars still around were the 1933 and later four-cylinder models, which were prized for their fuel economy during the gas rationing years.

1933 AMERICAN AUSTIN BANTAM
SERIES "2-75" ROADSTER (EARLY MODEL)
4 CYLS. 45.6 CUBIC IN. DISPLACEMENT
13 HORSEPOWER @ 3200 RPM
5.25 GEAR RATIO
2.2" x 3" BORE + STR. (5.10 TO 1 COMPRESSION)
75" WHEELBASE
3.75 x 18" TIRES   BODY BY
4-WHEEL MECHANICAL BRAKES   HAYES

© News Group Chicago, Inc., 1984

MFD. 1930-1941   5-6

TAP

CLIP and SAVE

VERTICAL HOOD LOUVRES ON MOST '33-4 TYPES.

ORIGINAL PRICE ONLY $335.⁰⁰ f.o.b., FACTORY *
(BUTLER, PA.)   * $445. IN '31
40 M.P.G.   50 M.P.H.

1933 American Austin Bantam

The American Austin made its debut in the U.S.A. in 1930—well suited for individuals who had to pinch pennies!

Later to be known as the Bantam, the American Austin was assembled in Butler, Pa., under license by Austin of Britain. Mechanically, it was similar to the famous little Austin "Seven" of England and many parts were interchangeable. (The Austin Seven was a great hit in England, where the average car was considerably smaller than its American counterpart.)

But, when the American Austin appeared, many would-be buyers laughed it off. The tiny car was the butt of many movie comedy scenes, and it was also part of circus acts where many clowns would emerge from an Austin!

The American Austin was too small for the average family. Only two-door models were offered, most with only one seat. But, the Austin was economical! Forty miles per gallon is more than twice what most other U.S. cars would deliver.

Incidentally, in 1933 the Austin Bantam cars changed from horizontal to vertical hood louvres; this early '33 roadster was one of the last holdouts for horizontal louvres in the line.

Some time ago, Larry Spindler, of Morris, N. Y., sent some helpful Austin information from the American Austin Bantam Club. Bantam was one of the early developers of the American Army Jeep vehicle, but they did not have facilities large enough to fulfill a big government contract, so the Jeep business went to Willys-Overland and to Ford, after less than 3,000 Jeeps were produced by Bantam.

TWELVE CYLINDERS!
1933 AUBURN V~12 12~165 "SALON"

"SALON" SERIES
new 1933 GRILLE HAS HORIZONTAL PIECES.

3~11~90

CLASSIC VALUE = $7000 ~ $25,000

12~165 "SALON" SERIES $1695.~$1845. ORIG. PRICE RANGE
133" WHEELBASE
391 CU IN. DISPL. V-12 ENGINE (LYCOMING) 3 1/8" x 4 1/4" B.+S.
160 H.P. @ 3400 RPM WEIGHT = 4870 LBS.
(AUBURN V-12 JOINED THE AUBURN STRAIGHT-8 IN 1932.)

AUBURN AUTOMOBILE CO., AUBURN, IND. (1900~1936)

1933 Auburn V-12

"Dual Ratio" was a unique feature found on 1932 Auburns and again on the 1933 models. Originated and introduced by Auburn, it was another concept of the two-speed rear axle.

In the old days, two-speed rear axles were sold as an accessory for some cars, but they were not as reliable as a conventional one-speed differential and not as good as the overdrive transmission that was soon to come. Auburn is one of very few makes that ever offered a two-speed rear end as a stock factory item.

Since the totally restyled 1931 Auburn was such a great success, the same look was continued in 1932 and 1933. However, extra-cost 1933 "Salon" models had new horizontal pieces in the V-shaped grille, dual trumpet horns below the headlights, V-shaped windshields, broadcloth upholstery in sedans, and other niceties that more than justified the slightly higher price.

Other interesting features of the 1933 Auburn: Bendix B-K vacuum-operated power brakes (on Salon V-12s); hydraulic brakes on all models; "Silent-second" transmission; "Free Wheeling," a coasting device used briefly in the early '30s until outlawed. The Bijur automatic chassis lubrication system was a feature of convenience offered by several quality cars in the 1920s; during the early '30s it was less frequently seen.

The "X-plus-A" steel chassis frame was sturdier than usual and considered twice as rigid as the previous year's basic X-frame.

It was written then that the new Auburn, priced well under $2,000, was just about the most car you could get for your money!

1930s

AL JOLSON'S 1933 CADILLAC V16 "ALL WEATHER PHAETON" 452-C SERIES

MECHANICAL VAC. BRAKES
4.64 GEAR RATIO
452 C.I.D.
16 CYLINDER OVERHEAD VALVE ENG. 165 H.P. @ 3400 RPM

AL JOLSON (1886~1950) LEGENDARY POP SINGER AND STAR OF BROADWAY, HOLLYWOOD, RECORDINGS AND RADIO. HIS 1927 MOVIE "THE JAZZ SINGER" (PART-TALKING) WAS THE FIRST FILM MUSICAL!!

THIS 6100-LB. ALL-WEATHER PHAETON WAS ORIGINALLY $8000., f.o.b.

ENGINE DETAILS V16
12-19

149" W.B.

V16 CADILLACS AVAIL. 1930 TO 1940. (V8 and V12 ALSO BLT. IN 1933.)

©1993 North America Syndicate, Inc. World rights reserved.

1933 Cadillac V-16 (Al Jolson's Car)

Classic automobiles once owned by celebrities are always popular at car auctions and shows. But, from time to time, frauds have been perpetrated by dishonest sellers who claim fictitiously that their car was once owned by some notable personality. Because of this, documented proof of original ownership is always a must should you ever plan to purchase a "celebrity car."

One of the most famous celebrity Cadillacs, other than Elvis Presley's convertibles of the 1950s, was this handsome 1933 16-cylinder convertible sedan known officially as an "All-Weather Phaeton." This car belonged to Al Jolson, once billed as "The World's Greatest Entertainer." Though Jolson passed on in 1950, he's still like Elvis Presley and Bing Crosby—a legendary performer. His memory remains in movies and on records.

Jolson's '33 Cadillac V-16 was one of only a few. For 1933, Cadillac had announced that it would limit production of its 16-cylinder models to just 400 cars. Because of the Depression, they fell short of that modest mark by nearly two-thirds! Sixteen-cylinder cars were not appropriate for Depression days, yet that's when most of them were built (since they'd been planned in more prosperous times). Some standard-type Cadillacs used Fisher bodies, but the 1933 V-16s came with deluxe Fleetwood bodies and, in a few cases, with custom-built bodies by other specialized coach crafters applied to bare chassis units bought to be completed to buyer's order!

The last 16-cylinder Cadillacs were built in 1940.

RARE !!

1933 ½ CHEVROLET "CC" SERIES

new "**STANDARD**" ECONOMY MODEL (INTRODUCED
107" WHEELBASE   MARCH, 1933)
6-CYL. OVERHEAD-VALVE 181 C.I.D. ENGINE
3 5/16" x 3½" BORE and STROKE
60 H.P. @ 3000 RPM   **70 M.P.H.**
5.2 TO 1 COMPRESSION

© News America Syndicate, 1986

new "STANDARD" MODEL GOT UP TO 27 M.P.G.

(note VERTICAL HOOD LOUVRES)
DIFFERS FROM MASTER / EAGLE
MODELS WHICH WERE INTRODUCED
EARLIER (DEC., 1932) WITH DOOR-
TYPE HOOD VENTS (3 EACH SIDE,)
A LONGER (110") WHEELBASE,
LARGER ENGINE, SYNCHROMESH, etc.

2 - PASS.
BUSINESS COUPE
$445.

1933 1/2 Chevrolet Standard

The Standard "CC" models of 1933 Chevrolet are so rare that many readers may not have known of their existence. The most noticeable exterior difference between the Standard and the better-known Eagle (renamed Master) models was in the hood side vents. On the more familiar Eagle Master, the vents consisted of three nearly-vertical doors near the rear end of each side of the hood. The Standard, however, had a row of plain, vertical louvres on each side.

The Standard was a mid-season model, introduced to supplement but not replace the more expensive series. The Standard was available at cut-rate prices as a two-door sedan ($455), three-window trunk coupe ($455), or three-window rumble-seat coupe ($475). The Eagle Master series offered a more complete variety of body types.

The Standard had a shortened wheelbase and a smaller-displacement engine, though it did offer the new-for-1933 Fisher Body "No-Draft Ventilation" built-in wind wings found on the costlier models. Braking surface was slightly smaller on the Standard series. (Chevrolets did not have hydraulic brakes until 1936.)

Chevrolet had adopted a synchro-mesh transmission in 1932, but on the 1933 1/2 Standard, the transmission was a less costly constant-mesh variety (with silent-second). No "free wheeling" on the Standard.

In May 1933, another midseason model was added (in the Master series), and this was the Town Sedan: a two-door coach with a built-in trunk bustle at rear (as differing from the usual "flat-back" sedan).

1930s

ONE OF THE RAREST OF ALL AMERICAN CARS OF THE 1930s!

1933 CONTINENTAL "ACE"
(WITH 6-CYL. CONTINENTAL ENGINE)
85 H.P.   3³/8 x 4" B·S

4.3 GEAR RATIO

114" W.B.   85 M.P.H.

3170 LB. DE LUXE SEDAN = $816.

1933 "BEACON" and "FLYER" MODELS ALSO.

MFD. 1933-1934 BY CONTINENTAL ENGINE CO. ("CONTINENTAL AUTOMOBILE CO.") OF DETROIT. THE CONTINENTAL WAS THE SUCCESSOR OF THE 1931-1932 DE VAUX CAR. ONLY 3310 UNITS PRODUCED IN 1933. (IN '34, ONLY THE 4-CYL. "BEACON" SERIES CONTINUED, WITH ONLY 953 SOLD.)
MECHANICAL BRAKES

TAP 12/18

©1988 North America Syndicate, Inc. All rights reserved.

1933 Continental "Ace"

When De Vaux went out of business, a large sum was owed to Continental for engines. The Continental Engine Co. decided to recoup the loss when De Vaux's receivers put the De Vaux assets up for sale. Continental purchased the De Vaux factory in Grand Rapids, Mich. and began manufacturing cars. The large, new Continental Ace model shared many mechanical features with the former 1932 De Vaux. The midrange Flyer model was a six on a 107-inch wheelbase. The low-priced Beacon was a four on a 101 1/2-inch wheelbase and sold, f.o.b., for only $355 and up! The Beacon was compact, and it would travel as far as 30 miles on a gallon of gas. It had a top speed of 60-65 m.p.h.

Reportedly, only 651 Ace models were built out of a total of 3,310 '33

Continentals. The Continentals used a Hayes body (like De Vaux), but the Ace bears somewhat of a resemblance to the Briggs-bodied Chrysler cars of 1933. All Continentals had "Flying Power" flexible engine mountings.

For 1934, only the little Beacon was continued, and it was re-named the "Red Seal" series. Continental tried a mail-order scheme for selling the cars, but it didn't work well. July 1934 marked the end of Continental automobile production—though Continental engines were continued as usual. (By 1932, Continental had already built more than 3 1/2 million engines, which had been used in more than 100 different makes of cars, in a generation!)

A PRIMITIVE "STREAMLINER!"

1933 "DOODLEBUG"
BY REO (EXPERIMENTAL)
WITH 4 CYL. "IXB"
HERCULES ENG.
20~25 HP

TOP SPEED = 60
3-SPEED REO TRANSMISSION.
MECHANICAL BRAKES.

©1992 by North America Syndicate, Inc. World rights reserved.

ENGINE IN REAR, MOUNTED
TRANSVERSELY (CROSSWISE),
WITH A RADIATOR AT EACH END
FOR MAXIMUM COOLING.
PLANNED PRICE OF ONLY
$400., TO COMPETE WITH
THE WILLYS "77."

REAR

UNIT BODY / FRAME CONSTRUCTION

1933 "Doodlebug"

One of the many independent auto manufacturers, Reo, got into the streamlining act in 1932, when the illustrated car was designed. It was completed by mid-1933, a hopeful pilot model for a proposed new line of $400 "Depression-beaters."

Reo's chief engineer and vice-president, H. T. Thomas, conceived this odd new car. Thomas also developed Reo's amazing "self-shifter" semi-automatic transmission in 1933, five years ahead of GM's famed "HydraMatic."

The $400 Reo "junior edition" was nameless, but it was nicknamed "Doodlebug" by H. T. Thomas and his son, Alden Peach Thomas. When he retired from Reo, H. T. Thomas purchased this car from the company.

From 1937 to 1941, the Doodlebug was used by Alden Peach Thomas. It performed well, except for one time when the motor actually fell out into the street! Improved motor mounts cured that defect. In '41, the Doodlebug was sold to a man in North Canton, Ohio, and within a few years it was no longer seen around town.

By the way, when the Doodlebug was first completed, the fuel tank was at the rear in the engine compartment. It was soon moved to the front for safety reasons.

The teardrop-shaped headlights were made for a '37 Ford. The original headlights on this car were round, but I had no photos of the original type. So, I decided to show the car as it looked in 1937, with the replacement lights. The car was originally painted two-tone brown, but in 1937 it was repainted light gray.

WHEN NEW, THIS CAR COST $20,000. IN THE 1950s, A MINT-CONDITION DUESENBERG WAS FOR SALE IN PALO ALTO, CALIF. FOR JUST $2000. IN 1991, ANOTHER 1933 DUESENBERG WAS PUT UP FOR AUCTION, AND A HIGH BID OF NEARLY 3 MILLION DOLLARS WAS _REFUSED_!!

420 CID LYCOMING STRAIGHT-8 ENG. 265 HP @ 4250 RPM ("J" SERIES)

12.8

A LEGENDARY CLASSIC!

142½" W.B.

1933 DUESENBERG "SJ" (320 HP w. SUPERCHARGER) "20 GRAND" SEDAN WITH ROLLSTON CUSTOM BODY DESIGNED BY GORDON BUEHRIG UP TO 129 M.P.H.

DUESENBERG MOTOR CO., INDIANAPOLIS, IND. 1920~1937

1933 Duesenberg "20 Grand"

Because of its name, some people have nursed the longtime misconception that Duesenbergs were made in Germany. Not so! The Duesenberg is a product of America's heartland—from the Hoosier state of Indiana.

In the early 1900s, Fred Duesenberg, a bicycle builder from Iowa, had been forced into bankruptcy over a debt of about $2,000. Shortly before World War I, he joined his brother August and formed the Duesenberg Motor Co. at St. Paul, Minn.—to build auto and marine engines.

After the 1920s began, the Duesenbergs had moved to Indianapolis and started the new Duesenberg Automobile and Motors Corp. The first commercially available Duesenberg automobile (1921-22) was the Model A, with a remarkable overhead-cam straight-8 engine, four-wheel hydraulic brakes, and other advanced features.

The company reorganized in 1925, and in 1926 E. L. Cord achieved control and decreed that an all-new and greater Duesenberg automobile must be built. For a brief interval, the A series became the Model X. This was replaced (1929) by the completely redesigned and inimitable J series, the gigantic classic Duesenberg familiar to many car buffs. A supercharged "SJ" version joined the "J" in 1932.

Of the "J" and "SJ" types, only about 480 were built, and a great many of them survive today because they were always admired. There were also a few "JN" models in the mid-1930s (with smaller 17-inch wheels, a longer wheelbase of 153 1/2-inches, and Rollston bodies)—as well as two short-wheelbase "SSJ" convertibles: one sold to Gary Cooper and the other to Clark Gable.

Early 1933 Essex-Terraplane 8

Hudson introduced its low-priced Essex companion car in 1919 and continued it into 1932. During 1932, it was decided that the name should be changed to Terraplane, meaning "earth-airplane," to denote speed. However, there was some confusion about the name change during 1932 and 1933, because some of the new cars were known as Terraplanes as early as 1932, and others were Essex-Terraplanes even in 1933!

True to its name, Terraplane's performance was superior. Good enough, in fact, to attract a notorious figure of the underworld: John Dillinger, Public Enemy Number One! For years it's been believed that Dillinger favored Ford V-8s for getaway cars to the point where Henry Ford I even received a personal note, allegedly from Dillinger, praising the performance of the Ford V-8.

However, Joe Pinkston, a former detective who—with Barton N. Hahn, former FBI agent—operates the unique John Dillinger Historical Wax Museum, says that FBI evidence has shown the letter to Henry Ford to be a fake. Though Dillinger may have used and liked the peppy Ford V-8s, his personal favorite was a '33 Essex-Terraplane 8 (as illustrated, complete with bullet holes).

Mr. Pinkston hastens to assure the public that the Dillinger Museum is a crime-fighting display and not one that glamorizes criminals. Other artifacts and wax figures of various gangsters, as well as of lawmen, are also on display.

As for the Terraplane, most of its subsequent models were sixes instead of straight-8s, and the name was phased out during 1938 in favor of "Hudsons only."

1933 Hudson "Major 8"

N o wonder 1933 Hudson 8s are rare! Less than 1,900 of them were built, including both series of 1933 Hudson 8s—Pacemaker "Standard" and "Major." The Standard had a shorter (119-inch) wheelbase.

Hudson's truly famous old models were the big "Super Sixes," available from the mid-'teens all the way to 1929. For 1930, Hudson offered nothing but their new straight-8s, though sixes were still the rule in Hudson's smaller Essex cars.

Because of many requests in the early 1930s to revive the Hudson Super Six, such a car reappeared in 1933, though it wasn't much larger than an Essex/Terraplane. Only 962 of the mousy '33 sixes were built, and Hudson skipped to 1935 before offering another six, the so-called Big Six, which really wasn't so big!

On the other side of the coin, the illustrated Major 8 was one of the largest, most impressive automobiles Hudson had ever built, with its lengthy 132-inch wheelbase in 1932 and 1933. Hudson offered nothing like it before or afterward! The 1933 models had Free Wheeling, "Startix," and an adjustable steering column.

The year 1933 was one of Hudson's weakest, with the company losing $4.5 million. This came after a nearly $5.5 million loss in 1932. What saved the day was the lower-priced Essex, which evolved into the Terraplane during 1932-33.

Reportedly, the Major 8 was one of the last cars to retain the old-fashioned vacuum-tank suction method of supplying fuel from gas tank to carburetor in conjunction with an updraft Marvel carburetor.

1933 Hupmobile "321"

The 1933 Hupmobile was the "25th Anniversary Model," since the Hupp Motor Car Co. had been founded in November 1908. Up to 1931, Hupmobile had been using letter model designations, but from 1932 to 1938 numbers were added. The first number of the model series designated the year, and the following two numbers stood for length of wheelbase. Thus, this 1933 "K-321" type had a 121-inch wheelbase.

The "new look" seen on some of the 1932 Hupmobile Eights was now shared by this 1933 Six (321). Improvements in 1933 included a more sloping grille with out-swept lower section; new, sloping vent doors on hood (instead of louvers as before); and a chrome molding that "ornamented the running board apron."

All early '33 models had an automatic choke, automatic manifold heat control, X-frame, and more. The three-speed "silent second" transmission had an available Free Wheeling unit.

The 1933 Hupmobile brakes were still mechanical ("Steeldraulic" type, originally developed by Hupmobile, used flexible sealed cables instead of brake rods).

Writer/actor Irvin S. Cobb, with his grown daughter Elisabeth, appeared in several Hupmobile magazine advertisements, discussing Hupmobile's quality features. Cobb portrayed Will Rogers' rival—the bushy-browed, stocky old steamboat captain—in the amusing 1935 movie *Steamboat 'Round the Bend*.

Hupmobile sales declined in the 1930s, and production temporarily ceased during 1936. The only so-called 1937 models were leftovers made of 1936 parts, though in 1938 Hupmobile got a new lease on life and continued to 1940. The final 1939 and 1940 Hupmobile Skylarks used '37 Cord body dies.

1933 1/2 Prosperity Cab

"**T**he Cab of the Future!" "A New Deal in Service!"

That's what the original advertising claimed when the all-new Prosperity Cab was announced in mid-1933. The Prosperity Cab Co. was located at 1775 Broadway, New York City and was affiliated with the Allied Cab Manufacturing Company.

During the 1920s and 1930s, several odd brands of taxis were manufactured in the United States. Checker was one of the best-known cab specialists, as was Yellow (which for a few years was a General Motors subsidiary). De Soto (a Chrysler product) probably built the largest volume of taxis between 1935 and the end of the 1940s.

Many odd taxi brands popped up here and there before that time, such as Luxor, Paramount, Parmelee, Moller, and many more. Most were rather strange looking, but the weirdest was this Prosperity Cab. Its mishmash styling gave it the appearance of some Frankenstein monster made from the pieces of many different kinds of cars.

At least it had headroom. The interior of the cab was fifty inches from floor to roof, though it would have been even more spacious had the body extended down to the running board level. The streamlined tail had a pronounced slope, and the backlight (rear window) was mounted in a strange, dormer-like extension!

The Prosperity Cab had two electric clocks: one for the driver, one for the passengers. Spare tires were carried in style in a wheel-well on each front fender. A luggage rack was placed at the rear. The three-blade leaf bumpers were anachronistic for 1933.

1933 STUTZ
DV 32
134½" OR 145" wheelbase

NO FAN BELT!

THERMOSTATIC RADIATOR SHUTTERS

322.1 CID OVERHEAD-CAM STRAIGHT-8 STUTZ ENGINE (3 3/8" x 4 ½" BORE and STROKE)

155.8 H.P. @ 3900 RPM

POWER BRAKES AUTOMATIC CHOKE $3295. UP

"PATRICIAN COUPE" WITH BODY BY BRUNN

BUILT AT INDIANAPOLIS, 1913-1934. A NEW "STUTZ" REVIVED IN 1970s

© Field Enterprises. Inc. 1983

.1-30

1933 Stutz DV-32

A true classic, but seldom ever seen, is this 1933 Stutz DV-32 Patrician Coupe—hand-built in extremely limited number!

Stutz Motor Car Co., in the early 1930s, was almost ready to close its doors. Because of the Depression, luxury car sales had slipped badly. Those still buying big cars were picking Cadillacs, Packards, Lincolns, etc., as they didn't want to take a chance on the other fine cars available.

Motor magazine, in January 1933, displayed a photo of the illustrated Patrician Coupe and revealed that "Stutz has made numerous improvements in its single- and dual-valve eights, including the adoption of a Bendix vacuum-operated clutch control, automatic choke, thermostatically-controlled hood doors, thermostatically-controlled shock absorbers, tandem mufflers (more silent than before), three-speed synchromesh transmission with silent second, push-button operation of starter, white-wall tires, drop center rims, trumpet horns."

Single-valve eight prices started at $2,595, the dual-valve (DV-32) eight at $3,295, and a six-cylinder series at $1,895. Among the lower-priced models was a new Challenger 8, though this did not get very far because of Stutz's financial problems.

However, a Pack-Age-Car small delivery vehicle was introduced by Stutz in 1933, and this managed to continue longer than did the automobile line.

Because of the mystique of the classic Stutz name, new cars bearing this name have been introduced in recent years, though not connected with the original manufacturer at Indianapolis.

THE RARE NON-AIRFLOW CHRYSLER 6 OF 1934.!!

ATTENTION WAS FOCUSED ON THE STREAMLINED NEW CHRYSLER AIRFLOW 8s, AND THIS CHRYSLER 6 RECEIVED COMPARATIVELY LITTLE ATTENTION AND WAS NEARLY FORGOTTEN LATER.!

1934 CHRYSLER "CA" BUSINESS COUPE (ONLY 1,650 BLT.)

INDEPENDENT COIL SPRING FRONT SUSPENSION

93 HP
L HEAD 6
241½ CID

4.11 GEAR RATIO

2879 lbs.
118" WB

6.50 x 16 TIRES

HYDRAULIC BRAKES

HIT SONGS OF 1934

BLUE MOON
MOONGLOW
LOVE IN BLOOM
LOVE THY NEIGHBOR • TRUE
I ONLY HAVE EYES FOR YOU
BOULEVARD OF BROKEN DREAMS
WAGON WHEELS • THE BEAT O' MY HEART
YOU OUGHT TO BE IN PICTURES • I SAW STARS
I'LL STRING ALONG WITH YOU • CHAMPAGNE WALTZ
LITTLE MAN, YOU'VE HAD A BUSY DAY • LOST IN A FOG
THANK YOU FOR A LOVELY EVENING • COCKTAILS FOR TWO
PARDON MY SOUTHERN ACCENT • ALL I DO IS DREAM OF YOU
THE VERY THOUGHT OF YOU • LOVE IS JUST AROUND THE CORNER
THE MOON WAS YELLOW • MY OLD FLAME • WINTER WONDERLAND
THE OBJECT OF MY AFFECTION • YOU'RE A BUILDER-UPPER
2 CIGARETTES IN THE DARK • THE CONTINENTAL

1934 Chrysler 6

Chrysler Corporation produced some very racy-looking, low-slung, five-window Plymouth and Dodge coupes in 1933 and 1934. People seeing them today often wonder if these stubby-cabbed coupes are "original"—because the tops are so low, they appear to be "chopped." But, that was the design!

As for the 1934 Chryslers, the new Airflows (8-cylinder) were the most widely recognized and publicized. Because of this, many old-timers may have forgotten that in 1934 Chrysler also built conventionally styled "CA" and "CB" sixes (with 118-inch or 112-inch wheelbases). The "CA" series included this illustrated business coupe with its body similar to the '33 and '34 Plymouths and Dodges.

Note the "steel artillery" wheels. These disc wheels (with a circle of holes that helped to ventilate the brakes) replaced the old-style wood or wire-spoked wheels and were briefly popular in the 1933-1936 era.

Car radios were gaining in popularity during 1934. Most new automobiles were "wired for radio," and many buyers decided to order a radio with their new car in order to be entertained while traveling. Factory installations were usually mounted in the dash, but many of the after-market accessory radios had control heads attached to the steering column. On the air in 1934, you were likely to hear the song hits listed on the lower portion of the accompanying picture.

A FRENCH CLASSIC!
WITH FRONT WHEEL DRIVE
1934 CITROEN 7~S CABRIOLET
114½" W.B.

4 CYL. 1303 cc DISPLACEMENT
(72 cm BORE, 80 cm STROKE)
THIS "TRACTION AVANT" SERIES WAS SO
SATISFACTORY, IT CONTINUED FROM '34 to '57!!

4-DR. SEDANS MORE
COMMONLY SEEN. THE
CABRIOLET AND THE
3-WINDOW COUPE ARE
SCARCE!

THESE
HOOD VENT DOORS
REPLACED BY LOUVRES
IN LATER 1930s.

ABOUT 7000 CITROENS BUILT IN 1934.

©1994 by North America Syndicate, Inc. World rights reserved.

TAP
7•3

PRE-WAR PRICES
AS LOW AS $895.
IMPORTED TO
LOS ANGELES.

MFD. BY
S.A.
ANDRE CITROEN
PARIS (SINCE 1919)

UNITIZED BODY/FRAME, WITH A
RIBBED "BELLY-PAN" UNDERSIDE.
GEARSHIFT LEVER ON DASH!

1934 Citroen "Traction Avant"

Andre Citroen was once a chief engineer for the manufacturer of the French Mors automobile. He established his own gear-making firm in 1913 and entered the auto manufacturing business in 1919. The Citroen car became a great success in the 1920s, and soon joined Renault and Peugeot as one of France's "Big Three."

The illustrated "Traction Avant" model was so well built and well received that it continued from its introduction in 1934 until 1957—interrupted only by World War II. The four-door sedan is the most common of this series, but only a limited number were sold in the United States because of a shortage of dealerships.

Running changes were made during the long production run of the "Traction Avant" Citroen. There were various model numbers, increases in engine size, and a six-cylinder model joined the line (the Model 15 having a 122-inch wheelbase). Early pre-war sedans had an outside spare tire at rear, but later models had a trunk with the spare tire concealed within.

Continuing into 1957, the "Traction Avant" was superseded in 1956 by the all-new radically streamlined "DS-19," a car that has a futuristic look even today!

The most popular Citroen was the little "2 CV" model, a flat-sided sedan with the homely shape of a roll-top desk! Designed just before World War II, the "2 CV" was in full production from 1948 to 1990. A rival to Volkswagen's famous Beetle, the "2 CV" had many friends but never equaled the phenomenal popularity of VW.

1930s

A RARE PRE-WAR JAPANESE CAR! FEW REMAIN.
1934
DATSUN
DETAILS THANKS TO BOB SNYDER YONKERS, N.Y.
78" WHEELBASE
24 x 4" TIRES
WT. = 1364 lbs.
5-GAL. GAS TANK UNDER COWL.
RESEMBLING A MINIATURE 1934 FORD, THIS EARLY DATSUN WAS MFD. BY NISSAN JIDOSHA KAISHA, LTD. AND EXPORTED BY MITSUBISHI SHOJI KAISHA, LTD., TOKYO. (UP TO 50 MPG)
4 CYL. NISSAN L-HEAD ENG (748 cc)
2.2" x 3" BORE/STR. 12 HP @ 3000 RPM
JAPAN'S AUTO INDUSTRY REMAINED SMALL UNTIL THE 1960s, WHEN THEIR EXPORT BUSINESS INCREASED.
ALL DATSUN MODELS KNOWN AS NISSAN SINCE 1984.
RIGHT HAND DRIVE
WITH A TOP SPEED OF ONLY 45 MPH! (6.5 TO 1 GEAR RATIO)
TAP 6~23
© 1991 North America Syndicate, Inc. All Rights Reserved

1934 Datsun

Because Japanese car manufacturers have grown so large and competitive in recent years, it's hard to believe that until the 1950s, Japan's motor industry remained stuck in its infancy. In the very late 1950s, Datsun and Toyopet (Toyota) began importing cars to the United States.

Japanese car history goes back a long way to the 1907 Takuri (and even a few earlier attempts at car building), but for half a century most Japanese cars were flimsy and underpowered. The illustrated 1934 Datsun had only 12 h.p. and would only do 45 m.p.h. at full throttle with its excessively low-geared 6.5 to 1 rear axle!

Nissan had big plans for the Datsun, even in 1934. That year, allied with Mitsubishi, Nissan claimed sales outlets in Australia, France, India, Iran, Germany, China, the Philippines, South Africa, England, Argentina, and elsewhere. A 1934 advertisement even stated that there were American sales distributors in Seattle, San Francisco, and New York City, though I've seen no record of any prewar Datsuns that were actually sold in the United States. However, Bob Snyder, of Yonkers, N.Y., owns a rare 1937 Datsun roadster. How it got to America, some years ago, is a mystery.

In the 1930s, in addition to their small sedans and roadsters, Nissan built a large Type 70 sedan (the "Special"), which was a copy of the American Graham of 1935-36. And, there was a 1935 Toyota that looked like a scaled down '34 Chrysler Airflow, though the Toyota had a one-piece windshield and pedestal headlights.

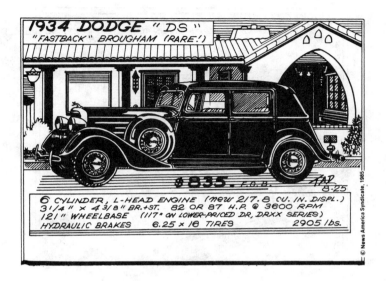

1934 DODGE "DS"
"FASTBACK" BROUGHAM (RARE!)

$835. F.O.B.

TAP
8-25

6 CYLINDER, L-HEAD ENGINE (new 2/7.8 CU. IN. DISPL.)
3 1/4" × 4 3/8" BR.+ST.   82 OR 87 H.P. @ 3600 RPM
121" WHEELBASE   (117" ON LOWER-PRICED DR, DRXX SERIES)
HYDRAULIC BRAKES   6.25 × 16 TIRES   2905 lbs.

© News America Syndicate, 1985.

1930s

1934 Dodge DS

The 1934 Dodges are scarce these days. And, even scarcer is this unusual "fastback" model: streamlined—but only at the rear!

Standard Dodges in 1934 had a 117-inch wheelbase, but the special DS series (also including a convertible sedan) rode on a 121-inch wheelbase. Moreover, there were variations in the arrangements of the long and shorter horizontal hood louvres.

The straight-eight models of Dodge, available since 1930, were no longer offered in 1934, leaving only the Dodge six. There were two cylinder heads available: With a cast-iron head, the 1934 engine developed 82 h.p., with a compression ratio of 5.6-to-1. An optional aluminum head of 6.5-to-1 compression boosted the h.p. to 87. For 1934, the crankshaft was enlarged, and there were now seven counterweights in place of the former four. "Floating

Power" engine mounting, available on Dodge since 1932, was successfully continued, giving amazing smoothness to the performance!

A new, independently-sprung, front-wheel suspension utilized coil springs. Improved leaf springs were continued at the rear.

The illustrated fastback Brougham carried luggage in the space between the back seat and tail. As there was no trunk lid, the luggage space was reached by moving the seat cushions.

An improved window vent system utilized swinging "butterfly" sections. Chrysler Corporation went one better than General Motors, providing butterfly windows that could be rolled down into the doors when not in use, thus eliminating the vertical pillar in front of the door window opening when the butterfly windows were in roll-down position.

1934 LA SALLE COUPE (WITH RUMBLE SEAT) $1595.
WITH new STREAMLINED BODY BY FLEETWOOD *119" W.B.*
new HYDRAULIC BRAKES *3815 LBS.*
new 240.3 c.i.b.
4.78 GEAR RATIO
@ 3700 RPM
90 HP
7.50 x 16
STRAIGHT 8 ENGINE
© News America Syndicate, 1986
WISHING YOU A
VERY MERRY CHRISTMAS!
TAD
12~21

1934 La Salle

F ew cars have ever changed so much in just one year as the La Salle did from 1933 to 1934! The '33 La Salle had closely resembled its sister car, the Cadillac, with the same big 353-c.i.d. V-8, and the price of a La Salle coupe in '33 was $2,245, just $450 less than Cadillac's coupe.

But, in 1934, La Salle was totally restyled, with a sleek new streamlined body and a long, narrow hood—graced along the sides with a row of five unusual bubble-shaped vent ports. The V-8 engine was replaced by a 240.3-c.i.d. straight-8 modified Oldsmobile engine, and the new wheelbase of 119 inches was the same as the Oldsmobile Eight's, down some from the former 130- or 136-inch wheelbase of '33!

The price was another attraction: the coupe was now only $1,595, while for $100 more, three other body types were presented: sedan, club sedan, and convertible coupe. Even though the early '30s were hard times, La Salle production more than doubled—from 3,482 (1933) to 7,195.

In the early '30s, General Motors had been discontinuing its "companion" cars. In '32 and early '33, La Salle appeared to be threatened. GM's styling whiz, Harley Earl (who'd designed the first 1927 La Salle), set to work with a talented team to whip up a real knockout for 1934!

The result: a beauty and a great buy, though there were gripes that the modified Olds engine, Olds transmission, and other chassis parts made it less than a Cadillac.

A CLASSIC CAR!

LEAPING GREYHOUND ORNAMENT

1934 LINCOLN BROUGHAM TOWN CAR (CHAUFFEUR-DRIVEN) $6800. WITH BODY BY BRUNN ONLY 15 BLT.!

TAP 6~4

145" W.B. • 5480 LBS. • 414 c.i.d. V-12 • 150 HP 3800

1934 Lincoln

In 1920, Henry Leland founded Lincoln. From the first, the Lincoln was a large, V-8-powered machine with towering coachwork and quality features.

The business recession of 1921 forced Mr. Leland to sell his Lincoln Motor Company to Henry Ford. From 1922 on, Lincoln was the prestige line of Ford Motor Company.

For 1932, Lincoln introduced a new V-12 of 448 c.i.d. to join its 385 c.i.d. V-8. Things were simplified for 1934: just one Lincoln engine choice was offered, a new 414 c.i.d. V-12. That displacement size continued until 1940 on the senior "K" type Lincolns.

There were two 1934 Lincoln model series: the 521 series "KA" with a 136-inch wheelbase, and the 271 series "KB" with a long 145-inch wheelbase.

New Lincolns were rare in 1934. The largest-selling 1934 Lincoln was the "KA" five-passenger Town sedan

(only 450 sold, at $3,450 each). The illustrated Brougham Town Car (by Brunn) was the lowest-selling of the regular production models, with only fifteen built. It was luxurious, but certainly not streamlined.

Interestingly, Lincoln returned to vertical-door hood vents in 1934, as they'd used in 1932. The 1934 fenders were now skirted, as they were on the later 1933s.

Most town cars had removable or slide-away roof sections to cover the driver's compartment in bad weather. Nevertheless, since the driver's compartment in a town car was often open at the top, the upholstery on the driver's seat was usually heavy leather. Battery-operated telephones, or simple speaking tubes, were frequently used for communication to the driver.

Mechanical detail labels within illustration: RETURN-TO DASH / ALAN & DOROTHY KLUG L.I., N.Y. / UP TO 85 M.P.H. / UP TO 18 M.P.G. / new 117¼" WB / 3210 lbs. / MECHANICAL BRAKES, CABLE-ACTUATED (BY BENDIX) / 6.00 x 17 TIRES / RUMBLESEAT CABRIOLET / $785., f.o.b. FACTORY / 4.55 GEAR RATIO / 1934 PONTIAC 8 / WITH STRAIGHT-8 L-HEAD ENGINE (NO PONTIAC 6 IN '33 OR '34) / 223.4 CID, 3 3/16" x 3½" BORE and ST. / 84 HP / © 1990 North America Syndicate, Inc. All Rights Reserved

1934 Pontiac

C ar performance was improving rapidly during the early 1930s. As that decade had begun, a typical new Pontiac 6 would barely exceed 60 to 65 m.p.h. top speed, even going downhill. Yet, by 1934, many six-cylinder cars were reaching 75 to 80 m.p.h., and more. New Pontiacs (straight-8s only in '33 and '34) were capable of at least 77 to 85 m.p.h. or more, depending on the body type and number of passengers.

What was featured on the 1934 Pontiac 8? The new model was larger, heavier, faster, more powerful, and easier-riding. Yet, increased compression (6.2 to 1), through a redesigned cylinder head, gave a ten percent boost in fuel economy. "Knee Action" independently sprung front wheels and fatter 6.00 x 17 tires helped smooth out the road. A few years later, cars with independently

sprung front wheels would lose considerable resale appeal because they required more frequent alignment.

The 1934 Pontiac hood had grown seven inches longer, covering more of the cowl. Painted headlight shells, pleasingly bullet-shaped, were five inches longer than before. And, the wheelbase had grown 2 1/4 inches. "Touring" sedans (two-door or four-door) had the advantage of a built-in trunk but a rather high, small trunk door.

Bendix mechanical brakes, with enclosed "steeldraulic-type" cables, were much improved for 1934. The accelerator pedal actuated the starter (puzzling some potential car thieves who weren't up on the latest developments), and the distributor could be manually set at different positions to best accommodate the octane rating of the gasoline used.

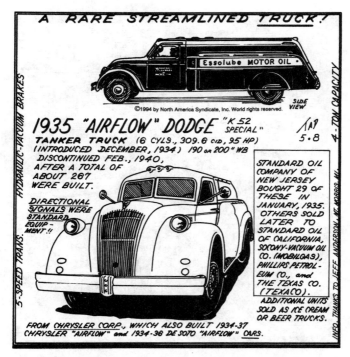

A RARE STREAMLINED TRUCK!

Essolube MOTOR OIL

SIDE VIEW

HYDRAULIC-VACUUM BRAKES

5-SPEED TRANS.

4 - TON CAPACITY

INFO. THANKS TO JEFF ANDERSON, MT. MORRIS, WI.

1935 "AIRFLOW" DODGE "K 52 SPECIAL"

TANKER TRUCK (6 CYLS., 309.6 CID, 95 HP)
(INTRODUCED DECEMBER, 1934) 190 or 200" WB
DISCONTINUED FEB., 1940,
AFTER A TOTAL OF
ABOUT 267
WERE BUILT.

DIRECTIONAL
SIGNALS WERE
STANDARD
EQUIP-
MENT!!

STANDARD OIL
COMPANY OF
NEW JERSEY
BOUGHT 29 OF
THESE IN
JANUARY, 1935.
OTHERS SOLD
LATER TO
STANDARD OIL
OF CALIFORNIA,
SOCONY-VACUUM OIL
CO. (MOBILGAS),
PHILLIPS PETROL-
EUM CO., and
THE TEXAS CO.
(TEXACO).
ADDITIONAL UNITS
SOLD AS ICE CREAM
OR BEER TRUCKS.

1 MPG
5.8

FROM CHRYSLER CORP., WHICH ALSO BUILT 1934-37
CHRYSLER "AIRFLOW" and 1934-36 DE SOTO "AIRFLOW" CARS.

1935 "Airflow" Dodge Tanker Truck

Most car buffs admire the streamlined Chrysler and DeSoto "Airflow" models, super-cars of the mid-1930s. Lesser known is Chrysler Corporation's streamlined series of Dodge "Airflow-style" trucks, built as 1935 to 1940 models.

Most of them were sold to major oil companies, but some were made into beer trucks—ordered by the Schlitz Brewing Company. Schlitz had special cargo bodies applied to these Dodge trucks by the Barkow Auto Body Co. of Milwaukee. Dairylea Ice Cream trucks were also adapted from these big Dodge "Airflows," sold to the Dairymen's League Cooperative Association of New York City.

Certain modifications appeared during the 1935-1940 production run: changes in wheelbases, increased engine size and power, new grilles, and other improvements.

Drivers loved these trucks! Though large, they were comfortable to handle, with soundproofed cabs and numerous safety features. The Dodge Airflow tanker truck was one of the earliest vehicles to include directional signals as standard equipment. Some of these trucks even included a courteous sign at the rear that read, "We'll Share the Road—Blow Your Horn."

Texaco probably made the greatest purchase of the Dodge Airflow tankers, and recently a scale model (of this type) has been offered for sale to interested collectors, through the Airflow Club of America (in Akron, Ohio). By now, the scale models are probably more plentiful than the real trucks!

1930s

1935 De Soto "Airflow"

During 1934, De Soto was only available in the new streamlined "Airflow" series. So radical were these new models that sales were disappointing. Some people were afraid to be seen in a car so different and so eye-catching!

Therefore, in 1935, a less streamlined "Airstream" model was also presented to the public.

Even though its snub-nosed aerodynamic styling scared off many conservative buyers, the Airflow was a sort of super-car: a good performer, extremely safe and well built, and a stable handler under any road conditions. In an accident, the sturdy unitized body/frame was almost indestructible, providing a protective cage around driver and passengers. All it lacked were seat belts (they were seldom used before the 1950s).

A six, the De Soto Airflow was more economical to operate than its straight-eight Chrysler counterpart. Both the new Chrysler and De Soto Airflows had been plain-looking in 1934, with slot-like "waterfall" grilles that followed the sloping contour of the hood. For 1935, styling in the front was improved with new protruding grille sections grafted on at the center.

Prices were lowered during the 1935 model year. De Soto Airflows were reduced from $1,195 early in the season to only $1,015 by June.

A total of 6,797 De Soto Airflows were built in 1935. But, over 20,000 of the new, less streamlined Airstreams were sold in 1935, demonstrating that the general public was not ready for cars as unique as the Airflows!

MFD. BY GRAHAM-PAIGE MOTORS CORP., DETROIT
(THE FINAL GRAHAM WAS THE 1941 MODEL. IT WAS THE
ANCESTOR OF THE POST-WAR KAISER FRAZER CARS.)
THE 1935 GRAHAM 6 HAD AN L-HEAD, 169.6 CID
6 CYL. ENGINE (3" x 4" BR. + STR.) 70 HP @ 3500 RPM
WITH 7 TO 1 HI-COMPRESSION ALUMINUM CYLINDER HEAD.
HYDR. BRAKES • 12 GAL. GAS TANK • SWIVEL VENT WINDOWS OPT.
CHOICE OF 4.55 OR 5.1 TO 1 GEAR RATIO
BACKGROUND = PACIFIC GROVE, CALIF.
MUNICIPAL SWIMMING POOL (OPENED 1935)

1935 Graham

In 1932, Graham cars made history by offering models with a sleek, semi-streamlined design. This '32 Graham (a.k.a. the "Blue Streak") introduced skirted front and rear fenders on a production car—and also a marvelous new optional color: "Pearlessence of Blue." The paint for this color was made, in part, of powdered fish scales, which were known for their iridescence.

Q: But, what was "different" about the 1935 Graham 6?

A: From 1932 to 1934, Graham had retained the successful "Blue Streak" profile. But, the 1935 Graham was slightly modernized, with a sloping tail on sedans, new hood louvers, and a narrower grille. The 1935 Graham lineup consisted of the new low-priced Six (illustrated) and also the Special 6, Eight, Special 8, Supercharged 8, and Supercharged Custom 8.

All but the basic Six carried the spare tire and wheel inside the trunk. On the illustrated model, the spare tire was exposed at the rear, and the luggage compartment was thus reached by moving the rear-seat back cushion.

Graham entered the 1935 season offering a new economy model that helped them to stave off bankruptcy. Designed to sell "in the lowest price range," the Graham 6 for 1935 sold for as little as $595 and up (at the factory, as of January 1935).

One exclusive and noteworthy Graham feature was the "outboard" leaf-spring suspension system. The springs were mounted outside and next to the frame, instead of directly underneath. This greater width between the springs on opposite sides increased road stability, especially when cornering at speed.

1935 Hispano-Suiza V12

Marc Birkigt, a well-known Swiss engineer, designed a car named the Castro that was manufactured in Barcelona, Spain from 1901 to 1904. The Castro had replaced the chain-driven La Cuadra automobile, but in turn the Castro was replaced by the Hispano-Suiza in 1904, when the company reorganized again.

In 1931, the new V-12 was added to the Hispano-Suiza line. The V-12 had overhead valves, and it was capable of 100 to 115 m.p.h., depending on the body type and weight. Six-cylinder models were also available. The V-12 was discontinued in 1938 when the Paris factory shut down.

The beautiful V-12 Sedanca Coupe is a sort of abbreviated town car and a most distinctive body style. This car (illustrated) is one of Hispano-Suiza's greatest classics, with custom body by Fernandez and Darrin. (Mr. Fernandez was the financier of this partnership, and "Dutch" Darrin was the stylist.) Back in the 1920s, Darrin was in partnership in Paris with Tom Hibbard, but the Hibbard and Darrin body manufacturing ceased when Hibbard returned to America in 1931 to work for General Motors.

Fernandez and Darrin produced some beautiful automobile bodies in the 1930s, and a car exactly like the illustrated model was custom built for the Baroness Rothschild of London. The baroness's well-heeled friends liked the looks of her new car so well that they also placed orders with Fernandez and Darrin. But, most of the other such bodies that Fernandez and Darrin supplied were on Rolls-Royce chassis, because Rolls-Royce was THE preferred luxury car in England.

1935 LINCOLN V-12 "K" SERIES
WITH CONVERTIBLE VICTORIA BODY BY BRUNN
(MODEL 547)   5135 LBS.   136" WHEELBASE
12 CYLINDERS   L-HEAD V-ENGINE
              (3 1/8" x 4 1/2")   150 H.P.
4.58 GEAR RATIO   FREE WHEELING
VACUUM POWER BRAKES
MFD. BY LINCOLN MOTOR CO. DIV. OF FORD MOTOR CO.

ORIGINAL PRICE, AT FACTORY   WISHING YOU A MOST
                              BLESSED CHRISTMAS!
$5500.00

18 BODY TYPES, INCLUDING COACHBUILT
SEMI-CUSTOM VARIETIES BY BRUNN,   12-23
JUDKINS, LE BARON, WILLOUGHBY, ETC.   News America Syndicate
                                       © News Group Chicago, Inc., 1984

1930s

1935 Lincoln K

The big, solid Lincoln K models of the 1930s were among the finest of classic cars! The K was the predecessor of the luxury Lincoln Continental, though in 1940 the final K was still available along with the first Continental and also the lower-priced Lincoln-Zephyr (which had been introduced for 1936).

At home in such elegant surroundings as Newport, Pebble Beach, Grosse Point, Beverly Hills, Palm Springs, etc., the Lincoln K was improved for 1935 with an engine set further forward on the frame, so rear-seat passengers now rode ahead of the rear axle and not over it as before. The center of gravity was lowered, and springs were softer. A new stabilizer held the rear end closer to the road. Shifting was now easier, and acceleration was swifter than in '34.

Horizontal vent louvre doors and horizontal bands of brightwork graced the sides of the hood on the '35 Lincoln. The radiator cap was now concealed beneath the front of the butterfly-type hood, with the traditional leaping-greyhound mascot in a fixed position.

Reportedly, there was a change in the position of the emergency brake lever during the 1935 model year. Early '35s had the lever at center; later '35s had the lever at left on the panel under the dash. Meanwhile, a space was made available on the dash for an optional radio.

The illustrated Victoria convertible had a 136-inch wheelbase, as did some other types, but limousines and certain others had a super-long 145-inch-wheelbase chasse.

1930s

1935 Pierce-Arrow

"**W**hy is it that certain thoroughbreds stand out against all the horseflesh in the world?

"Why do certain paintings call forth rhapsodies, when so many canvases are painted?

"Why does a Pierce-Arrow stir the pulse so strongly, with so many cars on the road?

"Perhaps it's because each of us yearn for perfection, and find it so rarely. Pierce-Arrow"

The above quote is from one of Pierce-Arrow's infrequent advertisements of 1935.

Since 1913, Pierce-Arrows were easily recognized by their distinctive headlights (sunken into the fenders). Only a few post-1913 Pierce-Arrows were built with conventional separate headlights, and that was only on special order.

For 1935, *Motor* magazine (January 1935) described the changes in Pierce-

Arrow for the new year: "The new Pierce-Arrows reveal a further modernization of the distinctive styles of the past year. Conspicuous refinements of exterior and interior design include handsome new hood louvers, improved fender skirts, new-type headlamp lenses, completely redesigned instrument board, special custom tailoring (upholstery), and a new range of colors. Front compartments are roomier."

Starting at only $2,795, f.o.b. Buffalo, N.Y., a new Pierce-Arrow in 1935 was a greater bargain than ever. Back in 1921, the price of a new Pierce-Arrow was $7,500 and up!

In the mid-'30s, Pierce-Arrow sought to diversify by manufacturing quality travel trailers in addition to its automobiles. But, because of low sales, the Pierce-Arrow went out of production in 1938.

1930s

1935 Pontiac

The year 1935 was the first for Pontiac's once-famous Silver Streak series, easily identified by the unique band of parallel chrome strips along the top of the hood. This identifying mark continued each year on Pontiacs until the mid-1950s. Some Pontiacs during those years also had a second set of chrome strips running down the rear deck.

The totally restyled 1935 model was advertised as "the most beautiful thing on wheels," and, indeed, it was singularly attractive. Body was all new and featured the new "Turret Top" one-piece steel roof, curvy streamlined styling, and a two-piece V-shaped windshield.

Starting in 1935, and continuing through 1954, there was a choice of a six-cylinder or straight L-head engine. (In 1933 and 1934, the only Pontiac choice had been the straight-8.) From the outside, the 1935 Six could be distinguished from the Eight because the Six had an Indian-head-in-circle hood ornament astride the row of chrome strips, while the Eight had a forward-leaping figure instead—and was slightly longer.

Both models had hydraulic brakes.

Regarding style, the 1935 and 1936 Pontiacs had much in common, though the 1935 had the infamous front "suicide" doors, which were hinged at the rear and swung open at the front. That type of door, seen on some 1932 to 1935 cars, got its bad name from the fact that if not closed tightly, it could whip open suddenly when the car was traveling fast with dire results! That type of front door was eliminated on the 1936 model.

1935 WILLYS "77"
MFD. BY WILLYS-OVERLAND, TOLEDO, OHIO

COUPE   2034 lbs.

ONLY $**395.**
f.o.b. FACTORY PRICE IN 1935

new "BUBBLE" HOOD PORTS

new GRILLE

BORE + STK. 3⅛" x 4⅜"
48 H.P. 70 M.P.H.
UP TO 30 MILES PER GALLON.

©1992 by North America Syndicate, Inc. World rights reserved.

4.3 GEAR RATIO

5.00 x 17" TIRES.
BENDIX MECHANICAL BRAKES

L-HEAD 134.2 C.I.D. 4 CYL. ENGINE

WILLYS INTRO. THE ECONOMICAL "77" IN 1933, with 3 HOOD VENT DOORS ON EA. SIDE, and STEEL-STAMPED ARTILLERY WHEELS. THE 1934 MODEL HAD WIRE WH. and SEMI-HORIZONTAL HOOD LOUVRES. (ARTILLERY WHEELS IN '36.)

100" WHEELBASE "FLOATING POWER" (BY ARRANGEMENT WITH CHRYSLER CORP.)

AAP 2-2

1935 Willys

Back in 1933, Willys-Overland went into receivership. The struggling company avoided imminent bankruptcy by canceling all its larger cars and concentrating on its new model: a cramped, homely, but very economical little "77" series. This car had a four-cylinder engine similar to the type used previously in Willys' budget-priced Whippet car ('27 to '31).

The "77" was America's lowest-priced family-sized car, and many families during the Depression could afford nothing more.

By license agreement with Chrysler Corp., the Willys "77" used the flexible "Floating Power" engine mounting system that had first been introduced on the new "PA" series Plymouth in mid-1931. This device virtually banished vibration!

The four-cylinder Willys car would be enlarged and totally restyled for 1937, thus doubling the sales from 30,826 to 63,467 in just one year! As for the illustrated 1935 model, it was the lowest-selling "77": only 10,715 Willys sales in '35.

When World War II and gas rationing came along in the 1940s, four-cylinder Willys models were in demand at the car lots. Also, the 1940s was a good decade for Willys-Overland because Willys was the greatest producer of military Jeeps.

At one time, used Willys "77" coupes were popular at the stock car tracks. Even with an original engine, the "77" was a good runner for its small size and would do 70-75 m.p.h.

On the sides of the '35 Willys hood, the new bubble-shaped vent ports were probably inspired by those on the beautiful 1934 La Salles.

A "MINI-CLASSIC"

EARLY 1936 CHEVROLET
4 DOOR CVT. PHAETON
RARE! ONLY 217 OF THESE
CHEVROLET PHAETONS BUILT
IN 1935, FOR $485. EACH,
f.o.b. FACTORY. EVEN FEWER
CHEVROLET PHAETONS BLT. AT
BEGINNING OF 1936 MODEL YR.,
BEFORE DISCONTINUATION.

THE FIRST CHEVROLET WITH HYDRAULIC BRAKES WAS THE 1936 MODEL.

6 CYLINDER, OVERHEAD-VALVE 206.8 c.i.d. ENGINE

TAD
9~25

ONLY A FEW 1936 CHEVROLETS
HAD THESE WIRE WHEELS. MOST
HAD THE NEW 1936-STYLE STEEL
"ARTILLERY TYPE" WHEELS.

5.25 x 17" TIRES
4.11 GEAR RATIO
2495 lbs. WT. ('35)

79 H.P. @
3200 RPM

109" W.B.
(STANDARD)
(MASTER = 113")

1936 Chevrolet Phaeton

Y ou could browse through classic and antique auto shows for years, and you'd be unlikely to ever find another 1936 Chevrolet phaeton like this one. It's among Chevrolet's rarest models of all!

The Phaeton—successor to the commonplace touring car of the 'teens and 1920s—was becoming a rare breed as the 1930s commenced. Chevrolet's last regular-production phaeton was the 1935 model, of which only 217 were built (on the Standard series chassis). Most 1936 Chevrolet listings mention the cabriolet (convertible coupe with roll-up windows) as Chevrolet's only convertible model that year. But, apparently, a mere handful of phaetons may have been put together in the early days of the 1936 model year—perhaps, 1935 cars with 1936 grilles tacked on?

A photo of the illustrated car appeared in the Jan./ Feb. 1982 issue of *Antique Automobile* magazine. It appears to be authentic and not a sedan with the top cut off, as some might suspect.

Hydraulic brakes were new to Chevrolet in '36. Of the "Big 3" low-priced cars, only Plymouth had offered them earlier.

Master DeLuxe models offered "Shockproof Steering" and $20-optional "Knee Action" independent front wheel suspension. However, the cheaper Chevys with the solid front axles were more trouble-free. "Knee Action," introduced by General Motors in 1933, had problems in its early years. Cars with this feature tended to "shimmy" and "wander" at highway speeds, and their resale value suffered.

QUESTION : WHAT DID SHIRLEY TEMPLE, BING CROSBY, JANET GAYNOR, GINGER ROGERS, JOAN BENNETT, CLAUDETTE COLBERT *and* WARNER BAXTER HAVE IN COMMON?
ANSWER : MOVIE STARDOM, *and a* 1936 DODGE!

1936 DODGE "D-2" STD. 4-DR. SEDAN
217.8 C.I.D., 6-CYLINDER L-HEAD ENGINE
3 1/4" × 4 3/8" BORE + STROKE
87 H.P. @ 3600 RPM   116" WHEELBASE
$735.°°, f.o.b., FACTORY   4.12 GEAR RATIO
WEIGHT = 2923 lbs.   18 TO 24 M.P.G.

CLIP AND SAVE!

© Field Enterprises, Inc. 1984

TAP   1-29

600 × 16
HYDRAULIC BRAKES

IN ORIGINAL ADVERTISING, FILM STARS ENDORSED 1936 DODGES, *and also* 1937 TO 1939 DE SOTOS, PLUS OTHER CARS.

1936 Dodge

Bing Crosby's singing and acting career was going great in 1936; and though he could have afforded a Duesenberg, he drove a new Dodge and gave his testimonial for the car in magazine advertisements. Little Shirley Temple, the movies' most popular child star (seen on the running-board of the illustrated car), was also a "'36 Dodge person," though the car was obviously registered to, and driven by, her daddy.

Several popular screen stars endorsed the new Dodge for 1936, stating that they owned and used one and were highly pleased! Whether or not Chrysler Corp.'s Dodge Division supplied these cars in exchange for the stars' endorsements is unknown; but even if the famous film personalities bought the cars on their own, they were surely reimbursed well for the use of their names and photographs in the ads that appeared.

Endorsements by celebrities may have helped to sell products in the '30s, but the 1936 Dodge was an excellent, dependable car that could sell on its own merits. One of its many fine engineering features was "Floating Power" (extremely flexible engine mountings used since 1932), which gave great smoothness to the car's performance and virtually banished vibration!

In 1937, Chrysler Corp. moved its celebrity endorsement ad campaign to its De Soto line, and added radio personalities and other notables to the roster of famous owners. By 1939, even the king of cartoonists, Walt Disney, owned a new De Soto and was photographed with it for a color advertisement.

1936 1/2 Ford

The '36 1/2 (or late '36) Ford had an improved engine, and there were more body types later in the season. The noteworthy mid-year model was the all-new Club Cabriolet, a convertible club coupe with a back seat inside the body and under the top. The ordinary '36 Ford Cabriolet had a rumble seat and a shorter top.

Only 4,616 of the Club Cabriolets were built in 1936, compared to over 14,000 rumble-seat Cabriolets, but then the Club model had not been available all year. Club Cabriolet sales nearly doubled when this model was continued in 1937.

By late 1936, there were three-window and five-window coupes (with or without rumble seats), a roadster, a phaeton, and various Tudor, Fordor, and Fordor Convertible sedans, available with or without a built-in trunk. More than 7,000 Ford "woody" station wagons were also built that year.

There were Standard and Deluxe models, the latter having "dual equipment" (two tail-lights, two horns, two inside sun visors) and other luxuries.

Originally, the '36 Ford instrument panels were finished in gray metallic pyroxylin. There were leather seats in convertible models (imitation leather in rumble seats), and some cabriolets were available with Bedford cord upholstery.

There were five different kinds of optional radios for '36 Fords. The windshield defroster (illustrated) was an odd little gadget that resembled a vacuum cleaner attachment.

How much is a '36 1/2 Ford Club Cabriolet worth (in 1986)? The price range is $4,500 to $25,000, depending on the car's condition.

BRITISH-BUILT
CLASSIC!

1936 ROLLS-ROYCE

new "25 / 30" series

LIMOUSINE 132"WB
BODY BY WINDOVERS

RIGHT-HAND DRIVE

©1992 North America Syndicate, Inc. World rights reserved.

6.00 x 19"
TIRES

4 SP. TRANS.
4.55 GEAR
RATIO

OWN 6 CYL. OVERHEAD-VALVE 259.8 c.i.D. ENGINE
APPROX. 115 HORSEPOWER @ 4500 RPM (4300 lbs. WT.)
3½" 4½" BORE and STROKE   SERVO-ASSIST. BRAKES

TOP SPEED   80 MPH

1936 Rolls-Royce "25/30"

"The Best Car in the World!" This slogan has been Rolls-Royce's for generations! Even if one has another favorite brand of luxury car, there's no denying Rolls-Royce's enviable reputation for hand-crafted quality since production began back in 1904.

Rolls-Royce is thoroughly British, though an American branch factory was also in operation at Springfield, Mass. from the early 1920s to the early '30s.

In 1936, Rolls-Royce offered the choices of the 20/25 series (1930-1937), the new 25/30 series, or the luxurious V-12 Phantom III (of which only 710 cars were built, between '35 and '39). The chassis price of the PIII was 2,600 pounds in British currency.

Bodies for Rolls-Royce chassis units were supplied by a number of quality coachbuilders—such as Hooper, Barker, Park Ward, Thrupp & Maberly, Freestone & Webb, James Young, H. J. Mulliner, Gurney Nutting, Rippon Bros., and several others, including Windovers on the illustrated car.

The 25/30 had a seven-main-bearing engine (cast iron block and aluminum crankcase) and a Zenith-Stromberg carburetor. It had more power than the 20/25 series, though the 25/30 was heavier and much of the extra power was spent in dragging around the added weight.

Before World War II, all Rolls-Royces had wooden-framed coach-built "composite" bodies. In fact, during the '20s and early '30s, there was a brief fad for flexible Weymann wood-framed, fabric-covered bodies, constructed in the manner of some early airplanes. But, such non-metallic body surfaces were prone to weathering and serious rot, as well as being dangerous in a collision.

1936 Terraplane Pickup

The Hudson Motor Car Co. was established in 1909 with the introduction of its early 1910 models. In 1919, the manufacturer launched a companion car to the Hudson Super Six, and that was the Essex (four cylinder). In '24, the Essex became a six, and in 1932-1933 it was renamed the Essex-Terraplane. The name was shortened to Terraplane from 1933 to 1938, as the Hudson cars also continued.

In addition, Hudson built pickups and commercial vehicles, such as this 1936 Terraplane 3/4-ton. Hudson pickups continued into the 1940s, but were dropped after the 1947 model, because the 1948 Hudson was totally redesigned with a body-frame "step-down" chassis not readily adaptable for a pickup conversion. The Hudson pickups could have continued with the 1947 design, of course, but low sales made that idea impractical. (I might add that the 1948 Hudson car was a great success!)

In 1936, according to *Automotive Industries* magazine (January 2, 1937), nearly 800,000 trucks had been sold in one year (a very small percentage of them being Terraplanes!).

Both trucks and cars were used in great numbers in fleet service. AT&T had the most in the 1935-1936 season with 12,970 trucks and 4,060 cars. Automotive Industries (February 22, 1936) published a list of nearly 100 organizations and the exact number of trucks and cars in their individual fleets. Prosperity was returning to the U.S.A. in the Mid-30s!

One peculiar feature of Hudson-built vehicles was the "wet" clutch, the plates of which were studded with cork and continually bathed in oil to reduce wear.

1930s

323.5 CID STRAIGHT-8 L-HEAD ENG. (3¼" × 4⅞") 130 H.P. @ 3400 RPM (4600 BLT. IN '37.)

DASH

1937 AIRFLOW C-17 BY CHRYSLER $1610. f.o.b. 128" W.B. 4300 lbs.

1937

4-8

C News Group Chicago, Inc., 1984   WAX

TAD

3.03 GEAR RATIO WITH OVERDRIVE

7.50 × 16" TIRES

1937 Chrysler Airflow

Beginning in 1934, Chrysler Corporation created a new sensation in automotive circles with the new "Airflow" models, in both the Chrysler and De Soto lines.

In spite of their startlingly new aerodynamic styling and many exciting mechanical features, the Chrysler and De Soto Airflows were not commercially successful. After 1936, De Soto dropped its Airflow model, and 1937 was Chrysler's final year for the Airflow (illustrated).

The Airflow was not only streamlined, but it was remarkably safe, with a roll-proofed body and frame unit that was welded together like a protective steel cage, with many reinforcing members under the metal "skin." A smooth, level ride was provided through a long wheelbase, improved suspension and balanced weight—by moving the engine forward over the front axle and by placing rear seat passengers ahead of the rear axle.

All Airflows, except a few of the costliest Imperials, had two-piece windshields, and both halves of the windshield could be cranked open.

A total of more than 55,000 Airflow Chryslers and De Sotos were built during the mid-1930s, but sales declined year by year because of customer resistance. In '37, only one series was offered, the Chrysler C-17 (in two-door and four-door body types).

After the passage of years, the Airflows were at last admired as the super-cars they truly are. But, the available supply of these cars, for appreciative collectors, is understandably limited!

THE new FORD "60" FOR 1937!
OFFERING A new **SMALL** V-8 FOR ECONOMY, A
60-HP MINI ENGINE OF ONLY 135.9 CID!
THIS ENGINE HAD BEEN USED IN THE
FRENCH FORD THE PREVIOUS YEAR.
THE FORD V-8 "60" ENGINE
WAS AVAIL. IN USA 1937 THROUGH
1940.

EMBLEM

4.44
GEAR RATIO

112" W.B.

1937 FORD "60"
COUPE   WT. = 2275 lbs.
$529., f.o.b.   6.75 COMPRESSION

LARGER 221 CID 85-HP
V8 STILL AVAIL. ALSO. (3.78 GEAR
RATIO)

("60" TOP SPEED ONLY 70 MPH)

1937 Ford "60" Coupe

Ford Motor Company had high hopes for the smaller 60-h.p. V-8 (just under 136 c.i.d) as an alternative to their full-sized 85-h.p. 221 c.i.d. engine. The '37 Ford with the little engine was the "74" series, and the 85-h.p. model was the "78." But, the small one was always better known as the "60."

The small engine was easy on gas, but "gutless" compared to the full-sized type. The "60" needed a 4.44 gear ratio differential (lower-geared than usual) to keep it from faltering when pulling torque. Its top speed of 70 was at least 15 m.p.h. less than the 85-h.p. model would do.

White sidewall tires look nice on this Ford "60" coupe, but most people who chose this "cheapie" model also settled for the less expensive black-sided tires. Tire size of the 1937 "60" was 5.50 x 16, while the 85-h.p. Ford came with 6.00 x 16s.

There were Standard and DeLuxe Fords. The Standard had a painted dash and window trim, instead of being woodgrain-decorated like the DeLuxe. The Standard did not have chrome on the windshield frame. Also, the Standard had a painted grille, and a plainer steering wheel. The Standard had only one windshield wiper. And, for several years, Standard Fords included only one taillight at left instead of "dual equipment."

Since the dimensions and overall design of the Standard and DeLuxe '37 Fords were the same, a "60" engine could be fitted in a DeLuxe Ford. Many Standards offered the 85-h.p. engine.

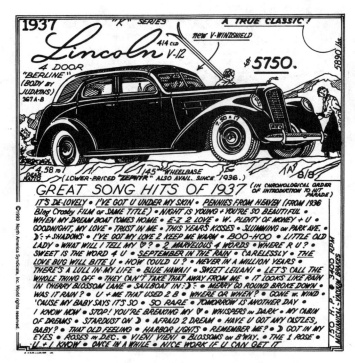

1937 Lincoln Model "K" Berline

Most readers are more familiar with the '37 Lincoln Zephyr than with the large Model K shown here. After all, the Zephyr (introduced '36) was a screaming bargain, priced in '37 at only $1,165 f.o.b. for a Lincoln with a streamlined body and a 12-cylinder engine! (V-12 engines were all that Lincoln offered from 1934 to 1948!) Because of its bargain price, the 122-inch-wheelbase Zephyr far outsold the expensive Lincoln "Ks"; the latter were much longer (136-inch or 145-inch wheelbase), much heavier (3 tons), and far more luxurious, even if more old-fashioned in appearance.

On the "K" series, new for 1937, were the sunken headlights protruding from the fenders in Pierce-Arrow fashion. And, on most of the "K" body types, there was a new two-piece V-shaped windshield.

From famous coach builders, there are many custom-ordered body types on the '37 "Ks." The lowest-priced "K" was the standard 354 A-B sedan (five- or seven-passenger), starting at $4,450. Other models were as follows:

136-inch wheelbase: Le Baron convertible roadster, $4,950; Le Baron coupe, $4,950; Willoughby coupe, $5,550 Brunn convertible Victoria, $5,550.

145-inch wheelbase (five-passenger): Brunn cabriolet, $6,750; Judkins Berline (illustrated); Le Baron convertible sedan (with or without partition), $5,450 or $5,650; Willoughby sport sedan, $6,850.

145-inch wheelbase (seven-passenger): Willoughby touring, $5,550; Judkins sedan limousine, $5,950; Seven-passenger sedan, $4,750; Seven-passenger limousine, $4,850; Willoughby limousine, $5,850; Brunn touring cab., $6,950; Brunn brougham, $6,750; Willoughby panel brougham, $7,050.

News America Syndicate
© News Group Chicago, Inc., 1984
12-2

1937 PACKARD 6, WITH STATION WAGON, WOODEN BODY

WAGON DETAILS THANKS TO JOHN WOODS, SACRAMENTO, CALIF.

TAD

L-HEAD 237 C.I.D. 6-CYL. ENGINE
3 7/16" x 4 1/4" BORE and STROKE
100 H.P. @ 3600 RPM
6.50 x 16" TIRES
115" W.B. - 4.36 GEAR RATIO
17-GALLON GAS TANK
1937 PACKARD 6 PRICES FROM
ONLY $895. (BUSINESS CPE.)
THE FIRST 6-CYL. PACKARD
SINCE 1928.
STRAIGHT-8 and V-12
MODELS ALSO IN '37.

A COLLECTOR'S CLASSIC!

1937 Packard Six

Some car buffs refer to this Packard Six as the model 110, but in 1937 its official designation was the Six, or the 115 (in reference to its 115-inch wheelbase). The Six was new for '37, since a six-cylinder Packard had not been available since 1928.

Packard had been saved from financial ruin by introducing the 120 eight in 1935. The 120 was a reasonably-priced, but high-quality, straight-eight costing only $995 and up. For 1937, Packard tried the price-beater formula again, giving the 120 its even lower-priced companion. Meanwhile, Packard was also building Super 8s and V-12s. The year 1937 turned out to be Packard's most prosperous!

In 1937, a special brochure was published for the new Packard station wagons, available in either the 120 or new Six lines. The 1937 wagon had safety glass in the windshield and front door windows, and transparent sliding curtains in rear doors and quarter windows. The back curtain was removable and could be stored in a pocket in back of the front seat.

Wagon seats were upholstered in "leatherette," an early predecessor of Naugahyde®. Genuine leather was reserved for Packard convertibles and certain other high-priced models, though if a buyer wished to pay the extra cost they could usually special-order leather upholstery.

Some Packard admirers disliked the 120 and Six, since they believed that Packard had desecrated its good name by adding "cheap" cars. But, Packard would surely have gone broke had they refused to include affordable models in their lineup during the price-cutting 1930s.

1930s

1938 Cadillac Fleetwood

With its imposing grille of many crisscrossed pieces, this '38 Cadillac Fleetwood looked majestic—coming at you, or from any angle! The Fleetwood V-8 (75 series) resembled the V-16-powered 90 series, except that the V-16 had long, teardrop-shaped horizontal hood vents.

The V-12 engine (introduced in 1931) was no longer available. The V-16 was now a slightly smaller, 135-degree, L-head replacement of the former O.H.V. version (introduced in 1930).

The V-8, mainstay of the Cadillac/La Salle line, was also of L-head design and would remain so until the 1949 models appeared.

Longest of all stock 1938 American cars was Cadillac's colossal V-16 Presidential Limousine with a 161-inch wheelbase!! The other V-16s and the 75 series shared a 141.3-inch wheelbase.

Quoting from a 1938 advertisement: "Few Cadillac-Fleetwood owners no matter the luxury and ease to which they have always been accustomed—can refrain from comment on the sense of restfulness and relaxation with which they arrive at a long journey's end.

"Every Cadillac-Fleetwood is deliberately built to add many additional miles—of solid comfort—to what is generally accepted as an ordinary day's journey. This is one of the many attributes of a Cadillac-Fleetwood that so endear this motor car to its owner."

The advertisement continued, reminding the reader that in addition to the uncommon comfort, "utter safety and incomparable luxury," there was also the prestige that Cadillac ownership confers.

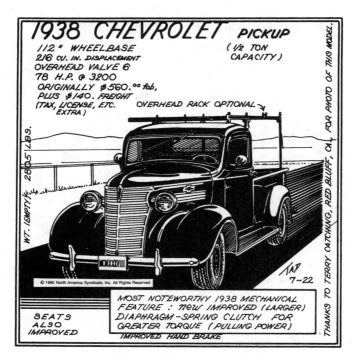

1938 Chevrolet Pickup

O ld Chevy pickups have been popular for years, and they appeal to a growing number of collectors as time goes by.

A bit of history: Following the Depression of 1929-1933, car and truck sales began to pick up again in the mid-1930s; 1936 was a good year, and so was 1937, but then a series of labor strikes and a new business recession hampered the production and sales of 1938 models. As a result, the 1938s have always been scarcer than the '37s and '39s.

In the October 23, 1937 issue of *Automotive Industries* magazine, the new Chevrolet trucks for 1938 were described. In the light delivery field, the Chevrolet passenger car chassis was used for the "coupe pickup" and "sedan delivery" models. Half-ton models, on

the other hand, used the truck chassis and included the pickup, panel-canopy express, and Carryall Suburban (a large, metal-bodied station wagon).

The 3/4-ton and 1-ton capacity Chevrolet trucks included pickup, stake, and panel models, on a 122 1/4-inch wheelbase. The heavy duty ton-and-a-half models included pickup, stake, canopy-express, and panel models on a 131 1/2-inch wheelbase, and high-rack, stake express, and stake models on a 157-inch wheelbase.

A 201-inch-wheelbase Chevrolet school bus chassis was also available in 1938.

One-and-a-half-ton models had heavy-duty steel artillery wheels with no hubcaps and with five semi-circular holes in them, which helped to keep the brakes cool.

1938 Chrysler "Royal 6"

The "Royal" name was first used to designate deluxe Chrysler sedans and coupes in the later 1920s, but Royal did not become a complete model series until 1937, when it was applied to the lower-priced Chrysler sixes.

The 1938 Chrysler products (Plymouth, Dodge, De Soto, Chrysler, and Imperial) were generally similar to the 1937s in profile, but there were numerous minor changes. Headlights now rested on the fenders, instead of being suspended above them. Grilles no longer extended all the way down the front, but rested on decorative and aerodynamic aprons. Windshields, which formerly swung open, were now stationary—with fewer noticeable frames. And, there was no longer a Chrysler Airflow series.

The recession year, 1938, followed a 1933-to-1937 era of gradual recovery from the Great Depression, under Roosevelt's New Deal. Strikes in the automotive industry and elsewhere reflected a growing unrest. Hitler's armies threatened world peace across Europe. The Imperial Japanese military forces were stirring up trouble in the Pacific.

In 1938, car sales fell well below those of 1937. There were 62,408 Chrysler Royal four-door trunk ("touring") sedans produced in '37, but that figure declined to less than 32,000 in '38. The four-door trunk sedan was by far the most popular Royal model, as other body types sold in only three- or four-figure numbers. The scarcest '38 Chrysler Royal was the fastback two-door Brougham (coach) with only eighty-eight built!

1938 Dodge

In the late 1930s, most American auto manufacturers sold two types of two-door and two types of four-door sedans. The models with the biggest trunks sold best, as there was only a few dollars difference in price.

Take the case of the '38 Dodge: Some 73,417 four-door "Touring Sedans" (with extended trunk) were produced, while only 714 of the illustrated "flatback" four-doors were built. That meant that more than 102 times as many "bustle back" as "flat back" four-door sedans left the Dodge factory in the '38 season! Let's look at the other '38 Dodge production figures:

Two-door Touring Sedan (bustle back) 17,282

Two-door Sedan (flat back) 999
Business Coupe (trunk) 15,552
Rumble Seat Coupe 950
Station Wagon (wood body) 375
Convertible Coupe 701
Convertible Sedan 132

Limousine (seven-passenger, with 132-inch wheelbase) 153

Seven passenger sedans were also built on the extended 132-inch wheelbase; some were used as taxis.

As on all Chrysler products for 1938 (including Plymouth, De Soto, and Chrysler), the Dodge had a new wraparound panel below the grille, which joined the front fenders as a single unit.

Reportedly, there were forty-seven improvements for 1938, including a lengthened body and a roomier front compartment. The emergency brake control was changed from a floor-mounted lever to a less-obtrusive "pistol-grip" handle just under the center of the dash. There were new "airplane-type" hydraulic shock absorbers, and new eleven-inch brake drums. Then there were the customary changes in grille, trim, instrument panel design, etc., as well as minor unseen mechanical improvements.

1938 FORD V-8
1-TON TRUCK
$660. f.o.b. FACTORY
new WATERPROOF, WASHABLE UPHOLSTERY in ROOMIER, RESTYLED CAB
(PICKUP 2902 LBS.)

4 WHEELBASES —
112" PICKUP, COMMERCIAL
122" 1-TON CAPACITY
134" OR 157" 1½ TON CAPACITY

FROM 1937 TO 1940, A SMALL 60-HP ECONOMY V8 (136 c.i.D.) WAS ALSO AVAIL. (2.6" x 3.2" BORE + STROKE, 60 HP @ 3500 RPM)

STANDARD "85" V8 HAD 221 c.i.D. and 85 HP @ 3800 RPM

1 TON CAPACITY FORD TRUCKS ARE *new* FOR 1938! 122" W.B.

TAP
1-30

MECHANICAL BRAKES.
1 TON AVAIL. AS PICKUP, PANEL, STAKE OR CHASSIS.

1938 Ford One-Ton Truck

When the 1938 Ford trucks were announced late in 1937, Ford Motor Co. revealed that it had already built more than four million trucks. Many of the older Ford trucks were still in daily use.

The big news for 1938 was the introduction of the new one-ton capacity Ford truck line to bridge the gap between the light-duty half-tons and the 1 1/2-ton heavy-duty models.

The front end was restyled for 1938 with a smart, more-rounded grille, new fenders, and new headlights. Cabs were larger and more comfortable.

One new model for 1938 was a panel delivery van, using either the 112- or 122-inch wheelbase Ford truck chassis. The body, however, was not by Ford but supplied to order by Transportation Engineers Inc. of Detroit. Body side panels and roof were made of Plymetl, and the one-piece floor was made of Phemeloid, supported by a pressed-steel underframe welded into one piece. The delivery van (a rarity) had sliding side doors.

Stake (flatbed) trucks were available in half-ton, one-ton, or 1 1/2-ton lines.

Anxious to sell more units in the recession year of 1938, Ford dealers offered to lend new trucks for an "on-the-job" test. A prospect could borrow, for free, a new Ford truck for a day's work.

The gear ratio of the one-ton model was a normal 4.11 to 1 with the 85 h.p. engine, but a cripplingly slow and low 6.67 to 1 if the little 60 h.p. engine was used.

A CUSTOM CLASSIC !   WISHING YOU A BLESSED CHRISTMAS !

1938 PHANTOM CORSAIR
BODY BY MAURICE SCHWARTZ

MECHANICAL COMPONENTS = CORD
SOUPED-UP 288 cid LYCOMING V-8
(190 HP)   20' OVERALL LENGTH

THIS PILOT MODEL COST
$24,000. TO BUILD !

TAD 12-20

THIS CAR WAS FEATURED IN THE FILM "THE YOUNG IN HEART" (1938.) IN THE MOVIE, THE CAR WAS KNOWN AS "THE FLYING WOMBAT."

A ONE OF A KIND CAR! TO BE PRICED AT $7,500 EACH, OTHERS LIKE IT WERE PLANNED, BUT AFTER THE ACCIDENTAL DEATH OF OWNER-DESIGNER RUST HEINZ (HEIR OF THE HEINZ "57 VARIETIES" FOODS EMPIRE), NO OTHER PHANTOM CORSAIRS WERE PRODUCED.

TOP SPEED = 115 TO 130.

125" WHEELBASE   FRONT WHEEL DRIVE

© 1992 by North America Syndicate, Inc. World rights reserved.

67" WIDE. 5 COULD FIT IN FRONT SEAT !

1938 Phantom Corsair

The Phantom Corsair was designed by 23-year-old Rust Heinz of Pasadena, Calif. He was the scion of the wealthy Heinz foods family, and though he'd studied naval engineering at college, he was keenly interested in creating an all-new automobile. The Phantom Corsair was conceived for his own use, but he had plans to have others built and sold.

Using many Cord mechanical parts, the Phantom Corsair was a radical design. It had a bit of the weird look of the cab-forward Stout "Scarab" of 1935-1936, but of course the Phantom Corsair had a very long hood and a rakishly sloping fastback. Visibility from inside the car was poor. The two-piece V-shaped windshield was too small, as were the windows in the doors—not to mention the split rear window high in the sloping tail.

The diamond-padded interior was of leather and partial broadcloth, and it resembled the handmade interiors of custom-car creations of the '40s and early '50s. Doors were opened by electric push buttons. Safety glass in windows was tinted green.

Under the car, the entire chassis was sheathed in sheet metal, to eliminate air drag and road noise.

In spite of his plans to build more Phantom Corsairs, young Rust Heinz did not live to see his plans materialize. He was killed in an accident (in another car). So the Phantom Corsair remained a one-off production.

In recent years, the Phantom Corsair has been on display at the famed Harrah's Automobile Collection (a.k.a. National Automobile Museum) in Reno, Nev.

1939 De Soto

What did Walt Disney, Myrna Loy, Carole Lombard, Ginger Rogers, Fredric March, Spencer Tracy, and Tyrone Power have in common? Of course, all of them were famous Hollywood celebrities. And, each one owned a 1939 De Soto.

All the celebrity cars were four-door sedans, even though De Soto also produced two-door sedans, business coupes, club coupes, and seven-passenger sedans and limousines in '39.

Speaking of seven-passenger cars, De Soto did a land-office business with their taxicab production from 1936 to 1948 (and even later). A great number of taxis in the United States during those years were De Sotos, including the mammoth Yellow Cab fleet! De Soto taxi production began in earnest late in 1935, but pre-'36 De Soto cabs are extremely rare.

The '39 De Soto was pleasingly restyled, with a large new two-piece V-shaped windshield, new fast-back rear on sedans, all-new front end with flashing three-piece grille sections, and stylized headlights sunken into the fender.

The new "Handy Shift" was up on the steering column, and the "Safety Signal" speedometer had a jeweled indicator light that changed colors from green to amber to red as it moved around the dial. The 1939 De Sotos offered optional overdrive with a total of five forward speeds! With all its features, it was hard to believe that the '39 De Soto was priced from only $870 (for the bottom-of-the-line De Luxe business coupe).

73788

420 '39 LA SALLE SEDANS
(2 DR. AND 4-DR.) HAD OPTIONAL
new "SUNSHINE TURRET-TOP"
SLIDING SUN ROOF!

1/31

1939

COUPE (WITH REAR
OPERA SEATS)
$1240.00
3635 lbs.

La Salle

MFD. BY GENERAL MOTORS'
CADILLAC DIVISION

322 CID V8 (L-HEAD)
125 HP @ 3400 RPM

3.92 TO 1 GEAR RATIO
COIL FRONT SPRINGS
120" WHEELBASE
(TOTAL LENGTH 202½")
7.00 × 16" TIRES

22-GAL. FUEL TANK

1939 La Salle

La Salle was a lower-priced companion to the Cadillac from 1927 to 1940. It used an L-head V-8 engine (except from 1934 to 1936, when it used a straight-eight similar to that used in the Oldsmobile). There were years when La Salle's styling was close to Cadillac's, and other years when it was even better!

"Get a La Salle!" an early '39 ad advised. "For Looks, La Salle sets the style pace again—no doubt about it! Wherever motor cars are discussed, you hear this freely admitted. There's nothing to compare with La Salle's trimness—its low-swung lines—its over-all balance. And La Salle is not only beautiful—it's different! It has individuality. … Yes, when you own a La Salle, you stand completely apart in the world of motordom. If you doubt it—ask your own eyes!"

The ad continued, telling of gorgeous upholstery (Nuvo Cord or Ribbed Broadcloth) in the finest custom manner, attractive hardware and fittings, and 25 percent greater vision with larger glass areas for 1939.

All windows had chrome reveals, and the 1939 La Salle was available either with or without running boards (according to the 1939 sales catalog). The '39 La Salle was identified at either end with "La Salle" script on the narrow center grille, as well as on the rear bumper.

The sliding sunroof (an available option on sedans) was an amazingly advanced feature, seldom offered on any American cars until the late 1960s!

1939 LINCOLN-ZEPHYR V-12   3-WINDOW COUPE (2500 BLT.) $1320. WT. — LBS.3520.

12 CYLINDERS

LINCOLN-ZEPHYR 1ST INTRODUCED FOR 1936 (BY FORD MOTOR CO.,) AS AN AFFORDABLE LUXURY CAR.

1936

UNIT BODY / FRAME

4.44 GEAR RATIO   125"WB

7.00-16

WITH 267.3 CID L-HEAD V-12 ENG. (2 3/4 × 3 3/4 " BR. + ST.) 6.70 TO 1 COMPRESSION 110 HP @ 3900 RPM

14 - 18 MILES PER GALLON AVG. new HYDRAULIC BENDIX BRAKES. CIRCULAR INSTR. DIAL at CENTER of DASH.

2/12

OVERDRIVE OPTIONAL

1939 Lincoln-Zephyr

The Lincoln-Zephyr was the most affordable of all 12-cylinder cars. When it first appeared for 1936, it bridged the wide price gap between the economical Ford V-8 and Ford Motor Company's costly Lincoln "K" series. (The Mercury did not appear until the 1939 model season.)

At first, only sedans were available in the Lincoln-Zephyr line. But, during the following years, coupes, club coupes, convertible coupes, convertible sedans, and even a limousine were added. By 1939, over 60,000 Lincoln-Zephyrs were on the road.

New features for the 1939 Lincoln-Zephyr: hydraulic brakes, a higher and longer hood, new vertical-piece "waterfall" split grille, new front bumper with center "air slots," and new concealed running-boards (hidden by a flared section at lower body sides).

Like Fords, the 1939 Lincoln-Zephyr used transverse leaf springs: one at front, one at rear—mounted crossways, 136 inches apart.

The unit body-and-frame consisted of steel panels welded to steel trusses, and was quite safe and rattle-free. Six passengers rode comfortably "amid-ships" in chair-height seats. A low center of gravity reduced side-sway on curves.

Though two-piece windshields were in vogue in 1939, Lincoln-Zephyr and Willys (Overland) clung to flat, one-piece windshields, which would come back into style in 1953 when other cars gave up split windshields.

The Lincoln-Zephyr name continued until 1942. After the war, a similarly designed 1946 model was simply called the Lincoln (to differentiate it from the exotic Lincoln Continental).

REPLACES 1936 TO 1938 "MACK JR." PICKUP

RARE!

BULLDOG HOOD MASCOT →

3 OR 4 SPEED TRANSMISSION AVAIL.

120½" OR 136½" W.B.

CHASSIS PRICES = $675. OR $810. f.o.b.
ALLENTOWN, PA.

WITH 6 CYL. 210 c.i.d.
CONTINENTAL ENGINE
67 H.P. @ 3000 RPM
1-TON CAPACITY

WT. 3125 lbs. and up
7800 lbs. G.V.W. (7.50 x 17's TIRES)

ONLY 2686
OF THESE BUILT
1938 ~ 1944

1939 MACK
MODEL "ED"

Mack PICKUP

6-21

1930s

1939 Mack "ED" Pickup

Mack is known primarily for building heavy-duty trucks, fire engines, and buses. But, there was a time when Mack also produced pickup trucks.

The slightly larger 1-ton "ED" (illustrated) replaced the "Mack Junior" (1938). The new "ED" was attractively styled and very solid-looking, with a rugged but up-to-date design.

The original Mack Bros. Co. began in Brooklyn, N.Y. in 1902, but moved to Allentown, Pa. in 1905. After a couple of corporate name changes (including International Motor Co., etc.), the firm became known as Mack Trucks, Inc. in 1922. One of the most famous old Mack trucks (introduced 1916) was the "AC" type, which had a sloping, Renault-style hood with a stylized "M" in a front vent hole. The radiator was mounted behind the engine, just ahead of the cab!

During the 1930s, Mack introduced a "limousine" fire engine, in which all the crew could ride comfortably inside, instead of having to cling to outside platforms as on other fire engines.

Mack buses were once common, and in the very early 1930s, they built many for Greyhound, prior to GMC doing so. From 1931 to 1934, and in the 1940s and 1950s, Mack also built city transit (flat-fronted) buses.

In 1966, Mack opened its new factory in Hayward, Calif., which became the center of operations.

In the late 1980s, Mack advertised that their trucks were available with Diesel V-8 engines of up to 500 h.p., known as the "Whispering Giants," with a three-year, 300,000-mile warranty with extension options!

≡1940≡

MERCURY 8

© Field Enterprises, Inc., 1984

WITH 239.4 C.I.D. V-8
(L-HEAD)
3 3/16" × 3 3/4" BORE and STR.
95 H.P. @ 3600 RPM (6.15 COMPR.)
116" W.B.   6.00 × 16" TIRES
2919 lbs.   3.54 GEAR RATIO
OVERDRIVE OPTIONAL

"SEDAN-COUPE"
(5-PASSENGER)

$970.,
f.o.b.,
FACTORY

3-4-84

TOP 1940 SONGS :

SCATTERBRAIN • ALL THE THINGS YOU ARE • CARELESS •
WHEN YOU WISH UPON A STAR • WOODPECKER SONG • IMAGINATION •
I'LL NEVER SMILE AGAIN • ONLY FOREVER • FERRYBOAT SERENADE •
MAYBE • TRADE WINDS • WE THREE • BLUEBERRY HILL •
FOOLS RUSH IN • MAKE-BELIEVE ISLAND • WITH THE WIND AND THE
RAIN IN YOUR HAIR • DARN THAT DREAM • INDIAN SUMMER

CLIP and SAVE

1940 Mercury

"Until the autumn of 1938, it was commonly accepted that you could have a big, powerful, comfortable car—or you could have economical performance. Never *both* in the same automobile. Then came the Mercury 8 [which began as a '39 model]." The 1940 ad we've just quoted claimed that 60,000 new Mercurys were sold in a year and that many drivers were getting 20 miles per gallon fuel economy from the V-8 engine!

The 1940 model was only slightly changed from the '39, with new sealed-beam headlights, altered grille, new blue-and-silver dash, new steering-column gearshift, and new front "butterfly" vent windows, etc.

The Mercury had a four-inch-longer wheelbase than the Ford and was slightly larger and roomier. The illustrated "Sedan-Coupe" was particularly attractive because of the brightwork around the side windows (giving the look of a "hardtop convertible" years ahead of its day, though center body pillars were full-height to the roof). This unique body type was available in 1939 and 1940, but in 1941 a more conventional style of five-passenger coupe (or "club coupe") appeared, without the chrome window frames.

One interesting new feature was the "battery condition indicator." Steering wheels were of modern two-spoke type. Unlike some of the earlier models, the windshields would not open. The swiveling "butterfly"-wing windows gave adequate ventilation, in most opinions.

From their first introduction, 1940 Fords and Mercurys bore a unique charisma and have long been popular among car enthusiasts and collectors.

1940 OLDSMOBILE
CUSTOM 8 CRUISER   3555 lbs.

SOME OF THE GREAT RADIO SHOWS
HEARD IN THE 1940s:

THE SHADOW • JACK BENNY.
THE ROMANCE OF HELEN TRENT.
NATIONAL BARN DANCE •
MARY MARGARET Mc BRIDE •
BOB HOPE • I LOVE A MYSTERY.
THE LONE RANGER
WALTER WINCHELL •
THE HAVEN OF REST.
TRUTH OR CONSEQUENCES •
AMOS 'N' ANDY • GANGBUSTERS.
BURNS AND ALLEN •
EDGAR BERGEN + CHARLIE McCARTHY
FIBBER McGEE + MOLLY •
MOLLÉ MYSTERY THEATER •
BREAKFAST IN HOLLYWOOD.
ABBOTT + COSTELLO •
LUX RADIO THEATRE •
RADIO BIBLE CLASS •
YOUR HIT PARADE •
GRAND OL' OPRY •
RUDY VALLEE •
INNER SANCTUM.
ELLERY QUEEN •
MA PERKINS •
BABY SNOOKS •
RED RYDER •
QUIZ KIDS •
SUPERMAN •
BLONDIE.   RADIO
TOM MIX •   AVAILABLE IN
BREAKFAST   THIS CAR, ALSO
CLUB •   "Hydra Matic" AUTO.TRANS.

110 H.P. @ 3600 RPM

STRAIGHT-8, L.HEAD ENG.
257.1 CID
124" W.B.
7.00 × 15" TIRES
4.3 GEAR RATIO
6-CYL.
ALSO
OFFERED

© News America Syndicate, 1987   2-22

1940 Oldsmobile

"Olds Covers a Lot of Ground—
Even When Standing Still!"
Extra length meant extra luxury
and status back in the 1940s, and we read
from an original advertisement: "seven-
teen and a half feet overall—that's the
length of the magnificent 110 h.p. Oldsmobile Custom 8 Cruiser. And it's
crowned by the longest, roomiest Unisteel
Turret Top body ever built by Fisher—a
body with a front seat five feet wide."

The most interesting feature of the
bigger and better 1940 Oldsmobile was
the four-speed automatic transmission:
GM's famous "Hydra-Matic." Believe
it or not, Hydra-Matic was optional for
only $57 extra on all models of the
1940 Oldsmobile (six or eight). Thus, it
was a popular feature that many
ordered. Gear shifting had discouraged
many beginners from learning to drive,
but an automatic transmission made it
all so much easier! Olds had an

optional semi-automatic transmission
since May 1937, but for 1940 it was
fully automatic!

Sealed-beam headlights were new
on this and most 1940 cars. Bulb and
lens were now one easy-to-change
unit. Sealed-beam lights stayed
brighter longer and provided "50 percent more light."

The "90" Series was an eight and
the "60" and "70" Series were sixes.
Each had L-head engines. The eight
did not have outside running boards,
and the Custom Cruiser four-door
sedan body was big and new, with no
rear quarter windows.

Note that the 1940 Oldsmobile
grille had the name Olds, rather than
Oldsmobile.

Two seldom-seen body types of
1940 Oldsmobile: the wooden-bodied
station wagon and the glamorous-look-
ing four-door convertible Phaeton.

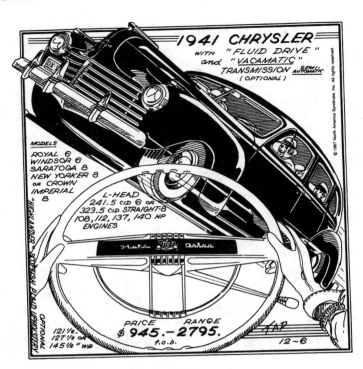

MODELS
ROYAL 6
WINDSOR 6
SARATOGA 8
NEW YORKER 8
OR CROWN
IMPERIAL
8

L-HEAD
241.5 CID 6 OR
323.5 CID STRAIGHT-8
108, 112, 137, 140 HP
ENGINES

"HIGHLANDER" SCOTTISH PLAID UPHOLSTERY OPTIONAL

121½,
127½ OR
145½" WB

PRICE RANGE
$ 945.—2795.
f.o.b.

12~6

1941 Chrysler

In 1941, Chryslers were pleasingly restyled and featured an optional semi-automatic four-speed transmission with "Fluid Drive" liquid clutch coupling. With the steering-column gearshift in "high" position, a smooth but slow start was made in third gear. It shifted to fourth when the foot was lifted above 15 m.p.h., and it dropped back into third for "passing gear" when the accelerator was stepped on hard at up to 53 m.p.h.

In low-range position, upward shift occurred at 8 m.p.h., and down shift occurred when the pedal was pressed hard at up to 27 m.p.h. High gear ratio was 3.54 to 1.

Fluid coupling with three-speed-and-overdrive was available on Chrysler straight-8 models. Chrysler bodies for 1941 were longer and wider. They rode lower on a new shallower but stiffer chassis frame, with box-section side rails welded together and box-type cross members welded to them. Two new body styles for 1941: a six-passenger Club Coupe with full-width rear seat, and a Town Sedan with no rear quarter windows (sedans with seven windows were also available).

There were fifteen body color choices and no less that twenty-three interior trim and upholstery combinations (plaids, stripes, two-tones, mohair, broadcloth, whipcord, or leather), so your 1941 Chrysler could be "tailored to taste!"

Two additional, exciting features available in the top-of the-line 1941 Chrysler Crown Imperial: electronically-operated windows, and All-Weather air control (with refrigerated air, if desired!).

A NOSTALGIC REMINDER OF THE 1940s!

ALUMINUM - ALLOY
1941 GREYHOUND *
"SILVERSIDES" INTER-CITY BUS
BUILT BY YELLOW COACH DIVISION
OF GENERAL MOTORS CORP.
THIS STYLE INTRODUCED APRIL,
1940 AND CONT'D. UNTIL THE END
OF THE 1940s. 591 BLT. IN 1940 ~
1941, and 2000 MORE BLT. FROM
MARCH, 1947 THROUGH 1948.

REPLACED 1936 ~ 1939 STYLE.
* A FEW SOLD TO OTHER BUS LINES AS WELL.

ONE OF THE MOST ATTRACTIVE, MOST COMFORTABLE, AND BEST-LOVED BUSES OF ALL TIME! A FEW ARE STILL RUNNING IN THE 1990s!

GMC/YELLOW BUSES AVAIL. with GASOLINE or DIESEL ENGINES

PDG-3701 IS EARLY 33' TYPE. 3751 IS 35' LONG.

LIMITED

COLOR:
BLUE, WITH BRIGHT METAL SIDES and WHITE TOP (WHITE DOG EMBLEM)

2-27

1941 Greyhound Bus

This is the typical style of the Greyhound "SuperCoach," which was new in the 1940s and in widespread use for up to three decades.

The most distinctive thing about the bus was its pleasing, colorful design, with aluminum alloy "silversides" and its bright blue front end with plenty of brightwork decoration. The origin of the Greyhound Bus Co. can be traced back to the founding of the Northland bus company of Hibbing, Minn. in 1914. There Andrew Anderson and Charles Wenberg purchased a 1913 Hupmobile touring car. Originally, they'd intended to become Hupmobile dealers. But, after failing to sell new cars, they decided to turn their demonstrator car into a jitney bus.

On the first day of their new jitney venture, Anderson and Wenberg netted $7.40 in fares, after expenses. The first route was from Hibbing north to Alice, Minn. and back, with the fare set at fifteen cents one way and twenty-five cents for a round trip.

Wenberg soon tired of the driving and sold his share to C. Eric Wickman. New partners were added to the business as it expanded, and by 1926 a full-sized Fageol bus was being used. In that year, the company's name changed from Northland to Northland Greyhound. By 1929, Greyhound and its partner, Yelloway Lines, were operating coast-to-coast, and the world's largest bus system was well on its way.

Greyhound buses were boxy in shape, with a large engine hood protruding in front (until the streamlined, art deco-style GM Super Coach was introduced in 1936).

1940s

© News Group Chicago, Inc. 1984

HUDSON 1941

"SUPER SIX"
6-CYL.
L-HEAD
ENGINE
212 C.I.D.
3" x 5"
BORE and
STROKE
3040 lbs.
4.11 TO 1
GEAR RATIO
$922. fob
PLUS EXTRAS

TAP
6-24

91,679
HUDSONS BUILT 1941.
HUDSON CARS AVAIL. 1909-1957.

121-INCH WHEELBASE

98 H.P.

LEARN ABOUT COLLECTORS' CARS OF ALL AGES.
CLIP AND SAVE "AUTO ALBUM" EVERY WEEK!

1941 Hudson

"Symphonic Styling" was emphasized in the 1941 Hudson, with attractive new interiors color-keyed (in some cases) to the exterior hues. The most striking example was the two-tone green model with two-tone green upholstery harmonizing inside.

Wheelbases were lengthened, with bodies 5.5 inches longer and two inches lower than in 1940. Deluxe running boards were optional. In 1941, many cars ditched the familiar old running board.

One truly great safety feature of the Hudson, one that many other cars should have adopted, was the mechanical reserve foot brake, which could automatically take over should the hydraulic system ever develop a leak and fail. Patented Auto-Poise Control assured a safe stop on a true course, should a tire blow out.

Independent front wheel coil springing gave a smooth ride on all roads and was included even on Hudson's lowest-priced Six (from $695, delivered in Detroit)! The 1941 Hudsons were economical with gas, too. Even the straight-8, 120-horsepower models could average over 20 miles per gallon!

During the 1941 season, optional overdrive and "Vacumotive Drive" became available. Vacumotive eliminated the necessity of using the clutch pedal in many situations.

Hudson cars, for years and years, used a cork-faced "wet" clutch immersed in oil, and it was claimed to be superior to the ordinary dry plate clutch used in most other cars.

Hudson had a prosperous year in 1941, showing a profit of almost $4 million. Defense contracts (from 1941 to 1945) helped the financial situation, and Hudson prospered until 1953.

Hudson and Nash merged in 1954 to form American Motors Corp.

FABULOUS "FASTBACK"

1941 OLDSMOBILE "DYNAMIC CRUISER" 2 DR. CLUB SEDAN

125" WHEELBASE
AVAILABLE WITH
238.1 CID 6 CYL.
ENGINE (100 HP)
OR 257.1 CID
STRAIGHT-8
(L-HEAD SIDE-
VALVES IN EITHER
ENGINE.)

WEIGHT =
3325 LBS.
(6 CYL. "76")
3420 LBS.
(8 CYL. "78")

$954.
UP

PARK CENTRAL HOTEL

AUTOMATIC HYDRA-MATIC TRANSMISSION OPTIONAL!

4-11

HAPPY EASTER!

1941 Oldsmobile Dynamic Cruiser

General Motors Corp. built some extremely attractive "fastback" sedans, two-door or four-door, in the 1940s. Some of their two-door fastbacks were known as "sedanettes," but the 1941 Oldsmobile version was known officially as the Club Sedan (in the mid-range Dynamic Cruiser series).

Oldsmobile's most outstanding feature in the 1940s was its fully automatic transmission, Hydra-Matic. Though Reo had introduced a "Self Shifter" automatic back in 1933, Oldsmobile was the first to popularize an automatic transmission and offer it on a grand scale. The first Olds automatic was available in 1938, and the better-known Hydra-Matic variation appeared in 1939.

From 1932 through 1948, Oldsmobile offered buyers a choice of either an L-head six or an L-head straight-eight engine. In 1949, the straight-eight would be replaced by a hot new "Rocket" V-8, which would make Olds history!

As for the 1941 Oldsmobiles, there were three basic model series: Special, Dynamic Cruiser, or Custom Cruiser. All were available with either the six or straight-eight. This illustrated Dynamic Cruiser Club Sedan (when offered with six-cylinder engine) was Oldsmobile's most popular '41 model, of which nearly 47,000 were sold. Least popular was the straight-eight Dynamic Cruiser single-seat business coupe, of which a mere fifty-one were recorded!

The Park Central Hotel in the background of this illustration is in Miami and reportedly dates back to 1937. A striking example of pre-war modernistic architecture, the Park Central has escaped the wrecker's ball because it is now a recognized part of Miami's illustrious Art Deco district.

1941 Pontiac

"For several years, Pontiac has shared the fruits of its success with Pontiac buyers by giving them more for their money than they could otherwise possibly expect. This year sees no change in this policy. However, because 1940 was the most successful year Pontiac has ever enjoyed, the 'extras' packed into 1941 Pontiacs far surpass all previous records. For example: All Pontiacs for 1941 are 'Torpedos,' with larger, safer bodies and greater overall length and width for increased passenger comfort. All are vastly more beautiful externally and more richly appointed within. For the first time in automobile history, you may have your choice of a six or an eight in any model ..."

Chassis and engine mounts were so designed that the six was interchangeable with the straight-eight and vice versa! Radiator position was the same regardless of the length of engine, so with the six installed, there was a greater distance between engine and radiator.

The three basic model series for 1941 Pontiacs were Deluxe Torpedo, Streamline Torpedo, or Custom Torpedo. (There was also a "Metropolitan Torpedo" close-coupled six- cylinder sedan.) There were eleven body types on two chassis lengths, including a "woody" wagon.

Running boards were now concealed beneath the flare at the lower body edge. Fresh air for the defroster was drawn in through a tube from behind the grille. Another futuristic touch was the two-spoke steering wheel with horn-actuating keys set into the spokes within easy thumb reach. (Horn buttons and horn rings were more typical of 1941!)

1942 BUICK 8

$990.—2545. PRICE RANGE

IN 5 SERIES: 40-A SPECIAL; 40-B EXTRA SPECIAL; 50 SUPER; 70 ROADMASTER; 90 LIMITED

ALL WITH STRAIGHT-8 VALVE-IN-HEAD 248 OR 320 CID

110 TO 165 HP

118" TO 139" W.B.

'94-'442 '42 BUICK'S BLACKOUT MODELS: BUILT FEB. '42 TO '33-'42 NO-CHROME "BLACKOUT" MODELS: BUILT FEB. '42

USA 1942

CIVILIAN CAR PRODUCTION SUSPENDED BECAUSE OF WARTIME, FROM 2-42 TO 7-45.

1~5

© News America Syndicate, 1986

1940s

1942 Buick

Though loaded with improvements and new features, the 1942 cars were not available for long. Introduced in the autumn of 1941, they arrived just in time for America's full involvement in World War II.

In 1941 the automobile industry was already deeply involved in military production. In an October 11, 1941 ad for the new '42 Buick, we read:

"It was no time to duck or dodge the facts. So we didn't try.

"Instead we said—these being the materials critical in the defense program—we'll do our planning for 1942 with that foremost in mind.

"Not merely for an 'acceptable' car—certainly not for any 'ersatz' number. We bowed our necks against that.

"No, we had to have a real representative Buick. One we could be

proud of. One able enough, active enough, durable enough to serve and delight its owners till that unscheduled time when annual new models are the rule again."

Buicks for '42 were restyled with broad new grilles, "fadeaway" front fenders, wraparound bumpers, and many improvements (such as a step-on parking brake).

Certain materials needed for defense production, such as zinc, aluminum, and nickel, were reduced in the new cars and replaced by more plastics, more cast iron, and metal stampings.

On the "50" and "70" series convertible coupes and two-door sedanets, fadeaway front fenders reached not only into the front doors, but all the way through them to taper back and meet the rear fenders!

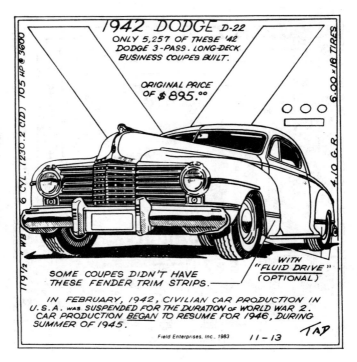

1942 DODGE D-22

ONLY 5,257 OF THESE '42 DODGE 3-PASS. LONG-DECK BUSINESS COUPES BUILT.

ORIGINAL PRICE OF $895.⁰⁰

6 CYL. (230.2 CID) 105 HP @ 3600

119½" WB

6.00×16 TIRES

4.10 G.R.

SOME COUPES DIDN'T HAVE THESE FENDER TRIM STRIPS.

WITH "FLUID DRIVE" (OPTIONAL)

IN FEBRUARY, 1942, CIVILIAN CAR PRODUCTION IN U.S.A. was SUSPENDED FOR THE DURATION of WORLD WAR 2. CAR PRODUCTION BEGAN TO RESUME FOR 1946, DURING SUMMER OF 1945.

Field Enterprises, Inc., 1983   11–13   TAD

1942 Dodge

If you enjoy Bill Cosby's entertaining monologues on records, you may have heard him speak of the "old '42 Dodge" he used to have. Bill Cosby's may have been a well-worn specimen by the time he bought it, but the 1942 Dodge, and all Chrysler products of the 1940s, were phenomenally reliable and durable! It just seemed that you couldn't stop these rugged Chrysler products of the '40s!

From 1941 through 1948, Chrysler, De Soto, and Dodge built some unusual-looking three-window coupes with uncommonly long, cavernous trunks! Since they were three-passenger models, they weren't much in demand later as used cars. But, their unusual profile makes them distinctive and highly "collectible" today.

The "Fluid Drive" semi-automatic transmission was easy to operate but sluggish in pick-up. Still, it was as reliable as most *manual* transmissions. Though it was featured on most Chryslers, Dodges, and De Sotos in the 1940s, Plymouth did not use it. Nor did Plymouth build a three-window coupe in those years.

The '42 Dodge engine had a new piston displacement of 230.2, with h.p. increased from 91 to 105. Gear ratio was changed from 4.30 to 4.10, resulting in more speed and less engine effort on the highway. There were two series: the De Luxe and the higher-priced Custom. The business coupe was available only in the De Luxe series.

Some of the '42 cars were "blackout" models, with a minimum of chrome trim, and painted metal strips where brightwork would normally be. These are now desirable because of their historical significance.

1942 HUDSON "SUPER 6"

6 CYL. L-HEAD 212 CID ENG.
3" x 5" BORE and STROKE
6.5 TO I COMPRESSION
102 HP @ 4000 RPM
(CIVILIAN CAR PRODUCTION CEASED
FEB. 1942, BECAUSE OF WORLD WAR 2,
AND RESUMED JULY 1945, FOR '46.)

PRESENTLY VALUED AT $350. TO $7700.
(RANGING FROM POOR TO PERFECT COND.)

←121" WHEELBASE→

3-PASS. COUPE
$1036. 2925 LBS.
40,661 1942 HUDSONS BLT. (6 and 8 CYL.)

© 1991 North America Syndicate, Inc. All Rights Reserved

1940s

1942 Hudson Super Six

In calendar year 1942, Hudson shipped only 5,396 of its more than 40,000 1942 models. The rest were built during the final months of 1941. In 1942, some sixty-seven Hudson commercial vehicles were also produced—mainly Hudson pickups, styled in front like the Hudson cars. February 5, 1942 was the date that civilian car production was suspended for the duration of World War II.

In 1942, Hudson offered the Six, Business Six, De Luxe Six, Super Six, Commodore Six, Commodore Eight, and Custom Commodore Eight. These models were "marked by longer, lower and more flowing body lines" (as shown on the illustrated Super Six coupe). "New front end and fender styling are stressed. Running boards are concealed." The additional horizontal chrome strip linking body and fenders on the Super Six made the car look longer.

Hudson didn't do much advertising of its '42 models, though in the September 22, 1941 issue of *Life* magazine there was a full-page ad, in black and white, showing various '42 Hudson features. One Hudson advantage was the optional "Drive-Master" semiautomatic transmission, which eliminated most gear shifting and clutch pushing.

Another option was the "Hudson Sleeper Kit," which allowed the rear seat to fold down into a bed. Hudson also offered "Double-Safe Brakes." On the Commodore Series featured in the *Life* magazine ad, there was a more elaborate decorative piece in the center of the grille and no chrome strip running down from the hood ornament (as found on the illustrated Super Six).

ORIGINAL PRICE
$1900.
1942 LINCOLN ZEPHYR V-12
12 CYLINDERS, WITH new 305 cid
PUSH-BUTTON DOOR-OPENERS INSIDE and OUT!
TAP 8-19
News America Syndicate © News Group Chicago, Inc., 1984
130 H.P. @ 3800 RPM
2 15/16" x 3 3/4" BORE and STR.
125" W.B.   3920 LBS.
OPTIONAL LIQUAMATIC TRANSMISSION

1942 Lincoln-Zephyr V-12

The most immediately-noticed mechanical feature on the new Lincoln Zephyr for 1942 was the unique method of opening the doors. Conventional door handles, inside and out, were totally eliminated in favor of new push-buttons! No other car had push-button doors, and Lincoln continued them on the 1946 models when production was resumed after World War II. However, the push-buttons could become troublesome, and after early 1947, only the Lincoln Continentals retained them.

The Lincoln Zephyr was powered by an L-head 12-cylinder engine, the only American-built V-12 since Cadillac and Packard had given up their versions. (Lincoln continued the V-12 to 1948.) One might suspect a 12-cylinder engine of gobbling twice as much gas as a six, but that wasn't so. Driven carefully, the V-12 could often squeeze 12 to 18 miles from a gallon!

The standard rear axle ratio was 4.22-to-1, but a 4.44 ratio was used when optional Liquamatic transmission and overdrive were combined. This semi-automatic arrangement provided *six* forward speeds, with the following overall gear ratios:

1—Low 10.32-to-1
2—Low overdrive 7.24-to-1
3—Second 8.08-to-1
4—Second overdrive 5.66-to-1
5—High 4.44-to-1
6—High overdrive 3.11-to-1

(These figures are from *Motor* magazine, October 1941, p. 236.)

The Liquamatic-equipped '42 Lincoln could be driven most of the time with the control lever set to high-gear position, unless low or reverse gears were needed. Speeds were changed by pressing or releasing the accelerator pedal at certain intervals at certain speeds.

1942 Studebaker "Champion"

For a few years, Studebaker's low-priced series was the Dictator model (introduced 1928). However, with the growing unpopularity of tyranny and dictators in the 1930s (the likes of Hitler and Mussolini), Studebaker decided, after 1937, to drop the Dictator name. In 1938, the 116 1/2-inch-wheelbase Commander 6 was made the low-price leader for Studebaker at $875 and up, f.o.b., factory. The Commander 6 continued in 1939, even after the budget-priced Champion was ready at $660 and up.

The Champion was a hit! In 1940, over 66,000 Champions were sold, and almost 85,000 were sold in 1941. The figure decreased to 29,678 Champions in 1942, but only because civilian car production was curtailed early in February 1942, due to the war. The year 1942 was the final one for the straight-8 President series. In 1946, when civilian cars returned, only the Skyway Champion 6 was available. Then, in the spring of 1946, Studebaker surprised the world by unveiling its totally restyled 1947 models in the Champion and Commander series, with excitingly futuristic styling from end to end!

The President name was laid to rest until 1955, when it reappeared briefly on a new top-of-the-line President V-8 series. Wisely, when Studebaker introduced the Champion in 1939, they included the Studebaker nameplate and referred to Champion only as a model series. Earlier, Studebaker had experienced disappointing results with two low-priced cars they did not call Studebakers: One was the Erskine (1927-1930), and the other was the Rockne (1932-1933).

1940s

1940s

3 ~ 22

1942 WILLYS 442 TYPE
"AMERICAR" COUPE
WITH L-HEAD, 134.2 C.I.D.
4-CYL. ENGINE (3 1/8" x 4 3/8"
6.48 COMPR. BORE and STR.)
63 H.P. @ 3900 RPM
2-PASS. CPE, 4 DR. SEDAN OR
STATION WAGON AVAIL.
(ALSO MILITARY "JEEPS.")

ADVERTISED AS "THE PEOPLE'S CAR."

TAD

22-35 M.P.G. GAS ECONOMY!

DURING WORLD WAR 2 GAS RATIONING, USED 4-CYL. WILLYS CARS (1933~1942) WERE MUCH IN DEMAND!

104" W.B.

5.50 x 16

AVAILABLE IN 3 SERIES:
SPEEDWAY = $ 737. UP
DELUXE 812. "
PLAINSMAN 863. "
(OVERDRIVE STANDARD ON PLAINSMAN, OPTIONAL ON OTHER SERIES.

4.44 GEAR RATIO

1942 Willys "Americar"

Joseph W. Frazer, later a partner in the Kaiser-Frazer industrial empire, was president of Willys-Overland Inc. in the early 1940s. In 1931, Willys had scored a fabulous success with its new Army Jeep. It was to be expected that the popular Jeep would be mentioned even in civilian Willys-Overland advertising.

"Those amazing Army 'Jeeps' built by Willys-Overland prove our leadership in engineering," read one advertisement that announced the 1942 "Americar" civilian models; and the simple, rugged L-head four-cylinder Willys "GO-Devil" engine was used in the Jeeps as well as in the civilian cars.

Pearl Harbor had not yet been attacked when Frazer wrote, "Whether the European War collapses tonight or drags on for years, this is my prediction: Today's over-size, over-weight, over-powered and over-dressed cars are on the way out now. They're too expensive to buy and to run for the great mass of the people."

However, Mr. Frazer's predictions did not come true as soon as he'd expected, because after the war ended in 1945, cars did NOT shrink! In fact, during the 1950s and 1960s, American cars grew bigger and more powerful by leaps and bounds. The Kaiser/Frazer cars Mr. Frazer himself was manufacturing after the war, with Henry J. Kaiser, were no small economy jobs themselves! It wasn't until the gas crunch of 1973-1974 put real fear into the heart of the American motorist that small cars began to come into their own.

1944 Plymouth

S ince civilian cars were not built in the United States between February 1942 and July 1945, was there such a thing as a 1944 Plymouth?

The answer is yes, if you consider an unsold, unused 1942 car as still new if it wasn't released for sale until 1944. A number of unsold 1942 cars—scarce as they were—were held in storage during the war years and released only to individuals in "essential" work who had managed to secure a "priority" to get a new car. A doctor, for example, or a specialized defense worker might have been eligible for a new-car priority in 1943, 1944, or 1945.

Wartime models as a rule were known as "blackout models." Bumpers were liable to be painted black or gray, and a few wartime cars had no bumpers at all, but merely planks of wood bolted on as a cheap substitute. A few patriotic individuals donated their car's bumpers to scrap drives and substituted wood planks by choice.

On the few station wagons released for sale during the war, the body wood might not be varnished in contrasting natural wood tones, but rather painted over for ease of maintenance.

An interesting feature on all Plymouth P-14 cars released during 1942-45 was the "safety-signal" speedometer. Its numerals and pointer changed colors at night as speed increased—from green to amber to orange and to red.

"A SWEDISH BEAUTY" — SLOGANS — "WHEN BEAUTY COMES TO TOWN"

1944 VOLVO "PV 444" (new)

BECAUSE OF WARTIME STEEL SHORTAGE, FULL PRODUCTION WAS NOT UNDER WAY UNTIL 1947. THE PV 444 (544 AFTER '58) WAS THE FIRST VOLVO SERIES EXPORTED OUTSIDE THE SCANDINAVIAN COUNTRIES. VARIATIONS OF THIS SERIES CONT'D. TO 1965.

PRICE = $1300. (EQUIVALENT)

40 HP

4 CYLS.

(440,000 OF THIS SERIES BUILT, BY 1965.)

GENERAL STYLING OF THIS CAR MAY REMIND YOU OF A FORD TUDOR SEDAN OF THE 1942~1948 ERA! (ESPECIALLY IN PROFILE)

3~7

HELPFUL DETAILS THANKS TO AB VOLVO, GÖTEBORG, SWEDEN

©1993 North America Syndicate, Inc. World rights reserved.

1944 Volvo

Some European nations had shut down peacetime assembly lines as early as 1939 or 1940! Sweden, then, was a rare exception when a new car was introduced in 1944.

Volvo's "PV-444" designation on the new model stood for "personvagn, 4-cylinder, 1944 model." It was displayed at a special exposition in Stockholm in September 1944. Some mechanical parts were Volvo-built, but others were American or British. There was a strong American influence in the design. From the side, the new model resembled a scaled-down Ford.

Steel shortages and a 1945 strike in Sweden prevented the PV-444 from going into mass production until the 1947 season, but once the assembly lines began rolling at full steam, the PV-444 was a great success! Volvo had been building cars for Sweden's domestic trade since 1927, but the PV-444 went worldwide and was the first Volvo to become available in the United States, in 1956. (The '56 was rated at 70 h.p., had 5.90 x 15-inch tires and a 102 1/2-inch wheelbase. Its 1956 price in the United States, at port of entry, was $2,170.)

Originally, in 1944, the planned price of this Volvo in equivalent dollars was $1,300. But, postwar difficulties and inflation pushed the cost up to $2,160 in 1947. Yet, Volvo honored 2,300 standing orders at the old $1,300 price, a most generous concession not often seen in the business world. Amazingly, the 1956 U.S. price of the Volvo was only $10 above its 1947 equivalent in Sweden!

THEY HELPED WIN THE VICTORY!

MORE THAN 360,000 BLT. DURING WW II.

6.00 × 16" TIRES

JEEP VEHICLES BUILT BY:
AMERICAN BANTAM = 1940-1941
WILLYS-OVERLAND = 1941-1962
FORD (ONLY DURING WW II EMERGENCY) SAME DESIGN AS WILLYS
KAISER JEEP = 1963-1969
AMERICAN MOTORS 1970-1986 CHRYSLER-1987 ON

1944 WILLYS
MILITARY JEEP 80"
4-WHEEL-DRIVE W.B.

TAD 2-21

TOP SPEED = 65
20 M.P.G.

2453-lb.
ROAD WEIGHT
(w. GAS, WATER)
132¼" LONG, 62" WIDE
69¾" HIGH w. TOP UP

HELPFUL DETAILS
THANKS TO
BILL KISH, N.Y.C.

1940s

1944 Willys Jeep

The sight of this Willys Military Jeep should stir a wave of nostalgia in anyone who has served in the U.S. Army during World War II or since then!

The Jeep came none too soon! It was first seen in 1940-1941, and the initial developer was the tiny American Bantam Co. of Butler, Pa. However, American Bantam was too small and too weak a company to meet the oncoming big demand for Army Jeeps, so government contracts were awarded to Willys-Overland. Even Ford Motor Co. produced a number of Jeeps for the government during the most difficult days of World War II, though the Ford Jeeps were duplicates of the Willys-Overland model so that all parts were interchangeable. Only the name was different. After the war ended in 1945, Willys-Overland realized it had a great winner and expanded the line of Jeep vehicles. In 1946, came the Jeep all-metal station wagon, followed (1948) by the sporty "Jeepster" convertible. Other new products included Jeep pickup trucks and other commercial varieties.

Kaiser and Willys merged in 1954, but the Willys name continued on all Jeep vehicles until the introduction of the Kaiser Jeep in the 1963 model series. In the 1970s and earlier 1980s, American Motors Corp. produced Jeep. After that, Chrysler purchased the venerable line from AMC/Renault.

The long-lasting popularity of Jeeps has been phenomenal! Resale value of military Jeep and CJ types has been high for many years.

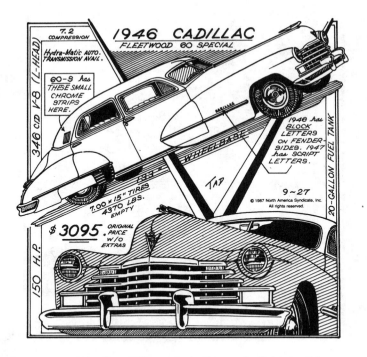

1946 Cadillac 60 Special (60-S)

The 60 Special Fleetwood series of Cadillac came in only one body style during most of its days: as a four-door sedan (illustrated). As many auto buffs may know, the 60 Special was introduced in 1938 by Cadillac and received rave notices for its styling because of its crisp, squared-off "continental" look.

For years afterward, the 60 Special was Cadillac's "sporty" sedan, and examples of the later 1940s had characteristic diagonal bands of small, parallel chrome strips on either rear quarter panel (as shown in the illustration).

Fleetwood bodies (as on the 60-S) were considered more exclusive than the standard GM Fisher body—even though Fleetwood was also a GM property.

Only 5,700 60-S sedans were produced in 1946, because of postwar shortages. The number increased to 8,500 in 1947. By 1949, new cars were much easier to get, and more than 11,000 60 Specials were sold, with 13,755 sold in 1950 and 18,631 sold in 1951.

Cadillac's greatest seller during these years, however, was the less-costly Series 62 four-door sedan (14,900 were sold in 1946, and by 1951 more than 55,000 of the Series 62 sedans left the factory!).

How good were the '46 Cadillacs? According to one 1946 advertisement, "because our V-type engine and Hydra-Matic drive were used throughout the war in the army's light tanks—enabling us to improve them even more than would have been possible in four years of peace—Cadillac's leadership is the greatest in history. There is literally nothing with which to compare this great new car."

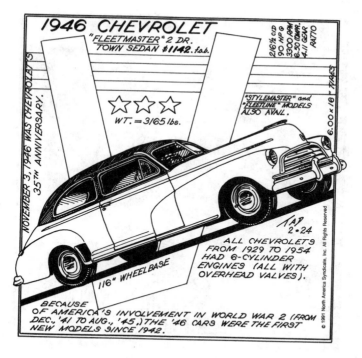

1946 CHEVROLET
"FLEETMASTER" 2 DR.
TOWN SEDAN $1142. f.o.b.

2 6½ C.I.D
90 H.P. @
3300 R.P.M.
6.50 COMP.
4.11 GEAR
RATIO

★ ★ ★
WT. = 3165 lbs.

"STYLEMASTER" and
"FLEETLINE" MODELS
ALSO AVAIL.

NOVEMBER 3, 1946 WAS CHEVROLET'S
35TH ANNIVERSARY.

6.00 x 16" TIRES

1AD
2·24

ALL CHEVROLET'S
FROM 1929 TO 1954
HAD 6-CYLINDER
ENGINES (ALL WITH
OVERHEAD VALVES).

116" WHEELBASE

BECAUSE
OF AMERICA'S INVOLVEMENT IN WORLD WAR 2 (FROM
DEC., '41 TO AUG., '45,) THE '46 CARS WERE THE FIRST
NEW MODELS SINCE 1942.

1946 Chevrolet

As peace was restored to the Pacific in August 1945, civilian car production was resuming. The new '46 models were hard to get, however. It wasn't until 1948 that the new-car supply was once again "plentiful."

Most 1946 cars continued with their 1942 profiles—but with new grilles, trim, instrument panels, and upholstery choices. Although prices were up, cars were still a great bargain, with many priced at less than $2,000 out the dealer's door.

Two-tone paint jobs were popular on GM cars. One popular '46 Chevy color scheme was brown above and cream on the lower body. In '47, dark green over cream was also available and became a fad for a few months. There were three available two-tone combinations on '46 Chevrolets, plus three solid colors (as of late '45, as the new season was getting under way).

A batch of lower-priced, Stylemaster, four-door sport sedans were first off the postwar Chevy production lines. Other models and body types followed, as additional facilities and materials became available.

The 1946 grille was new, with all horizontal blades. Bumpers were improved for fuller coverage. The '46 Chevrolet had a vacuum-powered gearshift, and the column-mounted shift lever could not be budged unless the engine was running. Characteristic of Chevrolets in the 1940s, this feature was a nuisance if the battery was dead and one was trying to push-start the car.

But, Chevrolets of the 1940s were reliable and very well built. Never were new cars received with such enthusiasm as when the postwar 1946 models appeared!

1946 DE SOTO "S 11"
"CUSTOM"
SUBURBAN
$2175.
WT.=4000 lbs.
DE SOTOS BLT. BY THE CHRYSLER CORP. (1929 TO 1961 MODELS)
SLOGAN= "8 OUT OF 10 SAY 'DE SOTO AGAIN'"
1946 TO EARLY 1949 CHRYSLER CORP. CARS SO GOOD THEY CONTINUED VIRTUALLY UNCHANGED FOR OVER 3 YEARS!
121½" WHEELBASE (139½" ON 7-PASSENGER TYPES)
TAD
6·20
7500 SUBURBANS BUILT 1946-1948
"WATERFALL" GRILLE
6 CYL. L-HEAD ENGINE
236.6 CU. IN. DISPL.
109 H.P.
FRONT DETAILS
WITH SEMI-AUTOMATIC GYROL FLUID DRIVE and TIP TOE SHIFT
©1993 North America Syndicate, Inc. World rights reserved.

1946 De Soto Suburban

Millions of Americans fondly remember the big De Soto sedans of the 1940s. Thousands of them were used in metropolitan taxi service. The seven-passenger De Soto sedan was used as a taxi more than any other kind of car throughout the 1940s.

A variation on the De Soto sedan was this "Suburban," sometimes thought of as a station wagon because it had a roof rack—as well as a back seat that could be folded or removed in order to provide a long cargo area, accessible from the trunk or side doors.

Notice the white "beauty rings" on the wheels of this car. Mounted between the hubcap and tire, the early postwar beauty ring was a clever idea from Chrysler Corp., which gave the look of a white sidewall tire without the added expense.

Fluid Drive was another feature of this De Soto. Though there was a Safety Clutch pedal, it was possible to drive the car without shifting gears in forward speeds. The gears automatically changed as the car reached certain speeds, accelerating or decelerating.

Weighing exactly two tons, the Suburban was big and heavy. Gas mileage averaged 14 to 17 miles per gallon, and top speed was in the neighborhood of 95 m.p.h.

Before 1952, all De Sotos were six-cylinder cars, with the exception of the rare De Soto straight-eights available in addition to the six in 1930 and 1931. In 1952, De Soto introduced its new "Fire Dome" V-8 engine (with overhead valves), and as the 1950s progressed, V-8s seemed to take over.

1946 Dodge 1-Ton Pickup

This particular style of Dodge truck was introduced in 1939, with its attractive two-piece V-shaped windshield and upper and lower split horizontal grilles. However, the 1939 model bore the Dodge name in small block letters above each side of the upper grille. From 1940 on, the name appeared on the side of the hood and on the heavy chrome piece running down the middle in front. There were slight modifications in grille, trim, etc. between 1939 and 1947. For 1948, Dodge trucks would be totally restyled—a year ahead of the Dodge cars and the other Chrysler products.

For 1946, four sizes of Dodge "Job-Rated" pick-ups were obtainable: the 1/2-ton or 3/4 ton models were 95-h.p. engines, or the illustrated 1-ton pickup with a 105-h.p. engine and with a choice of 120- or 133-inch wheelbases.

In this illustration, similar to an original 1946 Dodge truck ad, a route manager is delivering bundles of newspapers to boys to sell downtown. In the 1940s, most cities and towns had young newsboys who sold papers on busy corners. They usually yelled out the headlines to get attention. You see this now in old movies of the 1930s and 1940s, but seldom in real life. Boys (and girls) still deliver newspapers on bicycle or foot routes, though in many cities adult-operated motorized routes have gradually replaced the young carriers.

1946 (early) Ford Tudor Sedan

Americans took good care of their cars during World War II. Nearly everyone had to make do with used cars. The oldest cars commonly seen in the 1940s were 1929 models, and the majority of cars seen then were 1936 to 1942s.

Ford and Hudson were two of the first to reconvert to civilian production in July 1945. However, the war did not officially end until early September, and new '46 models were very hard to get.

After the war, Ford offered sixes and V-8s in De Luxe and Super De Luxe models, with a variety of body types: coupes, club coupes, two-door (Tudor) sedans, four-door (Fordor) sedans, wood-bodied station wagons, wood-bodied "Sportsman" convertibles, and steel-bodied convertibles.

Ford, in 1946, retained its old-fashioned transverse (crosswise) leaf springs, one set at front and one at rear. But, thinner leaves (and more of them) were now used for a smoother ride. New 1946 brakes were larger and required less pedal pressure. New "Silvaloy" bearings were advertised to last "up to three times longer."

Ford interiors boasted "colorful new fabrics, rich plastics, simulated leather trim."

One of the earliest postwar Ford ads I have found is a two-page color spread from *Life* magazine of October 8, 1945, which assured readers, "Today, these cars are rolling off the production lines in limited numbers. Next month and the month after there'll be more new Ford cars available ... and still more in 1946. So hold to your plan—don't settle for less. There is a Ford in your future."

1946 Lincoln V-12

T his handsome car was the moderate-priced companion to Lincoln's classic Continental—at about half the cost.

One of the postwar novelties of the Lincoln was the push-button door control, introduced in 1942. The buttons worked OK most of the time, but they weren't foolproof, and were replaced by handles before long.

Lincoln improvements for 1946 and the postwar era included: wider bumpers with larger bumper guards. The grille was new, with crisscross pieces in both top and lower sections and built-in fog lights. There were eight color choices. Upholstery patterns were new, and there was also a choice of colors for the instrument panel.

Most amazing feature: power-operated electric side windows. Most cars offered this—only as an option—ten years later. In the mid-'40s, power windows were absolutely futuristic.

Strangely, not much publicity was given to this advanced idea in 1946. The power windows were a standard feature on 1946 Lincolns, but in the near future they would become an "extra" and in most cases would be excluded. Gadgetry could be troublesome at times.

Christmas of 1946 was a happy time. U.S. servicemen were back from the Pacific and Atlantic theaters of war after many months of mustering-out. Many families treated themselves to a brand-new postwar car … IF they had been on a dealer's waiting list, or IF they were willing to pay an inflated black-market price for a readily available car.

Plastic, with its sweet, agreeable aroma, was used, increasingly, on the dash and interior of many automobiles. A new era had arrived!

THE WOODEN NASH (RARE!)

1946 Nash MODEL 4664 "AMBASSADOR" SUBURBAN with WOOD-PANELED BODY!

EVER SEEN ONE OF THESE UNIQUE "WOODY" SEDANS?

121" W.B. 6 CYL., 234.8 c.i.d. HORSEPOWER @ 3400 RPM VALVE-IN-HEAD ENGINE 6.8 COMPRESSION WT. 3470 lbs. $1804.°° f.o.b. MFD. BY NASH MOTORS, KENOSHA, WIS. AND DETROIT (1917-1957)

6.50 × 15

© Field Enterprises, Inc. 1983

1946 Nash Suburban

I n the 1940s, there were two basic Nash series: the Ambassador with overhead valves, and the lower-priced 600 with a smaller, L-head engine.

As World War II ended, there was a severe shortage of steel. This hampered auto manufacturers, but one partial solution was to include wood in portions of some car bodies, thus stretching the steel supply a bit. Wood looked "sporty" if waxed and varnished often.

Many manufacturers had already been building "woody" station wagons, and shortly before the war had begun, Chrysler had introduced a most-attractive wood-paneled Town & Country sedan.

When it was time to begin the post-war 1946 models, more woody cars were available than ever before! Chrysler had joined its Town & Coun-try sedan with a glamorous new Town & Country wood-bodied convertible. And, Ford Motor Co. not only offered its usual line of Ford and Mercury woody wagons, but also the new wood-paneled Ford and Mercury Sportsman's convertibles. (All-steel convertibles were also available from Chrysler, Ford, and Mercury.)

Studebaker planned a luxury wood-paneled station wagon for their all-new 47 series launched in May of 1946, but only a pilot model of the wagon was completed.

Of all the early postwar woody cars actually in production, the '46 Nash Suburban is one of the most rare. The only scarcer postwar woody is the steel-roofed, hardtop convertible version of Chrysler's Town & Country, of which less than eight were built and sold!

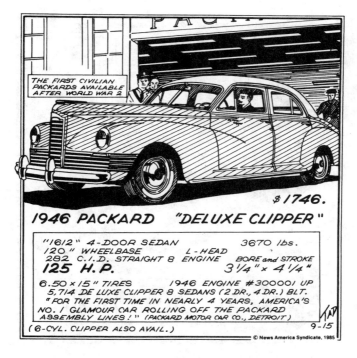

THE FIRST CIVILIAN
PACKARDS AVAILABLE
AFTER WORLD WAR 2

$1746.

1946 PACKARD   "DELUXE CLIPPER"

"1612" 4-DOOR SEDAN   3670 lbs.
120" WHEELBASE   L-HEAD
282 C.I.D. STRAIGHT 8 ENGINE   BORE and STROKE
125 H.P.   3 1/4" x 4 1/4"
6.50 x 15" TIRES   1946 ENGINE #300001 UP
5,714 DE LUXE CLIPPER 8 SEDANS (2 DR., 4 DR.) BLT.
"FOR THE FIRST TIME IN NEARLY 4 YEARS, AMERICA'S
NO. 1 GLAMOUR CAR ROLLING OFF THE PACKARD
ASSEMBLY LINES!" (PACKARD MOTOR CAR CO., DETROIT)
(6-CYL. CLIPPER ALSO AVAIL.)   9-15

© News America Syndicate, 1985

1946 Packard Deluxe Clipper

Admirers of the streamlined '41-'42 Packard Clipper were glad to see it return for '46, though many others regretted the complete disappearance of Packard's pre-war 160 and 180 series. After the war, luxury car buyers swung more and more to Cadillac, as they believed Packard had cheapened its image of exclusiveness by favoring affordable middle-class models. But, in spite of such complaints, Packard sold over 30,000 cars in 1946 and could have sold more if not for various materials shortages.

For 1946, the seventy-eight Packard improvements included restyled grille with heavier center pieces, new interiors, exterior detail changes, and minor mechanical betterments, according to *Motor* magazine, November 1945. The hood ornament was restyled, and top molding along the hood was removed for a smoother appearance. Bumpers were strengthened, as a bumper-type jack was now included with each car.

Packard offered opportunities for new dealers after the war, and reported in its advertising of a case where two men began negotiations with Packard on November 23, 1945, and were in business as new Packard dealers (in Coldwater, Mich.) on January 21, 1946! These partners were given a quota of twenty-eight new Packards, displayed their first car on February 1, and began taking advance orders on a grand scale (for a town of less than 8,000 population).

In the summer of '46, Packard advertising promised that the 1947 models would be unchanged, as that would eliminate retooling and make it possible to fill more orders sooner!

1940s

HELPFUL INFORMATION THANKS TO FRED K. FOX, DELHI, CALIF.

A RARE TRUCK!

© News America Syndicate, 1985

6.50 x 16" TIRES

2710 lbs. (EMPTY)

170 CU. IN. DISPL.
3" x 4" BORE and STROKE
L-HEAD 6-CYLINDER ENGINE

MODEL
M-5

4.82 GEAR RATIO

Coupe Express
HALF-TON
PICK-UP

1946
STUDEBAKER

$968.⁰⁰ f.o.b., FACTORY, SOUTH BEND, IND.
80 H.P. @ 4000 RPM 6.5 COMPRESSION

113" WHEELBASE

TAD 7-21

1946 Studebaker Pickup

How many remember that in the 1940s and 1950s, Studebaker built a good-selling line of pickups and other trucks! Studebaker trucks were available even earlier, but starting in 1937 they introduced the "Coupe Express," which was conceived then as a car-pickup (like the more recent Chevy El Camino and Ford Ranchero). In 1941, however, the so-called Coupe Express had become more like other pickups. The 1941 model looked very much like the illustrated '46, except that 1941 models were advertised with chrome on all grille pieces, and the 1941 had chrome belt-trim and car-like chromed hubcaps.

During World War II, Studebaker built various military trucks and vehicles, including the famous amphibious "Weasel."

Just after the war, many of the new Studebaker trucks had little chrome or ornamentation. The next major styling change in Studebaker trucks came in June 1948 on the new 1949 "R" series (a type continued through 1953). Other models followed, including the Transtar. In 1960, the "Champ" pickup appeared, styled after Studebaker's Lark compact cars. Studebaker trucks continued to 1964. In 1965 and 1966, following a shutdown at the South Bend plant, Studebaker's final cars were assembled at their Canadian plant.

The spirit of Studebaker lives, though, because the Avanti II—a continuation and refinement of Studebaker's sports GT of the early/mid-'60s—has been produced independently by a group that includes many former Studebaker employees.

A FLYING CAR!

1947 AIRPHIBIAN

(INTRODUCED 1946)
BLT. AT DANBURY, CT.,
BY CONTINENTAL, INC.
FOUNDED BY
ROBERT EDISON FULTON, JR.

AIR SPEED = 120 M.P.H.

ALUMINUM BODY

65 H.P.

6 CYLINDERS

CONVERTIBLE TOP

News America Syndicate
© News Group Chicago, Inc., 1985

1-13
TAP

PROPOSED PRICE = $6000.

READY FOR THE ROAD, WITH WINGS, PROP.,
REAR FUSELAGE and TAIL DETACHED.

55 M.P.H.
HIGHWAY SPEED

1947 Airphibian

In '46 and '47, Continental, Inc. (of Danbury, Conn.) attempted to manufacture a car/airplane aptly named the "Airphibian." If you'll pardon the pun, only "pilot" models were made of this flying car—even though it was hoped that 1947 production would approach a dozen units.

Designer and builder of the Airphibian was Robert Edison Fulton, Jr. This inventive individual was a descendant of both Robert Fulton and Thomas Edison. Among his other brainchildren were the "Aerostructor" flight simulator and the "Gunairstructor," built to train Naval aerial gunners in the early days of World War II.

The Airphibian wasn't the only flying car. There were the Waterman Arrowbile, the Aerocar, and others.

But, *why* a flying car? Fulton considered it a nuisance for a flyer to have to find surface transportation once he'd landed. With a flying auto, one could descend to an airport, and then have a handy little car.

Eventually, the Airphibian was sold to Taylorcraft, but there was little news about flying car development during the 1950s and 1960s. In the November 1957 issue of *Motor Trend*, Walt Woron mentioned that the only such project that appeared to be alive at the time was the Aerocar.

A more recent development (1973) was a flying Ford Pinto with an attachable pair of wings and a double tail like a P-38 fighter plane. However, as of June 1973, the car had only flown a short distance above the ground.

TEST YOUR FRIENDS ON THIS 1947 CAR!
DO THEY RECOGNIZE IT?
(ANSWER UPSIDE-DOWN AT LOWER LEFT CORNER
REMOVE "As" and "Os" TO REVEAL THE MAKE
OF THIS CAR.)

1947 PRICE RANGE = $1497.TO $3030.
WEIGHT RANGE =   F.O.B. (DELIVERED AT FACTORY)
3670 TO 4445 lbs.   (BUILT IN MICH., CALIF. OR N.J.)

121, 124 OR 129" W.B.

STRAIGHT-8 O.H.V.
ENGINE (1931~1953)
248 CID (110 HP)}
320.2 " (144 ")} 1947
COIL SPRINGS FRONT and REAR!

7~17

90 MPH
9 TO 17 MPG
ALMOST 283,000
BUILT IN 1947!

©1994 by North America Syndicate, Inc. World rights reserved.

ABOAUOIAACOKOA

1947 Buick

The 1942 to 1954 Buicks had a gleaming "waterfall"-style grille, with a large number of closely spaced, curving vertical pieces. In recent years, some new Buicks have featured grilles with modifications of this classic style.

In 1947, Buick's three model series were the "40" Special, "50" Super, and "70" Roadmaster. The latter had the larger of the two available straight-8 engines Buick had long championed. The Buick straight-8 (1931-1953) was probably the most popular engine of the long-extinct genre. Buick always used an overhead-valve engine. (The lone exception was the 1929-30 Marquette, a smaller car sold by Buick dealers but with an Oldsmobile-like L-head six.)

Notice the long "fadeaway" front fenders on this 1947 Buick. They were introduced on Buick's 1942 line, having been adapted from the same type of fenders seen on Harley Earl's experimental "Y-job" convertible show car of 1938, built by his GM styling dept.

The early postwar Buicks had the illustrated "bomb-sight" hood ornament: a missile passing through a ring. Unfortunately, these were so popular with teenagers that many were swiped off parked Buicks!

During the later 1940s, Buick's lower-priced "Special" series was rarely advertised or seen in Buick showrooms. The Super and Roadmaster were the big sellers. However, in the summer of 1949, the new 1950 Buick Special made its premature debut, featuring the weird buck-toothed bumper-grille that would also appear on the other 1950 Buicks when ready.

This 1947 model was the final Buick not to offer the option of an automatic transmission. Buick's new "Dynaflow" liquid automatic appeared in 1948.

1947 Chrysler "Town & Country" Sedan

The price of this car was supposedly $2,366, but most sold for well over $3,000—and some for as much as $4,500, depending on the supply and demand. Just after World War II, millions of prospective buyers were on waiting lists.

Moreover, steel was in short supply, so the real wood in the body was then a practical one. The wood was also a sign of luxury, having been used in stylish station wagons for many years. As early as 1941, Chrysler had offered a wood-paneled "Town & Country" sedan.

Chrysler's Town & Country series for '46 was expanded. In addition to the illustrated sedan (six-cylinder), there was also the popular straight-8 convertible, plus a few rare models such as the steel-top hardtop convertible, the roadster, and

two-door Brougham. These three were experimental, though seven of the hardtop convertibles were sold, and their upper profile was not unlike the 1950 Chrysler "Newport" two-door hardtop!

Dashboards of 1946, '47, '48, and early '49 Chrysler Corp. cars were beautiful. Speedometers changed colors as speed increased, and radio dials changed colors as the tone was adjusted from bass to treble.

Steering wheels and radio grilles were done in richly-colored plastic, usually harmonizing with exterior paint or interior upholstery.

The main drawback to a genuine "woody" collector's car is that you may become a slave to the wood. Frequent polishing, sanding, staining, etc. is necessary, unless you can keep the car indoors almost all of the time.

1940s

107,000 NASH CARS BUILT IN 1947.

"you'll be ahead with *Nash*". $1420.

6 CYLS. (172.6 c.i.d.)
3 1/8" × 3 3/4" BORE and STR.
82 HP @ 3800 RPM
7.1 to 1 COMPRESSION
112" W.B. 2826 LBS.

ECONOMICAL !
30 M.P.G.,
HWY !

new HOOD
ORNAMENT

1947 NASH "600"

HOW TO TELL THE '46,
'47 and '48s APART :
1946 HAS A NARROWER
UPPER GRILLE ; 1948
HAS HIGHER CHROME
BELT TRIM (CLOSER
TO WINDOW LEVEL.)

("AMBASSADOR" 6
HAS 112 HP, 121" W.B.)

© 1989 North America Syndicate, Inc. All rights reserved

1947 Nash 600

The postwar Nash cars of 1946-1948 were attractive and solidly built. From the side, they somewhat resembled Chevrolets (though without the "fadeaway" front fenders that continued into the front doors).

The grille, of course, was unmistakably Nash, with a wide, wrap-around lower section and a narrower upper section—all gleaming in chrome!

Changes for 1947 were minor, but could be seen. The upper front grille was 6 inches wider (with small extensions at either side). New wings were added to the ornamental hood figure, and eleven different body colors were now available. Inside, the former ivory-colored Tenite trim was changed to maroon, and door insert panels were changed from Tenite to chromium.

Since 1935, Nash sedans had fold-down seats that could convert to beds, and coil springs on all four wheels

"turned every road into velvet." The unitized body-and-frame combination eliminated squeaks and rattles and also reduced overall weight.

Twenty-five to 30 miles per gallon on the highway was much better mileage than most full-sized 1947 cars delivered (such as fifteen to twenty, and much less in the case of luxury cars), Nash's "Weather-Eye" conditioned air system was a Nash exclusive back in the 1940s—a very efficient heating/ventilating design.

In 1947 there were the "600" and "Ambassador" models, both sixes. The Ambassador featured an overhead-valve engine, with more power—and also a longer wheelbase.

Because they lacked fast "pick-up," Nash cars used to be called "the gutless wonders." But, because of their terrific fuel economy benefits, Nash owners "laughed all the way to the gas station!"

1947 Plymouth

"**O**ld Indestructible!" Of all the cars I've owned (about forty-five, so far), the most comfortable, durable, reliable, and trouble-free has to be the black 1946 Plymouth P-15 Special De Luxe club coupe that I bought used for $450 in December 1953.

I kept the car until 1976, and in those nearly twenty-three years I must have put about 300,000 carefree miles on it, with only one minor ring-and-valve job in all that time. The odometer mysteriously stuck at 41,000, and the car hardly seemed to age after that! In twenty-three years, it never even needed a tune-up. Since the radiator had anti-freeze in it when I bought the Plymouth, I never drained the water and only added a tiny bit every few months as I thought necessary.

The original L-head six was virtually silent at slow speeds and still very quiet at 70 or more! Passengers said they could not hear the engine at all when it idled or ran slow.

The only faults with the car: It burned a quart or two of oil every 1,000 miles, the front seat-backs eventually came loose at the hinges, and one afternoon the gearshift linkage came loose. I got it fixed within minutes.

The Plymouth P-15s were so good in the early postwar era that they were continued with almost no changes through 1946, 1947, 1948, and to February 1949. It may seem dull not to have drastic annual changes, but in Chrysler Corporation's case, they had more than three years to perfect an already good design.

1947 Studebaker Champion

In addition to the many *Auto Album* pictures and stories I've already released, there are still a few that I've previously drawn and held aside for various reasons. Here's an "oldie" from the vault of never-seen *Auto Album*s, which I drew in May 1982. A few of my older drawings I have never released because I wasn't satisfied with them. I liked this drawing well enough, but it was not intended to be a regular part of the series.

In 1982, I was asked to draw a special picture to use as a sample to send to newspaper editors unfamiliar with *Auto Album*. This was intended for that purpose. But, the '47 Studebaker "Starlight Coupe" (with its huge wraparound rear window) is such an interesting car that I thought it should be seen in the series.

The '47 Studebaker was introduced early, in May 1946, and it created a sensation! Radio comedians kidded about these all-new postwar Studebakers, how you couldn't tell which way they were going because the front and back ends looked alike! That, of course, was a gross exaggeration, and surely you'll have no difficulty knowing which end is which as you look at this picture.

The true (early) 1946 Studebakers, developed in 1945, were available for only a few months and were virtually forgotten after midyear when the totally restyled '47s appeared! The "forgotten" '46 Studebaker and its instrument panel are shown at upper left. Quite a change from that model to the redesigned '47!

1948 Buick "Roadmaster"

The big, wide, cushy Buick convertibles of the early postwar years have always been much admired, and good specimens are now approaching a value of $40,000! Buick's big news for 1948 was the new optional-on-Roadmaster "Dynaflow Drive" liquid-turbine automatic transmission. It made Buick fully acceptable to anyone who didn't like to shift gears or didn't know how. With Dynaflow, Roadmaster horsepower was upped from 144 to 150. Dynaflow-equipped Roadmasters were labeled as such on the rear deck ornament.

All four wheels rode softly on big "Quadruflex" coil springs. The suspension was "newly shielded against vibration" for 1948. "Vibra-Shielding" made tiring tremor build-up a thing of the past. General Motors was great for unique adjectives and catchy names for features in the '40s and '50s. The '48 Buick had "Taper-Thru Styling," "Road-Rite Balance," "Sound-Sorber Top Lining," "Flex-Fit Oil Rings," Straight-8 "Hi-Poised Fireball Power," "Safety-Ride Rims," and more! Buick's broad, heavy hood opened sideways, at the right, instead of at the front as on most other cars.

Buick's Dynaflow, according to *Popular Science* (Feb. 1948) was the first torque converter transmission on the road, replacing the usual three-forward gear speeds with "an infinite number of (Fluid) gear ratios." Chevrolet got a similar type transmission ("Powerglide") as a 1950 option, but Dynaflow and Powerglide transmissions were changed within a few years, after numerous complaints of slippage and wasted power.

1948 1/2 CROSLEY
4 CYLS. ONLY 44 C.I.D.!
2½" x 2¼" BORE and STR.

AMERICAN INDUSTRIALIST POWEL CROSLEY, JR., MANUFACTURER OF RADIOS, REFRIGERATORS, TVs, ETC., AND FOUNDER/PRESIDENT OF CROSLEY MOTORS (WITH OFFICES AT CINCINNATI, OHIO and FACTORY AT MARION, INDIANA)

MR. CROSLEY BELIEVED HE SHOULD GIVE BUYERS AN HONEST VALUE FOR THEIR MONEY, AND HONORED ALL OF HIS GENEROUS GUARANTEES!

Powel Crosley Jr.

1886~1961

NEW GRILLE and ODD CHROMED "SPINNER" NOSE IDENTIFIES 1948½ "NEW LOOK" SERIES

26½ H.P. @ 5400 RPM

ALMOST 29,000 SOLD IN 1948, ALONE! (28,734)

80" WHEELBASE

ONLY $869. f.o.b.

WT. 1280 LBS.

EASY ON GAS! UP TO 44 M.P.G.!

©1994 by North America Syndicate, Inc. World rights reserved.

CROSLEY MINI-CARS AVAIL. 1939~1942; 1946~1952. POWEL CROSLEY, JR. LOST $3 MILLION ON THIS VENTURE!

1948 1/2 "New Look" Crosley

Powel Crosley Jr., a wealthy Cincinnatian, made a fortune in the 1920s by producing low-cost radios and, later, other appliances. He also held a controlling interest in a radio station and the Cincinnati Reds baseball team. He had plenty of financial resources by the time he decided to build automobiles in 1939.

Crosley wasn't seeking huge profits, so he produced a tiny car for those who otherwise couldn't have afforded private transportation. The first Crosley cars were priced under $300, f.o.b., factory. At first they were available not from auto dealers but rather through large stores that sold other merchandise. Pre-World War II Crosleys had tiny two-cylinder engines and little power.

During World War II, Crosley directed his attention to military production, but in 1946 he switched back to small cars. This time the company produced a four-cylinder model with a little engine made of stamped steel, not cast metal, called the "Cobra" (copper-brazed) engine. But, when the engine proved unsuccessful over the long haul, Crosley developed a better cast-iron block ("Ciba") engine for 1949. He offered it for a mere $65 to owners of pre-1949 Crosley fours.

By making good on all his promises and guarantees, Crosley did not realize a profit on his automobile manufacturing business. By the time he ceased manufacturing automobiles in 1952, he had lost $3 million of his own money trying to keep the venture afloat. But, he was able to retire from it with a clear conscience, knowing he had done his best to run an honest company.

Field Enterprises, Inc., 1983

1948

6 CYL.
226.2 CID
100 HP 3600

FRAZER

123¼ W.B.

$ 2152. AND UP

FRAZERS AVAIL. IN 1947-1951 MODELS. BUILT BY KAISER-FRAZER CORP., WILLOW RUN, MICH. (CONTINENTAL ENGINE USED) HAPPY 4ᵀᴴ OF JULY !

4 BUMPER GUARDS (INSTEAD OF 2) AND CHROMED GRILLE ARE NEW FOR 1948.

7/3

1940s

1948 Frazer

S tyling of Kaiser-Frazer cars was ahead of its time, as they offered the slab-sided 1949 look as early as 1946 (when the '47 models were available). However, some thought Kaiser-Frazer styling austere, with little chrome ornamentation and a Spartan plainness of line. The 1947 Frazers, in fact, didn't even have chrome on their grilles!

Kaiser-Frazer cars were able to grab a lead in styling because they had no earlier (pre-war) models from which they'd have had to retool. It was a fresh start, though early Frazers were advertised as a product of Graham-Paige.

Kaiser manufactured steel, and was able to obtain this material when many other auto manufacturers periodically ran short. Also, Kaiser-Frazer was using the almost-new giant factory in Willow Run, Mich., which had been built to meet war-time production needs. After a slow beginning in 1946, production began to move along fast. Kaiser-Frazer sales flourished in 1947 and 1948, when there were plenty of new-car buyers eager to replace their pre-war transportation. But, in the 1949 season, credit was sharply restricted by government decree and a mild recession rattled the auto industry. After that, the boom was over for Kaiser-Frazer.

In early 1950, the totally and beautifully restyled 1951 Kaiser was introduced. It did fairly well because of its good looks, but the '51 Frazer received only a bizarre frontal facelift and was dropped not long afterward—phased out in favor of the compact Henry J and Allstate cars, new running mates to the Kaiser.

1940s

1948 "FUTURAMIC" OLDSMOBILE 8
$2256.
(OLDSMOBILE'S LAST STRAIGHT- 8)
"98"

127" WHEELBASE, 3745 lbs.

257.1 CID, L-HEAD, STRAIGHT-8 ENGINE (3 1/4" × 3 7/8" B. + ST.) 115 HP @ 3600 RPM 7 TO 1 COMPR.

TAD 9~11

HYDRA-MATIC AUTO. TRANS. WITH "WHIRLAWAY"

"FUTURAMIC"
THE 8-CYLINDER 1948 OLDSMOBILE HAD ALL-NEW 1949 TYPE STYLING. THE 1948 6-CYLINDER OLDSMOBILE GENERALLY RESEMBLED THE PREVIOUS 1947 MODELS, AS DID THE "DYNAMIC 8s."

1948 Oldsmobile "Futuramic 98"

Oldsmobile, in 1927, was first to feature chrome (instead of nickel plating). And, in 1948, only Cadillac (except for the "75" series) and Oldsmobile's Futuramic 98 series were available with the all-new 1949-style bodies a year ahead of time.

Because of its advanced styling, the Futuramic Olds captured much attention in 1948. Comparatively little notice was given to the more expanded line of "Dynamic" sixes and straight-eight Oldsmobiles because they looked more or less like warmed-over 1946 or 1947 models.

On the Futuramic 98, "whirlaway" was an added feature: a passing gear to provide a quick burst of acceleration.

Famous auto tester Tom McCahill, writing in the October '48 issue of *Mechanix Illustrated*, reported on the new Futuramic 98. He liked its looks, but the performance left him cold! He concluded that the automatic transmission was far too sluggish in its pickup (aside from the Whirlaway passing gear). It took him eighteen seconds to go from 10 to 60 m.p.h. in third gear of drive, and a lazy twenty-two seconds from 20 to 60 in fourth gear. Top speed of the car was supposed to be 90 m.p.h., but Tom was unable to find a suitable stretch of road on which to "hold it open" long enough.

In 1949, all Oldsmobiles got the new Futuramic styling, as well as large air-scoops under the headlights. Also, new for 1949 were the "Rocket" V-8 engine and the "88" series. Both the "98" and "88" had the new V-8, which replaced the straight-eight. The six ("76" series) continued into 1950.

new STREAMLINED "WOODY"

"OUT OF THIS WORLD... INTO YOUR HEART"

120" WHEELBASE

1948 PACKARD 8 STATION SEDAN

STEEL BODY with GENUINE BIRCH WOOD DECORATIVE PANELS!
(AVAIL. 1948 TO 1950)

4~26

"ASK THE MAN WHO OWNS ONE"

4080 lbs. WT.

$3425. WHEN NEW

STRAIGHT-8 ENGINE L-HEAD 288 CID
3¼" x 3¾" B+ST.
130 HP @ 3600 RPM
7.0 TO I COMPRESSION

NEARLY 8' CARGO SPACE WITH TAILGATE OPEN

1948 Packard 8 Station Sedan

During 1947, officials of the Packard Motor Car Company in Detroit decided that it was time for a new kind of postwar station wagon: an all-new 1948 model that would have a streamlined body of steel with some wooden paneling, with more wood in the tailgate than anywhere else.

However, the first 1948 Packards available were convertibles. Some welcomed the new convertibles. But, other Packard customers squawked loudly, because if they wanted a closed car, they'd have to settle for an available '47 instead of a '48. The problem didn't go away until the complete line of '48 Packard body types was ready.

Advertised as a "double-duty beauty," the new Station Sedan was described: "The stunning new Packard Station Sedan is truly an entirely new kind of car.

"Here, for the first time, sedan luxury is combined with the real carryall utility of a station wagon."

The new Station Sedan was "equally at home carrying six distinguished passengers to a summer theater opening, a formal country club dance, or skimming over a country highway loaded with farm produce or camping duffle." The rear seat folded forward, and the lower half of the tailgate could be folded down, providing space for skis, a small rowboat, or what-have-you.

When Packard restyled for 1951, the Station Sedan was not offered again. It would be Packard's only postwar station wagon until the era following the merger with Studebaker in 1954. A station wagon was offered in Packard's two final years: 1957 and 1958.

1949 Chevrolet

The 1949 Chevrolet was beautifully restyled and bore little resemblance to the earlier models. For '49, all General Motors cars except for the rare early series Buick Special and the Cadillac "75," had been thoroughly restyled. The "new look" for GM cars was bright and airy, with large windows, pleasing curves, and graceful pontoon fenders (front fenders were integrated into the body). The '49 sales brochure called the new Chevy, "The most beautiful buy of all!"

Ending an eventful decade, 1949 was the third full year of the postwar era—and, at last, new cars were becoming easier to get. In fact, there was grumbling throughout the auto industry because the government had tightened credit regulations and had thus driven off a portion of the new-car business.

There was absolutely no competition yet from the Japanese auto industry back then, though British cars were being imported to the USA since the war ended, and the ubiquitous German VW "Beetle" would make a bold sweep across the United States during the 1950s and 1960s.

The rosy glow of 1946 and 1947 optimism had deteriorated by 1949 into an uneasiness about the Cold War and unemployment. And, within a year, we'd be involved in a new war in Korea.

Popular music was doing well in this pre-rock era, and much was available on the new, little plastic 45-r.p.m. records. The 33 1/3-r.p.m. records, first available in the early 1930s, had been revived in 1948, and soon these L.P. (long-playing) ten-inch and twelve-inch discs took the place of the old-style 78s.

MANY THOUSANDS OF THESE DEPENDABLE OLD "CHEVY" PICKUPS STILL IN DAILY USE!

1949 CHEVROLET
PICKUP (½-TON CAPACITY)
6-CYL. OVERHEAD-VALVE
216.5 C.I.D. ENGINE
90 H.P. @ 3300 RPM
6.5 COMPRESSION
3½" × 3¾" BORE and STR.
116" wheelbase
4.11 GEAR RATIO
6.00 × 16 TIRES
3320 lbs.

$1205.⁰⁰ fob
PLUS TAX-LICENSE-ETC.

EXCEPT FOR CERTAIN SMALL DETAILS, THE 1948 THROUGH 1953 CHEVROLET TRUCKS LOOK VERY MUCH ALIKE.

TAP 3-13

© Field Enterprises, Inc., 1983

1949 Chevrolet Pickup

The Chevrolet truck line was totally restyled in the summer of 1947, as the 1948 trucks were revealed several weeks in advance of the usual fall introductions. The new '48 models were so popular that they continued almost unchanged through '53! To continue for six years, in a highly competitive field, a new model had to be good! Even now, numerous 1948-to-1953 Chevrolet trucks are still giving dependable service every day!

There were minor changes in these '48-to-'53 trucks during their long run. The earliest '48 pickups had the gas filler on the cargo box, rather than on cab side. Starting in '52, there were push-button outer door handles (replacing swing-down type), and the '53 models had 60-pound oil pressure gauges. Also, on the later trucks, there were model number designations accompanying or replacing the

"Chevrolet" sign on the sides of the hood. Periodic minor mechanical improvements were made between '48 and '53, and model letter designations were changed each year. We're grateful to Bryon Stappler of Kelowna, B.C., Canada, for sending helpful details concerning various minor changes within the '48-to-'53 model run.

These were known as the "Advance Design" Chevrolet trucks, with "the cab that breathes" (referring to the improved heating-ventilating-defogging system).

Windshield/window visibility had been increased twenty-two percent over that of previous models. On top of that, optional rear corner windows were also available. During the first year of this series, there were 107 models on eight wheelbases (changed to eighty-one models on nine wheelbases during 1949).

THE "SILVER ANNIVERSARY"
1949 CHRYSLER c46
" *TOWN and COUNTRY* " CVT.
(WITH *REAL* WOOD TRIM ON BODY.)
ONLY 1000 BUILT!
$3970.⁰⁰
BASE PRICE f.o.b.
© 1989 North America Syndicate, Inc. All rights reserved
TAP 8~20
323½ CU. IN.
HEMI-HEAD, STRAIGHT 8 ENGINE
8.20 × 15
"PRESTOMATIC" GYROL FLUID DRIVE TRANSMISSION
WT.= 4630 LBS.
THESE TOTALLY RESTYLED MODELS INTRO. FEB., 1949. ("EARLY 1949" CHRYSLER CORP. CARS WERE CONTINUATIONS OF THE 1946-1947-1948 MODELS.)
135 H.P. @ 3200 RPM
3.54 TO 1 GEAR RATIO   131½" WB
FRONT VIEW   20 GAL. GAS TANK
7.25 COMPR.

1949 Chrysler Town & Country

Chrysler's first wood-paneled Town & Country model appeared in March 1941, as a combination sedan/station wagon. Both six- and nine-passenger Town & Country sedans were available in 1941 and 1942.

The wood trim on the Town & Country was real! Much of the body was actually of white ash wood, with contrasting mahogany insert panels. But, real wood required much upkeep: frequent waxing and treatment with special preservative oils, as well as periodic varnishing (preferably after sanding away any blemishes). Weather was not kind to vulnerable wood bodywork. Neglected examples soon lost their original luster and began to look like old gray driftwood. And, without proper upkeep, wooden bodies grew rattly and rickety.

In 1947, Chrysler began to use imitation mahogany panel inserts, less costly and less perishable than genuine wood. The printed substitute material was called Di-noc.

In early 1949, all of Chrysler Corporation's cars were completely restyled (as illustrated). On the 1949 Town & Country, real wood was still used for the light-colored raised pieces, but Di-noc was used for the darker inserts on the first 300 cars. The other 700 of the 1949 convertibles had insert panels painted to match the individual car's body color.

All 1949 Chrysler Town & Country models were convertibles. The final year for the original series was 1950, but the Town & Country name was resumed later for some rather ordinary Chrysler wagons. The legend lived on, however, and Chrysler eventually resumed the series in 1983 with new convertibles and wagons (using convincing-looking plastic wood trim), and Town & Country minivans in 1990.

NO, FRIENDS, THIS ISN'T A CUSTOMIZED '49 FORD! IT'S A...

1949 METEOR * V8
BUILT BY FORD MOTOR COMPANY
OF CANADA. THIS WAS A FORD-
SIZED CAR OFFERED BY CANADIAN
LINCOLN-MERCURY DEALERS.

CANADIAN **FORD** DEALERS
OFFERED A MERCURY-SIZED
MONARCH (IN ADDITION TO FORD)
(STARTING 1946.)

* = new FOR
1949!
(ONLY $26. ABOVE THE
PRICE OF A FORD.)

CONVERTIBLE OR WAGON NOT
IN THE '49 METEOR LINE, BUT WERE
AVAILABLE IN 1950. THE 1949
METEOR SUPERSEDED THE LOW-PRICE
"114" MERCURY CANADIAN SERIES,
(WHICH WAS ALSO FORD-SIZED.)
239.4-CID L-HEAD V8 ENGINE
(100 HP) and OTHER SPECIFICATIONS
SIMILAR TO 1949 FORD.

© News America Syndicate, 1986

1940s

1949 Meteor

Until 1946, Canadian Ford products bore a close resemblance to the American versions. Then the Monarch was created, with its own unique horizontal-bladed grille, to be sold in the Mercury price field by Ford dealers in Canada.

Consequently, for 1949, the Lincoln-Mercury dealers of Canada got a new Ford-sized car to sell in the low-priced field, and this was the Meteor. Body-wise, it resembled a 1949 Ford, but had its own grille (resembling, generally, that of a Mercury). From 1949 to 1951, the Meteor had the same dashboard design as a Ford. But, from 1952 to 1954, a Mercury dash was used. Then in 1955, the Meteor returned to the Ford-style dash. Meanwhile, into the 1950s, the grille, side trim, taillights,

hubcaps, as well as interior trim and appointments were exclusively Meteor's own.

These Canadian Meteors and Monarchs of the 1950s are extremely scarce in the U.S.A., other than near the northern border. They were sold new only in Canada, and few were taken to the U.S.A. later and resold used.

Most American car buffs have, at one time or another, seen every year model of both Ford and Mercury from the 1950s, scarce as some of these are becoming now. But, a Canadian Meteor or Monarch is a rare sight outside maple leaf territory. These are not to be confused with the American Mercury Meteors of the early 1960s or the Mercury Monarchs of the later 1970s, which were commonly seen in the U.S.A.

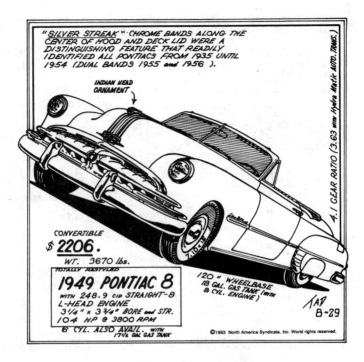

"SILVER STREAK" CHROME BANDS ALONG THE CENTER OF HOOD AND DECK LID WERE A DISTINGUISHING FEATURE THAT READILY IDENTIFIED ALL PONTIACS FROM 1935 UNTIL 1954 (DUAL BANDS 1955 and 1956).

INDIAN HEAD ORNAMENT

4.1 GEAR RATIO (3.63 with Hydra Matic AUTO. TRANS.)

CONVERTIBLE
$ 2206.
WT. 3670 lbs.

TOTALLY RESTYLED
1949 PONTIAC 8
WITH 248.9 c/d STRAIGHT-8
L-HEAD ENGINE
3¼" x 3¾" BORE and STR.
104 HP @ 3800 RPM
6 CYL. ALSO AVAIL. WITH 17½ GAL. GAS TANK

120" WHEELBASE
18 GAL. GAS TANK (WITH 8 CYL. ENGINE)

TAD
8-29

©1993 North America Syndicate, Inc. World rights reserved.

1949 Pontiac 8

In 1935, Pontiac drew many new buyers by not only offering the six or eight and all-new "Turret-Top" steel-roofed styling, but also by introducing its famous "Silver Streak" motif of parallel chrome strips along the top of the hood.

The Indian-head radiator ornament (or hood ornament) that bore the image of the historic Chief Pontiac, of Native American fame, was another noteworthy characteristic. In the later years of Pontiac's Indian-head figure, it was often made of clear amber plastic and illuminated by a small, concealed bulb.

In 1948, Pontiac joined the growing ranks of cars to offer an optional automatic transmission. And, in 1949, all Pontiacs were restyled with the attractive, new GM-Fisher "pontoon-type" body with graceful curves and fenders blended into the sides. From 1949 through 1952, Pontiac retained this general design. The grille, trim decorations, and interiors were slightly altered from year to year.

A July 1949 advertisement for the Pontiac convertible was entitled "When You Make a Sweetheart Your Own." It read, in part: "What happier day is anyone likely to know than a wedding day—always an occasion of complete joy, a time to be long remembered.

"And what finer companion for every happy couple than a beautiful new 1949 Pontiac? For here, truly, is the perfect car for perfect days.

"No smarter, more beautiful car will make its appearance before any church or cathedral. And no car will give greater satisfaction and pride to those who own it, than this great new Pontiac."

News America Syndicate
© News Group Chicago, Inc., 1984

10-21

TAP

4.09 GEAR RATIO
(3.18 WITH OVERDRIVE)

$ 2906. (ON WEST COAST)

1949 STUDEBAKER "COMMANDER" CONVERTIBLE
6-CYL. L-HEAD ENGINE (245.6 CID) 6.5 COMPR.
100 H.P. @ 3400 RPM   119" WHEELBASE

START YOUR "AUTO ALBUM" COLLECTION NOW!

1949 Studebaker Commander

Having pulled off a dramatic styling coup in mid-'46 (for the '47 model year), Studebaker offered only minor changes for 1948 and 1949. One noticeable change for 1949 on the illustrated "Commander" model was the addition of a vertical chrome trim piece down the center of the grille.

"Studebaker's the Stand-Out in savings that count and style that sings," proclaimed the manufacturer in 1949 advertising. "Make Studebaker your new-car buy word—and watch how fast you find yourself cash money ahead!"

Studebaker set a sales record for itself by selling more cars and trucks during the first three months of 1949 than it had in any previous quarter! In some of its advertising in the 1940s, Studebaker featured various father-and-son teams employed by its South Bend,

Ind. factory—to demonstrate the loyalty and perseverance of its workers. "You wait and see, Dad … you'll have grandsons on this Studebaker team someday!" quoted an August 1949 ad. However, such predictions didn't always come to pass, because Studebaker cut back production during the 1950s and 1960s, and in '64 moved its operations to its Canadian plant. Two years after that, the final Studebakers were built there.

But, there's encouraging news: The Avanti, a high-performance model from Studebaker first introduced during 1962, was revived in recent years by ex-Studebaker employees, as the Avanti II! And, many original Studebakers are now preserved and enjoyed by collectors who still say, "We'd rather fix than switch!"

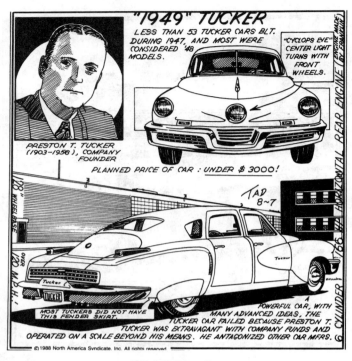

1949 Tucker

Preston Tucker had many remarkable new ideas, and he actually built more than fifty complete and running Tucker cars.

In many ways, the Tucker was a truly amazing car, years ahead of its time! But, Tucker bit off far more than he could ever chew by trying to compete directly against long-established, high-volume American manufacturers. No way could Tucker have realized a profit by selling his luxurious cars in the $2,500 to $3,000 range, as planned. However, if Tucker had started off small, limiting production to 500 or fewer cars a year and pricing them around $7,500 each, he might have succeeded.

His plans were too grandiose, and he was certainly an unwise steward when it came to his handling of the corporate money-bag. As the venture ran out of capital and banks declined to lend more, key Tucker executives began bailing out faster than rats leaving a sinking ship. Soon, Tucker was left virtually alone to face an S.E.C. stock mismanagement investigation.

As for his Chicago-built Tucker cars, they were true classics even from the first. And, most of them were bought and preserved by collectors who knew a good thing when they saw it.

Among the many Tucker features: turnable "cyclops" third headlight; padded dash and safety "crash cowl;" tapered safety frame, designed to deflect an impact from another car; a powerful rear engine (designed by Franklin for use in Bell helicopters!) and a "pop-out" safety windshield that would break loose on impact.

The story was told in a well-researched 1988 movie, "Tucker," still available on video!

1950 CHRYSLER C-49 Town & Country "newport" HARDTOP

© Field Enterprises, Inc. 1983

8 CYL., 323.5 CUBIC-IN., STRAIGHT-8 ENGINE/135 HP. @ 3200 RPM./7.25 COMPRESSION/ONLY 698 TO 700 OF THESE 1950 TOWN & COUNTRY HARDTOPS BUILT—RARE! (NO T & C CONVERTIBLE AFTER 1949.)/131½" WHEELBASE/WEIGHT = 4670 LBS./8.20 x 15" TIRES/WOOD TRIM/$4003.

TAD

CLIP and SAVE   10-16

1950 Chrysler Town & Country

Chrysler first introduced its wooden-bodied Town & Country sport model as a hatchback sedan in 1941. It was well liked by the public, though not sold in great numbers. Early in 1942, production stopped for the duration of World War II, but in 1946 the luxurious "woodie" Town & Country Chryslers reappeared as new two-door convertibles as well as new "bustle-back" utility sedans.

In February 1949 Chrysler products were totally restyled, and that year only a remodeled Town & Country convertible was offered. Early models had Di-noc woodgrain-style center panels on the doors (in addition to genuine wood border trim). Later '49s had painted metal center panels with real wood on edge trim as before. A single "Newport" two-door hardtop convertible was built in '49, as a pilot model; and for 1950, it was decided that the hardtop would replace the convertible in the Town & Country series.

A steel-bodied Town & Country station wagon continued to be available in the Chrysler line for many years (some with imitation wood trim and graining). Due to popular demand, late in 1982 the revived Town & Country convertible joined its cousin, the imitation-wood-grained-and-wood-paneled Le Baron Town & Country station wagon.

Thus, the romance of beautiful wood paneling was revived in Chrysler's Town & Country models, though with more durable imitation wood substitutes for the real thing.

Genuine wood has its charm, but on a car it requires time-consuming and expensive care.

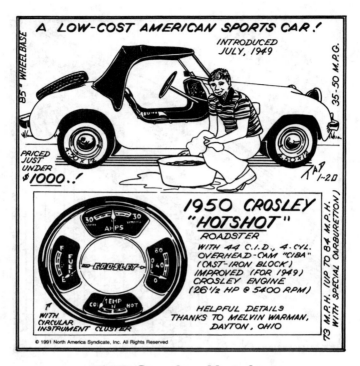

A LOW-COST AMERICAN SPORTS CAR!

INTRODUCED JULY, 1949

85" WHEELBASE

35-50 M.P.G.

PRICED JUST UNDER $1000..!

1950 CROSLEY "HOTSHOT" ROADSTER

WITH 44 C.I.D., 4-CYL. OVERHEAD-CAM "CIBA" (CAST-IRON BLOCK) IMPROVED (FOR 1949) CROSLEY ENGINE (26½ HP @ 5400 RPM)

73 M.P.H. (UP TO 84 M.P.H. WITH SPECIAL CARBURETION.)

WITH CIRCULAR INSTRUMENT CLUSTER

HELPFUL DETAILS THANKS TO MELVIN WARMAN, DAYTON, OHIO

1950 Crosley Hotshot

The Crosley car first appeared in 1939—as a tiny, two-cylinder convertible. Prewar Crosleys were much too small and underpowered to be popular, in spite of their great fuel economy, and less than 6,000 were sold from 1939 to 1942.

After World War II, Crosley returned (a little later than most other postwar cars) and featured a four-cylinder engine of its own. But, this new engine was utterly strange: It was a stamped metal engine, with sheet-metal parts copper-brazed together. It was known as the Cobra (for "copper-brazed") engine. Though it weighed only fifty-nine pounds and seemed practical, it proved to be exceptionally troublesome and was replaced in 1949 by the cast-iron CIBA engine.

The illustrated Crosley Hotshot was a true American sports car, simple as it may have been. It introduced genuine four-wheel disc brakes, decades ahead of the competition! But, its non-synchromesh "crashbox" transmission left something to be desired.

Headlights protruded from the sloping front end, as they would a decade later on the bug-eyed Austin-Healey Sprite. Sides were cut so low that doors were unnecessary.

Crosley provided a variety of body types in the postwar years, but tiny gas-sippers were not in fashion at a time when regular gas was twenty-one to twenty-three cents a gallon and easy to get.

For 1951, the Hotshot was renamed the Super Sports and got new, large, swing-open side doors as well as more complete interior upholstering.

Crosley cars were discontinued after 1952, but the manufacturer was also well known for radios, TVs, refrigerators, and other consumer products.

1950s

1950 De Soto "S-14" Series
"CUSTOM" 4-DR. SEDAN
WT. = 3640 lbs. 125½" W.B.
236.7 CID $2174. f.o.b. FACTORY
L-HEAD 6
(112 HP @ 3600 RPM)
136,203 DESOTOS BUILT IN 1950
custom
NEW WIDE REAR WINDOW
REAR VIEW
GYROL FLUID DRIVE
"TIP-TOE" HYDRAULIC SHIFT and
1950 GRILLE IS BISECTED BY NEW EMBLEM-BEARING PLATE.
© News America Syndicate, 1986
SLOGAN = "DRIVE A DE SOTO BEFORE YOU DECIDE."

1950 De Soto

The 1929 De Soto "K" was a great success, but other models (the straight-8 available in '30 & '31, and the 1934 Airflow-only models) were not popular. De Soto regained success as it began mass-producing taxis for Yellow Cab and other companies. The taxi business boomed from 1935 to 1949 (and especially in the early postwar years), but in early 1949 the Chrysler Corp. cars were totally restyled and the compact-bodied De Sotos after that time weren't as suitable for taxi use. In '57, De Soto again grew big, but by then De Soto taxis were usually older models (especially the seemingly-everlasting '46 to '48s).

De Soto prospered in 1949 and 1950, as far as sales to private owners were concerned; each year saw well over 100,000 units sold. Styling in 1950 was not drastically changed from '49, though the new grille contained heavier chrome pieces with an emblem plate at the center, and the rear window was widened. There were new taillights and other rear detail changes. There was a turn away from the usual wood-graining on the 1950 dashboard, but the graining returned on the '51s.

Throughout the industry, 1949 was a year of drastic postwar restyling, while 1950 proved to be a year of mechanical refinements and improvement. De Sotos remained in production until late 1960, when a few early '61 De Sotos appeared.

1950 FORD
"CUSTOM" SERIES
100 H.P., 239.4 CID V8 OR
95 H.P., 226 CID 6
(BOTH L-HEAD ENGINES)

STYLING SIMILAR TO 1949,
BUT 1950 FORD HAS
new KEYSTONE-SHAPED
FORD EMBLEM
ABOVE GRILLE,
INSTEAD OF
"FORD"
LETTERING.
(OTHER MINOR CHANGES
ALSO.)

"COUNTRY
SQUIRE" 2-DR.
STATION WAGON
(WOOD-AND-
GRAINED TRIM)
3511 LBS.
22,292 BUILT
$2028.

114" WHEELBASE

TUDOR
SEDAN
3015 LBS.
398,060 BUILT
$1511.

3.73 GEAR RATIO

17-GALLON GAS TANK

BUSINESS COUPE, 2-DR. and
4-DR. SEDANS AVAIL. IN
LOWER-PRICED "DELUXE" SERIES ALSO.

TAP
7-17

1950 Ford

In the spring of 1948, the all-new 1949 Ford, Mercury, and Lincoln cars were unveiled—and they were a sensation!! Ford Motor Co. had completely redesigned its products, showing the influence of young Henry Ford II, who took over the corporate reins from his aged grandfather in 1945 (Henry Ford I died in 1947).

The 1949 Fords were so new that little needed changing, in terms of style, in 1950. But, there were numerous mechanical and detail improvements.

The camshaft was redesigned for quieter valve action. Piston slap was reduced by new "Autothermic" pistons (fitting as close as .0005 inch), and an oil squirt hole was added in connecting rods to lubricate pistons. Synthetic rubber seals on the intake valve guides prevented oil from working through the

guides. The improved oil-bath air cleaner used a cork silencer. A new three-blade fan assembly was designed for quieter action.

The handbrake was redesigned, as was the double-walled glove-box door (mounted on a piano-type hinge). The "Magic Air" heater had improved controls. The interior light switch was moved from pillar to dash. And, there were other small improvements.

For 1950, Ford had its first million-car sales year since 1930 and the hey-day of the Model A! By now, the American public was used to the new look of the 1949 Fords, and with the mechanical improvements of 1950, they were even more convinced!

Ford's well-known "Keystone" emblem first appeared in 1950 and continued for many years.

SLOGAN : "NOTHING COULD BE FINER"

MODEL "OEH"

1950 LINCOLN "COSMOPOLITAN"

SPORT SEDAN 125" wheelbase
4293 lbs. (4349 lbs. with HYDRA-MATIC)
with 336.7 cid L-HEAD V8 ENGINE

152 H.P. @ 3600 RPM 7.0 to 1 COMPRESSION

21½-GALLON FUEL TANK

$3239.50 f.o.b., DETROIT

© News America Syndicate, 1985

HAPPY FATHER'S DAY! 6-16

8341 COSM. SEDANS BLT.

3.91 (3.31 with HYDRA-MATIC, 4.27 with OVERDRIVE) GEAR RATIO

THOUGH LINCOLN IS BUILT BY FORD MOTOR COMPANY, THIS 1950 LINCOLN WAS AVAILABLE WITH AN OPTIONAL "**HYDRA-MATIC**" AUTOMATIC TRANSMISSION BY GENERAL MOTORS CORP.! ($174.25 EXTRA)

LOWER-PRICED '50 LINCOLNS HAD V-WINDSHIELD AND MERCURY-TYPE BODY.

1950 Lincoln Cosmopolitan

In 1950, the luxurious Lincoln Cosmopolitan enjoyed its second season. This model had replaced the first series of Lincoln Continentals in 1949. The Cosmopolitan lacked the international styling and glamorous image of the Continental, but it was typically post-war American, with a broad "dollar grin" grille and a bulbous, fender-less body.

Little did anyone then know that for 1956 the Continental series would return to stay! The massive Cosmopolitan, in fact, was destined to be a highly individual luxury series only through 1951, becoming a less distinctive, lower-priced series when all Lincolns were totally restyled, downsized, and pepped-up in 1952.

During the "Cosmo's" initial three years, the only readily noticeable changes each season were rearrangements of the pieces in the toothy grilles. Instrument panels were redesigned in 1950, and there were taillight changes in '51. Beautifully luxurious as it may have been, the '49-'51 Cosmopolitan reminded some of a landlocked whale!

Advertised as "the First Car of the Land," the 1950 Lincoln Cosmopolitan was powered by an L-head V-8, as was the standard series of Lincoln from 1949; although from 1933 to 1948, all Lincolns had been V-12s.

In 1950, some 8,341 Cosmopolitan Sport Sedans were built. There was also a Cosmopolitan Coupe and a Cosmopolitan Capri padded-top Coupe. Rarest of all was the 1950 Cosmopolitan convertible, with only 536 built!

From 1950 to 1954, Lincoln used a General Motors Hydra-Matic as its optional automatic transmission.

135 H.P. @ 3600 RPM • 3 1/2" × 3 3/4" BORE and STR.

1950 PACKARD

EIGHT DELUXE MODEL 2362

HAPPY 4TH OF JULY WEEKEND!

$2383.

with L-HEAD, 288 c.i.d. STRAIGHT-8 ENG. (7 TO 1 COMPR.)

TAP 7-B

IN STD. 8 SERIES (SUPER 8 and CUSTOM 8 SERIES ALSO AVAIL.)

120" WHEELBASE 3840 lbs.

WITH "ULTRAMATIC DRIVE" AUTOMATIC TRANSMISSION (OPTIONAL) 3.9 GEAR RATIO (4.1 w. OVERDRIVE)

7.60 × 15" TIRES • 17-GALLON FUEL TANK

1950 Packard 8 Deluxe

This 1950 Packard was the final model in the three-year cycle of slab-sided postwar Packards that began with the '48.

For 1950, changes were minor, mostly relating to chrome trim, interior patterns and colors, and such. For several years afterward, the '48 to '50 Packards were considered unglamorous tanks, lacking the classic elegance and pizzazz of the prewar models.

How much gas mileage would you expect a big eight-cylinder (straight-8) car like this to deliver? Surprisingly, the advertisements promised 19 miles per gallon and more in a 1950 Packard with the 135-h.p. engine, if overdrive was included. In April 1950, Packard reported that thirty-three percent of more than 1,000 '50 Packard owners surveyed reported more than 19 m.p.g. (obviously at moderate highway cruising speeds).

Ultramatic Drive was Packard's own automatic transmission and a big sales feature in 1949-1950. There was no clutch pedal to be concerned with and no "jerk" or "clunk" as the automatic transmission changed gears underway. There was no slippage at cruising speeds or on steep grades. Ultramatic was considered to be a superiorly designed automatic transmission, its only fault was that low gears tended to wear out sooner than usual because they were automatically put into action so frequently.

The Custom 8, top of the line and identified by its crisscross grille pieces, had Ultramatic as standard equipment. Ultramatic was optional at extra cost on the other models (even on the lowest-priced standard eight, after the spring of 1950).

In 1950, more than half of the Packards built since 1899 were still in use!

1950 Plymouth

After a total restyling in 1949, few people expected noticeable changes in the '50 model. However, the 1950 Plymouth featured a new, large grille with fewer but larger pieces, a wider rear window, new taillights, and other changes inside and out.

Plymouth had a dowdy image in the early 1950s because of its plain styling. But, from 1949 to 1952, Plymouths did very well in various national stock car races, coming in second only to the V-8 Oldsmobiles in many cases! Lee Petty and Johnny Mantz scored numerous victories in Plymouths, which were considered underdogs in racing. In 1950, Johnny Mantz wrecked his Olds "88," replaced it with a Plymouth, and won the first Darlington Southern 500 Race! The winning Plymouth was a "cheapie" two-door fastback like the one illustrated here.

The 1950 Plymouths were easy to repair and maintain. One plus was the rear fenders. Though blending well with the body, they were fully detachable and thus easier to repair or replace than the integral rear fenders on many other makes.

As in the 1940s, Plymouth offered "Safety-Rim" wheels. When a tire blew out, it remained safely in place and did not flip-flop off the wheel at high speeds.

"Chair-height" seats and ample headroom assured riding comfort. The '50 Plymouths were also safe for little children, as the door lock buttons locked the inside door handles as well as the outside handles. Even if the door were unlocked, the inside handle had to be pulled upward to open it.

1950 STUDEBAKER SERIES R-5 EXPRESS PICKUP (1/2 TON)
170 c.i.d. 6 CYL. L-HEAD ENGINE
85 H.P. @ 4000 RPM (3" x 4" BORE and STR.)

$1262 and up (f.o.b.)
STUDEBAKER CORP.,
SOUTH BEND, INDIANA

ADVERTISED AS THE "FIRST TRUCKS TO OFFER OPTIONAL *OVERDRIVE!*"

WT. 2675 LBS.
112" WHEELBASE

(STYLING SIMILAR TO 1949)

1950 Studebaker Express Pickup

In 1949, Studebaker restyled its pickup line with a new postwar look, after totally restyling its line of cars in the spring of 1946 for the '47 season. The new '49 truck grille was inspired, in part, by the attractive grilles of the beautiful '47 to '49 Commander cars by Studebaker (which also includes the Land Cruiser).

The 1950 Studebaker trucks resembled the '49s, but they offered the added option of overdrive. As a 1950 advertisement read, "Make sure of long-lasting, long-range operating economy! Get Studebaker's thrift-assuring overdrive transmission, if you're thinking of buying a new half-ton or three-quarter-ton truck.

"This revolutionary Studebaker forward step in truck engineering is extra cost—but it starts paying its way right away in extra thrift.

"First trucks to offer gas-saving, engine-saving overdrive, Studebaker trucks are also first with real 'lift the hood' accessibility to engine ignition—instrument panel wiring. They're America's first trucks, too, with variable-ratio extra leverage steering for easier turnarounds and parking—first trucks with twist-resisting K-member frame up front."

Studebaker also featured an optional "Truck Climatizer" cab heating and ventilating system, the next-best thing to air conditioning in those days. Low cab floor was another Studebaker feature.

The 1950 Studebaker trucks came in the following capacities: 1/2 ton, 3/4 ton, 1 ton, 1 1/2 ton, and 2 ton. The 1/2 ton pickups had car-style wheels with hubcaps (as illustrated); 3/4-ton and larger trucks had utilitarian-looking steel artillery wheels with exposed lug nuts and six large semicircular vent holes.

1950 ZIS

T he Russian ZIS automobile originated in 1936, and the Model 101
of the later '30s resembled a large
American car of 1935 vintage, with an
engine somewhat like that of a Buick 8.
The manufacturer was the "Stalin
Works" in Moscow (officially known as
Zavod Imieni Stalina). Model 102
appeared as the 1940s began.

During World War II, Packard dies
were purchased by the Russians, reportedly on the "lend-lease plan," and the
resulting postwar ZIS "110" strongly
resembled the classic senior Packards
of '42. Only a close inspection would
reveal the minor differences.

A limited-production luxury car, the
ZIS was reserved for Communist Party
bigwigs and was a far cry from the plebeian Russian "people's cars:" Mosk-
vitch, Pobieda, Volga, Lada, etc.

In the Khrushchev era of de-Stalin-
ization, the ZIS was replaced in 1956
by the ZIL, as the factory was renamed
for Ivan A. Likhachev, former director
of the factory and a noted Russian automotive designer.

Meanwhile, there was a ZIM car
built since 1950 in Gorky at a factory
named for Molotov. The ZIM was a
luxury car, but smaller and less ostentatious than the flashy ZIS.

Russian cars are a mystery to most
Americans. Few have ever left Eastern
Europe, though in the 1970s, a ZIS
was transported on a trailer around the
United States and exhibited in some
cities for $2.50 a look. I saw it in San
Jose, Calif.

The Russian-built Lada was sold in
Canada for several years.

"NEW YORKER" SEDAN $3378., f.o.b., DETROIT
new V-8 OVERHEAD VALVES "FIREPOWER" 331.1 C.I.D. ENGINE
180 H.P. @ 4000 RPM 7.5 COMPRESSION 3¹³/₁₆"x3⁵/₈" BORE & STROKE
WITH CHRYSLER'S FIRST V8 ENGINE   11-18   4260 lbs.

1951 CHRYSLER V-8

new "ORIFLOW" SHOCK ABSORBERS

new POWER STEERING AVAIL.

8.20 x 15" TIRES

131½" WHEELBASE

News America Syndicate
© News Group Chicago, Inc., 1984

YEARS WHEN OTHER MAKES OF CARS INTRODUCED V8 MODELS:
1915-CADILLAC; 1921-LINCOLN; 1932-FORD; 1939-MERCURY;
1949-OLDSMOBILE; 1951-STUDEBAKER; 1952-DeSOTO; 1953-BUICK,
DODGE; 1955-CHEVROLET, PLYMOUTH, PONTIAC, HUDSON, NASH,
PACKARD .... AND THE V8 "CRAZE" WAS IN FULL SWING!!

1951 Chrysler

"**F**irePower' … 'Hydraguide' … 'Oriflow' … They're not just fancy names for minor improvements. FirePower is an entirely new type engine no standard passenger car ever had before. It gets more power from every drop of gas. It has the first practical Hemispheric Combustion Chamber ("hemi") in an American passenger car. An engineering ideal that makes it possible for us to give you 180 horsepower with great economy! …

"'Hydraguide' is the greatest development since the self-starter. It's power steering that does four-fifths of the work of steering and parking your car ... With it—even at a standstill—you can turn your wheels with one finger ….

"… 'Oriflow' is a brand new Shock Absorber with over twice the shock-absorbing power of the best you ever had. You'll find the car steady as you never believed a car could be. It literally paves the roughest road ahead of you—even if it's filled with ruts and potholes."

Chrysler's venerable straight-eight engine—first introduced in mid-1930 for the 1931 model year—was forthwith replaced by the new overhead-valve "FirePower" V-8, a remarkable improvement which drew much attention to Chrysler in '51.

The L-head six-cylinder engine was still available during the 1950s, but it was the V-8 that was drawing the attention at that time. The V-8 was so popular that similar engines were developed for De Soto (1952), Dodge (1953), and Plymouth (1955). By the time the 1955 season was under way, nearly every American make of automobile offered some kind of up-to-date overhead-valve V-8.

BUILT IN THE SOUTH,
FOR SOUTHERN BUSINESSES

1951 CORBITT 6

DIESEL HAULER   (CUMMINS DIESEL ENG.)
TOP SPEED = 80

ALL 6-CYLINDER
ENGINES
GAS = 330, 371,
427, 513, 572,
OR 602 CID
(100-200 HP)

DIESEL = 298, 404,
426, 529, 672,
OR 743 CID
(99 TO 200 HP)
137-160"WB

MODELS:
G 101 B
G 301 B
G 302 B
G 402 B30
G 601 B32
G 603 B34
G 101 T20
G 302 T22
G 402 T22
G 602 T27
D 202 T20
D 401 T23
D 402 T25
D 601 T27
D 800 Ser.
D 803 T32
(D-DIESEL
T-TANDEM)

* PRODUCTION
SUSPENDED
1953-1956

BUILT BY CORBITT CO., INC.
HENDERSON, N.C.
1912-1958 *

TAP
4-28

1951 Corbitt Truck

The Brown and the Corbitt trucks were each built in North Carolina, as recently as the 1950s, and they can still be found in use in some parts of the southeastern U.S.A.; in other parts of the country, few have ever heard of them.

The Corbitt was built in Henderson, N.C. from 1913 to 1952 and again from 1957 to 1958. Richard J. "Uncle Dick" Corbitt, who had previously bought and sold tobacco, founded the company. After losing out to a large tobacco trust, he founded the Corbitt Buggy Co. (1899) and did very well with it. Within a few years, Corbitt was manufacturing automobiles, and in 1913 he switched to trucks (adding buses in 1915).

In addition to becoming the South's largest truck manufacturer in the 1920s, Corbitt exported trucks to twenty-three foreign countries! In the mid-1930s, some of the lighter Corbitt trucks and school buses used front-end sheet metal from 1934 Auburns, giving them a "classic" look and probably fooling a few casual observers into believing that they were Auburn trucks.

In the 1930s and 1940s, Corbitt's survival was encouraged by orders from the U.S. Army for medium and heavy-duty vehicles. In 1952, because of his age, Uncle Dick at last decided to retire. But, without his leadership the company soon closed. After a dormant period, Corbitt Co. Inc., in 1957-1958, re-entered the truck business for a very brief interval.

Have you ever seen a Corbitt truck? How about a Brown? Perhaps you have, if you live in or near North Carolina.

1950s

1951 De Soto

As a collector's car, this 1951 De Soto has some good things going for it. First, it is a discontinued make (gone for over four decades), which adds a great deal to its interest.

Second, it's a convertible, and convertibles are always popular with collectors.

Third, it was built by Chrysler Corporation, and Chrysler products of the early '50s are dependable and particularly well-engineered. Another "plus" is its toothy chrome grille—a real eye-catcher!

De Soto-Plymouth dealers sponsored *You Bet Your Life* on both radio and TV, hosted by Groucho Marx. Known in Marx Brothers films as the wisecracking ringleader, and a master of the barbed insult and corny pun, Groucho planned to come on that way in his *You Bet Your Life* quiz show.

Contestants were picked for their weird appearance or occupation, so they could easily be put down. However, Groucho mellowed and treated his contestants and guests with more kindness and courtesy as time went on. Vintage episodes of *You Bet Your Life* are still being syndicated on television today!

Please note the list of top 1950-1951 TV shows, bordering the illustration. If you're wondering why the ever-popular *I Love Lucy* isn't included, it's because Lucy and Desi began their famous TV series on October 15, 1951, at the beginning of the 1951-1952 season. Ironically, Desi and Lucy had to spend $5,000 of their own money to make a pilot film of the show, because know-it-all bigwigs predicted it would be a resounding flop! They wouldn't even touch it, at first.

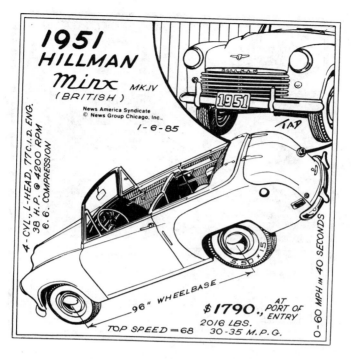

1951 HILLMAN minx MK.IV (BRITISH)

News America Syndicate
© News Group Chicago. Inc.,

1-6-85

4-CYL. L-HEAD, 77 C.I.D. ENG.
38 H.P. @ 4200 RPM
6.6. COMPRESSION

96" WHEELBASE

$1790., AT PORT OF ENTRY

2016 LBS.

TOP SPEED = 68   30-35 M.P.G.

0-60 MPH IN 40 SECONDS

5.50 x 15

1951 Hillman Minx

The first Hillman was the 1907 Hillman-Coatalen, so named since the earliest models were designed by Louis Coatalen. From 1908 to 1930, Hillman retained the same basic radiator shape, though it had been altered over the years. The Minx model name has been around since the early '30s, though the Hillman Minx known to Americans as the postwar type sold in the U.S.A. from 1949 until the mid-1960s, and the era of the Super Minx and Imp.

For years a member of the Rootes Group of British auto manufacturers, Hillman was affiliated with overseas Chrysler after 1964 when Chrysler Corp. gained a controlling interest in Rootes.

In March 1951, *Road and Track* magazine road-tested the Hillman Minx and gave it a generally good report—though they mentioned that the engine was a design from the early 1930s that had seen refinements over the years.

Early in 1949, as Hillman planned to launch its car in the U.S. market, *Forbes* magazine (March 1, 1949, page 15) reported that in 1947 only 1,124 British cars were sold in America, but that in '48 the figure had leaped to 21,854, and the British manufacturers hoped to sell 30,000 to 40,000 cars in America during 1949 while planning to sell 75,000 in Great Britain.

In typical British fashion, the top on the illustrated car could be set in three positions: up, down, or half-open (drop-head style) with only the rear quarters covered.

CLASSIC BRITISH LUXURY !

$4700. IN U.S.A.

TOP CAN FOLD TO HALF - WAY POSITION.

18 M.P.G. (HIGHWAY)   95 MILES PER HOUR

1951 JAGUAR MARK V

"DROPHEAD" CONVERTIBLE COUPE   120" W.B.
6 CYLINDERS (3½ LITRES DISPL.) 125 H.P.
INDEPENDENT TORSION BAR FRONT WHEEL SUSPENSION
0 TO 50 M.P.H. IN 9.8 SECONDS

News America Syndicate
© News Group Chicago, Inc., 1984   8-5

1951 Jaguar Mark V

In the early 1920s, in Blackpool, England, William Lyons and William Walmsley manufactured motorcycle sidecars, adding a coach-building business in 1927 to provide custom bodies for certain popular makes of British and European cars. This was to become known as the Swallow Coach-Building Co., Ltd.

In 1932 a Swallow "S.S. I" car was developed on a Standard chassis with some modification.

In 1936, the Jaguar name first appeared in the "S.S." line of cars (1932-1945), but Jaguar did not become an actual make of automobile until 1945 when S.S. Cars, Ltd. became Jaguar Cars, Ltd.

The stately Mark V (sedan or convertible) was offered from 1949 to 1951, and later in '51 it was joined by the improved Mark VII. There was

also the popular XK-120 Jaguar sports car, offered from '48 in roadster or coupe form. The Mark VII adopted the powerful dual OHC six engine used in the XK-120.

In an original Mark V ad, we're told that "The Jaguar is renowned, not only in Britain but throughout the world, for its unique combination of elegance and high performance...

" ... at 5 or 95 the Jaguar heralds its approach with the merest whisper; and in the deep-seated comfort of its real leather upholstery the driver has the magnificent feeling that he could steer this car through the eye of a needle."

The illustrated convertible could be driven with top "half open," as shown, and there was genuine polished walnut wood on the elaborate instrument panel and on garnish mouldings, etc.

1951 Nash *Airflyte* "AMBASSADOR"

6 CYL. (234.8 CID)
O.H.V. ENGINE
115 H.P. @ 3400 RPM
20-GAL. FUEL TANK
121" *wheelbase* © News America Syndicate, 1985

4-DR.
SUPER
SEDAN
$2330.
WT. = 3410 lbs.

LAST OF THE 1949-1951 "BATHTUB-BODIED" NASHES.
(LOWER-PRICED "STATESMAN" SERIES WITH LESS CHROME.)

RECLINING SEATS FOLD TOGETHER TO FORM A BED!

80 M.P.H. IN 15.3 SEC.

OVER 25 M.P.G.

new
REAR
FENDERS,
TAILLIGHTS.

new
VERTICAL
PIECES
IN
GRILLE.

new
RECTANGULAR
PARKING+
DIRECTIONAL
LIGHTS.

TAP 10-20

97 M.P.H. WITH OVERDRIVE

new
SIDE TRIM,
"GUARD RAIL" BUMPERS.

1951 Nash Ambassador

For 1951, Nash continued its ultra-streamlined fastback "Airflyte" sedans (two-door or four-door). Though the 1949 and 1950 models had looked virtually alike, there were several noticeable changes for 1951 (please check arrows in illustration).

In the 1951 Mobil Gas Economy Run, the Nash Rambler (compact model) got 31.05 m.p.g. (with overdrive), and the medium-priced Statesman got 26.12. Top-of-the-line Ambassador got 25.92, excellent economy for a big car!

"Weather-Eye" Conditioned Air System was not air conditioning as we know it today. It did not include a power-driven refrigeration unit, but it gave excellent hot and cool air circulation as desired—and was proudly mentioned in most Nash advertising in the 1940s and early 1950s.

"There's much of tomorrow in all Nash does today," was a Nash slogan in the early 1950s. Body and frame were one "welded, double-rigid unit" ... one of many advanced ideas in this car.

GM Hydra-Matic Drive (automatic transmission) was an available option in the 1951 Nash, even though Nash Motors was a part of Nash-Kelvinator Corp. of Detroit, Mich. and Kenosha, Wis. (and not affiliated with General Motors).

The convertible seat-to-a-bed was a Nash feature since 1935; in addition, front seats were adjustable to five reclining positions, so that passengers could rest or sleep en route.

One bizarre feature of the Nash Airflyte was the low-cut wheel openings along body sides. They looked good, but made tire-changing more of an effort and limited the turning radius of front wheels.

1950s

1951 Packard 400 Patrician

This was Packard's most luxurious model for 1951, available September 1950 with other '51 Packards from 200 series and up. For '51, Packards were totally and pleasingly restyled, with sturdy-looking new bodies that would still look good in the mid-1950s! Gone was the old narrow look of the 1940s. The '51 Packard had a bold, broad new grille, which managed to retain the traditional Packard fluted outline around its borders.

Packard and Pontiac were the final American cars to offer L-head straight-eight engines (as late as 1954), and the 1951 Packard eight came in a choice of two displacements: a new 288 c.i.d. or new 327 c.i.d., with 135 or 155 h.p. respectively. (The larger engine, if sold with a manual or overdrive transmission, was rated at 150 h.p.)

New shock absorbers were "direct-action" with special valves that automatically adjusted to all types of road shock. This was to compete with Chrysler Corporation's new "Oriflow" shock absorbers for 1951, which were heralded to be about the best that money could buy.

Packard window areas were enlarged. Rear window (backlight) was swept back stylishly, increasing vision by ninety-six percent! An entire twelve inches was added to the rear seat width! And, front seats were two inches wider than in '50. There were many more improvements, as well.

The lower-priced 200, with the smaller eight, managed to top 95 m.p.h. in a speed test. The 400 was heavier, but with its larger engine, it might have equaled or surpassed that figure.

1951 PLYMOUTH P-23
"CRANBROOK"
4-DR. SEDAN
3109 LBS.

$1826. f.o.b.
PRICE (at factory)
(TAX, LICENSE, DELIVERY, OTHER COSTS ADDED LATER)

6 CYLS.
(217.8 CUBIC IN. DISPL.)
97 HP @ 3600 RPM
7.0 TO 1 COMPR.

6.70 x 15 TIRES

ALSO AVAILABLE IN P-23 "CAMBRIDGE" SERIES (118½" W.B.,) OR IN P-22 LOWER PRICED (111" W.B.) "CONCORD" SERIES (INCLUDING "SUBURBAN" OR DELUXE "SAVOY" STATION WAGONS.) (BECAUSE OF '50-'53 KOREAN WAR, 1951 PLYMOUTHS INTRODUCED LATE : 1-13-51.)

WITH "SAFETY-FLOW RIDE," ENHANCED BY THE NEW IMPROVED "ORIFLOW" SHOCK ABSORBERS.

© News America Syndicate, 1986

1951 Plymouth

"**O**riflow" shock absorbers were the big news on Chrysler Corp. cars (Plymouth, Dodge, De Soto, Chrysler) in 1951, but there were other changes as well.

The grille on the new '51 Plymouth was a perfect example of the "toothy" faces of 1950s cars. This grille resembled a sad, droopy-cornered mouth, giving the 1951-1952 Plymouths a nickname among some as the "sad-mouthed Plymouths." Plymouth held its own in sales, but the lugubrious new grille did nothing to attract customers.

De Luxe and Special De Luxe model names were scrapped in favor of New-Englandy "Ivy League" model names of Concord, Cambridge, and Cranbrook on these staid family cars.

Inside, the dash was redesigned and upholstery patterns were new.

Other new features: waterproofed (rubber-covered) spark plugs and igni-tion system; constant-speed electric windshield wipers; narrower front corner posts and broader rear windows; new side trim; new "easy action" hand brake; improved foot brakes, etc.

Each year, usually around October, throngs of people flocked on down to their local car dealerships at new-model time. But, the Plymouth was late in 1951, not making its '51 debut until Saturday, January 13.

The 1951 and 1952 Plymouths were nearly identical twins, but the '52 appeared with a new circular hood badge instead of the shield badge, and with script lettering on fender-side model designations (instead of block letters as in '51).

The hardtop convertible (club coupe without center side pillars) was growing in popularity in '51, and Plymouth offered a new one in its top-line "Cranbrook" series in 1951: the "Belvedere."

1950s

Within the illustration: AN EARLY TYPE OF "TILT-CAB" TRUCK! BY WHITE MOTOR CO., CLEVELAND, OHIO. 85", 91" OR 109" WHEELBS. 1951 WHITE CAB-OVER-ENGINE 3000 SERIES. 4.75 70, 7.20 GEAR RATIOS. 6375 TO 8215 lbs. CHASSIS WT. White SUPER POWER 3000. 6 CYL. 318, 340 OR 386 CID. 114, 120 OR 135 HP @ 3000 RPM. 5-SPEED TRANS. 16½ TO 27 TONS GROSS WEIGHT. © 1988 North America Syndicate, Inc. All rights reserved.

1951 White 3000 Series Truck

"The Truck That Tips Its Cab To Service!" That was the White 3000 series cab-over-engine (c.o.e.) truck, tilt-cabs being a novelty back in the early 1950s.

"The first really major truck advance in years!" proclaimed an April 1951 White truck advertisement (running in *Fortune* and in *Collier's* magazines, to mention two publications). "From all lines of business, large and small ... from owners, fleet superintendents, mechanics, drivers ... the reports are the same: The White 3000 saves so much time in traffic ... Saves so much driver energy ... And is so quickly maintenanced ... That its dollar savings can be measured at the end of every day."

The new 3000 series c.o.e. was described and illustrated as early as May 1949 in *Motor* magazine, and within two years it seemed to be catching on with truckers and business owners. It was so easy to maintain, because the cab lifted up (with power assist) to make engine, chassis, and drivetrain easy to get at. A short wheelbase c.o.e. truck or tractor was more maneuverable for crowded, narrow city streets. The 3000 series, in fact, was particularly recommended for city service, whereas the White conventionals were suited for inter-city hauls.

The 3000 series was built lower to the ground, with a lower frame than most other c.o.e. trucks. Available as a tractor to pull trailerized cargos, or as a cab/chassis unit to which any number of specialized truck bodies could be fitted, the 3000 series was available in various wheelbase lengths and with three types of six-cylinder engines.

A RELIABLE "WORKHORSE"

1951 WILLYS "JEEP"
4-WHEEL-DRIVE PICKUP
MFD. BY WILLYS-OVERLAND MOTORS, TOLEDO, OHIO
"MAKERS OF AMERICA'S MOST USEFUL VEHICLES."

3062 LBS. (5300 GVW)

TAD 9·15

$1591. and up

© 1991 North America Syndicate, Inc.
All Rights Reserved

4 CYL.
134.2 CID
3⅛" × 4⅛" B+ST

118" W.B.

WILLYS "HURRICANE"
F-HEAD ENGINE had
OVERHEAD INTAKE VALVES AND
IN-BLOCK EXHAUST VALVES
(cutaway view)
5.38 GEAR RATIO (AVAIL. OVERDRIVE)
6.00 or 6.50 × 16 S TIRES

7.4 TO 1 COMPRESSION

72 HP @ 4000 RPM

1951 Willys Jeep Pickup

In the early postwar years, Willys produced the Jeep station wagon and the Jeep pickup (illustrated), in addition to the popular Jeeps. The Willys name continued on Jeeps and Jeep vehicles until 1962. In 1963, the totally restyled Kaiser Jeep vehicles appeared.

During the Korean War era, Jeep pickups were selling well. To quote a July 1951 magazine ad: "With farm labor so scarce, it is more important than ever to keep each season's work right on schedule. One of your biggest helps in doing that is the Four-Wheel-Drive Willys (Jeep) truck.

"This sturdy truck, with the extra traction of all-wheel drive, is your best assurance of getting jobs done on time, regardless of weather, bad roads, and tough driving conditions. It will pull through mud, sand, snow, and boggy fields that no ordinary truck could tackle. It has spectacular grade-climbing ability and stands up under rough cross-country travel.

"The Willys is powered by the sensational F-head Hurricane Engine, with a compression ratio of 7.4 to 1 (7.8 optional for high altitude). It has selective two- and four-wheel drive, with regular and special low gear ratios, giving you an operating range to meet all travel conditions."

In this Jeep pickup, there were three shift levers: the main three-speed shift lever; the transfer case lever (back for two-wheel drive, forward for four-wheel drive); and the low-range lever (move it forward to put into extra-low ratio in 4-W-D, for heavy pulling power).

1950s

THE FIRST WILLYS SINCE 1942 WHICH WAS NOT A "JEEP"!

new 1952 *Aero Willys*

108" WHEELBASE *new* FOR 1952, AND. AVAIL. IN 2 DOOR "AERO WING" ('52 ONLY) "AERO ACE CUSTOM" OR "AERO EAGLE" H/T MODELS. (NO 4 DR. SEDANS UNTIL 1953)

FROM $1989.⁰⁰ F.O.B., TOLEDO, OH.

6 CYL. L-HEAD
"AERO LARK DELUXE", "AERO FALCON" W/B.
ADDED IN 1953
161 CU. D.
90 H.P. @ 4400 RPM

UP TO 35 M.P.G. WITH OVERDRIVE!

Tad 2-4-90

ARE YOU INTERESTED IN CARS or TRUCKS (OF ANY MAKE) BUILT BETWEEN 1928 and 1965? IF SO, YOU'D LIKE THE C.H.V.A. (CONTEMPORARY HISTORICAL VEHICLE ASS'N.) FOR FREE DETAILS ON THIS EXCELLENT CLUB, JUST SEND A SELF-ADDRESSED, STAMPED ENVELOPE TO: C.H.V.A. (DEPT. A) 16944 DEARBORN ST., SEPULVEDA, CA. 91343

1952 Aero Willys

"Up to 35 miles on a gallon!" Willys-Overland, of Toledo, Ohio, assured prospective buyers that they could get such great fuel economy in a Aero Willys, at highway cruising speeds—with the optional overdrive.

Since 1943, Willys-Overland had been building nothing but Jeep vehicles. In the December 1946 issue of *Popular Science,* there was an announcement for a new postwar Willys-Overland 6-70 (non-Jeep) sedan with a 104-inch wheelbase. It was planned for mid-1947 introduction, but never reached the showrooms. Instead, Jeep vehicles continued to occupy all of Willys' production until the arrival of the 1952 Aero series.

True to its name, the new '52 car was aerodynamically designed with a "low 5-foot silhouette" minimizing wind drag. To make the car more maneuverable, especially when parking, fenders were high enough that the driver could see all four. Front and rear seats were each over five feet wide (61 inches, to be exact)—plenty of room for six adults!

The lowest-priced Aero Wing was dropped after '52, replaced by the Aero Lark. The Aero Eagle (top of line) didn't appear until later in '52. Various models were added or dropped as the Aero series continued through the '53, '54, and early '55 seasons.

The Aero Willys was not the only compact car available in the early '50s. Nash offered the Rambler, Kaiser offered the Henry J, and Hudson got into the act with its compact Jet.

Commonly seen in the 1950s, the Aero Willys is now scarce and most remaining examples are in the hands of collectors.

1950s

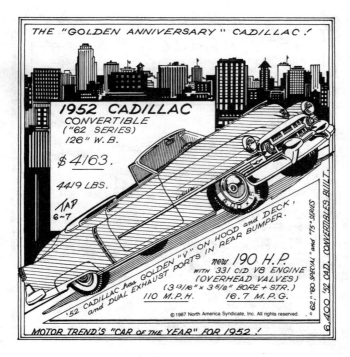

THE "GOLDEN ANNIVERSARY" CADILLAC!

1952 CADILLAC
CONVERTIBLE
("62 SERIES)
126" W.B.

$4163.

4419 LBS.

TAP
6~7

'52 CADILLAC has GOLDEN "V" ON HOOD and DECK, and DUAL EXHAUST PORTS IN REAR BUMPER.

new 190 H.P.
WITH 331 CID V8 ENGINE
(OVERHEAD VALVES)
(3 13/16" x 3 5/8" BORE + STR.)
110 M.P.H.   16.7 M.P.G.

6,400 '52 CAD. CONVERTIBLES BUILT. "62," "60 SPECIAL" and "75" SERIES

MOTOR TREND'S "CAR OF THE YEAR" FOR 1952!

1950s

1952 Cadillac

Because the first Cadillac had been built in 1902, General Motors' Cadillac Division pulled out all the stops to celebrate Cadillac's Golden Anniversary in '52. The new model looked only slightly changed from 1951: The V-insignias in front and back were now golden instead of chrome, and there was a new plaque with winged insignia at either side of the grille. In back, dual exhaust ports passed through the bumper.

Also noteworthy was the 30 h.p. increase in engine output. C.F. Arnold, Cadillac's chief engineer, explained specifically how the horsepower boost was accomplished: 15 h.p. increase for new carburetion; 9 h.p. for a new cylinder head with 1/8-inch larger exhaust ports; 2 1/2 h.p. for a new exhaust manifold; and 3 1/2 for a new intake manifold, bringing the total horsepower to 190 (from the 1951 figure of 160).

The Hydra-Matic Drive automatic transmission (standard equipment) was improved for '52, with an extra-power range for quick acceleration (ready at a "flick" of a finger).

The convertible was available only in the "62" series, which also included a four-door sedan, a coupe, and a Coupe de Ville hardtop convertible.

The 60 Special Fleetwood (easily recognized by its additional chrome trim) was available only as a sedan ($4,323, as opposed to $3,684 for a "62" sedan). The 60-S had a 130-inch wheelbase, and 16,110 were built.

The 146-inch-wheelbase "75" series offered two different eight-passenger models, and there was also a long 157-inch-wheelbase "75" "commercial chassis" available for special body applications (ambulances, funeral vehicles, or stretch limousines).

TRANS.) LOWER-PRICED "SPECIAL" HAS LESS CHROME.

1952 CHEVROLET

KK SERIES
STYLELINE DELUXE
SPORT COUPE

WITH 6-CYL. OVERHEAD VALVE ENGINE
216.5 C.I.D. (W. STD. TRANSMISSION)
(3½" x 3¾" BORE and STROKE) **92 H.P.** @ 3400 RPM

115" WHEELBASE
WEIGHT = 3100 LBS.
16-GALLON FUEL TANK

105-H.P., 235.5 C.I.D. ENGINE AVAIL. w. OPTIONAL "POWERGLIDE" AUTO. TRANS.
(SINCE 1950)

© News America Syndicate, 1985

5-26

4.11 GEAR RATIO (3.55 w. AUTO.

$**1730.** and up f.o.b.

OPTIONAL CHROME HERE

ABOVE SPORT COUPE DIFFERS FROM "BEL AIR"
2-DR. HARDTOP (W/O UPPER CENTER PILLAR), and NOT TO BE MISTAKEN
FOR THE 2-DOOR SEDAN (WHICH HAS LONGER CAB.)

1952 Chevrolet

Here's a car that nearly everyone likes! Though they were not spectacular performers (80 to 87 m.p.h., 14 to 24 m.p.g.), the six-cylinder Chevrolets of 1949 to 1952 were extremely dependable and attractive cars with clean, pleasing lines. The '52 was the final model in a four-year styling cycle that featured simple curves, pontoon-style rear fenders, and a two-piece curved windshield.

The '52 Chevrolet differed from the '51 most noticeably in that it had five, new raised pieces running down the center blade of the grille (as illustrated). There were other small changes as well.

For 1952, Chevrolet offered a choice of twenty-six colors and two-tone combinations, (with color-matched two-tone blue, green, or gray interiors in De Luxe models). They called this "Royal-Tone Styling."

"Power-Jet" carburetor was improved, with automatic choke on 105-h.p. Powerglide models. "Quick-Reflex" shock absorbers were improved, and new "Centerpoise Power" meant a better-balanced engine. Compression ratio: 6.6 to 1 (or 6.7 to 1 in 105-h.p. version).

Powerglide automatic transmission (introduced 1950) cost $178.35 extra (with prices varying in some areas). Other options: radio, heater-defroster, seat covers (plastic, fiber, or rayon), directional signals, back-up light, fog lights, electric clock, glare-proof mirror, license plate frame, ornamental steering wheel, outside visor, signal parking brake, front fender chrome pads, etc.

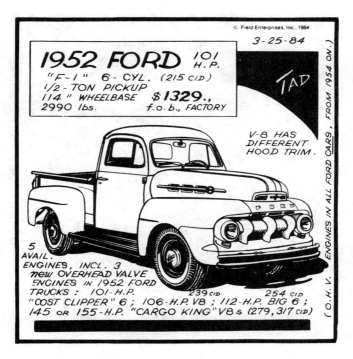

C. Field Enterprises, Inc., 1984

3-25-84

1952 FORD *101 H.P.*

"F-1" 6-CYL. (215 CID)
1/2-TON PICKUP
114" WHEELBASE **$1329.,**
2990 lbs. *f.o.b., FACTORY*

TAD

V-8 HAS DIFFERENT HOOD TRIM.

(O.H.V. ENGINES IN ALL FORD CARS, FROM 1954 ON.)

5 AVAIL.
ENGINES, INCL. 3 *new* OVERHEAD VALVE ENGINES IN 1952 FORD TRUCKS : 101-H.P.
239 CID
254 CID
"COST CLIPPER" 6 ; 106-H.P. V8 ; 112-H.P. BIG 6 ; 145 OR 155-H.P. "CARGO KING" V8s (279, 317 CID)

1952 Ford Pickup

Thousands of reliable Ford pickups from the 1950s are still in regular service. Chances are, you've seen one or more around town, even recently!

The 1948-1952 Ford pickup had, basically, the same body shape, though the 1951-1952 had a broader, bolder (and more ferocious-looking) grille than did its predecessors. In 1953, came many changes, a general restyling, and a redesigned cab with a wider hood.

In 1952, the big news in Ford trucks was the addition of three new "low-friction" short-stroke engines to the line, making five engines to choose from! These new engines offered overhead valves, two years before the Ford *cars* dropped the once popular L-head arrangement.

Among other improvements was a redesigned "full-flow" oil filter.

There were 275 series power combinations, with a wide choice of engines, transmissions, axles, and tire sizes. Gross capacity ratings ranged from 4,000 to 41,000 lbs., depending on the model. These were from Ford's famous "F" series, beginning with the standard 1/2-ton F-1 pickup shown here. In 1953, the 1/2-ton pickup changed to the more familiar F-100 designation.

Looking for an old car to buy? Don't ignore the possibilities of owning an old pickup truck! Sometimes one can find a real bargain in one of these, and they're built heavy to last!

1950s

FAMOUS "STEP-DOWN" BODY / FRAME DESIGN INTRODUCED BY HUDSON (ON 1948 MODEL)

2-DR. CLUB CPE.

© 1989 North America Syndicate, Inc. All rights reserved.

4-DR.

124" WHEELBASE

1952 HORNET "CUSTOM" CLUB COUPE 3550 LBS.
$2742.⁰⁰, fob,
HUDSON MOTOR CAR CO., DETROIT

(PACEMAKER 6, WASP 6, COMMODORE 6 or 8 ALSO AVAIL. FROM HUDSON, 1952.)

OVERDRIVE OR= AUTOMATIC TRANSMISSION OPTIONAL.

"YOU SEE THE NEW STYLE ... COME TRY THE POWER!"

1952 HUDSON "HORNET
"HOTTEST" SIX OF THE 1950s!!

WITH **BIG 308** CU. IN. **6 CYL. ENGINE!**
(L - HEAD)
145 HP @ **3800** RPM
7.2 10 1 COMPRESSION
(3 13/16 × 4 1/2" BORE + ST.)
20 GALLON FUEL TANK
4.1, 4.55 or 3.58 GEAR RATIO

7.10 × 15

TAP
11~5

1952 Hudson "Hornet"

In 1952, the Hornet (and Wasp) featured "Twin H-Power," an improved carburetion system that thoroughly vaporized the gasoline equally in all cylinders and assured the utmost power from every drop of fuel. "Twin H-Power" also gave the 1952 Hornet more pickup in high gear, even from a low speed.

The Hornet used the Hudson H-145 engine, while the new, lower-priced '52 Wasp used the H-127 engine (also a six).

Road & Track magazine (July 1952) described the Hornet as "obviously bulky, yet low ... and the bumblebees plastered at various vantage points leave no doubt that this is a Hornet. Chrome seems to swirl about with little rhyme or reason..."

Top speed of the Hornet in the *Road & Track* test report was over 97 m.p.h.

Gas mileage varied from 15 m.p.g. (at 30 miles per hour) to eleven (at eighty).

Hudson interiors were judged roomy and luxurious, and the V-shaped windshield was set far ahead of the dashboard (a feature that the reviewer didn't like).

Motor Trend (August 1952) also tested a Hudson Hornet, and got it up to 105 m.p.h.! In "D-4" drive range, *Motor Trend* testers observed over 21 m.p.g. at 30 miles per hour, and 13.1 in city traffic. *Motor Trend* mentioned that the imitation "mother-of-pearl" background on the speedometer dial made the figures difficult to read.

Hudson, back in 1932, was a pioneer in replacing dash gauges with so-called "idiot lights," and in 1952 there was no oil pressure gauge or ammeter—but simply red warning lights to indicate trouble.

A VARIETY OF ROSE IS NAMED FOR THE CHRYSLER IMPERIAL!

CHRYSLER *Imperial*

131½" WHEELBASE

ADVERTISED AS "THE FINEST CAR AMERICA HAS YET PRODUCED!"

"NEWPORT" 2-DR. H/T LESS THAN 475 BUILT!

ORIGINALLY PRICED $4224.⁰⁰ fob, DETROIT CURRENTLY WORTH $550. TO $18,000., (POOR TO LIKE-NEW)

W. 4365 lbs.

331.1/ C.I.D. V8 180 HP OVERHEAD VALVES 2ND YEAR FOR CHRYSLER'S V8 ENGINE

1952

HAPPY THANKSGIVING!

TAP 11•24

1952 Chrysler Imperial

I f you're a horticulturist or a grower of roses, you may be familiar with the "Chrysler Imperial" strain of prize roses. Back in 1952, Chrysler Imperial featured roses and jewelry in its delightful series of new magazine advertisements.

Because of the successful reception of Chrysler's restyled 1951 models, many with the all-new 180-h.p. "Fire-Power" overhead-valve V-8 engine, little change was deemed necessary for '52.

As in '51, the 1952 Chrysler lineup included the Windsor (with a traditional L-head "Spitfire" engine) and the V-8-powered Saratoga, New Yorker, Imperial, and Crown Imperial models.

"Hydraguide" power steering was a feature available on all 1952 Chryslers, having been introduced for the first time on the 1951 Imperial and New Yorker models. Though Chrysler was the pioneer of power steering, GM

jumped on the bandwagon in 1952 with such a blaze of advertising fanfare that many assumed it was a GM exclusive!

Disc brakes were another advanced feature of the '51-'52 Imperials, with forced-air cooling to reduce brake temperatures thirty-five percent and prolong life.

In *Fortune, Holiday, Saturday Evening Post*, etc., Chrysler Imperials were advertised in '52 more frequently than before—with such quotes as, "More and more of the people who can afford any car in all the world are today selecting the Chrysler Imperial," and "The Imperial by Chrysler has become the ultimate expression of taste and judgment."

Top-of-the-line was the 145 1/2-inch wheelbase Crown Imperial Limousine. But, the truly sporty Imperial for '52 was this "Newport" two-door hardtop, since no convertible was offered.

1952 Kaiser Manhattan

In early 1950, the 1951 Kaisers appeared—totally restyled and introduced with a colorful splash of advertising. Frazer was discontinued after 1951, and its final '51 model had a bulbous, strange-looking grille but a plain-looking body similar to the '47-'50 series. Frazer's main claim to fame for '51 was that it had a variety of models that included a four-door convertible. Otherwise, it was all Kaiser's show!

Kaiser was unanimously reported as the best-looking car of 1951, and throughout the early 1950s Kaiser was the prettiest! For '52, there were a few modifications: The 1952 windshield was one-piece instead of divided at the center, and taillights were considerably enlarged, a noteworthy safety feature!

Other improvements for 1952 included a more comfortable front seat with heavier padding over springs; an accelerator pedal requiring less pressure than before; improved suspension; a quieter engine; a bumper combined with the lower portion of the grille; and much more. Kaiser's stylist was Howard "Dutch" Darrin, a well-known automotive designer who had designed the Kaiser-Darrin sports car for Kaiser-Frazer. One safety feature Darrin included in his designs was a padded dash.

In a *Motor Trend* test, a '52 Kaiser did over 95 m.p.h.! Great work for a six-cylinder car that could also get up to 20 or 25 miles per gallon of gas! *Motor Trend* reviewers were really pleased with the '52 Kaiser, noting that many of the suggestions they had made for improvements in 1951 had been followed through.

new 317.5 C.I.D. OVERHEAD-VALVE V8 ENGINE
0 - 60 MPH IN 16.67 SECONDS
9 TO 19.7 M.P.G.
4235 lbs.
123" WB

ALL FORD-BUILT CARS TOTALLY RESTYLED FOR 1952.

1952 LINCOLN "CAPRI" HARDTOP

7.5 TO 1 COMPRESSION

160 H.P. @ 3900 RPM

$35/8.

8.00 X 15

TAD 3-2

100 M.P.H. TOP SPEED,
BUT WITH HIGH-SPEED REAR AXLE,
OVER 130 M.P.H. WAS REACHED!
LINCOLN WON GREAT VICTORIES IN THE
MEXICAN ROAD RACES!

© News America Syndicate, 1986

GM SUPPLIED THE DUAL-RANGE "Hydra-Matic" AUTOMATIC TRANS.

1950s

1952 Lincoln

The totally-restyled Lincoln, for 1952 (in look-alike Cosmopolitan or Capri series), was advertised as the car designed for "modern living" and was illustrated in magazines on colorful single- and dual-page spreads, shown against up-to-date backdrops of Spartanly-simple modernistic homes, apartments, and office buildings. In some cases, it was even shown indoors, with simple 1950s-modernistic furniture.

All Ford Motor Co. cars were redesigned for '52 and looked completely new. Partially because of the 1950-1953 Korean War, rival automobiles changed very little in 1952, so Ford products stole a lot of thunder! The Lincoln and Mercury, both heavy and bulbous-looking during 1949-1951, had been trimmed down and didn't look much larger than the Fords! But, the new lean look was well received.

The 1952 Lincoln was the first Ford Motor Co. car to add overhead valves to its redesigned V-8 engine—and performance was exceptional.

Automatic transmission was standard on Lincoln for '52. Though (since 1951) Ford had an optional "Ford-O-Matic" and Mercury a "Merc-O-Matic," the Lincoln Division chose to buy "Hydra-Matic" units from their competitor, General Motors, for a few years.

Suddenly, Lincoln was a road-racing car! In the second, third, and fourth Carrera Panamericana, south of the border, Lincoln was at the top of the "International Standard" Class, taking top five places in 1952, top four in 1953, and top two in 1954. And, in '52, a Lincoln finished the 2,000-mile ordeal from Juarez, Mexico to the Guatemalan border an hour sooner than the sport Ferrari that had won in '51!

A RARE CANADIAN CAR!

1952 METEOR

"MAINLINE"

2-DOOR "RANCH WAGON" WITH L HEAD 239 CID V8 (110 H.P. @ 3800 RPM)

new 115" W.B.

4.09 TO 1 GEAR RATIO (4.27 w. O.D.; 3.54 w. A/T MERC-O-MATIC)

© 1990 North America Syndicate, Inc. All Rights Reserved

BUILT BY FORD MOTOR CO. OF CANADA AND AVAILABLE ONLY FROM CANADIAN LINCOLN-MERCURY DEALERS. NOT SOLD IN THE U.S.A.

DATA THANKS TO WALLACE WEBSTER, KIRKLAND, WA.

AAP 7-29

"MAINLINE" SERIES DASH

("CUSTOMLINE" HAS 255 CID V8 AND MERCURY STYLE DASH.)

1952 Meteor "Mainline"

In 1952, Ford Motor Co.'s Canadian Meteor was available in a two-model series: "Mainline" and the more expensive "Customline." The latter had ten more horsepower and a chrome strip along the side (running back to almost the rear edge of the front door). Wheel covers of either model were the same, but the Customline had a more unique dashboard, resembling that of the 1952 Mercury.

Like the American-built Ford Motor Co. cars, the Canadian Meteor and Monarch also had the all-new body styling for '52. Of the so-called "Big Three," Ford was ahead in 1952 styling, because '52 GM and Chrysler Corp. cars were changed but little from '51; they'd be restyled in '53. However, Nash introduced an all-new "Golden Airflyte" model with Pininfarina styling for '52, and the '52 Willys Aero was a totally new car! Studebaker got rid of its '50-'51 "bulletnose," but retained its former body style one more year and added a new two-door "hardtop convertible."

Generally speaking, most 1952 cars are very simple and reliable. They didn't have many of the automatic gadgets found on some cars of the later '50s, and were better off without them since the gadgetry had a marked tendency to cause electrical and mechanical problems after a few years of use.

120" WHEELBASE
239.2 CID 6 OR 268.4 CID 8
1952 Pontiac
OPTIONAL "DUAL RANGE" HYDRA-MATIC TRANS.
3.08 GEAR RATIO (AUTOMATIC)
3.9 GEAR RATIO
122 HP @ 3600 RPM (STRAIGHT 8)
7.10 x 15
$ 1956.~$2772.
ORIGINAL 1952 PRICE RANGE
4.1 GEAR RATIO
102 HP @ 3400 RPM (6) OR

© 1990 North America Syndicate, Inc. All Rights Reserved

3~4~90

INTERESTED IN A GOOD PONTIAC CLUB? FOR DETAILS, SEND A SELF-ADDRESSED, STAMPED ENVELOPE TO: PONTIAC-OAKLAND CLUB, P.O. BOX 4789, CULVER CITY, CA., 90230-4789

1952 Pontiac

The big news for '52 in GM's Pontiac line was the improved automatic transmission: the new, optional "Dual-Range" Hydra-Matic. *Motor Trend* reviewers liked it, stating, "It's been a long time since anything as good as the "Dual-Range" Hydra-Matic transmission happened to drivers who like automatic transmissions."

Motor Trend contended that the "Dual-Range" was "the best compromise between the stick shift (with its full driver control) and the fluid coupling (with its convenience)." With ease, it could be hand-shifted back and forth between third and fourth speed, "giving you the advantage of engine braking, at the same time allowing you to accelerate upgrade without fear that it will automatically change to fourth as you're trying to pass another car."

With this improved automatic, a new higher-speed rear axle (differen-

tial) was used (3.08 instead of 3.63 to 1), for more economical high-speed cruising in fourth.

The new "Dual-Range" Hydra-Matic started off in second gear, but flooring the gas pedal brought in first (low) for heavy-duty pulling, steep hills, etc.

Not only was the '52 Pontiac more economical on fuel than the '51, but it was also faster: over 95 m.p.h. in some tests!

Because of certain industry restrictions brought about by the 1950-1953 Korean War, styling changes on the '52 model were minor: The "Pontiac" name above the grille was now in block letters instead of in script. Just below the 1952 nameplate, there were four very small horizontal slots in the upper piece of the grille. Side trim was slightly changed from 1951, as were hubcaps, interior details, etc.

1950s

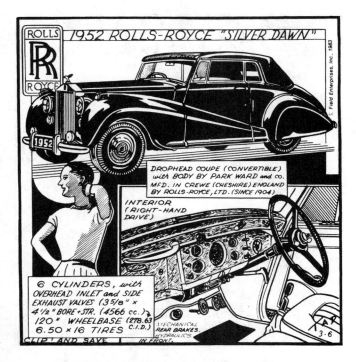

1952 ROLLS-ROYCE "SILVER DAWN"

© Field Enterprises, Inc. 1983

DROPHEAD COUPE (CONVERTIBLE) with BODY BY PARK WARD and CO. MFD. IN CREWE (CHESHIRE) ENGLAND BY ROLLS-ROYCE, LTD. (SINCE 1904)

INTERIOR (RIGHT-HAND DRIVE)

6 CYLINDERS, with OVERHEAD INLET and SIDE EXHAUST VALVES (3 5/8" x 4 1/2" BORE + STR. (4566 cc.) 120" WHEELBASE (278.63 C.I.D.) 6.50 x 16 TIRES

MECHANICAL REAR BRAKES. HYDRAULICS IN FRONT.

CLIP AND SAVE

3-6

1952 Rolls-Royce Silver Dawn

Long entitled "the best car in the world," the magnificent Rolls-Royce is known everywhere for its impeccable quality. Over fifty percent of the Rolls-Royces built (from 1904 to 1983) are still registered and in use! Rolls-Royce is considered "the car that never wears out," and justifiably so.

The Silver Dawn series was first introduced in 1949, and for a time was built for export (including an available left-hand drive). The illustrated 1952 model was available in its home country of England, as well as elsewhere.

Several years ago, I acquired a most attractive, original 1952 Silver Dawn catalogue for which I'm ever grateful! In the 1952 catalogue, the Silver Dawn was described as "a car that has been developed to conform with the changing needs of the times," as it was designed to be owner driven. Uniformed private chauffeurs were becoming a disappearing breed after World War II.

Silver Dawn saloons (sedans) had all-steel bodies built by Rolls-Royce, but the illustrated convertible had a body by Park Ward and Co. Most of the more expensive varieties of Rolls-Royce automobiles had made-to-order bodies.

Like more costly Rolls-Royces, the Silver Dawn had a dashboard and interior trim of genuine, hand-finished polished wood.

With an eighteen-gallon fuel tank, the Silver Dawn averaged fourteen to 16 miles per gallon. The sedan weighed 4,132 lbs. and cost over 4,605 pounds in British currency (including tax). Prices were upwards of $10,000 in the U.S.A.

BLT. BY BROWN TRUCK AND EQUIPMENT COMPANY, CHARLOTTE, NORTH CAROLINA (1939 TO 1953)

MODEL "LS"

TAD 8/28

10.00 × 20" TIRES
4 OTHER PREVIOUS BROWN TRUCK MFRS. SINCE 1912!

5-SPEED TRANS.	*1953 BROWN*	18½-TON GROSS VEHICLE WT.
6.16 TO 5.28 GEAR RATIO	CAB-OVER-ENGINE TRUCK-TRACTOR "LT" and "LP" MODELS HAVE 6-CYLINDER, 743 C.I.D. CUMMINS DIESEL ENGINES (LT=200 HP; LP=175 HP) "LS" HAS 6-CYL. BUDA "6-DC-844" ENG. 844 C.I.D. (210 HP @ 2100 RPM)	

1950s

1953 Brown Truck

Here's a rare hauler, hailing from North Carolina. The Brown truck of 1939-1953 was seen mostly in the Southeastern states.

These truck-tractors were originally created for the exclusive use of Horton Motor Lines, and were designed by J. L. Brown (chief engineer of Horton Motor Lines). In 1942, Horton merged with six other companies to form Associated Transport.

After the war, an improved Model 513 Brown truck was made available to the general public. In the late 1940s, Cummins diesel engines became an option. Brown trucks were built in conventional (long-hood) models, as well as in the illustrated c.o.e. (cab-over-engine) type.

If they were successful in the Southeast, then why were the Brown trucks discontinued in 1953? Associ-ated Transport officials decided they could save money by ordering lower-priced, mass-produced trucks from major manufacturers. With the loss of its major customer, Brown Truck & Equipment Co. had little encourage-ment to continue production, though apparently the factory continued for some years to service and supply parts for its older units.

An interesting feature of the final Brown trucks of 1953 (and late 1952) was their use of aluminum —to add "2,300 lbs. extra payload" to the new Brown c.o.e. tandem tractor! According to a November 1952 advertise-ment in *Motor Transportation* magazine, Brown's latest design, the illustrated "LS" model, had over thirty aluminum parts. Totaling 2,140 lbs., they "saved more than their own weight" in this heavy-duty tractor.

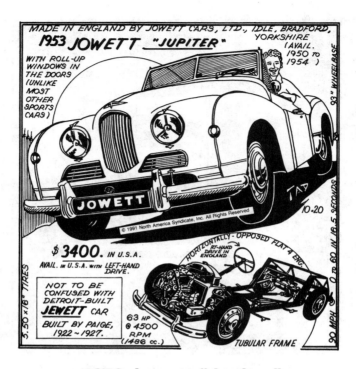

MADE IN ENGLAND BY JOWETT CARS, LTD., IDLE, BRADFORD, YORKSHIRE

1953 JOWETT "JUPITER" (AVAIL. 1950 to 1954)

WITH ROLL-UP WINDOWS IN THE DOORS (UNLIKE MOST OTHER SPORTS CARS)

93" WHEELBASE

JOWETT

TAD

10-20

© 1991 North America Syndicate, Inc. All Rights Reserved

$3400. IN U.S.A.

AVAIL. IN U.S.A. WITH LEFT-HAND DRIVE.

5.50 x 16" TIRES

NOT TO BE CONFUSED WITH DETROIT-BUILT JEWETT CAR BUILT BY PAIGE, 1922~1927.

63 HP @ 4500 RPM (1466 cc.)

HORIZONTALLY - OPPOSED FLAT 4 ENG.

RT-HAND DRIVE IN ENGLAND

90 MPH. 0 TO 60 IN 16.5 SECONDS

TUBULAR FRAME

1953 Jowett "Jupiter"

This 1 1/2-liter car scored many track triumphs in the early '50s. In 1951, the Jowett Jupiter won both first and second place at the Monte Carlo Rally, and took first place at the Lisbon Rally, Bremgarten Sports Car Race, Rheineck/Walzenhausen Hill Climb, Le Mans 24 Hour Grand Prix, Watkins Glen Meeting (1 1/2-Liter Race), Rallye de l'Isrean, and won first and second at the R.A.C. Tourist Trophy Race!

This kind of performance was amazing, considering the smallness of the most unusual flat-four horizontally opposed Jowett engine (1,468 cc., 90.6 c.i.d.), and the Jupiter managed to average 25 miles per gallon in combined city and highway driving!

After World War II, Jowett produced the Javelin, a fastback family sedan that resembled a scaled-down Lincoln Zephyr, with many sophisticated mechanical features. The Javelin was an excellent car, except for a somewhat temperamental transmission. The Jupiter sports car joined the line in 1950, and some 1,200 were built between then and '54.

Increasing competition hurt many small manufacturers during the 1950s. Also, Jowett depended on Briggs Motor Bodies of Dagenham, England for their supply of car bodies. Jowett could not afford to continue buying the large quantities of bodies that Briggs preferred to sell, and so the price of the individual bodies was thus increased. After briefly considering the problem, Jowett officials decided to call it quits.

Nevertheless, after Jowett production ceased in 1954, the prices of the leftover cars remained the same. There were plenty of seriously interested buyers waiting for Jowetts, so a price-chopping "distress sale" was unnecessary.

1953 Maverick

During the early 1950s, I lived in Los Altos, Calif., just blocks from the new home of Maverick Motors. Noticing some very unusual-looking new roadsters being hand-built in and around a small factory, I stopped in to look around.

H. Sterling Gladwin Jr. was the guiding light of this small manufacturing operation, and he and his assistants allowed me to watch them at work on their new sports cars. It was Gladwin's idea (years ahead of its time) to build a glamorous, nostalgic-looking roadster with pre-war styling—using a fiberglass body that could be adapted to many different available chassis.

The bodies were sold, alone, for $950 "in the rough" (plus $200 for floorboard assembly, $200 for fiberglass hard top, $350 for instrument panel assembly, and $100 for windshield assembly). Maverick bodies and floorboard assemblies, used together, were not jigged to suit individual chassis frames, because they covered the wheelbases of some 400 different models of cars! Any 120- to 128-inch wheelbase chassis would fit, by using Maverick's cleverly adaptable floorboard assembly.

The Maverick used reconditioned pre-war La Salle grilles and post-war Lincoln headlights. The styling of the Maverick was "1939," though the boat-tailed rear made it look even older in back. A powerful Cadillac V-8 engine was used, in most applications.

"Put your brand on a Maverick!" was the sales slogan.

The Maverick venture lasted only until 1955, and from 1953 to 1955 as few as seven complete cars may have been built (plus a number of separate bodies, to be applied to chassis owned by purchaser).

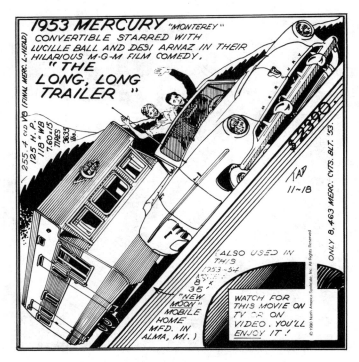

1953 Mercury

In 1953, actress Lucille Ball and her Cuban-born bandleader husband, Desi Arnaz, co-starred in a new movie. Married in real life since 1940, Lucy and Desi were already famous from long careers in, respectively, movies and Latin-American dance music. In the 1950s, Lucy and Desi were particularly famous for their wildly popular "I Love Lucy" TV show.

Their 1953 movie was *The Long, Long Trailer.* Lucy and Desi played a married couple who bought a 35-foot-long New Moon house-trailer and attempted to haul it cross country with their new Mercury convertible. Lucy and Desi ran into one frustrating problem after another, hauling the behemoth behind their car, up and down grades as steep as what you see in this illustration. (It was a job for a heavy truck, not a car.)

The '53 Mercury was changed only slightly from the totally restyled '52 model, but there were a few visible differences (new grille, etc). And, 1953 was the final year that Fords and Mercurys used the old-style L-head V-8s. In 1954, both would switch to overhead-valve V-8 engines.

The popularity of New Moon trailers was greatly enhanced by the movie. New Moon's manufacturer (formerly Redman, but changed to New Moon in '53 to match the brand name) proudly advertised that their trailer was selected for the movie over "200 others." The 1952-1955 New Moons had the distinctive front-end styling you see here, and they were instantly recognizable, even from a distance. Many of these are still found in older trailer and mobile home parks across the U.S.A.!

1953 METEOR *
SEDAN DELIVERY
115" WHEELBASE
with L-HEAD V8 ENGINE
(239.4 CU. IN. DISPLACEMENT)
110 HORSEPOWER
@ 3800 RPM
7.2 TO 1 COMPRESSION RATIO
* BUILT BY FORD MOTOR CO.
OF CANADA.
DURING THE 1950s, THE METEOR WAS A FORD-SIZED CAR
AVAILABLE AT LINCOLN-MERCURY DEALERS IN CANADA. AND
THE MONARCH WAS A MERCURY-SIZED CAR AVAILABLE AT
FORD DEALERS IN CANADA.
EACH HAD GRILLES
AND TRIM UNLIKE
FORD OR MERCURY
CARS.
CARGO COMPARTMENT 39" HT.
RARE! SELDOM SEEN OUTSIDE OF CANADA.
STANDARD, OVERDRIVE, OR AUTOMATIC TRANSMISSION.
TAP
C Field Enterprises Inc 1983
2-6

1950s

1953 Meteor Sedan Delivery

In Canada, the Monarch was introduced in 1946 and the Meteor in 1949. These were introduced so that Ford dealers and Lincoln-Mercury dealers in Canada would have more varieties of cars to offer their customers. The Meteor was a Ford-sized model sold through Lincoln-Mercury dealers in Canada, and it differed from a Ford in its grille design, trim, and other minor details, but used the regular Ford engine. (Likewise, the Monarch, sold by Canadian Ford dealers, shared engines and body designs with the Mercury, but had its own unique grille and trim.)

The illustrated Meteor sedan delivery offered the styling, performance, and easy handling of a car, but provided over 100 cubic feet of cargo space, with a swing-open rear door. The American-built Ford offered a similar model. In the later 1950s, Ford's sedan delivery model was called the "Courier." Later (in 1972), the Courier became the name of the new small truck that Toyo Kogyo (Mazda) of Japan began building and importing for Ford Motor Co.

Getting back to the 1953 Meteor in the illustration, we learn from original advertising that the cargo compartment measured 79 inches in length, 59 inches wide, and 39 inches in height. The rear door was 46 1/2 inches wide, and the large single window in that door accounted for nearly half the door's area, supplying "picture-window visibility." In addition, there was extra storage space in the front compartment, to the right of the single driver's seat.

"HANDI-PAK" NET CARRIER

AUTO. TRANS. AVAIL.

NEW POWER STEERING

1953 *Nash* Airflyte

"AMBASSADOR CUSTOM" COUNTRY CLUB HARDTOP $2829.

PININ FARINA OF ITALY (STYLIST)

7·5·92

121¼" WHEELBASE

252 CID 6 120 OR 140 HP 3550 lbs.

©1992 by North America Syndicate, Inc. World rights reserved.

REAR

1953 Nash

Ever since the mid-1930s, Nash was an extremely comfortable and economical car, delivering as much as 30 m.p.g. on the highway. Since 1935, Nash also featured folding seats that could be made into beds—for those who wished to save hotel or auto-court costs by sleeping in their car. In addition to this, Nash offered remarkable quietness from the engine.

But, old Nashes didn't appeal to all. Some called them "the gutless wonders," and others thought they were too plain-looking or even downright ugly, as in the case of 1935 and 1936 models, which reminded some people of "sea turtles from outer space"! (No offense intended to collectors of these unusual-looking '35s and '36s!)

Most everyone will agree that the best-looking Nashes of all time were the '52 to '54 models. For 1952, there was a complete change from the big fastback streamliners of '49 to '51. The '52 was totally restyled by Pinin Farina (his picture and trademark shown here). The early 1950s witnessed a strong Italian influence in the styling of American cars, and Italian design studios such as Ghia, Pinin Farina, etc. were kept busy!

Among the unique touches on the illustrated '53 Nash were the broad one-piece windshield with the lower edge contoured to arches of hood and fenders; and the distinctive row of decorative stamped "paddings" along the body sides, just below window level.

The illustrated "Country Club" hardtop was part of Nash's top-line Ambassador series. There were also the Statesman and compact Rambler models.

WITH O.H.V. 252.6 C.I.D. NASH "DUAL JETFIRE" ENGINE

A SPORTS CAR CLASSIC!

STYLED BY PININ FARINA

40 H.P. @ 4000 RPM
8 TO 1 COMPRESSION

108" WHEEL BASE

20-GALLON FUEL TANK

NASH-HEALEY AVAIL.

$3899

1953½ (JUNE, 1953)

NASH-HEALEY AVAIL. 1950 (DECEMBER) TO 1954.

Nash-Healey

"LE MANS" HARDTOP (GENUINE LEATHER UPHOLSTERY)

HELPFUL INFO. THANKS TO MILTON PLANTIN, LAKEWOOD, CALIF.

102" W.B. CONVERTIBLE ALSO AVAIL.

3-SPEED TRANSMISSION WITH OVERDRIVE   2970 lbs.

1953 1/2 Nash-Healey

Donald Healey, director of the Donald Healey Motor Co. of Warwick, England, had built a special sports car using a souped-up Nash Ambassador straight-6 overhead-valve engine and Nash drive train. Healey entered this car in the July 1950 Le Mans 24-hour endurance race. It did well (finished in fourth place), and Nash Motors of Kenosha, Wis. commissioned Healey to build more of these sports cars for export to the United States.

In December 1950, some thirty-six cars were built, and sixty-eight more were produced in January, February, and March of 1951. Originally, only convertibles were available, painted in either "Champagne Ivory" or "Sunset Maroon."

From April 1951 to January 1952, there was a hiatus in Nash-Healey production. Then came a new '52 roadster (convertible) with Italian body by Pinin Farina of Turin (or Torino, as the famous Italian motor city is also known). One hundred fifty of the 1952 models were produced.

In 1953, the convertible was joined by the new Farina-designed hardtop (illustrated).

An outstanding mechanical contribution to these cars was the Healey KW independent front suspension with coil springs and stabilizer bar. Another unusual feature: a steering mechanism of "walking beam" type.

This "Le Mans" hardtop was shown in the 1953 1/2 Nash-Healey catalog, of which 50,000 copies were published in June 1953. No doubt, many of the catalogs found their way into the hands of auto literature collectors, because the Nash Healey was a "collectors car" from the time it was still in production!

DELUXE "CHIEFTAN" SEDANS FROM $2119., f.o.b.

3396 lbs. (6)

268.4 CID STRAIGHT-8 (118 HP @ 3600 RPM) OR 239.2 " 6 (115 HP @ 3800)

new CURVED 1-PIECE WINDSHIELD

"DUAL-STREAK" TWIN ROWS OF CHROMED HOOD STRIPS USED 1953 ONLY.

new 122" WHEELBASE

3.08 GEAR RATIO WITH AUTO. TRANS. Hydra-Matic

TAP 7-8

News America Syndicate © News Group Chicago, Inc., 1984

POWER STEERING AVAILABLE

"Dual-Streak" *1953* **Pontiac**

1953 Pontiac

Restyled for 1953, Pontiac continued the chrome strips along the hood and deck that had been its trademark since 1935; but for '53 only, the strips were now in a dual set, thus the "Dual Streak" designation. A one-piece windshield was new (the first undivided windshield on Pontiac since 1934), and bodies were longer and wider than in '52, with a lengthened wheelbase.

The new "Panorama-View" instrument cluster featured an arc-shaped speedometer at left (above small, rectangular gauges); horizontally-arranged radio and heater controls at center; and a very large, circular radio speaker grille at the right end of the panel (with an optional circular clock at center of the speaker grille). The instrument panel was illuminated at night in a greenish glow, said to be restful to the eyes.

Many "goodies" were available at extra cost, such as the new "Autronic Eye," which automatically dimmed headlight beams as oncoming cars approached; power steering; Dual-Range Hydra-Matic automatic transmission; underseat heater and defrosters; back-up lights; illuminated Indian head hood ornament; lights in trunk, under hood, and in glove compartment; horizontal grille guard above the front bumper; windshield washers; directional signals; glare-free adjustable rear-view mirror; hand brake alarm signal; and more!

Because of shortages created by the Korean War of 1950-53, the chrome plating on many '52 and '53 cars was inferior to earlier chrome; on the '53 Pontiac, the brightwork was protected from oxidation by a coating of clear enamel that tended to peel off in a few years.

BUILT IN COVENTRY, ENGLAND, AND SOLD IN CANADA WITH LEFT-HAND DRIVE. NOT AVAILABLE IN THE U.S.A. *

1953 VANGUARD "VOYAGEUR"
BY STANDARD MOTOR CO., LTD. (1903~1963)
127.6 C.I.D. STEEL SLEEVED 4-CYL. O.H.V. ENGINE
68 HP @ 4200 RPM 7 TO 1 COMPRESSION
"50 YEARS OF PROGRESS" ANNIVERSARY YEAR

LOCKHEED HYDR. BRAKES

WT. 94" WHEELBASE
2625 lbs. £590.
(BRITISH VERSION) (BRITISH PRICE)

OPTIONAL LAYCOCK DE NORMANVILLE HYDRAULIC OVERDRIVE
RADIO and WHITEWALL TIRES ALSO OPTIONAL
OVER 235 DEALERS IN CANADA (BRITISH COLUMBIA, ALBERTA,
SASKATCHEWAN, MANITOBA, ONTARIO, QUEBEC, NEW BRUNSWICK,
NOVA SCOTIA,
PRINCE EDW. ISLAND, OLDER FOREIGN CARS ARE
and NEWFOUNDLAND.) HIGHLY COLLECTIBLE TODAY!
WITH SPECIAL THANKS TO DICK SCHROEDER, ELGIN, ILLINOIS, FOR
SENDING IN A RARE CANADIAN ORIGINAL AD FOR THIS CAR!
* SOME OTHER STANDARDS HAVE BEEN IMPORTED TO U.S.A.

1950s

1953 Vanguard Voyageur

Standard automobiles were manufactured in England from 1903 to 1963, but only a small number of them were ever sold in the United States, though Standard's "partner car," the Triumph, did fairly well in America.

Standard's Vanguard model was introduced in 1947 for the Canadian market; the sedan had a smooth fast-back profile through 1952. In 1953, it was restyled with a more conventional type of "bustle-back," with a trunk section protruding at the rear.

We're grateful today to Dick Schroeder, of Elgin, Ill., for sharing a rare double-sided Canadian advertising page for the Vanguard Voyageur from *The Toronto Star's* weekly magazine section of May 30, 1953.

"Arrive safe and refreshed, with money to spend," the colorful ad is captioned, with the illustrated car shown in blue. The text reads: "Now, travel relaxed, arrive in style in the beautiful new Vanguard! It's a dream to drive—a delight to ride in. Vanguard's exclusive high power 'Steel Sleeved' engine thrills to super highways. Its superb springing smooths out the roughest country roads. It corners, climbs, cruises with effortless ease ... handles with assurance in big city traffic."

The ad also extolled the economy of the car.

On the back of the May 30, 1953 ad was a list of more than 235 dealers in Canada and its provinces, but the ad also proclaimed "Over 400 Dealers Coast to Coast," which apparently included a number of Standard-Triumph dealers south of the border in the United States.

Cadillac 1954

PLEASINGLY RESTYLED (WITH NEW "PANORAMIC" WRAPAROUND WINDSHIELD, also FEATURED ON 1954 OLDS and BUICK and on ALL '55 GM CARS)

331 CID OHV V8 (230 HP @ 4400 RPM.)

WITH "HYDRA-MATIC" TRANS, STD.

"62" SERIES COUPE DE VILLE 2 DR. H/T 4405 lbs.

216.4" TOTAL LENGTH

$4261., f.o.b. AT FACTORY (17,170 BLT.)

NOW VALUED AT $1200. TO $32,000., DEPENDING ON CONDITION.

129" WHEEL BASE

TAD 5-5

© 1991 North America Syndicate, Inc. All Rights Reserved

1954 Cadillac

A new styling cycle for Cadillac was begun in '54, most notably with the wraparound windshield. In 1955, Ford and Mercury also offered it, along with Packard, Nash, and Hudson, and—in a modified degree—Chrysler Corp. cars.

Driver/passenger comfort was enhanced by a dual heating system (one for the front seat compartment, one for the rear), and a '54 Cadillac equipped with the optional luxury of air-conditioning could be spotted by the streamlined air-intake bubble on the rear deck, just behind the rear window. Electric front-seat option made the seat adjustable horizontally and vertically. Cadillac had offered optional electric windows since the late 1940s.

According to an original '54 Cadillac advertisement: "If a motorist wanted to make the move to Cadillac solely for the car's prestige, he would most certainly be justified in doing so. For the rewards, which grow out of Cadillac's unprecedented public acceptance, comprise the rarest and greatest satisfaction in all motordom—an inescapable feeling of pride, a wonderful sense of well-being, and a marvelous feeling of confidence and self-esteem.

"Those who presently enjoy these unique Cadillac virtues will tell you that they (the feelings) are, in themselves, worth the car's whole purchase price. Of course, most motorists would hesitate to take such a step purely for their personal edification.

"But in Cadillac's case, this wonderful prestige is actually a 'bonus,' so to speak—an extra dividend that comes with every Cadillac car ... in addition to its breath-taking styling, its magnificent performance and its superlative luxury."

1954 Chrysler

The 1954 Chrysler New Yorker, New Yorker DeLuxe, Custom Imperial, and Crown Imperial were ahead in the great horsepower race in 1954, claiming the highest-powered engine for the year, with a new 235 h.p.!

Air conditioning was now available, too. But, strangely, not all '54 Chrysler advertisements mentioned it once the season was in progress. Perhaps there were "bugs" to be ironed out! (For years already, however, Chrysler Corp. had been supplying "Airtemp" air-conditioning units to offices and homes.)

Incidentally, it was in 1954 that Chrysler Corp. decided to classify its top-of-the-line Imperial series as a make unto itself, rather than as a Chrysler.

The new '54 dashboard had a pair of large dials at left, mounted in a pod with an attractive machine-turned metal panel. The dash was partially padded for passenger safety.

One-piece curved windshield and rear window provided good visibility, and Solex heat-and-glare-reducing glass was optional. The painted gas filler cap was located conveniently at the rear, near the left side, below the deck opening.

The quadrant for the Powerflite Automatic Transmission was lettered "R-N-D-L" (reverse, neutral, drive, low). There was no "Park" position, but the T-handled parking brake lever under the dash controlled an emergency brake.

Though the '54 Chrysler attained 118 m.p.h. on the track, there is at least one documented case (Chelsea, Mich. 1954) where a new Chrysler New Yorker exceeded 125 m.p.h. (And, a Chrysler V-8 engine in a Kurtis-Kraft racing chassis developed 447 h.p. and reached an amazing 182.554 miles per hour!)

1954 Dodge

Dodge joined the "V-8 rebellion" in 1953, as more and more makes of cars introduced new high-powered models with new V-8 engines during the early and mid-1950s.

Times changed during the 1950s. The early years of the decade—marred only by the Korean War of 1950-1953—were comparatively innocent, idealistic, and bucolic.

Most cars in the early 1950s were bland, six-cylinder models, and there were still a few straight-8s. In 1950, the V-8 field was dominated by Ford Motor Co. cars and by GM's Cadillac and Oldsmobile 88 and 98. But, in '51, Chrysler and Studebaker got V-8s. One by one, other makes jumped on the V-8 bandwagon, and the last straight-8s were produced in 1954 by Packard and Pontiac. It was in 1955 that Chevrolet and Plymouth finally

offered V-8s as well as their usual sixes, so that all the "low-priced three" had been "won over."

The 1954 Dodges were similar in profile to the '53s, but there were various changes in grille, side trim, interior details, etc. Well-advertised for 1954 were the colorful new Jacquard fabric upholstered interiors.

In addition to considerable newspaper and magazine advertising, Dodge also sponsored a new radio show starring Roy Rogers on NBC and two TV shows: *Break the Bank* with Bert Parks (ABC-TV), and *Make Room for Daddy* with Danny Thomas (ABC-TV). As the 1950s went on, many companies found it more economical to co-sponsor several shows with other types of companies, rather than to fully sponsor a single show.

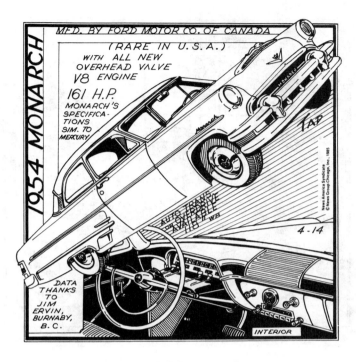

MFD. BY FORD MOTOR CO. OF CANADA

(RARE IN U.S.A.)
WITH ALL NEW
OVERHEAD VALVE
V8 ENGINE

161 H.P.

MONARCH'S
SPECIFICA-
TIONS
SIM. TO
MERCURY

1954 MONARCH

AUTO TRANS.
AVAILABLE
118" WB

4-14

DATA
THANKS
TO
JIM
ERVIN,
BURNABY,
B.C.

INTERIOR

News America Syndicate
©News Group Chicago, Inc. 1985

1950s

1954 Monarch

Ford motor Co. of Canada produced some very interesting variations on the usual American Fords and Mercurys of the 1950s!

After World War II, Ford Motor Co. decided to operate *two* dealer chains in Canada: one for Fords and the other for Lincoln-Mercury. However, the Canadian Ford dealers also wanted a Mercury-type car to sell, and the Lincoln-Mercury dealers eventually wanted a smaller, Ford-sized car to include in their wares. What should they do? Well, that's why the Monarch was created (1946)—to give the Ford dealers a Mercury substitute.

In 1949, the smaller Meteor was added for Lincoln-Mercury dealers to sell. Monarchs and Meteors had grilles and side trim that differed considerably from those of the regular Mercury and Ford cars. Some Americans who may have, at some time or another, seen one of these unique Canadian models may have thought they were customized cars.

A good many American car collectors, especially fans of Ford products of the 1950s, would undoubtedly be delighted to find an old Monarch or Meteor they could buy now. Yet, few of them have ever found their way into the U.S.A., except with Canadian tourists, and it would be safe to venture that ninety-eight percent of those reading this column have never seen this particular car in real life. Perhaps fifty percent or more never knew about the Monarch until Lincoln-Mercury dealers made the name available in the U.S.A. (1975), on a companion car to Ford's Granada.

THE "MOTORAMIC"
1955 CHEVROLET or V8
235½ cid 6 (123 or 136 HP)
new 265 cid V8
(162, 170, 180 HP)
150 210 or
BEL AIR SERIES

115" WHEELBASE

COLOR:
PINK and
DARK GRAY

©1992 by North America Syndicate, Inc. World rights reserved.

$ 2583.
BEL AIR V8 CVT.
41292 BLT. 3240 LBS.

AJ
5-31

1955 Chevrolet

T he Concours d'Elegance at Pebble Beach, Calif., has been an annual event since the 1950s. Exotic, classic, and antique cars are displayed on a Sunday in August on the oceanside greens behind the famous Del Monte Lodge.

One of Chevrolet's 1955 advertisements featured a new Chevrolet Bel Air convertible among the rows of rare old and import cars at the Pebble Beach Concours. The colorful ad was captioned, "Blue-Ribbon Beauty That's Stealing the Thunder from the High-Priced Cars!" For a dozen years, I've had this attractive ad (May 1955) displayed on the wall by the stairway leading up to my studio. Several visitors mentioned they liked this ad, and so I decided to use it as a model for today's *Auto Album* illustration, with only minor changes.

Dark gray over salmon pink (official color names: Shadow Gray over Coral) was a very popular color combination on '55 Chevy Bel Airs, yet this color is infrequently seen on '55 Chevys today.

The totally restyled '55 Chevrolet was a sales sensation, and '55 was a very good year for Detroit in general. Many makes offered new or recently introduced V-8 engines, including Chevrolet. And, the latter 1950s became the era of the big, high-powered V-8 American car that was loaded with all kinds of electrical gadgets and luxuries.

The 1955, 1956, and 1957 Chevrolets have differing grilles and trim, but similar profiles. This three-year cycle of '55 to '57 models was to become known as the "Classic Chevys," and these cars are still wildly popular with collectors.

1955 CORVETTE BY CHEVROLET

FIRST 'VETTE TO OFFER AN ENGINE CHOICE OF V8 or 6. (1953 and 1954 CORVETTES HAD 6 CYL. ONLY.) 674 BUILT IN 1955 MODEL YEAR.

SUPER-DETAILED SCALE MODELS OF THIS --- AND MANY OTHER FAMOUS "COLLECTORS' CARS" ---- CAN NOW BE FOUND AT HOBBY AND SPECIALTY SHOPS, OR BY MAIL ORDER.

WITH DECK LID OPEN

$2799. (6)
2934. (with new V8)

102" WHEELBASE

CHEVROLET EMBLEM

FIBERGLASS BODY

3~13

1955 Corvette

Chevrolet's high-performance Corvette sports car has been so popular for so long that it's difficult to believe it wasn't a smashing success at the very start.

The Corvette, the first successful American sports car with a fiberglass body, was launched in the latter months of 1953, when only 300 were sold.

For its first two seasons, the Corvette was available only with the six-cylinder Chevrolet "Blue Flame" engine (105 h.p.). In a lightweight car like the Corvette, the six performed well but was no match for most of the hot, new, overhead-valve V-8 engines that so many other cars began to feature during the 1950s.

As the 1955 model year began, Chevrolet offered Corvette buyers the option of a new V-8. However, 1955 Corvette sales were dampened by the debut of Ford's new Thunderbird sports roadster, a direct rival of the Corvette. The Thunderbird had a steel body, and some buyers were leery of buying a "plastic car" like the Corvette.

In time, Thunderbird wandered away from its original concept as a sports roadster and headed toward the luxury GT-type market. The Corvette remained a true "hairy" type of sports car, sticking with roadsters and coupes.

There were rumors in 1970, and at other times, that Corvette was going to abandon fiberglass and create a steel body, but those stories were unfounded. Production-model Corvettes have always carried fiberglass bodies. White was the only color available on the earliest Corvettes, but soon blue, red, and other colors appeared.

The Corvette got its first restyling in 1956.

1950s

1955 Hudson

The Hudson car, a great "independent" marque of Detroit since its debut in 1909, became a near-clone of the Nash, following the 1954 merger of the two. Gone for good was Hudson's famous "step-down" body design of 1948 to 1954, which had featured a very broad, low look—with the body sunken into the chassis frame for a low center of gravity and for protection from side collisions.

Interestingly, the new V-8 engine and the Ultramatic transmission in the '55 Hudson were not built by Hudson or Nash, but by Packard. A Hudson six, with a Hudson-built engine, was still offered as well.

"Deepcoil" suspension on the '55 Hudson was a system that placed the coil springs on a slant and at a high level in the car.

Hudson seats were six inches wider than those in most other cars, and three inches more headroom was available. All-season air conditioning was located under the hood and dash, thus freeing trunk space. (Some early air conditioning units were at the back.)

A '55 Hudson V-8 would do at least 105 miles per hour and zero to 60 m.p.h. in 12.1 seconds. Famous auto reviewer Tom McCahill rated the top speed at 106 to 109 m.p.h.

Hudson's mechanical reserve brake system, which was automatically activated if the hydraulic brakes should fail, was still an exclusive safety feature that had for a long time won many buyers.

1955 Monarch

Ford Motor Co. of Canada was established in 1904, a year after Ford Motor Co. of Dearborn, Mich., went into business and sold their first cars. The first Canadian Fords were identical to the American models, because the parts were manufactured at the Dearborn factory and sent to Canada for final assembly.

But, as time went on, many parts for the Canadian Fords were made in Canada—and there were variations from the American models. The greatest differences between American and Canadian Ford products came in the 1950s.

Shortly after World War II, the Monarch was introduced up north. It was a car in the Mercury price class, built to be sold in Canadian Ford dealerships for those who wanted something a bit fancier than a regular Ford. Its grille and trim details differed from both Ford and Mercury.

Then, in 1949, the Meteor was introduced: a Ford-sized car to be sold at Lincoln-Mercury dealers in Canada, for those who wanted an economical car of that size. (Lincolns and Mercurys had grown big in '49!)

Through the 1950s, these two Canadian variations maintained their distinctiveness from the more common American-style Fords and Mercurys also sold up there.

In 1955, this Monarch "Richelieu" was advertised as "Dramatic!" It featured a new, restyled body with panoramic, wrap-around windshield, "new longer, lower, sleeker lines" (with an "urgent forward sweep" to the hooded headlights, and a "new crispness" of its massive rear fender treatment). Improved ball-joint front suspension provided "the smoothest ride and the easiest steering you've ever enjoyed."

1950s

1950s

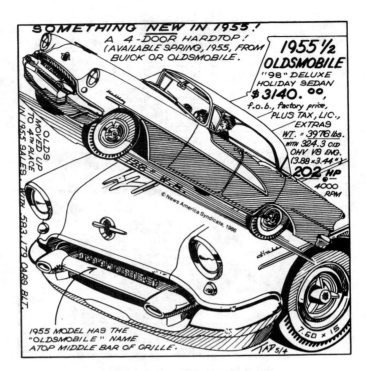

SOMETHING NEW IN 1955!

A 4-DOOR HARDTOP! (AVAILABLE SPRING, 1955, FROM BUICK OR OLDSMOBILE.

1955 1/2 OLDSMOBILE "98" DELUXE HOLIDAY SEDAN $3140.00, f.o.b., factory price, PLUS TAX, LIC., EXTRAS WT. = 3976 lbs. WITH 324.3 CID OHV V8 ENG. (3.88 x 3.44") 202 HP 4000 RPM

OLDS MOVED UP TO 4TH PLACE IN 1955 SALES, WITH 583,179 CARS BLT.

© News America Syndicate, 1986

1955 MODEL HAS THE "OLDSMOBILE" NAME ATOP MIDDLE BAR OF GRILLE.

7.60 x 15

TAP 5/4

1955 1/2 Oldsmobile

The "1955 1/2" development was the new four-door, pillar-less hardtop sedan, introduced in the spring of 1955 on Oldsmobile and Buick. (The three other GM cars—Chevrolet, Pontiac, and Cadillac—would get four-door hardtops the following year.)

When the four-door hardtop was introduced, Oldsmobile gave theirs a good advertising campaign: "Here's the first completely new body type since the introduction of the hardtop coupe. And naturally it comes from Oldsmobile." (Buick did not get credit in this ad for its 1949 Riviera hardtop coupe, because though it was also a General Motors product, the various GM divisions were highly competitive with one another.)

The four-door Holiday Sedan (hardtop) was available in all three Oldsmobile model series: "88," "Super 88," and "98."

Interestingly, four-door hardtops weren't really new in '55, just forgotten from an earlier era. In the mid-'teens, several manufacturers built four-door sedans without center pillars, one of the best-known being the Hudson. But, in the frantic '50s, only the historians and old-timers remembered this.

Since the '54 Oldsmobile had been dramatically restyled, the 1955 was merely "face-lifted," with changes in grille, trim, interior, etc. (called the "Go-Ahead" look).

"Flying Colors" was the advertised designation for Oldsmobiles' new paint schemes, the majority of them in two-tone varieties. There were attractive hues such as a Shell Beige, Coral, Panama Blue, Glen Green, Grove Green, etc. even a blue-and-gray Oldsmobile that could sell on either side of the Mason-Dixon line!

PLYMOUTH 1955

"P-26" (6) or "P-27" (V8s)

230 C.I.D. L-HEAD 6 (117 HP @ 4000 RPM)
241 or 260 CID O.H.V. V8s
(157, 167 or 177 HP @ 4400 RPM)
"POWERFLITE" AUTOMATIC TRANSMISSION AVAIL.
3.54, 3.73 or 4.1 GEAR RATIOS

BASE PRICE RANGE→
1639-2424.
F.O.B.

115" W.B.

V8: 99 MPH

0-60 MPH in 14½ SECONDS   21.8 MPG at 30 MPH

1955 Plymouth

Automotive writers accused Plymouth of having dowdy, uninspiring styling in the early 1950s. Since 1932, Plymouth had been the third of the famous "Big 3" low-priced American cars. But, in 1950, Buick (with its weird "buck-toothed" bumper-grille that year), managed to take third place from Plymouth.

Plymouth dropped behind Buick again in 1955, but no longer could Plymouth be accused of looking dumpy. The all-new 1955 Plymouth was a completely restyled beauty that featured Chrysler Corporation's new "wrap-around" windshield—a better design than the Chevrolet or Ford versions because the Plymouth windshield pillars swept back and not forward, avoiding those awkward "dogleg" posts that continually got in the way.

Plymouth was no longer short and plain-looking; it was a fresh, new seventeen-foot-long "butterfly," just out of the cocoon. Plymouth was now the "biggest car in the lowest-price field!" It was advertised as "a great new car for the young in heart"; an up-and-coming looking young couple was pictured in the lower right corner of most '55 Plymouth ads.

The 1955 Plymouths were available in Plaza, Savoy, and Belvedere models (listed in ascending price order and in the increasing quantity of chrome trim).

The PowerFlite automatic transmission had its "Flite-Control" Drive Selector protruding from the instrument panel. Beginning the following year, Chrysler Corp. cars would carry on a long flirtation with push-button transmission controls on the dash.

Power assists were abundant options: power steering, power brakes, power seats (up-and-down and back-and-forth), and power window controls. "Airtemp" (air conditioning) was another option.

1955 Studebaker

In 1953, Studebaker had dramatically restyled all their new cars, and, in 1955, the most noticeable change was the bold, new grille, heavily framed in chrome and encompassing the parking/turn signal lights.

The President model series returned. It had been missing from the Studebaker line since the last straight-8 Studebaker was made in 1942. Studebaker had built only sixes from 1946 to 1950, but had included an overhead-valve V-8 in their selection since '51.

The '55 model series: Champion 6 (Custom, Deluxe, Regal); Commander V-8 (Custom, Deluxe, Regal); President V-8 (Deluxe, State).

The State President lineup included a two-door hardtop coupe in both the standard ($2,456) and special 1955 1/2 sports "Speedster" versions. The Speedster cost $3,252 and up.

State President sedans had gold-plated hardware with gold-plated Mylar plastic trim plates behind the door hardware. The lower section of the instrument panel was gold finished, while the radio grille was in gold with a chrome frame—giving this series the look of luxury!

Power brakes were optional, as were power steering, power seats, electric window lifts, and air conditioning. Available overdrive gave a fourth speed forward and enhanced Studebaker's fuel economy. A 1955 Commander V-8 averaged 27.4 miles per gallon in the 1,323-mile Mobligas Economy Run!

Since the mid-1930s, Studebaker had an available feature called "Hill Holder." As the name implied, it prevented rollbacks on steep hills when the driver wanted to move ahead from a standing stop. V-8s with standard transmission included this device; it was optional on other types.

1950s

"76-R" ROADMASTER RIVIERA 2-DR. 48B *
(*=12,490 BUILT)
1956 BUICK
8.3597.
322 C.I.D. V-8
4 x 3.2 BR. + ST.
9.5 COMPR.
255 HP
4400 rpm
8.00 x 15
4-BARREL CARB.
127" WHEELBASE
TAP 6-17
HAPPY FATHER'S DAY!
© News Group Chicago, Inc. 1984
ROADMASTER'S DIFFERS FROM OTHER 1956 BUICKS' REAR DECK TRIM.
ROADMASTER
AUTO. TRANS. and POWER STEERING

1956 Buick

For 1956, "Best Buick yet!" That year, Buick presented eighteen body styles in four model series: Special, Century, Super, and the mighty Roadmaster. Safety was a selling point in 1956. Seat belts were available, and the dash was padded with foam rubber.

All '56 Buicks had a 332 c.i.d. overhead-valve V-8 engine (unlike 1955, when the Special had a smaller engine). Tom McCahill, for *Mechanic Illustrated*, road-tested a Century four-door hardtop and said it would do almost 120 m.p.h.!

Shock absorbers with three times the oil volume of the old ones, and all coil springing, provided a "Deep-Oil-Cushioned" luxury ride. Brake linings were grooved along their full length to prevent overheating. The rear axle was completely redesigned. Air-conditioning unit (optional) was simplified. The Dynaflow automatic transmission was improved for "Variable Pitch," better acceleration, and gas mileage. Front grilles were widened and slightly V-shaped. Rear fenders were longer and sharper, with less chrome around the taillights.

Some models had attractive three-tone paint, with one color for top, another for hood, deck and belt area, and a third color below the sweep chrome trim along the side.

Non-Roadmaster Buicks for 1956 had the year model at both ends on a round emblem, but some customers squawked at having their cars dated in such a way, thinking that it smacked of "planned obsolescence."

LEFT TAIL-LIGHT OPENS FOR GAS FILLER

1956½ CHEVROLET
"BEL AIR" 2-DR. SEDAN
3195 lbs.   115" W.B.
$2120.
O.H.V. 265 cid V8
(3¾" × 3")
TOP H.P. RAISED
TO 225 DURING
SPRING, '56.

"BLUE FLAME
140" 6 CYL.
ALSO avail.

TAD

1~20

News America Syndicate
© News Group Chicago, Inc., 1985

"210" and "150"
MODEL SERIES ALSO

1956 1/2 Chevrolet

As though 205 h.p. wasn't enough for Chevrolet in 1956, the h.p. figure of Chevy's hottest V-8 was raised to 255 in mid-season, as in this late '56 (or '56 1/2) model.

Luxury options were plentiful on Chevrolets during '56. There was "Power Touch" power steering; power brakes; power windows; and power seats (each available for Bel Air or "210" models); Powerglide automatic transmission; "Touch-Down" overdrive (which reduced engine speed twenty-two percent in highway cruising); "All-Weather" air conditioning; and more.

In the years that have passed since the 1955-1957 Chevrolets were new, these cars have attracted a large group of admirers and collectors. The 1955-1957 models are often referred to as the "classic" Chevrolets because they were great performers, good looking, and have outlasted many newer models. There's a mystique about these Chevrolets, which has grown stronger with the passage of time.

Of the three models, the '57 is the most popular—perhaps because of the many performance options that year and because of the sharp new tailfins and Buick-styled front end. The '55 is also well-liked, as it's the first of the hot, new V-8s and the most cleanly styled of the three. The illustrated '56 is not as popular as the other two, yet, in this writer's opinion, it's the most attractive, particularly because of its broad expanse of chrome in front.

As I was putting the finishing touches on this week's article, I glanced out the window just in time to see a snow-white '57 Chevrolet—restored to perfection—drive past the house!

The illustration contains the following labels:

1956 CHRYSLER

"NEW YORKER ST. REGIS"
2-DOOR HARDTOP
4175 LBS. $3889.
WITH PUSH-BUTTON AUTOMATIC TRANSMISSION

"C~72~2"
OPTIONAL CBS "HIWAY HI-FI" RECORD PLAYER (new)

21-GAL. GAS TANK
3.94 x 3.63" BORE and STR.
9.0 COMPRESSION
3.54 or 3.73 GEAR RATIOS

THE PRESENT ADDRESS OF THE WPC CLUB (FOR FANS OF CHRYSLER PRODUCT CARS) IS 5204 COLONY WOODS DR., KALAMAZOO, MI., 49009. (DUES $20. YR.) (FOR INFO. ON CLUB, SEND THEM A SELF-ADDRESSED STAMPED ENVELOPE.)

126" WB

354 CID V8
280 HP @ 4600

REAR FIN DETAILS

1956 Chrysler

The San Francisco, Calif. *Call-Bulletin* for Monday, October 10, 1955 heralded the new '56 model Chrysler products with a full-page ad that featured the new push-button automatic transmission control. Along with a large picture, the ad proclaimed, "Just think! You can now select your driving range with a touch of your finger to a button on the dash at your left—where only you can touch it."

"Press D and you're in Drive. Step on the gas and away you go, with PowerFlite, best combination of smoothness and acceleration among all automatic drives. To reverse, simply push R, for Low, push L, and for Neutral, press N."

The "Forward Look" of 1955 was accentuated by the new 1956 "Flight Sweep" of the taller, new rear fenders.

Seat belts were optional. Back in the mid-1950s, they were just coming into fashion. They would not be mandatory for several years to come.

In the 1956 Chrysler line, the Windsor had a grille with three heavy horizontal pieces, while the costlier New Yorker series had a grille with more numerous, thinner, horizontal pieces, as illustrated. The St. Regis had the decorative mini-louvers on the back upper portion of the rear fenders, as shown.

How much is this 1956 Chrysler New Yorker St. Regis two-door hardtop currently worth, on the collector's market? According to a Gold Book listing, not long ago, it would go for $2,645 to $6,300, depending on condition (fair to excellent). The Windsor and New Yorker convertibles are worth even more: $10,000+ each, if in excellent condition.

1956 Dodge La Femme

Here is one of the very rare models of the 1950s: the La Femme, a special edition of the Dodge, which was intended to appeal to women only. The series was introduced in the spring of 1955 and again in 1956. An interesting curiosity, the La Femme was not a sales success, as women didn't like to be told that they must prefer pink cars.

In 1954, Chrysler Corp. (manufacturer of Dodge) had built special La Comtesse and Le Comte show cars, designed, respectively, for women and for men. The idea was pursued further in the spring of '55, when the new La Femme was available in limited numbers to the buying public. At this time, Dodge also offered a macho Texan model, in two-tone brown with special upholstery and added horsepower.

Reportedly, only about 1,100 La Femme Dodges were produced in 1955-1956, and they are certainly collector's cars! Not only did they have special paint jobs, but the interiors were done (in '56) in orchid Jacquard upholstery trimmed with gold Cordagrain vinyl. The '56 La Femme had a pair of special containers on the backs of the front seats. The 1955 La Femmes had harmonizing purses, compacts, combs, cigarette holders, raincoat and cap, and other special matching accessories to please the gals. A rain cape and cap and umbrella were also included with the '56 La Femme. And, I mustn't forget to mention the special gold-and-gray cardboard box that was also supplied to store some of the small accessories.

1956 INTERNATIONAL "S" SERIES PICKUP (REPLACES "R" SERIES OF 1953 TO 1955)

6 CYL. "S 100"

$1662. and up, F.O.B. INTERNATIONAL HARVESTER CORP. CHICAGO

new GRILLE and HIGHER HEADLIGHTS "COMFO VISION" CAB

ACME APPLIANCES

S100

3310 LBS.

115" WHEELBASE (½-TON CAPACITY) (127" W.B. ON ¾-TON PICKUPS

©1992 by North America Syndicate, Inc. World rights reserved.

OVERDRIVE, AUTOMATIC TRANSMISSION OR POWER STEERING OPTIONAL. 10 DIFFERENT GASOLINE OR LPG ENGINES AVAIL. MODELS AVAIL. UP TO 33,000 LBS. GVW

1956 International "S" Pickup

1950s

The first International Harvester Co. motor vehicles were 1907 "Auto Buggies," high-wheeled two-cylinder horseless carriages. Primitive though they may have been, they lasted many years. (In 1951, International announced that one million International trucks—more than half its total output since 1907—were still in service at that time!) Some of these early International cars and trucks are now in the hands of appreciative collectors.

In 1909, the International "Auto-wagon" appeared; and in 1912, a more conventional Model "M" truck.

For 1915, International introduced light- and medium-duty trucks with a sloping Renault-style hood and a radiator behind the four-cylinder engine. A larger two-ton, cab-over-engine, flat-front truck was also offered at that time.

By the mid-1920s, several new International truck types had appeared, and after '23 the sloping-hood models were unavailable.

Over the years, International trucks changed with the prevailing styles. A design was usually good for three or four years. For example, the "C" series was built from '34 to early '37. The streamlined "D" series ran from 1937 1/2 to 1940, and then the "K" series appeared in '41. The early postwar model was the "KB."

The "L" series came in 1950, and in 1953 the "R." The illustrated "S" was introduced in late '55 and continued to early 1957.

In the mid-1970s, International discontinued their line of light-duty pickups and concentrated on heavy duty trucks with the exception of the small RV-type "Scout," made from 1961 to 1980, plus medium-duty, chassis-cab units, etc.

A RARITY FROM CANADA!

FEW EVER SEEN IN U.S.A.!

©1993 North America Syndicate, Inc. World rights reserved.

TAD 2-21

'56 *Meteor*

"RIDEAU" 2-DR. HARDTOP

MFD. BY FORD MOTOR CO. OF CANADA

"MERC-o-MATIC" AUTO. TRANS. OPTIONAL, PLUS POWER ASSISTS.

INSTRUMENT PANEL and MECH. SPECS. SIMILAR TO '56 FORD.

V8 ENG. (6 CYL. NOT AVAIL. EARLY IN YR. IN CANADIAN MODEL.)

"FASHION AT ITS FINEST"

HELPFUL DETAILS THANKS TO BRYON STAPPLER, KELOWNA, B.C.

1956 Meteor

Meteors and Monarchs were popular Ford Motor Co. products in Canada during the 1950s. Fords and Mercurys were also produced in Canada at that time, and Lincolns were imported from the United States.

In 1946, Canadian Ford dealers and Lincoln-Mercury dealers became separate entities, so Ford dealers wanted a Mercury-sized car to sell, and Mercury dealers wanted a Ford-sized car in their own line. In 1946, the new Monarch (a Mercury with a different grille) was introduced for Ford dealers to sell. Lincoln-Mercury dealers got a shorter Mercury "114" series to sell along with the costlier Mercury 118 (model numbers referring to wheelbases). In 1949, when all Ford Motor Co. cars were totally restyled (introduced early, in mid 1948) the Mercury "114" was replaced by the new Meteor: another Ford-sized car for Lincoln-Mercury dealerships.

Americans sometimes mistake these Monarchs and Meteors for "customized" Fords and Mercurys, since they had their own unique grilles, side and rear trim, taillights, interiors, model series names, etc. All this makes these Canadian variations of great interest to American collectors of Ford cars of the '50s.

In addition to the costlier Rideau series, Meteor for a time offered a lower-cost Niagara.

Interestingly, when Ford introduced its new compact Falcon for the '60 model year, a Canadian version was known as the Frontenac (for 1960 only), and it had its own special grille and trim.

In 1961, the Mercury Meteor became an American model, while the Comet replaced the Frontenac in Canada.

3.75 × 3.13 B+S   *187 HP @ 4400 RPM*
277 CID V8 ENG.
"FURY" HIT INTRO. IN 1956 SEASON.
115" WB
"BELVEDERE" 4 DR. HT. $2326.   3415 LBS.
1956 PLYMOUTH V8
"P-29"
PUSHBUTTON CONTROLS FOR "POWERFLITE" AUTO. TRANS.
11 TO 17½ M.P.G.
93 MPH
new TALL REAR FINS START ON 1956 MODEL.
6-29
FROM

© News America Syndicate, 1986

1950s

1956 Plymouth

"**A**erodynamic Plymouth '56. Push-Button Driving. First on Plymouth in the low-price 3." Just a finger-tip touch on a button and PowerFlite fully automatic transmission took over! This was the important new feature for the 1956 Plymouth.

Style-wise, those new, sharp, high tailfins were definitely in vogue during the later 1950s. The tailfin fad had its beginnings with the 1948 Cadillac, though Cadillac's early tailfins were low, rounded, and definitely subdued. But, 1956 was the year that Chrysler Corp. went overboard with high fins, and much of the competition soon followed suit, climaxing with the monstrous daggers found on the rear of 1959 Cadillacs.

What other features did the '56 Plymouth include? There was the "Hy-Fire" overhead-valve V-8 engine (Plymouth offered a choice of six or V-8, beginning in 1955), "Full-Time Power Steering," power brakes, push-button power seat, push-button power windows, and other options.

Safety plusses: SafeGuard door latches, Safety Rim wheels that held the tire in place after a blowout, and dual brake cylinders in each front wheel, as well as the widest front seat of all three low-priced cars, and the most head and leg room.

Models (in ascending order) were Plaza, Savoy, and Belvedere. And, during the '56 season came the powerful new Fury sport hardtop.

Interestingly, back in 1956 Chrysler Corp. had abandoned an experimental OHV V-6 engine on which they had been working—because it demanded a costly additional mechanism to keep the crankshaft in balance. But, GM came along with a more successful V-6 in the early 1960s.

© News America Syndicate, 1986

HOW MANY OF THESE 1957 POPULAR SONGS DO YOU KNOW?
I'M GONNA SIT RIGHT DOWN AND WRITE MYSELF A LETTER (1936 REVIVAL)
WAKE UP, LITTLE SUSIE • THAT'LL BE THE DAY
BANANA BOAT SONG (DAY-O) • TAMMY
1957 CADILLAC V8 "FLEETWOOD 60 SPECIAL"
4-DOOR HARDTOP 4755 lbs. $5614. fob
HAPPY EASTER!
VIEW POINT ELEVATION 1800 FT.
365 C.I.D. O.H.V. V8 ENGINE (4" x 3 5/8" BORE + STROKE)
300 H.P. @ 4800 RPM 133" W.B.
10 TO 1 COMPRESSION
SONG HITS OF 1957: AROUND THE WORLD
A WHITE SPORT COAT • SO RARE (1938 REVIVAL)
LOVE LETTERS IN THE SAND (1931 REVIVAL) • TILL
IT'S NOT FOR ME TO SAY • ALL THE WAY • APRIL LOVE

1957 Cadillac

Dramatic restyling, a new lower silhouette (created in part by a new tubular center X-frame, with body secured to outrigger mountings instead of on side rails), and many other improvements created a very new Cadillac in 1957!

The new 300-h.p. engine could put out 325 h.p. with the addition of twin four-barrel carburetors.

Among the more minor improvements were the rubber tips on the bumper guards. Cadillac and Buick retained 15-inch wheels in 1957, while other GM cars tried the new 14-inch size.

Twenty-four thousand of the illustrated Fleetwood "60" Special four-door hardtops were built in the '57 model year, making it outsold only by Cadillac's "62" series hardtop sedans and coupes.

Certain advertisements in 1957 suggested that the reader take an hour-long test drive of a new Cadillac in order to be convinced that this was the "car of cars." After an hour at the wheel, the prospective buyer who could afford a Cadillac might well be persuaded to buy the Cadillac so that the luxurious experience could continue. And, surely, the salesman who went along for the ride was busy extolling the many automatic and power-operated luxury options that were available.

An hour's demonstration ride seems somewhat long and leisurely for this day and age, when many salesmen are in a big rush to surpass their sales quotas. Some might even try to sell a car without any demonstration drive. However, a salesman with real class will take that little extra time to make his prospect feel comfortable and at ease.

375 H P @ 5200 RPM OR 390 H P @ 5400
WITH 392 C/D V8 ENGINE (OVERHEAD VALVES and HEMI. COMBUSTION CHAMBERS)
4" x 3.9" BORE/9TR.
126" WB
4390 LBS.
COMPRESSION 9.25 or 10 to 1
TAD 8-11
© News America Syndicate, 1985
'57 CHRYSLER "300 – C" $5359.
145 M.P.H. POSSIBLE! THE "300" WAS HORSEPOWER KING UNTIL OUTDONE BY A 410 H.P. 1962 PLYMOUTH
"LETTER" SERIES 300s AVAIL. 1955-1965. STD. 300 to 71.

1957 Chrysler 300-C

Chrysler introduced its "300" series in '55, as a performance car. For '56, there were few noticeable changes in the "300-B," but for '57, the "300-C" had grown, with an all-new body, taller grille, quadruple headlights, larger tailfins, and all the trappings of those times!

To quote an original advertisement, "Here are the thrills of sports car motoring without the limitations. Enjoy the stirring surge of 375 horsepower putting the bite to the wheels, the feel of sure-footed cornering. The kind of control that makes a car and its master almost one.

"Sounds like a sports car, and it is, in terms of sheer driving pleasure. But here's the difference: No bundling to the ears to go around the block. No tears and red faces from the merciless wind. No acrobatics to get in and out.

"For the mighty Chrysler 300-C has the same spacious interior as any new Chrysler model, magnificently finished in rich sports-car leather."

There were two four-barrel carburetors; a special high-output camshaft; ball-joint, anti-dip-rubber-isolated torsion-bar front suspension; special nylon racing-type tubeless tires on 14-inch wheels; and a choice of convertible or two-door hardtop bodies in the 300-C line.

The height of the car was 54.7 inches, and it was 219.2 inches long. One problem with the big cars of the later 1950s was that they would not easily (if at all) fit into the short, narrow one-car garages of houses that were built in the 1940s or earlier. Consequently, the houses built since the mid-1950s usually have large garages to accommodate large cars.

1950s

NEW "SWEPT-WING" STYLING!
"STEP INTO THE WONDERFUL WORLD OF AUTODYNAMICS!"

1957 DODGE "ROYAL LANCER" 2 DR. H/T
$2769. and up, f.o.b. FACTORY
3585 LBS.

3.73 GEAR RATIO (3.36 w. AUTO. TRANS.)
11.8 to 20½ M.P.G.
ONLY 4½' HIGH

8.00 x 14" TUBELESS TIRES

NEW "TORSION-AIRE" RIDE

325 CID V8 WITH 245 TO 310 HP (138 HP @ AVAIL.)

122" WHEELBASE

EARLY 1957 DODGES HAVE THESE 6 UPRIGHT "TEETH" ATOP FRONT BUMPER.

OPTIONAL "D 500-1" 354 CID V8 WITH 340 HP @ 5200 RPM and 10 TO 1 COMPRESSION

©1992 by North America Syndicate, Inc. World rights reserved.

1957 Dodge

Laden with most available extras, your '57 Dodge could have had a gas-gulping V-8 engine, power steering, power brakes, power-adjustable seats, power windows, and push-button torque-flite automatic transmission, plus more! All these goodies were nice when new, but they spelled potential repair problems down the road.

A 1957 advertisement originally proclaimed, "Detroit automobile critics are buzzing about the buying surge to the new 'SweptWing' Dodge ... powered by a unique aircraft-type engine rated up to 310 h.p.. Autodynamic advances include a new revolutionary suspension system (Torsion-Aire), which virtually eliminates road-sway and brake-dip, [and] isolates vibration..." Torsion-Aire used torsion bars for front suspension, and conventional leaf springs at rear.

According to the ad, Dodge's price range in Detroit ran from $2,165 (including taxes) to $3,600. And, "every 45 seconds, someone buys a new Dodge."

In 1955, Chrysler Corp. cars had been dramatically restyled with a finely finished, solid appearance. The 1957 models, totally restyled, may have looked newer, but they possessed a slipshod, tinny, flimsy look in spite of all the broad expanses of sheet metal and brightwork and bright two-tone paint jobs. The 1957s didn't age well, either, and with any kind of hard use they began to loosen at the seams and limp around like sick dinosaurs. But, now that they're so scarce, 1957 Dodges have great appeal to those who fancy "1950s funk."

The six "fangs" on the front bumper (as illustrated) made the '57 Dodge appear too "toothy" in front; most later '57s appeared without them.

1957 GMC Pickup

"**F**rom half-ton to 45 tons, GMC makes the full family of trucks. Both gasoline and Diesel engine models, every one a Blue Chip GMC moneymaker!" —to quote a 1957 advertisement.

Some of General Motors Corp.'s large diesel models had new turbocharged engines and new air suspension. The latter feature appeared on some GM cars the following year, but was not considered successful; the air suspension bellows were prone to leakage.

At one time, GM had built Chevrolet, Pontiac, Oldsmobile, Buick, Cadillac, and GMC trucks (though not simultaneously). Until 1953, Pontiac sedan delivery trucks were still available, and Cadillac ambulances and hearses were seen everywhere (with bodies by Henney, Hess & Eisenhardt, and others). But, in '57, General

Motors' principal lines of trucks bore either the GMC or Chevrolet name. Chevrolet trucks were sold through Chevrolet dealers, and GMCs were handled by dealers who sold one of GM's four other makes.

The illustrated '57 GMC pickup had up to 206 h.p. with the available V-8 engine. While '57 GMC pickups are still quite popular, because of their flashy car-like grille and other features, they're not so easy to find.

If you enjoy reading about old trucks of all types and ages, you'll be fascinated with the excellent *Wheels of Time*, a well-illustrated magazine issued bimonthly by the American Truck Historical Society. You need not own a truck to belong to this club, but anyone who appreciates old trucks of any kind should look into this!

1950s

1957 ½ INTERNATIONAL
new "GOLDEN ANNIVERSARY"
A-100 3-DOOR TRAVELALL WAGON
$2364.

DURING THE 1950s, OPEN-SIDED "CARPORTS" WERE AS POPULAR AS GARAGES.

© News America Syndicate
© News Group Chicago, Inc., 1984

TAD 8-26

6 CYLINDERS O.H.V. 240 CID 140 H.P. 114" W.B. 4015 lbs. GAS TANK FILLER BEHIND DRIVER'S DOOR

"A-100" INTRO. SPRING, 1957.

2 DOORS AT CURB SIDE, ONLY 1 DOOR ON DRIVER'S SIDE! MFD. BY INTERNATIONAL HARVESTER, CHICAGO

1957 1/2 International Travelall

Spring 1957: The "Golden Anniversary" line of International trucks made its bow with considerable fanfare, commemorating a half-century of International Harvester vehicles. (Early '57 models were basically a continuation of 1956, but the "Golden Anniversary A Series" was "new from road to roof" and successfully continued into 1958.)

International Harvester (of Chicago, Ill.) produced a wide variety of 1957 trucks of all sizes, from pickups to heavy haulers. They also built International buses, crawler tractors, construction equipment, and a line of McCormick farm machinery and Farmall tractors.

In addition, International produced Travelall station wagons in 1/2-ton or 3/4-ton capacities. Travelall was similar in front-end styling to the International pickup of the same year, and carried eight passengers.

An unusual feature of the illustrated '57 1/2 Travelall was the three-door body! For the safety of children in the back seat, there was only one door on the left (driver's) side, but two on the right (in addition to the tailgate/hatch at rear).

In 1961, Travelall was joined by the new, smaller International Scout, a recreational-type vehicle that doubled as a pickup or a mini-wagon (with a removable top). After 1975, International no longer listed new pickups and Travelalls but did continue the Scout and the various heavy trucks, etc. In the early 1980s, during the automotive recession, production was suspended for a brief time. But, International has come on strong again, reorganized, and revitalized with an all-new series of trucks.

A "HOT LITTLE 'BOMB!'"
1957 1/2 (AVAIL. IN USA, MAY, 1957)
XK-SS
BY JAGUAR

U.S. PRICE $5600.

6 CYL. 210 CID
DUAL OVERHEAD CAM
ENGINE (3442 c.c.)
260 HP @ 6000 RPM (or 262)
9 TO 1 COMPRESSION
6.00 x 16" TIRES
90.6" WHEELBASE
2230 LBS. (W/O FUEL)

MADE IN ENGLAND

4 TH-GEAR RATIO = 3.54 TO 1
*O TO 60 MPH IN ONLY 5.2 SECONDS!
TOP SPEED = 149 M.P.H.!
10 - 14 MPG   DISC BRAKES

REAR DETAILS

*4.2 SECONDS IN OUR TEST! #

6-12-94

1950s

1957 1/2 Jaguar "XK-SS"

This fast, little car was a "screamer" in every sense of the word, with a muffler so loud that it was illegal in many populated areas! You can see this notorious muffler under the left side of the car.

The XK-SS roadster was described by Jaguar as a "dual purpose car," suitable for use on the street or competition on the track. But, most reviewers found it suited only to competition driving. It was noisy and hard-riding. With the top up, the driver's compartment was cramped to the point of claustrophobia!

The little car was so packed with power that it was difficult not to spin the rear wheels unintentionally. And, it would be easy to spin out and fly off the road on a curve taken at speed!

But, *Motor Life* magazine, April 1957, described the hairy little Tasmanian Devil as "Coventry's answer to Corvette and Mercedes in the high-performance sports car bracket." The design, according to *Motor Life*, resembled the competition-model Jaguar "D" racing roadster, except that the XK-SS had a top and side curtains.

It's a wonder that Jaguar was able to produce and deliver any cars that season, for on February 12, 1957, its Coventry factory was hit by a fire so severe that steel girders were melted and collapsed in a large portion of the complex! But, the people of Jaguar rose to the occasion. The wreckage was quickly cleared away, and a new building was constructed in just nine weeks!

1957 MASERATI TIPO 52 (200-S)
SPORTS CAR with ONE-OF-A-KIND CUSTOM BODY BY SCAGLIETTI (ONLY 32 OTHER CARS IN THIS SPECIAL SERIES, BUILT APR.,1956 TO JULY, 1958.)

MASERATI CARS MADE IN MODENA, ITALY SINCE 1938 (AND ORIGINALLY MADE IN BOLOGNA, ITALY, 1926-1938.)

ONLY 39.2" HIGH

95" LONG

58" WIDE

TOP SPEED: **150 MPH** (250 KILOMETERS PER HOUR)

4 CYLS. (119.6 CU.IN. DISPL.) (1993 cc) 3.7 × 3" BORE AND STROKE (92 mm × 75 mm) 9 TO 1 COMPRESSION RATIO **186 H.P.   7500 RPM** 88" WHEELBASE   26.4-GAL. FUEL CAPACITY

TAD 3—15

© News America Syndicate, 1987

1957 Maserati

Ferrari, Lamborghini, and Maserati are three long-famous builders of Italian luxury cars, and because they have each produced so many different models and variations within those models, there is no really "typical" example of each!

In the case of Maserati, however, the reader may think of a luxury touring sedan, as that is what Maserati has chiefly exported to the U.S.A. during the 1980s. In 1981, for example, the Maserati "Quattroporte" (four-door) was selling in America for over $56,000 and would go 123 m.p.h. in third gear. This was later joined by the Maserati two-door "Biturbo," priced just below $27,000.

Maserati's trident insignia was inspired by the traditional symbol of Bologna, Italy, the city where the Maserati originated in 1926. The company founder was the late Alfieri Maserati.

In addition to Ferrari and Lamborghini, other Italian cars sold in the United States in recent years include Alfa Romeo, Lancia, and Fiat. The latter has been withdrawn from the American market since 1983.

Maserati, over the years, has built cars with 4-cylinder engines, as well as straight 6, V-6, V-8, straight-8, V-12, and even V-16 engines! The first Maserati V-16 was the mighty "Tipo V-4" (don't let the model name fool you!), and though this multi-cylindered powerhouse had a relatively small displacement for its sixteen cylinders (just 221.4 c.i.d.), it boasted 305 h.p. at 5,500 RPM, and in 1929 it set a speed record in Italy of 152.9 miles per hour!

1957 Monarch

During the 1950s, Ford Motor Co. offered two additional makes in Canada that were not available in the USA. These were the Meteor and the Monarch. Each of these unique makes had their own grille designs, different taillights, and different side trim, etc. from the usual Ford and Mercury (also available there).

This attractive 1957 Monarch shows its close relationship to the Mercury. But, note that the Monarch has horizontal grille pieces, while Mercury's are vertical.

In *Maclean's* magazine (Canada) for January 5, 1957, a '57 Monarch was advertised. Bryon Stappler of British Columbia was kind enough to send me a photocopy of this rare ad. I certainly wish I could find more Canadian car advertisements, either originals or photocopies, because they're virtually impossible to find in the U.S.A. These Canadian variants are of great interest to *Auto Album* readers and to me! *Maclean's* was one Canadian magazine that frequently advertised cars, but nobody seems to have old copies of that magazine around.

Just a handful of these older Canadian cars have found their way to this country, and when they are seen here, they are sometimes mistaken for "custom jobs."

Ford wasn't the only one to build special Canadian editions. The Acadian Beaumont was a General Motors car seen only in Canada (in the 1960s). And, Chrysler Corp. made a Dodge Kingsway in Canada only, as well as other unusual variations. In the later 1940s, there was a Canadian Dodge that had the crisscross grille of the 1946-1948 Dodge, but the small body of a 1946-1948 Plymouth!

"STAR CHIEF" CONVERTIBLE
347 C.I.D. V8 ENGINE (O.H.V.)
(3.94" × 3.56" BORE + STROKE)
270 HORSEPOWER
@ 4800 RPM
10 TO 1 COMPRESSION
Hydra-Matic AUTO.TRANS.
20-GALLON FUEL TANK
3860 LBS.

$3105.,
f.o.b.,
FACTORY

'57 Pontiac

optional
"CONTINENTAL"
STYLE
REAR SPARE
TIRE / WHEEL with
EXTENDED BUMPER

124" W.B.

8.00 × 14"
TIRES

PONTIAC

© Field Enterprises, Inc., 1983

TAP 4-17

1957 Pontiac

"Star Flight" body styling was GM's description for Pontiac's new 1957 look. Overall length was increased 1.2 inches, and the grille was an attractive new convex "waterfall" type with plenty of air-scoop space just above. This was an improvement over the "gaping" look of '55 and '56 front ends! The hood was lower, and visibility was markedly improved. There were eighty-six changes for 1957!

The illustrated "Star Chief" was the top line for the new year, and 1957 was the season that Pontiac finally eliminated the parallel chrome strips along the hood (a Pontiac trademark since 1935). Other '57 Pontiac series included Super-Chief and Chieftan, these latter two came on a shorter (122-inch) wheelbase.

The "Strato-Streak" V-8 engine was larger than in '56, with increased horsepower, larger manifolding, larger valves, re-designed carburetors, etc. Distributor, starting motor, and ignition control were also re-designed. Performance: from zero to 60 in 8.3 seconds, top speed 110 or more!

Pontiac proudly stated that "one of the nation's largest state highway patrols" tested six different makes of cars and then purchased 300 new Pontiacs for police cruisers. *Hot Rod* magazine wrote, "Pontiac is no longer grandma's car, because we don't think granny could stand the acceleration built into this torpedo without blacking out."

Hot Rod continued, "When the transmission hits third gear and the throttle hits that third carburetor, you'll think you've been catapulted from a carrier deck."

During 1957, Pontiac introduced the first of its "Bonneville" models, a high-performance convertible with fuel-injected engine.

"MORE THAN A CAR!" "MORE THAN A TRUCK!"

new 1957 RANCHERO

BY FORD (THE FIRST RANCHERO!) 116" WB

$2149. "CUSTOM" SERIES HAS THIS SIDE TRIM STRIP.

POWER STEER., BRAKES, SEATS, WINDOWS OPTIONAL

292 CID V8 (212 HP) (190 HP 272 V8 OR 144 HP 223 6 AVAIL.) FORD O MATIC, OVERDR., OR 3-SP. MANUAL TRANS.

TAD 10/14

1957 Ranchero

Back in the late 1930s, Studebaker built vehicles that were half car, half truck known as "Coupe-Expresses." There were other such vehicles as well. Remember Hudson's car-like pickups of the 1940s? Or, Ford's Model A "roadster-pickups?"

However, the idea seemed new again when Ford introduced its sporty Ranchero in the 1957 model year. The Ranchero was designed for beauty and comfort as well as for utility. It resembled a two-door Ford station wagon, minus the upper rear superstructure.

Advertised as "the only pickup that rides, handles and feels exactly like a car," Ranchero featured body sides that were little more than three feet above the road, which meant that loading and unloading was a cinch! Its half-ton-plus payload capacity put it in the league of standard-sized pickups.

There were two models: Ranchero (standard) and Custom Ranchero (as illustrated). The Custom Ranchero was comparable to Ford's Super Deluxe Fairlane line of cars. Strangely, the "Custom" line in Ford cars had eventually become the "cheapie" series, minus the chrome pizazz of a Custom Ranchero.

Ranchero appealed to anyone using one vehicle for both business and pleasure. You could haul lumber in it and later drive it to a dinner-dance at the country club!

In 1960, the Ranchero would shrink, as it moved from the full-size Ford line to the new compact Falcon series.

The 1957 Ranchero colors (single-tone) included Raven Black, Dresden Blue, Starmist Blue, Colonial White, Cumberland Green, Willow Green, Silver Mocha, Doeskin Tan, Woodsmoke Gray, Gunmetal Gray, and Flame Red.

LAST OF THE CLASSIC 3-PASSENGER THUNDERBIRDS!

$3408. and up

NARROWER, SHARPER TAIL FINS ON 1957 MODEL

SIDE VENT ADDED IN 1956.

new 7.50 x 14 TIRES

THANKS TO RALPH FINLEY, SARATOGA, CA., FOR HELPFUL PHOTOS.

1957
THUNDERBIRD
292 OR 312 C.I.D. V8

212, 245 OR 270 H.P. *
FORD-O-MATIC TRANS. AVAIL.
* 285 H.P. OPTION
(OVERDRIVE ALSO AVAIL.)

FIRST T-BIRD WAS THE 1955. JUST ONE 3-PASS. T-BIRD ('57 STYLE) WAS BUILT, EXPERIMENTALLY, IN 1963...BUT FORD MOTOR CO. DECIDED TO OFFER THE MUSTANG INSTEAD.

3.10, 3.56 OR 3.70 G.R.

12-11 TAP

1957 Thunderbird

This is, unquestionably, one of the most popular collectors' cars of the 1950s! The ultimate personal car (according to many), the three-passenger Thunderbird (1955-57) combined the performance of a sports car with the luxury of a Lincoln in a compact, easy-to-handle package.

Thunderbird power was increased, and the instrument panel was new—a hooded cluster of circular gauges. Instead of the formerly circular parking/directional lights, the 1957 counterparts were made rectangular and moved down into the bumper. The new front bumper had a pronounced center dip, better displaying the grille.

An unusual new accessory was marketed for the 1957 Thunderbirds (or for any other convertible it would fit), and that was the "Birdnest," a rumble seat that fit into the trunk space to accommodate additional passengers. That was the first rumble seat available since the

beginning of the 1940s. But, its market would suddenly dwindle when the four-passenger Thunderbird was introduced for 1958.

The rear-quarter side porthole, introduced on the removable T-bird hardtop in 1956, was again available. You could also get the removable fiberglass hardtop without the port-hole—or a manually folding fabric top, if preferred.

The top could be ordered in a color contrasting the body color, if desired, and the following top/body colors were offered in the 1957 brochure: flame red, raven black, gunmetal gray, colonial white, starmist (light) blue, willow (light) green, coral sand (orange), Inca gold (yellow-green), Thunderbird bronze, and dusk rose (pink). Thirty-four two-tone combinations were illustrated! (Many purchasers ordered single colors, though.) Interiors were color-keyed to exterior finish.

1958 Corvette

"**V**ROOOMMMM!!" As usual, the new Corvette for '58 was one of America's hottest performers, as the sports car excitement continued. The most noticeable of the new 1958's physical features were the new quadruple headlights, typical of all new GM cars that year.

Chevrolet's Corvette had been introduced during 1953, and it quickly became America's most successful fiberglass-bodied car. It was a true sports car, though in '53 and '54 only six-cylinder engines were available. As soon as a V-8 appeared for 1955 (a few of the 1955 Corvettes were sixes), performance took off and continued to climb as the years passed and bigger and better engines came along.

The '58 Corvette, like its predecessors and followers, had a "glass-fiber-reinforced plastic body, painted with polished acrylic lacquer." Buyers had a choice of manual folding fabric top (power top optional) or easily removable plastic hard top. Power windows were optional.

In 1958, four Chevrolet V-8 engine choices were offered—two of them with fuel injection. Three transmissions were available: powerglide automatic, three-speed manual, or four-speed manual. To operate the four-speed manual, a lever had to be pushed to the far left and then forward for reverse. Low gear position was where reverse would normally be in a three-speed manual transmission.

A carburetor was eliminated on models with the Ramjet Fuel Injection, as fuel was then "pressure-injected directly at each cylinder intake port." Fuel injection was a novelty in the 1950s, but it's found on several makes of cars today.

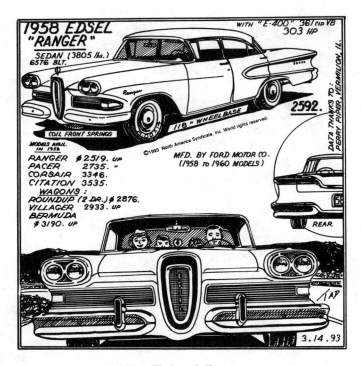

1958 Edsel Ranger

The smaller Edsels—like this Ranger, the Pacer, and the Roundup—shared many mechanical components with the Ford, while the larger Edsels were akin to the Mercury.

The only flaw in the Edsel was its "Teletouch" transmission button control in the hub of the steering wheel. These buttons were wired to electric motors that did the work of changing transmission speeds. Problems arose in the wiring that twisted through the steering column, in the buttons, and in the electric motors. The touchy Teletouch was included in higher-priced Edsels and optional in some of the smaller models. It proved troublesome enough that it wasn't included in the 1959 or 1960 Edsels.

The Edsel was unveiled in September 1957 for the 1958 model year, just as a sharp, yearlong recession had begun! At that time, most buyers were looking for low-priced economy cars, and most of the Edsels were in the medium-priced range. None were gas-sippers, either, for all '58 Edsels were V-8s!

TV comedians and dealers of Ford Motor Co.'s competitors made up a number of clever but cruel Edsel jokes, writing off the car as a loser and failure just as it was getting on the market. Some would-be buyers were discouraged from selecting an Edsel for fear of ridicule!

The 1960 Edsel had new '60 styling, with an all-new split grille, somewhat reminiscent of a '59 Pontiac, but in November 1959 orders went out to stop the Edsel. Those '60 models became an instant rarity!

1958 Ford Pickup

Today, there are numerous collectors of older pickup trucks (in addition to car collectors). While some light trucks of fifteen years of age or older can still be bought for a low figure, others have considerably increased in value.

Fans of older Ford pickups are divided as to the years they particularly like. Some prefer the pre-World War II models. Others like those of the early postwar years. Still others have a preference for the rather gaudy models of the late '50s, such as the illustrated 1958 model.

Beginning in '57, Ford pickups began to put on a bit of flab and glitter, in keeping with the passenger car trend of that time. Dual sets of headlights, large grilles, fancy sculptured moldings, etc. were all in vogue in 1958.

The Styleside wide-bed on the pickup was standard. The comfortable "driverized" cab offered Hi-Dri ventilation, Lifeguard steering wheel, suspended foot pedals, inboard steps, and woven plastic upholstery with non-sag seat springing. This was one reason Ford named itself "Number One Farm Pickup" in '58. Other reasons included the twenty-three percent greater load-space than competing half-ton pickups, the superior suspension that gave a car-like ride, and the "short-stroke" power of Ford's overhead-valve straight-6 or V-8 engines.

A "12-million truck study" proved the longevity of Ford trucks. In the '50s, there were still Model A and AA Ford trucks of 1928-1932 vintage in daily service on farms and in small businesses everywhere!

1958 Meteor

C anadian Fords and Mercurys were similar to their American counterparts, but the Meteors and Monarchs were distinctively Canadian; they were never sold in the United States. Rarely seen outside of Canada, they are now scarce in their own home country.

For 1958, twenty "sparkling new body colors" were available in the "Magnificent Meteor" line. Styling was somewhat like the 1958 Ford, but with a different grille, side trim, and other detail changes. Meteor's "Niagara" and "Rideau" model series were distinctly Canadian.

New "Luxury Lounge" interiors and a "Safety-Curve Control Center" dash were designed to "make motoring fun." The deep-center safety steering wheel was a feature also seen on American Fords since '56.

New "Finger-Touch Ball-Race" steering had a 27 to 1 ratio. The Meteor had a forty-foot turning diameter.

"Quadri-Beam" (four) headlights were a new Ford feature for 1958 on both sides of the border. And, the front-hinged hood was a new safety feature, as this hood could not be whipped open accidentally.

A former product of the Mercury-Lincoln-Meteor Division of Ford Motor Co. of Canada, the Meteor is a choice collector's item for anyone who likes Fords of the '50s. Its appearance at car shows—even in Canada—is a rare occurrence.

Should you ever buy a Canadian Meteor, you'll probably never see another exactly like it. And, be prepared to hear people say, "Hey, some car! But what is it?"

1958 Oldsmobile

"**O**ldsmobility!" That was just what the new '58 Olds offered you, according to advertising that year. General Motors' ad writers were always coming up with catchy sales names and slogans back in the '50s! Designed for "the rocket age," the new model combined "mobility" with Oldsmobile high technology, so why not call it "Oldsmobility"?

GM had its Golden Anniversary in 1958, and all the stops were pulled out in a new advertising campaign to promote the new cars in the midst of a biting recession that had begun in mid-1957. For the new year, all GM cars had become totally restyled, with a new look that was for 1958 alone. And, despite differences in size, grille design, trim, etc., the GM cars all bore a close family resemblance to one another that year.

Available in Dynamic 88, Super 88, and 98 models, all 1958 Oldsmobiles were generously plastered with chrome strips and embellishments from end to end. Though chrome strips seldom perform an important function, they do brighten up a car. At that point in time, the chrome era was reaching the zenith of its glory.

Overall average fuel consumption was 12-to-14.2 m.p.g. (city and highway combined), and the 0-to-60 m.p.h. pickup was achieved from 8.6-to-10.2 seconds, depending on which model and engine you were using.

The air suspension system option was new. It was discontinued in a matter of months because of air leaks that caused many of these cars to creep along the ground like tired old reptiles.

THE "KISSING PANHARD"

1958 "DYNA" PANHARD

MADE IN FRANCE AND PRICED IN
THE U.S.A. AT $*1995.* and up
(DISTRIBUTED BY CITROEN)

SMALL GRILLE
RESEMBLES A
PAIR OF
PUCKERED LIPS!

42 HORSEPOWER AT 5000 RPM

© News America Syndicate, 1985

TAD
7/14

TO 40 M.P.G. (30-34 AVERAGE)

ONLY
2
CYLINDERS!

"150DYNE" SUSPENSION
101.2" WHEELBASE
WEIGHT = 1880 LBS.
4.71 GEAR RATIO (4TH GEAR)
BY 1958, 2000 "DYNA"
MODELS LIKE THIS WERE
BEING USED AS TAXIS IN PARIS.

AIR-COOLED
OVERHEAD-VALVE
ENGINE (51.9
CU. IN. DISPL.)
(850 CC)

(PANHARD CARS
PRODUCED 1890
TO 1967.)

TOP SPEED = 85 MILES PER HOUR

1958 "Dyna" Panhard

The front end of this unique French Panhard may remind you of a fish face, if not a pair of kissing lips! Since this was an air-cooled car with a front engine, you may wonder, as I do, why the grille opening wasn't larger.

Unlike other French cars, Panhards were not imported to the U.S.A. for many years at a time, other than for brief intervals in the very early days and in the 1920s. But, in 1955, French Motor's Inc. of Los Angeles made an attempt to promote and sell Panhards in the United States.

With only two cylinders, a "Dyna" Panhard won the French Mobil Gas Economy Run in 1957 by delivering 55.17 miles per gallon of gas! And, in 1958, Panhard advertised that it had won "800 Sports Car Victories," including a record-breaking six wins at the 24 hour Le Mans event! By Spring 1958, Panhard had gathered a list of 100 dealers and ten distributors coast-to-coast in the U.S.A. Because of this, it's surprising that "Dyna" Panhards have always been scarce on these shores!

Panhard importing fizzled out after 1959, but in the early 1960s new models were available elsewhere, such as the "24-CT," which resembled a modified Corvair from the rear and a miniature Ferrari or Maserati from the front! The "24" series was the last to leave Panhard's factory, for sales had fallen from 30,000 in 1964 to less than 500 in 1967, Panhard's final year.

At the time of its discontinuance, Panhard was the oldest remaining French make of automobile.

DRIVE-IN MOVIES WERE AT A PEAK OF POPULARITY IN 1958, WITH OVER 4000 IN THE U.S.A.!

BECAUSE OF HIGH LAND COSTS, MANY DRIVE-INS REPLACED BY HOUSING TRACTS OR SHOPPING CENTERS.

1958 PONTIAC BONNEVILLE
2 DR HARDTOP
122" WB
370 CID V8
255 310 HP
20-GAL. GAS TANK

9144 BUILT

8.00 x 14" TIRES

$3481.
F.O.B., FACTORY PRICE

3710 lbs.

FRONT END

1958

1950

1958 Pontiac Bonneville

"A new kind of car is born! Meet the bold new Pontiac ... A revolution on wheels ..." The adjectives flowed fast in Pontiac's 1958 advertising campaign. Sales literature and ads promised blazing power and a thrilling ride. Pontiac, and all GM-built cars, were totally restyled for 1958, though this new "bulbous-curvy" look would continue only for that season, replaced for 1959 by another new look: the "linear" look.

The 1958 Pontiacs had an optional "Ever-Level Air Ride," though air suspension was later to be called off as a deflated balloon, once several manufacturers had toyed with it in the late '50s.

The Bonneville (a.k.a. Bonneville Custom) was Pontiac's top-line model and bore the designation "Bonneville" on the hood and rear deck. The Bonneville was first available during 1957

as a convertible. The illustrated two-door hardtop was added for 1958.

Pontiac's model series for 1958, in ascending order: Chieftan, Super Chief, Star Chief Custom, and Bonneville (or Bonneville Custom). All Pontiacs since 1955 had been powered by overhead-valve V-8 engines, and for 1958 there were seven horsepower variations!

Notice the drive-in movie theater in this scene. The first drive-in theater was opened in New Jersey in 1933. The fad didn't catch on until shortly after the end of World War II. In the late 1940s and through the 1950s, drive-in theaters opened in most suburban areas of the United States. During the 1950s and 1960s, drive-ins appeared to be replacing indoor theaters, but in the 1970s, many drive-in operators found it more profitable to sell out to a developer.

1958 Rambler American

Rambler was a venerable name on the American auto scene, dating back to 1897! In 1914, the Rambler had been replaced by the Jeffery, which in turn made way for the 1917 Nash. But, years later, in 1950, Nash revived the Rambler for its all-new line of 100-inch-wheelbase compact cars. During the 1950s, Rambler grew in size, and by 1957 it was a 108-inch wheelbase intermediate.

But, 1958 was a recession year, and it was back-to-basics again. A revived 100-inch wheelbase model returned to the line, restyled and re-titled the Rambler American. It lacked frills, though a Flash-O-Matic transmission was available as an option.

The American was a wise innovation. Its name stirred up the loyalty of those who resented the invasion of the small, foreign cars. And, this new model was truly a gas saver. Advertised to get 30 miles per gallon on the road, the American outdid itself on an official Los Angeles to Miami economy run. With overdrive, it got an amazing 35.39 m.p.g.!

Total Rambler sales for 1958: 135,606 cars, a 76.5 percent increase over the 76,827 cars sold in the '57 fiscal year! Rambler moved from twelfth place up to seventh in automotive sales. Since Nash and Hudson had been struggling when they'd merged just four years earlier, *Motor Age* magazine mused, "How long will the success ride continue?"

In addition to the '58 American, Rambler also offered the 108-inch wheelbase Deluxe, Super, and Custom Six; Deluxe, Super, and Custom Rebel V-8; and the 117-inch-wheelbase Super and Custom Ambassador V-8.

1959 ASTON-MARTIN "DB4"
6 CYL. DOHC (3670 cc) ENG. 263 HP @ 5700 RPM
TOP SPEED 145 M.P.H. 2884 lbs.
ITALIAN-STYLED BODY (BY TICKFORD)
(MK. III MODEL ALSO AVAIL.)

REAR VIEW

nearly £4000. IN ENGLAND

($9770. IN U.S.A.)

2/9

O TO 100 MPH and BACK TO FULL STOP IN ONLY 26.2 SECONDS!!

98" W.B.   DB4 1959

DISC BRAKES   14~17 M.P.G.

1959 Aston-Martin

Because of Ian Fleming's fictional character James Bond (Agent 007), many people think of the Aston-Martin as a "secret agent's car." In the 1964 James Bond movie *Goldfinger*, an Aston-Martin DB-5 coupe (quite similar to the illustrated DB-4) was rigged with special equipment, such as parking-light machine-guns, telescoping front and rear bumper guards for ramming the villains' cars, tire-cutting hub extensions, and a bullet-proof rear screen that popped up from the rear deck through a slot—like a piece of toast!

The movie car, with optional fighting equipment supplied by the British Secret Service, cost $45,000. Even the illustrated DB-4 of 1959 cost nearly $10,000, a high price for a car back then—when $10,000 would fully pay for a good three-bedroom house!

The illustrated car had a "superleggera"-type Italian-style body with tubular framework, designed by Touring of Italy and built by Tickford of England. The hot 3,670 cc engine (224 cubic-inch displacement) was considerably faster than the 202-h.p. one in the lower priced Mk. III series, though the Mk. III was no slouch on the highway!

Aston-Martin Lagonda Ltd. was forced into receivership and the factory closed on the last day of 1974; but two Aston-Martin fans (one from the United States and one from Canada) bought the factory in mid 1975, and regular production soon began anew. By late 1978, the price of a new Aston-Martin Lagonda V-8 was up to $75,000, and would soon run to well over 100K—because of all the sophisticated electronic equipment on board!

1950s

1959 Buick

Spurned as "gas-guzzling dinosaurs" in the mid-1970s, the giant-sized American cars of the late '50s are now of considerable value to a growing list of admirers all around the world.

Back in the 1950s, broad, imposing grilles—and globs of chrome everywhere—were "in." And, 1959 marked the grand climax of the "bigger and bigger and better than ever" school of automotive design. (In the 1960s, we owned a super-wide 1959 Pontiac Bonneville Vista flat-top, similar to the Buick illustrated, which would seat five adults in front!)

Some Americans resent their dear old chrome dreamboats being "Sold down the river," but foreign collectors are often willing to pay more than domestic buyers will offer. Many of our cars from the 1950s are being shipped to Japan or Germany, but even smaller countries are interested. In Finland, for example, there's an excellent publication called *V-8* magazine, which features glamorous, glossy color photos of older American cars that have found new lives with Finnish collectors.

But, in most European and Asian countries, gas prices are outrageously high. So, these old American cars have become "big toys" for those who can afford to send for restored specimens. Even the big cars of the 1960s and 1970s are climbing in value. Naturally, condition and authenticity have much to do with what a specific older car may be worth, not to mention the popularity of that particular model.

1959 De Soto "Explorer" Wagon

On the 1959 De Soto, one could order the following extras: Four-Season "Airtemp" pushbutton air conditioner (with heavy duty ceiling-mounted unit for station wagons), power brakes, "Constant Control" power steering, power windows, six-way power seat, Solex anti-glare glass, electric clock, pushbutton heater/defroster/vent, Dual-Jet windshield washers, Station-Seeker radio (transistorized, with toe-operated station selector), Touch-Tuner radio (transistorized, with conventional finger push-buttons), rear-seat radio speaker, automatic headlight beam changer (light-activated), dual radio antennas (on rear fenders), padded dash, remote control outside mirror, Mirror-Matic rearview mirror or three-way Prismatic rearview mirror (both anti-glare adjustable), triad (three-tone) horn, dual exhausts, ash tray light, trunk light (or rear dome light in wagons), map and glove box light, variable speed windshield wipers, and even more! The extras could be ordered at discount in various accessory group packages listed in the sales folder.

One of the special new features also available: Sports Swivel seats, which rotated to the side for easy entrance or exit. These were available on most models, an exclusive feature of Chrysler Corp. cars.

The 1959 De Sotos were available in four series: Firesweep, Firedome, Fireflite (illustrated), or the special Adventurer. The Adventurer sported golden trim, including gilt-toned wheel covers, grille, and side spear, plus gold-colored hues inside the car.

The 1961 model was the final De Soto, although Chrysler Corp. continued the name on a line of small trucks sold overseas.

1959 EL CAMINO *new from CHEVROLET!*

MODEL 1180 = 6-CYL. (235½ c.i.d.) 135 H.P. WEIGHT = 3605 lbs.
" 1280 = V8 (283 c.i.d.) 185 OR 230 H.P.
3.55 GEAR RATIO (STD.) (3.36 AUTO TRANS.) (4.11 OVERDRIVE)
PICKUP BED is 76¼" LONG, 64¼" WIDE, 12¾" DEEP
17-GALLON FUEL TANK   PRICES BEGIN (f.o.b.) AT $2470.

A NEW COMBINATION PICKUP/CAR, INTRO. TO COMPETE WITH FORD RANCHERO. (10-16-58 DEBUT)

NO 1961-63 EL CAMINO. IT RETURNED IN *new* 1964 CHEVELLE LINE.

14" WHEELS   119" WHEELBASE   © Field Enterprises, Inc., 1983

TAP 2-13

1959 El Camino

In 1957, Ford introduced its Ranchero pickup car. Not to be outdone, Chevrolet (in 1959) brought forth the new El Camino (illustrated).

Studebaker and Hudson each built pickup cars before World War II. Hudson's continued until 1947. But, then pickup cars were forgotten in the U.S.A., though they were produced during the 1950s in Australian auto factories (where they were called "Utes"). By the later 1950s, such vehicles were "new" to the U.S.A., again.

Chevy's El Camino was dropped in '61, but returned in 1964. GMC trucks eventually introduced an El Camino twin, the Sprint, for GMC dealers to handle.

One ad of 1959 stated: "Ideally, El Camino is for work days and weekends both: five days earning its keep on the payroll, two days doubling as a personal car."

Also, "Your favorite sport or do-it-yourself project could easily call for El Camino's all-steel, half-ton capacity pickup box. Here you have plenty of space for sports gear or tools and materials—wide-open workable space for long loads or high ones."

As the '59 model year progressed, as many as eight V-8 choices were available (up to 335 h.p.) in addition to the six! Powerglide or Turboglide automatic transmissions were each optional.

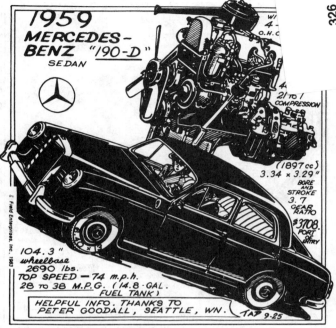

1959
MERCEDES-BENZ "190-D"
SEDAN

W
4 -
O.H.C

4
21 TO 1
COMPRESSION

(1897 cc)
3.34 x 3.29"
BORE AND STROKE
3.7 GEAR RATIO

$3708.
PORT OF ENTRY

104.3"
wheelbase
2690 lbs.
TOP SPEED — 74 m.p.h.
28 TO 38 M.P.G. (14.8-GAL. FUEL TANK)
HELPFUL INFO. THANKS TO PETER GOODALL, SEATTLE, WN.

© Field Enterprises, Inc. 1983

9-25

1959 Mercedes-Benz 190-D

"**D**aimler-Benz's 'Program for Every Need' has now experienced an important broadening," declared the original sales literature. "Taking its place beside the reliable, economical and truly world famous diesel passenger car 180-D is the new 55 h.p. 190-D. This elegant touring car offers many of the advantages of the [gasoline powered] 190: the snug, comfortable interior and costly fittings, the excellent driving performance, plus the unrivaled economy of the modern, powerful diesel engine. With a 190-D the pleasure of an especially comfortable diesel vehicle will be found in 'your' car."

Several options were available: wide, white-sidewall tires; leather upholstery; bucket seats; radio; fog lights; etc. American-sold models had directional signal lights below the headlights.

Other '59 Mercedes-Benz models included the gasoline powered 190 already mentioned, the 190-SL roadster, 220, 220-S, 220-SE, 230-SL, 300, 300-SE, 300-SL sports car, 300-h.p. "600," and the magnificent 600 "Grand Mercedes" Pullman Limousine with a super-long 153 1/2-inch wheelbase.

These, and other model series of older Mercedes-Benz autos, include many that are now considered "classics." And, in spite of today's high prices, the current Mercedes-Benz models enjoy great popularity in the United States as well as in their native Germany!

1959 Moretti

Is it news to you that there was a 1959 Moretti? Few people know much about this one. It's a limited production Italian marque that never sold in high numbers.

In its advertising, Moretti traced its roots back to 1926. Its actual car production began in 1945, as Italy was still reeling from the devastation of World War II. The first Moretti car was the La Cita, a two-cylinder mini that was said to be capable of 60 m.p.h. and 80 miles per gallon! Four-cylinder models joined the Moretti line, and by 1954 there was a good selection of models.

Buyer financing was harsh: The company required a fifty percent down payment with each order! That was understandable, though; a manufacturer that small could not afford to gamble with cancellations.

Originally, Moretti built their own mechanical components and bodies, and there was much high-quality, old-fashioned hard work in the modest factory. In 1957, Fiat conversions were included in the line, and from 1960 on, Fiat chassis were used on virtually all Morettis.

At the time the illustrated Coupe Turismo was advertised, there was just one Moretti distributor for the entire United States, the J. F. R. Co. in Massachusetts.

Moretti also built custom bodies on special order for most of Europe's leading automobile manufacturers. Moretti took great pride in their meticulous body-making processes. Bodies, paint jobs, and upholstery work were produced almost exclusively by hand—no automation there!

WITH THE NEW "LINEAR" LOOK
1959 OLDSMOBILE
SUPER 88 4-DR. HOLIDAY SPT. SEDAN
123" W.B.
$3405., fob

WITH 394 C.I.D. V-8 (O.H.V.)
4.13" × 3.69" BORE + STR.
315 H.P. @ 4600 RPM
9.75 TO 1 COMPRESSION
9.00 × 14" TIRES

3.23 GEAR RATIO WITH Hydra-Matic

5-13
© News Group Chicago, Inc., 1984
HAPPY MOTHER'S DAY!

1959 Oldsmobile

Though GM's 1958 models had all-new bodies and unique styling in '58, it was quickly decided that the 1959 models must, again, be all-new—in order to stimulate sales. And, happily, 1959 was a much better year for the industry!

As the 1959 Oldsmobile sales catalog explained, this was the start of a new styling cycle. "There's new figure and form, with a new 'Linear Look' in all three series (88, Super 88, 98) ... a new outlook, with nearly 40 percent greater total glass area.

"Olds' new 'Linear Look' is best exemplified by the Holiday Sport Sedan's unique, fleet roof line (a flat look), and full wrap-around rear window. Exceptional visibility makes this smart style note a rousing success from the passenger's point of view."

Olds' famous Jetaway Hydra-Matic transmission (automatic) was standard equipment on the big 98 series and optional on the 88 and Super 88.

Optional power assists included Roto-Matic Power Steering, Pedal-Ease Power Brakes, Six-way Power Seat, electric window lifts (and even electrically controlled butterfly vent windows, if desired), electric radio antenna (raised and lowered by a switch inside the car), and (in the Fiesta station wagon) an electrically-controlled tailgate window.

A "Safety Sentinel" on the speedometer could be set as desired so that a warning light and buzzer alerted the driver when the speed limit was exceeded. Also, the conventional speedometer needle had been replaced by a horizontal, thermometer-type sliding bar indicator that changed from green to amber and then to red as speed increased.

1950s

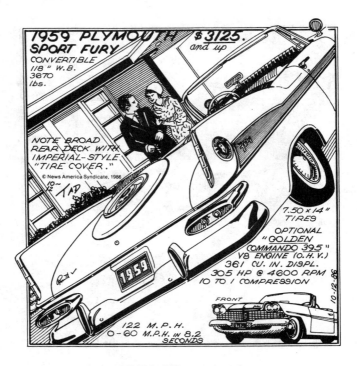

1959 Plymouth

"Today's best buy ... Tomorrow's best trade." "If it's new, Plymouth's got it!" The 1959 Plymouth included many improvements—in styling, as well as available features!

The broad rear deck on this new Sport Fury was enhanced by the new Imperial-style imitation spare tire cover; and up front, the quadruple headlights appeared to "float" below their chromed brows, against a blacked-out background. The grille was parted at the center by a new medallion.

Inside, new swiveling bucket seats made it easier to get in or out. Push-button heating and ventilating controls were an improvement, and warm air was quickly provided when the heater was turned on. An optional, new "electronic" Mirror-Matic rear view mirror automatically reduced glare from the headlights of following cars.

A new "compound Star View" windshield in hardtops and convertibles gave added visibility, as it curved up AND around.

The L-head six-cylinder Plymouth was last offered in 1959. The new, inclined "slant-6" of 1960 would have overhead valves (as the Plymouth V-8s already had).

Plymouth models for 1959: Savoy, Belvedere, Fury, Sport Fury (new for '59), and Suburban wagon (Deluxe, Custom, or Sport).

The low-priced Plaza series of 1958 was not continued.

Plymouth sought to give the public what they wanted at the time: a big, luxurious-looking car at a modest price.

1959 Rambler "Ambassador"

While in charge of American Motors, George Romney sought to give the buyers a more economical, more practical, easier-to-park, and easier-to-handle car than those his rivals were offering.

During the '59 model year, AMC magazine advertising often included clever cartoons ridiculing cars that were "gas-guzzling dinosaurs" (no names mentioned), and leading cartoonists such as Eldon Dedini, George Lichty, Irwin Caplan, George Price, Barney Tobey, "Claude," and others lent their efforts for a reasonable sum. (Cartoonists' work in auto advertising continued in the early 1960s, most notably with Charles Schulz's "Peanuts" characters in the Ford Falcon ads.)

"Have bigger '59 models 'sized' you out of a new car?" asked one ad for the Rambler Ambassador. This model was presented as a Personalized Luxury Car in an easy-to-manage compact package. The Ambassador was the top-of-the-line AMC car, but considerably smaller than a Cadillac, Lincoln, or Imperial, and it cost considerably less! With 270 h.p., it would get out and move, if necessary! Nash had first used the Ambassador name in the late 1920s, and after the final Nash was built in 1957, the name continued with Rambler and AMC until 1974.

As for Romney, he was born in 1907, served as president of AMC from 1954 to 1962, and served as governor of Michigan from 1963 to 1969. He was a delegate to the Republican conventions of 1964, 1968, and 1980. In 1968, he was seriously considered as a possible nominee to run for president!

1959 "Mystery Car"

A famous automobile name was discontinued in England in 1963 when the Standard marque was dropped.

The Standard nameplate was also used on six different (unrelated) American-built makes, the best known being the one built by the Standard Steel Car Co. (which also built railroad cars) at Butler, Pa. from 1912 to 1923. Two German makes and one Italian make were also built bearing the name of Standard.

As for today's subject, an original 1959 British Standard ad (from *The Autocar* magazine, October 24, 1958) stated: "This famous car has been restyled to combine the best of British and Continental lines with new harmonizing color tones and a superb exterior and interior finish. This is certainly a car you will have to see at the Motor Show."

Among the 1959 improvements: new grille, larger windscreen (windshield) and rear window, opening butterfly vent windows on the front and rear doors, padded dash, lockable glove-box door, and much more!

In addition to the illustrated Vignale Vanguard, the 1959 Standard line also included the Vanguard Estate Car (deluxe station wagon), Standard Ensign, Pennant, Ten, Eight, and Companion (wagon) models.

It is written that Triumph-Standard may have dropped the "Standard" nameplate, since it sounded too plebeian (the opposite of "De Luxe") in some people's minds.

The final 1963 Standard Luxury Six looked almost identical to the car you see here—except that the word "Six" appeared just below the emblem at the front of the hood.

PASSENGER SEAT AVAIL. AT EXTRA COST.

5½-GAL GAS TANK

©1992 by North America Syndicate, Inc. World rights reserved.

5CWT VAN

HYDRAULIC BRAKES

REAR DETAILS

3·8·92

4.429 TO 1 GEAR RATIO

1959 **THAMES** "5 CWT VAN"
MADE IN ENGLAND BY FORD MOTOR CO.
LTD., DAGENHAM.
2400 lbs. WITH LOAD (¼ TON CAP'Y.)
1172 cc
4 CYL. L-HEAD ENGINE (71.55 CID)
36 HP @ 4500 RPM (7 TO 1 COMPR.)
5.60 x 13" TIRES
* PRONOUNCED "TAMS" (A LARGE RIVER IN ENGLAND)

WITH SPECIAL THANKS TO
WALLACE WEBSTER, KIRKLAND, WA.,
FOR CONTRIBUTING AN ORIGINAL
BROCHURE ON THIS RARE IMPORT.

1959 Thames

O nly a few readers can recall ever seeing a Thames truck in the United States. They're rare on this side of the Atlantic because only a few were imported in the late '50s and early '60s.

The 1957-1962 era is an interesting one for small import cars. Many unusual, little vehicles were brought to America from England and Europe to be offered to those who preferred economy over luxury. The American Crosley was no longer available from '53 on, and the smallest domestic car in the later '50s was the American Motors (ex-Nash) Metropolitan, which was actually made of British mechanical parts.

British cars dominated America's import scene in the 1950s, though Germany's VW was coming on stronger and stronger! In the United States, imports were available from England, Germany, France, Italy, and even (for a time) Czechoslovakia! Japanese car imports began in the late 1950s, but no one took them seriously for a few years. Toyopet (Toyota) and Datsun (Nissan) were the first Oriental cars to arrive in large numbers.

Some who may remember the Thames may not have known that it was a product of Ford Motor Co.'s English division. Had it been labeled "Ford," its American sales might have been much better.

Though called a van, this little truck may also be considered a sedan delivery or panel-type.

The "7 CWT" model resembled the illustrated "5 CWT" vehicle, except that the other type had a grille with all-vertical pieces.

1959 Volkswagen Double-Cabin Pickup

Though Volkswagen trucks were first imported to the USA in the 1950s and 1960s, the older ones are scarce and many readers will be surprised to know that they made both single-cabin (three-passenger) and double-cabin (six-passenger) pickups. A pickup with a back seat was a novelty when VW began importing that particular type into the USA in 1959. But, various American manufacturers imitated the idea in the 1960s, just as they also copied the clever idea of a small cab-forward truck, van-type station wagon, and other ideas VW had introduced here.

For added convenience, the sides and tailgate of the VW pickup box could be lowered (as illustrated) or removed. There was also added storage space under the pickup bed on the right-hand side of the single-cab model.

Under the removable rear bench seat in the double-cabin model was a chest for the storage of tools, equipment, etc. Stakes and a canvas canopy top (covered-wagon style) were available for the pickup box, for added versatility. VW pickups were shipped to the USA until 1971.

Several years later (late 1979 to early 1983) VW re-introduced a pickup truck in its best-selling line, but decided after a time not to continue the pickup because of increased competition from small Japanese trucks and then from small American trucks such as Chevy's S-10, GMC's S-15, Ford's Ranger, etc.

1960 B.M.C. Mini

In 1959, when British Motor Corporation developed their tiny new Mini, they expected it to be a success but probably had no idea how far reaching its unique new features would become!

By 1960, Volkswagen's Beetle had captured a sizeable share of the international small-car market. But, in America, gas was inexpensive and easy to get, and the typically large, gaudy, V-8 powered car was still king. In Europe and England, however, little cars had been popular for many years—as they were better suited to the narrow roads and the higher fuel and licensing costs in that part of the world.

In 1960, when the Austin and Morris 850 mini-twins were introduced to the USA, they enjoyed some attention but gained no overwhelming popularity. They seemed like "Dinky toys" to many Americans! And, they were introduced here too soon for their time. After 1973 and the Arab oil embargo, American tastes in cars began to change. Small cars were now "in," as gas prices escalated and long, tedious lines formed at filling stations. But, by that time (the mid-1970s), British car imports to the United States had declined to a sorry state because of Britain's inability to compete with the new flood of Japanese imports—in the face of excessive demands from Britain's labor unions. In the mid-1970s, the Austin had become the last, small British car available in America. After that, Rolls-Royce, Jaguar, and a few pricey exotics were the only British representatives available here, other than sports cars.

new "SKYLIGHT ROOF" on 1960 NASHUA 10' x 50' MOBILE HOME
PRICE WHEN NEW, UNDER $5000

1960 BUICK V8
$2756-$4300 fob PRICE RANGE
123" OR 126.3" WHEELBASE
19 MODELS AVAIL. IN LE SABRE, INVICTA, ELECTRA, OR ELECTRA 225 SERIES

LE SABRE has 364 CID V8, 250 HP. OTHERS: 401 CID, 325 HP.
7.60 OR 8.00 x 15 TIRES

TURBINE DRIVE AUTOMATIC TRANSMISSION

News America Syndicate
© News Group Chicago, Inc., 1965

1960 Buick

"The turbine drive Buick "60"— Buick's all-time best!" That was the catch phrase in Buick advertising for '60. The best-selling individual Buick model that year was the low-priced Le Sabre series four-door hardtop; nearly 36,000 of these alone were sold!

Buick produced 253,807 cars in 1960; down from 284,248 in 1959 (a year of a big styling change). The 1960 figure was also less than the 276,754 they'd sell in 1961, when Buicks were again restyled and had a new compact Special/Skylark series. In 1960, Buick's only small car offering was GM's German Opel, sold in the U.S.A. by Buick dealers to meet the growing demand for compact cars.

Among the features of the '60 Buick were fin-cooled aluminum brake drums, improved Turbine Drive automatic transmission, and a MirroMagic non-glare instrument panel that "tilted to eye level" by moving the mirror that reflected the reverse-image gauges. There was also the new, optional "Twilight Sentinel," which turned the headlights on automatically, after dark. An automatic transmission was optional on the Le Sabre models.

Illustrated with the '60 Buick is the Nashua mobile home for 1960, with new raised "skylight roof" section. After the mid-1950s, trailers for permanent residence became known as "mobile homes," and grew from eight feet wide to ten-wide (and later to twelve-wide, fourteen-wide expando, double-wide, and more)! In the early 1960s, a growing number of families and individuals chose mobile home living as an economical alternative to conventional housing. Some of the better mobile home parks were like luxurious resorts.

"THE SUPERLATIVE"
1960 CHEVROLET
IN BISCAYNE, BEL AIR or IMPALA SERIES

"BEL AIR"
2-DOOR SEDAN
119" WB   3430 LBS.
7.50 x 14" TIRES
$2384.
WITH
236 CID O.H.V. 6
135 HP @ 4000 RPM

283 or 348 CID V8s AVAIL. 170, 230, 250 or 280 HP 3.96, 3.55, 3.70 GEAR RATIOS AVAIL.

TAD
12~31
HAPPY NEW YEAR!

1960 IMPROVEMENTS:
MORE CONSERVATIVE STYLING THAN 1959 ; REAR DECK OPENS 1½" LOWER ;
IMPROVED BRAKES (LARGER FRONT CYLINDERS, PARKING BRAKE RATCHET
IMPROVED); CARB. RECALIBRATED FOR FUEL ECONOMY ; STD. V8 NOW
    HAS LOW-LIFT CAMSHAFT ; NEW PAINT and UPHOLSTERY
    CHOICES, ETC.
    5 AVAILABLE TRANSMISSIONS = 3 SP. 4 SP.
    OVERDRIVE, POWERGLIDE or TURBOGLIDE A.T.

X-FRAME and
FULL COIL SUSPENSION
IMPALA HAS 6 REAR LTS. (INCLUDING 2 BACKUP LTS.

1960 Chevrolet

T he party was over! The gigantic tailfins, the ever-escalating horsepower race, the chrome-plastered excesses, and the "big-big-bigger" craze had reached its climax in 1958-1959.

Because of the sharp business recession of 1958 and because of the invasion of foreign economy cars (VW and many others) on the American scene, Detroit got the message and started toning down for 1960. Even greater changes, plus downsizing, would take place in 1961 and 1962 on most American cars. But, the '60 Chevy reflected the beginnings of the new trend to economy and simplicity, without changing too much at a time.

The lowest-priced Biscayne had a minimum of chrome trim (almost none), and the area around its taillights was painted to match the body color. Biscayne interiors were also the plainest.

The Bel Air (Chevrolet's top model in the 1950s, until the '58 Impala made its bow) was the middle-range Chevrolet (illustrated). The heavy chrome trim, extra rear lights, fancy interiors and gadgetry were reserved for the Impala series.

The dashboard of the '60 Chevrolet contained an arched, hooded cluster of instruments at the left, with a large circular speedometer flanked on either side by pairs of smaller circular instruments. The oblong radio was placed at the very center of the dash, with the glove compartment to the right. As could be expected, the Impala had the flashiest-looking dash and a fancier steering wheel, plus the best-looking interior choices.

1960s

THE LOW-PRICED BIG DODGE!
1960 DODGE "DART" (new!)
"PIONEER" WAGON
122" wheelbase
$2792. and up,
F.O.B.

News America Syndicate
© News Group Chicago, Inc., 1984
10-14

DART BECAME A COMPACT CAR IN 1963, WAS REPLACED IN 1976 BY THE ASPEN.

new 225 CID "SLANT 6" ENGINE (145 HP @ 4000 RPM) OR 318 CID V-8 (230 HP @ 4400 RPM) 3.54 to 1 GEAR RATIO 3.31 (w. AUTO. TRANS.) 3820 TO 4065 lbs.

1960 Dodge Dart

If you're under forty years of age, you might not have known that the Dodge Dart originated, for 1960, as a large car. It was big, like the "regular" Dodges. In 1961 and '62, Dodge offered a compact Lancer, which was similar in many ways to Plymouth's Valiant compact.

However, the Lancer name never caught on, so Chrysler Corp.'s Dodge Division dropped the Lancer after '62 and shrank the Dart to compact size for '63. The change worked wonders! Dart was a great seller as a compact, and it continued until 1976, when it was replaced by the Aspen (later to become the Aries).

In the big '60 Dart line, there were twenty-four different models (with V-8 or new "slant-six" engines) in three basic series. There was the low-priced Seneca series, the middle-range Pioneer, and the luxury Phoenix.

Though the illustrated wagon had a 122-inch wheelbase, the other body types (two-door and four-door sedans, two-door and four-door hardtops, and convertibles) had 118-inch wheelbases.

The '60 Dart was built for those who wanted the look and size of luxury with a modest price tag and economical performance. Come to think of it, who wouldn't want such a combination?

Options included automatic Swing-Out Swivel Seats, which turned when doors were opened; "TorqueFlite" or "PowerFlite" push-button automatic transmissions; power steering; and other "goodies" that could push the price up another $1,500 or $2,000! Truly, economy never looked so good!

Were you surprised to read there was once a *big* Dodge Dart? A nice, clean one today would be a collector's creampuff!

1960 FRONTENAC
AVAIL. 1960 ONLY, FROM FORD MOTOR CO. OF CANADA.
"COUSIN" TO FORD FALCON.
(REAR)
EXTREMELY SCARCE!
11.7 GAL GAS TANK
144 C.I.D. 6 (90 H.P.)
3⅝"×2⅜" BORE-STR.
8.7 to 1 COMPRESSION
3.10 to 1 GEAR RATIO WITH STANDARD or AUTO. SPEED TRANS.
DETAILS THANKS TO PHIL SKINNER, FULLERTON, CALIF.
Frontenac
SELF-ENERGIZING HYDRAULIC BRAKES (9" DRUMS)
19 60
AP JUNE 27
©1993 North America Syndicate, Inc. World rights reserved.

1960 Frontenac

Unless you're in Canada, you're not likely to see one of these. It was built to resemble a 1960 Ford Falcon with a different grille, but only for Canada! This is the 1960 Frontenac from Ford Motor Co. of Canada, available for only one year. It was on the market between the time that the first Ford Falcon was introduced and the time that Lincoln-Mercury's new compact Comet appeared (later in 1960).

This Frontenac bears no relationship to the 1932 Canadian Frontenac illustrated previously in *Auto Album*. The 1932 car was a product of Durant Motors, during Durant's final year of production.

The 1960 Frontenac was painted in "lustrous baked enamel" and offered in nine single colors and fourteen two-tone combinations. Basic colors: Raven Black, Corinthian White, Montecarlo Red, Skymist Blue (light), Belmont Blue (medium), Adriatic Green (light), Meadow Vale Green (medium), Sultana Turquoise, and Platinum.

The '60 Frontenac had a manual choke pull-knob (young drivers may not know what a manual choke is, since most cars now have an automatic choke), which cut off a part of the air supply to the carburetor so the car would run smoothly during the warm-up period. Once the engine was at operating temperature (over 140 degrees), the choke knob could be pushed in, giving more air to the carburetor.

Independent front suspension featured coil springs, with five-leaf, semi-elliptical springs at the rear.

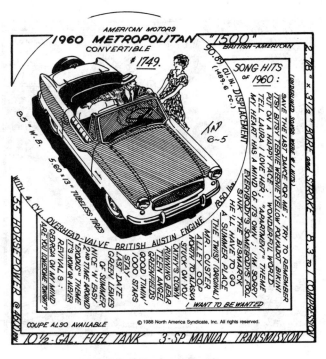

1960 Metropolitan

The diminutive 1960 AMC Metropolitan convertible (shown here) measured 149 1/2 inches long, 61 1/2 inches wide, 55 inches high, and weighed only 1,850 lbs. (The hardtop coupe weighed an additional forty lbs.)

This little car originated in 1950 as Nash Motors' "N.X.I." convertible: an experimental, one-of-a-kind mini sports car on a Fiat chassis with an 18-h.p. Fiat engine.

Nash/AMC's production version, smaller than their popular Rambler, became available to the public in 1954 as the Metropolitan (coupe or convertible). It was an American-designed car, built in England for an American company—a new idea at the time. British Motors Corp. supplied the Austin four-cylinder engine and the Fisher & Ludlow body. The cars were shipped to the U.S.A. and sold by AMC dealers. Until 1957, there were both Nash and Hudson dealers affiliated with AMC. The "Hudson Metropolitan" is indeed a rarity!

In 1956, the Metropolitan received a new mesh grille, new scoopless hood, new side trim, two-tone paint schemes, and other improvements. The same design continued from 1956 on. However, in 1959, the "Met" got an opening trunk hatch on the rear deck. Until then, moving the back of the rear seat provided the only access to the trunk. Another 1959-1960 improvement was the addition of butterfly, swinging vent windows on the doors.

In tests, Metropolitans could get up to almost 35 m.p.g. highway mileage, under favorable driving conditions. The top speed was 70 m.p.h., and after 1956, performance was slightly improved.

← OTHER BRITISH CARS AVAILABLE IN 1960 →

1960 MG-A "1600"

4-CYL. OVERHEAD-VALVE ENGINE (1588 c.c. DISPL.) 2.968 × 3.5 BR.+STR. 79½ H.P. @ 5600 RPM 8.3 COMPRESSION (TWIN-CAM O.H.C. ENG. AVAIL. WITH 108 H.P. @ 6700 9.9 COMPR.)

94" wheelbase
5.60 × 15 TIRES
(5.90 × 15 ON
TWIN-CAM MODELS)
4.3 GEAR RATIO
WT. = 2004 lbs.
10-GAL. FUEL TANK
TO 27 M.P.G.
TO 100 M.P.H.

COUPE: $2734. P.O.E.

THE FIRST MG-A WAS THE 1956 (INTRO. SEPT., '55)

MGA 1600

Field Enterprises, Inc. 1983

1960 MG-A-1600

The old MGs were not dramatically changed since the first MGs of the 1920s. But, the MG-A, first introduced for the 1956 season, was a thoroughly streamlined departure from the quaint, nostalgic MG "midgets."

In 1960, further improvements were made, and the "A" became the "A-1600" series (in 1600-c.c. class), with a beefed up engine and new fade-resistant front-disc brakes. New body colors were also featured.

The roadsters were more commonly imported to America than was the illustrated coupe. The coupe had genuine leather upholstery and sold in England for 724 pounds, plus 302.15.10-pound tax. It carried a twelve-month warranty.

American auto reviewers liked it, but they disliked the dinky foot pedals placed so close together and the inadequate ventilating system.

The higher-priced Twin Cam model boasted hotter performance, but was labeled as "noisy and an oil-drinker" by one British reviewer, writing in *Motor Sport* magazine.

That same reviewer, though he enjoyed driving the standard MG-A-1600, considered it mechanically outdated (save for the disc brakes in front) and listed a few specific points of criticism. The metal dash had sharp, crude lower edges, and the horn button and directional signal control on the dash seemed inconvenient. The reviewer disliked the wire pulls that opened the doors from the inside; if a wire should break, the door wouldn't open.

"Safety Fast" was the traditional MG sales slogan. The manufacturer was MG Car Company Ltd., Abingdon-on-Thames, Bershire, England.

The letters "MG" originally stood for Morris Garages, as the MG was an offshoot from the Morris.

1960s

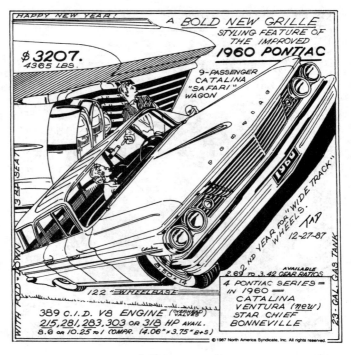

HAPPY NEW YEAR!

A BOLD NEW GRILLE STYLING FEATURE OF THE IMPROVED 1960 PONTIAC

$3207.
4365 LBS.

9-PASSENGER CATALINA "SAFARI" WAGON

3 RD. SEAT

2 ND YEAR FOR "WIDE TRACK" WHEELS.

TAP
12-27-87

WITH FOLD-DOWN

122" WHEELBASE

389 C.I.D. V8 ENGINE (OVERHEAD VALVES)
215, 281, 283, 303 OR 3/8 HP AVAIL.
8.8 OR 10.25 TO 1 COMPR. (4.06" × 3.75" B+S)

AVAILABLE 2.69 TO 3.42 GEAR RATIOS

4 PONTIAC SERIES = IN 1960 —
CATALINA
VENTURA (new)
STAR CHIEF
BONNEVILLE

23 GAL. GAS TANK

© 1967 North America Syndicate, Inc. All rights reserved.

1960 Pontiac

After introducing its fabulous, big, new "wide-track" models for 1959, GM's Pontiac Division rode the crest of a swelling wave of popularity all through the '60s!

The excitingly new "wide-track" '59 Pontiac was a tough act to follow, but for 1960, Pontiac restyled the front end with a pleasingly bright, horizontal V-grille. Rear fenders were also restyled.

The cooling system was redesigned, and the Hydra-Matic transmission had a new narrower case with a shallower oil pan, enabling the drive tunnel in the front seat compartment to be reduced in size correspondingly. Several other minor mechanical changes were made throughout the chassis for 1960, including an improved intake manifold on the engine. An oil filter (formerly $9 extra) was now standard equipment.

For 1960, there were fifteen solid and sixty two-tone "Magic-Mirror Finish" exterior paint choices for the buyer! The illustrated station wagon had "gorgeous yet tough" Jeweltone Morrokide upholstery inside. The Bonneville Custom Safari wagon closely resembled the illustrated Catalina Safari, but had a roof rack and a few other little luxuries.

An interesting extra on some '60 Pontiacs: the dash-mounted "GuideMatic" unit, which dimmed headlights automatically when cars approached from the opposite direction. Here's how it worked: Bright beams (all four) faded down to a soft glow, signaling the other driver to dim his lights. An instant later, the inboard beams turn off, restating ... with greater urgency ... a safety message that can't be ignored. Once you've passed in perfect safety, all four lamps switch back to bright.

A RARE SPORTS CAR FROM CZECHOSLOVAKIA!

1960 SKODA
"FELICIA"

4 CYLINDERS
66½ CU. IN. DISPL.
53 HP @ 5500 RPM

WEIGHT 2050 LBS.
(WITH FUEL)

4-SPEED TRANSMISSION

TOP SPEED 84
UP TO 39 MPG
$2700. IN USA (PRICE LATER CUT DUE TO POOR SALES)

5.90 x 15" TIRES

THANKS TO JOSEPH A. CLEMENTS, CLEMENTS PRECISION CO., RICHMOND, INDIANA, FOR HELPFUL INFORMATION! (HE BOUGHT ONE OF THESE CARS NEW)

94.1" WHEELBASE

TAD 11-7

1960 Skoda "Felicia"

S koda was a major industrial corporation of the Austro-Hungarian Empire. Following the November 11, 1918 armistice ending World War I, Skoda's factories became situated in what was the new republic of Czechoslovakia (in the cities of Pilsen and Mlada Boleslav). In 1923, automobile production began at Skoda with the building of Hispano-Suiza cars under license with that company (using bodies built by Skoda). In 1925, cars with the Skoda nameplate began to appear.

As for the Skodas, they were briefly imported into the United States by Motokov, which represented various Eastern European brands of cars during the late 1950s and early '60s.

Auto Album reader Joseph A. Clements was one of the few purchasers of a new 1960 Skoda Felicia convertible, as illustrated. He noted that in 1961, many citizens of the New York town where he lived were strongly opposed to the sale of "Communist cars" in America.

In a desperate move, the hapless dealer drastically slashed the prices of the new Skoda convertibles from $2,700 down to a mere $875. Clements said he still owed more than that and regretted not having waited until after the unexpected price drop to buy his. He added that little things started breaking and going wrong on his car in a very short time. After only three years, he stopped driving it. After sitting idle on the family property for a long time, the Skoda was finally sold off cheap "as is." I hope it was eventually restored, as it's a rare model today.

1960s

1960 Thunderbird

T he 1960 Thunderbird was the last of the so-called Squarebirds that had replaced the original 1955-57 two-seater roadsters in 1958. Ford Motor Co. executives decided that for 1958, the T-bird must "grow up" and provide more passenger space under the roof.

In a sense, the redesigned 1958-60 Thunderbirds were like little Lincoln Continentals in styling as well as in horsepower. In the 1958-60 "Squarebird" cycle only, the big 430 c.i.d. Lincoln Continental V-8 engine was available for Thunderbird as an option to the 352 c.i.d. V-8.

Admittedly, the "Squarebird" was less of a sports car than its 1955-57 predecessors. But, Ford officials had firmly decided that the Thunderbird must offer luxury and comfort for its affluent buyers and not remain a college kid's car.

At the time, the majority agreed. Sales rose from 21,380 in 1957 to 37,892 in 1958. In 1959, the figure rose to 67,456, and in 1960 some 92,843 T-birds were sold.

The 1958-60 "Squarebirds" had a solid-looking "unibody" (body and chassis frame as a single unit) and a classic formal roofline. They somewhat recalled the 1956 and 1957 Continental Mark II two-door luxury models.

On the "Squarebirds," grilles and trim changed each year: mesh grille in 1958, horizontal slats in 1959, and three vertical and one horizontal bar in front of mesh in 1960.

When this *Auto Album* picture and story appeared, the market value of a 1960 Thunderbird hardtop coupe ranged from $750 in poor condition up to $22,000 in perfect (like new) condition.

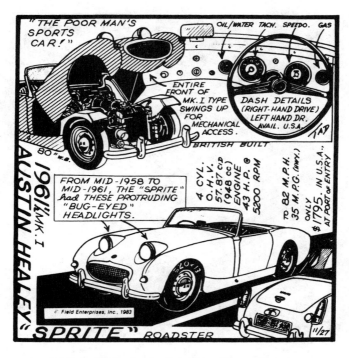

1961 1/2 Austin-Healey Sprite

This was known, unofficially, as "the poor man's sports car," because it was priced even lower than many small import sedans!

Austin-Healey also sold a larger sports car (the 100-six), which was joined by the little Sprite in mid-1958. This first series Sprite (Mark I) was continued to early 1961, with its unusual, hinged "smiling face" front end that opened as a unit. It was remembered for its raised headlights. These headlights, reportedly, were placed high on the hood in order to conform to American safety standards of that time; a good number of the Sprites were exported from England.

In mid-1961, the Sprite was restyled for 1962, and the new Mark II type had a face-lifted front end with a separately-hinged hood (much easier to lift!) and headlights at the upper front of fenders as on other cars.

A product of British Motor Corporation, Ltd., the Sprite came from the same family as the Austin, M.G., Morris, Riley, etc., and shared the small four-cylinder o.h.v. engine used in most BMC products (a similar engine was used in AMC's British/American Metropolitan). The Sprite shares many characteristics of the M.G. Midget.

In September 1983, a neighbor put a "FOR SALE" sign on his 1961 Sprite. No price was listed on the sign, and at first I hesitated to inquire. But, curiosity prevailed, and when the neighbor told me how little he wanted for the car, it was an offer I couldn't refuse. A deal was soon completed!

1960s

1961 Cadillac

The 1961 and 1962 Cadillacs represented a brief return to "reality" after several years of ever-growing and ever-more-powerful cars—and after years of more and more chrome plastered about!

Conservative styling of the 1961 Cadillac was undoubtedly dictated by the sharp business recession of 1957-1958. The mood of many 1961 cars—especially GM products—was restrained. For '61, Cadillac even made a sawed-off "Town Sedan" with a very short trunk and rear-fender section (a full seven inches shorter than the 1961 Cadillac Sedan De Ville). Still, many buyers liked the larger trunks and longer rear fenders of the illustrated Coupe De Ville, which was 215 inches long.

In spite of the trim down, bodies were said to be roomier and easier to get in and out of than before, with the tops of the doors heightened, and narrowed door sills. The awkward "dogleg" corners of the previous year's panoramic windshield were eliminated. Rear doors were six inches wider and swung open seven inches further than before. Headroom was increased two inches over the 1960 models, and drivetrain tunnels in front and rear compartments were now lower (because of changes in placement of the engine and transmission).

Air conditioning was $473.60 or $623.70 extra, depending on the type ordered. Air suspension (considered a "flop") was available (at $214.60), and Cruise Control was $96.60. Other options: Deluxe "Eldorado" engine ($134.30 more), door guards, "E-Z Eye" glass, fog lamps, six-way seat adjusters, Guide-Matic headlamp control, heaters ($128.70 or $178.50), etc.

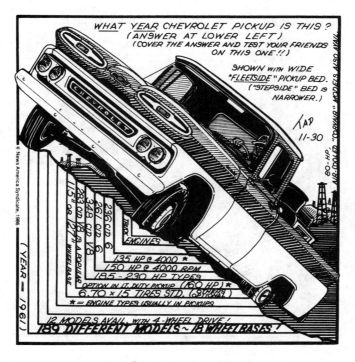

WHAT _YEAR_ CHEVROLET PICKUP IS THIS ?
(ANSWER AT LOWER LEFT)
(COVER THE ANSWER AND TEST YOUR FRIENDS
ON THIS ONE !!)

SHOWN WITH WIDE
"FLEETSIDE" PICKUP BED.
("STEPSIDE" BED IS
NARROWER.)

TAD
11-30

© News America Syndicate, 1986

(YEAR = 1961)

135 HP @ 4000 ★
150 HP @ 4000 RPM
185 - 230 HP TYPES
OPTION IN LT. DUTY PICKUP (160 HP) ★
6.70 x 15 TIRES STD. (6 PLIES)
★ = ENGINE TYPES USUALLY IN PICKUPS

12 MODELS AVAIL. WITH 4-WHEEL DRIVE !
189 DIFFERENT MODELS ~ 18 WHEELBASES !

1961 Chevrolet Pickup

This alligator-snouted Chevy pickup may look grotesque by today's standards, but in the early '60s it was right in style. The design was somewhat similar to the '60 pickup, which had carried the Chevrolet name lower on the grille. But, for '61, cabs were improved and most of them now had a lower driveshaft floor tunnel for added roominess.

I.F.S. (Independent Front Suspension) was carried over from 1960, and ads claimed that Chevrolet trucks now could travel 30 m.p.h. on rough roads that formerly limited speed to five to 8 m.p.h.! The ads also promised 55 m.p.h. on roads where ordinary, solid-front-axle trucks would have to hold it down to thirty! Chevrolet claimed its I.F.S. "smothered as much as

seenty-eight percent of all objectionable road shock and vibration."

For 1962, Chevrolet pickups would be restyled in the front, with a more conventional grille and with only two headlights. Small rectangular parking/directional lights were to appear at the front of the hood above the grille, replacing the former "pods." So, the odd "alligator snout" look was to be banished forever to that land where tall, sharp tailfins, toothy grilles, breast-like bumper protrusions, jet-plane hood ornaments, and all the garish trappings of the 1950s eventually went!

The survival rate of Chevrolet trucks of the 1960s is excellent; many are still serving on farms and in businesses all across the U.S.A.

1960s

1961 Chrysler Newport

"**P**ositively ... No Junior Editions!" This slogan referred to the fact that although Chrysler Corp. offered a small Plymouth Valiant and Dodge Lancer in 1961, there were no "little" Chryslers. The budget-priced Chrysler Newport, a new model series for 1961, was a full-sized Chrysler with the same 122-inch wheelbase as the Windsor series, and with seats that were five feet wide!

The Newport retained the sweeping tailfins that had evolved from Chrysler's "Forward Look" era of the middle and late '50s; but front-end styling was new, with a fan-shaped grille and canted pairs of headlights.

"Lustre-bond" exterior enamels came in several pleasing colors, and the body-frame unit ["Unibody"] of the Newport was sprayed with over ninety lbs. of sound deadener and "padded with enough material to make a 10-foot-x-10-foot rug!" This enhanced the quiet ride!

Chyrsler Corp.'s efficient and compact new "alternator" replaced the conventional type of generator, and it was more effective at charging the battery while the engine was idling.

Torsion-bar suspension was used, and "double-weave" upholstery fabrics were advertised to be durable. The car was well engineered and long-lasting.

Other Chrysler models for 1961: the medium-priced Windsor, the luxury New Yorker, and the performance-oriented "300-G." The Saratoga model had been discontinued, and the top-bracket Imperial existed at that time as a make unto itself, above the various Chrysler series.

The illustration includes the following handwritten notations:

new for 1961 · FORD Econoline "STATION BUS"

© Field Enterprises, Inc. 1983

144 C.I.D., O.H.V. 6 with 85 H.P. @ 4200 RPM 3.5 × 2.5 BORE and STROKE · 3.5 OR 4.0 GEAR RATIO

90" WHEELBASE

WT.: 2843 lbs. · CARRIES 8 PEOPLE (OR 204 CU. FT. OF CARGO)

BUNK BED KIT $170. EXTRA · FROM $2130., fob

TAP 5-1

1961 Ford Econoline Station Bus

For 1961, Ford added the "Econoline" series, compact in size and with engines similar to what they were using in the compact Falcon car. In the Econolines, the engine was sunken into the cab floor and covered with a soundproofed shroud. Because the engine was not out front as in conventional trucks, the Econolines were cab-over-engine types with flat noses as were the VW trucks and microbus wagons.

For their short wheelbase, the Econolines offered a great carrying capacity. Compact pickup trucks, freight vans, and passenger vans comprised the Ford Econoline series. Under ideal conditions, these vehicles were capable of 30 m.p.g. fuel economy (with the 144 c.i.d. six), though the wind resistance built up by the boxy shape of the Econolines, plus the added weight of freight or passengers (or both), usually meant less mileage than the ideal. For more power, a 101 h.p., 170 c.i.d. six was also available.

The illustrated "Station Bus" was a particularly interesting member of the new Econoline family. It could seat eight people, or the seats could be moved to make space for added cargo or a special bunk bed kit that provided sleeping accommodations for four! With the $170 accessory bunk kit in place, two people slept above each other, lengthwise along the left; one slept lengthwise in the center; and a fourth person slept on a slightly raised section, lengthwise at right (as illustrated, top view).

1961 OLDSMOBILE "F-85"
(OLDSMOBILE'S FIRST COMPACT CAR) (new)

REAR DETAILS

DELUXE 4-DOOR SEDAN
MODEL 3119   2547 lbs.

112" W.B.   6.50 × 13 TIRES
ALUMINUM "ROCKETTE"
215 C.I.D. V8 ENGINE
3.50 × 2.80 BORE and STROKE
155 HP @ 4800 RPM

8.75 TO 1 COMPRESSION
3.07 STD. GEAR RATIO
(3.23 WITH HYDRA-MATIC)
16-GALLON
FUEL TANK

$2519.

19/10 29½ M.P.G.

95 M.P.H.

SLOGAN:
"...EVERY INCH AN OLDSMOBILE!"

© News America Syndicate, 1985

TAD 9-1

F-85-61

1961 Oldsmobile F-85

General Motors Corp. had released its all-new compact Chevrolet Corvair for 1960, and since compact cars were riding a new crest of popularity, for 1961 GM offered compact editions of Buicks, Oldsmobiles, and Pontiacs as well!

Buick's compact was the new Special, Pontiac's was the new Tempest, and Oldsmobile's was the new F-85. These models were soon joined by, and subsequently superseded with, deluxe editions—named, in respective order, Skylark, Le Mans, and Cutlass.

"Not too Big ... Not too Small ... Just Right For You!" declared a mini-brochure for the F-85. The brand-new aluminum "Rocket" V-8 engine was designed just for that model.

As compact-car fever was high in '61, even the full-sized GM cars were somewhat downsized, with fins and excess chrome trimmed down in reaction to the growing popularity of Germany's Volkswagen and other imports.

F-85 options: Hydra-Matic, power steering, back-up lights, clock, white sidewall tires, deluxe steering wheel, chrome door window frames, oil filter (and, for the station wagon, a luggage carrier).

With a total length of 188.2 inches overall, the F-85 was described as "a 'honey' to handle and a 'peach' to park!" During the 1961 model year, the deluxe new Cutlass Sports Coupe joined the F-85 line, and, eventually, various Cutlass models replaced the F-85 altogether.

1960s

1961 Valiant

Chrysler Corp. introduced its new, compact Valiant for 1960. For 1961, the same unique Valiant styling was retained, though the '61 grille was simplified. The Valiant had an imported look, even though it was entirely American. It was truly distinctive in appearance, except that the shape of the grille was somwheat like that of Studebaker's compact Lark.

The January 1961 *Sports Car Illustrated* reported that 20,000 aluminum-block engines would be available (at no extra cost) in about one out of every ten '61 Plymouths and Valiants. GM had also tried aluminum engines in some of its smaller '61 cars, with disappointing results.

Aluminum-block engines were conceived to save weight, but they developed many problems: aluminum shavings in the oil, adverse reactions to certain coolants and other chemicals, early failures, etc.

Another interesting Chrysler idea in the early '60s was the gas turbine engine. A few hundred were actually built.

Welded "Unibody" (unitized body-frame) construction eliminated most potential squeaks and rattles. Rust proofing was remarkably thorough!

Valiants were available in the "V-100" series. Two-door models were new for '61. The new two-door hardtop (pillar-less) was available only in the "V-200" series.

In 1963, Valiant would be totally restyled, making its appearance more conventional.

Champ '62 Pickup

MODELS
7E5 – 7E7
7E10 – 7E12

PICKUP

BY STUDEBAKER (RARE!)
"7E5" MODEL has
OWN 6-CYL. "I-E" (O.H.V.)
170 C.I.D. ENGINE.
3" × 4" BORE + STR.
8 TO 1 COMPRESSION

CHASSIS WEIGHT = 2485 LBS.

112" W.B.
4.27 TO 4.55 GEAR RATIO

© News America Syndicate, 1986

110 H.P. @ 4500 RPM
PICTURE and CERTAIN DETAILS
THANKS TO FRED K. FOX, DELHI, CALIF.
STUDEBAKER BLT. CARS UNTIL 1966 and TRUCKS UNTIL 1964.

1962 Champ Pickup

1960s

By 1960, Studebaker truck sales were slipping badly. The compact Studebaker Lark car, introduced 1959, was doing very well, thank you. But, Studebaker dealers in general were reluctant to promote Studebaker's line of trucks, because of intense competition from Ford, Chevrolet, Dodge, GMC, and International.

For 1960, the Studebaker Corp. (of South Bend, Ind.) chose to introduce an all-new economy pickup with cab and front-end sheet metal borrowed from the popular Lark. Prices would start at well below $2,000 (only $1,855 and up, during '60 and '61).

Before long, Champ pickups were using some pickup boxes purchased from Dodge (to save production costs). The Champ was a better seller than the Transtar and other Studebaker truck models, but much of the business was by word-of-mouth referrals from satisfied Studebaker owners. The Champ was not well advertised, as Studebaker was operating on a tight budget and its horizons were shrinking each year of the early '60s. On a sad day in December 1963, Studebaker's board of directors voted to cease production of all models except a Lark-based car. No more trucks, no Hawk, and no Avanti.

In 1965 and 1966, Studebaker cars were built only at the Canadian factory, the original South Bend factory having shut down in 1964.

Have you ever seen a Studebaker Champ pickup? They are scarce. Even scarcer are Studebaker's heavy-duty trucks of the early 1960s.

1962 Chevrolet Impala

C hevrolet Impala and Impala SS convertibles and two-door hard-tops are much in demand from car collectors these days! Perhaps the most popular Chevrolet of all time is the 1957. Many a school kid who can't remember any new cars built before the 1990s can, nevertheless, identify a '57 Chevy on sight!

Opening an original '62 Chevrolet sales brochure, we read: "An elegant blend of the tried and the new: Here is a car that does justice to its tradition ... the '62 full-sized Chevrolet. It's the new beauty with Jet-smooth ride. In it, you will see many of the enduring qualities that have consistently made Chevrolet America's most popular car. You'll see the same concern for craftsmanship, inside and out. You'll find the same basic engineer-ing excellence. Even the same sensible size people liked so much last year. But you'll have to look mighty hard to find anything that isn't brand-spanking new in its clean-lined looks and luxurious appointments."

New engines were available. Chevrolet's De Luxe Air Flow Heater and Defroster was standard equipment for 1962. New inner fenders, in front, protected against rust, and new exhaust mufflers were corrosion-resistant.

A new touch on Bel Air or Impala Sport Coupe (two-door hardtop) was a sculptured steel roof with creases to give it a "ragtop" look.

Since 1960, Chevrolet also offered the low-priced compact Corvair, with rear engine, and 1962 saw the debut of the intermediate-compact Chevy II, a.k.a. Nova.

"THE NEW LEAN BREED OF DODGE"
1962 DODGE "POLARA 500"
CONVERTIBLE
$3268. f.o.b. EAST
$3600. ON WEST COAST

DRAMATICALLY RESTYLED, THIS CAR WAS TOO FAR AHEAD OF ITS TIME, and ONLY 12,268 '62 POLARA 500s SOLD. 1962 DART HAD SIMILAR STYLING, SAME 116" WHEELBASE.

WINDSHIELD IS CURVED, THOUGH IT DOES NOT APPEAR SO WHEN VIEWED FROM THIS ANGLE.

TAP 5-22

116" WHEELBASE

361 C.I.D V8 (305 HP)

7.00 x 14" TIRES

20-GAL. FUEL TANK   4 BUCKET SEATS   3430 lbs.

1962 Dodge Polara 500

1960s

Though the big Dodge "880" continued from '61 with few changes, the mid-sized Dart 330 and 440 and the Dodge Polara 500 shared this exciting new design! It was daringly different, unlike anything else on the road. What a shame, that it was not a greater seller at the time. Buyers often do not respond well to radical styling changes. Yet, when Chrysler Corp. had gone in for bloated excesses and giant fins, in the later 1950s, the public responded well for a few years.

The bloated excesses were "out" on the '62 Dart and Polara, however! As the sales catalog accurately stated, "Dead weight has gone right out the window."

Also, "... Gone is useless sheet metal, overhang and chrome. Gone is flashiness and fat. What's left is pure muscle—nearly two tons of hard, lean, lusty road machinery."

Racing driver Don Garlits managed to do 0-60 in 8.1 seconds, in the V-8-powered model, and Buck Baker got a Dart "440" up to 130 m.p.h. on the Utica Proving Grounds circular track. Baker said the Dart was still picking up speed at 130, and he could have gone faster if he'd tested the car somewhere where there was more straightaway!!

The Dart was first introduced in 1960 as Dodge's lowest-priced model series, though it was as big as the "big" Dodges. In 1962, the size was trimmed on both Dart and Polara, and in 1963 the Dart grew even smaller and became a compact car, while the other Dodges began to grow again as the 1960s moved along.

1962 Falcon Futura

Ford's economical, compact Falcon was introduced late in 1959 for the 1960 season. Sales were good. Total Falcon sales, since the first 1960 model, reached a million in two years.

During 1961, the deluxe Falcon Futura coupe was added to the line. However, 1962 was a quiet year in the automotive industry. Most dealers complained about a lull in sales, and even in the popular Falcon array, sales of this Futura coupe slipped from 44,470 in 1961 to only 17,011 in 1962.

After 1962, the final year that all Falcons were sixes, the Falcon would include a Sprint hardtop coupe, powered by a small (260 c.i.d.) V-8 engine, while also continuing the two sixes (144 or 170 c.i.d.).

In the middle of the 1962 season, a new Falcon Sports Futura coupe was added, with squared-off vinyl-covered top "in the Thunderbird style." It was a five-window coupe, like the illustrated model, but the roofline was definitely different. Because it was fancier than the illustrated "standard" Futura, you're more likely to find a surviving Sports model in the hands of a collector today. All 1962 cars seem to be scarce, ever since the 1970s, and this 1962 Falcon Futura is seldom seen.

Many new- and used-car dealers have found that having an unusual car displayed in the showroom, or at the front of the lot, attracts attention and generates new business. Some dealers have added to their regular income by successfully buying and selling a large number of clean or restored old cars.

"AMERICA'S MOST CAREFULLY-BUILT CAR"

1962 IMPERIAL "CROWN"
4-DR. SOUTHAMPTON HARDTOP
129" W.B.   227.1" LONG
WITH O.H.V. 413 C.I.D. V8 ENGINE
340 HORSEPOWER @ 4600 RPM
4.18 × 3.75   10.1 TO 1 COMPR.
BORE + STR.

$5949.⁰⁰

8.20 × 15" TIRES

23-GAL. FUEL TANK

"FREE-STANDING" CHROMED HEADLIGHTS PROTRUDE.

CHRYSLER DEALERS CONTACTED THOUSANDS OF PROMINENT ATTORNEYS, BANKERS, BUSINESS EXECUTIVES, DOCTORS, ETC., IN 1962, OFFERING THEM THE USE OF A NEW IMPERIAL FOR AN EXTENDED TEST DRIVE.
(3 SERIES = CUSTOM, CROWN, and LE BARON.)   TAP

4770 LBS.

© 1987 North America Syndicate, Inc. All rights reserved.   8~16

1962 Imperial "Crown"

Let's look at an original 1962 Imperial sales brochure. We read: "The Crown series includes two- and four-door Southamptons (hardtops), and a convertible. Imperial Crowns are more completely equipped than Customs, and include all the equipment listed below...

"Standard equipment: Power window lifts. 6-way power seat Constant-Control power steering. Total-Contact power brakes. TorqueFlite automatic transmission with pushbutton drive selector. Dual headlamps. Air-foam padded seat cushions, front and rear. Center arm rests. Electroluminescent instrument lighting. Padded safety steering wheel. Safety cushion instrument panel. Floor carpeting. Vanity mirror. Map light. Luggage compartment light. Step-on parking brake. Windshield washer. Electric clock. 3 cigarette lighters." And much more...

Fourteen body colors were available, plus ten interior decors (leathers, cords, and metallic-accented fabrics) in the Crown series. Some of the body color names were: Rosewood, Cordovan, Silver Lilac, Oyster White, Alabaster, Willow Green, and Sage Green.

Unlike some of the other Chrysler products, which had been using body/frame unitized construction, the Imper-ial still had a separate body and chassis frame.

Since 1957, Imperial had been using a torsion-bar suspension system, said to eliminate the "mushiness" of conventional coil suspension.

Available extras included: automatic headlamp dimmer, touch-tuner radio, tinted glass, auto-pilot (pre-set speed control), power door locks, pushbutton heater and air conditioner, power vents, rear window defogger, sure-grip differential, and remote-control rearview mirror.

"THE PRIDE OF WISCONSIN!"

$2635.

BUILT IN KENOSHA, WISCONSIN, AMERICAN MOTORS' RAMBLER REPLACED BOTH NASH AND HUDSON AFTER 1957. (THE RAMBLER NAME WAS REVIVED BY NASH IN 1950, AFTER THE ORIGINAL RAMBLER HAD BEEN MISSING FROM THE SCENE SINCE 1914 WHEN REPLACED BY THE JEFFERY CAR. *)

* THE JEFFERY WAS REPLACED BY THE 1917 NASH.

1962 RAMBLER "AMERICAN"

"400" CONVERTIBLE WITH 125 H.P. O.H.V. 6 (190 H.P. L-HEAD 6 AVAIL. ON LOWER PRICED AMER. "DELUXE" and "CUSTOM" SERIES). "CLASSIC" 6 and "AMBASSADOR" V8 .. ODEL SERIES ALSO OFFERED.

©1992 by North America Syndicate, Inc. World rights reserved.

1962 Rambler American

The early 1960s was a good era for American Motors' Rambler.

Sales approached a half-million in 1960, and though they dropped to less than 375,000 in '61, Rambler at least managed to capture third place in sales that year, behind Ford (1,338,790) and Chevrolet (1,318,014), squeezing in ahead of Plymouth and Pontiac.

Rambler went down to fifth place in '62, but sold more cars (423,104). The '61, '62, and '63 Rambler American had a boxy but very distinctive body style—unlike anything else on the road. They could be recognized two blocks away! They looked much larger and heavier than their '60 and earlier counterparts, and they offered "sculptured" styling with stiffening/decorative creases and mouldings stamped into the sheet metal, in place of the usual chrome decorative strips. This "sculpturing" was a brief fad in the early 1960s, in an attempt to avoid the shiny excesses of the 1950's automotive dreamboats. In the case of the '61-'63 Rambler Americans, however, the new look reminded some people of a desert box tortoise!

American Motors Corp. Convertibles have always been scarce, and this 1962 Rambler American convertible is seldom seen. In spite of that, it has recently been valued at from $200 in poor condition to $6,000 in mint condition, which makes it an affordable collector's car.

I'm not in the old-car appraisal business, but, if you wish to know the value of your older car, there are now various price-guide books with those values listed. They're available at most local bookstores or public libraries.

SPORTS CAR FROM OAKLAND, CALIFORNIA!

1963 APOLLO *(RARE!)*

ONLY 200 BUILT PER YEAR, BY INTERNATIONAL MOTOR CARS INCORPORATED, 444 HARRISON ST., OAKLAND, CALIF. (1962 ~ 1966)

0 - 60 MPH IN 7.7 SECONDS! BORG-WARNER 4-SPEED GEARBOX
140 M.P.H.!

PRICE $6597. (FALL, 1963)

97" WHEELBASE • WEIGHT = 2200 LBS.
BUICK V8 ENGINE (3524 cc, 200 HP @ 5200 RPM)

STEEL BODY HAND-FORMED IN ITALY.
FACTORY-INSTALLED AIR CONDITIONING

TAD 7~19

DURING 1973, GM's BUICK DIVISION INTRODUCED ITS OWN COMPACT "APOLLO" CAR, (with BODY SIMILAR TO CHEVROLET NOVA, PONTIAC VENTURA, and OLDSMOBILE OMEGA.)

1963 Apollo GT

1960s

The Apollo GT sports car of the early 1960s! It was built in Oakland, Calif. by International Motor Cars Incorporated, using Italian bodies shipped over for completion and sold only through a few West Coast dealers in exotic or luxury cars.

A few auto historians and collectors remember the car, and it's mentioned in a handful of books. One account says that the Apollo changed its name to Vetta Ventura during 1964, and afterward it was manufactured in Dallas, Texas.

Originally, the Oakland-built version was known as the Apollo 3500 GT (Gran Turismo Sports Coupe) and was a sleek fastback with solid rear quarter panels. Sometime in '63, rear quarter windows were added for greater visibility.

The early model was priced at $5,987, with a 190-horsepower aluminum Buick V-8 engine. Weight was 2,200 lbs., and the car was 51 inches high, 66 inches wide, and 180 inches long (with a 97-inch wheelbase). It carried a 21-gallon tank for a sizable cruising range, and could be equipped with an optional Buick Special automatic transmission. Early models came with a manual Buick Special three-speed gearbox as standard, but the four-speed Borg-Warner gearbox was optional (and later standard).

A convertible (roadster) was also available during some of the time the Apollo GT was on the market.

In an October 1963 Laguna Seca Racing Program from Monterey, Apollo sales outlets were listed for Oakland, San Jose, and Monterey, Calif., and Reno, Nev.

INSTRUMENT PANEL

TOP SPEED UP-TO **161** *M.P.H.!*

1963 PRICE: **$4589.** *NOW VALUED AT $1500-42,000. (POOR TO MINT COND.)*

WITH 327 *CID OHV* V8 250, 300, 340 *OR* *FUEL INJECTED* 360 HP

CONCEALED HEADLIGHTS

2-PIECE REAR WINDOW ON 1963 MODEL ONLY.

1963 CORVETTE 98" *W.B.* *STING RAY* *BY CHEVROLET* (10,594 BLT., PLUS 10,919 CONVERTIBLES)

6.70 x 15" TIRES

THE FIRST CORVETTE WAS THE 6-CYLINDER 1953 MODEL. FIBERGLASS BODIES (ON ALL)

1963 Corvette "Sting Ray"

The legendary '63 Corvette Sting Ray coupe has continued to grow in popularity over the years.

Noted automotive tester and reviewer, Tom McCahill, actually drove a new '63 Corvette an amazing 161 miles per hour! The '63 Sting Ray, a new model, was the first "fastback" Corvette, all previous models having been convertibles with canvas tops or removable hard tops.

A June 1963 advertisement was aimed at fans of performance cars: "Our new Corvette Sting Ray's rearward weight bias chassis design and three-link independent rear suspension scotches the hop. With more weight on the driving wheels, and these wheels separately suspended for maximum road grip, the Corvette goes where you point it. Rides firmly but gently. This blissful security is abetted by a more-than-merely-blissful 327-cubic-inch

Corvette V8 and steering that flatters your driving sense.

The '63 Corvette was shortened from its 1962 predecessor. Wheelbase dropped four inches from its former 102, and overall length shrunk from 176.7 inches to 175.3. Width narrowed from 70.4 inches to 69.6, and height was trimmed from 52.9 inches to 49.8. Headroom in the car was increased, however, from 35.8 inches to 38.1 inches in the convertible and 37.0 in the new Sting Ray.

One reason Corvette's base price was not increased for '63 is that General Motors began using standard front suspension parts from its other brands on the Corvettes—instead of the costly, limited-production suspension parts formerly made only for Corvettes.

A new '63 Corvette feature was the adjustable steering wheel. Power steering was optional, as was air conditioning.

1960s

A COMPACT PICKUP 20 YEARS AHEAD OF ITS TIME!

1963½ INTERNATIONAL MODEL "900" PICKUP (new) 4-CYLINDER, 93.4 HP "COMANCHE" ENGINE (ALSO USED IN "SCOUT")

1100-LB. GROSS CAPACITY

6-FOOT BED

107" WHEELBASE

© News America Syndicate, 1986

TAD 2~2

LARGER 1000-1300 SERIES 6-CYL. and V8 PICKUPS ALSO AVAIL. ($2098. UP, 119" WB UP) ALSO HVY. TRUCKS, VANS, ETC.

INTERNATIONAL HARVESTER CO., CHICAGO (SINCE 1907)

1963 1/2 International 900 Pickup

1960s

"It's the new, low-cost International Model 900 Pickup!

Designed to handle small loads at low cost, it wastes no space ... wastes no power ... wastes no money. You don't have to pay for a bigger pickup than you need.

"This is the new International pickup that's low in initial cost, economical in operation—the very latest (mid-1963) addition to a great line of light-duty trucks."

And, the new 900 was a great idea, compact in size and using the four-cylinder engine also found in International's compact Scout. But, the 900 was a decade ahead of its time, introduced too soon to enjoy the new popularity of small trucks in the early 1970s!

The International 900 small pickup is a rarity today. After 1975, in fact, International Harvester Co. discontinued its pickups (except for the Scout, discontinued in 1981), and concentrated on the heavy-duty vehicles in which it now specializes.

Though the 900 is a rarity, there are thousands of the standard-sized International pickups, Travelall wagons, and small Scouts still on the road. Most of their owners are quite pleased with them and hope that someday International might again build a small truck!

1963 KAISER JEEP

" WAGONEER "

(REPLACES 1962 WILLYS JEEP SERIES)
4 WHEEL or 2 WHEEL DRIVE

FROM $3279. (4WD) (2 DR.)
" $ 3332. (ILLUSTR. 4 DR.)

new "TORNADO" ENGINE (AMERICA'S
ONLY OVERHEAD-CAM ENGINE IN 1963)
140 HP @ (4 CYL. ALSO AVAIL.)

TOTALLY RE-DESIGNED !

NEW AUTOMATIC TRANSMISSION OPTIONAL

110" WHEELBASE

9~13

OPTIONAL POWER STEERING and POWER BRAKES.

3623 LBS

MFD. BY
KAISER JEEP CORPORATION
TOLEDO, OHIO

©1992 by North America Syndicate, Inc. World rights reserved.

1963 Kaiser Jeep Wagoneer

Many readers know that the Jeep originated as a military vehicle shortly before World War II, and it became one of the Army's most valuable resources during the long conflict.

After peace was declared, Willys-Overland had planned to resume a new series of civilian cars, but instead it decided to create an expanded line of Jeep vehicles for civilians and for the military as well. Joining the military-type Jeep (now also available for farm use, etc.) was the new 1946 all-metal Jeep station wagon. Also, Jeep pickups and panel trucks were added to the line. And, in 1948 came the sports-model "Jeepster."

The Willys Jeep station wagon was a utilitarian but popular vehicle, and it kept its stubby profile for many years, though there were changes in grille, side trim, and other details. In 1954,

Willys merged with Kaiser, and after 1955 no more Kaiser cars were built in the United States.

For 1963, when an all-new series of larger Jeep wagons and pickups joined the line, it was soon decided that they would be known as Kaiser Jeeps instead of Willys Jeeps. After 1962, the Willys name was not generally used domestically, though it appeared elsewhere, such as on the 1963 Brazilian Willys, illustrated some time ago in this series.

The new Kaiser Jeep Wagoneers offered passenger-car comfort, roominess, and greatly improved performance. Before long, V-8s and V-6s would be available, and during the 1960s and 1970s the Jeep Wagoneer gradually changed from an economical utility car to a more costly status symbol for "outdoors" people.

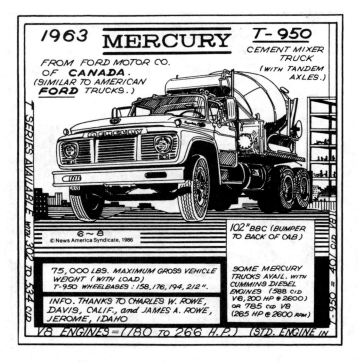

1963 Mercury (From Ford Motor Co. of Canada. Similar to American Ford trucks.) *T-950 Cement Mixer Truck* (with tandem axles.)

T SERIES AVAILABLE with 302 TO 534 CID

6~8

© News America Syndicate, 1986

102" BBC (BUMPER TO BACK OF CAB)

75,000 LBS. MAXIMUM GROSS VEHICLE WEIGHT (WITH LOAD)
T-950 WHEELBASES : 158, 176, 194, 212".

INFO. THANKS TO CHARLES W. ROWE, DAVIS, CALIF., and JAMES A. ROWE, JEROME, IDAHO

SOME MERCURY TRUCKS AVAIL. with CUMMINS DIESEL ENGINES (588 CID V6, 200 HP @ 2600) or 785 CID V8 (265 HP @ 2600 RPM)

407 CID = T-950

V8 ENGINES = (180 TO 266 H.P.) (STD. ENGINE IN

1963 Mercury Cement Mixer Truck

"Quality built to last longer," Ford's Canadian Mercury trucks were guaranteed for 24,000 miles or two years (standard warranty). The Mercury trucks, like their American and Canadian Ford counterparts, were available as pickups, conventionals, and cab-over-engine types. There were even a few vans.

For 1963, a new "Perma-tuned" transistorized ignition system option was available on all "Super Duty" V-8 engines (401, 477, or 534 c.i.d.), and these engines were guaranteed for up to 100,000 miles against defective parts.

Seven different Cummins diesel engines were also available on order for these trucks: the V-6 "200," V-8 "265," and the in-line 6-cylinder NH-180, NHE-180, NHE-195, NH-220, and NH-250, the numbers referring to horsepower ratings. The gigantic NH-250 had a bore and stroke of 5 1/2 inches x 6 inches, and a displacement of 855 cubic inches!

The Mercury name appeared on Canadian Ford trucks sold by Lincoln-Mercury dealers in Canada from 1946 to 1967. After '67, Lincoln-Mercury dealers sold Ford trucks, as the Canadian Ford dealerships had been doing all along.

Interestingly, some of the early Mercury trucks were fitted with slide-open rear windows, though the trucks with the Ford name did not offer this option until a few years later.

During the 1960s, Ford's compact Econoline trucks and vans were also available in Canada with the Mercury name.

"WIDE TRACK" "LUXURY"!

388.9 cid V8
303 HP @
4600 RPM
10:25 to 1 COMPR.
HYDRA-MATIC
AUTO. TRANSMISSION
3.23 to 1 GEAR RATIO

72,959 BUILT • 108 MPH • 0-60 in 9.9 SECONDS

1963 PONTIAC

GRAND PRIX
2 DR. HARDTOP
$3489.

THANKS TO AUGIE HARTUNG,
REDLANDS, CALIF., FOR CONTRIBUTING
HELPFUL PICTURES AND DETAILS.

25-GAL. FUEL TANK

5/15

1963 Pontiac "Grand Prix"

Pontiac's first "wide track" model was the '59. Unusually low and wide, it was the peak of 1950s flashiness. The new wide-track Pontiacs could seat four abreast on a bench seat. Those models also seemed impossible to tip over.

Meanwhile, Pontiac's Grand Prix sport/luxury two-door hardtop made its bow in 1962. But, some fans consider the 1963 a much improved and more noteworthy model. Featuring GM's new "clean look" for the mid-1960s, the '63 Grand Prix relied on angular, sculptured surfaces, and a minimum of chrome, for its beauty.

The Grand Prix was based on the lower-priced Pontiac Catalina series, but had the big engine of the Bonneville. The Grand Prix had bucket seats in front, with a center console. General Motors Corp. claimed that the rich floor carpeting in the Grand Prix

"may never wear out," as its factory testers were unable to wear out the material in a lengthy series of grueling hard-use tests!

Continuing the Pontiac trend, four headlights and a recessed horizontal split grille were featured, with Pontiac's wide-track V-shaped emblem at the center of the nose. A pair of directional signal/parking lights, mounted in front of the grille, resembled the "rallye lights" of foreign sports cars.

With its many improvements for 1963, the Grand Prix sold 140 percent more units than in 1962! From 1962 to 1969, Pontiac pushed Plymouth out of third place in nationwide sales.

On 1963 1/2 Grand Prixs, an even larger V-8 engine was optional, with 421-cubic-inch displacement and 353 h.p. with four-barrel carburetor, or 370 h.p. with three two-barrel carburetors.

1960s

'63 RAMBLER AMBASSADOR "990" "THE NEW SHAPE of QUALITY"

"CLASSIC" and "AMERICAN" MODELS ALSO.

WITH V8 ENGINE (250 HP @ 4700 RPM) (270 HP AVAIL.)

TAD 3-3

new 112" WHEELBASE
3158 LBS.   7.50 x 14 TIRES
$2929. with "TWIN STICK" 3-SPEED and OVERDRIVE TRANS.
$3034. with AUTOMATIC TRANS. (MANUAL ALSO AVAIL.)
"LIFETIME GUARANTEED" CERAMIC ARMORED MUFFLER
SEPARATE SAFETY FRONT and REAR BRAKE SYSTEMS

News America Syndicate
© News Group Chicago, Inc., 1985

1963 Rambler Ambassador

T he 1963 American Motors Rambler won the Motor Trend "Car of the Year" Award for "outstanding design achievement and engineering leadership." Rambler's Ambassador and Classic line had been totally restyled, and, on the outside, the two models closely resembled one another, each with the new concave grille with matching headlight openings that looked like gaping fish mouths.

The Ambassador had a long, horizontal strip of brightwork running the length of the car's lower body, plus a smaller parallel strip above the front fenders that ran back to the middle of the front doors. The Classic had *one* strip, full-length, above the fenders. These differences were the easiest ways to tell the two models apart. At first, all '63 Ambassadors were V-8s, and all Classics were sixes. But, due to popular demand, V-8s became available in the Classic as options in spring '63.

The restyled '63 Ambassador/Classic lines shed their old distinctive and more easily identifiable look. But, no doubt about it, the restyled '63s were destined to look pleasing and up-to-date, even in the 1970s! Over 428,000 Ramblers were sold in 1963.

Worthy of note on this '63 Ambassador is the optional new "Twin Stick" shift setup. One could "whiz through six gears in a flash." Overdrive control was now actuated by a second stick, next to the main floor-shift lever.

In 1963, a new series of number designations was enacted. The Americans were in 220, 330, or 440 series; the Classics came in 550, 660, or 770 series; and the Ambassadors came in 800, 880, or 990 series.

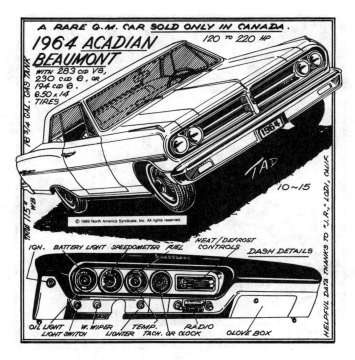

A RARE G.M. CAR SOLD ONLY IN CANADA.
1964 ACADIAN BEAUMONT
120 TO 220 HP
WITH 283 cid V8, 230 cid 6, or 194 cid 6.
6.50 x 14 TIRES
16 3/4 GAL. GAS TANK
115" WB
10~15
© 1989 North America Syndicate, Inc. All rights reserved.

HELPFUL DATA THANKS TO "J.R.," LODI, CALIF.

IGN. BATTERY LIGHT SPEEDOMETER FUEL HEAT/DEFROST CONTROLS DASH DETAILS

OIL LIGHT W. WIPER TEMP. RADIO
LIGHT SWITCH LIGHTER TACH. OR CLOCK GLOVE BOX

1964 Acadian Beaumont

Liberty magazine was famous in the United States three generations ago, and it was briefly revived in more recent years. In the 1960s, this was also the title of "Canada's young family magazine," which sold for only ten cents a copy.

Inside the front cover of the May 31, 1964 issue of the Canadian *Liberty* magazine was a full-color ad for General Motors' Acadian Beaumont, available only north of the border at Acadian-Pontiac-Buick dealerships.

Quoting from the ad: "Sportier performance, longer looks, stylish family room.

"The Acadian Beaumont is all new this year! Never before [have there been] so many wonderful new features, so much room and comfort, all on a bigger 115-inch wheelbase. Never before, such clean, sculptured styling. And Beaumont has great new performance to match! Select from two thrifty 6's, two sizzling V-8's. See Beaumont—the new size, the YOU size of value from General Motors."

In addition to the hardtop coupe shown here, and the aforementioned convertible, the 1964 Beaumont line also included sedans and a station wagon. The frontal styling bore a resemblance to the 1964 American Pontiac Tempest, but the rear end appearance was more akin to the Chevy II. Trim and decorative features were unique to Canada, however. That's what makes these Canadian variations so interesting!

Each of the two available V-8 engines were of 283-cubic-inch displacement, but the two-barrel model had 195 h.p. at 4,800 rpm, while the four-barrel V-8 developed 220 h.p. at 4,800. Compression ratio on each V-8 was 9.25 to 1—and 8.5 to 1 on the sixes.

INTRODUCED SPRING, 1964

1964½ BUICK

SKYLARK
SPORTS WAGON
with PANORAMIC
OVERHEAD
"SKYROOF"
WINDOWS (new!)

(ALSO AVAILABLE ON
OLDSMOBILE's
"VISTA CRUISER".)

SkyTop INN

AP 7~31

120" WHEELBASE 3648 LBS.

7.50 × 14"
TUBELESS TIRES

225 CID V-6 ENGINE (3.75 × 3.40" BORE + STR. 9 TO 1 COMPRESSION
115 H.P. @ 4400 RPM (3.36 TO 1 GEAR RATIO) V8s ALSO AVAIL.

1964 1/2 Buick

Introduced during the spring of 1964, the Buick Skylark Sports Wagon (illustrated) featured an all-new set of upper "Skyroof" windows. They were great for mountain or big-city scenic tours! The idea was no doubt inspired by the railroads' popular "Vista-Dome" passenger coaches and diner lounges, which afforded wide, new high-level viewing.

General Motors also provided the new roof windows (of the same type) on its Oldsmobile Vista-Cruiser, but Chevrolet, Pontiac, and Cadillac never used it.

The Buick Skyroof Sports Wagon continued through 1969, after which time the Sports Wagon got an ordinary flat, solid roof. However, the Oldsmobile version continued longer: The attractive roof windows were available through the 1972 season. For 1973, the Vista-Cruiser provided only a small glass sunroof vent over the front seat.

In the automotive world, a styling idea becomes "old hat" in just a few seasons, and the manufacturers strive to lure the buyers with something new. But, the raised roof windows on these GM-built wagons were uniquely attractive and offered better scenic visibility, as well as added headroom for rear-seat passengers. This is one idea that ought to be revived today!

As for the Buick and Oldsmobile wagons with these panoramic roof windows, they can occasionally be found today—for reasonable prices. But, as time goes by, and they become scarcer and scarcer, these wagons may well increase considerably in value!

A VERY POPULAR CHEVY! = EVEN in 1993!

1964 CHEVROLET IMPALA
4-DR. HARDTOP "SPORT SEDAN"
3490 lbs.
$2850.   0-60 MPH IN 9.3 SECONDS.
110 MPH.
230 cid 6
OPTIONAL 283,327 OR 409 cid V8s
UP TO 425 H.P.!

9 TO 22 M.P.G. (DEPENDING ON SIZE OF ENGINE and SPEED)

©1993 North America Syndicate, Inc. World rights reserved.
2-28

FRONT DETAIL

7.00 x 14" TIRES

JET-SMOOTH CHEVROLET

CHEVROLET

1964 CH

119" WHEELBASE

LOWER-PRICED BISCAYNE and BEL-AIR MODELS ALSO AVAILABLE.
2,348,965 new CHEVROLETS SOLD in 1964 ALONE!

1964 Chevrolet

In 1964, a Chevrolet showroom customer could choose between four individual sub-makes in addition to the regular Chevrolet line. There was the sporty Corvette (since 1953), the rear-engined, compact Corvair (since 1960), the conventional compact Chevy II (since '62), and now the new intermediate-sized Chevelle.

Today we look at the regular, full-sized Chevrolet Impala four-door hardtop. In addition to this model, the Impala series included a two-door hardtop (Sport Coupe), convertible, four-door sedan, and six- or nine-passenger station wagons. There was also a special Impala SS (Super Sport) series that included a two-door hardtop and a convertible.

In the '64 Impalas, foam-cushioned seats were finished in decorator fabrics and trimmed with leather-grain vinyl and tufted cloth. According to the 1964 Chevrolet sales catalog, other standard luxuries included extra-long armrests with fingertip door releases, back-up lights, parking brake warning light, electric clock, and more! Seven interior color schemes were available, including black, in the SS line.

The 1964 Chevrolets gave a ride of luxury. They were insulated at over 700 points for reduction of noise and vibration.

"Flush-and-dry" rocker panels (body sills) and inner fenders were designed for greater resistance against rust and corrosion.

A six-cylinder engine was known as the "Turbo-Thrift," and the V-8s were known as "Turbo-Fire." Three-speed, four-speed, overdrive, or Powerglide automatic transmissions were available.

In 1964, the final year of a three-year styling cycle, hardtops had a crisply sculptured "convertible profile."

A DEPENDABLE "WORKHORSE!"

1964 CHEVROLET C SERIES
"FLEETSIDE" PICKUP
with FULL-WIDTH CARGO BED
115 WHEELBASE (with 6½' long BED)
127" " (with 8' long BED)
WEIGHT = 3175 LBS. and up

O.H.V. 230 cid & 1140 H.P.) STANDARD
170 H.P., 292 cid 6 OPTIONAL
(V8s ALSO AVAIL.)

ORIGINAL
f.o.b., FACTORY
PRICES FROM $2007.

("STEPSIDE" MODELS
HAVE NARROWER CARGO BEDS.)

INDEPENDENT FRONT SUSPENSION

TAD 3~19

© 1989 North America Syndicate, Inc. All rights reserved.

6.70 × 15" TIRES   3.73 GEAR RATIO (4.11 OR 3.07 OPTIONAL)

1964 Chevrolet Pickup

From 1963 to 1966, there were few outward changes in Chevrolet pick-ups. This C series, from the mid-'60s, is one of Chevy's best.

Stepside and Fleetside models were available. The '64 Fleetside with the optional "Custom" cab is shown (easily spotted from the outside by the strip of horizontally grooved bright metal just behind the upper portion of each side door). The Custom cab boasted such deluxe features as a full-depth foam cushion seat with inserts of striped nylon fabric, trimmed at the sides with red or beige vinyl leatherette. Also included: arm-rest on driver's door, right-hand-door lock, chrome-trimmed control knobs, cigarette lighter, two sunshades, horn ring, and a long Chevrolet nameplate along the lower edge of the glove-box door.

Chevrolet's light pickups had coil springs on all four wheels, and the high torque 6-cylinder or V-8 engines were of lighter-than-usual weight, made possible by reduced thickness in many uncritical areas.

Pickup box floors were made of wood, with protective metal strips running full length. The Fleetside box was seventy-two inches wide (fifty inches wide between wheel wells) and nineteen inches deep. The Stepside box was fifty inches wide at all points, and it was 17 1/2 inches deep. The Stepside had a full-width tailgate, but the Fleetside tailgate was sixty-five inches wide (seven inches less than maximum box width).

In addition to the pickups, Chevrolet commercial vehicles in '64 included vans, panel trucks, high-bodied Step-Vans, stake trucks, tandem-wheeled flat beds, gas or diesel heavy-duty cab-and-chassis (or tractor units for use with trailer combinations), tilt-cab trucks, and many others!

"THE BIG DODGE," THE RARE "880" SERIES, WAS ONLY AVAILABLE FROM EARLY 1962 TO 1965, and HAD PRE-1962 BODY STYLING. IT WAS NOT WIDELY ADVERTISED, AND MANY PEOPLE DO NOT KNOW THAT THE DODGE "880" EVEN EXISTED!!

GRILLE

1964 DODGE
"880" SEDAN
122" WHEELBASE 3790 lbs.
$3299. f.o.b., FACTORY

© News America Syndicate, 1986

TAP 3-9

OVERHEAD VALVE 361 CU. IN. V8 ENG. STANDARD, WITH **265 HP** @ 4800 RPM (383 CID V8 OPTIONAL) 3-SPEED MANUAL TRANSMISSION STD., OR OPTIONAL "TORQUE-FLITE" AUTOMATIC TRANS. (4-SP. MANUAL " OPTIONAL WITH 383 V8.)

23-GALLON FUEL TANK 8.00 × 14 TIRES

HELPFUL DETAILS THANKS TO LYNN JOHNSON, SEATTLE, WASH.

1964 Dodge 880

Browsing through a '64 Dodge sales catalog, we read: "Although a lot has changed in the last half-century, that same tradition of dependability has been handed down to the 1964 Dodge line. The '64 Dodges have been designed for the growing needs of a new and modern age. Here are three different size Dodges, in three distinctive styles. All handsome. All spirited. All dependable."

For 1962, the standard-sized Dart/Polara types had been totally restyled and somewhat downsized. As the 1961 model year drew to a close, it appeared that Chrysler Corp. was not planning to continue the large, pre-1962 type car in the Dodge line.

But, sometimes a company can change its corporate mind. The Chrysler people changed theirs, and conceived the big Dodge 880 to join the other '62 models (though the 880 didn't go into production until January 22, 1962, many weeks after the other models).

The first 880 of '62 shared many components with the old, big '61 Dodge Polara, as well as with the '62 Chrysler Newport. The body was a continuation of the large 1960 bodies used by Chrysler Corp. when they introduced unitized body/frame construction on their cars that year. No major retooling was necessary in this case. All '62s in the new 880 series were "Custom 880s," but a standard 880 also appeared in the '63 and '64 model years.

On the illustrated '64, small pylon-shaped ornaments with the Dodge emblem appeared atop the forward end of each front fender. The Custom 880 had more brightwork around the side windows than the standard 880.

1960s

1964
Ferrari
4 - SPEED TRANS.

250 GT "BERLINETTA LUSSO"
COUPE
(BODY BY PININFARINA)

2540 lbs.
V-12 ENGINE (180 C.I.D. or 2953 C.C.)

TAP
9-29

$ 12,900.
AT PORT OF ENTRY,
NEW YORK

0 - 60 IN SECONDS!

14 - 22 M.P.G.

150 MILES PER HOUR

DISC BRAKES
94½" W.B.
250 H.P. @ 7500 RPM

TRADITIONAL
PRANCING -
HORSE FERRARI
TRADEMARK

BUILT AT MODENA, ITALY (SINCE 1940)

© News America Syndicate, 1985

1964 Ferrari 250-GT

Ferrari's founding father, Enzo Ferrari, is a colorful figure and a strong personality who played a prominent part in the company that bears his name. Ferrari, born in 1898 in Modena, Italy, became a racing driver in his younger days, though his father owned a metal shop and had wanted his son to become an engineer.

Ferrari got acquainted with many famous racing drivers, and opportunities arose for him to drive in races during the early 1920s, particularly for Alfa Romeo.

In 1923, after a June 17 racing triumph, Ferrari met the father of the famous late Italian air ace, Francesco Baracca. The elder Baracca admired Ferrari's winning driving, invited him to his home, and gave Ferrari his son's special yellow-and-black prancing horse emblem, which had been removed from his airplane.

Honored by this gift, Ferrari began to use the prancing horse emblem on his race cars and eventually on his Ferrari automobiles, which first appeared in the late 1940s. Most of the early Ferraris were race cars, and even the later passenger cars (GT coupes and roadsters) were suited to racing.

Ferrari's first company was AAC (Auto Avio Contruzione). During the early 1940s AAC was involved with war production. The first three Ferrari Type 125 V-12 engines were completed late in 1946, with the first Ferrari race cars built in 1947. The V-12 is the most typical Ferrari engine, but there have also been V-6, V-8, and even flat-12 types!

Most Ferrari bodies were designed by Pininfarina and built, with only a few exceptions, either by Pininfarina or Scaglietti.

1960s

$ 3233. 1964 FORD
"GALAXIE 500 XL"
2-DR. HARDTOP

5/25

© News America Syndicate, 1966

3622 LBS.

AUTOMATIC TRANS.;
OVERDRIVE AVAILABLE.
7.50 x 14" TIRES.
119" WHEELBASE.

TOP ENGINE AVAILABLE = 427 O.I.D. V8 (425 HP)
(ALSO 223 CID 6; 289, 352 OR 390 CID V8s)

1964 Ford

In addition to the standard-sized Ford (illustrated), there were also the compact Falcon (since 1960), compact/intermediate Fairlane (since 1962), sport/luxury Thunderbird (since 1955), and the new Mustang "pony car" (introduced April 1964 and generally considered a 1965 model).

For 1964, Ford was restyled and improved. After considerable experience in various racing events the previous year, suspension was improved. And, though the '64 Ford was lower, headroom inside was increased. Every standard-shift '64 Ford had a Synchro low gear, which meant that the driver could make a clash-less downshift to low, even when the car was in motion. A new optional three-speed automatic transmission gave more passing ability for highway driving, and the transmission tunnel "hump" on the floor was lowered.

In the illustrated Galaxie 500/XL, "Twin footlights in the door automatically shine inward to light your entry and outward to warn oncoming traffic your door is open." The glove compartment and ashtray were also lighted, not to mention the enlarged, lighted, and "handsomely lined" trunk.

In the Galaxie 500/XL, deep-pile wall-to-wall carpeting was standard, (as it was in many new homes and apartments that year)! Foam-padded shell bucket seats were comfortable, and various vinyls were used in the upholstery.

Maintenance costs were cut, as the '64 Ford needed a major chassis lubrication only once every 36,000 miles or three years. Oil changes and minor lubes were recommended every 6,000 miles or six months. Radiator coolant-antifreeze was good for 36,000 miles or two years.

1964 Imperial

Chrysler Corporation's prestigious Imperial was totally restyled for 1964, and it came up looking much like a Lincoln Continental. This resemblance was not so surprising; the stylist for the '64 Imperial was Elwood Engel, who'd previously designed the 1961-and-later Lincoln Continentals for Ford Motor Co. The Continentals were well liked, so Engel decided to try a similar appearance for Chrysler's Imperial.

With more than 23,000 sold, Imperial did better in '64 than it had the previous few seasons. The Continental look was continued in '65 and '66, with some modification.

Besides good looks, the '64 Imperial also offered maximum quietness in a new car. Over 154 different engineering improvements made the '64 Imperial—according to its sales catalog—the "quietest motorcar produced in America ... permanent evidence of the new precision and performance built into an incomparable fine car."

The Imperial was amply rust proofed by means of seven dip baths and six spray treatments during body construction. Nine coats of paint were then applied, all but the final coat being hand-sanded to achieve a remarkably smooth finish. The ninth coat was machine buffed "to provide a lasting luster impossible to achieve by hand."

On the assembly line, 1,650 quality-control evaluations were made on each new Imperial. Each completed car was carefully road tested and inspected.

What extras were available? There was "Auto-Pilot," cruise control, AM/FM radio, air conditioning, vinyl-covered roof, power door locks, adjustable steering wheel, etc.

1964 Plymouth

"**G**et up and go Plymouth!" (1964 slogan)

In 1964, Plymouth introduced the sharply wedge-shaped rear-quarter window section on some of its two-door hardtops (as illustrated). This Sport Fury was Plymouth's top-line model in 1964, and it was available in two-door hardtop or convertible body styles.

Though V-8s were extremely popular in the 1960s (when gas was under thirty-five cents a gallon, and there were four gas stations at some busy intersections), the "slant-six" (introduced 1960) was the best and longest lasting of Plymouth's engine choices. The slant-six was a vastly superior design and was used for years in some Valiants, Plymouths, Dodges, Darts, and Lancers, as well as in some more recent models.

The choice of seven different engines offered by Plymouth in 1964 was a wasteful idea! It raised production costs and caused various complications as these cars got older. Most American makes of cars competed hotly in the 1960s to offer "something for everyone," thus spawning a vast array of engines, transmissions, options (including power assets of all types), body types, paint and upholstery combinations, etc., which seemed almost endless each year and in nearly any model line!

On the other hand, Volkswagen, with a simple little two-door model (initially), made great inroads into the American market in the late 1950s and throughout the 1960s!

1960s

1964½ SUNBEAM "TIGER"
=SPORTS CAR=

RESEMBLES 4-CYL. "ALPINE" MODEL, BUT WITH A 260 C.I.D., 164 H.P. FORD V8 ENGINE!

ORIG. PRICE = **$3598.**

2565 LBS. CURB WT.

(6 OTHER RATIOS AVAILABLE)

86" WHEELBASE

5.90 x 13" TIRES
118 MILES PER HOUR!
0-60 MPH IN 7.8 SEC.
20 M.P.G. AVERAGE

© 1987 North America Syndicate, Inc. All rights reserved.

TAP 8-2

2.88 GEAR RATIO

BUILT IN ENGLAND BY ROOTES MOTORS, LTD. (A CHRYSLER CORP. AFFILIATE IN LATER '60s)

1964 1/2 Sunbeam "Tiger"

The four-cylinder Sunbeam Alpine sports car was a more than adequate performer for its size (would do 100 m.p.h.). But, starting in early 1964, when it was also available as the Sunbeam Tiger with Ford V-8 engine, it was HOT! Carroll Shelby masterminded the engine conversion. The small-displacement Ford V-8 engine would fit in, once the firewall was slightly altered. (Pilot models were first named "Thunderbolt.")

Sunbeam's British history harks back to 1899. Sunbeam was one of the early British imports to the United States, advertised and available here in limited numbers on the East Coast, even back in the early '20s! After that interval, Sunbeams were not imported here for many years, until the early postwar era.

There was a $1,100 difference between the price of the standard Alpine sports car and the V-8 Tiger. The Tiger had a heavier-duty suspension to accommodate the added weight load of the V-8 engine. (By moving the engine back, no more than 100 extra pounds were laid on the front axle, however.) Some advertisements (such as in the *British Motor Sport* magazine for April and May, 1965) claimed the Tiger would do over 120 m.p.h.! And, a souped-up version reached 160!

Rack-and-pinion steering was standard.

The Sunbeam Tiger chalked up a respectable number of wins at various races and track events. It was last available in the United States in the '67 model year; any sold after that time were apparently leftovers.

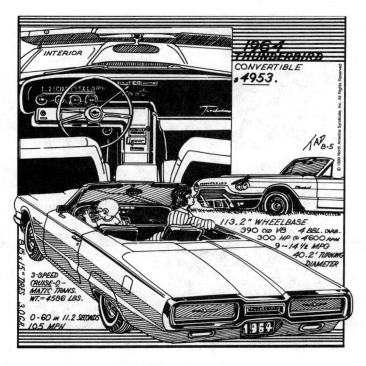

1964 Thunderbird

O ne of the most striking features of this '64 Thunderbird is the huge, flashy-looking pair of rect-angular taillights, housed in a bumper-like plated frame. From end to end, the restyled '64 T-bird was singularly attractive, and many new sales were won by its looks alone.

The '64 Thunderbird was available as a hardtop coupe, Landau Coupe (vinyl-covered top and extra trim), or convertible (as illustrated).

The fourteen-inch wheels of '63 were replaced by fifteen-inch wheels, for better brake cooling.

Thin-shell front bucket seats allowed for more rear legroom and had optional headrests. In the rear compartment, upholstery wrapped around the sides with a cafe-booth curve of luxury. A long console ran down the center floor, separating all four seats, making this Thunderbird strictly a four-passenger model. There was, however, loads of luggage space in the big, new trunk!

In the two closed models, "Silent-Flo" ventilation pulled fresh air through the entire car, even with the windows closed. An available "Swing-Away" steering wheel gave easier access to the front seat.

A low-slung, relatively heavy car, the '64 T-bird handled nicely in all kinds of weather and was at an advan-tage in heavy crosswinds that sent other cars rocking or wandering dan-gerously.

This was not an economy car; one could seldom expect more than four-teen miles per gallon in fuel con-sumption. But, to be able to travel in such luxury and elegance, the fuel expense was well worth it in the days of inexpensive gas!

1965 Cadillac

Even today, the 1965 "Caddy" is a pleasingly fancy, very long and luxurious dreamboat that symbolizes power and prosperity. The big, broad grille is an outstanding styling feature. Europeans who thought U.S. cars to be excessively ostentatious called such generous flashes of frontal chrome "the dollar grin" back in the 1950s. Maybe they were right, but some of *their* cars looked like plain potatoes.

The 1965 Cadillac was heralded in its sales brochure as "the most dramatically new Cadillac in 16 years!"

A new frame and suspension design created "incredible steadiness and levelness of ride." And, even when the car was in motion, "there was a quiet beyond anything you imagined possible in a motor car."

"Craftsmanship a creed ... Accuracy a Law" was a principle at the Cadillac factory, where the cars were built "exclusively in one plant by workers who share their skills with no other car, and who have spent an average of more than ten years producing to Cadillac standards."

In 1965, the selection included the top-line Fleetwood 75 long-wheel-base nine-passenger sedans and limos, Fleetwood Eldorado convertible, Fleetwood 60-Special sedan and vinyl-topped Brougham, popular DeVille series (various body types, including the illustrated convertible), and the new lower-cost Calais series that replaced the former "62," at prices starting at $5,224, f.o.b., factory.

An interesting feature: "Twilight Sentinel," which turned headlights on and off automatically, according to light conditions outdoors.

Air conditioning was a $495 option, but many other features were standard, even in the Calais series.

"NO OTHER CAR IS BUILT LIKE CHECKER."

1965 CHECKER "MARATHON"

283 CID V8 (195 HP) 327 CID V8 (250 HP)

BUILT BY CHECKER MOTORS CORP., KALAMAZOO, MI. (1922~1982) (MORRIS MARKIN, FOUNDER)

INTERIOR

120" WB

8.75 x 15 TIRES

$2793. and up, F.O.B., FACTORY 1965 PRODUCTION 6/136

DATA THANKS TO HOWARD AUSTIN MOTORS OF SAN JOSE CALIF.

STARTING 1965, CHECKER'S FORMER 226 CID CONTINENTAL ENGINE (6 CYL.) WAS REPLACED BY A *new* CHOICE OF CHEVROLET 6 OR V8 ENGINES.

MOST CHECKER CARS WERE TAXIS, BUT FROM '60 ON, THEY WERE ALSO AVAIL. TO *PRIVATE* INDIVIDUALS. NO MAJOR STYLING CHANGE AFTER 1956!

230 CID 6 (140 HP)

TAP 7·28

1963 Checker Marathon

For many years, Checker built only taxis. But, as the 1960s began, Checker Motors Corp. decided to sell cars to the general public as well. Many people who had ridden in Checker cabs had been impressed with the roominess, comfort, and easy access and exit. Checker began marketing the Checker Superba. This was soon joined, and then replaced, by the Marathon series.

Because of the old-fashioned styling, some people thought the Checker could be a Russian car. I happened to see part of a TV series rerun in which Soviet agents were driving a Checker in Czechoslovakia! But, this was no "Czech Checker!"

New York City and other large metropolitan areas have long used great fleets of Checker cabs. But, the supply of new ones was cut off after 1982,

because Checker, a small company, could not meet the increased demands of the autoworkers' union as larger manufacturers could afford to do.

For Checker, 1962 appears to have been a banner year, with 8,173 units produced. This was the 40th anniversary year, and a 5,000-pound Town Custom limousine was added to the line, with a nine-inch-longer wheelbase and a price of $7,500.

Checker found 1965 to be a more prosperous year in general than '62, but production was down to 6,136. Production of cars and station wagons continued to decrease in the 1970s, with shrinking figures of less than 1,000 per year. In 1982, with no progress made at the union bargaining table, Checker decided to give it up. The last Checker cab was built Monday, July 12, 1982. Its color was green and ivory.

1960s

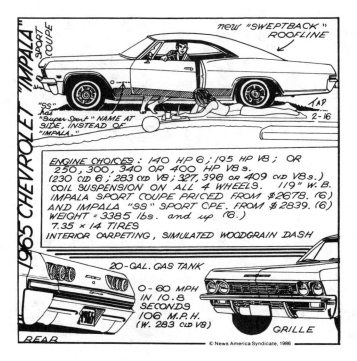

Drawing annotations: 1965 CHEVROLET "IMPALA" — SPORT COUPE. new "SWEPTBACK" ROOFLINE. "SS" has "Super Sport" NAME AT SIDE, INSTEAD OF "IMPALA." ENGINE CHOICES : 140 HP 6; 195 HP V8; OR 250, 300, 340 OR 400 HP V8's. (230 CID 6; 283 CID V8; 327, 396 OR 409 CID V8's.) COIL SUSPENSION ON ALL 4 WHEELS. 119" W.B. IMPALA SPORT COUPE PRICED FROM $2678. (6) AND IMPALA "SS" SPORT CPE. FROM $2839. (6) WEIGHT = 3385 lbs. and up (6.) 7.35 × 14 TIRES. INTERIOR CARPETING, SIMULATED WOODGRAIN DASH. 20-GAL. GAS TANK. 0-60 MPH IN 10.8 SECONDS. 106 M.P.H. (W. 283 CID V8). REAR. GRILLE. TAP 2-16.

© News America Syndicate, 1986

1965 Chevrolet

L ike its rivals, Ford and Plymouth, Chevrolet was also totally restyled for 1965. Bigger and broader, with a new semi-fastback roofline on the Sports Coupe models, the '65 looked bigger and better than ever! Wider-track ("Wide-Stance") wheels and full coil suspension gave a pleasing new ride. And, there were numerous options for those who desired luxury, convenience, and performance (six engines available).

The new Chevrolet was unveiled at dealers on Thursday, September 24, 1964, along with the Chevelle, Chevy II and Nova, Corvair, etc. That night, the skies in most cities were lit up with swinging searchlight beams, as multitudes hurried down after work to see the new models.

Since 1958, the Impala series was Chevy's top-of-the-line. Later, in the 1965 model season, the new Caprice name would appear, first as a four-door hardtop luxury package and before long as a new top model series.

There were "standard" Impalas, and there were "SS" (Super Sport) variations for the performance-minded. There were nearly 200 items that could be added as options to the "SS," so such a car could wind up costing thousands more!

Plainest-Jane of the full-sized Chevrolet models was the simple Biscayne, with two-door priced from $2,363. Then there was the Bel-Air from $2,465. (Respective West Coast prices on these were $2,615 and $2,717.)

1965 CHRYSLER STD. **300** 4-DR. HARDTOP, A BODY TYPE NOT AVAIL. IN 300 "LETTER" SERIES SPORT MODEL. 12,452 BUILT 124" W.B. 4210 lbs. 383 CID V8 (315 HP) OR 413 V8 (360 HP) 8.55×14 TIRES

$4061., fob

CHRYSLER

5-20

SPEC. SPORT 2-DR. H/T and CVT. (letter) "300" MODELS BUILT :

'55	300	1725
56	300-B	1102
57	C	2402
58	D	809
59	E	690
60	F	1212
61	G	1617
62	H	558
63	J	400
64	K	3647
65	L	2845

1965 Chrysler Standard 300

Much has been written about Chrysler's famous 300 (letter) series, which began in 1955. The '56 model became the 300-B, the '57 the 300-C, and so forth. (After the 300-H of '62, the '63 became the 300-J, as Chrysler Corp. thought the letter "I" might be confused with a Roman Numeral one.)

A new, standard (non-lettered) 300 line of Chryslers joined the prestigious, high-performance letter series, beginning in 1962, when the standard 300 replaced the former Windsor series.

Some 300 fans were dismayed to see their favorite model number cheapened by putting it on a less exclusive series, but it helped Chrysler to sell more cars! For the purist in '62, there was still the performance model 300-H, though only 558 of those were sold, in contrast to over 25,000 of the standard 300s!

The standard 300 for '65 had a four-barrel carburetor and 10-to-1 compression. "It really moves," the catalog promised! Three-speed manual transmission was standard, with option choices of either four-speed manual or three-speed automatic. In 1965, the standard 300 bore a close resemblance to the sport 300-L, except that the standard type had a narrower red cross-type insignia on cross-shaped grille trim, and the 300-L had a flatter front bumper with a pair of small rubberized vertical rub strips. There were a few other small differences, but the "L" was the last of that famous letter series, while the standard 300 continued on.

CONVERTIBLES OF THE 1960s ARE IN DEMAND!

1965 FALCON *"FUTURA" CONV'T.*
109 ½" WHEELBASE
WEIGHT 2782 LBS. (6); 3056 LBS. (V8)
6.50 x 13" TIRES
(OVERHEAD-VALVE SIXES OR V8)
3 SPEED AUTOMATIC TRANS.
AVAILABLE (Cruise O matic)

CONVERTIBLE PRICE
$**2717.** UP (6)
2881. (V8)

2.80, 2.83, 3.20 or 3.50 GEAR RATIO

ENGINE CHOICES:
170 CID 6
(101 HP @ 4400)
200 CID 6
(120 HP @ 4400)
289 CID V8
(195 HP @ 4400 RPM)

FORD MOTOR CO.'s FALCON WAS AVAILABLE FROM THE 1960 TO 1970 MODEL YEARS.

TAD 2~25~90

1965 Falcon

Ford's compact Falcon was introduced in 1960, and a few of the early models are still in use! The early Falcons were somewhat underpowered, though economical. In 1963, a V-8 engine was also available, joining the sixes. And, by the mid-1960s, the little Falcon had grown brawnier, better looking, and more powerful.

In 1965, a new 170 c.i.d. six replaced the 144 c.i.d. six as the basic engine, with twenty extra horsepower, yet better fuel economy (up to a fifteen percent increase) because of the efficient design. "Low profile tires" reduced road friction and increased mileage.

The new 200 c.i.d. had seven main bearings, an unusual feature in an "economy" engine.

The 289 c.i.d. V-8 replaced the former 260 c.i.d. version. And, a new alternator was used (instead of a generator).

In a *Consumer Reports* test, a '65 Falcon Futura delivered 27 m.p.g. at 30 miles an hour, and 20 1/2 at 60 m.p.h. In traffic, the figure fell to 15 1/2 m.p.g. This test was made in a car with a 3.0 to 1 rear axle (gear) ratio.

Because no stock American-built convertibles were produced from 1977 to 1981, the value of older convertibles has escalated. Most convertibles are now worth about thirty percent more than their enclosed counterparts, even though convertible tops need periodic replacements.

In only fair condition, a '65 Falcon convertible such as this would be worth $2,200 to $2,500. In perfect condition, its value could be $5,700 to $7,500, depending on its features, extras, etc.

1960s

1965 JAGUAR
4.2 SEDAN
$6990. AT PORT OF ENTRY
BRITISH-BUILT
"A DIFFERENT BREED OF CAT"
DUAL OVERHEAD-CAM 6-CYL. ENGINE
258.4 C.I.D.
3.63 x 4.17 BORE + STR.
© 1991 North America Syndicate, Inc. All Rights Reserved
JAGUAR
123 MILES AN HOUR
11 TO 22 M.P.G. AVG.
LEATHER UPHOLSTERY (SEATS) WITH WALNUT DASH
BORG-WARNER AUTO. TRANS.
3.54 TO 1 GEAR RATIO
24-GAL. GAS SUPPLY (2 TANKS)
DUNLOP 14" TIRES and 4-WHEEL DISC BRAKES!
BENDIX POWER STEERING
WEIGHT=3920 LBS.
TAP 3-24
HAPPY EASTER!
265 HORSEPOWER @ 5400 RPM

1965 Jaguar 4.2 Sedan

The 3.8-liter Mark X Jaguar sedan was upgraded to 4.2 liters for 1965, yet automotive reviewers assure all that there would be little if any decrease in gas mileage because the larger engine displacement would add more torque with its greater bore. Top speed was boosted up into the 120s! However, horsepower rating remained at 265, as before.

According to *Autocar*, the British magazine, the new '65 Jaguar 4.2 sedan would do 0 to 60 m.p.h. in less than ten seconds—just a hair quicker than Ford's V-8 Falcon "Sprint." The overall average fuel consumption was 14.5 miles per gallon.

The new Marles/Bendix "Varamatic" power steering was considered a "revelation" by *Autocar* reviewers. "Scarcely perceptible movements of the wheel hold the car to a dead-straight course at three-figure speeds," the reviewers wrote. "On twisting roads, the steering takes so little effort that this big car can be whisked around tight corners with little more than finger-pressure on the wheel rim."

Jaguar brakes—already good—were further improved on the 4.2 sedan. A "mere 25-lb. load on the pedal gives a near-50 percent stop," and "this heavy car stops all-square within 29 feet from 30 m.p.h." (In other words, in less than twice the car's length!) Front and rear hydraulic systems were independent, with a brake-fluid-level warning light on the dash.

The safety hood was hinged at the front, opening at the rear. Heating and ventilating systems were improved.

Other '65 Jaguars: 3.8-liter MK II and "S" sedans, and the XKE roadster and coupe.

1965 Oldsmobile 4/4/2

For 1964, Oldsmobile's F-85 Cutlass models had been available with a new 330 c.i.d. V-8 engine; and for 1965, another new V-8 (400 c.i.d.) was included in the "4/4/2" performance package option.

What did the numbers stand for? Reportedly, they signified four speed (or else 400 c.i.d.,) four-barrel carburetor, and two exhausts. Lightweight, high-performance muscle cars were "in" during the middle and later sixties, and the 4/4/2 would prove a popular series for a few years!

The '65 4/4/2 was available either as a convertible or sports coupe. In addition to its hot engine and dual exhausts, the 4/4/2 also featured a heavy-duty frame and suspension (four coils), front and rear stabilizers, nylon redline tires, etc. It could be identified by the red-and-white 4/4/2 grille, deck, and side insignias. The sport wire wheel covers lent an added dash of pizzaz!

In a Spring 1965 promotional compaign, Olds sponsored a "GOLF-O-RAMA" contest. Entry forms were available at Olds dealers or at participating golf pro shops until June 5, and entrants did not need to play golf to win. Top four prizes: a new Olds 4/4/2! There were 442 other prizes of a scale model Oldsmobile with a transistor radio built in. This writer has a scale model (1/25 size) of a '63 Cadillac with such a built-in radio, but has never seen one of the rare prize model Oldsmobiles. The collecting of scale-model cars, especially in 1/25 size, has grown in popularity, until a *toy* has become as valuable as the actual prototype was only a few years earlier!

The cartoon illustration contains the following handwritten text:

426 CID V8 OPTIONAL) 119" WHEELBASE

1965 PLYMOUTH
" FURY III " HARDTOP
$ **2968.** and up, f.o.b.
(6-CYL.)
WT. 3510 lbs. "

(330-H.P.) 383 CID V8 OR 365-H.P.

7.75 x 14" TIRES

© News America Syndicate, 1985

LOWER-PRICED 1965
PLYMOUTH "BELVEDERE"
HAS ONLY 2 HEADLIGHTS,
AS DOES VALIANT.

HAPPY THANKSGIVING!

225 CID 6 OR 318 CID V8 STD.

25-GALLON FUEL TANK

3.23 GEAR RATIO (V8) (2.93 w. AUTO. TRANSMISSION)

1965 Plymouth Fury III

Gasoline was cheap in the 1960s, so few people complained that the '65 Plymouth Fury III, with the standard 318 c.i.d. V-8, got only 10.7 to 16.4 miles per gallon with a 13.7 average. With the 318 engine, the car would do 102 m.p.h. and 0 to 60 in 11.6 seconds. The screamingly powerful 426 c.i.d. "hemi" V-8 engine (optional) would push a Fury up to 120 m.p.h., but at a cost: only 8 to 14 m.p.g. on premium (ethyl) gas.

For '65, the Fury series was available as Fury I, Fury II, Fury III, or Sport Fury, and was the largest Plymouth built (up to that time), being three inches longer, three inches wider, and an inch higher than its 1964 predecessor.

Priced below the Fury series were the Belvedere I, Belvedere II, and the plush Belvedere Satellite. In the compact line, Plymouth offered the Valiant and the sport Barracuda.

A '65 Plymouth Sport Fury convertible was the official pace car of the 1965 Indianapolis 500 automobile race.

The '65 unit-construction body eliminated most squeaks and rattles, and Fury models were sprayed in a new acrylic enamel finish, which could safely be buffed.

Power steering, power brakes, air conditioning, and various power assist accessories were optional.

Plymouth, once in third place in sales behind Chevrolet and Ford, was struggling to make fifth place (behind Buick) in 1965.

In all fairness, we must add that Dodge, another Chrysler product, was a popular car that captured many sales that would otherwise have gone to Plymouth. Dodge built full-sized models as well as the compact Dart.

1960s

A "MUSCLE-CAR" CLASSIC!

1965½ SHELBY GT-350

108" WHEELBASE
289 c.i.d FORD V8 ENGINE ("R" VERSION SHELBY MODIFIED TO 328 HP @ 7000 RPM) (STD. 306 HP @ 6500 RPM)

SHELBY ALUMINUM WHEELS with GOODYEAR 7.75x15" TIRES

32-GAL. FUEL TANK
WT.: 2800 lbs.
FRONT DISC BRAKES (WIDE REAR DRUM "")

A TOTAL OF 13,765 SHELBY MUSTANGS AVAIL. 1965~1969. FINAL CARS SOLD AS "1970" MODELS.

with BORG-WARNER "T-10" 4-SP. MANUAL TRANS.

CARROLL SHELBY AND ASSOCIATES * MODIFIED THESE FORD MUSTANG 2+2 FASTBACKS FOR STREET OR TRACK PERFORMANCE. (562 BUILT IN 1965) MID-1965 PRICE = $4428.

* - "SHELBY AMERICAN"

AAP 4-18

3.89 :1 GEAR RATIO

STD. COLOR = WHITE w. BLUE STRIPES (OTHER COLORS AVAIL. LATER)

©1993 North America Syndicate, Inc. World rights reserved.

1965 1/2 Shelby GT-350

Carroll Shelby left Texas to become a world-famous race driver, but when doctor's orders forced him to give up racing in 1960, he decided to build performance cars.

Shelby first offered his expertise to GM, but most of Corvette's design and engineering staff were reluctant to work with an outsider.

Then Shelby learned, in 1962, that British A. C. sports car production was facing possible cessation because Bristol was no longer building six-cylinder engines for them. Ford Motor Co. had just developed a new, lightweight 221 c.i.d. V-8, and Shelby got hold of one of them. He bored it out to a mightier 260 c.i.d., and then he got A. C. to install it in one of their roadsters.

Before long, "Shelby American" was organized and grew to a workforce of about 700. Not only were V-8-pow-ered A. C. cars converted to Cobras there, but on January 27, 1965, Shelby formally announced his new souped-up version of the Ford Mustang, known as the Shelby GT-350 (illustrated).

Shelby and a few knowledgeable partners made Shelby American a success story, with performance conversions of the A. C. Cobra, Sunbeam "Tiger" sports car, Cobra 427, Ford GT-40, and Ford Mark IV—not to mention variations on the Mustang. In mid-1967, Shelby turned the production of the Mustang variations over to Ford Motor Co.

The GT-350 got its name not because of horsepower or engine displacement, but simply because it was "350 feet from Shelby's factory to the building across the street!" This amusing anecdote was related in *Motor Trend* magazine for November 1977.

The illustration contains the following hand-lettered notes:

'65 Rambler AMERICAN
440H 2-DR. H/T (MODEL 6509-7)
2555.00
f.o.b., FACTORY, AMERICAN MOTORS CORP., KENOSHA, WIS.
ONE OF THE "SENSIBLE SPECTACULARS" FOR 1965.
125 H.P. @ 4200 RPM
232 CID 6 ALSO AVAIL.
1965 AMERICAN HAS NEW SIDE TRIM AND 3 NEW VERTICAL "BREAKS" IN THE GRILLE.
196 (195¾) CID O.H.V. 6 3⅛" x 4¼" BORE + STROKE
2.73 GEAR RATIO (OTHERS OPT.)
106" WHEELBASE 2650 LBS.
THE OLD-STYLE L-HEAD (FLAT-HEAD, SIDE-VALVE) 196 C.I.D. 6 WAS STILL AVAILABLE (WITH 90 HP) ON AMERICAN 220 and 330 SERIES.
16-GALLON FUEL TANK
TAD 7~3

1965 Rambler American 440-H

Nearly 325,000 American Motors Corp. cars were built in 1965—down from almost 380,000 in '64, and better than 1966 and 1967 (when 265,712 and 237,785, respectively, were produced).

AMC/Rambler products got a major re-styling for 1964. Thus, 1965 saw only minor face-lifts for the Rambler American, Classic, and Ambassador.

During the mid-1960s, AMC cars had three-digit model series numbers: the first two numbers were alike, and the third number was always "zero." In the American line, there were the 220, 330, 440 series (and also the illustrated 440-H hardtop, a notch above the regular 440 hardtop).

The Classic line included the 550, 660, and 770 series (and also a special 770-H hardtop). Ambassadors included the 880 and 990 series.

The new fastback Marlin hardtop, closely related to the Classic in '65,

didn't have a three-digit designation. If it had, it might have been "770-M."

There were numerous available extras for 1965 AMC cars: automatic transmission, overdrive, floor shift, air-conditioning, various AM or AM/FM radios, a "Vibra Tone" rear speaker, and "Duo-Coustic" twin stereo-sound rear speakers.

You could order a parking brake "on" warning light, back-up lights, trunk lights, dual courtesy lights under the dash (to light the floor), glove compartment light, windshield washer, spotlight, vertical bumper guards, door-edge guards, door window vent shades, remote-control outside mirror, rooftop luggage carrier, compass, tissue dispenser compartment, litter box, various wheel covers (including simulated wire wheels), and more!

On the American convertible, an old-fashioned, manually-operated top was standard equipment.

FIRST YEAR MODEL OF FORD BRONCO!

new **1966 BRONCO**
(BY FORD)*
4-WHEEL-DRIVE
92" WHEELBASE

170 c.i.d. SIX
105 H.P. @
4400 RPM
2750 LBS.

$2356
U-130
"ROADSTER"
ILLUSTRATED.
ALSO AVAIL. IN
PICKUP OR
2-DR. WAGON
STYLE.

14-GAL. FUEL TANK   4.11 OR 4.57 GEAR RATIOS

* IN 1960, IN GERMANY, THE 4-W-D, 3-CYL. AUTO UNION
"1000" BRONCO SOMEWHAT RESEMBLED THIS VEHICLE.

HELPFUL DETAILS THANKS TO GEORGE REICHOW, of W. MILWAUKEE, WI.

1966 Bronco

International launched its Jeep-like Scout in 1961. Noting the success of that car (as well as that of the Jeep), Ford Motor Co. entered that category with its new Bronco for 1966. (GM followed suit three years later with the Chevy Blazer, and Chrysler Corp. introduced its own versions in 1974: the Dodge Ramcharger and Plymouth Trail Duster.)

An early 1966-season ad (from October 1965) explained Ford's reasons for entering the four-wheel-drive recreational field: "Want to get away from it all? From the roads? From the crowds? Get a Bronco—Ford's new kind of four-wheel-drive excitement! Takes you over beach sand in summer, through snow in winter. Into the woods for hunting. Right up to streamside for fishing, camping. Up hills too steep for roads.

"Bronco gives you features never combined before. Frisky six-cylinder power. Clashless gear shifting. Smooth coil-spring ride. Lots of ground clearance. Tight 34-foot turning diameter. No annoying whine in two-wheel drive. Choice of Roadster, Wagon, or Sports-Utility (pickup truck). It all adds up to new fun—for mountain hopping or family shopping. So bust loose in a Bronco—from your Ford dealer's corral!"

Far-traveling Bronco owners who weren't satisfied with the range of the standard fourteen-gallon gas tank could order an optional second gas tank to be installed under the driver's seat. The second tank held an extra eleven gallons. Filler pipes for both tanks were located on the left side of the body (note the dual filler caps in the illustration).

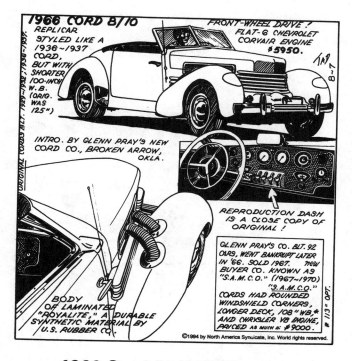

ORIGINAL CORDS BLT. 1929~1932 - 1936~1937.

1966 CORD 8/10
REPLICAR
STYLED LIKE A
1936~1937
CORD,
BUT WITH
SHORTER
100-INCH
W.B.
(ORIG.
WAS
125")

FRONT-WHEEL DRIVE!
FLAT-6 CHEVROLET
CORVAIR ENGINE
$5950.

INTRO. BY GLENN PRAY'S NEW
CORD CO., BROKEN ARROW,
OKLA.

REPRODUCTION DASH
IS A CLOSE COPY OF
ORIGINAL!

BODY
OF LAMINATED
"ROYALITE," A DURABLE
SYNTHETIC MATERIAL BY
U.S. RUBBER CO.

GLENN PRAY'S CO. BLT. 92
CARS, WENT BANKRUPT LATER
IN '66. SOLD 1967. NEW
BUYER CO. KNOWN AS
"S.A.M.C.O." (1967~1970)
"S.A.M.C.O."
CORDS HAD ROUNDED
WINDSHIELD CORNERS,
LONGER DECK, 108" WB,
AND CHRYSLER V8 ENGINE,
PRICED AS MUCH AS $9000.

113" OPT.

1966 Cord "8/10" Replicar

As a young boy in Oakland, Calif., I traveled several miles by bus in order to get my first look at a Cord automobile. It was a yellow-and-black 1937 Cord coupe, and had been advertised for sale in the local newspaper for $400. This coupe, though I didn't know it then, was one of only two '36-'37 Cord coupes ever built! It had a black, leather-padded top with a tiny split rear window as on the Cord sedans. I drew a picture of this car, and, at the age of eleven, I thought it turned out very well. Sadly, I lost the drawing.

Glenn Pray was a Tulsa, Okla. schoolteacher who was a longtime fan of the '36-'37 Cords. In 1960, with the help of Wayne McKinley, he was able to purchase the remaining assets of Indiana's Auburn-Cord-Duesen-berg Co., along with the legal right to use the Cord name on future replicars.

The first pilot model was completed in 1964. It was called the Cord 8/10 because it was eight-tenths the length of the original "810." Five more pilot models were built. Pilot model No. 1 was given free to Gordon Buehrig, designer of the original 1936-1937 Cords. Production stopped in June 1966, after nearly 100 of the "8/10" replicars had been built.

The original Cords are still more valuable than the replicars, but the supply of the replicars is also very limited and they, too, have escalated in value in recent years.

I'm grateful to Stephen D. McClure, a reader from Highland, Calif. He sent me much helpful information on the Cord replicars.

1960s

THE "LITTLE" DODGE VAN "A-100" COMPACT SERIES OF 1964 TO 1970

© 1989 North America Syndicate, Inc. All rights reserved

KAP 5~21

1966 DODGE SPORTSMAN VAN WAGON 5 TO 8 PASSENGERS

DODGE

Dodge

A 100

DEPENDABLE 170 C.I.D. SLANT "SIX" ENGINE, 101 HORSEPOWER @ 4,000 RPM, 3.4" x 3.125" BORE & STROKE. COMPRESS. 8.5 TO

MANY OF THESE FAITHFUL COMPACT VANS ARE STILL IN DAILY SERVICE!

90" WHEELBASE, WITH 21-GALLON FUEL TANK 6.50 x 13" TIRES 3055 LBS. EMPTY $2567. and up, f.o.b. FACTORY

1966 Dodge "A-100" Sportsman

The Volkswagen Microbus began the mini-van fad. The VW bus of the 1950s could carry far more inside than any conventional station wagon—with no space wasted on a front hood or rear deck, and with considerably more headroom.

Noting Volkswagen's success, Ford got the mini-van idea in '61 with its compact Econoline pickups and vans (the pickups were cab-forward types, like the vans). Chevrolet introduced the Corvair rear-engine pickup and Corvair Greenbrier van. Chevrolet brought out the Chevy-Van in 1964—the same year that Dodge introduced the dependable A-100 series, similar to what is illustrated here. The A-100 line included small vans and cab-forward pickups.

After the '50s ended, Chrysler Corporation's "slant-six" engine replaced the old L-head six. The slant-six had overhead valves and a large, free-breathing exhaust system made possible by tilting the engine to one side from its former upright position. The slant-six proved to be a remarkably economical, efficient, and long-lasting engine.

In the A-100 series, there was the illustrated Sportwagon; a Custom Sportwagon with two-tone paint and deluxe interior; a windowless freight van with windowless double doors on the right side; and a Panel Van that was also windowless, without the double side doors. There was also an A-100 compact, cab-forward pickup (same frontal design as the vans), which was available with or without two-tone paint and with or without a pair of wraparound rear quarter windows.

Camper tops could be ordered for the A-100 pickups, or pop-top camping conversion roof units for the passenger vans.

1960s

THE FIRST CHARGER!
(37,344 BLT.)
$3122. UP

1966 DODGE CHARGER

117" W.B.

©1994 by North America Syndicate, Inc. World rights reserved.

CHARGER

RETRACTABLE
HEADLTS.
IN
GRILLE

318, 361, 383 or
426 cid V8 (to 425 HP.!)

120 M.P.H.
0-60 IN 7.8 SEC.
12~16 ML PER GALLON
19-GAL. FUEL TANK 3.23 G.R.
7.35 x 14" TIRES (AUTO. TRANS.)

DODGE

4·10

1966 Dodge Charger

From the great era of pony cars, muscle cars, and specialty cars comes the first of the Dodge Chargers—the 1966 "fastback." The Charger was based on Dodge's popular "Coronet" series, but vive le difference!

From February 1966, we read: "Charger! ... new leader of the Dodge Rebellion.

"This beautiful new bomb comes from the drawing board to your driveway with all the excitement left in. It's Dodge Charger, and it's loaded. With fresh ideas, eye-tempting styling, explosive performance.

"'What a handsome home for a Hemi!' you say? We thought you would—so a big, bad 426 Street Hemi is optional ... in a package deal with a heavy-duty suspension to keep you firmly in control. Plus 11-inch (drum diameter) brakes and four-ply nylon Blue Streak tires for extra safety. Add

to the package with options like heavy-duty TorqueFlite automatic transmission (set for full-throttle shifts at 5500 RPM) or a competition-type four-speed manual gearbox. Check out Charger, the hot new one from Dodge that proves sports cars can also be luxurious."

One popular color combination was a silvery-gray paint job on the body with a red vinyl interior and four horizontally pleated bucket seats. Rear bucket seats could be folded down, wagon style, to provide space for skis and additional luggage. Four large circular dials graced the left end of the dash, including a tachometer! An optional swivel clock could be mounted on the floor console.

Notice the broad taillight expanse across the rear: a safety "plus" that Ford's Thunderbird also featured in the mid-1960s.

1966 Ford Camper Special Pickup

Back in the 1960s, Ford pickup trucks were easy to identify because they featured a new and different grille each year.

In 1966, Ford Motor Co. advertised that independent tests had proven "Ford pickups ride best." This good ride was due mainly to Ford trucks' twin I-beam suspension, which made use of dual front axles and large coil springs. Each of the two forged steel I-beam front axles worked independently to dampen road shocks before the driver or passengers could feel them.

The illustrated Camper Special pickup had a long wheelbase, large 6 or V-8 engine, and "all the heavy-duty features you need to carry a big camper body." This pickup had the wide Styleside bed with outer walls that were flush with the cab sides.

In 1966, Ford painted all new Ford engines blue. Why? To make them readily identifiable. "We want you to know the instant you see a Ford-blue engine in a car, truck or tractor it's powered by Ford—built to the highest standards of engineering excellence."

"...You've heard of green giants... white tornadoes ... so why not blue horses?"

By '66, Ford had built and sold over 35 million V-8 engines, more than any other manufacturer since the first mass-production Ford V-8 was introduced in 1932. Actually, Ford had built V-8 engines back in the 1920s, too—in their high-quality Lincoln automobiles.

Pickups with campers on them are quite affordable and have been extremely popular since the 1960s. Some camper bodies can be easily removed when the truck needs to be used as a truck.

1960s

108" WHEELBASE   6.95 x 14" TIRES   16-GAL. GAS TANK

2 + 2
35,698 BUILT

SHELBY 350 GT RESEMBLES 2 + 2, BUT HAS REAR QUARTER WINDOWS, 306 HP, and TOP SPEED OF *133* MPH !

new 1966 GRILLE HAS ALL HORIZONTAL PIECES.

$2606.
TO
$3642.
PRICE RANGE

THE FIRST FORD MUSTANGS WERE SOLD IN APRIL, 1964.

CONVERTIBLE
72,119 BUILT

HARDTOP
499,751 BUILT

MUSTANG

1966

MANUAL OR CRUISE-O-MATIC TRANSMISSION

200 C.I.D. 6
120 HP @ 4400

or 289 C.I.D. V8
200 HP @ 4400
or 271 HP @ 6000

TAP
8~21

1966 Mustang

S o remarkably popular was the 1965 Mustang that it was a tough act to follow! Therefore, Ford Motor Co. stylists decided not to spoil a good thing. Only minor styling changes appeared on the '66 model.

The most noticeable change on the '66 Mustang was the set of all horizontal pieces in the grille, replacing the mesh pieces in the previous models.

Lee Iacocca, who was then with Ford, helped conceive and plan the Mustang. As early as 1961, he'd planned a personal-sized Ford: a sporty, young people's car, reminiscent of the early T-birds, which would sell at least 100,000 units a year. The Mustang did even better than expected! Between April 1964 and January 1965, nearly 700,000 were sold—and during 1965, the million-car mark was passed!

In 1966, Ford advertised: "What do you do after you build a million Mustangs? Start on the second million!" In 1966, well over half a million additional units were sold! With an amazingly large selection of options from which to choose, one could almost create a one-of-a-kind personal car—not to mention color and upholstery variations.

During the 1965 season, the 170-c.i.d., 101-h.p. six was dropped in favor of the beefier 200 c.i.d. six (120 h.p.). The small V-8 (260 c.i.d., 164 h.p.) was dropped for 1966, but 200-, 225-, and 271-h.p. versions of the 289-c.i.d. V-8 could be had—not to mention the hot Shelby special!

1960s

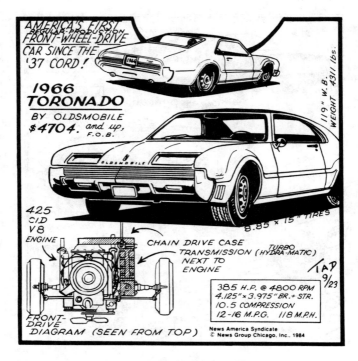

AMERICA'S FIRST *REGULAR-PRODUCTION* FRONT-WHEEL-DRIVE CAR SINCE THE '37 CORD!

1966 TORONADO

BY OLDSMOBILE
$4704. *and up,* F.O.B.

119" W.B. 4311 lbs.

425 C.I.D V8 ENGINE

8.85 x 15" TIRES

CHAIN DRIVE CASE
TRANSMISSION (HYDRA-MATIC)
NEXT TO ENGINE
TURBO

FRONT-DRIVE DIAGRAM (SEEN FROM TOP)

385 H.P. @ 4800 RPM
4.125" x 3.975" BR.+ STR.
10.5 COMPRESSION
12 -16 M.P.G.   118 M.P.H.

1966 Toronado

Some so-called "automotive experts" around Detroit predicted that Oldsmobile's all-new front-wheel-drive Toronado for 1966 would be "an expensive flop." "Front-drive offers no real advantages on big, U.S.-style cars," they were quoted as saying.

But, in spite of the negative predictions for the new Toronado, it was well received and continued for years! GM considered it successful enough that for the following year (1967), Cadillac launched a new front-wheel-drive in the El Dorado series.

In addition to front-wheel drive, the '66 Toronado boasted of other special features: radical new styling with the look of a racing GT and headlights that were concealed behind doors by day; full-length side windows that eliminated the long-popular butterfly vents; completely flat floors inside (since there was no driveshaft to the rear wheels nor the necessity of a driveshaft tunnel); ultra-wide doors; drum-type speedometer; etc.

The '66 "Toro" was available in only one body type: two-door hard-top, though there was a deluxe edition with new "Strato Seats" that had a fold-down center armrest and available headrests, plus other luxuries.

Motor Trend magazine liked Toronado's radical new features and voted it "Car of the Year" for '66, giving it much coverage in the December 1965 issue. This was the first time Olds had won the *Motor Trend* award since it was begun fourteen years earlier.

Note: a "preview" Toronado was shown to eager GM executives in Arizona in 1964, and they readily gave their approval to get this new car on the market in less than two years!

1966 Trabant

"**B**acteria being sought to gobble little lemons!" In April 1991, an *AP* news release revealed that the Trabant, formerly the "people's car" of East Germany, was now a four-wheeled pariah that was filling Germany's scrap heaps.

In the spring of 1991, both the Wartburg and Trabant cars were discontinued, after freedom had come, at last, to East Germany and most of the Iron Curtain nations. East Germans were now able to purchase better cars than the homegrown variety they had put up with since the 1950s.

Nicknamed "Trabi," the Trabant lost its resale value in one fell swoop. In fact, the final useful act of many a Trabant was to carry its owners to freedom in West Germany during a mass exodus in 1989.

As the communist system came unglued, many East Germans looked upon their noisy, smoke-belching little Trabants with scorn. But, scrapping the "Trabis" posed a serious problem: the bodywork contained much cellulose resin and phenol-formaldehyde resin, which produce toxic smoke when burned. If buried, these plasticized bodies could pollute the soil!

A group of German scientists patented a bacteria that could devour most of a Trabant body in three weeks, leaving only a harmless, disintegrated mush. Perhaps the solution was to "throw it to the bugs."

Americans and other foreigners visiting or working in Germany became interested in the little throwaway cars, and a handful have been shipped home. A million have already been scrapped, but that's only a third of the total output.

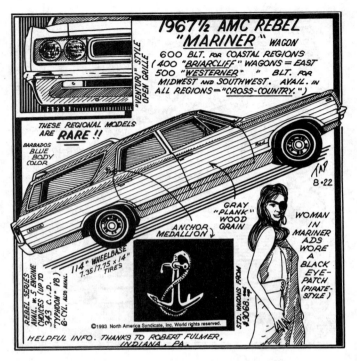

1967½ AMC Rebel "Mariner" Wagon

600 BLT. for COASTAL REGIONS (400 "BRIARCLIFF" WAGONS = EAST 500 "WESTERNER" " BLT. for MIDWEST and SOUTHWEST. AVAIL. in ALL REGIONS = "CROSS-COUNTRY.")

"VENTURI" STYLE OPEN GRILLE

THESE REGIONAL MODELS ARE RARE!!

BARBADOS BLUE BODY COLOR

TAP 8·22

GRAY "PLANK" WOOD GRAIN

ANCHOR MEDALLION ↓

WOMAN IN MARINER ADS WORE A BLACK EYE-PATCH (PIRATE-STYLE)

114" WHEELBASE 7.35/7.75 x 14" TIRES

REBEL SERIES AVAIL. W. 5 ENGINE CHOICES (UP TO 343 C.I.D. "TYPHOON" V8) 6-CYL. ALSO AVAIL.

STD. WAGONS FROM #3068.

©1993 North America Syndicate, Inc. World rights reserved.

HELPFUL INFO. THANKS TO ROBERT FULMER, INDIANA, PA.

1967 1/2 AMC Rebel Mariner

R egional models of automobiles, available only in certain parts of the United States or overseas, are scarce, but not new. Back in 1934, for example, a certain green-and-black color combination on Ford V-8 sedans was only available in or near the state of Florida. On other occasions, certain colors or color combinations have been designated for release in certain states, cities, or even for certain individual dealerships.

During the later 1967 season, American Motors Corp. introduced a "1967 1/2" series of "regional" station wagons. In my part of the country (coastal), I saw a few Mariner station wagons from AMC, but never any of the Westerner or Briarcliff wagons (which had differing styles of decorative trim).

With its nautical theme, the Mariner was sold only in coastal regions. On each side of the car, just in back of the rear door side window, there was a tiny anchor decoration. Though most station wagons in the 1960s had either plain painted sides or optional brown wood-grain effects (imitation mahogany or walnut, etc.), the sides of the Mariner were finished in a whitish-gray material that simulated bleached teakwood. And, the horizontal dark-painted strips suggested the sides of a wooden boat. The standard body color was "Barbados Blue," and inside the car, color-coordinated upholstery featured "star-and-anchor" embossing.

It's regrettable that AMC didn't continue these interesting models. They were available for only a matter of weeks, and when all were sold there were no others.

1960s

1967 Amphicar

The Amphicar was assembled in Germany, starting in 1960, and distributed in the U.S.A. until 1967. That year, stringent new government safety regulations made it impossible for some small manufacturers to comply. Amphicar was such a victim. In 1967, since the Amphicar used a British Triumph engine, Amphicar officials hoped that the U.S. government would certify the engine for Triumph, thus granting Amphicar more time to comply with other items. However, Triumph submitted a different engine for certification, which didn't do a bit of good for Amphicar! The final 1968 sales were outside the U.S.A.

In 1963, Amphicar's American distributor (Amphicar Corp. of America) issued a sales folder entitled "Welcome Aboard! Amphicar." On the split front cover, a blue Amphicar convertible was shown in the water—with top down. When the two halves of the front cover were spread open, the Amphicar was shown on land, with top up.

When in water, the Amphicar's front wheels acted as rudders. The car rode fairly low in the water, with the waterline close to the side rub rail. Therefore, the double seals on the side doors had to be completely secure in order to prevent dangerous leaks. The same precaution also applied to propeller shaft seals and to any point where water might seep in. The car came equipped with a small bilge pump.

If you should ever be interested in buying an Amphicar, check it carefully for rust, and make sure all of the seals are tight. If there are any leaks, you'll find out fast!

TOTALLY RESTYLED !! 1967 CHEVROLET PICKUP ½ TON SERIES 10

115" WHEELBASE (127" AVAIL.)
78" OR 98" BED LENGTH
2 OR 4-W-D AVAIL.
20-GAL. FUEL TANK

(WIDE-BED
"FLEETSIDE" TYPE)
283 OR 327 CID
V8
(175 OR 220 HP)

8.15 × 15" TIRES
(6.50 × 16" OPTIONAL)
OTHER SIZES ALSO

6 CYL. OR V8

250 OR 292 CID
6
(155 OR 170 HP)

3.73,
3.07 OR 4.11
GEAR RATIO
3 OR 4-SP., O.D.,
OR AUTOMATIC
Turbo-HydraMatic
OR Powerglide
TRANS.

5~24

1967 Chevrolet Pickup

"What's a Nice Truck Like You Doing In a Place Like This?" That was the eye-catching caption of a 1967 Chevrolet pickup advertisement that appeared in various magazines. It pictured an orange pickup wallowing gracefully through a city dump (similar to this illustration, with mounds of debris all around). The ad continued: "The way it looks, the '67 Chevy pickup should stay out of dumps. In fact, judging by those dashing lines, this one should do only nice, polite things like helping suburban ladies with their daily chores or squiring campers on holidays.

"But the way it works is some-thing else.

"Because, looks aside, there's never been a tougher Chevy pickup than this. Dumps won't faze it; nor trackless farmland nor expressway hustle. It's built to last longer with new body sheet metal that fights rust; and with a pickup box made of double-walled steel ..."

The October 4, 1966, issue of *Look* magazine gave the new Chevy pickup a gigantic three-page spread, showing an ivory-colored Fleetside, one of twenty-six new Chevrolet pickup models for '67, and pointing out the many new fea-tures (one of which was an unusually attractive new car-like two-toned instrument panel with a trio of circular gauge clusters).

The Stepside pickup (with narrow box and separate rear fenders) was still available. But, during the 1960s, most of Chevrolet's truck advertising was focused on the more glamorous wide-box Fleetside.

As well as restyling its pickups, Chevrolet also added a new 108 (108-inch wheelbase) van to its exist-ing line of ninety-inch wheelbase Chevy Vans.

PONTIAC'S FIRST FIREBIRD!
1967½ FIREBIRD
FROM $3017.
INTRODUCED FEBRUARY 23, 1967

THESE SIDE VENT WINDOWS NOT FOUND ON 1968 FIREBIRDS.

"400"

1967½ FIREBIRD PRODUCTION: COUPES = 67,032 CONVERTS. = 15,528

TAD 4-17

AVAILABLE IN 5 MODELS:

FIREBIRD	"SPRINT"	"326"	"HO"	(ILLUSTRATED) "400"
O.H. CAM	O.H. CAM	O.H.V.	O.H.V.	O.H.V.
230 CID 6	230 CID 6	326 CID V8	326 CID V8	400 CID V8
165 H.P.	215 H.P.	250 H.P.	285 H.P.	325 H.P.
9 TO 1 COMP.	10.5 TO 1	9.2 TO 1	10.5 TO 1	10.75 TO 1
1-BBL. CARB.	4-BBL.	2-BBL.	4-BBL.	4-BBL.

108" WHEELBASE   E 70 x 14 WD TIRES AVAIL.   FROM 3093 lbs.

1967 1/2 Firebird

Appearing on the scene in February 1967, "The Magnificent Five" Firebird models were as follows: the standard Firebird and the Sprint (both sixes); the "326," "HO" (High Output), and the "400" (V-8s).

Quoting from a March 1967 advertisement: "Leave it to Pontiac to design an exciting new sports car and make it in five versions for every kind of driving.

"Firebird 400 is our thriller. For action lovers. With 325 hp under a twin-scooped hood. Loaded down with special suspension …

"Firebird 326 is for regular-gas lovers who still want 250 hp worth of V-8. And Firebird (standard) boasts a 165 hp Overhead Cam Six—also using regular."

The mighty 400 was available with a three-speed stick manual gearbox, a four-speed, or three-speed Turbo HydraMatic automatic transmission. There was a special variation of the "400," the Rain Air 1, which had functioning hood scoops and a few engine modifications (though officially rated at 325 hp like the regular 400).

Because of the numerous options available, you could practically custom-tailor your own car to suit yourself, and it has been written that no two surviving early Firebirds appear to carry the exact same equipment!

The early Firebirds (the 1967 1/2 models) can be readily identified by the presence of "butterfly" swinging quarter vent windows in front doors. This feature was eliminated for 1968.

The Firebird was an early user of a collapsible spare tire, to conserve trunk space.

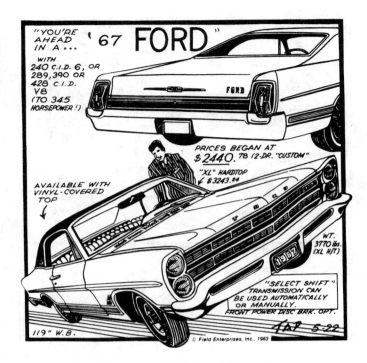

"YOU'RE AHEAD IN A... '67 FORD"

WITH
240 C.I.D. 6, OR
289,390 OR
428 C.I.D.
V8
(TO 345 HORSEPOWER!)

PRICES BEGAN AT $2440.78 (2-DR. "CUSTOM"

"XL" HARDTOP $3243.84

AVAILABLE WITH VINYL-COVERED TOP

W.T. 3770 lbs. (XL H/T)

"SELECT SHIFT" TRANSMISSION CAN BE USED AUTOMATICALLY OR MANUALLY. FRONT POWER DISC BRK. OPT.

119" W.B.

© Field Enterprises, Inc., 1983

1967 Ford

Quoting from the original Ford sales catalog: "A wave of better ideas puts you ahead in the '67 cars from Ford. These are the newest Ford Engineering Magic ideas."

A new dual brake system had two master cylinders and separate lines to front and rear brakes, so that all brakes could not lose hydraulic fluid at once. Power front disc brakes were available, and transmissions (Select Shift) could be operated manually or as automatics! A convenience control panel warned the driver when the door was ajar, fuel was low, the parking brake was left on, and when to fasten seat belts.

New LTD models were available, including a vinyl-topped variety. Another available feature from Ford Motor Co. was Automatic Speed Control, which allowed the driver to set freeway cruising speed at a fixed rate. If the brake was pressed, the device was automatically disengaged.

Weather stripping and other interior silencing aids were improved to enhance the inner quietness of the new Ford, and in the mid-1960s Ford advertised that its cars (luxury models) were "quieter than a Rolls-Royce." This was a big change from the days of the fast-but-noisy Ford V-8s of the 1930s!

Safety features included collapsible steering columns and steering wheel spokes that bent on impact, as well as doors that wouldn't open from inside unless locking buttons were raised (and an optional vacuum door lock which kept doors locked at any speed over 8 m.p.h.). Even the armrests were "energy-absorbing," though energy-absorbing bumpers had disappeared after the 1930s and would not return until the 1970s.

TV and FILM STAR DANNY THOMAS APPEARED IN 1967 JEEPSTER ADS.

"THE RETURN OF THE "JEEPSTER!"

ORIGINALLY INTRODUCED IN 1948 BY WILLYS.

TAD

10~19

© News America Syndicate, 1986

1967 JEEPSTER
BY
KAISER JEEP CORP.,
TOLEDO, OHIO,
OAKLAND, CALIF., and
WINDSOR, ONT., CANADA
101" WB, 2835 lbs.
WITH 134.2 C.I.D. F-HEAD 4-CYL.
"HURRICANE" ENGINE
(75 H.P. @ 4000 RPM)
OR 225 C.I.D. "DAUNTLESS"
OVERHEAD-VALVE V-6
(160 H.P. @ 4200 RPM)
4-WHEEL-DRIVE
(AUTO. TRANS. AVAIL. AS OPTION
WITH V-6 ENGINE.)
POWER-OPERATED TOP
OPTIONAL.

7.35 x 15" TIRES

1967 Jeepster

The Jeepster returns, by popular demand! ... This was big news on the 1967 automotive scene! By the mid-1960s, the original Willys Jeepsters (from the late '40s and early '50s) had become desirable collector's items, and the supply did not meet the demand. Since 1963, Kaiser had been producing Jeeps (and would continue to do so until 1969, after which AMC would take over for 1970).

Kaiser Jeep executives, noting the lasting interest in, and market for, the older Jeepsters, decided to revive this specialty car in 1967. Four Jeepster models were brought forth: the convertible; Jeepster Commando station wagon; Jeepster Commando half-cab pickup; and Jeepster Commando roadster.

Even in 1967 (as today), owning a remote-area four-wheel-drive car was an "in" thing, and thus the new Jeepster included such. Turbo Hydra-Matic was optional. Fuel capacity was fifteen gallons.

Film star Danny Thomas—who had starred in a popular TV series from 1953 to 1965 and again in 1970 and 1971—was between shows in 1967, and he was hired to star in numerous Jeepster advertisements. "Holy Toledo, what a car!" he'd exclaim, while seated at the wheel of the new Jeepster. More recently, Thomas has become associated with St. Jude's Children's Research Hospital, a worthy institution for the treatment and examination of children with various malignant illnesses.

The final year for the Jeepster (of the style illustrated) came in 1971, though it had become the Jeepster Commando, usually seen with a rigid top.

1960s

1967 Marlin

The Marlin was one of the most interesting cars made by American Motors Corp., but it was only available from 1965 to 1967. The 1965 1/2 model was shown in *Auto Album* in January 1984, and the 1966 model resembled that in many ways. However, the illustrated 1967 model, presented to you today, was considerably changed from its predecessors and was larger than before, having moved from the "Classic" chassis to the big "Ambassador." (In '67, the intermediate "Classic" series became the new "Rebel" series.)

Though some sources report $3,315 as the starting price for the '67 Marlin, an American Motors comparison shopping catalog for '67 lists the same car (with standard transmission) for as little as $2,963, f.o.b. factory. Its closest rival in appearance was the fastback Dodge Charger (introduced 1966), which cost $3,128 and up, according to the AMC book. Please note: Prices tend to fluctuate during most model years, and sometimes there can be a difference of a few hundred dollars!

Though the distinctive Marlin was dropped during '67, it was replaced in 1968 by two even hotter sports models: the sleek Javelin, and the peppy little AMX!

The Marlin was offered only as a two-door hardtop fastback and never in any other body type. It is a car of growing appeal to collectors!

1967 PONTIAC "EXECUTIVE" WAGON
400 C.I.D. V8   290 TO 350 H.P.   4360 LBS.

WITH *new* HIDDEN WINDSHIELD WIPERS

FROM $4019.

8.55 × 14" TIRES

TAP
12-16

new SAFETY FEATURES: ENERGY-ABSORBING STEERING COLUMN; 4-WAY HAZARD FLASHER; DUAL MASTER BRAKE CYLINDERS; FOLDING SEAT BACK LATCHES, *and* MORE

"EXECUTIVE" REPLACED FORMER "STAR CHIEF" SERIES.

News America Syndicate
© News Group Chicago, Inc., 1984

1967 Pontiac Executive

1960s

The Pontiac Executive Series was new for 1967, replacing the former Star Chief between the Catalina and larger Bonneville series. (Top of the line was the Grand Prix, introduced in 1962, and the Grand Prix hardtop coupe was now joined by a genuine convertible.)

On all full-sized Pontiacs, windshield wipers were recessed behind the hood and were out of sight when not in use. Much advertising hoopla was directed toward this point, though there were several other improvements in the 1967 Pontiacs.

With 400 or 428 c.i.d. V-8 engines, the big Pontiacs (121-inch or 124-inch wheelbase) were not particularly "gas sippers." A 26.5-gallon fuel tank was provided.

The illustrated wagon, with two-tone paint and wood-grained lower panels, was known as the Executive Safari. Pontiacs sold very well in the 1960s, with attractive big-car styling and a massive wide-track stance. (The first wide-track Pontiac was the '59 model, which launched Pontiac to new sales heights!)

Pontiac also offered, in '67, compact models such as the Tempest, Sprint, Le Mans, GTO, and Firebird, so Pontiac had come a long, long way since 1926 when GM's new brand offered only a coupe or two-door sedan in just one basic model series!

The Catalina series was available with one of the highest-geared differentials yet known. The gear ratio was a fast-cruising 2.29-to-1, indeed a far cry from the low-geared Essex cars of the 1920s, which crawled around with 5-to-1 and even lower gear ratios!

LASTINGLY POPULAR!

1967 WINNEBAGO "F-19"
19' MOTOR HOME
$6838.
AND UP

HUNDREDS OF BRANDS
OF MOTOR HOMES
HAVE BEEN BUILT SINCE
THE 1960s, OF WHICH
WINNEBAGO IS ONE OF THE
TOP SELLERS!

© 1991 North America Syndicate, Inc. All Rights Reserved

1967 Winnebago Motor Home

Instead of an old car, today we present a bit of motor-home lore. The Winnebago has long been a leading seller in its field. Some of the less popular brands have gone "belly up" in the face of price-cutting, boom-and-recession business fluctuations, etc.

In 1966, Winnebago manufactured "Life-Time" motor homes, but in '67 they built all their products under the Winnebago name. Since then, "Big W" has branched out with various subsidiary brands and models.

The 1960s was the decade when motor homes became nationally popular. What did you get in a nineteen-foot Winnebago in '67? There was a Robertshaw thermostatic 25,000 BTU space heater, four-burner "Holiday" range with hood light and fan, gas refrigerator (electric was optional), and a double kitchen sink.

A 27-inch by 35-inch mini bathroom featured overhead fan, shower, wash basin, medicine chest, and hopper-type marine toilet. For $151.25 extra, a Monomatic airplane-type commode could be substituted.

With a second upper bunk over the dinette, the nineteen-footer would sleep up to six! The 1967 Winnebagos were built in seventeen-foot, nineteen-foot, twenty-two-foot, and twenty-seven-foot lengths. They featured "Thermopanel" construction with laminated wall panels and built-in insulation.

1968 Cadillac

GM's Cadillac introduced a huge new engine in 1968, a V-8 with a displacement of 472 cubic inches. As one reviewer wrote in *Motor Trend* magazine, "Things are bound to happen when you crack the throttle!" The reviewer found that a '68 Cadillac would go from zero to 60 m.p.h. in one full second less than its '67 predecessor had.

What's equally amazing is that the performance of the '68 Cadillac was superior even though it was saddled with new built-in, government-mandated, anti-smog gadgetry.

In its April 1968 issue, *Fortune* magazine published an interesting article by Robert Sheehan entitled "A Cadillac is a Cadillac is a Cadillac." In the article, Cadillac history was reviewed, and the latest Cadillacs were discussed in detail. Mr. Sheehan reported that in the early 1950s, Cadillac executives had considered limiting Cadillac's yearly production to no more than 100,000 cars in order to keep it "exclusive" rather than make Cadillac "popular." Fortunately, the final decision was that Cadillacs were popular, and raising production goals would not compromise the quality of the cars. Cadillac, and its parent company, General Motors, prospered in the 1950s and 1960s, as new sales records were made!

Cadillac's lowest-priced model (starting just below $6,000) was the Calais series. The De Ville series, however, outsold the Calais by a long shot. Above the De Ville, there was the line of various Fleetwood Cadillacs: the Brougham, 60 Special Sedan, the sport Eldorado, and the "75" luxury limousines and sedans.

Surprisingly, nearly all '68 Cadillacs were priced below $10,000, f.o.b., except for the "75" sedan ($10,791) and limousine ($10,930).

1960s

SS 396 Chevelle 1968

"TURBO JET"
396 CID V8 (325 TO 375 HP AVAIL.)
F70 x 14 RED-STRIPE
TIRES (WIDE OVAL)
20-GAL. FUEL TANK

112" W.B. ON H/T CPE. OR CONVERTIBLE

2 DR. H/T
$3249.

WT.= 3510 lbs.

TAJ
12-9-90

AM/FM RADIO and 8 TRACK TAPE (4 SPEAKERS) AVAIL.

HELPFUL INFO. THANKS TO
SCOTT RYGH, OF
SACRAMENTO, CALIF.

1968 SS

UP TO 105 MPH

1968 Chevelle "SS-396"

After more than three decades, the '68 Chevrolets and Chevelles are still popular with Chevy fans. Especially desirable to collectors is the Super Sport SS-396 series, as illustrated here.

Back in 1964, the Pontiac GTO was GM's hot, new "muscle car," but the same year, 100 Chevelle SS-396s were built. Chevy boss Pete Estes was pleased with the new model, and ordered it into full production starting in 1965.

The '68 SS-396 received good reports from most reviewers. There were a few minor complaints: small trunk, cramped rear seat. Also, the Muncie four-speed transmission in the SS-396 had a shifter that was connected to the transmission *and* to the transmission cross member. When the engine torqued, it misaligned the shifting mechanism and spoiled the shifting action. A Hurst shifting linkage was recommended as a substitute. And then, the stock tachometer was considered hard to read, and it tended to stick at certain points. Recommended: a better grade of tachometer, available at any speed equipment shop.

Basic horsepower for the SS-396 (with 396 cubic inch V-8 as standard equipment) was 325. However, 350-h.p. and 375-h.p. versions were available.

In the Chevelle line for '68, coupes and convertibles had a 112-inch wheelbase chassis, but sedans and wagons used a 116-inch wheelbase.

New for '68 were the long-hood, short-deck restyled body, and the "Hide-a-Way" concealed windshield wipers. The exhaust emissions controls were made more efficient, in compliance with new regulations.

In 1968, American cars also were required to have side marker lights and/or headlights and taillights that could be seen from the side.

1968 1/2 CONTINENTAL Mark III

(INTRODUCED SPRING, 1968)
$7423.   4739 lbs.   117.2" WB

OPTIONAL VINYL ROOF

WITH SELECT-SHIFT AUTOMATIC TRANSMISSION
POWER BRAKES WITH FRONT DISCS
POWER STEERING • POWER WINDOWS
POWER SEAT • CONCEALED DUAL HEADLAMPS
DUAL EXHAUSTS • NYLON CARPETS
INDIV. ADJUSTABLE VENTILATION SYSTEM
POWER FOLDING ARMRESTS
REAR LAMP MONITOR SYSTEM
DUAL BRAKE SYSTEM
4-WAY EMERGENCY FLASHER

OPTIONAL AUTO TEMP CONTROL
TILT STEERING WHEEL
SPEED CONTROL
AM-FM STEREO RADIO
AM RADIO WITH TAPE
ELECTRIC REAR DEFROST
6-WAY POWER SEAT WITH RECLINING PASS. SEAT

HOOD 6' LONG!

460 C.I.D. V8 ENGINE

365 HP @ 4600 RPM

TAD
6~28

BOLD NEW UPRIGHT GRILLE IDENTIFIED THE MARK III.

1968 1/2 Continental Mark III

Revealed to the public through the news media in early February, the new Continental Mark III, a personal luxury motor car with long hood and short deck, was available at Lincoln-Mercury dealers starting in April 1968. Some car buffs call this a 1968, others say 1969, but since it was unveiled after the 1968 model year was well underway, let's call it a 1968 1/2.

The First Mark III Continental had been the gigantic 1958 model, which few had liked as well as the trimmer 1956-1957 Mark II. In 1959, came a Mark IV, and in 1960 there was a Mark V. Then the "Mark" designations were shelved until this new model appeared in 1968 as a sporty companion to the regular series of Lincoln Continentals.

Ignoring the lesser-esteemed Mark III, IV, and V of '58-'60, Ford's Licoln-Mercury Division named the new '68 1/2 the Mark III, "The most authoritatively styled, decisively individual motor car of this generation." True to the original Continental tradition of the 1940s, there was a bulge in the deck lid to suggest the rear spare tire that had once marked the Continentals.

There were twenty-one choices of exterior colors, plus an array of interior combinations and two choices of simulated wood on the dash, steering wheel, and door panels. The instrument panel had a row of five large gauges set in the simulated wood strip.

Though the Mark III was shorter than the standard series Continentals, it appeared huge in front because of the extra-long hood and upright center grille, lending to it a classic status from the very first!

1960s

LEAVES MOST OTHER CARS ...

...IN ITS

DUST!

1968

12~10

1968 1/2 DODGE CORONET "SUPER BEE"

FROM THE DODGE "SCAT PACK"

117" WB

REAR STRIPE DETAIL

© 1969 North America Syndicate, Inc. All rights reserved.

STD. 383 CID V8 (4 BBL. CARB.) 10 to 1 COMPRESSION WITH SPECIAL CAMSHAFT, HYDRAULIC VALVES, EQUAL LENGTH 4-BRANCH LOW RESTRICTION INTAKE MANIFOLD, DUAL EXHAUSTS 335 H.P. @ 5200 RPM ALSO AVAIL=426 CID HEMI V8 WITH 10.25:1 COMPR. and 425 H.P. @ 5000 RPM

DETAILS THANKS TO BOB MARTIN, WAUWATOSA, WI.

1968 1/2 Dodge Coronet "Super Bee"

"**B**eware the hot-cammed, four-barreled 383 mill in the light coupe body. Beware the muscled hood, the snick of the close-coupled four speed, the surefootedness of Red Lines (red-lined tires), Rallye-rated springs and shocks, sway bar and component 11-inch drums. Beware the Super Bee. Proof you can't tell a runner by the size of his bankroll." —so read an original Super Bee ad in the March 1968 *Hot Rod* magazine.

The Dodge Super Bee was introduced in February 1968, in the '68 1/2 season, to accompany another hot, new Chrysler product: Plymouth's new Road Runner.

We're grateful to Bob Martin of the National Hemi Owners Association for sending us historical details on Chrysler Corp. "muscle cars" —the Dodge Super Bee in particular.

According to Bob's report, all the earliest Super Bees were pillared coupes, but in 1969 a pillarless two-door hardtop was available, as well as the coupe. Later in '69, a "Six Pack" Super Bee was available with a 440 c.i.d., high performance, 390 h.p. V-8 that had three two-barrel carburetors. The "Six Pack" Super Bee also featured a fiberglass lift-off hood.

For 1970, the Super Bees offered a few sheet-metal changes. In 1971, the Super Bee moved from Dodge's Coronet series to its Charger line. The final year for the Super Bee was 1971, as it was for many a muscle car! In 1972, "muzzled" cars seemed to prevail, as government regulations specified tough new smog controls, engine de-tuning, and a sharp decrease in the horsepower of most engines.

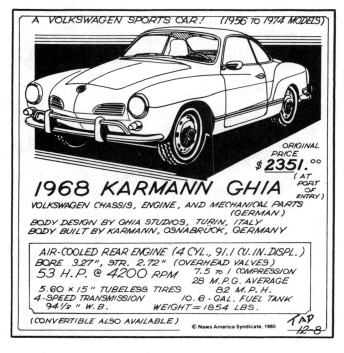

A VOLKSWAGEN SPORTS CAR! (1956 TO 1974 MODELS)

ORIGINAL PRICE
$2351.°°
(AT PORT OF ENTRY)

1968 KARMANN GHIA

VOLKSWAGEN CHASSIS, ENGINE, AND MECHANICAL PARTS (GERMAN)
BODY DESIGN BY GHIA STUDIOS, TURIN, ITALY
BODY BUILT BY KARMANN, OSNABRÜCK, GERMANY

AIR-COOLED REAR ENGINE (4 CYL., 91.1 CU. IN. DISPL.)
BORE 3.27", STR. 2.72" (OVERHEAD VALVES)
53 H.P. @ 4200 RPM   7.5 TO 1 COMPRESSION
28 M.P.G. AVERAGE
5.60 × 15" TUBELESS TIRES   82 M.P.H.
4-SPEED TRANSMISSION   10.6 - GAL. FUEL TANK
94½" W.B.   WEIGHT = 1854 LBS.

(CONVERTIBLE ALSO AVAILABLE)   © News America Syndicate, 1985   TAP 12-8

1968 Karmann Ghia

The German coach-building firm of Karmann was an old and respected one. In 1874, according to their literature, they built one-of-a-kind horse-drawn coaches for the European nobility. Later, they built auto bodies for early-day models of Adler, Hanomag, Hansa, Mercedes, and others.

In the late 1960s, production of Karmann Ghia was deliberately limited to 208 or less units per day. There was much quality handwork involved. At this time, Karmann was also building bodies for the Volkswagen Kabriolett (German spelling) and for certain Porsches.

All but the very first Karmann Ghias had gas gauges, but the standard VW beetle didn't get this feature until late 1961, with the advent of the '62 series.

In 1968, the Karmann Ghia catalog claimed that the cost of this deluxe sports coupe was only about $550 more than the price of a VW sedan! Two-tone paint was about $20 additional. The '68 Karmann Ghia had a dual brake system, with front discs.

There was a rear seat, but the car was best suited for only two passengers (driver included), because when the fifteen-position-adjustable front seats were pushed all the way back for utmost legroom, little space was left for anyone behind them.

As many as 46,000 Karmann Ghias were built a year during good times, though only a third of that number went to the U.S.A. in any one year.

Older Karmann Ghias had painted instrument panels, but in 1967 and later, imitation teak woodgrain paper was applied. In 1968 several mechanical changes were made, some to satisfy the strict new U.S. government safety and emission standards.

A RARE "WOODY" HARDTOP!
1968½ MERCURY "PARK LANE"

INTRODUCED ITS WOODGRAIN EFFECTS ON SIDES DURING THE 1968 MODEL YEAR (PLAIN-SIDE H/Ts ALSO AVAIL.)

FROM $3575.

WEIGHT: 3955 lbs.

123" WB

390 OR 428 CID V8

2584 BLT. (INCLUDING PLAIN-SIDE)

SOME SONG HITS OF 1968:
LOVE IS BLUE
I'VE GOTTA BE ME
CAB DRIVER • HONEY
LITTLE GREEN APPLES
SCARBOROUGH FAIR • DELILAH
MacARTHUR PARK • SIMON SAYS
THE GOOD, THE BAD, AND THE UGLY
HARPER VALLEY P.T.A. • THOSE WERE THE DAYS
LES BICYCLETTES DE BELSIZE • WICHITA LINEMAN
SITTIN' ON THE DOCK OF THE BAY • 1-2-3 RED LIGHT

© News America Syndicate, 1985

9-8

1968 1/2 Mercury Park Lane

"**M**ercury's got it—the 'competitive edge.' Mercury '68 with the fine car touch." So proclaimed Mercury advertising copy during the course of 1968, as the big M offered an automobile with much of the massive luxury of the Lincoln Continental.

This late arrival in the '68 season—the 68 1/2 Park Lane sweptback hardtop with woodgrained sides—was heralded as the "first hardtop with yacht-deck vinyl paneling." The walnut-tone outer vinyl paneling was also available on a new Park Lane convertible, a Brougham hardtop and, of course, on the successful Colony Park station wagon as before.

To add to the "fine car touch," the '68 Mercurys carried 123 pounds—and nineteen kinds—of sound insulation "to give you the luxury of silence." Nylon interior carpeting was as rich and

durable as that in a fine home. Eighteen-inch-deep seats were padded with 2.5 inches of foam.

The rear window in the illustrated car measured "a whopping 1,755.9 square inches," bigger than anything in its class (but, of course, not equaling Plymouth's older Barracuda fastbacks)! New "Comfort Stream" ventilation sent forced air through the car when desired and completely refreshened the air with each mile.

In 1968, Mercury temporarily superseded its compact Comet with a new, more luxurious Montego. Mercury also offered the sporty Cyclone line, featuring a super-fast screamer with a hopped-up version of the 427 V-8, which jammed out an amazing 600 to 625 h.p., when driven an average of over 143 m.p.h. by Cale Yarborough in the Daytona 500!

1960s

The illustration contains the following handwritten labels:

1968 MUSTANG "CALIFORNIA SPECIAL" CS/GT COUPE

MORE THAN 4800 OF THESE ASSEMBLED AT FORD'S MILPITAS, CALIF. FACTORY, FROM 10-67 THRU MOST OF 4-68.

ORIGINALLY INTENDED FOR SOUTHERN CALIFORNIA, THE CS/GT BECAME AVAILABLE ELSEWHERE IN THE WEST.

CS/GT PACKAGE INCLUDES = SIDE SCOOPS, SPOILER, QUARTER PANEL EXT., LOWER BACK PANEL, FOG LAMPS, SPECIAL HOOD w. EXT. LOCKS, SPEC. TAPE STRIPES, HORIZONTAL "COUGAR" TYPE TAILLIGHTS, POP-OPEN GAS CAP, ETC.

(A FEW 6s ALSO BLT.) CHOICE OF VARIOUS V8s.

FANS OF THE MUSTANG "CALIFORNIA SPECIAL" WOULD ENJOY THE: GT/CS REGISTRY, (CRAIG ZIELINSKI,) c/o MUSTANG MONTHLY P.O. DRAWER 6320, LAKELAND, FL. 33807.

DETAILS THANKS TO PAUL M. NEWITT OF DAVIS, CALIF.

© News America Syndicate, 1986

1968 Mustang "California Special"

This unusual car was conceived as a "poor man's Shelby Cobra." With its fiberglass body additions and special trim, etc. it did resemble the Shelby Mustangs to a great degree! Yet, its price was not much above the standard Mustang range.

In spite of its mean looks, the "California Special" was not usually powered by the mighty 427 c.i.d. "Cobra" (390 h.p.) Ford V-8 engine. Most of the "California Specials" (CS/FT) used the 289 or the standard 302 V-8.

In addition to the California Special, there was a variation known as the "High Country Special" built for Colorado and the rocky Mountain territory.

All '68 Mustang colors were available, and the special CS/GT stripes were made in black, white, red, dark blue, light blue, or medium green. A few of these CS/GTs had optional black or white vinyl-covered tops.

The Marchal brand rectangular fog lights (in grille) were ruled illegal in California, and Ford dealers soon notified all CS/GT buyers that they would replace them with Lucas Square eight-inch lamps (which were acceptable). The California Special grille was a plain, black grid type with no filled-in center area for mounting a Mustang horse emblem.

The "High Country Special" sold in the Colorado region had a shield decal instead of the "CS/GT" on the side scoop.

The CS/GT or High Country Specials are all of much interest to collectors. Unfortunately, a few have been faked; so today's buyer of such a car must determine that the grille, body decals, etc., are authentic!

1968 Oldsmobile

Because Oldsmobile is America's longest-established existing car company (since 1897!), General Motors' advertising department decided to promote the Olds line as "The Youngmobiles" in 1968. There was nothing "old" about Oldsmobile anymore, and GM sought to erase the image of an Oldsmobile as the car for real estate saleswomen, elderly doctors, and professors.

"Think young. Live young. Go young ... with the new generation of Rockets," advised the 1968 sales brochure. "Rocket" referred to the Rocket overhead-valve V-8 engines used by Oldsmobile so successfully since 1949.

"Brighten your life in a brisk new world of performance. Young movement, young ride, youthful feeling. Stamp your '68 Olds with your own modern image: Choose from a wide selection of transmissions, action accessories, power assists and trim options."

There were numerous Oldsmobile models in 1968: the F-85, Cutlass, Cutlass Supreme, 4-4-2, Delmont 88, Delta 88, Delta Custom, the 98, Toronado, and the Cutlass and VistaCruiser wagons. And, in the late 1960s, so many models and combinations of engines, transmissions, paint colors, upholstery patterns and options were available that the number of possible variations simply boggles the mind.

The Cutlass "S" Holiday Coupe (hardtop) was similar in many ways to the Cutlass Supreme Holiday Coupe, except the Supreme had brightwork rocker panel trim (along the lower edge of the body sides). The "S" touted its sporty-looking pair of louvered panels toward the rear of the hood, unusual to find on a "price leader" model! The "S" sold for $3,076 and weighed 3,282 pounds, while its Cutlass Supreme counterpart was priced at $3,257 and weighed 3,312.

ADVERTISED AS "THE GREAT ONE"
1968 PONTIAC "GTO"
2-DR H/T COUPE (77,704 BUILT)

112" WHEELBASE
G77 x 14 TIRES
3506 LBS.

112 M.P.H.
O TO 60 IN
6.6 SECONDS
9-12 M.P.G.

CONCEALED HEADLIGHTS

new 400 C.I.D. V8 ENGINE
360 H.P. @ 5400 RPM *with* "RAM AIR" OPTION
4.12 x 3.75 BORE *and* STROKE
4-SPEED TRANSMISSION   3.9 TO 1 GEAR RATIO
21½-GAL. GAS TANK   © 1989 North America Syndicate. Inc. All rights reserved.

$3101. *and up*

TAD   5~28

1968 Pontiac GTO

1960s

The GTO joined the Tempest line in 1964. The first Tempest had been the mechanically radical 1961 model with a slant-four front engine that was half of a Pontiac V-8, coupled by a flexible torque-drive tube with an unusual rear transaxle combination!

The GTO won *Motor Trend* magazine's 1968 "Car of the Year" award, the fourth such award for Pontiacs. The '68 GTO had an all-new body, giving it a sportier look with a longer hood and shorter rear deck. The semi-fastback roofline was in style, but some automotive writers criticized its "blind spot" in the rear quarter panel.

The rubberized plastic "Endura" bumper-grille was a new idea for '68. It could absorb a minor dent and return to its original shape on its own, or perhaps with the help of a Pontiac dealer's ser-vice department. Also, it could be painted to match the car, which meant that the flashy chrome look was missing from the front end, for a change.

Concealed headlights were a GTO option. The concealed windshield wipers, new on the "big" Pontiacs of 1967, were now standard on the GTO and optional on other '68 Tempest models.

The two-door had a 112-inch wheelbase in 1968, yet four-door Pontiacs in this compact class had a 116-inch wheelbase.

In addition to the V-8 engines, an overhead-cam six was available. V-8 valves and combustion chambers were redesigned to reduce emissions. In 1968, new U.S. government safety standards meant more smog controls, marker lights, safety padding, improved seat belts, etc.

A SWEDISH-BUILT   "GT" SPORTS CAR
WITH FIBERGLASS
2-PASSENGER
COUPE
BODY
WITH INTEGRAL
ROLL-BAR.

1968 SAAB "SONETT"

WITH GERMAN FORD V-4 OVERHEAD-VALVE ENG.
1498 c.c. DISPLACEMENT (91.4 CU. IN.)
73 HORSEPOWER @ 5000 RPM   PRICE IN U.S.A.:
FRONT-WHEEL-DRIVE   **$3795.**
85" WHEELBASE
WEIGHT = 1720 LBS.
155-15" PIRELLI CINTURATO TIRES
97 M.P.H. TOP SPEED   AVERAGES 27 M.P.G.
0-60 IN 13.7 SEC.

15.8-GAL. FUEL TANK

4-SPEED TRANS.

HELPFUL DATA COURTESY OF DANIEL A. PETIT

SAAB-SCANIA of AMERICA, INC., ORANGE, CT., DISTRIBUTOR IN U.S.A.

1968 SAAB "Sonett"

1960s

Sweden's SAAB automobiles enjoyed a good year in 1968.

For one thing, their first attractively styled model, the 1969 "99" type, was unveiled.

Another big development for '69 was the availability of Saab's new fiberglass-bodied sports car, the Sonett V-4 (also known as the Sonett II, since it used a German Ford V-4 engine rather than the old-type Saab engine of the very first Sonett). During 1967, 455 Sonett II models had been produced. (The first Sonett prototype sports car had been shown to the press on February 4, 1965.)

In addition to manufacturing their own engines, Saab had begun to buy V-4 engines from Ford of Germany. The hood of the Sonett had to be enlarged and "bubbled" in order to squeeze in the V-4 engine.

Road and Track magazine gave good coverage of the Sonett V-4 in their September 1968 issue. They liked the handling and performance of the little car, but thought its looks left much to be desired. Everything seemed tacked on as an afterthought; the styling was not integrated from one end of the car to the other. The seats were awkwardly placed too low in the car, with doorjambs too high off the floor and doors too little. Speaking of doors, there were none on the glove box. Going up a hill, everything usually fell out on the floor!

For 1970, the Sonett II was replaced by a redesigned Sonett III. The final Sonett (III) was the 1974 model. Sonett production ceased in the autumn of 1974.

The illustration reads: 1969 CAMARO "SS" CONVERTIBLE BY CHEVROLET. V8 ENGINES UP TO 396 CID (TO 325 HP) OR 230 CID, 140 HP SIX. 108" wheelbase. 18-GAL. FUEL TANK. TAD 9-9. News America Syndicate © News Group Chicago, Inc., 1984. 3160 lbs. (6). E78 x 14 TIRES. CONCEALED HEADLIGHTS. (THE FIRST CAMARO WAS THE 1967 MODEL.) IN '69, CHEVROLET WAS PLEASED TO REPORT THAT CAMARO WAS TO BE THE "INDIANAPOLIS 500" PACE CAR FOR THE 2ND TIME IN 3 YEARS! FROM $3172. (6-CYL.)

1969 Camaro SS

"**C**amaro, 'The Hugger.' Look how it all hangs together. No tacky gingerbread anywhere.

"The interiors are also more of a delight. The ride is quieter and the car feels more solid than ever before.

"The power range is formidable. Standard V-8 (as of November 1968) is 210 hp (327 cid). (A 307 cid V-8 also appeared.) There's a new one you can order at 255 hp that moves on regular fuel.

"SS engines available up to 325 hp. And for that added SS (Super Sport) sock, you get striping that flanks the nose and then charges up the side, special hood, power disc brakes and wider wheels with wide oval tires to hug the road even tighter.

"Go on, other sportsters, gnash your gears and look tough. Maybe it will help." The preceding text was typical of many Camaro ads.

The headlights, concealed by day, were cleaned by built-in water jets. A new Hurst-linkage four-speed transmission was available. The steering column locked to foil would-be thieves.

The grille was new, parking lights were below bumpers, and the rear end was restyled with a "softer look," bearing the triple horizontal taillight unit in the rear bumper.

Various models of Camaro for '69 included a standard type, SS, RS (Rally Sport), and Z-28. With the variety of colors and options, one could almost order a "custom-built" Camaro from the factory!

Later '69 Camaros could be ordered with a "Super Scoop" hood that carried a mean-looking center bulge and an open, rear-facing vent at the back end, just ahead of the windshield.

1969 Corvair

For 1960, each of the "Big Three" introduced a new compact car. Ford had the new Falcon, and Chrysler-Plymouth the new Valiant. But, Chevy's Corvair was America's one and only rear-engine, air-cooled car at the time.

Before that, America's last attempt to popularize a rear engine had been the much-admired, but ill-fated, Tucker of the late 1940s. The last air-cooled American car of any consequence was the 1934 Franklin.

The Corvair got off to a good start in '60, and, in 1961, trucks and van-wagons were added to the line.

The 1965 Corvair made its only major styling change, so the 1960-64 and the 1965-69 models are the only two basic cycles. True Corvair fans, however, can spot minor yearly differences.

The Corvair was discontinued in 1969 as a result of the wave of unfavorable publicity in the mid-'60s created by Ralph Nader's best-selling book, "Unsafe at Any Speed." Much of the book was a direct and hard-hitting attack on Corvairs, declaring them prone to spinouts and loss of control in various situations due to their odd suspension design and heavy rear end.

GM had already made corrections in the Corvair suspension, etc., but as the 1960s continued, Corvair sales fell off sharply, and the choice of models was systematically narrowed. The compact Chevy II (introduced 1962) and the intermediate-sized Chevelle (Malibu), introduced 1964, were considerably more popular than the rear-engine Corvair.

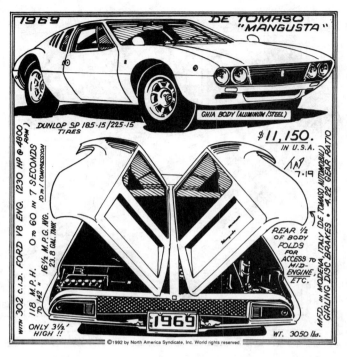

1969 De Tomaso "Mangusta!"

Back in 1969, my wife and I were driving from San Jose to Sacramento. On the hilly portion of the highway east of Livermore, we were passed by an exotic, yellow car with an extremely low-slung body and a pair of huge rectangular backlights (rear windows) on its fastback deck. We had just seen our first De Tomaso Mangusta!

This unusual Italian vehicle was conceived by Alessandro De Tomaso, who was also in charge of Carrozzeria Ghia (Ghia Body Co.) of Turin. The Ghia body was designed by Giorgio Giugiaro, one of Italy's famed stylists. These cars were always scarce. Production averaged but one car a day in 1969.

De Tomaso himself was a native of Argentina, but pursued a career as a racecar driver on the circuits of Europe.

In October 1959, he opened his small factory in Modena, Italy and began to build racecars.

The Mangusta was developed in 1966 and reviewed in the automotive press in 1967. At that time, it used an aluminum-block V-8 engine by De Tomaso. That 4,778-c.c. V-8 delivered 418, 437, or 506 h.p., depending on the carburetor or fuel injection system used. By 1969, the Mangustas had switched to Ford V-8 engines, which were much easier to service, with parts available everywhere.

In a *Road and Track* test, a '69 Mangusta did an easy 118 in a fifth gear run. In an average of four runs through a measured meter, the Mangusta reached 142 m.p.h., more typical of an exotic speed car than a mere 118!

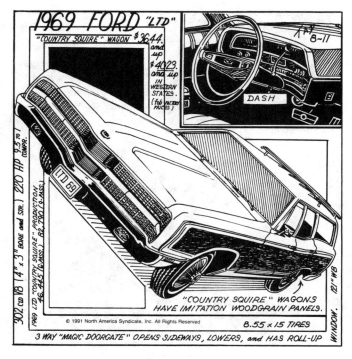

1969 FORD "LTD"

"COUNTRY SQUIRE" WAGON $3644. and up $4023. and up IN WESTERN STATES. (fob factory prices)

DASH

LTD 69

"COUNTRY SQUIRE" WAGONS HAVE IMITATION WOODGRAIN PANELS.

302 cid V8 (4" x 3" BORE and STR.) 220 HP 9.5 to 1 COMPR.

1969 LTD "COUNTRY SQUIRE" PRODUCTION 46,445 (6-PASS.) 82,790 (9-PASS.)

WINDOW. 121" WB

8.55 x 15 TIRES

3 WAY "MAGIC DOORGATE" OPENS SIDEWAYS, LOWERS, and HAS ROLL-UP

© 1991 North America Syndicate, Inc. All Rights Reserved

1969 Ford Ltd

The 1969 Ford LTD was a truly impressive machine, with its broad, roomy body—wide hood and intricate grille—and stylishly concealed headlights. Country Squire station wagons featured the illustrated grained paneling reminiscent of the genuine "woody" wagons of the 1930s and 1940s.

For efficiency and visibility, the instrument panel was placed at the far left, in a protruding unit just above the steering column (see illustration).

The new '69 Fords were unveiled to the public at showrooms on Friday, September 27, 1968. Ford Motor Co. promoted new sales by circulating their annual *Buyer's Digest* as well as a multi-page advertising supplement

in many newspapers and magazines. The *Buyer's Digest* was a colorful catalog of all the various Ford-built cars. Not only were the car prices quoted, but also included were the specific prices of the dozens of "extras" one could order! Air conditioning was one of the costliest options: $388.74, and only available on Fords with V-8 engines.

Speaking of engines, the most powerful 429 c.i.d. V-8 (360 h.p.) was only $237.07 on the option list. You couldn't buy an engine alone for such a low price, but that's what it would cost if substituted for one of the lesser engines in your new Ford. The 390 c.i.d. V-8 (265 h.p.) was only $58.34, if substituted for the 302 c.i.d.

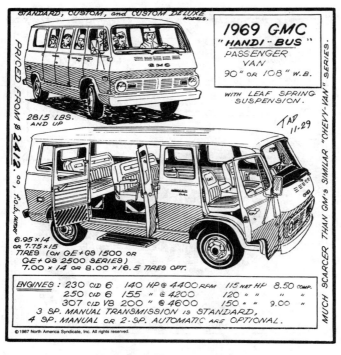

1969 GMC Handi-Bus

T he popularity of Volkswagen's "Microbus" passenger van helped to spawn a variety of new American-built van-wagons in the 1960s. In an earlier *Auto Album*, we showed you Ford's Econoline Station Bus of 1961. Chevrolet followed suit before long with its own series of small "Chevy-Vans." Since Chevrolet and GMC trucks, buses, and vans are all products of General Motors Corp., GMC was bound to introduce its own small van, too. It was a twin to the Chevy-Van, except in name. Chevrolet dealers sold the Chevy-Van; dealers in other GM cars or trucks sold the GMC version.

The illustrated 1969 Handi-Bus had seating for up to eight passengers, "with a variety of seating options" available. The freight version, minus the side windows and extra seating, was known as the Handi-Van. These models were low-slung for their type, having a floor level just two feet above the ground. Available in 90-inch or 108-inch wheelbases, these vans provided up to 256 cubic feet of space in a vehicle measuring a compact 15 3/4 feet in total length! Some Handi-Vans were produced with windows along the right side (but not on the left).

The Handi-Bus came in three models, the Custom and Custom DeLuxe having full interior upholstery and vinyl-coated jute headlining with bright-metal roof bows. The Custom DeLuxe model provided chromed bumpers, bright-metal hub covers, full-length bright-metal side moldings, carpeted driver's area, and other niceties. All Handi-Bus mode's had a padded dash, plus several other safety features.

1960s

1969 Renault 16

Some individuals thought this car was an ugly one when introduced to American shores; though one writer seriously contended that at least the roof would not be damaged if the car should turn upside-down, since the side walls of the Renault 16 rose noticeably above the level of the roof and were capped with tough chrome strips! The sides were built that way to add to body strength.

With rear seats in place, it carried extra passengers. But, rear seats could give way to cargo space when required. And, as on many old Nash cars, front and rear seats could be folded down and joined to form a double bed!

If you think the sides-above-roof look of the 16 is strange, you'll be even more surprised to learn that this car had two wheelbases in one! The left-hand wheelbase was 2 3/8 inches longer than the right-hand wheelbase! Sounds crazy! But, this odd development was made necessary because of the novel design of the torsion-bar suspension, and there was no adverse effect on steering or handling, surprising as that may seem!

Disc front brakes were another advanced feature.

The engine had a cast aluminum block, five main bearings, and a sealed liquid cooling system as featured on many cars since.

The Renault 16 was voted "Car of the Year" following its European introduction during 1965. It beat out such biggies as Rolls-Royce (whose new "Silver Shadow" got second place) and the Oldsmobile Toronado (third place).

"THE FROG-FACED BUBBLE CAR!"
1969 SUBARU "360" 2-DR.
2-CYL., 2-STROKE 21.7 CU. IN. DISPLACEMENT
AIR-COOLED REAR ENGINE (25 HP @ 5500 RPM)
$1,297.□
AT PORT OF ENTRY
MADE IN JAPAN BY FUJI HEAVY INDUSTRIES
(A TINY SUBARU TRUCK AND WINDOW VAN ALSO AVAILABLE)
UP TO 66 MILES PER GALLON!
CRUISES AT 51 MPH
TOP SPEED 68~69
THIS MODEL AVAIL. IN JAPAN SINCE 1958.
IMPORTS TO U.S.A. START 1968.
70.9" WHEELBASE
6.6 GAL GAS TANK
360
9~19
©1993 North America Syndicate, Inc. World rights reserved.

1969 Subaru "360"

This unusual, little car with the cutesy face was available in its native Japan as early as 1958. It was one of many different makes of "bubble cars" (tiny, utilitarian gas savers) that proliferated in Europe and Asia during the later 1950s. However, Subaru was a relative latecomer to the shores of the States, not appearing here before mid-1968.

The weight of the '69 Subaru "360" was only 925 pounds. The tiny two-cylinder engine was linked to a four-speed manual transmission. This type of minicar was not suitable for use on American freeways, which is why the earlier "bubble cars" appearing here did not succeed.

Subaru's "360" had an unusual pair of running-mates: a minuscule flatbed truck and a window van. These utility vehicles are even scarcer than the

"360," which did enjoy a brief flurry of attention in late '68 and '69 because of its low price ($1,297, p.o.e.) and much-touted gas mileage.

For 1970 and 1971, Subaru imports featured the more substantial four-cylinder "Star" series (two-door, four-door, and wagon, which were priced at $1,699, $1,799 and $1,899).

Changes came fast, as Subaru upgraded its wares for American consumption. The 1972 models were known as the "G" series (and GL "Coupe Leone").

Two-cylinder imports such as Honda's '71 and '72 coupes and Subaru's "360" were certainly easy on gas, but too underpowered and toy-like for general American use. Nevertheless, promoters of bubble cars did not give up forever.

1960s

1970 "Automodule"

As a rule, *Auto Album* subjects are old cars or trucks that were factory produced. Many of them are models that are well known or remembered, and others are obscure. Occasionally, we show you a one-of-a-kind "dream car" or an "oddball" vehicle of experimental nature, such as the glass-box 1968 Quasar, or the "plastic polliwog" Fascination, previously seen in the series.

Today's featured car qualifies as an "oddball" in every sense of the word: It's odd, and truly ball shaped!

It was built in France by a "Paris press agent," according to a picture article in a back issue of *Life* magazine.

Among its special features was the Automodule's globular shape, its four, small, outboard wheels (meeting the ground in a "diamond" pattern like the 1945 Gordon Diamond), and the Automodule's ability to "pirouette" on those "caster-like wheels."

The engine type and horsepower remain a mystery in this case. But, because its top speed was about 25 m.p.h., it would appear that the Automodule was propelled by an electric motor.

Hopefully, this strange vehicle has not been dismantled or destroyed. If no longer in the builder's possession, perhaps it is being preserved in some collection or museum—for future generations to stare at.

I would appreciate hearing from anyone who may have further documented information on this amazing vehicle, and/or its whereabouts!

1970 BMW "2800"
SPORTS COUPE 106" WB

TAD
2-3

News America Syndicate
©News Group Chicago, Inc., 1985

125 MILES per HR.

0-60 IN 9.2 SECONDS

192 H.P.

4-SP. TRANS.
(AUTO. TRANS. and
POWER STEER. AVAIL.)

3.54 GEAR RATIO
POWER DISC BRAKES

DR. 70 × 14" TIRES

OVERHEAD CAM, 6-CYL.

MODELS and PRICES

1600	2-DR.	— $2727.
2002	"	— 2982.
2000	4-DR.	— 4140.
2500	"	— 5284.
2800	"	— 6284.
2800 COUPE		— 7480.

PRICE RANGE INCREASED TO $3015. TO $8453.,
(AT PORT OF ENTRY) DURING 1970.

MADE IN GERMANY
BY
BAVARIAN MOTOR WORKS
(SINCE 1928, WHEN
BMW/DIXI CAR INTRODUCED)

170.1 C.I.D. (3.386" × 3.150" BORE and STROKE) 9 TO 1 COMP.

1970 BMW

The BMW 2500 and 2800 models were introduced to the USA during 1969 and were so named because the model numbers approximated the displacements of their six-cylinder engines (in cubic centimeters). They had a six-inch-longer wheelbase than the already-established 1600-2000 four-cylinder series. The complicated shape of the new combustion chambers on the BMW sixes made it impossible for them to meet U.S. emission control standards without any add-on devices!

By the 1970s, Mercedes-Benz was feeling the heat of competition for the luxury import market from BMW. BMW was a tough runner that was growing rapidly in favor among Germany's affluent young executives—and also among American buyers. In the late '60s, the "2002" was particularly liked in the USA because it was a hot performer, yet a very affordable import, priced just a hair below $3,000.

In 1972, the illustrated 2800 Sport Coupe was replaced by the comparable 3.0 CS Coupe, increasing in price from $8,803 in 1972 to $11,730 in 1973.

During the 1970s, the fame of the BMW grew in the USA, as did the price. By 1977, the new six-cylinder BMW 630 CSi Coupe was priced at $23,600. p.o.e., New York. In 1978, this model had become the 633 CSi, by 1980 its price had escalated to $33,530, and by 1983 it reached $39,985!

One consolation to the inflation was that the prices of used BMWs had risen, also. Some BMWs the age of the car in today's feature had become worth more used than they had sold for when new!

1970s

DASH

1970 BUICK

WILDCAT CUSTOM
4-DOOR HARDTOP
12,924 BUILT
$3997. EAST
4892. WEST

4187 LBS.

WITH new
455 CID
V8
370 HP
@
4600 RPM

2.78 GEAR RATIO, with
3-SPEED MANUAL OR
TURBO HYDRAMATIC 400
TRANSMISSIONS AVAILABLE.

124" WHEELBASE   H78×15 TIRES   AAM 9~22

1970 Buick "Wildcat Custom"

Seemingly with a car for everyone, Buick's '70 selection was as follows: Skylark, Skylark 350, Skylark Custom, GS, GS 455, Sportwagon, LeSabre, LeSabre Custom, LeSabre 455, Wildcat Custom (illustrated), Estate Wagon, Electra 225, Electra Custom, and the Riviera!

The Wildcat Custom featured "AccuDrive" suspension, a major refinement that enabled the car to "track straight and literally claw its way around corners," as the 1970 Buick sales catalog put it.

Four-door hardtops (without the upper center pillar between doors) are becoming scarce these days. They were legislated out of production during the early 1970s in a government safety campaign. By the mid-1970s, all new sedans were required by law to have full-height center pillars and greater body reinforcement.

This 1970 Buick Wildcat Custom was one of the last cars of GM's big models to require premium (leaded Ethyl) fuel. In 1971, seeing the handwriting on the wall regarding the coming of unleaded fuel, GM began building new '71 models that were advertised to run on either regular leaded or unleaded!

Readers often ask me what they can do about obtaining the proper fuel for their high-powered '50s and '60s collector's cars, which were designed to use premium leaded Ethyl gasoline. Fortunately, there is a solution: Most auto supply stores now sell a liquid leaded compound that can be mixed in the tank with modern unleaded fuel. Using the additive, you can change unleaded gas into something approximating the old-fashioned Ethyl that is now so hard to find.

1970s

*"MONTE CARLO" COUPE $ 3123.**
(400 or 454 C.I.D. V8s ALSO AVAIL.)
* MFR'S. SUGGESTED RETAIL PRICE

1970 CHEVROLET
WITH 350 C.I.D. V8 (250 HP @ 4800)
9 TO 1 COMPRESSION

COLORS: COBI BEIGE · TUXEDO BLK.
ASTRO BLUE · FATHOM BLUE
CHAMPAGNE GOLD · MISTY TURQUOISE
GREEN MIST · FOREST GREEN
CORTEZ SILVER
CRANBERRY RED
W/3 SURPRISE
CLASSIC WHITE
2-TONES

116" WHEELBASE   G/8 × 15 TIRES
20-GALLON FUEL TANK

CHEVY'S
FIRST
MONTE CARLO!

2-26-84

© Field Enterprises, Inc., 1984

1970 Chevrolet "Monte Carlo"

"On the move: the Chevrolet '70s." It was bound to come: a special-series personal luxury coupe for Chevrolet, comparable in appeal to what GM's four other divisions had already been offering.

Pontiac started it in '62 with the Grand Prix. Then, in '63, Buick introduced its Riviera luxury coupe. For '66, came the Olds Toronado, and for '67, Cadillac's Eldorado. Each of these featured front-wheel drive.

Chevrolet's entry in the luxury coupe field came for 1970 with the all-new Monte Carlo. It appeared on September 18, 1969, with many of Chevrolet's other 1970 models, but captured most of the attention! This was a conventional rear-wheel-drive car, but it reeked of elegance and had the longest hood of any "Chevy" yet built! The name Monte Carlo was a masterful choice, for it suggested the luxury and excitement of the French Riviera.

Instead of the quadruple headlights so popular in that era, the Monte Carlo sported two, large, simple-looking, high-intensity headlights, surrounded by generous spaces of sheet metal.

And what about chrome? A Monte Carlo advertisement (*Life*, October 3, 1969) compared excess chrome to "cheap costume jewelry," and declared that Monte Carlo would avoid such "tinsel."

Quality and quietness were emphasized in this tasteful new car, with all sound-admitting "holes" sealed. The plastic instrument panel was finished in imitation Carpathian-burled elm wood grain.

1970s

AN <u>ALL-NEW</u> MODEL FOR 1970 !
1970 DODGE "CHALLENGER"
R/T 2-DR. HARDTOP $3226. f.o.b.
($3649. WEST COAST)

W: 3405 lbs.

SPECIAL OPTIONAL SUSPENSION PACKAGES

110" WHEELBASE or 15" TIRE SIZES AVAIL.
VARIOUS 14" or 15" TIRE SIZES AVAIL.
18-GALLON FUEL TANK
150-MPH SPEEDOMETER !

9
DIFFERENT
ENGINE
CHOICES !!
225 cid 6 (145 HP)
318 cid V8 (230 HP)
340 cid V8 (275 HP)
3 TYPES of 383 cid V8s
MAGNUM 440 cid V8 (375 HP)
440 cid 6-PACK V8 (390 HP)
or HEMI 426 cid V8 (425 HP)
3 SP. or 4-SP. MANUAL or
3 SP. TORQUEFLITE AUTOMATIC TRANS.
AVAILABLE
AN 3-28

STD.
F70/14
TIRES ON
R/T MODEL

1970
SLOGAN: "**YOU** COULD BE
DODGE MATERIAL !"

©1993 North America Syndicate, Inc. World rights reserved.

1970 Dodge Challenger

In pony car tradition, the new Challenger came with a very long hood, short deck, and a low profile. Most 1970 Challengers were two-door hardtops, but a R/T convertible was available. One of Challenger's popular colors was a purple known as "Plum Crazy!"

Standard engines: 225 c.i.d. six or 318 c.i.d. V-8, with seven larger V-8s optional. Two modern touches were concealed windshield wipers (below the rear upturned lip of the hood) and vent-less, one-piece door windows. Steering wheel was finished in simulated walnut, and floors were covered with deep-pile carpeting.

Letter designation "R/T" stood for "road or track," and "SE" meant "special edition."

In accordance with government safety standards, a four-way emergency flasher Hazard Warning System was standard equipment, as were front shoulder belts in the two-door hardtops.

As the 1970 sales brochure put it, "Take a studied look. Let all the differences start happening. The stance: It's wide for greater stability and security. The doors: Deeply molded and indented. Thicker, with side-impact protection. Flush door handles, inside and out. The unusual but comfortable bucket seats with built-in head restraints. Challenger comes nine different ways. You can order the Challenger R/T and power it up with a race-ready 440 Magnum V-8 or the new 440 Six Pack V-8 (with triple two-barrel carburetors).

"Or go formal and drive 'the little limousine'—Challenger SE—with rich touches like vinyl-covered formal roof, rich vinyl bucket seats, and matching door trim. No matter which Challenger gets to you, it's designed to compete with the pony cars."

GALAXIE 500

1970 FORD

1970 ENGINE
CHOICES :
240 CID 6
(150 HP)
302 CID V8
(220 HP)
351 CID V8
(250 HP)
390 CID V8
(265 HP)
429 CID V8
(320 OR 360 HP)

121" W.B.
3586 LBS.
$**3573**. UP (WEST)
$ 3094. fob

© News America Syndicate. 1986

DEAR
FRIENDS :
HAVE A HAPPY
THANKSGIVING!

F 78 x 15"
TIRES

1970

TAY
11-23

SELECT SHIFT CRUISE-o-MATIC TRANS. AVAILABLE

THESE SONGS WERE HITS IN 1970, WHEN THIS CAR WAS NEW :
RAINDROPS KEEP FALLING ON MY HEAD • WITHOUT LOVE •
RAINY NIGHT IN GEORGIA • BRIDGE OVER TROUBLED WATER •
HEY THERE, LONELY GIRL • EVERYTHING IS BEAUTIFUL •
TENNESSEE BIRDWALK • CLOSE TO YOU • UNITED WE STAND •
THE WONDER OF YOU • WE'VE ONLY JUST BEGUN • SNOWBIRD

1970 Ford Galaxie 500

By 1970, there was a proliferation of fifty Ford models! In addition to the Falcon, the new Maverick, the Fairlane, Torino, Mustang, and the Thunderbird, there were more types of "standard" Fords with varying grille designs and styling! In ascending order, these were: Custom, Custom 500, Galaxie 500, XL, LTD, and LTD Brougham.

For 1970, quiet luxury was emphasized; Ford engineers were said to have made possible an almost totally quiet ride by "designing quietness in," so to speak—a far cry from the noisy, rough-riding early Ford V-8s of the mid-1930s!

There were two varieties of Galaxie 500 two-door hardtops: the illustrated Formal Roof hardtop (with vinyl-covered top) and the semi-fastback "Sports roof" type.

Optional equipment included Select Shift automatic transmission (which could be manually controlled when desired); automatic speed control; tilt steering wheel; Stereo-Sonic tape/AM radio; electric rear window defroster; Select Aire conditioner; power front disc brakes; trailer hitch and connections, and more!

The final year for Ford's compact Falcon was 1970, as the Maverick was taking its place. But, strangely, there were two completely different Falcons that year: first, an early '70 *small* Falcon, which resembled the '69. This was soon dropped, and later replaced by a *big* 70 1/2 Falcon, which looked like the Fairlane and Torino models! This '70 1/2 Falcon is a scarce car.

As for 1970 American-built cars in general, they have already passed their low point in value and are "coming back." Good specimens appeal to today's collectors!

RARE 1970½ FALCON!
THE "BIG" FALCON, SIMILAR TO FORD'S 1970
FAIRLANE / TORINO SERIES (AND THE LAST
OF THE FALCONS!)

WISHING
YOU A
SAFE AND
HAPPY
4TH OF JULY!

67,053 BUILT =
(26,071 2-DRS.,
30,443 4-DRS.,
and 10,539 WAGONS)

6 CYL.
$2827.
and up

2 DR.
3242 lbs.

TAP
7~2

AVAILABLE ENGINES : 250 CID 6 (155 HP);
302 CID V8 (220 HP); 351 CID V8s (251 OR 300 HP);
429 CID V8 (380 HP); 429 CID "COBRA" V8 (370 HP)
117" WB (114" ON WAGON)   E78/G78 × 14 TIRES

22 GAL. GAS TANK (18 IN CALIF.)

© 1989 North America Syndicate, Inc. All rights reserved.

1970 1/2 Falcon

Ford Motor Co. introduced its first Falcon late in '59, for the 1960 season. Falcon's competition in the compact line was Studebaker's Lark (introduced for '59), Chevrolet's Corvair, and Plymouth's Valiant (both making their debuts for '60).

Falcon got a minor facelift each year, but remained a simple compact car. After 1968, Falcon's styling didn't change. During 1969, Ford tried to drop the Falcon—since they had introduced its replacement, the 1970 Maverick, in April 1969. Also, locking steering columns were newly required by government safety standards, and Ford executives didn't want to spend the money to bring their "outdated" compact up to standard.

An early 1970 Falcon (available in 1969) was virtually unchanged from before, and then suddenly it was dropped. Many people squawked, so Ford Motor Co. hastily tacked the Falcon name on a larger car based on the newer intermediates, Fairlane and Torino. This new "big" Falcon was officially known (even in showroom literature) as the "1970 1/2" model. It, too, was available for only a few months, with less than 70,000 sold.

For 1971, Ford's compact Maverick would be joined by a new subcompact Pinto. The Torino would continue, but there was no place in 1971 for a Falcon.

Few people are aware that these 1970 1/2 Falcons ever existed. They were scarcely advertised, and I didn't even have a sales brochure for one until a few years later.

Should you see one of the 1970 1/2 Falcons, you might mistake it for a Torino. The resemblance is very close, but the Falcon has less side chrome.

A HOT-PERFORMING "COLLECTORS' CAR!"
1970 "HEMI-'CUDA"
(PLYMOUTH BARRACUDA)

108" WHEELBASE
FROM $3527.06
3.23 TO 4.1 GEAR RATIOS

GOODYEAR
F70 x 14 TIRE SIZE

WITH "SHAKER HOOD"
AND QUIVERING
COLD AIR GRABBER

TAP
1-1-89

HAPPY NEW YEAR!

9 TO 17 M.P.G.

340, 383, 440, OR 426 CID "HEMI" V8 ENGINE 8-BBL
275 HP @ 5000 TO 425 HP @ 5000 RPM

1970 "Hemi-'Cuda"

High-powered "muscle" ponycars of the late 1960s and early 1970s are much in demand—highly prized by collectors who remember them from their youth. But, good, clean, original condition specimens are hard to find! Most "muscle cars" had the wheels virtually run off them before they were two or three years old. Their young drivers demanded much from them, and some couldn't take it for long!

This is how the new 'Cuda was described in that catalog: "...in the beginning, most ponycars were designed to be little more than personalized compacts. And despite the demands of car enthusiasts for something gutsier, many ponycars still cling to their spindly-legged ancestry.

"We figured it was time someone gave equal time to the ponycar's dark side: its chassis—the suspension, brakes, driveline and so on. We figured our ponycar ought to begin life as nothing less than a bona fide Sports/GT car.

"The result of our efforts is called simply, 'Cuda."

All 'Cudas carried crash bracing that was designed on the same principle as the roll cages in Trans-Am and Grand National race cars—offering protection from side impacts as well as from rollovers.

'Cuda had a long list of special high-performance features and options. One could literally create a custom street racer from the equipment available!

If you own an older muscle car and are thinking of having it repainted, be sure that the original decals are not obliterated unless they can be replaced. These cars are worth considerably more when they bear all the original decals. Some of the old decals are unavailable.

1970s

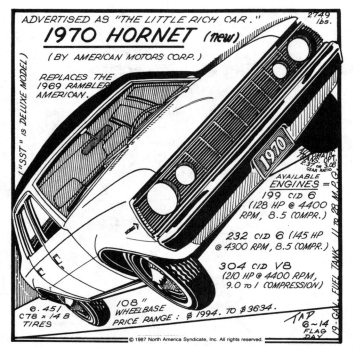

ADVERTISED AS "THE LITTLE RICH CAR."

1970 HORNET (new)

(BY AMERICAN MOTORS CORP.)

REPLACES THE 1969 RAMBLER AMERICAN.

("SST" IS DELUXE MODEL)

2749 lbs.

AUTOMATIC TRANS. OPT. 2.37 or 3.08 GEAR RATIO

AVAILABLE
ENGINES =
199 CID 6
(128 HP @ 4400 RPM, 8.5 COMPR.)

232 CID 6 (145 HP @ 4300 RPM, 8.5 COMPR.)

304 CID V8 (210 HP @ 4400 RPM, 9.0 TO 1 COMPRESSION)

19 - GAL. FUEL TANK

6.451
C78 x 14 B
TIRES

108"
WHEELBASE
PRICE RANGE : $ 1994.70 $3634.

TAP
6 ~ 14
FLAG
DAY

1970 Hornet

"The car you're looking at is the American Motors Hornet. It took about 40 million dollars, three years, and one million man hours to get it to this page. It's an entirely new car idea. The Hornet is the first car in America designed to prove that the word small doesn't automatically stand for cheap." This is a quote from American Motors' 1970 catalog.

AMC had a banner year in 1970! It was the company's first full year as the new builder of the famous civilian and Army Jeep (AMC purchased Jeep from Kaiser Motors in 1969). The Hornet was a new car for 1970 and so was AMC's, soon-to appear, 1970 1/2 Gremlin.

The Hornet name was revived from the early 1950s, when Hudson had applied it to its high-performance big six.

The 1970 Hornet had vent-less front windows, a black anodized aluminum grille, anti-theft single lock for transmission, ignition, and steering column, and twin ball-joint suspension.

When coupled with the Shift Command automatic transmission, the 145 h.p. big six was upped to 155 h.p.

Variable-ratio power steering and Twin-Grip differential were optional.

Other AMC cars available in 1970 were the Javelin, AMX, Rebel, and the top-of-the-line Ambassador.

In the next few years following 1970, the Matador, Concord, Spirit, Eagle, etc. came into being.

1970 1/2 Oldsmobile Cutlass S Rallye 350

"**W**ouldn't it be nice to have an escape machine? Oldsmobile: Escape from the Ordinary." That was Oldsmobile's sales slogan for 1970, and several Oldsmobile magazine advertisements that year depicted frustrated workers in humdrum jobs, longing to escape from it all in a new Olds!

Then there were those strange "other" Oldsmobile ads! High-performing models (like the one illustrated) were often shown in comical-looking posed ads with the seemingly mad scientist "Dr. Oldsmobile" and his weird crew of misanthropic stooges.

The March 1970 *True* magazine carried a more restrained Dr. Oldsmobile ad, without the oddball assistants, showing the new Sebring Yellow and Black Rallye 350 (illustrated). Some of its features: four-barrel carburetor and air induction with dual scoops on the fiberglass hood, new urethane-coated

yellow bumpers, blacked-out sport grille, heavy-duty "FE-2" suspension (developed from the 4-4-2 type) with front and rear stabilizer bars, superwide G70 x 14-inch bias belted blackwall tires on Sebring Yellow sport wheels, custom sport steering wheel, sports-styled outside mirrors with remote control of left-hand mirror, Rallye 350 decals, and more!

The Rallye 350 option was available on three models: F-85 Sports Coupe, Cutlass S Holiday Coupe, or Cutlass S Sports Coupe.

As for Dr. Oldsmobile, he appeared (more sedately and unaccompanied by monstrous assistants) in a February 1971 *Motor Trend* ad, featuring a blue "4-4-2 W-30." But, the fun and games were over by 1972, when tough government antismog restrictions and devices took the muscle out of the muscle cars and drastically cut horse power on most new models, across the board!

1970 PLYMOUTH "FURY" GRAN COUPE
120" W.B.
STANDARD EQUIPMENT = V-8 ENG.,
AIR CONDITIONING, AUTO. TRANS.,
POWER STEERING, TINTED GLASS,
POWER BRAKES, VINYL ROOF,
AM RADIO, WHITE SIDEWALL
TIRES,
AND MORE !

STANDARD
3/8 CID V8 has
230 HP @ 4400 RPM.

340, 383, 428 and
440 CID V8s ALSO AVAIL.,
WITH UP TO 425 HP !!
PLYMOUTHS PRICED FROM $2409 (DUSTER 6) TO $4177 (SPT. SUB'N. WAGON V8)

F78/G78 x 15 TIRES

TAP
6~19

1970 Plymouth "Fury"

Chrysler Corporation's Plymouth Division presented an amazing variety of models and nameplates in 1970! They'd built the Valiant (in the compact field), and for 1970, it was joined by the new Duster and the performance oriented Duster 340 (V-8).

Then there were the hot "pony cars," the Barracuda (since '64), and the new 'Cuda.

Intermediate-sized Plymouths included the Belvedere, Satellite, Sports Satellite, the Road Runner, the GTX, and the dramatic-looking Road Runner "Superbird" with the face of a Corvette and the hind end of a P-38 plane! Truly, the Superbird is a very valuable and sought-after collector's car, with its unusual twin tail and its blazing performance!

The "big" Plymouth was the Fury series (in all its variations, such as Fury I, Fury II, Fury III, Sports Fury, Fury Gran Coupe, etc.).

"Plymouth Makes It!" was a 1970 sales slogan. Indeed, Plymouth did make it, as far as variety was concerned!

The Fury Gran Coupe was advertised for its many standard features, most of which were not included on its rivals, Ford LTD or Chevrolet Caprice. Yet the Gran Coupe was priced $233 less than the LTD and $348 less than the Caprice, according to Plymouth advertising.

Since the 1970s and 1980s, there's been a strident trend among most manufacturers (of all products) to "knock" the competition in advertising. Back in the old days, Plymouth used "comparison charts," to list its features not found in competing makes, but the rival brands were only identified as "Low-Priced Car 2" and "Low-Priced Car 3." That was a gentle way of comparing.

1970 THUNDERBIRD

OPTIONS INCLUDE AM / FM STEREO, POWER WINDOWS, TILT STEERING WHEEL ETC. 117"-WB 4-DR. ALSO MFD. BY FORD MOTOR CO. (SINCE '55)

4360 lbs.

$5531.

LANDAU 2-DR.

429 CID V8 ENGINE 7 TO 18 M.P.G. 360 H.P. @ 4600

215 R15 TIRES

TAP 7-22

News America Syndicate © News Group Chicago, Inc., 1984

1970 Thunderbird

"1970: Year Of The Great Birds" "There have been great Birds before. But none like this Bird. This Bird flies higher. Sweeps longer. Rides lower. Stands wider. Takes you where others don't go. With standards others charge extra for: Power steering. Power ventilation. Power front disc brakes. Radial-ply tires. 429-CID V8 and Cruise-O-Matic transmission. No Bird before has ever been so dependable. Its systems are backed by space-age technology. Its smooth ride was designed by computer.

"And no Bird before has given you so much choice. Bench seats or buckets. Two doors or four. Sunroof or no. The luxury list goes on and on. See your Ford dealer and this rarest of all Birds, today." Thus read the copy of a Thunderbird advertisement in the early spring of 1970.

Incidentally, an AM radio and a clock were also included as standard equipment. The two-door Landau with vinyl top is illustrated, but a model with plain, painted top could be had, for less.

The most distinctive styling feature of the new 1970 Thunderbird was the long, pointed hood with its protruding front center grille section. The long "nose" was extremely impressive, but highly impractical. Several owners reported that minor end-to-end parking bumps were causing grille damage resulting in three-figure repair bills. And, the rear seat lacked sufficient leg room and head room.

Some thought the '70 T-bird looked too "GM-ish," with the long-nosed look reminding many of a Pontiac Grand Prix. The array of power accessories was luxurious when new, but created many annoying electrical problems as time passed.

1971 Cricket

"Chirp! Chirp! It's the Little Car that Can!" This was the new Cricket for 1971, brought to the U.S.A. by Chrysler Corp. from their Hillman affiliate in Great Britain. Volkswagen had already achieved great success with its world-famous Beetle. Hudson and AMC had each offered a Hornet, and Dodge had recently offered a Super Bee. So why not another insect, if that's what the people demanded? (Still, some people didn't like insects and might shy away from certain bug names.)

Regardless, Cricket was the chosen name. Hillman was no longer exporting cars to the U.S.A. since the 1960s, but they were able to supply a "captive import" for Plymouth dealers in 1971 and 1972, since Plymouth had no sub-compact car of its own to compete with Ford's new Pinto and Chevrolet's new Vega.

As Hillman supplied the Cricket to Plymouth dealers, Mitsubishi of Japan simultaneously supplied its Colt to Dodge dealers. The Colt was a greater success; its overhead-cam engine was peppier-and-quieter. The British Cricket was an adequate car, but it offered no new and exciting ideas, and when fitted with an automatic transmission it seemed "gutless."

During 1971, Cricket only came as a four-door sedan. In the spring of 1972, a station wagon became available; but it was too little, too late. Dodge Colts sold well and were continued, but in '73 the Cricket was no longer imported, though it was still available in Puerto Rico in the later 1970s.

1971 FORD "LTD" 2-DR. HARDTOP (BROUGHAM TYPE)

4079 LBS.

WITH 351, 390, 400 OR 429 CID V8

$4116. PLUS TAX, LICENSE, EXTRAS

121" WB / F78 G78 × 15 TIRES / 240 TO 360 HP

LEARN HOW TO IDENTIFY OLDER CARS. CLIP and SAVE "AUTO ALBUM" EACH WEEK.

1972 FORD FRONT END, SHOWING DIFFERENCE.

News America Syndicate © News Group Chicago, Inc., 1985

1971 Ford LTD

At a glance, the 1971 and 1972 Fords may look very much alike. Both have long hoods and narrow, pointed grilles. But, as you'll note by the illustration, the grille of the '71 is *above* the bumper, which dips near the middle. The '72, however, has a straight-across bumper and the lower part of the grille is visible through an opening in that bumper. Next time you see one of these Fords on the road, take a good look at the front end—with this identifying tip in mind.

Prospective '71 Ford buyers were advised to "Take a quiet break" with Ford, because Fords were engineered for quiet smoothness at all speeds. One Ford ad went so far as to warn readers how "Studies show that excessive noise can bring on anxiety, bizarre body sensations, and personality disintegration. For fast, fast relief … the quiet '71 Ford LTD!"

Extras included SelectShift automatic transmission; air conditioning with automatic temperature control; Tilt steering wheel adjustable to five positions; Fingertip Speed Control; High Back seats; Stereo-sonic tape system with front and rear speakers; cornering lights; etc.

All LTD's for '71 included, as standard equipment, a 351 c.i.d. V-8; front power disc brakes; new protective steel guard rails in doors; nylon carpeting; Uni-Lock safety harness; and a self-regulating electric clock. As of October 1970, there were eighteen new '71 models of Ford from which to choose, including an all-new luxury LTD convertible (replacing the convertible in the discontinued XL series). The LTD convertible was to become a collector's item, available only in 1972.

1970s

1971 Lamborghini "Countach" LP-600

This new car was so radically advanced in 1971 that it still looks like a future design today!

The founder, Ferrucio Lamborghini, was born April 28, 1916, in a little farming community in Italy (namely, Renazzo di Cento, in the province of Ferrara). During World War II, he was a mechanic for the Italian Air Force on the island of Rhodes. Then he was captured by the British and held as a prisoner of war until hostilities had ended.

Back home in Italy in 1946, Lamborghini converted surplus war vehicles into "Carioca" farm machines. In 1947, he modified a little Fiat Topolino for racing, and he also souped up several other Fiats, on special order. In 1949, he founded Lamborghini Trattici and built farm tractors for many years—even after he began manufacturing autos, in 1963.

The 350 GTV (1963) and 350 GT (1964) were among his earliest performance-car creations. In 1963, Mr. Lamborghini declared, "In the past I have bought some of the most famous gran turismo cars, and in each of these magnificent machines I have found faults. Too hot, or uncomfortable, or not sufficiently fast, or not perfectly finished. Now I want to make a GT car without faults. Not a technical bomb. Very normal, very conventional, but a perfect car."

In 1974, the illustrated Countach went into regular production, somewhat modified from the pilot model.

The interior of the Countach was a great departure from the ordinary, from its unique steering-wheel hub, its various coded lights and switches, to its left-mounted illuminated diagram of the complicated tubular chassis.

1971 MERCEDES-BENZ
LP-1113 DIESEL TRUCK
CAB-OVER-ENGINE TYPE

M-B HWY. TRUCKS NEWLY AVAIL. IN U.S.A.

WITH 6-CYL. MERCEDES-BENZ 346 CID DIESEL ENG.

12-TON GROSS VEHICLE WEIGHT

© 1990 North America Syndicate, Inc. All Rights Reserved

4~1~90

MADE IN GERMANY.

M-B ——BUILT THE FIRST DIESEL TRUCK (1923)

1971 Mercedes-Benz Truck

In addition to luxury cars—for which they are most famous—Mercedes-Benz has also built, for many years, trucks of various types, and even a passenger van.

However, Mercedes-Benz trucks are not commonplace in the United States and were not imported here regularly until 1970, just before this 1971 model appeared. Even then, they were available only in the East.

In answer to my written inquiry in 1977, Mercedes-Benz of North America informed me that their trucks, at that time, were "sold only in 23 Eastern states and in some selected areas in the Midwest." With their letter, they also sent me a brochure on their 1977 conventional trucks (with hoods in front), which then included the diesel-powered L-1113, L-1116, and L-1316.

When Mercedes-Benz advertised the 1971 LP-1113 cab-over-engine truck (as illustrated), they used the following caption: "Mercedes-Benz introduces the two-penny mile to America." The advertisement, a two-page spread in the July 1970 *Trucking Business* magazine, stated that parts and labor maintenance expenses amounted to no more than two cents a mile. As for the 346 c.i.d. diesel engine, "It gets upward of 10 miles per gallon" and should last "200,000 miles or more."

Mercedes-Benz designed, developed, tested, manufactured, and guaranteed every major component in their trucks, so that "you'll never find 'a little bit of this and a little bit of that.'" Our trucks are pure Mercedes-Benz."

1970s

A BRITISH FAVOURITE!

IMPORTED BY BRITISH LEYLAND MOTORS (U.S. OFFICE=LEONIA N.J.)

$3259. AT PORT OF ENTRY

1971
MG-B
SPORTS CAR
105 M.P.H.
0 TO 60 IN
11.8 SECONDS

©1992 by North America Syndicate, Inc. World rights reserved.

STEEL BODY w. ALUMINUM HOOD
FRONT DISC BRAKES

155" x 14" TIRES
4 CYL. O.H.V.
1798 cc 92 HP @ 5200 RPM
8.8 COMPRESSION
4 SP. TRANS.
14 GAL. FUEL TANK
FINAL MODEL: 1980

109.8 CID ENGINE
3.909 a.r.

(82" W.B. 62 HP "MG MIDGET" SERIES ALSO AVAIL.)

1971 MG-B Sports Car

MG stands for "Morris Garages," and the MG—originally a byproduct of the Morris—has been around since the mid-1920s. The wire-wheeled, 1931-styled MG "TC" roadster was exported to the United States after World War II and became universally popular.

The TC was replaced by the disc-wheeled TD in 1950. During '54, the TD was in turn replaced by the TF, which had headlights sunken in the fenders and other minor changes.

For '56, the streamlined MG-A made its bow. In '63, the MG-B appeared, following the introduction of the smaller MG Midget the previous year. (I might add that over the years, various small sedans were added to, and pulled from, the MG line.)

The 1971 MG-B was available as a roadster (illustrated) or as a GT coupe.

A 12-volt electrical system was used, as on other cars, but according to a 1971 review, a pair of six-volt batteries were linked together (instead of one 12-volt type)!

Average fuel consumption: 25 M.P.G.

On May 27, 1971, the 250,000th MG-B was produced. To celebrate the occasion, MG dealers sponsored a drawing to give car No. 250,000 away to some lucky winner. The drawing, naturally, brought more prospects into MG showrooms.

At the 1970s progressed, the cost of the MG-B soared! By 1977, the price was $5,150, and by 1980 it was $7,950. The 1980 model was the final one. But, in 1981, magazine advertisements were still being seen for the previous year's leftover cars.

The MG name continued on other models, in England.

1971 PLYMOUTH "ROAD RUNNER"
new SHORTER 115" WB
new BODY

SOME WITH PAINTED LOOP BUMPER GRILLE.

RR 1971

A POPULAR "MUSCLE CAR"
STANDARD ENGINE = 383 CID V8
300 GROSS HP @ 4800 RPM (250 NET HP)
3-SP MANUAL TRANSMISSION with FLOOR SHIFT
3.23 GEAR RATIO
TORSION BAR FRONT SUSPENSION and
FRONT STABILIZER BAR. LEAF REAR SPRINGS
F 70 x 14 TIRES (G70 x 14 AVAIL.)
(6" x 14" RIMS) 11" BRAKE DRUMS
(DISC FRONT BRAKES OPTIONAL)
3640 lbs. (440 6 bbl. or HEMI V8 OPT.)
$3535.
and up, f.o.b.

TAD
11-4

0 TO 60 MPH in 6.7 SECONDS.

1971 Plymouth Road Runner

During the late 1960s, compact, high-powered V-8 "muscle cars" were at the crest of their popularity. After 1971, however, it was tough sledding for V-8 screamers, because strict new safety and fuel-economy standards pointed the way to smaller cars, smaller engines, and much less horsepower. Chevy's Corvettes and Camaros and Pontiac's Firebirds and Trans-Ams were among the very few performance cars still in production after the other "tigers" had been de-fanged or killed off.

In 1971, Plymouth advertising referred to its lineup of muscle cars as its "Rapid Transit System," and in addition to the illustrated Road Runner there were also the Duster 340 and 'Cuda (with 108-inch wheelbase), the 115-inch wheelbase GTX, and the 120-inch wheelbase Sport Fury GT.

Performance V-8 engine choices came in 340, 383, 440, or special Hemi 426 c.i.d. sizes, with horsepower ratings as much as 425 at 5,000 rpm (in the Hemi).

Plymouth's Road Runner had been introduced during the 1968 season, and it derived its name from the clever bird in the "Road Runner" series of movie and TV cartoons who continually out-smarted the pursuing coyote. The animated cartoon "road runner" bird made a "beep-beep" noise, and this style horn was also adapted to some degree by Plymouth for its car of the same name. "It still goes beep-beep," proclaimed a 1971 ad, which continued, "And it still has fat tires, high-flow cylinder heads, four-barrel carburetion and heavy duty brakes and suspension."

For '71, rear track (distance across, between the rear wheels) was length-ened 3.2 inches for improved stability.

1970s

1971 Vega

The Chevrolet Vega (introduced for 1971) had an all-new, long-stroke aluminum engine. The cylinder head was of iron, but the entire block, even the piston cylinders, was of an aluminum-silicon alloy which was considered tough enough that cylinder sleeves were unnecessary.

Vega was produced in a semi-automated factory near Lordstown, Ohio, and new robot welders helped to put the car together. The car was highly touted by John Z. De Lorean, who at that time was general manager of GM's Chevrolet Division.

One of the first problems came from the car washes! Shock absorbers and under-car housing were being torn off. Also, exhaust pipes were in danger. Most car wash conveyors required 5 1/2 inch clearances, but Vega's was only 4 1/2 inches. By cutting off the lower part of a bolt on the rear shock absorbers, the clearance could be raised, and dealers were advised by special bulletin to make this alteration on their unsold stock.

The aluminum-block engine proved to be other than trouble-free. And, while most of the workers were earning about $4.50 an hour plus fringe benefits (quite adequate by 1971 standards), they hated the fast pace, the pressure, and the monotony of the semi-automated Vega assembly line. This mounting pressure fanned the labor strife, which soon made Lordstown—and the Vega—notorious!

Eventually the labor problems were somewhat resolved, and in 1974 the Vega received a front-end facelift and many improvements, in spite of original plans to leave it unchanged through 1975.

1970s

1972 Capri

Back in the early 1950s, the Capri name designated a series of Lincolns. The name obviously refers to the Isle of Capri, known as a Mediterranean point of interest to wealthy tourists.

In the July 1963 issue of *Motor Sport* magazine, a British Ford Capri GT was described and illustrated, though it bore only a superficial resemblance to the German-built model you see here. By 1969, the British Ford Capri 1600 GT XLR Coupe was more like the illustrated car. Originally, this British Capri was to be called the Colt, but Mitsubishi of Japan wound up getting the use of that name. The Colt/Capri had some characteristics of the original Mustang, and in 1969, Capri sold well overseas: 70,000 were built in England, and 150,000 in Germany.

In 1970, when the Capri was first imported to the USA, the 1,600-cc.

four-cylinder English Ford engine and four-speed English Ford transmission would be used, but the car would be built in Ford's German factory at Cologne, because there was more space for production.

The sport instrument panel was more elaborate than the standard type shown here, with additional gauges. In 1970, in the USA, the Capri was advertised as priced "from under $2,300"; but with inflation, the price was up to "under $2,600" in 1972.

The restyled Capri II was introduced for 1975, but by March of that year it was designated a "1976" model. For 1979, Capris were redesigned again, with those sold in the USA now being built in the USA.

Sales declined during the 1980s, however, and the Capri was discontinued here during 1986.

1972 Dodge Polara

I n the automotive world, 1972 may be remembered as the year when most American cars were "de-tuned" and decreased in horsepower by various anti-smog devices and low-lead fuel requirements. But, 1972 was a great year for Dodge cars and trucks, as sales set new records.

Dodge offered an amazing variety of vehicles in 1972. They wooed the compact-car buyer with low-priced Dart, Demon, Swinger, and Swinger Special series, as well as with the Japanese-built Dodge Colt by Mitsubishi.

Then there was the Dodge Challenger, as well as the Rallye, Charger, and Coronet in the intermediate line.

The big Dodges were represented by the Polara (illustrated) and the Monaco (which had concealed headlights).

In addition, there was a very popular line of Dodge freight and passenger vans. Tradesman vans were usually designed for cargo hauling, but were sometimes customized for personal use. The Sportsman passenger vans were designed for family use, with full rows of side windows, and they were considerably roomier than Dodge's standard lines of station wagons.

Dodge also offered a variety of pickups and other trucks. Thus, many segments of the market were covered by Chrysler's Dodge Division alone.

The 1972 Polara was considerably restyled inside and out, and the standard engine was now a 318 cubic-inch V-8 (an option in 1971, when a six was also available in that series).

DESIGNED FOR TRAILER HAULING IN CROWDED FREIGHT YARDS.

1972 FLEXI-TRUC BY IBEX

93" TALL!

NARROW 1-PASSENGER TILT-CAB!

CHOICE OF 361 CID FORD V8 (249) or DETROIT DIESEL 4-53 ENGINE.

SHORT 82" WHEELBASE. (TURNS IN A SMALLER-RADIUS CIRCLE THAN A PORSCHE 911-T, A JAGUAR, or MOST SPORTS CARS!)

12~13~87

© 1987 North America Syndicate, Inc. All rights reserved.

NAMED FOR AN AGILE ASIATIC MOUNTAIN GOAT, IBEX TRUCKS HAVE BEEN MFD. IN SALT LAKE CITY, UTAH SINCE 1964.

10.00×20 TIRES (12-PLY)

41-GALLON FUEL TANK

6-SPEED ALLISON POWER STEERING and AUTOMATIC TRANSMISSION. 10.47 to GEAR RATIO

1972 Ibex "Flexi-Truc"

"What is shorter than a Porsche, makes tighter turns than a Jag, and hustles trailers 24 hours a day without breathing hard? The new Flexi-Truc, by Ibex!" So claimed the original sales brochure for the 1972 Flexi-Truc, which stated that the new model would "run rings around every other yard tractor in existence!"

Some Flexi-Trucs were run on-the-job for 144 consecutive hours, three shifts a day, Monday morning to Saturday night, for a nonstop six-day work week—with no adverse effects!

The curved right corner rear window slid open, giving the driver easy access from the one-man cab to the accompanying trailer's air and electrical terminals. The all-steel cab could be tilted forward for easy access to engine, chassis, and mechanical components.

The Flexi-Truc was a subsidiary of Flexi-Van, Inc., and the manufacturer was the Ibex Division of Jelco, with factory/headquarters at 847 W. 1700 South, Salt Lake City. There were business offices at 330 Madison Ave. in New York City, and also in Chicago, Los Angeles, and San Francisco.

"Free demonstration." The Flexi-Truc could be tried on a short-term rental, and could be bought on lease-purchase or outright sale. The similar-looking model, which had preceded it in 1971, had been known as the "Eager 'I' Tug," which had an even shorter (80-inch) wheelbase.

Ibex also made large, conventional style (hood-in-front) truck-tractors, as well as large flatbed pipe carriers and other specialized types.

1970s

1972 Javelin-AMX

Since AMC was considerably smaller than the "Big 3" (GM, Ford Motor Co., and Chrysler Corp.), it decided to stimulate sales by periodically changing model series names. The Marlin was an interesting sports fast-back (1965-1967), but was not popular enough to be continued. In its place for 1968, AMC offered the all-new Javelin, a model in the "pony car" image of Mustang/ Camaro, etc. The Javelin did well; 56,000 units reportedly left the factory the first year.

In mid-1968, the Javelin was joined by another sporty AMC product, the new, smaller AMX, which was more of a true GT performance car. The hot, little AMX was produced as a separate entity from mid-1968 to 1970, and then it was incorporated into the Javelin line starting with 1971. The illustrated 1972 model was advertised as the "Javelin-AMX." It had a V-8 engine, but the lower-priced Javelin "SST" was available with either a six or V-8.

Though well over 23,000 Javelin "SSTs" were built in 1972, the Javelin and Javelin-AMX were not continued after 1974. For 1975, AMC pulled another new model out of the corporate hat—the egg-shaped Pacer, a totally new adventure in advanced styling. Among other AMC cars that appeared and disappeared between the 1960s and 1980s were the Rebel, Hornet, Gremlin, Matador, Concord, Spirit, etc.

Interestingly, in 1971, Mark Donohue raced a specifically prepared Javelin-AMX to "seven victories over Mustang and Camaro," and he secured AMC's first SSCA Trans-Am racing championship!

"THE PICKUP CAR"

News America Syndicate
© News Group Chicago, Inc., 1984

1972 RANCHERO (BY FORD) IN "TORINO" SERIES

ENGINES:
250 CID 6
(95 HP)
302 CID V8 (140 HP)
ALSO AVAILABLE:
351, 400, OR
429 CID V8s
E70 × 14 TIRES

STD.
"500"
MODEL SHOWN

("GT" and
"SQUIRE"
ALSO AVAIL.)

THE FIRST RANCHERO WAS THE 1957 MODEL.

1972 ENGINES REDUCED IN H.P.,

ABLE TO OPERATE ON 91-OCTANE "REGULAR" GAS.

11-11

1972 Ranchero

Though the first Ranchero appeared in 1957, two years before the debut of the El Camino, both truck/cars were beaten to the draw by Studebaker's Coupe-Express of 1937-1939, a true truck/car in the same manner. And, there were other such pioneers, with Hudson and others offering coupes with pickup boxes in place of trunks back in the '30s.

The 1972 Ranchero is one of the most distinctively styled of this line, with a new long hood and narrow grille. It was a part of the Torino series (though Ranchero had begun as a standard-series Ford in '57, shrunk to a compact Falcon truck/car in 1960, and later moved up to the Fairlane line, which evolved into the Torino).

Wheelbase was increased four inches over 1971, and though there were six engine choices for 1972, speed and power left much to be desired. The late 1960s may have been the era of the high-powered "muscle car," but 1972 became the year of the "muzzled car," as strict U.S. government safety standards and smog controls decreed a drastic reduction in power, especially with cars sold in California, where smog controls were more stringent than any other place!

Example: A 1971 Ranchero 302 c.i.d. V-8 had 210 h.p., and the 250 c.i.d. six had 145. For 1972, the respective h.p. of these engines was slashed to only 140 and 95! In 1972, most auto advertising had precious little to say about horsepower—for a change!

1970s

A NEW COMPACT CAR FROM GENERAL MOTORS' BUICK DIVISION

1973½ APOLLO
BY BUICK
(INTRO. APRIL 5, 1973)
250 CID 6 or 350 CID V8
100 HP   150 HP

3317 LBS. (CURB WT.)

SIMILAR TO CHEVY NOVA, PONTIAC VENTURA and OLDS OMEGA.
111" WHEELBASE

FRONT END

4-DR., COUPE, or HATCHBACK COUPE AVAIL.

ONLY
$3200., EQUIPPED WITH V8,
HYDRA-MATIC AUTOMATIC TRANS.,
E78 × 14 WHITEWALL TIRES,
POWER STEERING, OTHER EXTRAS
3.08 GEAR RATIO (2.73 with AUTOMATIC)

NOW RARE!
DISCONTINUED AFTER 1975.

1973 1/2 Apollo

1970s

During 1973, General Motors used the Apollo name for Buick's new compact car. Pontiac and Oldsmobile had each introduced Nova-based compacts, and Buick needed one also, since the only small car Buick dealers had recently been offering was the German-built Opel.

Buick launched a sales blitz for its new Apollo during April of 1973, and many major newspapers carried a colorful four-page supplement devoted to that car. In the text of the supplement, Buick's new Apollo was compared to other small cars as well as to larger ones. Other small cars cost less and were fun to drive, related the advertisement, but they were often inadequately powered for passing on the highways, unsuitable for carrying an entire family or for use on rough roads. On the other

hand, large cars were costly and harder to park. Buick's Apollo promised the convenience and economy of a small car with the smoothness, power, roominess, and luxury of a large model!

Buick claimed that the Apollo, with the V-8 engine choice, weighed about 450 lbs. more than a comparable compact car, providing greater comfort and road stability.

Because of 1973 inflation, Apollo prices climbed to $3,877 and up during 1974, and $4,306 and up in 1975. In 1976, Isuzu of Japan (which built the Chevy "LUV" mini-pickup truck), produced a new "Opel," which could be sold by Buick dealers for $3,282, and this replaced both the Buick Apollo and the German Opel imports, though the German Opel continued as usual in Germany and in other parts of the world.

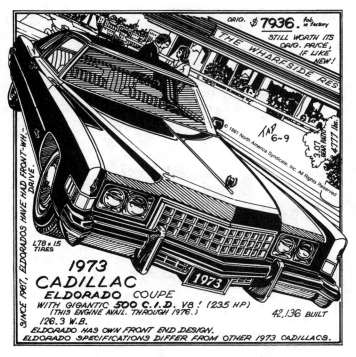

1973 Cadillac Eldorado

These days, older luxury cars are expensive to buy, but sometimes you can still get good deals on cars of the 1970s. The 1973 Cadillacs were attractive and luxurious. This Eldorado coupe is a case in point, with its gleaming grille, expansive hood, and attractive opera windows just behind the side doors.

The Eldorado coupe was a popular part of Cadillac's 1973 roster, with over 42,000 produced. It was outsold only by the '73 rear-wheel-drive De Ville two-door hardtop (112,849) and the De Ville four-door hardtop (103,394).

In 1973, Cadillac also offered the lower-priced Calais series, which replaced the "62" in 1965, but at $5,771 and up the Calais wasn't much cheaper than the De Ville and didn't sell as well.

The Fleetwood 50 Special Brougham Sedan was available at $7,765, with a longer 133-inch wheelbase. Biggest of all 1973 Cadillacs was the grand "75" series (sedans and limos), riding on an unbelievably long 151 1/2-inch wheelbase and priced in the $12,000 range.

The Eldorado was the only '73 Cadillac with the 500 c.i.d. V-8; others shared the standard 472 c.i.d. V-8 with 220 h.p. But, in 1975 and 1976, the giant 500-cuber was standard in all Cadillacs, except the new compact Seville.

In spite of the energy crisis, gas lines, price hikes, and the recession of the mid-1970s, Cadillacs stayed large until 1977, when GM pared inches and pounds off most of their cars in a "downsizing" campaign. There were no 500-cubic-inch V-8s from 1977 on.

1970s

1973 De Witt

When you see the date "1973" on this picture, you may at first wonder if there's been a big mistake! But, it's correct. This was the pilot model of a small series of replicas of the 1909 De Witt horseless carriages.

Believe it or not, nearly 375 different makes of motor vehicles have been built in the state of Indiana since the late 1800s. The best-known Indiana cars are Studebaker, Auburn, Cord, Duesenberg, Marmon, and Stutz.

The De Witt is one of the lesser-known Indiana cars, as it was only available in 1909 and 1910.

In 1908, the North Manchester (Indiana) Industrial Association paid Virgil L. De Witt (a Swiss immigrant a few year earlier) $1,500 cash and the deed to a vacant lot worth $600 in exchange for establishing his small factory there. De Witt had worked in the Kiblinger factory, and his new car was a high-wheeler like the Kiblinger.

On April 15, 1909, De Witt production began. A month later, Mr. De Witt fired an employee for damaging a car in a 45-minute speed run. Other employees conducted a sympathy strike. The strike was settled in a month, but the following year (1910) a fire wrecked the factory—after a total of about 200 cars and trucks had been built.

The next De Witt cars—replicas—were built in the same city by Russell "Pudge" Egolf, starting some sixty-three years later—at 802 West South St., just a few blocks from the site of the original De Witt factory.

WEST BROMWICH, ENGLAND (CARS SINCE 1936)
1973 JENSEN "INTERCEPTOR III"
(THIS TYPE INTRO. 2-72)
PRICED FROM $13,950., AT WEST COAST PORT OF ENTRY

REAR DETAILS
(LARGE HATCHBACK WINDOW)

MFD. BY JENSEN MOTORS, LTD., OF

JENSEN

STYLING BY VIGNALE

105" WHEELBASE   135 M.P.H.
440 C.I.D. CHRYSLER V8 ENGINE and
3-SPEED "TORQUEFLITE" AUTOMATIC TRANS.
2.88 TO 1 GEAR RATIO   215 H.P.
24-GALLON GAS TANK.   AIR-CONDITIONED.
GIRLING 4-WHEEL DISC BRAKES.
ALUMINUM ALLOY WHEELS with GR70VR15
WT.: 4000 lbs.   PIRELLI TUBED TIRES

AD 2/9

* 17,850 IN '74

© News America Syndicate, 1986

(JENSEN-HEALEY SPORTS CAR ALSO AVAIL.)

1973 Jensen Interceptor III

Though Jensen began building automobiles in the 1930s, its earliest history harks back to 1875, at which time W. J. Smith, Ltd., was established. Smith, in those early days, built horse-drawn coaches and carriages. In 1931, Richard and Alan Jensen joined the company, and by this time, motorcar bodies were a bill of fare.

Within three years, the Jensens acquired control of the company and changed the name to Jensen Motors, Ltd. During 1935, the first Jensen cars went into production (1936 models), and by 1937 they were gaining considerable notice as quality sports touring cars. Early Jensen cars used Ford V-8 engines, and some prewar models were fitted with Nash straight-eights.

In 1957, Jensen was one of the early manufacturers to include disc brakes on all four wheels.

For 1963, Jensen began using Chrysler V-8 engines for its own car, the new C-V8. This car looked sleek, except for the overly large set of canted quadruple lights, which looked very much out of place on such a machine. Production ceased for a time in 1967.

In 1970, Kjell Qvale, a San Francisco imported-car distributor, purchased a controlling interest in Jensen Motors. He reorganized the company and gave the chairmanship to Donald Healey (formerly of Austin-Healey). Within two years came the new Interceptor III (February 1972) and also the Jensen-Healey sports car.

Production ceased in 1976 because of financial difficulties, and by the end of that year hopeful new plans were announced for a 4-W-D on-or-off-road vehicle of four- or six-wheel configuration, aimed at military application.

1970s

1973 OPEL "GT" COUPE $3712 AT PORT OF ENTRY 4 CYLINDERS (1.1 OR 1.9 LITRES) 77 OR 102 HP 113 MPH (WITH 116 CID DELUXE ENGINE) 27½ MPG 165 HR-13 TIRES. 95.7" WHEELBASE 2120 LBS. WT. 13.2 GAL. FUEL TANK. CONCEALED HEADLIGHTS MADE IN GERMANY BY GENERAL MOTORS' OPEL DIV. STYLED LIKE A "LITTLE CORVETTE" SPECIAL THANKS TO SHELDON and GENIE OLSON, FRESNO, CAL., FOR PROVIDING ORIGINAL '73 OPEL BROCHURE. TAP 7-23 AVAIL. 1969 TO 1973 AT 2200 BUICK DEALERS. © 1989 North America Syndicate, Inc. All rights reserved.

1973 Opel GT

"The iron fist in a velvet glove!" That's how the new Opel GT was described when advertised in England in *Motor Sport* magazine in October 1968. It will "pull you along at the best part of 120 mph," the ad promised.

The Opel GT reached the United States not long afterward. According to *Road & Track*, the body of the new German GT model was built by a French company, Brissoneau & Lotz. Windtunnel experiments, before production, contributed to the smooth, aerodynamic design.

The smaller of the two engines available (1.1 liter) pushed the GT to 95 m.p.h.

During the late 1960s, Opel's Kadett series was imported to the United States by Buick dealers, and the GT shared a few of its mechanical components. The GT made its dramatic appearance in American Buick showrooms during the spring of 1969. It was advertised in the April 1969 *Motor Trend* as one of Buick's "automobiles to light your fire." The 1969 price was just under $3,500—not cheap, then, for a small car. But, the GT was special, and many thought of it as a "baby Corvette."

The new GT was strictly a two-passenger model. Since there was no outside deck lid, luggage had to be slipped in behind the seats.

The 1970 GT offered a choice of an automatic transmission or the four-on-the-floor manual, previously standard equipment. GT wheel styles changed. The older ones had silvery deep-dish wheels with four rectangular vent slots to cool the brakes. The '72s were illustrated with artillery-style wheels, and the '73 appeared as illustrated here.

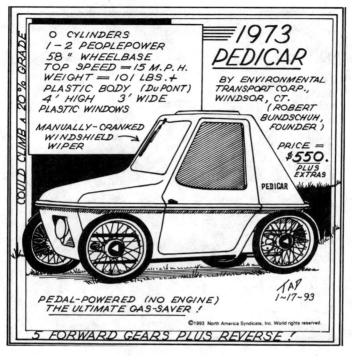

O CYLINDERS
1 - 2 PEOPLEPOWER
58" WHEELBASE
TOP SPEED = 15 M.P.H.
WEIGHT = 101 LBS. +
PLASTIC BODY (DuPONT)
4' HIGH   3' WIDE
PLASTIC WINDOWS

MANUALLY-CRANKED
WINDSHIELD →
WIPER

COULD CLIMB A 20% GRADE

*1973
PEDICAR*

BY ENVIRONMENTAL
TRANSPORT CORP.,
WINDSOR, CT.
(ROBERT
BUNDSCHUH,
FOUNDER)

PRICE =
$550.
PLUS
EXTRAS

PEDICAR

PEDAL-POWERED (NO ENGINE)
THE ULTIMATE GAS-SAVER !

TAP
1~17~93

5 FORWARD GEARS PLUS REVERSE !

1973 Pedicar

Here's the most economical kind of car you could imagine: no fuel required and no batteries needed, except to occasionally light the single headlight!

With a pilot model fully developed and displayed in 1972, the Pedicar was slated to go into regular production in early 1973. It was publicized in an October 11, 1972 article in the *Milwaukee Journal*, as well as in *Newsweek* (December 4, 1972) and *Popular Science* (February 1973).

The ultra-lightweight plastic Pedicar came equipped with bucket seats, seat belts, safety reflectors, and a rear view mirror. A speedometer, radio, sunroof, and turn signals were optional. The object was to keep the Pedicar lightweight, so only the bare essentials were included as standard equipment.

The Pedicar had a three-way pedal system. The driver could pump with one foot, use both feet alternately, or for "an extra surge of power," pump both pedals simultaneously.

In the June 1976 *Popular Mechanics*, a reader wrote to bicycle columnist Eugene A. Sloane to complain that the manufacturer of the Pedicar had not replied to his letters of inquiry. Sloane replied that the company had not remained in business for long, and added that he and his teenaged son had tried a Pedicar and were disappointed because they both had to put out much effort to pedal it just a few blocks.

Was the hoopla about the Pedicar being easy to pedal and "requiring little more effort than walking" just hot air? Or, did Sloane and his son happen to try out a sample that was out of adjustment?

THE "EAGLE-BEAKED" GRAND AM!

THE AGGRESSIVE-LOOKING "BEAK" OF THE 1973 GRAND AM, AN ALL-NEW SPORT MODEL FROM PONTIAC, GAVE THE APPEARANCE OF HIGH PERFORMANCE.

14½ M.P.G. 3.08 OR 3.23 G.R.

© Field Enterprises, Inc. 1983

TAD 6/26

1973 GRAND AM (MODEL 2H37) COLONNADE H/T COUPE 112" *wheelbase* 400 OR 455 C.I.D. V8 (TO 310 H.P.) WT. 4092 LBS. GR70 × 15 TIRES $4969. f.o.b.

GrandAm INSIGNIA

1973 Pontiac Grand Am

"**L**et's say you've always driven American cars ... always been intrigued with imports. Perhaps you've envied the handling ... the real wood in the interior ... the comfortable bucket seats. Whatever.

"We think you'll find our first Grand Am a more-than-acceptable alternative," continued the original advertisement.

"The suspension was designed for the standard steel-belted, wide-base radial tires. With thick front and rear stabilizer bars, it keeps Grand Am level and controlled in corners. Power front disc brakes and fast, variable-rate power steering are standard.

"Grand Am responds with a 400 V-8 and three-speed Turbo Hydra-Matic. Three other V-8s and a four-speed manual transmission are available."

Introduced within the Le Mans series as a sedan or as a coupe with either vinyl or painted steel roof (as illustrated), the Grand Am was Pontiac's answer to the challenge of quality German imports! The hood was very broad at the rear, but tapered to a sharp point at the front. The protruding nose of the car, at the center, reminded one of an eagle's beak! The bird-beaked Grand Am's snout was functional: It was of a flexible plastic material that usually rebounded after an impact. In one reported case, a Grand Am was sideswiped across the front by another car traveling 40 m.p.h. through an intersection. The total repair bill for the Grand Am was only $30!

The Grand Am interior was luxurious. The instrument panel and console were decorated with genuine African crossfire mahogany, with rally instruments. Reclining bucket seats were deep contoured, upholstered in wide-wale corduroy or all Morrokide.

AN *AFFORDABLE* PORSCHE OF THE 'SEVENTIES!

MADE IN GERMANY

TOP SECTION LIFTS OFF

WITH 102.3 CID, 4 CYLINDER FLAT MID-ENGINE (1679 cc) 76 HP @ 4900 (69 HP IN CALIF., WITH SMOG CONTROL DEVICES.) (120.3 CID, 91 HP ENGINE IN "914-9.") 5-SP. TRANS.

$4749.
and up
(AT PORT OF ENTRY)

PORSCHE "914" (1973)

AR 11~13

106 MPH 28 34 M.P.G.

© 1988 North America Syndicate, Inc. All rights reserved.

155 SR-15 TUBELESS TIRES

96½" WHEELBASE

4.429 to 1 GEAR RATIO

WT. = 2138 LBS.

(ONLY $3695, WHEN INTRODUCED FOR 1970.)

1973 Porsche 914

Beginning in the 1970 model year, the 914 was great news for all who desired a Porsche but had been unable to afford one. Prices for the new 914 began at just $3,695—a great buy, especially in view of the fact that the new 914 offered a mid-engine (placed just behind the front seats). Until then, mid-engined cars had been rare and terribly expensive!

With its mid-engine, the 914 cornered and handled beautifully, as the car's weight was not concentrated at either end.

For a few months in 1970, the 914 was available as a four or a six. Then, only a four was offered in that series. In 1973, there were two engine choices, both fours.

The 914 had two trunks: one in front, and another in back, because of the central placement of the engine.

The 914 was listed and advertised until sometime in 1976. By that time, its base price had increased to $7,425, with only the larger 120.3 c.i.d. four available in this model. Its speed was now up to 112 m.p.h.

Porsche kept coming out with new models during the 1970s. In 1976, the new four-cylinder 912 was priced at $11,020. The 911-S six was $14,020 and up. The most expensive Porsche in 1976 was the all-new, high-performance $26,025 six-cylinder 930 Turbo Carrera coupe.

Why the stationary rear roof and quarter panel? Simply for safety; it was a built-in "roll bar." A few people squawked about the looks of that feature in 1970, but it was put there for their own good!

1970s

Text visible in illustration: ©1992 by North America Syndicate, Inc. World rights reserved. / 1974 / Mustang II BY FORD / new SMALL EDITION OF THE MUSTANG (4 CYL. OR V~6) 96.2" W.B. / HARDTOP, GHIA, 2+2 OR MACH I / FRONT END / "THE RIGHT CAR AT THE RIGHT TIME." / $3480. IN EASTERN STATES / 0 TO 60 MPH IN 13½ SEC. (V6) / 100 MPH TOP SPD. / 170 CID 105 HP / (140 CID 4 HAS 88 HP) / 13 GAL. FUEL TANK / AP 3/22 / $3982. IN WEST / GHIA COUPE (SLIDING OPT. SUNROOF) / 2927 LBS. / THIS STYLE AVAIL. 1974 to 1978

1974 Mustang II

According to Jim Dunne, *Popular Science* magazine's Detroit Editor, the 1974 Mustang II was the "best news from Ford since the original Mustang" a decade earlier. The car was previewed in *Popular Science*'s June 1973 issue.

The original '65 Mustang was 181.6 inches long, but it grew. By 1973, the Mustang had become much heavier and considerably longer (193.8 inches). For '74, everything was to be trimmed back, bringing the Mustang II down to 175 inches overall length, with a much-shortened 96.2-inch wheelbase almost thirteen inches less than in '73.

Hot V-8s were "out" in this new economy car. Some Pinto parts were used, but much of the Mustang II was new. No longer a "muscle car," the new breed of Mustang for the mid-1970s depended on economy for its sales appeal in a time of bitter recession.

A four-speed manual transmission was standard, with three-speed automatic optional. The gear ratio was 3.55 to 1 with either type.

The Hardtop and Ghia had the notchback body (as illustrated), with hatchback/fastback bodies on 2+2 and Mach I.

Road & Track magazine reported that as early as 1968, a woman at Ford Motor Co.'s stockholder's meeting asked Lee Iacocca (then president of Ford Motor Co.) why the company was no longer building cars like her well-liked '65 Mustang. Iacocca took her seriously and called for such a new model at a November 1969 management meeting. What was to become the Mustang II was soon planned and developed.

1974 Chevy Nova

Chevrolet's Nova originated in 1962 as the Chevy II. It was an intermediate-sized compact, one step above the rear-engined Chevrolet Corvair, which was available from 1960 to 1969.

The top line of the early Chevy IIs was the "Nova" series, and Nova soon became synonymous with "Chevy II." Officially, the Chevy II name was scrapped in favor of Nova as the 1969 model year began.

The Nova continued, with only minor changes, to 1979; and advertisements often claimed that the car was so good it needed only periodic improvements. A new grille was featured in 1973. The Nova was replaced early in '79 by the all-new 1980 Citation.

The joint GM/Toyota venture at GM's Fremont, Calif., factory produced a new Japanese-American Nova from 1985 to 1988. It was replaced by the 1989 GEO Prizm, also a product of GM/Toyota.

The original Chevy Nova of the 1960s and 1970s built an enviable reputation for durability and economy, and these cars are still in demand for reliable transportation. Nova also built sporty models like the "SS," which are becoming collector's cars.

Further Nova history: The hatchback Nova was new for 1973. The '74 was heralded in a May 1974 ad as "Nova the Thirteenth" and was shown with a first-year '62 Nova in the background. Except for the grille change in '73, there were little yearly differences in the Nova from '68 on. Chevy had a good thing; why rock the boat?

1970s

1970s

BUILT 1971 TO 1979 in VOLKSWAGEN'S BRANCH FACTORY in MEXICO!
SOLD IN U.S.A. 1973 and 1974.

1974 VOLKSWAGEN "THING"
TYPE 181
4-DR. CONVERTIBLE
$2750. AND UP, AT PORT OF ENTRY

1974 "ACAPULCO" THING HAD SURREY TOP, OPEN SIDES, BLUE and WHITE PAINT SCHEME, RUNNING

FLAT 4-CYL. AIR-COOLED ENG. (96.7 cu.)
46 H.P. @ 4000 RPM
7.3 TO 1 COMPR.
94½" W.B.
4.12 GEAR RATIO
TOP SPEED = 73 MPH
0 - 60 MPH in 23.2 SECONDS
21 M.P.G. AVG.   10.6 GAL. GAS TANK

IF INTERESTED IN THE VW THING ASSN. (CLUB), PLEASE SEND A SELF-ADDRESSED STAMPED ENVELOPE TO LARRY AUSTIN, 5340 WHITNEY BLVD., ROCKLIN, CA., 95677, FOR CLUB DETAILS.

TND 5~7

HELPFUL INFO FROM LARRY AUSTIN, ROCKLIN, CALIFORNIA

1974 Volkswagen "Thing"

Although it's not a 4-W-D vehicle, VWs Thing (Model 181) doubles as an outdoors trailbuster. Light in weight with high clearance and fairly good traction, the Thing can handle most backwoods roads.

As the original sales literature proclaimed, this vehicle had "Removable top and doors, and a windshield that snaps down for dune buggy fun. A double-jointed rear axle to keep the wheels in contact with the ground, even over the roughest terrain. Four-wheel independent suspension for rough terrain use. And of course, an air-cooled rear-mounted engine for extra traction."

The Thing was based on Germany's World War II military Kübelwagen, but modified for civilian use. Just as the American Jeepster differed from the military Jeep, so the Thing differed from the original Kübelwagen.

There were 25,000 VW Things sold in the United States in '73 and '74, the two years that they were imported here, though they were available in Mexico since 1971. Standard color choices were orange, white, yellow, or green. The 1973 models had a gasoline-fed heater, but '74s had the typical Volkswagen hot-air type. Top speed varied from 68 to 73 mph., depending on who was doing the testing and how brave they happened to be!

In 1974, an "Acapulco Thing" was also offered, having a canopy "surrey" top and no side doors. A rope across each open doorway was supposed to afford protection from falling out!

Reportedly, the bodies of a '73 Beetle (two-door sedan) and a VW Thing could be interchanged simply by unfastening eighteen bolts on each side!

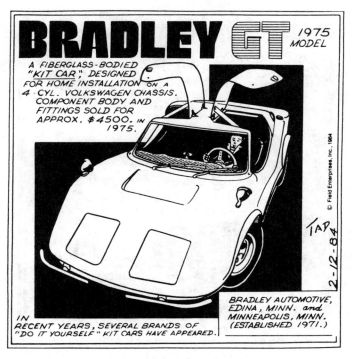

A FIBERGLASS-BODIED "KIT CAR", DESIGNED FOR HOME INSTALLATION ON A 4-CYL. VOLKSWAGEN CHASSIS. COMPONENT BODY AND FITTINGS SOLD FOR APPROX. $4500. IN 1975.

BRADLEY **GT** 1975 MODEL

© Field Enterprises, Inc., 1984

TAD 2-12-84

BRADLEY AUTOMOTIVE, EDINA, MINN. and MINNEAPOLIS, MINN. (ESTABLISHED 1971.)

IN RECENT YEARS, SEVERAL BRANDS OF "DO IT YOURSELF" KIT CARS HAVE APPEARED.

1975 Bradley GT

It's not a Corvette. It isn't a Bricklin, not a "Gullwing" Mercedes, nor an Opel GT, though it may remind you of one of these. It's the Bradley GT, a car designed for "do-it-yourself" home assembly on a new or used Volkswagen "beetle" chassis.

To quote a Bradley advertisement, "If you want a car that looks like a (high-priced) racing GT, there are several ways to go about it. One way is to buy a (high-priced) racing GT. Another way is to buy a Bradley GT fiberglass body and drop it onto a stock VW chassis. That way, you can have a car that looks like a million, but costs very little.

"It's surprisingly easy. You don't need any special tools, and there's no welding. Your Bradley GT kit includes all the parts you need and a fully-illustrated step-by-step assembly manual.

"And because the final product is lighter and has a lower center of gravity, you can actually get better mileage and performance than a stock VW! Up to 35 m.p.g. And up to 100 m.p.h., if you're into breaking speed limits."

The Bradley kit included a "jet cockpit" dash, steering wheel, seats and upholstery, 11 1/2 gallon fuel tank, headlights and taillights, and many other special components.

In 1977, the GT-II joined the Bradley line, with new bumpers, hood slots, and other refinements. And, in 1978, the standard GT was on sale for just $3,295. For the '80s, came the Bradley GTE Electric.

1970s

CHEVY'S LAST BIG CONVERTIBLE OF THE 1970s! RARE!

1975 CHEVROLET "CAPRICE CLASSIC"

IBN-67 CONVERTIBLE

$5640., f.o.b. AT FACTORY
STD. 350 cid V8 (145 NET H.P., 2 BBL. CARB.)
(CALIFORNIA REQUIRED A 4 BBL.
CARB., GIVING 155 NET H.P.)
ALSO AVAIL. 400 cid V8
(175 NET H.P.) OR 454 cid V8
(215 NET H.P.)

GEAR DETAILS

IAP 6~19

ALL '75 CHEVROLETS HAVE A CATALYTIC CONVERTER AND USE UNLEADED FUEL ONLY!

HR 78 x 15 RADIAL TIRES

WEIGHT 4451 lbs.

(2.56, 2.73 OR 3.08 GEAR RATIO AVAILABLE) AUTOMATIC TRANS.

121' 1/2" WHEELBASE

AN "AUTO ALBUM" SAFETY HINT
NEVER LEAVE SMALL CHILDREN ALONE IN A
CAR=ON A HILL, OR WITH THE KEYS IN THE CAR!
BETTER YET, DON'T LEAVE THEM ALONE IN A CAR AT ALL !!

1975 Chevrolet Caprice Classic

1970s

Recently I had the opportunity to ride around town in a nicely restored 1975 Chevrolet Caprice Classic convertible—the kind illustrated here. The owner had purchased it some years ago, driven it as a "transportation car," and then let it sit idle in a shed until he decided to restore the car.

In 1975, Chevrolet's full-size (large) series included the modestly priced Bel-Air, mid-range Impala, and the luxury Caprice Classic. The latter reminded many of a Cadillac!

"Chevrolet makes sense for America" was the 1975 slogan, as the 1973-1974 gas shortages and long lines at the pump had created a big demand for increased fuel economy. Chevrolet's new 1975 "Efficiency System" included high-energy ignition, the new catalytic converter (to reduce harmful exhaust emissions), carburetor air induction, early fuel evaporation system, the use of unleaded fuel in all engines, and radial tires (designed for "less rolling resistance").

The high-energy ignition system featured a new, smaller ignition coil housed in the distributor. Ignition "breaker points" and condenser were eliminated, and the redesigned system made possible a spark that was up to eighty-five percent hotter than before!

There was also an optional economy gauge that was called an "Econominder." Its needle swung through a semi-circle of various color strips as the gas pedal was pressed, held steady, or released. Keeping the needle in the green zone resulted in the best gas mileage.

All 1975 Caprice Classics had automatic transmission, power steering, power front disc brakes, and heavy insulation for a quiet ride. Power windows and power door locks were optional.

SOMETHING NEW FOR 1975   97" WB

DEAR FRIENDS:
HAVE A
HAPPY
THANKSGIVING!

$ 4250.
(4 CYL.)
$198. EXTRA
FOR V8

TAD
11-19

1975

0 TO 60 MPH IN 13.7 SECONDS

1975
Chevy Monza 2+2
WITH AVAILABLE 262 C.I.D. OHV V8 ENGINE
110 HP @ 3600 RPM
8.5 COMPRESSION
2.56 GEAR RATIO

18½ GAL. GAS TANK

1975 Chevy Monza

For 1974, Ford introduced its new, downsized Mustang II. Chevrolet's Camaro, introduced back in 1967 to compete with the original Mustang, was to retain its intermediate size. But, to compete with the new "little" Mustang, Chevrolet launched the 1975 Monza. The Monza name had been resurrected from Chevrolet's former rear-engine Corvair line, which had ceased in '69.

The illustrated Monza 2 + 2 fastback/hatchback bore a resemblance to the Mustang II Mach I coupe. And, the 1975 1/2 Monza "Town Coupe," introduced in midseason, looked much like the Mustang II Ghia notchback in many ways, and was even better looking!

The illustrated Monza 2 + 2 had a most unusual-looking front end—completely unlike the Town Coupe—with quadruple rectangular headlights and ventilating slots instead of a conventional grille. It looked somewhat like a racing car, even to the ten-holed sport wheels. Much of Monza's bizarre front end was made of resilient urethane plastic material, to minimize denting and scratching.

Steel-belted radial ply tires and a sports suspension system, which included stabilizer bars and a rear torque arm, enhanced handling.

In the hatchback, the rear seats could be folded flat to provide added cargo space. Inside, the 2 + 2 was fully carpeted (cut-pile) and cloth or vinyl upholstery was available in six different color choices.

The 1975 cars are now old enough to arouse the interest of a few collectors, and a Monza like this ought to have growing appeal. The next time you're on the freeway, or driving around town, watch for a Monza—in case one happens to pass your way.

1970s

1975
FORD "ELITE"
(new) $5309.
" A MID-SIZED CAR IN THE THUNDERBIRD TRADITION "

OPTIONAL
"MOONROOF"

VINYL PADDED TOP STD. EQUIPMENT

WITH
114"
WHEELBASE
351 c.i.D. V8
150 H.P. (154 @
3800 RPM)
8.2 COMPRESSION
26½ GAL. FUEL TANK
HR 78 x 15 STEEL-BELTED
RADIAL PLY TIRES
A/T, POWER STEER. + BRAKES STD.
COMPLETELY EQUIPPED = 4359 lbs.

11 TO 16 MILES PER GALLON

© 1991 North America Syndicate, Inc. All Rights Reserved

LIKE MOST 1975 CARS, HAS NEW CATALYTIC CONVERTER AND USES UNLEADED GAS.

1·27

1975 Ford Elite

In 1975, automotive writers observed that buyers were flocking to the intermediate (middle-sized) American cars and were less interested in full-sized models. Money was tight and gas prices had escalated since the first "Arab oil crisis" of mid-1973.

The 1975 models were the first American cars to be specifically designed for those bleak years. In creating the new Elite, Ford Motor Co. was offering luxury in a fairly compact package. The Elite was a glamorized Torino with the profile of a new Thunderbird! The Elite has its own distinctive grille, and, like the new Ford Granada, just two headlights instead of four. The Elite was pro-

duced only as a two-door hardtop with a vinyl-padded roof. It sported a small pair of distinctive "opera" quarter-windows on each side.

In advertisements, the new Elite was compared to other specialty cars such as Chevrolet's Monte Carlo and Chrysler's Cordoba. The Elite was "styled to keep you out of the crowd" and "priced so you can enjoy it now."

Most 1975 cars included the new catalytic converter, a muffler-like device on the exhaust line, between the engine and muffler, which was designed to cut emissions. Along with this, unleaded fuel was mandatory.

Note: The Elite and the Torino were replaced in 1977 by the LTD II.

1970s

1975 FMC

MOTOR HOME
BUILT BY FOOD MACHINERY CORP.
(FMC) OF SANTA CLARA, CALIF.
THE FMC MOTOR HOME WAS A
TOP-QUALITY UNIT WITH
MANY LUXURIOUS FEATURES.

INTRO. AS A '73 MODEL WITH 440 C.I.D. CHRYSLER "2900-R" V8 ENGINE. REAR. 29' LONG, 8½' HIGH, 4-WHEEL INDEPENDENT SUSPENSION. ORIGINALLY $29,500.

TAP
7-29

News America Syndicate
© News Group Chicago, Inc., 1984

1975 FMC Motor Home

How long have motor homes been on the American scene? Good question! Though mass-produced motor homes did not "catch on" until the 1960s, early variations of motor homes (or "house cars," as they were called long ago) were occasionally seen in the 1920s and even before. The early varieties were custom-built or home-made, often using a converted truck as the basic unit.

By mid-1972, when the first FMC "2900-R" was previewed to the press, motor homes were popular items, with many manufacturers in the competition. Most available brands were built on Dodge, Ford, Chevrolet, or International truck chasses.

Two notable, new luxury units of the mid-1970s, however, were the GMC (General Motors Corp.) and the FMC (Food Machinery Corp.) motor homes. These were longer and cost-lier than most rivals, with more luxurious features throughout. Both the GMC and FMC motor homes were newly designed from the ground up, not simply adapted to already-existing chassis units.

FMC, a company based in the greater San Jose area of California, had once specialized in the manufacture of mechanized cannery equipment, thus their original name of Food Machinery Corp. Later they became involved in many government-contracted projects for national defense and in the production of military vehicles, etc. Their entry into the motor home field for '73 seemed well timed at first, but the unexpected "gas crunch" of 1973-1974 set the motor home and RV industry back hard, for a time. Within a few seasons, FMC and GMC both dropped their luxury motor homes, to the regret of those who had admired these fine products.

1970s

BUILT IN IDAHO IN THE 1970s ; LOOKS LIKE A EUROPEAN CAR OF 1950 !

(LEATA MEANS "LITTLE" IN NORWEGIAN, ACCORDING TO MFR.)

1975 LEATA COUPE (SMALL CAR)

4 CYLINDERS   UP TO 50 MILES PER GALLON (ON REGULAR LEADED GAS)

MFD. IN POST FALLS, IDAHO BY DONALD E. STINEBAUGH, HIS 3 SONS, and 12 EMPLOYEES.

FIBERGLASS BODY

DIAMOND-PLEATED NAUGAHYDE INTERIOR

PRICED BELOW **$3000.**,

INCLUDING A RADIO, ELECTRIC SPEEDOMETER, WATER TEMP., GAS, OIL PRESSURE, and BATTERY OUTPUT GAUGES.

PRODUCTION RATE = ONE A DAY.

EASILY CONVERTS TO A SNOWMOBILE OR DUNE BUGGY !

LEATA

TAD 4~8

DETAILS THANKS TO WALT THAYER, WENATCHEE, WA.

ALSO AVAIL. AS A SMALL PICKUP TRUCK.

1975 Leata

A t first glance, this might appear to be a British or French car from the early 1950s—or even the late '40s. The heavy-looking wheels, of course, don't look "original" from that era.

In actuality, this car dates only to the mid-1970s, and it's American! Unless you happened to live in Idaho or in the Spokane, Wash. area in the 1970s, chances are that you never knew the Leata existed. Advertising for the car is virtually nonexistent.

The Leata was "fully licensable" in the Northwest, but it's likely that it might not have passed California's stringent smog and safety regulations, which ruled out many small cars at that time. Donald E. Stinebaugh, the manufacturer of the car, originally designed the Leata's engine. The engine design was then sold to a "commercial manufacturer who has refined the product and is mass producing it." Though the Leata's name and styling seem European, Stinebaugh was quoted as having designed it with the look of a 1941 Lincoln Continental in mind (evident mainly by the shape of the windshield). The Leata was in the planning stage for two years.

In 1975, Stinebaugh was quoted as having 1,000 standing orders for what his employees termed "the cutest car around."

The interior of the Leata had a customized look, with its two-toned, diamond-pleated Naugahyde and its row of five dark-faced circular gauges set in a somewhat rectangular panel directly above the small, racing-style steering wheel.

Stinebaugh hoped to increase production from one to three cars a day. He'd have to, in order to fulfill 1,000 orders in less than three years!

1970s

VARIOUS SONG HITS OF 1976 :
MUSKRAT LOVE • NADIA'S THEME • MISTY BLUE
NEVER GONNA FALL IN LOVE AGAIN • DECEMBER, 1963
YOU'LL NEVER FIND ANOTHER LOVE LIKE MINE • SHANNON
PALOMA BLANCA • THEME FROM S.W.A.T. • DREAM ON
WELCOME BACK KOTTER • I WRITE THE SONGS • CONVOY
DISCO DUCK • GAMES PEOPLE PLAY • 5TH OF BEETHOVEN
JUNK FOOD JUNKIE • YOU MAKE ME FEEL LIKE DANCIN'
(NOT LISTED IN ORDER OF POPULARITY)

1976 Aspen

Chrysler Corp. had two excellent compact cars, the Plymouth Valiant and the Dodge Dart, in the 1960s and early 1970s. These cars were virtually trouble-free—so good that they hardly needed to be advertised.

However, by the mid-1970s, the automobile business in the U.S.A. was lagging because of the "Arab oil crisis" and its resulting business recession. Chrysler Corp. officials decided it was time to give the old Valiant and Dart new images, as well as new names. They would become, respectively, the Volare and the Aspen: slightly larger, restyled, and more luxurious in appearance. (For a time, all four compact cars were available!)

The new Aspen and Volare featured new Isolated Transverse Front Suspension (crossways-mounted torsion bars), which was claimed to give a smoother ride and lessen road shock. Visibility from the inside of these cars was improved, and soundproofing was increased. These cars were covered by "The Clincher:" Chrysler Corporation's one-year guarantee in parts and labor for any repairs caused by defects.

Speaking of defects, the Aspen was good, but not as reliable as the Dart it replaced—when it came to necessary repairs. As with many new designs, there were built-in problems. Among the specific complaints from new owners were squeaking brakes; fast idling, stalling, and hard starting; shallow trunk space; poor body workmanship; less gas mileage than advertised; and so on.

But, in spite of the complaints, the majority of owners were pleased. Aspen and Volare captured *Motor Trend* magazine's "Car Of The Year Award" for 1976.

The Slogan: "For A Small Car At A Small Price, It's Unbelievable."

1970s

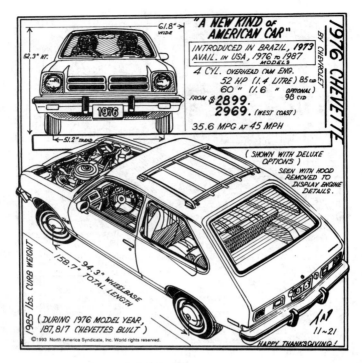

The illustration contains the following hand-lettered notes:

- 61.8" WIDE
- 52.3" HT.
- "A NEW KIND OF AMERICAN CAR"
- 1976 CHEVETTE BY CHEVROLET
- INTRODUCED IN BRAZIL, 1973
- AVAIL. IN USA, 1976 to 1987 MODELS
- 4 CYL. OVERHEAD CAM ENG.
- 52 HP (1.4 LITRE) 85 CID
- 60 " (1.6 " OPTIONAL) 98 CID
- FROM $2899.
- 2969. (WEST COAST)
- 35.6 MPG AT 45 MPH
- 51.2" TREAD
- (SHOWN WITH DELUXE OPTIONS)
- SEEN WITH HOOD REMOVED TO DISPLAY ENGINE DETAILS.
- 94.3" WHEELBASE
- 158.7" TOTAL LENGTH
- 1985 lbs. CURB WEIGHT
- (DURING 1976 MODEL YEAR, 187,817 CHEVETTES BUILT)
- 11~21
- HAPPY THANKSGIVING!
- ©1993 North America Syndicate, Inc. World rights reserved.

1976 Chevette

The Chevette was brought into the U.S. market to replace Chevrolet's controversial Vega subcompact car late in 1975 for the 1976 season. The Vega, however, did continue into 1977, so there was some overlapping of the two cars.

In 1973, General Motors introduced Chevette in Brazil, and it did well there. It was no surprise that it was then groomed to become the eventual successor to the Vega.

In the United States in 1976 and later, the Chevette offered a barebones economy model, the Scooter, which was a two-passenger version with no back seat and no frills. Though the Scooter's price was considerably less, it sold in much fewer numbers than the more deluxe editions: Only 9,810 Scooters were sold in 1976, compared with 178,007 of the costlier Chevettes.

Chevrolet's Chevette competed directly with Ford's Pinto. The Pinto had been launched in 1970, for 1971, as had the Vega. However, the Pinto was discontinued after 1980. The Pinto and Ford's economical front-wheel drive Fiesta, which had been introduced in Europe in 1976 and in the United States, starting with the 1978 season, bowed to the all-new 1981 Ford Escort, which also offered the popular, new front-wheel drive.

In spite of the front-wheel drive mania of the 1980s, Chevette continued with its tried-and-true rear-wheel drive all the way into 1987, when it was finally discontinued and displaced by Chevrolet's Japanese-American Sprint, Spectrum, and (Toyota) Nova. Starting with the 1989 season, Chevrolet's various Japanese-American cars banded together under the new "GEO" name.

1976 Chevrolet

America celebrated its Bicentennial Year with considerable fanfare, when this 1976 Chevrolet was new. But, things had changed on the automobile front.

Defending its big models, Chevrolet ads emphasized that gas mileage had been improved twenty-one percent since the 1974 models (using the 350 c.i.d. V-8 as an example for comparison). The 1976 advertising for the big Impala and Caprice models declared that buyers appreciated six-passenger legroom and elbowroom, comfort, and plenty of luggage space, with captions such as, "There's No Such Thing As Too Much Comfort," "Chevrolet Makes Room For America," and "Why Owning A Full-Size Chevrolet Still Makes Sense."

In a survey, Chevrolet determined that its 1976 customers preferred these colors on the Impala: 1-Light Blue, 2-Saddle (Brown), and 3-White.

There were 6,030 Chevrolet dealers in America as the 1976 season began, and they offered an amazing selection of models from the all-new Chevette sub-compact to the big Caprice Classic. Also available: Vega; Monza; Camaro; Corvette; Nova; Concours (a deluxe Nova); Chevelle Malibu; Monte Carlo; and, of course, the Impala (which had originally been introduced for 1958, bumping the Bel Air from the top of the line. The Impala was, in turn, bumped from the top of the line by Caprice, during 1965). While listing available 1976 Chevrolet types, we must not overlook the Blazer, Suburban, or the various Chevrolet trucks.

Chevrolet in 1976 also offered a de-chromed Impala "S" sedan at $4,507, a full-sized car with no frills. But, most buyers who still wanted big cars wanted more luxurious goodies than the "S" included.

1976 Ramcharger

Dodge's Ramcharger had been introduced early in 1974, which was certainly not a favorable time for anything but dinky, little gas-sippers. This 1976 Ramcharger wasn't much different from the earlier models, but the times had improved, and there was a more favorable market for big toys like 4-W-Ds and RVs.

Back in the 1930s, Dodge had adopted a mountain ram as a radiator ornament, so Ramcharger seemed an appropriate name for a wagon that would climb like a mountain goat! The 1976 advertising depicted a new Ramcharger in a scene much like the one illustrated: on a mountaintop, among the mountain goats. The best-known 1976 Ramcharger ad told us: "The world doesn't stop at the end of

the highway. And the new Dodge Ramcharger doesn't stop there, either.

"When you want to beat your way through the brush and up into the foothills before daybreak, you're not about to let some rocks and logs or a stream or two stop you. Ramcharger's full-time four-wheel drive and 318 V8 make short work of most anything in your way."

But, why all the interest in cars for country trails? Well, many an office worker was tired of the daily grind in the city and wanted to get away from it all on the weekends—maybe to go hunting, fishing, boating, water skiing—or maybe just to explore the wilderness and go camping.

One goody available on the '76 Ramcharger was a console beverage chest that kept contents "hot or cold for hours." Any camper would welcome that!

1976 SCOUT "Spirit" (384 BLT.) BY INTERNATIONAL

A RARE MODEL, SOLD DURING AMERICA'S BICENTENNIAL YEAR.

BASE PRICE $5438. f.o.b., INTERNATIONAL HARVESTER CORP., CHICAGO

4 CYL.

SCOUTS AVAIL. 1961~1980.

© 1992 by North America Syndicate, Inc. World rights reserved.

100" WB. 4 WHEEL DRIVE.

COLORS = WHITE WITH BLUE and RED TRIM BLUE TOP and INTERIOR

11-29

GREAT NEWS !!

IF YOU LIKE INTERNATIONAL SCOUTS, TRUCKS, TRAVELALLS, TRACTORS, or NAVISTARS, THIS CLUB IS FOR **YOU** :

THE SCOUT AND I.H. TRUCK ASSOCIATION, WANDA RAY, MEMBERSHIP SECRETARY 4026 SENOUR RD. INDIANAPOLIS, INDIANA 46239

WRITE THEM FOR DETAILS

DUES = $25. PER YEAR CLUB MEMBERS RECEIVE THE EXCELLENT MAGAZINE "INTERNATIONAL HAPPENINGS," PLUS NEWSLETTERS.'

1976 Scout "Spirit"

International Harvester Co. of Chicago has long been a manufacturer of heavy-duty trucks, as well as farm equipment. Until 1975, they also built pickup trucks; and from 1961 to 1980, they produced the popular Scout.

The Scout was conceived as a more up-to-date rival to Willys' Jeep in the growing sports/utility field. The Scout caught on well, and before long, Ford Motor Co. introduced its similar Bronco in mid-1965 for the 1966 season. By 1969, GM had entered the field with the Chevrolet Blazer, followed in 1970 by the GMC Jimmy.

Chrysler Corp. entered the field later (1974) with the Dodge Ramcharger and Plymouth Trail Duster.

With the growing competition, International needed a new gimmick to help Scout sales by 1976. Thus, the special-edition Scout (Scout II) "Spirit" (illustrated), painted Winter White with horizontal color bands of red above blue. The convertible top was of blue denim, and there was a color-keyed roll bar. Only 384 of these rare models were produced, and there was an even scarcer Patriot hardtop model available briefly in the Traveler, Terra, or Scout II series.

Over the years, Scout chassis units were sold to other companies as a base for specialty cars. In 1966, hundreds of Scout units were sold as a foundation for the new "Glassic" replicar, which was styled like a Ford Model A of the early '30s. In 1969, Stutz Bearcat replicars were made in Tulsa, Okla., also using Scout engines and parts.

As IHC decided to concentrate on heavy trucks, the last Scout was built on October 21, 1980.

1970s

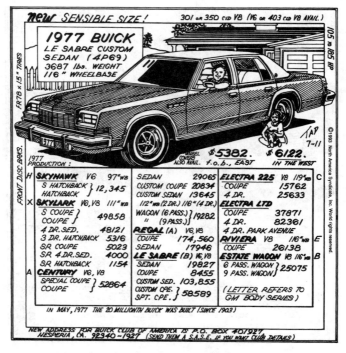

1977 Buick Le Sabre Custom

When an "energy crisis" hit the United States in mid-1973, American motorists were shocked as gasoline prices skyrocketed, and they had to wait in long lines to buy gasoline. Big gas-eating cars became hard to sell. Dealers selling small, foreign cars, especially from Japan, had a field day!

The handwriting was on the wall: Americans could no longer rely on a supposedly inexhaustible supply of low-priced gasoline. Domestic refineries didn't produce enough petroleum to meet the big demand at home. American cars would have to shrink and run on less fuel.

Retooling could not occur immediately, but for 1977, General Motors managed to "downsize" most of its cars. The change in the "big" Buick models from 1976 to 1977 was dramatic. In the Le Sabre line, some 800 pounds were trimmed per car, and there was a change from a 124-inch to a 116-inch wheelbase.

The long, bulbous look of the 1976 big Buicks changed to a trim, angular profile that would remain in style on some GM-built models for well over a decade.

In the 1980s, I bought my wife a used '77 Buick Le Sabre Custom sedan (similar to the illustrated car, except that ours had wheel covers instead of the "sport" wheels shown here). We used this car daily, and it was very comfortable and dependable.

An unusual feature of this model: the silver-faced, round, analog speedometer and gauges, which have an appearance more like 1937 than 1977!

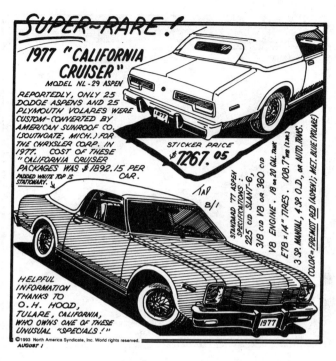

1977 "California Cruiser"

The first Dodge Aspen of 1976 was previously illustrated in *Auto Album*. Though the 1977 model featured little change, there was also a limited-production "California Cruiser" Aspen and Plymouth Volare variation, which were quite unique.

No stock American convertibles were made between 1977 and 1981, and some cars during that interval introduced "T-bar" roofs with a rigid center top section and removable side panels above the doors, giving a "convertible feel" from inside the car. The '77 Aspen, in fact, was available with a new T-bar roof option. But, the illustrated model looked more like a convertible, even though its padded white top covering was rigid.

Key Chrysler-Plymouth and Dodge dealers were to receive these special models: twenty-five Plymouth Volare conversions and twenty-five Dodge Aspen conversions. The regular coupe top was recovered with the padded material (to resemble a convertible top) and the opera windows were covered over. Inside the illustrated car was pleated, off-white leatherette upholstery with a padded, off-white headliner. The effect was sporty, especially with the wire wheels and old-fashioned, wide, white sidewall tires (out of fashion since the early 1960s, but lookin' good again!). Stock Aspen/Volare side trim was removed, as was the name above the grille.

The fifty sample cars did not sell rapidly enough to warrant further production. But, they are certainly interesting, scarce, and are bound to become more and more valuable as time goes by!

THE NEW "DOWNSIZED" CHEVROLET!

THE COMPLETELY RE-DESIGNED

1977 CHEVROLET

"CAPRICE CLASSIC" 4-DR. SEDAN

250 CID 6 (110 HP), 305 CID V8 (145 HP), OR 350 CID V8 (170 HP)

AVERAGE OF 11" SHORTER and 700 LBS. LIGHTER THAN 1976 CHEVROLETS!

new 116" WHEELBASE (121½" IN '76)

$5967.

TAD 6~26

2.56, 2.73 OR 3.08 GEAR RATIOS
EPA—UP TO 22 MPG (HWY.) OR 17 MPG (CITY) (6 CYL.)

21-GAL. FUEL TANK
FR 78-15" TIRES
3774 LBS.

FRONT DETAILS
212" LONG   76" WIDE   51½" HIGH

1977 Chevrolet

"The handwriting was on the wall.

"It clearly said that the time had come for a new kind of six-passenger car—one that would be more efficient in its use of this earth's space and materials than full-size cars of the past—one that would use a new standard engine that is smaller and more fuel efficient.

"Tall order.

"And we made it all the tougher by vowing that the new efficiency would not come at the expense of room, ride, comfort and security."

"So we started from scratch and created a car that meets today's needs without abandoning yesterday's desires." (The foregoing is from original sales literature on the 1977 Chevrolet.)

The new 1977 Chevrolet was "downsized," in keeping with the popular demand for economy and efficiency. Exterior dimensions of the 1977 model were decreased from 1976, and the new Chevrolet would turn in a three-foot-smaller diameter than its predecessor. Yet, inside the car, there was more headroom and rear-seat legroom than in the 1976 Impala/Caprice sedans and coupes! Trunk space was increased, as well!

More rust protection was applied: oil-base coatings on the frame, tough acrylic paint on the body, and the use of corrosion-resistant "Zincrometal," galvanized, and aluminum parts in areas normally rust-prone.

Unlike the Impala, the 1977 Caprice Classic had a rich-looking "textured" grille of fine pieces (as illustrated).

There were numerous options available: AM/FM and AM/FM stereo systems by Delco-GM, speed control, power door locks, and much more!

1970s

1977 Datsun F-10

Sensing the growing demand for a front-wheel-drive car, Datsun (Nissan) hurried the new F-10 into production and had it ready for the public in the summer of 1976. The F-10 used the same economical four-cylinder engine as Datsun's very popular B-210.

Two types of F-10 hatchbacks were available: the illustrated fastback coupe and a small, low-slung two-door wagon.

Japanese cars were first imported to be sold in the U.S.A. late in 1958. The Toyopet (Toyota) and the Datsun were the first to appear.

During 1981, it was decided that the Datsun name would be phased out in favor of Nissan (the manufacturer's name). Nissan executives in Japan had wanted to make the name change for several years. They believed that calling all their cars Nissans would upgrade the image, since "Dat" in Japanese means "rabbit," and "son" means "to lose money."

For a time, during the changeover, both the Datsun and Nissan names appeared on some cars and trucks.

Meanwhile, a new $600 million Nissan branch factory in Smyrna, Tenn. was built in 1981 and 1982, and it turned out its first American-assembled pickup truck in June 1983. This truck was sent to the Tennessee State Museum in Nashville.

As for the Datsun F-10, will it become a collector's car? Quite likely, since it existed for only 2 1/2 model years, having been replaced early in 1979 by the 310 model. In other countries, the F-10 was known as the Datsun "Cherry."

1970s

FIBERGLASS BODY, AVAIL. IN 7 COLORS.

1100 LBS.

ELCAR

7' LONG, 4½' WIDE

REAR DETAILS

HELPFUL INFORMATION AND PICTURES THANKS TO ROBERT A. JEAN, MILWAUKEE, WISCONSIN

1977 ELCAR ELECTRIC

RUNS ON 8 WET-CELL STORAGE BATTERIES.

UP TO 40 MPH TOP SPEED.

TRAVELS UP TO 50 MILES ON ONE FULL CHARGE.

$3220.
PRICE IN U.S.A.

ELCAR

KNOWN IN EUROPE AS "ZELE."

145 × 10" TIRES

© News America Syndicate, 1986

TAD 3-23

IMPORTED FROM ZAGATO OF ITALY, 1974-80, BY ELCAR CORP., ELKHART, INDIANA

1977 Elcar Electric

Dedicated antique car buffs have no doubt heard of the Elcar automobile from Elkhart, Indiana, available 1916 to 1930. This famous name was revived in the 1970s, with the arrival of the little Elcar Electric. The two cars were related in name only, though the new Elcar Corporation's American headquarters also happened to be in Elkhart.

Leon Shahnasarian was president of the new Elcar Electric venture, and he was quoted as saying, "The time is right for electric cars, or it never will be." In September 1974, when the first contingent of Elcar Electrics was shipped over from Italy, owners of gasoline-powered cars (that's nearly all of us) were tired of those months of long gas lines and shortages, and we were tired

of escalating gas prices. Could a simple electric car be the answer to all these vexations? Electrics seemed suitable for those many short, local trips—business, shopping, taking the kids to and from school, etc.

The electric car needed no gas, but of course batteries could be expensive when, eventually, they'd need to be replaced. And, an electric car needed to be recharged after about fifty miles of use, so its range was limited. Some motorists felt that the frequent recharging of batteries—which could become a nightly occurrence with frequent use of the car—could prove to be more trouble than it would be worth. This—plus the feeble performance of most electric cars—is the reason why electrics have remained only a novelty for so many years.

1977 Jeep Cherokee

In June 1977, *Motor Trend* magazine reported that American Motors' Jeep Corp. division was producing more units than all the other AMC makes combined. The latest increase in Jeep production was the eleventh since AMC had acquired Jeep from Kaiser, seven years earlier.

In 1972, only 275,000 four-wheel-drive vehicles were sold industry-wide, but 1977 projections were for 700,000!

The Jeep Cherokee competed with similar-type vehicles such as the Chevy Blazer, Dodge Ramcharger, Ford Bronco, etc. The Cherokee, however, boasted of such advantages as a higher ground clearance with a lower overall height, lower tailgate loading and passenger entry point, a standard integral steel roof for safety, cushioned headliner (ceiling upholstery), front bucket seats and an easy-to-remove folding rear seat, floor coverings throughout the entire interior, and other advantages born of Jeep's longtime experience with 4-W-D.

Jeep's Cherokee, claimed American Motors, offered many standard features available only as options in competing RVs. Also, with the introduction of a four-door Cherokee, Jeep possessed the only four-door model in that class. (Actually, the four-door Cherokee wagon looked quite similar to Jeep's long-established Wagoneer—but with fewer luxuries, and with a lower price tag.)

Available with a three-speed automatic transmission (along with the four-wheel-drive), the Cherokee carried a big twenty-two-gallon fuel tank to give it a greater cruising range. It was just as well, because average fuel economy for the Cherokee was only 14 1/2 miles per gallon, city or highway. These vehicles were built for off-road fun, not for economy.

"THE PINTO WITH PORTHOLES"

1977 PINTO
"CRUISING WAGON" (AVAIL. 1977-1980)

140 cid 4 (89 HP)
OR 171 cid V6
(93 HP)

PINTOS AVAIL. 1971 to 1980 MODEL YEARS, FROM FORD MOTOR CO.

TAD
9~28

© News America Syndicate, 1986

BASIC
WAGON
WEIGHT:
2624 lbs.
$3579.
UP

PINTO WAGONS ALSO AVAIL. WITH
CONVENTIONAL (RECTANGULAR)
SIDE WINDOWS (GRAINED
OR PAINTED SIDES.)

94 1/2" WHEELBASE
(14-GAL. FUEL TANK
IN WAGONS)

PANEL DELIVERY TYPE BODY (CARPETED CARGO AREA)

1977 Pinto Cruising Wagon

Popular in the 1930s and 1940s, the panel-truck type sedan delivery car had become a thing of the past by the 1970s. Though in the '70s, both Chevrolet's Vega and Ford's Pinto offered such a model.

Pinto's was the later arrival, beginning with the 1977 season. The September 1976 issue of *Popular Mechanics* carried a small photo of the car, with the announcement: "The look of a bigger van will come in a compact package in October with Ford's introduction of its new Pinto Cruising Wagon. It's offered with a sports rally(e) package."

In the 1977 Pinto catalogue, the Cruising Wagon was described as a "striking little fun car that may start a whole new trend in mini street vans." The prediction failed to come true,

though roomier mini-vans with greater *vertical* inside space have indeed become a new fad!

The Cruising Wagon was continued into 1980 (Pinto's final year), but it was an odd model, more suitable as a pizza delivery car than as a van. It was small and low, lacking the headroom of a van.

Along with a facelift for 1977, Pinto got more plasticized parts, such as the front shells around the headlights (a critical rust area in times past). An electro-dip priming process for Pinto gave each body a thorough dip in a prime-coat paint vat at the factory, to assure better protection against corrosion.

For 1981, Ford's domestic-built Pinto and European-built Fiesta sub-compact cars were replaced in the U.S. by the new Escort (though the Fiesta is still available outside the US).

The illustration contains the following handwritten labels:

1977 PONTIAC "CAN-AM"

112" WHEELBASE
400 C.I.D. V8 ENGINE
4.1212 x 3.750" BORE + STR.
200 H.P. @ 3600 RPM
8 TO 1 COMPRESSION
3.23 GEAR RATIO
TURBO-HYDRAMATIC AUTOMATIC AVAIL.
STANDARD COLOR: WHITE
MPG: 15 (CITY), 20 (HWY.)
ONLY 1,377 CAN-AM'S BUILT IN '77. ALSO AVAIL. IN 1978 MODEL

THANKS TO DEAN AND CINDY PUGH, FRESNO, CALIF., FOR HELPFUL DETAILS.

G70 x 15 TIRES

c News Group Chicago, Inc., 1984

1977 Pontiac Can Am

After the 1972 government-mandated horsepower decreases, the "energy crisis," and the resulting gasoline shortages of 1973-1974, gas-guzzling, high-performance "muscle cars" were "out" for a time. But, the muscle cars were destined to return, even if, at first, timidly.

Pontiac's Firebird Trans-Am was still available through the '70s, and in 1977 came an interesting variation, the "Can Am." Based on a Pontiac Le Mans sport coupe, the Can Am featured a high-torque, low-compression 400-c.i.d. V-8 and heavy-duty suspension. There was a "shaker" hood scoop, rear deck "spoiler," and—of course—decals.

Because of mandatory exhaust emission control equipment (PCV, ERG, catalytic converter, etc.), performance was not what it would have been before muscle cars were defanged in 1972. Yet, some Can Ams were clocked at 116 m.p.h.—not bad for a car with a speedometer that only went up to 80!

Brakes were superior, with discs on the front wheels. The suspension was an independent SLA type with coil springs, 1 1/8-inch steel stabilizer bars, direct double-action hydraulic Delco shock absorbers with one-inch piston diameter, and so forth. The frame was a separate, perimeter-type with "swept hips."

All '77 Can Ams were painted white with flat, black lower panels and multi-color stripes; 5,000 were planned for 1977, but only 1,377 were actually built (according to the Pontiac Division of General Motors Corp.). However, the Can Am was offered again, with few changes, in 1978.

1970s

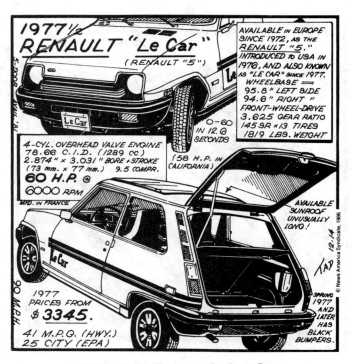

The illustration includes the following hand-lettered notes:

1977½ RENAULT "Le Car" (RENAULT "5")

AVAILABLE IN EUROPE SINCE 1972, AS THE RENAULT "5." INTRODUCED TO USA IN 1976, AND ALSO KNOWN AS "LE CAR" SINCE 1977. WHEELBASE = 95.8" LEFT SIDE 94.6" RIGHT " FRONT-WHEEL-DRIVE 3.625 GEAR RATIO 145.9R x 13 TIRES 1819 LBS. WEIGHT

0-60 IN 12.8 SECONDS

4-CYL. OVERHEAD VALVE ENGINE 78.66 C.I.D. (1289 cc) 2.874" x 3.031" BORE + STROKE (73 mm. x 77 mm.) 9.5 COMPR. 60 H.P. @ 6000 RPM

(58 H.P. IN CALIFORNIA)

MFD. IN FRANCE

AVAILABLE SUNROOF UNUSUALLY LONG!

© News America Syndicate, 1986

SPRING 1977 AND LATER HAS BLACK BUMPERS.

1977 PRICES FROM $3345.

41 M.P.G. (HWY.) 25 CITY (EPA)

90 M.P.H.

Le Car

1977 1/2 Renault Le Car

The Le Car (Renault 5) is probably the most distinctively shaped and one of the peppiest of all the so-called "econobox" small cars of the later 1970s, and its wheelbase is long enough to provide the smooth ride of a larger car.

"Thank Heaven For Little Cars!" proclaimed the ads for the Renault 5, when it finally appeared in the USA in 1976 (four years after its European introduction). In 1977, it was nick-named "Le Car," and the designation stuck. The early 1977 Le Car was shown in catalogs and ads with alumi-nized bumpers, but in the spring of '77, the bumpers were of black polyure-thane and stayed that way.

The '77 Le Car was available as "TL" or "GTL" (deluxe) model. Stan-dard body colors that year were: Glen Yellow, Chipper Orange, Rally Red, Sebring Green, Dune Beige. GTL col-ors included Moonlight Black, Metallic Beige (brown), Metallic Blue, and Metallic Silver.

By the end of 1978, Renault reported that more than 2 million Le Cars had been sold worldwide.

Le Car's optional sunroof had a much longer opening than other sun-roofs, enabling both front and rear pas-sengers to fully enjoy the sunshine and fresh air en route.

The custom sport aluminum wheels shown on the illustrated car were an option that added much to Le Car's unique look.

Though it had front-wheel drive, the Le Car did not have the transverse (crossways) engine mounting of several other f-w-d cars. The success of the Le Car helped Renault buy a sizeable share of American Motors Corp.

1977 Toronado "XSR"

Not since the 1947 Studebaker Starlight Coupe or the '64 Barracuda fastback has any American car introduced such a broad wraparound backlight (rear window)—until the Toronado XSR came along for 1977!

The XSR rear window was unique, since it appeared to be a three-piece type, but it was simply creased in two places to form a broad, squared-off "C." Another interesting touch was the pair of high-up brake-light slots—nine years ahead of the rear window brake light that would become mandatory on all 1986 and later American cars.

After Cadillac had built its final 1976 Eldorado "ragtop," production convertibles were "out" until 1982. But, the gap was filled by the new "T-top," "T-bar," or "T-roof" type of coupe, as illustrated. Removable or slide-in sections above the side doors gave an "almost-convertible" effect, and since

there was some rigid support between windshield and roof (at the center), the "T-roof" was deemed safer than a full convertible and could legally be produced. The "T-roof" was optional on the Toronado.

There was also a lower-priced ($8,134) Toronado Brougham Coupe, which had a narrower rear window, a vinyl-padded top, and small "opera" rear-quarter windows.

Toronado standard equipment in '77: power steering, power brakes, Turbo Hydra-Matic automatic transmission, driver's door armrest control console, air conditioning, digital clock, cornering lamps, velour upholstery with "loose-cushion"-style seats, and other luxury features. A new "Misar" on-board minicomputer continuously adjusted spark timing for utmost efficiency.

Oldsmobile's 1977 slogan: "Can We Build One for You?"

1970s

1977 1/2 Volkswagen "Beetle" Convertible

The first Volkswagens were designed by Ferdinand Porsche, who got the commission in 1934. The first three pilot models were completed in 1936, but none were sold to the public until 1939.

After World War II, British Occupation Forces controlled the VW factory, and most early postwar VW Beetles were produced for the British Army. In 1949, England released the factory to German administration. That year, the first convertible version of the Beetle was produced for the public.

In 1971, a more powerful "Super Beetle" became available, and a specially trimmed "Sports Bug" appeared in 1973. Other special Beetle variations came and went. In 1975, VW's Rabbit (a.k.a. Golf) appeared in the United States. This was the water-cooled, front-engined, front-wheel-drive, conventionally-styled car that would soon replace the long-running Beetle series.

The final two-door sedan Beetles were produced for the U.S. market in 1977, priced at $3,699.

The convertible version had sold for $4,195 in 1975, $4,545 in 1976, $4,799 early in 1977, and shot up to $5,695 by year's end! The convertible was available two more years. And, in the 1980s and later, VW Beetles were available south of the border, but not in the United States, where new safety codes had helped to run them off.

The 1980s saw a "Beetle convertible mania," as resale prices of these little ragtops skyrocketed! Good VW convertibles are still in demand and bring much more than most other cars of their age. (Restyled "Beetle" two-door sedans have been available again since 1998.)

NOT A "MONKEY," BUT A "BEE"! *

1978 APE "600"
3-WHEEL LIGHT DELIVERY
MFD. BY PIAGGIO/CO.,
SPA, GENOA, ITALY
(ESTAB. 1947)
(ALSO MFR.
OF VESPA
SCOOTERS
and MOTOR
VEHICLES.)
40 MILES PER HR.

MODELS WITH 200 TO 1200-LB. CAPACITIES

4-SPEED TRANSMISSION

UP TO 79 MPG!

AVAIL. WITH
1 CYL. ENGINE
(WITH AS LITTLE AS
50 cc DISPLACEMENT)
* "APE" MEANS "BEE"
IN ITALIAN. (VESPA MEANS WASP)
THESE SCOOTER TRUCKS ALSO SOLD
UNDER VESPA NAME.

EARLY
MODELS WITH
HANDLEBAR STEERING!

1978 Ape Light Delivery Truck

Y ou may have heard of the "bubble cars" of the 1950s and 1960s—tiny cars, usually foreign-made, that were amazingly small, even in comparison to our domestic sub-compacts.

Here is a "bubble truck," in the same utilitarian genre as the bubble car. This little three-wheeled vehicle from Genoa, Italy, ranks among the smallest of motor vehicles.

Piaggio Co. is the manufacturer of both the Ape and Vespa mini-vehicles, as well as a huge output of motor scooters and mopeds. The Piaggio scooter was named the "Vespa" (Italian for "wasp"). Within a few years, it was a world-wide success, even well known in the United States.

"Ape" ("Bee" in Italian) was the name chosen for Piaggio's lightweight scooter-trucks, although in English-speaking countries they were Vespas. Notwithstanding the difference in pronunciation, who would want to buy, in the United States, a "1978 Ape?"

Early Apes had a chain-driven differential and a one-cylinder, 4 h.p. engine of 125 cc displacement. These tiny engines were the simple two-cycle type and ran on a mixture of gasoline and oil.

From 1958 to 1961, two-cylinder Vespa cars (four-wheelers with coupe bodies) were built in France.

As of 1978, Ape/Vespa engines varied in size, from 50 cc to 187 cc.

Vespas or Vespa-based vehicles have also been produced in England, France, and Yugoslavia.

1970s

FIRST YEAR FOR OMNI!

$4135. AS SHOWN (PLUS TAX, DESTINATION CHARGES) CANOE NOT INCLUDED.

13-GALLON FUEL TANK

S.S. BARNACLE-BAIT

39 MPG HWY, 25 CITY (EPA)

FRONT WHEEL DRIVE

new 1978 DODGE OMNI
4-DOOR HATCHBACK
99.2" WHEELBASE
104.7 cid 4 CYL. ENG.
70 H.P. @ 5600 RPM
TRANSAXLE RATIOS:
   3.3 MANUAL   3.4 AUTOMATIC
   3.5 "   3.7 " (IN CALIF.)
8.2 COMPRESSION (UNLEADED FUEL)
P155/80R x 13 TIRES (P165/75R x 13 AVAIL.)

(NEW PLYMOUTH HORIZON SIMILAR)

3~25~90

© 1990 North America Syndicate, Inc. All Rights Reserved

1978 Dodge Omni

America's automobile industry was caught off guard when the first Arab oil embargo and resulting "energy crisis" hit back in 1973-1974.

The sudden shortage of gasoline was a rude awakening. Sales of imported cars soared, as Detroit slowly got the message that "gas sippers" were needed. When the next fuel shortage came in 1979, American manufacturers were better prepared.

Chrysler Corp. introduced the Dodge Omni and Plymouth Horizon for 1978. They were small, but didn't look or feel "cheap." The latest fad was front-wheel drive, and Omni and Horizon included it! Volkswagen supplied the manual transmission for these cars, but the automatic transmission was Chrysler-built. Engine blocks and cylinder heads were VW-built, but modified by Chrysler Corp. with longer strokes, greater displacement, "Lean Burn" electronic ignition, etc.

Motor Trend magazine named Omni/Horizon "Car of the Year" for 1978, but *Consumer Reports* didn't agree, giving these two a "Not Acceptable" rating in emergency handling situations. However, the Omni/Horizon cars were built for comfort, not for sports car use. With wheelbases of nearly 100 inches, they were not classified as subcompacts like the Rabbit or Fiesta.

Since bad publicity about handling had finally killed off the Chevrolet Corvair in 1969, Chrysler Corp. didn't want such a thing to happen to their new economy cars. Fortunately, most of the buyers of these cars were well pleased, and customer satisfaction is what counted in the long run.

Another Omni/Horizon "plus": four doors, when most "econoboxes" had just two. The hatchback could be considered a fifth door.

A "NEO-CLASSIC" CAR, RECALLING THE STYLE OF THE GREAT CLASSIC 1920s TO 1930s MERCEDES-BENZ AUTOS.

454 CID CHEVROLET V8 ENG.
215 NET HP @ 4000 RPM
3 SP. TURBO Hydramatic AUTO. TRANSMISSION

1978 EXCALIBUR III
PHAETON

30-GALLON NYLON FUEL TANK.
GENUINE LEATHER UPHOLSTERED SEATS.
4350 LBS.

MFD. (SINCE 1964) BY EXCALIBUR AUTOMOBILE CORP., WEST ALLIS (MILW.) WIS., SOLD RECENTLY TO MICHAEL TIMMER OF GERMANY, FOR $1.33 MIL. (CONTINUATION PLANNED)

EXC-SS

112" WHEELBASE
GR 78 x 15 TIRES
(GOODYEAR RADIAL PLY)
POWER DISC BRAKES

HELPFUL INFO. THANKS TO DON REIMAN, WEST ALLIS, WISCONSIN, and BERNIECE M. SPRINGER, GREENFIELD, WISCONSIN.

1978 Excalibur III

Brooks Stevens was the designer of the Excalibur, which was intentionally styled to resemble a vintage Mercedes.

Brooks Stevens had designed an earlier Excalibur (1952-1953) using a Henry J engine and that of an Alfa Romeo, in one car. Three prototypes were to be raced in '53, and if the early Excaliburs had gone into production then, the price would have been $2,000. Plans were shelved for a decade.

Then Brooks Stevens designed a second Excalibur series, also in Milwaukee, which SS Automobiles, Inc. (later known as Excalibur Automobile Corp.) would put into limited, but regular, production, starting in 1964.

In addition to the original roadster, a more conservative-looking four-passenger phaeton (illustrated) joined the line early on. Changes were made in the Excaliburs from time to time, as improvements were incorporated and safety features tacked on. But, the basic look was "Old Mercedes." The exhaust pipes through the hood gave an appearance of power. With a hot, Chevrolet V-8 engine, the car was powerful!

Production was usually around 250 cars per year. In June 1990, Excalibur Automobile Corp. was plagued with financial woes—many big, unpaid bills—and in September 1990 sought protection from creditors under Chapter 11 of the federal bankruptcy code.

Since that time, Michael Timmer, who'd been in the auto sales, leather, and grocery store development business in Germany, took a fancy to the foundering Excalibur operation. He'd been handling Excalibur cars in Germany, and decided to buy the factory. For all he got, $1.33 million is a screaming bargain!

1970s

1978 FIESTA

BUILT IN EUROPE BY FORD MOTOR CO. SINCE 1976. (1978, 1979 and 1980 FIESTAS AVAIL. IN UNITED STATES.)

4-CYL. TRANSVERSE 1.6-LITRE ENGINE 40-66 H.P. AVAIL. 97.5 CID 8.5 comp.

4 SP. MANUAL TRANS with F.R. WHEEL DRIVE

OPTIONAL "DECOR" "SPORT" or "GHIA" TRIM

TO 101 M.P.H.

BUILT IN GERMANY, ENGLAND AND SPAIN.

BASE PRICE FROM $3680.

"SPORT" DASH

0-50 IN 8.8 SEC.

30-46 MPG

90 MPH

1978 Fiesta

Ford Motor Co. introduced its new Fiesta in Europe during 1976. It was an $800 million gamble, because the world car market already seemed glutted with mini-cars and subcompacts.

The Fiesta offered front-wheel-drive, a transversely (crossways) mounted engine, and many other up-to-date features. It wasn't a rehash of an older type of small car; it was all new! To simplify matters, the only available transmission was a four-speed manual, and the only body choice a three-door hatchback. But, there were various engine horsepower options, and variety was also provided by the four basic trim packages: Standard, Decor, Sport, and Ghia. There were numerous extras, and numerous upholstery and paint combinations.

The Fiesta has been a resounding success in Europe ever since 1976, and during the 1978-1980 model years, it was also available in the U.S.A. Though it has continued overseas, the Escort replaced the Fiesta in the U.S. market in 1981.

Most reviews of the Fiesta were full of praise for the dependable, little car. Robert Lutz, head of Ford's German operations, said in 1976 that the Fiesta would be "the Tin Lizzie of the future," a car that could become as universal as the famous old Model T!

In June 1979, this writer bought a new '79 Fiesta. Like so many other Ford Fiestas, it provided several years of dependable and economical transportation, with exceptionally good headroom and visibility.

The American-market Fiesta is shown here. The European version has rectangular headlights and an oval Ford emblem at center of grille.

"JEEP WROTE THE BOOK ON 4-WHEEL DRIVE"
1978 JEEPS PRICED FROM
$4995.

1978
JEEP CJ-5
"RENEGADE"
83½" W.B. (93½" ON CJ-7)

WITH SAFETY "ROLL BAR"

258 cid 6 (or A 304 cid V8 for $86. extra)

Renegade

CJ-7 WITH "QUADRA TRAC" OPTIONAL 4 WHEEL DRIVE 2659 lbs. (3750 G.V.W.)

1978 Jeep CJ-5 Renegade

The first Jeeps were produced by American Bantam (1940-1941) and then by Willys-Overland (1941-62). During World War II, Ford also built Jeeps that matched the Willys Jeeps in every respect but the name. From 1963 to 1969, Kaiser built Jeep products, and in 1970, American Motors Corp. (AMC) acquired Jeep as a vital new addition to their line. In the later 1980s, Chrysler Corp. purchased AMC/Jeep from Renault. But, back in 1978, Jeeps were handled by AMC, and contributed greatly to the total sales of that small company.

In addition to the Renegade sport package, there was also a Golden Eagle version of the CJ Jeep—as well as the garden-variety standard model.

All 1978 CJ series Jeeps came with a folding windshield, electronic ignition, energy-absorbing steering column, passenger-side mirror, front passenger bucket seat, H78 "Suburbanite" tires and transmission/fuel tank skid plate.

Levi's seats and soft tops were available options, and the CJ-5 could be had with a metal cab (and CJ-7 with fiberglass top). Fabric tops were available for either model. In addition to the CJ type "universal/military" Jeeps in 1978, there were also the Cherokee wagons, Wagoneer luxury wagons, and J-10 and J-20 Jeep pickups.

The first sporty, non-military Jeep had been the Jeepster, which appeared in 1948.

Because CJ Jeeps were often driven hard and wild on tough, mountainous trails, rollovers were a real danger. Roll bars were added for the protection of driver and passengers, but those who failed to fasten their seat belts were usually thrown from these vehicles in the event of accidents.

1970s

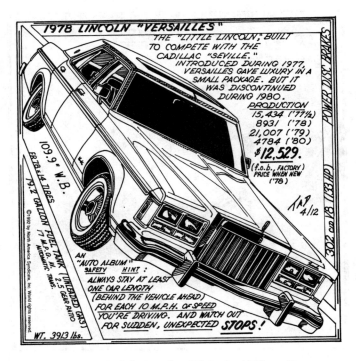

The illustration contains the following handwritten labels:

1978 LINCOLN "VERSAILLES"

THE "LITTLE LINCOLN," BUILT TO COMPETE WITH THE CADILLAC "SEVILLE." INTRODUCED DURING 1977, VERSAILLES GAVE LUXURY IN A SMALL PACKAGE. BUT IT WAS DISCONTINUED DURING 1980.

PRODUCTION
15,434 ('77½)
8931 ('78)
21,007 ('79)
4784 ('80)

$12,529.
(f.o.b., FACTORY)
PRICE WHEN NEW ('78)

109.9" W.B.

FR. 78x14 TIRES

79.2 GALLON FUEL TANK (UNLEADED GAS)
17 M.P.G. AV.
AUTOMATIC TRANS.
2.5 GEAR RATIO

©1992 by North America Syndicate, Inc. World rights reserved.

POWER DISC BRAKES

302 cu. in. (133 HP)

AN "AUTO ALBUM" SAFETY HINT:
ALWAYS STAY AT LEAST ONE CAR LENGTH (BEHIND THE VEHICLE AHEAD) FOR EACH 10 M.P.H. OF SPEED YOU'RE DRIVING. AND WATCH OUT FOR SUDDEN, UNEXPECTED *STOPS!*

WT. 3913 lbs.

1978 Lincoln "Versailles"

Because of GM's quick success with Cadillac's scaled-down Seville, Ford Motor Co. decided to produce a luxury compact of their own: the Lincoln Versailles. Like the Seville, it was available only as a sedan and loaded with "extras" in a small package. The Versailles was introduced during the 1977 model year.

During its three-year run, there were only minor changes. The 1977 1/2 came with a 135-h.p. 351 c.i.d. V-8, or with a 302 c.i.d. V-8 in California. Only the 302 V-8 was available on the 1978-1980 Versailles.

According to the 1978 catalog, many features were borrowed from the big Lincoln Continental Mark V and "applied to a Lincoln two and a half feet shorter" (meaning the Versailles). The Versailles contained over 100 lbs. of sound insulation. There was even a rubber insulator on the accelerator cable, to screen out engine sound or vibration from the driver's compartment. Sophisticated shock absorbers (gas-filled) and suspension design helped to create a smooth, quiet ride—as you'd expect in a car much larger! Eighteen-ounce interior woven carpeting was "molded over thick padding."

The 1978 Versailles had a new, computerized Electronic Engine Control system, which monitored engine temperature, air temperature, barometric pressure, and throttle plate position.

The Versailles was the first American car with German-style "Clearcoat" enamel finish. This was created by applying a base coat of high pigment enamel, followed by a second coat of clear acrylic enamel to bring out and hold a high gloss.

1978 Zephyr

F ord Motor Co. cars went through a year of transition in 1978. It was the final year for the large-sized Ford LTD and Mercury Marquis, and the first year for a new breed of compacts: the Ford Fairmont (replacing the Maverick) and the Mercury Zephyr (replacing the Comet). The Comet had been around since the spring of 1960, originally introduced as the running mate to Ford's new 1960 Falcon.

According to the 1978 Zephyr sales catalog, "The new Mercury Zephyr, innovative in its breezy, sporty styling, is a car planned to suit the now generation of drivers. It is one of the most efficiently designed domestic cars ever offered by Lincoln-Mercury—conceived through the most extensive computer technology ever used for a Mercury."

The catalog went on to tell of Zephyr's fuel economy, interior roominess, smooth-riding adaptation of McPherson strut-type suspension, rack-and-pinion steering, etc. Its "DuraSpark" solid-state ignition never needed adjustment!

Models available included: the illustrated sedan, a four-door station wagon (grained or ungrained sides), a two-door sedan, and a very attractive "Z-7" coupe (clone to Fairmont's Futura, with unusual-looking rear quarter windows and panels).

The Zephyr and Fairmont were designed around a space-efficient interior, rather than trying to stuff passengers into a styled exterior/interior package. The trunk was very wide and long, but not very deep, leading to a few complaints that filled grocery sacks, if large, could not be placed upright in the trunk. Another complaint spoke of a small glove box and flimsy ashtray, but these faults were trifling in comparison with the high overall quality of the Zephyr and Fairmont.

1970s

1979 Chrysler New Yorker "5th Avenue Edition"

On August 22, 1991, I completed my illustration of the '79 Chrysler New Yorker "5th Avenue Edition" sedan. After finishing the drawing, I went downtown to the post office. When leaving the post office, I could hardly believe what I saw parked outside: the same rare model I'd just drawn!

Delighted to see this one-in-a-million car, I studied it carefully, making mental notes of as many small details as possible. I talked with the owner when he returned to his Chrysler. He said he'd bought it late in '79, and though it was an early '80 model, it was just like a '79 except for the carburetor, different fender light lenses, and other minuscule differences. It was even the same color as a '79: "Designer's Cream/Designer's Beige." According to the 1980 brochure I checked later, that color scheme was continued in 1980, and a second choice

was added: "Black Walnut Metallic" monotone, which was a dark brown.

The 1979 was the first Chrysler New Yorker to be "downsized," following the success of the scaled-down Chrysler Cordoba (1975) and Le Baron (1977). But, the '79 New Yorker was still a big car. The New Yorker would shrink again in 1982.

What was included as standard equipment on each 5th Avenue Edition? Inside: champagne-colored leather and vinyl upholstery, reclining seats (to several adjustable positions), leather-wrapped tilt steering wheel, 20-ounce pile carpeting and a dash full of gauges and switches.

In the early 1980s, many Chrysler Corp. and other brands of cars would include vocally recorded commands. Such "talking cars" would actually tell you what to do!

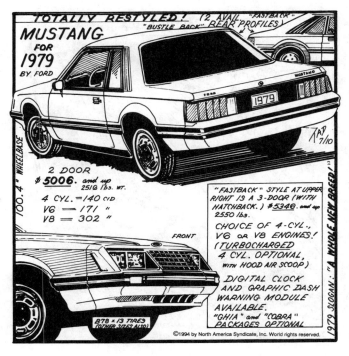

TOTALLY RESTYLED! (2 AVAIL "FASTBACK" REAR PROFILES)

"BUSTLE BACK"

MUSTANG FOR 1979 BY FORD

MUSTANG

1979

100.4" WHEELBASE

2 DOOR
$5006. and up 2510 lbs. WT.

4 CYL.=140 CID
V6 = 171 "
V8 = 302 "

FRONT

B78 x 13 TIRES (OTHER SIZES ALSO)

"FASTBACK" STYLE AT UPPER RIGHT IS A 3-DOOR (WITH HATCHBACK.) $5348. and up 2550 lbs.

CHOICE OF 4-CYL., V6 or V8 ENGINES! (TURBOCHARGED 4 CYL. OPTIONAL, with HOOD AIR SCOOP)

DIGITAL CLOCK AND GRAPHIC DASH WARNING MODULE AVAILABLE.

"GHIA" and "COBRA" PACKAGES OPTIONAL

1979 SLOGAN: "A WHOLE NEW BREED."

1979 Mustang

By '73, many complained that the Mustang had grown too large. So, in a drastic about-face, Ford replaced the Mustang with the little "Mustang II" for 1974. Now it was too small, and some were referring to the Mustang II as a "glorified Pinto."

The little Mustang II series continued through 1978, though dropping the "II" designation along the way. For '79, it was time for a new Mustang: longer, wider, and roomier .

Chrome was now "out," and cheap-looking black plastic trim was "in." There were only two basic body styles for '79 Mustangs: a two-door coupe or a three-door hatchback (the latter with semi-fastback profile).

This bland selection was spiced up with a wide variety of paint, trim, and upholstery choices, not to mention vari-ous "extras." And, the Ghia or Cobra package options provided a sporty flair. Of the various Mustangs of that year, the '79 Mustang Cobra is probably the most desirable to collectors.

But, the '79 Cobra was a toothless tiger compared to some of the mighty muscle cars of the late 1960s. The '79 Mustang Cobra touted roadability and sport suspension, rather than high speed or horsepower.

The Turbo 4, as delivered in most '79 Mustang Cobras, was a good per former compared to most contemporary small engines, but it could not outrun those powerful big V-8s of yore. However, the hood air-scoop on the '79 Cobra, along with aggressive-looking hood decals a la Pontiac Firebird, gave some satisfaction to the sporting driver.

1970s

1979 PONTIAC "GRAND AM" $6656.

18.1 GAL GAS TANK
231 c.i.d. V6 BUICK ENGINE STANDARD, with
105-115 HP @ 3400 rpm
(OTHER V6 or V8 ENGINES AVAILABLE, from GM's BUICK,
PONTIAC or CHEVROLET DIVISIONS.)
3.08, 2.56 or 2.41 GEAR RATIO AVAIL.
WEIGHT = 3289 LBS.
DASH = BLACK CIRCULAR GAUGES-
and-VENTS in ALUMINUM-
COLORED OBLONG PANEL-

108" WHEELBASE

COLONADO

IF YOU LIKE PONTIACS, YOU'LL *LOVE* THE PONTIAC-OAKLAND *CLUB* (BOX 4789, CULVER CITY, CA 90230-4789) JUST SEND THEM A SELF-ADDRESSED STAMPED ENVELOPE, FOR INFORMATION ABOUT THE CLUB.

205/70R 14" TIRES

1979 Pontiac "Grand Am"

Pontiac's first Grand Am was the popular 1973 model. The Grand Am was not to be confused with the Grand Prix, which originated in 1962 as a much-larger luxury Pontiac. The Grand Am was a sport model and a part of the intermediate Le Mans/Grand Le Mans series for '79. They're scarce, according to officers of the Pontiac-Oakland Club. In 1979, some 4,025 Grand Am coupes and 1,865 four-doors were built.

"Designed by Enthusiasts, for Enthusiasts," read a 1979 Grand Am ad. "No. Grand Am isn't for everyone. But if you're a driver who loves tight, responsive steering, Grand Am's got it. Just 3.3 turns of the wheel lock-to-lock. And a weight distribution that makes you feel you're at the center of the action."

The Grand Am featured "Rally Radial Tuned Suspension," including front and rear stabilizers and steel-belted radial tires.

The Pontiac line for '79 was a broad one. It included the Sunbird, Phoenix, Phoenix LJ, Le Mans, Grand Le Mans, Grand Am (illustrated), small Safari Wagon (in Le Mans series), Firebird (including standard Firebird, Esprit, Formula, and Trans Am variations), Grand Prix, Catalina, Bonneville, Bonneville Brougham, big Safari, and Grand Safari wagons.

In the spring of 1979, the restyled 1980 Phoenix appeared, making the true 1979 Phoenix relatively scarce. Other 1979 Pontiac models continued until late in the year.

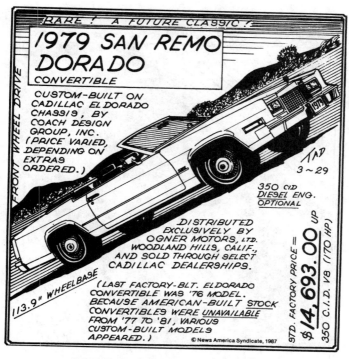

RARE! A FUTURE CLASSIC!

1979 SAN REMO DORADO
CONVERTIBLE

FRONT WHEEL DRIVE

CUSTOM-BUILT ON CADILLAC ELDORADO CHASSIS, BY COACH DESIGN GROUP, INC. (PRICE VARIED, DEPENDING ON EXTRAS ORDERED.)

TAD
3~29

350 CID DIESEL ENG. OPTIONAL

113.9" WHEELBASE

DISTRIBUTED EXCLUSIVELY BY OGNER MOTORS, LTD. WOODLAND HILLS, CALIF., AND SOLD THROUGH SELECT CADILLAC DEALERSHIPS.

(LAST FACTORY-BLT. ELDORADO CONVERTIBLE WAS '76 MODEL. BECAUSE AMERICAN-BUILT STOCK CONVERTIBLES WERE UNAVAILABLE FROM '77 TO '81, VARIOUS CUSTOM-BUILT MODELS APPEARED.)

STD. FACTORY PRICE = $14,693.00 UP

350 C.I.D. V8 (170 HP)

© News America Syndicate, 1987

1979 San Remo Dorado

During the 1970s, all American auto manufacturers phased out their convertibles. Manufacturers claimed there was a low demand for open cars, since many people ordered air conditioning for their cars.

"Convertibles are unsafe!" said many. "What happens if they turn over?" Most American convertibles were so low, wide, and heavy that the possibility of a rollover was remote. Nevertheless, convertibles did have disadvantages, among them was the high cost of replacing the top when it wore out or became torn.

As used convertibles shot up in value to meet the demand for open cars, etc., stepped into the gap with special conversions. They could take a stock coupe, chop off the roof, brace the weakened body with additional supports, and install a folding convertible top, specially tailored for the job.

One of the more attractive of these convertible conversions was the San Remo (Cadillac) from Ogner Motors, Ltd., in southern California. These conversions were made "under the discerning eye of Master Coach Builder Andre de Stefanis of Torino, Italy." Production was said to be limited to "only 200," and at present the total number of these cars is not known. They are rare, and in most cases were special-ordered through one of a few select participating Cadillac dealerships. The buyer would have to wait for his or her special car to be built and shipped.

1970s

1980 CHEVROLET CAMARO "RALLY SPORT" "T-TOP" COUPE

THE FIRST CAMARO WAS THE 1967 MODEL.

new V-6 ENGINE (229 C.I.D.) (231 C.I.D. IN CALIF.) (V8s ALSO AVAIL.)

Z-28, BERLINETTA, SPT. CPE. MODELS ALSO

$7116. (PLUS EXTRAS)

P-205/75R × 14 STEEL-BELT. RADIALS

TAD 10-30

© 1988 North America Syndicate, Inc. All rights reserved.

3464 LBS.

E.P.A. MILEAGE = 20 CITY 26 HWY.

115 H.P.

108" W.B.

1980 Camaro "Rally Sport"

"Energetic. Electrifying. Economical. ...For 1980, Camaro Rally Sport offers you something that's becoming increasingly rare: a combination of good, solid economy and show-stopping good looks.

"Camaro has always been one of Chevy's most aerodynamic cars. It moves through the air easily, and that helps you conserve fuel. But, for over 2 million people, Camaro's styling is more than that. It's a magical shape. It's 'The Hugger.'" (Camaro had advertised itself as "The Hugger" ever since 1967, its first year. The term refers to its road-hugging qualities.)

The 1980 Camaros sold in California were available only with the automatic transmission. But, manual transmissions were available in the other states and in other countries.

Notice the optional T-top roof, with its two removable panels (panels are removed in this illustration). Since there were no stock-built American convertibles between 1977 and 1981, the T-top roof became a desirable option on some sporty coupes. The center bar gave rigid support, for safety—and the removable panels on either side provided more light and fresh air than a sunroof.

Convertibles came back on the American scene in 1982, by popular demand—but at much higher prices than ever before! The T-top coupe is an interesting substitute for a full convertible.

The older and scarcer they become, cars such as this 1980 Camaro Rally Sport coupe are bound to keep increasing in appeal to collectors.

RETURN OF FORD'S CROWN VICTORIA!
ORIGINAL "CROWN VICTORIA" AVAIL. 1955 and 1956.
1980 FORD LTD CROWN VICTORIA
5 LITER (302 CID) V-8
130 HP
BAND WRAPS OVER ROOF
WT. 3524 lbs.
21,962 BLT.
16 M.P.G. (EPA) CITY, 27 HWY.
19-GAL. FUEL TANK
SLOGAN: "HERE'S THE CROWN VICTORIA."
114.3" WHEELBASE
P205 75 R14 TIRES
$7763. ($7900. WEST COAST)
©1992 by North America Syndicate, Inc. World rights reserved.
TAP 6-28
LARGE FORDS "DOWNSIZED" IN 1979.
OVERDRIVE OPTIONAL   140 HP (351 CID) V8 OPTIONAL

1980 Ford "LTD" Crown Victoria

F ord's 1980 model was nearly identical to its downsized '79, but for 1980 the Crown Victoria was revived as the new top line in Ford's LTD series. A Crown Victoria coupe was also available.

What were the differences between the 1979 and 1980 models? The '79 had a tall, narrow hood ornament, whereas the 1980 had either a low-wide ornament or none at all (depending on which series). The lower-priced LTD "S" sedan had its own grille design with parking lights mounted in the grille.

The available, new overdrive automatic transmission was a gas-saver, because at 40 mph in Drive, it would shift into a fourth (overdrive) speed.

A variety of LTD interiors were available in 1980: velour cloth; all-vinyl; or genuine leather seating surfaces. A "DuraWeave" vinyl option had the dull, rough look of heavy-duty cloth and was a Ford "exclusive."

Early in the '80 model year, only the station wagon had a twenty-gallon fuel tank; later, all '80 LTDs had one (instead of nineteen-gallon). The LTD with 5.0 liter V-8 and "SelectShift" automatic transmission got 17 mpg (EPA figure) and 24 on the highway with varying figures, depending on what type of V-8 and transmission combination was tested.

Strangely, the larger (5.8 liter) V-8 with overdrive got the highest LTD highway mileage estimate (27 mpg).

Figures were lower in California because of stringent smog control attachments.

In 1980, official labor charges in Ford garages were $21.35 an hour. Back in the 1920s, according to old repair manuals, the cost of a complete engine overhaul for a Model T Ford was only $25!

BY CADILLAC = A FUTURE CLASSIC?

1980 *Seville* V8

$23,055.00

THOUGH OLDER CARS ARE USUALLY SEEN IN "AUTO ALBUM," WE PRESENT THIS MODEL WHICH REPRESENTS A SIGNIFICANT MILESTONE IN STYLING HISTORY, AND BRINGS BACK THE ELEGANCE OF CARS BUILT BEFORE THE "ENERGY CRISIS" OF THE 1970s!

5.7 LITRE DIESEL ENG. 1980 (GAS V8 OPT.)

THE CLASSIC ROLLS-ROYCE-LOOK OF **new** DISTINCTIVE "KNIFE-EDGED" REAR STYLING

SEVILLE

TAP

2.4L GEAR RATIO 105 H.P.

4-21

News America Syndicate
© News Group Chicago, Inc., 1985

3911 LBS.
23 GAL FUEL TANK

1980 Seville

Cadillac introduced the downsized Seville model during 1975, for the '76 season. Though it cost more than most other Cadillacs, it was smaller. Then why was it more expensive? It came equipped with so many luxury features as standard equipment.

For 1980 (and up to 1985), Cadillac engineers decided to give the Seville a more luxurious profile, with a new sharply creased, sloping "knife edge" rear treatment. It was immediately reminiscent of classic Rolls-Royces and other quality British cars of the late 1940s and early 1950s! It was the freshest new design for 1980.

The Seville for 1980 was the first car to offer a diesel V-8 engine as standard equipment. But, for those who didn't like the rattling sound of a diesel or the more limited availability of refueling stops, there was an optional gasoline-powered six-liter V-8 with digital electronic fuel injection (at no extra cost). And, in California, there was an available 5.7-liter "EFI" V-8.

Because of the growing popularity of front-wheel drive, the '80 Seville included it. Other standard features: four-wheel independent suspension, four-wheel disc brakes, electronic level control (automatically adjusts to changing loads), new on-board computer diagnostics and mpg sentinel (with fuel-injected engines), electronic cruise control, twilight sentinel (automatically turns lights on and off), and much more. The list in the original catalog is amazing, and too long to include here!

Saddle leather seats were available (optional), in ten color choices. At the top of the Seville line: the "Elegante," painted in two-tone lacquer, with chrome-plated wire wheel covers and other goodies.

¡DE MÉXICO!
SOLD IN MEXICO BY VEHICULOS AUTOMORES MEXICANOS
(AMERICAN MOTORS' MEXICAN AFFILIATE)
INSIGNIA

TRANSLATION: (THE POSSIBLE DREAM)

1980 V.A.M. AMERICAN GT

112 NET H.P.

6 CYL. 232 PCD

©1993 North America Syndicate, Inc. World rights reserved.

10~17

4.38 MANUAL TRANS. DR70 × 14 TIRES.

FRONT DETAIL   VAM

FANS OF AMC + RAMBLER CARS (SINCE 1958) SHOULD LOOK INTO THE AMERICAN MOTORS OWNERS ASSOCIATION! FOR DETAILS ON THE CLUB, SEND A S.A.S.E. TO: DARRYL A. SALISBURY, 6756 CORNELL PORTAGE, MI. 49002

SLOGAN: "EL SUEÑO POSIBLE"

1980 V.A.M. American GT

American Motors Corp., for a time, offered a special line of cars in Mexico, and they're scarcely ever seen north of the Rio Grande!

The GT was a sporty, duck-tailed, two-door fastback/hatchback done in black with white sport wheels. It featured a black vinyl interior with reclining, cloth-faced bucket seats and a "four-on-the-floor" console. The black plastic dash sported panels of plastic woodgrain, and the small, racing-type steering wheel had three perforations in each of its three silvered spokes, with a small circular hub. Looking lean and mean, the GT was available with a tachometer.

This American GT was illustrated on the cover of the 1980 Spanish language catalog of Vehiculos Automores Mexi-

canos, AMC's Mexican affiliate. Other models in this catalog included the American coupe; a four-door sedan; American GFS coupe with vinyl-covered top and etched glass opera windows; American woodgrained "Camioneta" four-door wagon (also available with plain, painted sides and with a roof rack).

The Mexican catalog for 1980 also offered the Rally AMX hatchback, Gremlin, Gremlin X, and a full line of Jeeps: the Renegade, standard Jeep, Jeep pickups, and Wagoneers (with or without wood-grained sides).

As cars of the late 1970s and early 1980s get scarcer and become of greater interest to younger collectors, considerable excitement should be generated by any of these rare Mexican models that may turn up!

1980s

REVIEWED IN 4-81 ISSUE OF POPULAR MECHANICS, PAGE 130

1981 BEDE WITH 47 H.P. 1000 c.c. KAWASAKI MOTORCYCLE ENGINE. 2:1 BELT— REDUCTION DRIVE

ELECTRIC-MOTOR REVERSE

AD 6/18

REAR PROPELLER DRIVE, with SAFETY SHROUD

ALUMINUM CHASSIS FRAME

FIBERGLASS BODY

TOP SPEED OF ONLY 51, BUT GOT 117½ M.P.G. IN TESTS!

FROM BEDE AVIATION CO., WICHITA, KANSAS

PRICE IN KIT FORM)

$8000. (PLANNED)

1981 Bede

In the early 1980s, with rapidly rising gas prices and threats of "$3.50 a gallon" in the future, there were many experimental economy cars in the works.

The Bede Aviation Company was in the throes of bankruptcy when this new Bede "BD-CAR" was publicized. But, founder Jim Bede hoped he could get this unusual vehicle onto the market for about $8,000, in kit form. (An earlier and unsuccessful Bede idea was the BD-5 kit-built airplane.)

With its rear propeller and fuselage-style body, the Bede car had a somewhat aeronautical look. Certainly, it was aerodynamic in its styling! The illustrated car used a 1,000-c.c. Kawasaki motorcycle engine, mounted behind the two seats.

More or less a fan-driven car, the Bede used an electric motor for driving in reverse.

Naturally, the terrific draft from such a giant rear fan/prop would create problems on city streets. So, the protective louvers at the rear were designed to direct the big gusts upward—until the car reached road speeds.

Because of the lightweight, aerodynamic design (which used thin, motorcycle-type disc wheels for light weight and minimal "drag"), Jim Bede claimed that in three test runs he averaged 117 1/2 miles per gallon in fuel economy!

The Bede was tested at the Ohio Transportation Research Center track near Marysville. It had little if any pulling power, and top speed was less than 52 m.p.h. That would have crimped many a sale had this unusual car made it into full production.

Nevertheless, it's another interesting attempt to provide the American public with fuel-efficient personal transportation.

PRICED FROM $*14997.* and up, f.o.b. at FACTORY

121.4" WHEELBASE 2.41 GEAR RATIO (V8s)

1981 CADILLAC COUPE DE VILLE

ON BOARD COMPUTER DIAGNOSTIC SYSTEM

INTERIOR

AVAIL. WITH new 368 C.I.D. V8~6~4* ENGINE (A V8, WITH ELECTRONIC FUEL INJECTION) THAT CAN ALSO RUN ON 6 OR 4 CYLINDERS FOR FUEL ECONOMY. (252 CID V6 OR 350 CID 105 HP DIESEL V8 ALSO OFFERED.)

WT. 4151 LBS. AUTOMATIC TRANSMISSION

P215/75R15 TIRES

1981

* 140 HP

©1994 by North America Syndicate, Inc. World rights reserved.

1981 Cadillac V8-6-4

W hat was the "V8-6-4" engine? Here's how it was described in 1981 Cadillac advertising:

"As you leave your driveway, all eight cylinders in your gasoline-powered 1981 Cadillac are in operation. Then, as you reach intermediate speeds on a street or avenue and your power requirements lessen, the car automatically switches to six cylinders. And then when you reach cruising speeds and your power needs decrease further, the car automatically switches to four-cylinder operation."

By pushing a button, the driver of a 1981 Cadillac V8-6-4 could get a digital display on the instrument panel showing how many cylinders were in use at the moment, plus an "MPG Sentinel" reading that indicated both the instantaneous miles per gallon and the average figure.

Back in 1916-17, a few expensive V-12-powered automobiles could be run on six cylinders at the driver's control, but the new 1981 Cadillac's system of shutting down unneeded cylinders was far more sophisticated. And, the system was designed so that inactive cylinders would not be a drag on those still working.

The V8-6-4 engine was designed to save fuel. In May 1981, however, *Road & Track* magazine reported that the V8-6-4 engine might be phased out because it got 23 m.p.g. at cruising speeds with four cylinders engaged, but could only get an overall average of 17 m.p.g. In 1982, the Environmental Protection Agency would be demanding an average of 18.5.

1980s

A "COLLECTOR'S CAR" FROM THE START! PRODUCED 1981-1982

1981 DE LOREAN "DMC-12"

ASSEMBLED IN IRELAND BY DE LOREAN MOTOR COMPANY.

"GULL-WING-" SWING-UP DOORS

WITH 174 CID V6 RENAULT ALUMINUM-BLOCK O.H.C. REAR ENGINE 8.8 COMPR. 130 NET H.P. @ 5500 RPM

NCT 235/60 HR 15 REAR

94.8" W.B.

NCT 195/60 HR 14 FRONT

BODY OF BRUSHED STAINLESS STEEL OVER FIBERGLASS

WT.=2712 LBS.

130 M.P.H. 0~60 M.P.H. IN 8½ SEC. 13.2 GAL FUEL TANK

GOODYEAR TIRES USED 22 MPG AVG.

3.44 GEAR RATIO 5-SP. MANUAL TRANS.

1981 De Lorean

John Z. De Lorean enjoyed a most successful career with General Motors Corporation. In the 1960s, under his direction, GM's Pontiac Division's sales quadrupled! Later, De Lorean assumed a similar position at the Chevrolet Division and also worked wonders there. But, growing restless in a big corporation that tended to stifle his individuality, he left GM in 1973; and in two years he'd begun work on a new car that would bear his name.

De Lorean planned a factory in Puerto Rico. But, the British Government made him a better offer: considerable financial backing if he'd build the factory in Northern Ireland, where there was twenty-two percent unemployment. The De Lorean car generated much excitement: It was all new from an all-new company!

Unfortunately, the debut of available cars was delayed too long. Pilot models were around in 1977, but full production didn't begin until the factory was open in 1981. Inflation had upped the price. In '77 it was to sell for $10,000. In '81, the cost was $25,000 and going toward $40,000 or more! There were over 500 dealer outlets (many of them also selling Cadillacs), but De Lorean stepped up production to a point where he had hundreds of excess cars to sell off. The British Government and other creditors wanted their money. In the fall of '82, the factory in Ireland was shut down. A firm in Columbus, Ohio bought up the stock of De Lorean cars and sold them at reduced prices.

1980s

1981 Imperial

The reorganized New Chrysler Corp., under the able leadership of Lee Iacocca (formerly with Ford Motor Co.), forged ahead for 1981 with some excitingly different new models.

The Imperial, which had been discontinued since 1975, was once again available—but only as a club coupe. It had a most attractive "knife-edged" rear deck treatment, not unlike that of the successful 1980 to 1985 Cadillac Seville.

Several prices were quoted for the 1981 Imperial when it was new, all of them in the $18,000 or $19,000 range. No one seemed sure of just what a 1981 Imperial should sell for, since all sources disagreed. As for Chrysler Corp. advertising, price was not mentioned, so the $18,822 price given in the illustration was mid-range among the varying prices given in the different trade publications of the day. The 1981

Imperial contained nearly every luxury feature imaginable as standard equipment—even a remote-control garage door opener and a leather-wrapped steering wheel. Seats were available in a choice of Mark Cross leather or Yorkshire Cloth. The only factory option that cost extra was a sunroof.

Original 1981 Imperial colors: Sterling Silver Crystal Coat; Day Star Blue Crystal Coat; Nightwatch Blue (looked black unless seen in a strong light); Light Auburn Crystal (a Navy gray); Mahogany Starmist; Light Seaspray Green Crystal Coat; Spice Tan Starmist (a deep brown); Manila Cream; Morocco Red; Pearl White; Formal Black.

The standard-equipment "Triad" horn had three notes.

This limited-production automobile was available only for 1981-1983.

1980s

1981 Plymouth Reliant

The 1981 model-year introduction of the practical, gas-sipping "K cars," (Dodge Aries and Plymouth Reliant) along with the 1984 triumph of the new Dodge Caravan and Plymouth Voyager van-wagons, brought new success to Chrysler Corporation.

In 1973, gas was only 36.9 cents per gallon in Dallas; 39.6 in Atlanta; 41.9 in Louisville, Ky. and Boston; 42.2 in Chicago; 44.9 in Saginaw, Mich.; and at its highest (summer '73) of 58.9 in Fairbanks, Alaska.

By February 1981, self-service regular (leaded) gas was up to $1.21 a gallon in the West, $1.14 in the Southwest, and $1.18 in many Eastern states, with a U.S. average of $1.18. Self-service unleaded averaged $1.24, with full-service unleaded about five cents a gallon more.

According to reports published monthly in *Automotive Fleet* magazine, in March 1981, prices had climbed in just four weeks to an average of $1.38 for self-service unleaded!

Prophets of gloom were howling that we'd be paying $3.50 or maybe $5 a gallon for gas later in the 1980s, but fortunately their predictions did not come true. As of November 1989, self-service unleaded was down to 85.6 cents a gallon in Pasadena, Calif., and it was in the 90s in most parts of the country. However, the price was $1.45 in Maui, Hawaii, and $1.50 in Juneau, Alaska.

The 1981 Reliants (and Aries) came in three body types: two-door coupe, four-door, or four-door wagon with grained or ungrained sides.

This illustrated "SE" series coupe with vinyl-covered rear top was a luxury model. Basic no-frills Reliants were advertised for as little as $5,880.

1981 "Thrust 2"

C an you imagine driving a motor vehicle 650 miles an hour on land? That's the approximate speed of most jet airliners! At that speed, one could drive coast to coast in less than five hours.

This Thrust 2 required a 300-foot turning circle. Also, it required a trio of heavy parachutes—in addition to disc brakes—to slow it down once it really got rolling on an open desert stretch.

The February 1985 issue of *Car and Driver* magazine contained a fascinating article (with pictures) on the Thrust 2, brainchild of a British racing driver and adventurer, Richard Noble.

Noble said that he caught the racing bug back in 1952, at the age of six, when his dad took him to see John Cobb's jet racing boat, Crusader, at Loch Ness in Scotland. Cobb was killed just days later when his Crusader cracked up and disintegrated at 240 mph. (because its front water ski was cracked and Cobb couldn't wait to get it fixed properly).

In spite of the misfortune, Richard Noble was now keenly interested in racing, and worked with airplane engines during his college years.

Eventually he built a Thrust 1 racer, completing it in 1976. In 1977, he rolled it over at 140 m.p.h. and it was "totaled." But, soon he was at work on Thrust 2. Little did he dream, then, that he would break many speed records with it a few years later.

1980s

"NEO-CLASSIC" ELEGANCE!
THE IRRESISTIBLE
1982 **ZIMMER**
"GOLDEN SPIRIT"
CABRIOLET
WITH ELECTRONIC FUEL INJECTION
and AIR CONDITIONING

"74" WIDE!"

4-SP. AUTO. TRANS. WITH OVERDRIVE

BLT. on A FORD MUSTANG CHASSIS STRETCHED TO 142" W.B.

302 CID V8
W.B. 142"
53½ × 180

MFD. SINCE 1980 BY ZIMMER
MOTOR CARS CORPORATION
POMPANO BEACH, FLORIDA
(AVAIL. THROUGHOUT
MOST OF THE 'EIGHTIES)
PAUL H. ZIMMER, founder

/AD

P235/75R15 TIRES

$59,500. *SUGGESTED RETAIL PRICE, 1982*

4~24

HELDBILL DATA THANKS TO JOHN E. LLOYD, MOUNTVILLE, PA

1982 Zimmer

We recently received an inquiry regarding the unusual Zimmer luxury car, a costly "neoclassic" of the 1980s.

As the name implies, a neoclassic is a modern car designed with deliberately old-fashioned styling—often recalling something of the "classic look" of the 1930s.

A neo-classic differs from a "replicar" in that a replicar closely imitates the design of some specific make and model of an older car. A neoclassic, on the other hand, is not meant to exactly imitate a previous design.

Paul H. Zimmer, at the tender age of twenty, went into business with his brother in 1949 to manufacture mobile homes. In the ensuing years, Zimmer mobile homes gained an enviable reputation of quality!

In 1976, Zimmer bought a new Excalibur roadster for $22,000. Noting the admiration it drew, Zimmer decided to build something along that general line and market it himself. "We can do that!" he declared, eager to tap into a seemingly booming new market.

In 1980, the new Zimmer "Golden Spirit" became available to the public. Zimmer soon learned that there was more profit in producing these luxury cars on a limited scale than in the crowded mobile home and motor-home markets. The Zimmer mobile and motor homes continued to roll out of the factory, but for a time, the neoclassic car was Zimmer's pet project.

In 1982, Zimmer offered both closed and convertible models, with such standard luxury features as a leather-covered dash; six-way, power Recaro seats; imported Mouton carpeting throughout; 24-karat, gold-plated, tilting Nardi steering wheel; and so much more!

The following text appears within the cartoon illustration:

A TALKING CAR!

"ELECTRONIC VOICE ALERT" GIVES SPOKEN WARNINGS CONCERNING :
• KEY IN IGNITION SWITCH (DOOR OPEN)
• HEADLIGHTS ON   • (" ")
• SEAT BELTS UNFASTENED (w. IGNITION ON)
OIL PRESSURE LOW
ENGINE OVERHEATING
ELECTRICAL SYSTEM LOW VOLTAGE
PARKING BRAKE ON
WASHER FLUID RESERVOIR LESS THAN 1/4 FULL
DOOR AJAR
FUEL TANK LESS THAN 1/8 FULL
● = VOICE SAYS "THANK YOU" WHEN CONDITION WARNED ABOUT IS CORRECTED .
SAYS "ALL MONITORED SYSTEMS ARE FUNCTIONING" IF NO PROBLEMS AS CAR STARTS .

1983 CHRYSLER "TOWN & COUNTRY" CONVERTIBLE "MARK CROSS EDITION"

$18833.

REAR

"THANK YOU !! "

THE FIRST TOWN & COUNTRY CONVERTIBLE SINCE 1950!

VOICE SYSTEM ALSO ON 1983 CHRYSLER "E", DODGE "E", 600 "ES", OPT. on SOME OTHERS.

99.9" WB 4 CYL. 2.2L 96 hp

WHAT OTHER "TALKING CARS" DO YOU KNOW OF ? PLEASE WRITE AND TELL US THE YEAR AND MAKE, WHAT IS SAID, and WHETHER MAN'S or WOMAN'S VOICE HEARD.

1983 1/2 Chrysler Town & Country Convertible

Chrysler's famous "Town & Country" wood-paneled series began in 1941 as a combination sedan/station wagon. In 1946, there was both a straight-8, wooden-bodied convertible and a six-cylinder sedan. In 1949, the Town & Country convertible was still available, with a totally restyled body, but in 1950 the Town & Country appeared only as a glamorized, two-door Newport hardtop convertible with wood trim.

After that, the Town & Country name was used only intermittently on various Chrysler station wagons. But, by 1983, the lasting popularity of the old Town & Country convertibles from the 1940s—as valued collector's items—induced Chrysler Corporation to revive the Town & Country "ragtop."

However, the mid-year 1983 1/2 model was a vastly-shrunken little four-cylinder vehicle. The '83 1/2 Town & Country convertible had paneling of plastic imitation wood, more practical than the genuine but perishable wood of the original 1940s models.

The "Mark Cross" optional package on 1983 Chrysler convertibles consisted of genuine leather upholstery and various other luxury features. Without the Mark Cross package, the Town & Country convertible was base-priced at $15,595.

During the mid-1980s, there was a fad for "talking cars," as some American and import makes gained a voice of their own, through computerized electronic systems. Though it wasn't a set rule, American cars often spoke with a man's voice. Japanese cars frequently spoke with the more seductive tones of a woman.

I think these talking cars of the 1980s have great potential as collector's cars, and a study of which cars said what (and for how many years) would be a fascinating project.

1980s

1984 Caravan

T he Dodge Caravan and its sister vehicle, the Plymouth Voyager, were introduced as 1984 models and filled a great demand for those who wanted something smaller than a full-sized van but roomier than a full-sized station wagon.

Since 1984, most other automakers—American and foreign—have introduced their own versions of the minivan. But, after years of continual popularity and refinements, Chrysler Corporation's minivans continue to be leaders in their field.

Back in 1984, the new Dodge Caravan was advertised as a "transportation revolution: Not as long as a full-size station wagon, yet it holds 40 percent more cargo. And it's about the same height as the average American woman. It has front-wheel

drive, gets incredible mileage, and is backed by 5/50 protection" (five years or 50,000 miles limited warranty on engine, power train, and outer body rust-through, with minor deductible).

If only two adults were seated in the Caravan, up to 125 cubic feet of cargo space was available. As a full seven-passenger model, two people could be seated in front, two in the center seat and three in the full width back seat. There was a swing-up hatchback door at the very rear, and only one door on the left side of the vehicle for the driver. The center seat was only for two, in order to provide an aisle on the right for access to the back seat. The second door on the right side slid back and forth—safer for children than a swing-out door.

1984 Del Rey

For many years, as far as American car buyers are concerned, the vast Brazilian automobile manufacturing industry has been a "sleeping giant." Though Brazil exports cars to other nations, only a small percentage of its sizable output has ever reached the United States. Exceptions are few, such as certain recent models of Volks-wagen and the Lafer MP (a fiberglass-bodied Brazilian replica of England's MG-TD sports car of the early '50s).

Many Americans don't realize how large Brazil's cities and industries have become. Sao Paulo, a hub of heavy industry in Latin America, is a vast Brazilian megalopolis where one can look from a skyscraper and view miles and miles of equally tall buildings for as far as the eye can see!

Ever hear of a car called the Marajo? ... or the Pretty Car? ... or the Comodoro? These are just a few made in Brazil.

Ford's Del Rey is an attractive car, and the illustrated model was available even back in 1981. Its long, low, broad hood, fine-looking grille with vertical pieces, and broad headlights gave it a distinctive "face."

Should you take a trip to Brazil, you'll see many strange cars and trucks you never heard of before, and many look like nothing you've seen here. Only a small number of Brazilian cars are diesels, but a great many of them operate on "alcool" (alcohol fuel) instead of conventional gasoline.

1980s

ALL-NEW.!!
1984 TOPAZ
(BY MERCURY)
(MECHANICALLY SIMILAR TO FORD'S NEW TEMPO.)

84 HP @ 4600 RPM

PRICED FROM $ 9144.

FRONT WHEEL DRIVE

4 CYL. 140 CID ENG.

99.9" WHEELBASE

14-GAL. GAS TANK
175/80 R13"
TIRES

THE TOPAZ and TEMPO
REPLACED THE 1978~1983 ZEPHYR
and FAIRMONT.

GS OR LS MODELS

M.P.G. = 28 EPA, 43 HIGHWAY

TAP 4/14

© 1991 North America Syndicate, Inc. All Rights Reserved

1984 Topaz

In the 1980s, the traditional October model-change in the auto industry nearly became a thing of the past. American and foreign car manufacturers are now introducing new models at various times of the year, instead of saving everything until fall.

An example: When Ford Motor Co. launched its two, new front-drive compacts, the Tempo and Topaz, for 1984, it chose an early (May 1983) introduction date. Ford would later introduce a pair of larger Ford and Mercury front-drive cars for 1986, and these would be the Taurus and Sable. Changes were also to come in Ford's luxury Lincoln/Continental line.

The Tempo and Topaz had much in common, but weren't exactly alike. For example, Tempo had a seven-window sedan available, but all Topaz sedans appear to be five-window types. And,

the Topaz has a much more attractive front-end design than the early Tempo, with its gaping grille.

The 1984 and 1985 Topazes look very much alike, but in 1986 a heavy "upper lip" was added to the grille, which looks rather strange at first sight. Most unusual of all Ford Motor Co. front ends of the 1980s is that of the 1986, and later, Mercury Sable, with its unique "glass grille" (actually, a clear plastic "light bar" that extends headlight illumination all the way across the car).

The '84-'85 Topaz was available in two-door and four-door models, in the "GS" and more deluxe "LS" series. The $9,144 price applies to Western states, but in various areas, advertisements promised lower starting prices, sometimes even below $7,000 in special cases.

1980s

Inside illustration:

MADE IN BRAZIL

STYLING SIMILAR TO 1952 MG-TD

1985

©1993 North America Syndicate, Inc. World rights reserved.

MP LAFER

GLASS SIDE WINDOWS

LUGGAGE SPACE UNDER HOOD

ONE OF THE MOST POPULAR MODERN "REPLICARS" BASED ON FAMOUS COLLECTOR CARS! FIBERGLASS BODY ON A 1600 cc 4 cyl. AIR-COOLED VOLKSWAGEN CHASSIS. REAR ENGINE. 30 M.P.G.

$14,000. and up, IMPORTED TO U.S.A. DATA THANKS TO BREMEN MOTOR CORP., BREMEN, INDIANA (FORMER IMPORTER OF THE LAFER MP) BRAZILIAN PRICE=Cr.$5,436,000.

AVAILABLE IN 20 DIFF. COLORS!

1985 Lafer MP

During the past two decades, several small companies have produced—in limited numbers—a variety of replicars of different classics of the past. There have been reproductions of Cord convertibles, Duesenberg roadsters, Auburn boat-tailed speedsters, plus many others—including MG-TD sports cars, which were originally built from 1950 to early 1954.

Some half-dozen companies have tried their hand at manufacturing MG replicars similar to the type illustrated. One of the best-selling of the MG replicars was this Lafer MP, made in Brazil for many years and exported to the United States during the 1980s.

Most replicars have relied on readily available mechanical parts from better-known makes of cars, and the Lafer MP is no exception. It used a "remanufactured" Volkswagen chassis with a rear engine, the type used on the VW Beetle. With the engine in the rear, the long hood of the Lafer MP provided ample storage space. The hood was not the original "butterfly" type (hinged down the middle), but was hinged at one side so it swung open from the right, giving access to luggage and gear.

The fiberglass body on the Lafer MP was of superior quality, and it was claimed that a grown man could stand atop the front fender and not break it!

Features of the Lafer MP included top-grain leather reclining bucket seats, AM-FM radio with stereo cassette player, Rosewood steering wheel and dashboard, three sport lights, full instrumentation in a dashboard shaped like the original, glass side windows, a fire extinguisher and other accessories.

1980s

Index

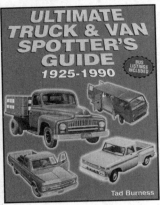

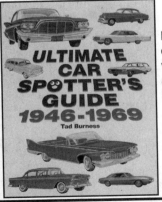